ΨΑΛΜΟΙ ΣΟΛΟΜΩΝΤΟΣ
Psalms of the Pharisees, commonly called The Psalms of Solomon

Ancient Texts and Translations

K. C. Hanson, Series Editor

Robert William Rogers
*Cuneiform Parallels to the
Old Testament*

D. Winton Thomas, editor
*Documents from
Old Testament Times*

Henry Frederick Lutz
*Early Babylonian Letters
from Larsa*

Albert T. Clay
Babylonian Epics, Hymns, Omens, and Other Texts

Daniel David Luckenbill
The Annals of Sennacherib

A. E. Cowley
*Aramaic Papyri of the
Fifth Century B.C.*

G. R. Driver
Aramaic Documents of the Fifth Century B.C., rev. ed.

Adolf Neubauer
*The Book of Tobit:
The Text in Aramaic, Hebrew,
and Old Latin with English Translations*

August Dillman
The Ethiopic Text of 1 Enoch

R. H. Charles
*The Apocrypha and Pseudepigrapha
of the Old Testament*

R. H. Charles
The Book of Enoch

R. H. Charles
The Book of Jubilees

R. H. Charles
*The Testaments of the
Twelve Patriarchs*

R. H. Charles
The Apocalypse of Baruch

Herbert Edward Ryle
& Montague Rhodes James
*The Psalms of the Pharisees,
commonly called
The Psalms of Solomon*

B. Harris Cowper
The Apcryphal Gospels

H. B. Swete
The Gospel of Peter

Bernhard Pick
The Apocryphal Acts

Richard Adelbert Lipsius
& Max Bonnet
*Apocryphal Acts
of the Apostles (3 vols.)*

ΨΑΛΜΟΙ ΣΟΛΟΜΩΝΤΟΣ
Psalms of the Pharisees commonly called The Psalms of Solomon

Herbert Edward Ryle
and
Montague Rhodes James

New Foreword and Bibliography by
K. C. Hanson

Wipf & Stock Publishers
Eugene, Oregon

ΨΑΛΜΟΙ ΣΟΛΟΜΩΝΤΟΣ PSALMS OF THE PHARISEES,
COMMONLY CALLED THE PSALMS OF SOLOMON
The Text Newly Revised from All the Mss.

Ancient Texts and Translations

Copyright © 2006 Wipf & Stock Publishers. All rights reserved.
Except for brief quotations in critical publications or reviews, no part
of this book may be reproduced in any manner without prior written
permission from the publisher. Write: Permissions, Wipf & Stock, 199
W. 8th Ave., Eugene, OR 97401.

ISBN: 1-59752-626-6

Cataloging-in-Publication data

Ryle, Herbert Edward, 1856–1925.

    Psalmoi Solomontos = Psalms of the Pharisees, commonly
    called the Psalms of Solomon / edited, with introduction,
    English translation, notes, appendix, and indices by Herbert
    Edward Ryle and Montague Rhodes James, with a new
    foreword and bibliography by K. C. Hanson.

    Ancient Texts and Translations

    xxxiii + 176 p.; 23 cm.

    1. Psalms of Solomon. 2. Psalms of Solomon—Commentaries.
    3. Psalms of Solomon—English and Greek. I. James, M. R.
    (Montague Rhodes), 1862–1936. II. Hanson, K. C. (Kenneth
    C.). III. Title. IV. Series.

    BS1830 P7 2006

Manufactured in the U.S.A.

Series Foreword

The discoveries of documents from the ancient Near Eastern and Mediterranean worlds have altered our modern understanding of those worlds in both breadth and depth. Especially since the mid-nineteenth century, chance discoveries as well as archaeological excavations have brought to light thousands of clay tablets, stone inscriptions and stelae, leather scrolls, codices, papyri, seals, and ostraca.

The genres of these written documents are quite diverse: receipts, tax lists, inventories, letters, prophecies, blessings and curses, dowry documents, deeds, laws, instructions, collections of proverbs, philosophical treatises, state propaganda, myths and legends, hymns and prayers, liturgies and rituals, and many more. Some of them came to light in long-famous cities—such as Ur, Babylon, Nineveh, and Jerusalem—while others came from locations that were previously little-known or unknown— such as Ebla, Ugarit, Elephantine, Qumran, and Nag Hammadi.

But what good are these remnants from the distant past? Why should anyone bother with what are often fragmentary, obscure, or long-forgotten scraps of ancient cultures? Each person will answer those questions for herself or himself, depending upon interests and commitments. But the documents have influ-enced scholarly research in several areas.

It must first be said that the documents are of interest and importance in their own right, whatever their connections—or lack of them—to modern ethnic, religious, or ideological concerns. Many of them provide windows on how real people lived in the ancient world—what they grew and ate; how they related to their families, business associates, and states; how they were taxed; how and whom they worshiped; how they organized their communities; their hopes and fears; and how they understood and portrayed their own group's story.

They are of intense interest at the linguistic level. They provide us with previously unknown or undeciphered languages and dialects, broaden our range of vocabularies and meanings, assist us in mapping the relationships and developments of languages, and provide examples of loan-words and linguistic influences between languages. A monumental project such as *The Assyrian Dictionary,* produced by the Oriental Institute at the University of Chicago, would have been unthinkable without the broad range of Akkadian resources today.[1] And our study of Coptic and early gospels would be impoverished without the Nag Hammadi codices.[2]

The variety of genres also attracts our interest in terms of the history of literature. Such stories as Athra-hasis, Enumma Elish, and Gilgamesh have become important to the study of world literature. While modern readers may be most intrigued by something with obvious political or religious content, we often learn a great deal from a tax receipt or a dowry document. Hermann Gunkel influenced biblical studies not only because of his keen insights into the biblical books, but because he studied the biblical genres in the light of ancient Near Eastern texts. As he examined the genres in the Psalms, for example, he compared them to the poetic passages throughout the rest of the Bible, the Apocrypha, the Pseudepigrapha, Akkadian sources, and Egyptian sources.[3] While the Akkadian and Egyptian resources were much

---

[1] I. J. Gelb et al., editors, *The Assyrian Dictionary of the Oriental Institute of the University of Chicago* (Chicago: Univ. of Chicago Press, 1956–).

[2] James M. Robinson, editor, *The Nag Hammadi Library in English,* 4th ed. (Leiden: Brill, 1996).

[3] Hermann Gunkel, *Einleitung in die Psalmen: Die Gattungen der religiösen Lyrik Israels,* completed by Joachim Begrich, HAT (Göttingen: Vandenhoeck & Ruprecht, 1933). ET = *Introduction to the Psalms: The Genres of the Religious Lyric of Israel,* trans. James D. Nogalski, Mercer

more limited in the 1920s and 1930s when he was working on the Psalms, his methodology and insights have had an on-going significance.

History is also a significant interest. Many of these texts mention kingdoms, ethnic and tribal groups, rulers, diplomats, generals, locations, or events that assist in establishing chronologies, give us different perspectives on previously known events, or fill in gaps in our knowledge. Historians can never have too many sources. The Amarna letters, for example, provide us with the names of local rulers in Canaan during the fourteenth century BCE, their relationship with the pharaoh, as well as the military issues of the period.[4]

Social analysis is another area of fertile research. A deed can reveal economic structures, production, land tenure, kinship relations, scribal conventions, calendars, and social hierarchies. Both the Elephantine papyri from Egypt (fifth century BCE) and the Babatha archive from the Judean desert (second century CE) include personal legal documents and letters relating to dowries, inheritance, and property transfers that provide glimpses of complex kinship relations, networking, and legal witnesses.[5] And the Elephantine documents also include letters to the high priest in Jerusalem from the priests of Elephantine regarding the rebuilding of the Elephantine temple.

Religion in the ancient world was usually embedded in either political or kinship structures. That is, it was normally a function of either the political group or kin-group to which one belonged. We

---

Library of Biblical Studies (Macon, Ga.: Mercer Univ. Press, 1998).

[4] William L. Moran, *The Amarna Letters* (Baltimore: Johns Hopkins Univ. Press, 1992).

[5] Bezalel Porten et al., editors, *The Elephantine Papyri in English: Three Millennia of Cross-Cultural Continuity and Change,* Documenta et Monumenta Orientis Antiqui 22 (Leiden: Brill, 1996); Yigael Yadin et al., *The Finds from the Bar Kokhba Period in the Cave of Letters,* 3 vols., Judean Desert Studies (Jerusalem: Israel Exploration Society, 1963–2002) [NB: vols. 2 and 3 are titled *Documents* instead of *Finds*].

are fortunate to have numerous texts of epic literature, liturgies, and rituals. These include such things as creation stories, purification rituals, and the interpretation of sheep livers for omens. The Dead Sea Scrolls, for example, provide us with biblical books, texts of biblical interpretation, community regulations, and liturgical texts from the second temple period.[6]

Another key element has been the study of law. A variety of legal principles, laws, and collections of regulations provide windows on social structures, economics, governance, property rights, and punishments. The stele of Hammurabi of Babylon (c. 1700 BCE) is certainly the most famous. But we have many more, for example: Ur-Nammu (c. 2100 BCE), Lipit-Ishtar (c. 1850 BCE), and the Middle Assyrian Laws (c. 1150 BCE).

The intention of Ancient Texts and Translations (ATT) is to make available a variety of ancient documents and document collections to a broad range of readers. The series will include reprints of long out-of-print volumes, revisions of earlier editions, and completely new volumes. The understanding of ancient societies depends upon our close reading of the documents, however fragmentary, that have survived.

—K. C. Hanson
Series Editor

---

[6] Florentino Garcia Martinez, *The Dead Sea Scrolls Translated: The Qumran Texts in English,* 2d ed., trans. Wilfred G. E. Watson (Grand Rapids: Eerdmans, 1996).

Foreword

Following the numerous discoveries in the late nineteenth and early twentieth centuries of noncanonical literature written by ancient Judeans and early Christians, there was much initial excitement and a flurry of publishing. These ancient works came down to us in the forms of small fragments, scrolls, and codices. This resulted in the publication of individual documents and eventually larger collections. *The Apocrypha and Pseudepigrapha of the Old Testament in English*[7] and *The Apocryphal New Testament*[8] are certainly the most important of these early collections. But some of these ancient documents had already been known for centuries, including the *Psalms of Solomon*. Some of them had been preserved in particular church traditions (for example, the Ethiopian Orthodox Church, the Coptic Church) or in the libraries of monasteries.

The study of the noncanonical literature has exploded in the past several decades. This renewed interest was at least partially fueled by the discovery of the Dead Sea Scrolls in the late 1940s and 1950s. To name but two influential figures, Professors Robert A. Kraft of the University of Pennsylvania (now emeritus), George W. E. Nickelsburg of the University of Iowa (now emeritus), and James H. Charlesworth of Princeton Theological Seminary have been leaders in the revival of interest in the Pseudepigrapha; see

---

[7] R. H. Charles, editor, *The Apocrypha and Pseudepigrapha of the Old Testament in English*, 2 vols., Ancient Texts and Translations (1913; reprinted Eugene, Ore.: Wipf & Stock, 2006).

[8] Montague Rhodes James, trans., *The Apocryphal New Testament* (Oxford: Clarendon, 1924).

especially Charlesworth's review of the literature,[9] as well as his editing of a new set of translations with notes and introductions,[10] and Nickelsburg's important textbook.[11]

But works such as the present volume have by no means been made irrelevant by on-going research. Ryle and James were important philologians who advanced our knowledge of the linguistic, historical, and theological dimensions of the *Psalms of Solomon*. And by writing such a detailed commentary with an extensive introduction, they led the way in approaching this literature in a comprehensive manner.

—K. C. Hanson

---

[9] James H. Charlesworth, *The Pseudepigrapha and Modern Research with Supplement,* Septuagint and Cognate Studies 7S (Chico, Calif.: Scholars, 1981).

[10] James H. Charlesworth, editor, *The Old Testament Pseudepigrapha,* 2 vols. (Garden City, N.Y.: Doubleday, 1983, 1985).

[11] George W. E. Nickelsburg, *Jewish Literature between the Bible and the Mishnah: A Literary and Historical Introduction, 2nd ed.* (Minneapolis: Fortress, 2005).

Select Bibliography

I. Editions and Translations

Baars, Willem. "Psalms of Solomon." In *Canticles or Odes; Prayer of Manasseh; Apocryphal Psalms; Psalms of Solomon; Tobit; 1 (3) Esdras.* The Old Testament in Syriac pt. 4, fasc. 6. Leiden: Brill, 1972.

Brock, Sebastian P. "Psalms of Solomon." In *The Apocryphal Old Testament,* edited by H. F. D. Sparks, 649–82. Oxford: Clarendon, 1984.

Gray, G. Buchanan. "Psalms of Solomon." In *The Apocrypha and Pseudepigrapha of the Old Testament in English,* edited by R. H. Charles, 2:625–52. Oxford: Clarendon, 1913.

Harris, J. Rendel. *The Odes and Psalms of Solomon.* 2d ed. Cambridge: Cambridge University Press, 1911.

———, and Alphonse Mingana. *The Odes and Psalms of Solomon.* 2 vols. Manchester: University of Manchester Press, 1916, 1920.

Jonge, Marinus de. "The Psalms of Solomon." In *Outside the Old Testament,* edited by Marinus de Jonge, 159–77. Cambridge Commentaries on Writings of the Jewish and Christian World 4. Cambridge: Cambridge University Press, 1985.

Lana, Maurizio. "Salmi di Salomone." In *Apocrifi dell'Antico Testamento,* edited by Paolo Sacchi, 2:39–146. Classici delle Religioni. Sezione seconda: La religione ebraica. Brescia: Paideia, 1989.

Rahlfs, A. "Psalmi Salomonis." In *Septuaginta,* 2:471–89. Stuttgart: Priviligierte Württembergische Bibelanstalt, 1935.

Viteau, J. *Les Psaumes de Salomon: Introduction, Texte Grec et Traduction.* Documents pour l'etude de la Bible. Paris: Letouzey et Ané, 1911.

Wright, Robert B. "Psalms of Solomon." In *Old Testament Pseudepigrapha,* edited by James H. Charlesworth, 2:639–70. Garden City, N.Y.: Doubleday, 1985.

II. Research

Aberbach, Moses. "Historical Allusions of Chapter IV, XI, and XIII of the Psalms of Solomon." *Jewish Quarterly Review* 41 (1951) 379–96.

Abrahams, I. "The Psalms of Solomon." *Jewish Quarterly Review* 9 (1897) 539–49.

Atkinson, Kenneth. "Herod the Great, Sosius, and the Siege of Jerusalem (37 B.C.E.) in Psalm of Solomon 17." *Novum Testamentum* 38 (1996) 313–22.

———. "Toward a Redating of the Psalms of Solomon: Implications for Understanding the *Sitz im Leben* of an Unknown Jewish Sect." *Journal for the Study of the Pseudepigrapha* 17 (1998) 95–112.

———. "On the Herodian Origin of Militant Davidic Messianism at Qumran: New Light from *Psalm of Solomon* 17." *Journal of Biblical Literature* 118 (1999) 435–60.

———. "On the Use of Scripture in the Development of Militant Davidic Messianism at Qumran: New Light from *Psalm of Solomon* 17." In *The Interpretation of Scripture in Early Judaism and Christianity,* edited by Craig A. Evans, 106–23. Studies in Scripture in Early Judaism and Christianity 7. Sheffield: Sheffield Academic, 2000.

———. *An Intertextual Study of the Psalms of Solomon.* Studies in the Bible and Early Christianity 49. Lewiston, N.Y.: Mellen, 2001.

———. "Theodicy in the Psalms of Solomon." In *Theodicy in the World of the Bible,* edited by Antti Laato and Johannes C. de Moor, 546–75. Leiden: Brill, 2003.

———. *I Cried to the Lord: A Study of the Psalms of Solomon's Historical Background and Social Setting.* Journal for the Study of Judaism Supplements 84. Leiden: Brill, 2004.

Baars, Willem. "An Additional Fragment of the Syriac Version of the Psalms of Solomon." *Vetus Testamentum* 11 (1961) 222–23.

———. "A New Fragment of the Greek Version of the Psalms of Solomon." *Vetus Testamentum* 11 (1961) 441–44.

Begrich, Joachim. "Der Text der Psalmen Salomos." *Zeitschrift für die neutestamentliche Wissenschaft* 38 (1939) 131–64.

Berrin, Shani. "Pesher Nahum, Psalms of Solomon and Pompey." In *Reworking the Bible: Apocryphal and Related Texts at Qumran,* edited by Esther G. Chazon et al., 65–84. Studies on the Texts of the Desert of Judah. Leiden: Brill, 2005.

Charlesworth, James H., assisted by P. Dykers and M. J. H. Charlesworth. *The Pseudepigrapha and Modern Research with a Supplement.* Septuagint and Cognate Studies 7S. Chico, Calif.: Scholars, 1981.

———. "Pseudepigrapha, OT." In *Anchor Bible Dictionary,* edited by David Noel Freedman 5:537–40. New York: Doubleday, 1992.

———. "Messianology in the Biblical Pseudepigrapha." In *Qumran-Messianism: Studies on the Messianic Expectations in the Dead Sea Scrolls*, edited by James H. Charlesworth et al., 21–52. Tübingen: Mohr/Siebeck, 1998.

Davenport, Gene L. "The 'Anointed of the Lord' in Psalms of Solomon 17." In *Ideals Figures in Ancient Judaism. Profiles and Paradigms,* edited by George W. E. Nickelsburg and John J. Collins, 67–92. Septuagint and Cognate Studies 12. Chico, Calif.: Scholars, 1980.

Delcor, M. "Psaumes de Salomon." In *Dictionnaire de la Bible Supplément,* 48:214–45. Paris: Letouzey et Ané, 1973.

Dimant, Devorah. "A Cultic Term in the Psalms of Solomon in the Light of the Septuagint." *Textus* 9 (1981) 28–51. [Heb.]

Efron, Joshua. "The Psalms of Solomon, the Hasmonean Decline and Christianity." *Zion* 30 (1965) 1–46. [Heb.]

Embry, Brad. "The *Psalms of Solomon* and the New Testament: Intertextuality and the Need for a Re-Evaluation." *Journal for the Study of the Pseudepigrapha* 13 (2002) 99–136.

Falk, Daniel. "Prayers and Psalms." In *Justification and Variegated Nomism*. Vol. 1, *The Complexities of Second Temple Judaism*, edited by Donald A. Carson et al., 7–56. Wissenschaftliche Untersuchungen zum Neuen Testament 2/140. Grand Rapids: Baker Academic, 2001.

Frankenberg, W. *Die Datierung der Psalmen Salomos: Ein Beitrag zur jüdischen Geschichte.* Beihefte zur Zeitschrift für die alttestamentliche Wissenschaft 1. Giessen: Ricker, 1896.

Franklyn, P. N. "The Cultic and Pious Climax of Eschatology in the Psalms of Solomon." *Journal for the Study of Judaism* 18 (1987) 1–17.

Gebhardt, Oscar von. *Die Psalmen Salomo's: Zum ersten Male mit Benutzung der Athoshandschriften und des Codex Casanatensis.* Texte und Untersuchungen zur Geschichte der altchristlichen Literatur 13. Leipzig: Hinrichs, 1895.

Hann, Robert R. *The Manuscript History of the Psalms of Solomon.* Septuagint and Cognate Studies Series 13. Chico, Calif.: Scholars, 1982.

———. "The Community of the Pious: The Social Setting of the Psalms of Solomon." *Studies in Religion* 17 (1988) 169–89.

Hilgenfeld, Adolphus. "Die Psalmen Salomo's und die Himmelfahrt des Moses, griechisch hergestellt und erklärt." *Zeitschrift für Wissenschaftliche Theologie* 11 (1868) 133–68.

———. "Die Psalmen Salomos." *Zeitschrift für Wissenschaftliche Theologie* 14 (1871) 383–418.

Holm-Nielsen, Svend. "Erwägungen zu dem Verhältnis zwischen den Hodajot und den Psalmen Salomos." In *Bibel und Qumran: Beiträge zur Erfarschung der Beziehungen zwischen Bibel und Qumranwissenschaft*, edited by S. Wagner, 112–31. Berlin: Evangelische Haupt-Bibelgesellschaft, 1968.

———. *Die Psalmen Salomos.* Jüdische Schriften aus hellenistisch-römischer Zeit 4/2. Gütersloh: Mohn, 1977.

Jonge, Marinus de. *De toekomstverwachting in Psalmen van*

Salomo. Leiden: Brill, 1965.

———. "The Expectation of the Future in the Psalms of Solomon." In *Jewish Eschatology, Early Christian Christology, and the Testaments of the Twelve Patriarchs: Collected Essays of Marinus de Jonge*, 3–27. Novum Testamentum Supplements 63. Leiden: Brill, 1991.

Kaiser, Otto. "Beobachtungen zur Komposition und Redaktion der Psalmen Salomos." In *Das Manna fällt auch heute noch: Beiträge zur Geschichte und Theologie des Alten, Ersten Testaments—Festschrift für Erich Zenger*, edited by Frank-Lothar Hossfeld and Ludger Schwienhorst-Schönberger, 362–78. Herders biblische Studien 44. Freiburg: Herder, 2004.

Kuhn, Karl Georg. *Die älteste Textgestalt der Psalmen Salomos*. Beiträge zur Wissenschaft vom Alten und Neuen Testa-ment 73. Stuttgart: Kohlhammer, 1937.

Lane, W. L. "Paul's Legacy from Pharisaism: Light from the Psalms of Solomon." *Concordia Journal* 8 (1982) 130–38.

Lattke, Michael. "Psalms of Solomon." In *Dictionary of New Testament Background*, edited by Craig A. Evans and Stanley E. Porter, 854. Downers Grove, Ill.: InterVarsity, 2000.

———. "Titel, Überschriften und Unterschriften der sogenannt-en Oden und Psalmen Salomos." In *For the Children Perfect Instruction: Studies in Honor of Hans-Martin Schenke on the Occasion of the Berliner Arbeitskreis für koptisch-gnostische Schriften's Thirtieth Year*, edited by Hans-Gebhard Bethge et al., 439–47. Nag Hammadi and Manichaean Studies 54. Leiden: Brill, 2002.

Lindblom, Johannes. *Senjudiskt Fromhetslif enligt Salomos Psaltare*. Uppsala: Almqvist & Wiksell, 1909.

Mowinckel, Sigmund. "Psalms and Wisdom." In *Wisdom in Israel and in the Ancient Near East Presented to Professor Harold Henry Rowley*, edited by Martin Noth and D. Winton Thomas, 205–24. Vetus Testamentum Supplements 3. Leiden: Brill, 1955.

Nickelsburg, George W. E. "The Psalms of Solomon." In *Jewish Literature between the Bible and Mishnah: A Historical and Literary Introduction,* 2d ed. with CD-ROM, 238–47. Minneapolis: Fortress, 2005.

O'Dell, Jerry. "The Religious Background of the Psalms of Solomon (Re-evaluated in the Light of the Qumran Texts)." *Revue de Qumran* 3 (1961) 241–57.

Perles, Felix. *Zur Erklärung der Psalmen Salomos.* Berlin: Peiser, 1911.

Pokorny, Petr. "Concerning the Eighteenth Psalm of Solomon." *Krest'anska Revue* 42 (1975) 151–57. [Czech.]

Schröter, Jens. "Gerechtigkeit und Barmherzigkeit: Das Gottesbild der Psalmen Salomos in seinem Verhältnis zu Qumran und Paulus." *New Testament Studies* 44 (1998) 557–77.

Schüpphaus, Joachim. *Die Psalmen Salomos: ein Zeugnis Jerusalemer Theologie und Frömmigkeit in der Mitte des vorchristlichen Jahrhunderts.* Arbeiten zur Literatur und Geschichte des hellenistichen Judentums 7. Leiden: Brill, 1977.

Swete, Henry Barclay. *The Psalms of Solomon, with the Greek Fragments of the Book of Enoch.* Cambridge: Cambridge University Press, 1899.

Torijano, Pablo A. *Solomon the Esoteric King: From King to Magus, Development of a Tradition.* Journal for the Study of Judaism Supplements 73. Leiden: Brill, 2002.

Trafton, Joseph L. *The Syriac Version of the Psalms of Solomon: A Critical Evaluation.* Septuagint and Cognate Studies 11. Atlanta: Scholars, 1985.

———. "The Psalms of Solomon: New Light from the Syriac Version?" *Journal of Biblical Literature* 105 (1986) 227–37.

———. "Solomon, Psalms of." In *Anchor Bible Dictionary,* edited by David Noel Freedman, 6:115–17. New York: Doubleday, 1992.

———. "The Psalms of Solomon in Recent Research." *Journal for the Study of the Pseudepigrapha* 12 (1994) 3–19.

Tromp, Johannes. "The Sinners and the Lawless in Psalm of Solomon 17." *Novum Testamentum* 35 (1993) 344–61.

Vermes, Geza. "The Psalms of Solomon." In *The History of the*

Jewish People in the Age of Jesus Christ, edited by Emil Schürer, Geza Vermes, Fergus Millar, and Martin Goodman, 192–95. Edinburgh: T. & T. Clark, 1986.

Winter, P. "Psalms of Solomon." In *Interpreter's Dictionary of the Bible,* edited by George A. Buttrick, 3:958–60. Nashville: Abingdon, 1962.

Wright, Robert B. "The Psalms of Solomon, the Pharisees and the Essenes." In *1972 Proceedings: International Organization for Septuagint and Cognate Studies and the SBLPS,* edited by Robert A. Kraft, 136–54. Septuagint and Cognate Studies 2. Missoula, Mont.: Scholars, 1972.

TO THE

RIGHT REVEREND BROOKE FOSS WESTCOTT, D.D.,

LORD BISHOP OF DURHAM,

THE FIRST HONORARY FELLOW OF KING'S COLLEGE,
CAMBRIDGE,

THIS BOOK

IS DEDICATED BY

TWO FRIENDS

MEMBERS OF THE SAME SOCIETY.

PREFACE.

THE *raison d'être* of this book is to be sought for partly in the fact that the Psalms of Solomon recently formed one of the subjects selected for the Theological Tripos by the Special Board of Theological Studies in the University of Cambridge, and partly in the fact that existing editions and commentaries were in many respects unsatisfactory, and difficult of access. It is hoped that the present edition will meet the needs of English students, at all events until the publication of the long-promised work of Dr Oscar von Gebhardt.

To the Syndics of the University Press we would express our sincere thanks for the publication of our book. We wish it were more worthy of the privilege thus accorded to it.

In respect of our other obligations, we have great pleasure in calling the attention of our readers to the help we have received from Dr Chr. Bruun, Librarian of the Royal Library at Copenhagen, from the Archimandrite Wladimir, of Moscow, and from M. l'Abbé Pierre Batiffol, of Paris. Our obligations to previous writers upon the Psalms of Solomon we have endeavoured to express in our Introduction.

The text of this edition is based on collations of three MSS. unknown to previous editors, together with a fresh collation of the two remaining authorities. Passages in which the LXX. version appears to have suggested words or phrases are printed in uncial type.

The translation aims at being literal.

The notes are intended to be useful to students of a not very advanced type. We venture to hope that the Indices will be found serviceable. The somewhat full Table of Contents is intended to obviate the necessity of an *Index Rerum*.

A joint Editorship, while productive of most real pleasure, is yet peculiarly favourable to the survival of errors of the press. For such of these as remain uncorrected in the present work we would apologise to our readers.

H. E. RYLE.
M. R. JAMES.

KING'S COLLEGE, CAMBRIDGE,
    March, 1891.

CONTENTS.

INTRODUCTION. § i. *Editions*. . . . . . . page xiii
    Cerda. Fabricius. Whiston. German version. French version. Akibon. Hilgenfeld's first and second editions. Geiger. Fritzsche. Hilgenfeld's last edition. Schmidt's conjectures. Wellhausen. Pick. Gebhardt's proposed edition. Writers who have treated of the Psalms. Nieremberg. Ferrandus. Janenski. Huet. Ernest Bengel. Movers (Kaulen). Ewald. Stanley. Grimm. Hitzig. A. Geiger. Langen. Delitzsch. Keim. Dillmann. Carriére. Vernes. Grätz. Drummond. Stanton. Schürer. Edersheim. Holtzmann. Girbal.

§ ii. *History of the book* xxi
    Early mentions of it. Stichometries. Pseudo-Athanasius. Nicephorus. The 'Sixty Books.' The Codex Alexandrinus. Council of Laodicea. Zonaras and Balsamon. The 'Pistis Sophia.' Ambrose. Lactantius. Vigilantius. The supplementary odes. Their probable origin and length. Versions of the Psalms in other languages.

§ iii. *The MSS.* xxvii
    The Augsburg MS. (A). Its history. The Vienna MS. Its contents and history. The Copenhagen MS. (K). Description. History. Contents. The Moscow MS. (M). Description by the Archimandrite Wladimir. The Paris MS. (P). Contents. Relation of the MSS. to each other. Readings peculiar to A. Probable errors of Cerda. Readings peculiar to V, K, P, M. Readings in which any two MSS. agree. Provisional pedigree. Possible identity of AV. Table of the Titles. Error in numeration of the Psalms. Close resemblance of all the MSS. to each other. Similarity of P to M. Provenance.

CONTENTS.

§ iv.   *Date and Authorship of the Psalms* . . . page xxxvii

    Historical position described in the Psalms. The foreign invader. Conjectured to be Titus, Antiochus Epiphanes, Herod the Great. The true solution; Pompey. Objections. Allusions to drought and famine. Date of the Psalms. Extreme limits of date.

§ v.   *Jewish Parties: and the Religious Thought of the Psalms of Solomon* xliv

    The title 'Psalms of the Pharisees.' The origin of the Pharisaic party. The Asmonean princes. The Sadducees. Identification of these with the party attacked by the Psalmist, as usurpers, unclean, indulging in foreign vices, oppressive. Attitude of the Psalmist characteristic of a Pharisee. Theocratic idea. The Law. Providence and Free Will. Retribution. Eternal life. Doom of the wicked. Angels. The Messiah.

§ vi.   *The Idea of the Messiah in the Psalms of Solomon*   lii

    Main outline. The time of Messiah's coming. His origin. Mission. Character of his rule. Distinctive characteristics. The title of Christ. Davidic descent. Subordination to God. King and priest. No Divine element. Resemblance to Solomon. Traits drawn from O. T. Special significance of this representation of the Messiah (a) in the history of the doctrine. Daniel. Enoch. Sibylline Oracles. (β) Significance in the history of the people.

§ vii.   *Place of writing, Authorship, Purpose, Style, Title of the Psalms of Solomon* lviii

    Place of writing, Jerusalem. Author a Pharisee, perhaps a priest. Purpose mainly polemical, perhaps liturgical. Style simple: resemblance to the 'Songs' in St Luke. Title pseudonymous; reasons for the choice.

§ viii.   *The Psalms of Solomon and Jewish Literature* . . lxii

    Relation to Psalmic Literature. Allusions to O. T. history. Relation to Ecclesiasticus. To Sib. Orac. iii. To the Book of Enoch. To the Parables of Enoch. To the Book of Jubilees. To the N. T. To IV. Esdras. To V. Esdras. To the Apocalypse of Baruch. To the Assumption of Moses. To the Testaments of the Twelve Patriarchs. To the Pirqe Aboth. Relation of Ps. xi. to Baruch iv., v. examined in detail. Other resemblances to Baruch.

CONTENTS.

§ ix. *The Probability of a Hebrew original* . . . page lxxvii

Antecedent Probability. Passages explicable on the hypothesis of corruption in a Hebrew text. Possible instances of mistranslation, from erroneous pointing, and from confusion of consonants. Structure of the Greek. Confusion of tenses. Misuse of the Hebrew Imperfect. Duplicate renderings. Literal reproductions of Hebrew in respect of Substantives, Verbs, Prepositions, the Negative, etc. Hypothesis of Greek original. Relation of the Psalms to the Book of Wisdom.

§ x. *The character of the Greek Translation* lxxxvii

Instances of obscure phrases. Words only found in these Psalms. Noteworthy Substantives, Adjectives, Verbs, Adverbs. Use of Prepositions.

§ xi. *The Date of the Greek Translation* xc

Not later than A.D. 100. Absence of Christian touches. Phrases indicative of date. Resemblances to the 'Songs' in Luke i. ii.

Additional Note on Cod. V xcii

THE PSALMS OF SOLOMON. TEXT, TRANSLATION, AND NOTES   1

APPENDIX. THE ODES OF THE 'PISTIS SOPHIA' . . . 155

NOTE ON SYRIAC APOCRYPHAL PSALMS . . 161

INDICES. I. OF GREEK WORDS 163

II. OF PREPOSITIONS 173

III. OF PASSAGES IN THE LXX. VERSION . . 174

INTRODUCTION.

§ i. *Editions.*

THE eighteen Psalms contained in this book have already been edited in one form or another some ten times, and to each of these ten editions we propose to devote a few words.

The Editio Princeps appeared in 1626 at Lyons. Its editor was one John Louis de la Cerda, a Spaniard, of the Society of Jesus, born at Toledo cir. 1560, died at Madrid 1643. His magnum opus was a commentary on Virgil in three folio volumes. The work with which we are concerned is entitled 'Adversaria sacra, opus varium ac veluti fax ad lucem quam multorum locorum utriusque Instrumenti, Patrumque et Scriptorum quorumcunque: Christianae antiquitatis et sacrorum rituum pancarpia: politioris denique literaturae thesaurus multiplex. Accessit eodem autore Psalterii Salomonis ex Graeco MS. codice pervetusto Latina versio et ad Tertulliani librum de pallio commentarius auctior.' The Adversaria are 187 chapters devoted to the discussion and illustration of obscure words occurring in the Vulgate and Latin Fathers. Among Cerda's favourite authors are Tertullian and St Aldhelm.

By way of appendix to this he adds two tracts, one the Psalterium Salomonis, the other Tertullian de Pallio. The latter is presented in an amended text, and is furnished with critical notes. We are only concerned at present with the former.

It is entitled simply 'Psalterium Salomonis.' In a short note 'Ad Lectorem,' Cerda merely says that he received the Psalms from the Rev. Father Andreas Schott, and that they had been recently found 'in membranis antiquissimis Bibliothecae Augustanae.' These words taken by themselves leave it an open question whether Cerda actually had the MS. in his hands or only a copy of it. From some of Cerda's 'Scholia,' however, one would rather gather that he had the MS. before him; see e.g. on ii. 4, iv. 19 ('obscure in meo Graeco Codice'), 21,

v. 16 ('in Codice quem vidi'); vii. 9 ('vix permittit Graecum legi') etc. Fabricius, however (p. 973), says that Cerda 'apographum se accepisse profitetur' from Schott. On the further history of the MS. see section iii., p. xxvii.

On the merits of Cerda's edition it may be well to say something. His MS. was either in a damaged condition or had been defectively copied for him, and his conjectures are not often convincing. In some few passages his Greek text gives one reading and his Latin version adopts another, because, probably, he had imperfectly revised the former. His view of the book is this:—that if not the work of Solomon, the great objection to such a view being the silence of ages concerning the document, it is at any rate the production of a man well learned in the Scriptures. He rejects the idea that it is a forgery, or that the author was a real Solomon, distinct from the king. His explanation of what he considers it to be is not easy to understand, 'quia induceret illum (Solomonem) loquentem et psallentem, ac parens David fortasse etiam accederet ut ipse auctor diceretur Solomon, nisi id fecisset Nepos episcopus,' etc. Elsewhere he speaks of himself as kindly inclined to the hypothesis of genuine Solomonic origin.

His notes are not very suggestive; he quotes from the classics a good deal, and interprets allusions occasionally. Psalm ii. is referred to a king of Babylon. He designedly assimilates his Latin version to the language of the Vulgate, which he has evidently studied with great care.

The Psalms appeared next in the *Codex Pseudepigraphus Veteris Testamenti* of Jo. Alb. Fabricius, Hamburg and Leipsic, 1713, pp. 914—999. Fabricius, whose services to Apocryphal literature can hardly be over-estimated, gives us here merely a reprint of Cerda's text version and scholia, prefixing an extract from Huet (*Demonstr. Evang.* IV. p. 397), and adding a few notes of his own. Some errors of the press are to be found in his reprint; his conjectures, which are few in number, can only be sustained, it seems to us, in two cases (iv. 2 $\sigma\eta\mu\epsilon\iota\omega\sigma\epsilon\iota$ and xviii. 4 υἱούς). The rest may be seen in our Apparatus Criticus.

The next two appearances of our Psalter were in translations. The first is Whiston's, which is to be found in that curious person's *Authentick Records*, Vol. I. p. 117—161. (London, 1727.)

We have here a version made, it seems, more on the authority of Cerda's Latin than on that of the original Greek. Its value is, as nearly as possible, nothing. But Whiston's theory of the authorship of the Psalms is so eccentric as to deserve mention. He regards them as the work of a certain Solomon, distinct from the king of Israel, of whom he finds mention made in 4 Esdr. x. 46, 'and after thirty years Solomon built the city and offered sacrifices' [thirty being here a misreading for three thousand]. Solomon, then, was an otherwise unknown leader who lived during the period of the Persian Captivity, in the days of Artaxerxes Mnemon.

The one service which Whiston has rendered seems to be that of introducing our book to English readers: but we cannot find that his work had much effect. He is also the first (and only) editor who calls attention to the passage from Lactantius (see p. xxiii.).

Geiger (p. 6) cites Fabr. *Bibl. Gr.* xiv. p. 162, as mentioning a German translation of these Psalms which appeared in 1716 at Leipzig.

Here may be also mentioned the French version inserted in Migne's *Dict. des Apocryphes*, Vol. I. col. 939—956 (1856). Nothing but a short prefatory note accompanies the translation, which is not particularly faithful.

Dr Akibon (mentioned by Geiger, p. 6) produced a German version in 1857.

All these editors had only Cerda's text to go upon. We now come to a series of editions which aim at presenting an emended text.

First come the two editions of Hilgenfeld, which are practically identical. The first appeared in his *Zeitschrift für Wissenschaftliche Theologie* xi. pp. 133—168 and 356. The second in his *Messias Judaeorum*, Leipzig, 1869, pp. xi.—xviii., 1—33.

His text is based on Cerda, and on Jos. Haupt's collation of the Vienna MS. He introduces also a good many emendations of his own, and some of Dr Paul de Lagarde's. Many of his own conjectures are ingenious, many very wild; all will be found in our Apparatus Criticus, but not many have been adopted into our text. Those by Lagarde are nearly always interesting, some, e.g. $\dot{\epsilon}\pi\epsilon\nu\kappa\tau\dot{\eta}$ viii. 18, seem to us undoubtedly right. This great scholar is, it may be incidentally mentioned, a believer in a Hebrew original of the Psalms (Hilg. on ii. 23).

Hilgenfeld's views may be shortly summarized here. He places the date shortly after Pompey's death in 48 B.C., and regards the book as an original Greek composition. The writer, he thinks, made use of the Wisdom of Solomon and the 3rd Book of the Sibylline Oracles. The writer of 4 Esdras, on the other hand, made use of the Psalms. Lastly, Hilgenfeld believes them to have been written in Egypt.

The next edition is that of Father Edward Ephraem Geiger, of the Convent of St Stephen at Augsburg. This book appeared in 1871 at Augsburg. It is an octavo of 168 pages, *Der Psalter Salomo's herausgegeben und erklärt*, etc. (Prolegomena, pp. 1—25. Text and German translation, pp. 28—79. Critical notes, pp. 80—94. Commentary, pp. 95—166.) His text is based on the same materials as Hilgenfeld's, but he does not adopt many of H.'s conjectures. He devotes much of his Introduction and Notes to the consideration of the Hebrew original, in which he is a firm believer. His general view of the date and situation agrees with that of Hilgenfeld and others: on certain questions, such as the relation of Ps. xi. to Baruch, he says little or nothing. On the whole, his book is a valuable and instructive one, and considerable use has been made of it in this edition.

Fritzsche, in his *Libri V. T. Pseudepigraphi selecti* (1871) has presented our book in a most convenient and accessible form (pp. 1—21). We have here a Greek text simply, with a short prefatory note. The editor is conscious of Hilgenfeld, but apparently not of Geiger. He uses no more MSS. than his predecessors. His collation of Cerda is not complete; the conjectures which he adds are not as a rule successful in our judgment, and he often prefers patent error in Hilgenfeld's company to possible correctness along with the MSS.

The last edition produced by Hilgenfeld calls for some remark. It is in the form of a translation with critical notes, and is to be found in Hilgenfeld's *Zeitschrift für Wissenschaftliche Theologie* for 1871, pp. 383—418. The immediate occasion for it was the appearance of Geiger's edition, and his strong advocacy of the Hebrew original of the Psalms. Hilgenfeld, disbelieving in this Hebrew original, takes occasion to review Geiger's arguments in critical notes attached to each Psalm. There is, further, a second set of critical notes, in which Geiger's readings are reviewed, and new conjectures of Hilgenfeld or of other scholars are added. This second set of notes is, in our opinion, the most important part of this edition, and the best of the new conjectures are by Maur. Schmidt; Hilgenfeld gives us no reference to any article or publication in which these conjectures may have been advanced, so that we are left to conclude that they were communicated privately to the editor. These conjectures are three in number:

i. 2.   εἶπα Ἀκούσεται.
xvi. 2.   ναρκᾶν.
xvii. 38.   ἐλέγξει for ἐλεήσει.

All these are remarkable, and it is much to be wished that Mr Schmidt should have occupied more time in elucidating the text of our book.

The new conjectures advanced by Hilgenfeld himself cannot be

INTRODUCTION. xvii

said to add much to the value of the work. The best is perhaps ἐπὶ ὁρίων ii. 30, for ἐπὶ ὁρέων. Others, not so good, are

iv. 15. ἐντατῇ for ἐν ταύτῃ.
viii. 9. ἐν παρορισμῷ for ἐν παροργισμῷ.
xii. 3. παροινία...φλογὶ ζήλους for παροικία...φλογιζούσης.
xvi. 8. ὑποκαιομένου for ὑποκειμένου.
xvii. 14. ζήλους for κάλλους.   37. ἀσπίδας for ἐλπίδας.

One passage is puzzling, viz. iv. 11 ἀλλήλων. Hilgenfeld's note here is 'ἀγγίλων ändere ich in ἀγγέλων (vgl. 2 Kön. (Sam.) 14, 20).' We have been unable so far to find any trace of a reading ἀγγίλων in either MSS. or editions, nor are we able to suggest what meaning could attach to it if it existed. On the other hand the alteration into ἀγγέλων is an extremely obvious but also a very important one, and is adopted by Wellhausen. It would therefore be very desirable to know the precise history of the reading.

Lastly in his *Zeitschrift* for 1876, pp. 140—2, Hilgenfeld reviews Wellhausen's translation of the Psalms with the approval it deserves, and takes occasion to defend once more his theory of the Greek original. None of the arguments he adduces in this article seem quite worth repeating.

The translation and notes which Wellhausen has given as an appendix to his book *Die Pharisäer und Sadducäer*, 1874, Greifswald, form by far the most important contribution to the study of this book which recent years have supplied. Some of Wellhausen's conjectures are exceedingly felicitous; all will be noticed in their proper places. But the great feature of his work is the view which he gives of the historical and religious position of the writer of the Psalms.

He speaks of having made a Hebrew version of the book, but we gather from Professor Robertson Smith, who was kind enough to communicate with him on the subject, that he has not committed it to writing.

The most recent edition of the Psalms is that by the Rev. Bernhard Pick, Ph.D., of Alleghany, Penn., which appeared in the *Presbyterian Review* for October, 1883, pp. 775—813. The form of this edition is extremely convenient; we first have a short Introduction (taken largely from Hilgenfeld, Geiger and Wellhausen) and a Bibliography taken chiefly from Schürer. Then from pp. 785—812 we have the text and English translation of the Psalms in parallel columns. The Apparatus Criticus and text of course depend on the work of previous editors, though the former is by no means complete, and no conjectures are advanced on Dr Pick's own responsibility. But the weak point of the

b 2

whole is the translation, and the defects of this seem to emanate partly from an imperfect knowledge of English, and partly from the fact that he sometimes prints one text and translates another. A few instances will serve to show this:

i. 4. διέλθοι εἰς filled.
ii. 2. κατεπάτουν. They have walked up and down in it.   6. ἐν ἐπισήμῳ ἐν in the sight of.   7. ὅτι ἐγκατέλιπεν. That He left them.   13. ἀντὶ πορνῶν. Because of the prostitutes.   15, 6. For all these things my heart mourns.   26. They will bring this to an end.   28. ἐν ἁρπάγματι like furies.   35. κοιμίζων stilling.
iii. 6. He looks out, where will come etc.
iv. 2. surpassing in words, surpassing in indolence all. ? insolence.   11. ἀλλήλων of others.   13. succeeded to scatter.
v. 3. After having called to Thee.   6. against thy discrimination. παρὰ τὸ κρίμα σου.   7. wilst (ix. 19).   9. we shall not cease.
viii. 1. ἠχούσης, calling to.   2. great pillar of fire.   7. fut. in txt, pres. in trans.   13. away from all kinds of impurity.   15. ἐπέρασεν sent upon them.   16. the Hardstricker.   36. μὴ ὄντος λυτρουμένου, irretrievably.
ix. 6. τῶν ὁσίων σου. Thy pious.
xi. 8. ἐλάλησεν ἀγαθόν, has promised salvation.
xii. 4. συγχέαι, to bring together.
xiv. 4. Who loved the day in the participation of their sins.
xv. 7. every substance of sinners.   6. as a persecuting hunger.   15. ἐλεηθήσονται, shall be pitied.
xvi. 1. I almost fell into a stupefaction.   8. nor of any who is controlled by unprofitable sin.
xvii. 16. As the heathen do for their idols.   32. He will exalt the Lord exceedingly in all the earth.
xviii. a gift beyond price.
etc. etc.

We cannot, in the face of this, affirm that Dr Pick has contributed much that is valuable to the study of these Psalms, though he has undoubtedly done a good work in bringing them before the notice of a fresh circle of students in a convenient and accessible form.

Had Dr Oscar von Gebhardt given his promised edition to the world, there would probably have been neither room nor demand for ours. But it may well be the case that English students will be glad to have an edition in their own language, which shall unite as far as possible all the results of criticism on the important document before us. No doubt Dr von Gebhardt will have many valuable solutions of critical and historical problems to offer: we heartily hope that he may be more successful than we have been in dealing with some of them.

We must now attempt to enumerate the principal notices of the Solomonic Psalms other than separate editions.

The first writer after Cerda who says anything much about them is, we believe, John Eusebius Nieremberg, S. J. In his work *De origine S. Scripturae*, Libri xii. fol. Lyons, 1641, et al. he devotes some space to a notice of our book; lib. IX. c. 37 (pp. 337—342). He prints Pss. i. and xviii. in Greek and Latin, and Ps. xvii. 23—51 in Latin only. He also gives a list of the headings. He decides against the Solomonic authorship, alleging, exempli gratia, two points from the Psalms he selects. (i) The mention of 'persecution' in Ps. i.; (ii) the χριστὸς κύριος in Ps. xviii.; and he adds the mention of a battering-ram in Ps. ii. 1, and the fact that no father alludes to the book at all.

Of the two next authorities we have not been able to furnish any account from personal inspection. They are (1) Lud. Ferrandus, who makes some mention of the Psalms of Solomon in his commentary on the Psalter, Paris 1683, and (2) G. Janenski, who wrote a special dissertation *de Psalterio Solomonis*, published under the auspices of J. G. Neumann, Wittenberg, 1687.

Huet (Pet. Dan.), Bp of Avranches, the well-known critic, has a notice of our book in his *Demonstratio Evangelica*, IV. p. 397, which Fabricius quotes. He attributes it to a Hellenist familiar with the LXX., living not long after our Lord; and he doubts whether any imposture was intended.

Probably other notices might be found in the works of eighteenth century scholars, but the next whom we are able to cite is Ernest Bengel, who, in his posthumous *Opuscula Academica*, Hamburg, 1834, examines the views of our writer on (1) the future life, p. 178, (2) the Messianic hope, p. 394. He gathers from Pss. ii. and xi. that the date of composition was posterior to the destruction of Jerusalem, and mentions a theory of Bretschneider's that the Psalms, originally written in Hebrew after the Exile, were rendered into Greek after A.D. 70.

An article by Movers in Herder's *Kirchenlexicon*, 1847, s.v. *Apokryphen* (revised by Kaulen for the recent edition by Wetzer and Welt), marks an epoch in the history of the criticism of our book. Movers is the first to assign the period of Pompey's invasion as the date of it, and, further, he believes in the Hebrew original. He speaks of the book as a pearl among Apocryphal documents.

Ewald in his *History of Israel* (followed by Stanley, *Jewish Church*, IV. 303), assigns the book to the time of Antiochus Epiphanes. Elsewhere he suggests the probability that some of the Psalms, e.g. i. and ii., are wrongly separated, and offers at least one conjecture on the text (xvii. 13).

Grimm (C. L. W.), in his *Erste Buch der Maccabäer*, p. xxvii., agrees in this view of the date, and mentions with favour the idea of a Hebrew original.

Hitzig, *Gesch. d. Volkes Israel*, p. 502, attributes the book to a Sadducaean author. Among his reasons for adopting this singular position are these, (1) that the description of the menpleasers in Ps. iv. resembles that of the Pharisees in the Gospels, (2) that the doctrine of freewill expressed in Ps. ix. 7 is Sadducaean, (3) that the Davidic Messiah of Ps. xvii. owes his revival to the existence of the Asmonean house.

Geiger (Abr.) in the *Jüd. Zeitschr. f. Wissensch. u. Leben*, VI. fasc. iii. 240, 1868, quoted by Hilgenfeld, calls the book a colourless production of the controversy between Pharisees and Sadducees—colourless, in the sense that it is difficult to date precisely.

Langen, *Jüdenthum im Zeit Christi*, p. 64, devotes some space to enunciating views which are practically those of Movers, and opposes Ewald's position.

Delitzsch, on the Psalter, II. 381, and Keim, *Jesu v. Nazara*, I. 243, name the reign of Herod the Great, or the time of his accession, as the probable date.

Dillmann, in Herzog's *Realencyklopädie*, s.v. *Pseudepigraphen d. A. T.*, has a notice on the subject. Since the publication of the first edition this critic has altered his views. At that time he supported Ewald's theory of the date. In the more recent editions he adopts Wellhausen's results. Oehler in the same work, s.v. *Messias*, has a short notice.

Carriére (Aug.) has written a special dissertation in Latin, Strasburg, 1870. We have not been able to see a copy of it.

Vernes (Maurice) in his *Histoire des Idées Messianiques*, 1874, 121—139, discusses the book at length with reference to his main subject, the doctrine of the Messiah. We are indebted to him for some few references.

Grätz, *Gesch. d. Jud.*, III. 489, assigned the Psalms to a Christian author, on the very slightest grounds. In the latest editions the statement is omitted.

Drummond, *The Messiah*, 1877, 133—142. This book gives a useful summary of previous criticisms, and a statement of the author's own view, which agrees for the most part with that of Movers, etc.

Stanton (Professor V. H.), *The Jewish and Christian Messiah*, Cambridge, 1884, has a short notice: he does not attempt to determine the date of the Greek version.

Schürer, *Palestine in the time of our Lord*, Eng. Trans., III. 17, gives

INTRODUCTION. xxi

by far the best and fullest account that has yet appeared of the book, its MSS. and editions. He gives a list of references to authors who have written on the subject: of these, most have been noticed in the preceding pages; a few remain whom we have not been able to consult.

Dr Edersheim (*Life and Times of Jesus the Messiah*, I. p. 79, 146) gives an appreciation of the book, and contributes a suggestion that the successive Psalms should be read in connection with the correspondingly numbered Psalms in the Davidic Psalter.

Holtzmann (Oscar), (*Gesch. d. Volkes Israels*) in part 153 of the Berlin *Allgemeine Geschichte*, edited by W. Oncken, pp. 448—56, gives an excellent résumé of the character and contents of the Psalms. He adopts the standpoint of Wellhausen, and quotes copiously from his translation.

A Montauban programme by M. Jules Girbal (Toulouse, 1887) seems intended to prepare the way for a new French edition of these Psalms, but offers little that is new towards the understanding of them.

§ ii. *History of the book.*

The history of the Psalms before us, so far as it is to be gathered from early criticisms, 'testimonies,' or quotations, is very short and scanty indeed. Of passages where direct and undoubted mention is made of the collection, we have but six in all, and four of these are mere lists of books, while the two others form practically but a single one, for they are couched in identical words. Of passages where the reference is doubtful, or only by implication, we have three. It will be as well, we think, to put together these passages at once, and see what information we may fairly deduce from them. We will divide them into two classes, those whose reference is clear and unmistakable being placed in the first, those of less certain import in the second.

First come three well-known catalogues of Canonical and Uncanonical books, that called by the name of Athanasius (Synopsis S. Scripturae), that of Nicephorus (A.D. 806—814), and that which may be conveniently cited as the list of the Sixty Books.

Credner (*Zur Geschichte des Kanons*) investigates the relations of these first two lists. He concludes that the one attributed to Nicephorus is really the earlier, and originated in Syria in 500 A.D., and that the Athanasian one, whatever its date, is an abridged form of this (omitting the στίχοι), and is of Alexandrine origin.

Schürer, Vol. III., p. 123, also gives the text of the lists, and a similar estimate of their relations one to another. With reference to the 3rd, he adds that it is for the most part a rearrangement of that of Nicephorus. Each has one item peculiar to itself.

Credner's conclusions are traversed by Zahn, with his usual ability (*Gesch. d. Neutest. Kanons* II. i. p. 295, etc.). According to him, Nicephorus's list is a document reduced to its present form at Jerusalem cir. 850, while the *Synopsis* was compiled in the sixth century.

(1) 'Athanasius' (T. II., p. 154 of the Paduan edition) in § 74 of the Synopsis, following on an analysis of the Apocalypse, gives a list which is the prototype of that of Nicephorus.

He enumerates (for the second time) certain ἀντιλεγόμενα of the O. T., viz. Wisdom, Ecclesiasticus, Esther, Judith and Tobit, and adds σὺν ἐκείνοις δὲ καὶ ταῦτα ἠριθμήνται.

Μακκαβαϊκὰ βιβλία δ'.
Πτολεμαϊκά.
ψαλμοὶ καὶ ᾠδὴ Σολομῶντος. (Fabricius and others read ᾠδαί.)
Σωσάννα.

(2) Nicephorus (Patriarch of Constantinople A.D. 806—814) rearranges this list, and adds the number of στίχοι to each item. He also omits one, the Πτολεμαϊκά (which, as Credner suggests, perhaps = 3 Macc. Zahn would read πολεμικά, and connect the word with Μακκαβαϊκά).

The entry in his Stichometry is as follows (v. Westcott *On the Canon of the N. T.*, no. XIX., App.):

καὶ ὅσαι ἀντιλέγονται τῆς παλαιᾶς αὗται εἰσίν.
1. 3 books of Maccabees.
2. Wisdom of Solomon. (Here one MS. inserts no. 4.)
3. Ecclesiasticus.
4. ψαλμοὶ καὶ ᾠδαὶ (v. l. -ή) Σολομῶντος, στίχοι ͵βρ'. (2100).
5. Esther.
6. Judith.   7. Susanna.   8. Tobit.

(3) The list of the 'Sixty Books,' which is found appended to Anastasius Sinaita's *Quaestiones et Responsiones*, has been often printed; from a Royal MS. at Paris by Cotelier, *Patr. Apost.* I. p. 196, from a Coislin MS. by Montfaucon, *Bibl. Coisl.*, p. 194, from the Baroccian MS. no. 206 in Hody *de Bibliorum Textibus*, and Westcott *On the Canon of the N. T.* App. no. XVII., from a Vatican MS. by Pitra *Juris Eccl. hist. et mon.* I. 100, and lastly by Zahn, l. c. p. 289. It contains an appendix to the canonical books in two sections. (1) ὅσα ἔξω τῶν ξ', which consists of nine Deuterocanonical books. (2) ὅσα ἀπόκρυφα, twenty-five pseudepigrapha of Old and New Testament arranged in an order partly corresponding to the dates of the supposed authors.

INTRODUCTION. xxiii

No. 8 is Ἀνάληψις Μωϋσέως. No. 9 is Ψαλμοὶ Σολομῶντος. No. 10, Ἡλίου ἀποκάλυψις. This list is closely related to that of Nicephorus.

(4) Next in order comes the well-known catalogue of the contents of the Alexandrine MS. Here our book appears in the following connection:

ἀποκάλυψις Ἰωάννου
Κλήμεντος ἐπιστολὴ αʹ
Κλήμεντος ἐπιστολὴ βʹ
ὁμοῦ βιβλία (number illegible)
Ψαλμοὶ Σολομῶντος ιηʹ.

We may note here that it seems possible that the Sinaitic MS (ℵ) originally contained our book on six leaves now lost at the end. Such is Mr Rendel Harris's conjecture.

(5) The LIXth canon of the Council of Laodicea (c. 360 A.D.) provides ὅτι οὐ δεῖ ἰδιωτικοὺς ψαλμοὺς λέγεσθαι ἐν τῇ ἐκκλησίᾳ, οὐδὲ ἀκανόνιστα βιβλία, ἀλλὰ μόνα τὰ κανονικὰ τῆς παλαιᾶς καὶ καινῆς διαθήκης. On this Joannes Zonaras (in 1118) and Theodorus Balsamon (about 70 years later) have the following note (see Beveridge's *Synodicum*, I. p. 480), quoted by Fabricius and others; ἐκτὸς μὲν τῶν ρνʹ ψαλμῶν τοῦ Δαβὶδ εὑρίσκονται καί τινες ἕτεροι λεγόμενοι τοῦ Σολομῶντος εἶναι καὶ ἄλλων τινῶν, οὓς καὶ ἰδιωτικοὺς ὠνόμασαν οἱ πατέρες καὶ μὴ λέγεσθαι ἐν τῇ ἐκκλησίᾳ διετάξαντο. Balsamon merely copies Zonaras, as is his wont.

These are all the undoubted references to our book which the united industry of previous editors has been able to collect, and we are unable to add anything to them.

(6) The *second* class of references is headed by the evidence of the book 'Pistis Sophia' (composed in Greek in Egypt during the period 200—250 A.D., and extant in the Thebaic dialect). This evidence must be examined in detail later on; at present it may suffice to say that ᾠδαί of Solomon are mentioned in four places, and in one passage (p. 75 of the Latin, 116 of the Thebaic) a nineteenth ode of Solomon is cited.

(7) Ambrose, *Praef. in Lib. Psalmorum* (quoted by Geiger), 'seems to show a consciousness of uncanonical poems attributed to Solomon,' where he says, 'Salomo ipse David filius licet innumera cantica cecinisse dicatur, unum tamen *quod ecclesia receperit* canticorum canticum dereliquit.'

(8) Lactantius, *Div. Inst.* IV. 12, *Epit. Div. Inst.* c. xliv., has the following passage: 'Salomon ita dicit; Infirmatus est uterus Virginis,

et accepit foetum, et gravata est, et facta est in multa miseratione mater Virgo.' In the Epitome the same words occur thus introduced, 'Apud Salomonem ita scriptum est.' So the passage runs in the ordinary text, but several MSS. add the source of the citation. In the Paris edition (Le Brun and Du Fresnoy) of 1748 we find the following note, 'Inter caeteros alii addunt *in Ode undevigesima;* alii *in Psalmo undevigesimo:* duo *in Psalmo vigesimo.*' Whether these words should stand in the text or not, they are all-important for our purpose. The fluctuation between *Psalmus* and *Ode* seems to point to the fact that different scribes added the reference from their own knowledge of the source quoted, and by consequence, to show that the words are a gloss. As to the conclusions to be drawn from the whole passage, they will be best reserved till a later period. Whiston (*Auth. Rec.* I. 155) is the first and only editor who called attention to this passage.

(9) That Vigilantius, the adversary of Jerome, who made use of the 4th Book of Esdras, made use likewise of an Apocryph under the name of Solomon seems certain from the following words of Jerome *adv. Vigilant.* (quoted by Geiger): 'in commentariolo tuo quasi pro te faciens de Salomone sumis testimonium quod Salomon omnino non scripsit, ut qui habes alterum Esdram habeas et Salomonem alterum.'

That this 'second Solomon' is to be identified with the book used by Lactantius is at any rate not unlikely. More than this it would hardly be safe to say.

These are all the Patristic references, certain or supposed, to the Psalms of Solomon; what may fairly be adduced from them?

Generally, we may gather that the book attained only a very limited circulation. This is a necessary conclusion from the paucity of Patristic references. On the other hand, where it was read, it seems to have been read with respect. It is the solitary instance of an Old Testament book, which from being merely ἀντιλεγόμενον became ἀπόκρυφον. It is the one book which the scribe of A thought fit to add to the Canon. It is not, we think, possible to draw any instructive conclusion as to the Churches which received it most freely. Our evidence is fairly well scattered: one authority is Egyptian (perhaps two), one Syrian, three Latin, one Byzantine. But if Zonaras is right in his guess that the council of Laodicea had the Psalms of Solomon in their minds when they forbad the use of ἰδιωτικοὶ ψαλμοί in church, we should gain a striking proof of their popularity in Asia in the IVth century. We believe, however, that Zonaras only instances our book because it was the one uncanonical collection of Psalms known to him.

Going more into detail, we gather that the book was existing about

A.D. 500 in two forms. There was, first, the collection now extant, the eighteen 'Psalms of Solomon.' There was also, however, an Appendix to this collection of ᾠδαὶ Σολομῶντος, almost equalling the first part in length, it may be. It is true that the latest editions of the lists of Ps.-Athanasius and Nicephorus read ψαλμοὶ καὶ ᾠδὴ Σ., but against this we have to set the earlier evidence of the Pistis Sophia, which uniformly speaks of the 'Odes of Solomon.' This appendix of Odes was, if not entirely Christian, at any rate interpolated with distinctively Christian matter. We hope to show, later on, that some of the Odes in the Pistis Sophia are, in fact, not necessarily Christian at all; but the passage which Lactantius quotes is unmistakable in its character. It is a curious coincidence that another fragment of the same Ode should be quoted in the Pistis Sophia: in that fragment the Christian element is not so apparent.

The Odes, whatever their origin, were most likely a later addition to the eighteen Psalms. Why were they added? Partly, no doubt, on the strength of the 1005 odes mentioned in the Book of Kings; but also, as we believe, because the original collection was obviously imperfect at the end. We venture to suggest that a possible history of the collection is the following. The original collection, of at least nineteen complete Psalms, and perhaps more, is circulated during the first century in Palestine. With the destruction of Jerusalem it narrowly escapes extinction, and is eventually propagated by the Christian community of Palestine, from an archetype of which the last leaf (or leaves) had disappeared. By way of restoring, or supplementing the gap, certain Odes are added, either Jewish ones already in circulation as detached pieces, or Christian ones composed for the purpose, and into the 2nd part Christian interpolations are introduced to an extent not now discoverable. However, copies of the original eighteen Psalms are still in circulation without the added Odes, and it is from these copies that our present text is derived. The scribe of A, and probably the author of the 3rd List of Books, was in possession of the shorter collection: Nicephorus, Lactantius, and the author of the Pistis Sophia, used the longer one. This is, of course, mere conjecture, and it may be urged that one feature in the particular is not probable, namely, the idea that the copies of the book had at one time all disappeared save one, and that a mutilated one. We should answer that it is most improbable that many copies of the Greek Version of this book were in existence before A.D. 70. The Psalms, according to most critics, were written in Hebrew for liturgical use. They probably would not be so used save in the near neighbourhood of Jerusalem, and in the city itself, and the majority of men who knew them at all would not require any Greek version of them. Hence the Greek copies would be few in number, and probably not dispersed over at all a wide area; for the Psalms are strongly Palestinian in character, and would not possess nearly the same amount of interest for a resident at Rome or Alexandria as for one living at or near the centre of political and religious life.

As to the length of the additions to the Psalms, we have only two facts to go upon. Nicephorus gives the length of Psalms and Odes together as 2100 στίχοι. The MSS. of the Psalms say that they contain 1000 ἔπη. It has been suggested by previous editors, that the ἔπος is much longer than the στίχος, and therefore that the 2100 στίχοι might be amply accounted for by the eighteen Psalms *plus* the five Odes. Any such hypothesis is, however, put out of court by the investigations of M. Ch. Graux (see his article in the *Revue de Philologie, &c.* n. s. II. 97), who has shown that στίχος and ἔπος are synonymous terms for a fixed quantity, and that the στίχος had an uniform length of 34 to 38 letters. According to him, the stichometry of our book is corrupt. The 18 Psalms contain nearly 24,000 letters; and this means that they would yield about 700 στίχοι. But though the number 1000, given by our MSS., may be wrong for our present text, it does not follow that it was necessarily wrong when the calculation was made. It may refer to a slightly longer recension than we possess—one, for example, in which the last Psalm existed in a complete form. Still less can we conclude that the stichometry of Nicephorus is incorrect in allotting 2100 στίχοι to the Psalms *and Odes* of Solomon. This much is clear; that the five Odes in the Pistis Sophia would not nearly make up the difference between 1000 and 2100 lines. Besides this, we must remember that there is nothing to show that the five Odes were all that existed under Solomon's name,—indeed, the evidence points in the other direction. We believe then that the added portion was quite twice as long as our present collection, and it is much to be wished that some further remains of it should be recovered. The number of στίχοι attributed to the whole by Nicephorus gives us a book of the same length as Joshua. The canonical Psalms, according to the same authority, contain 5100 στίχοι.

A word as to possible versions of our book in other languages than Greek. We cannot assume the existence of a Thebaic version from the evidence of the Pistis Sophia, for the whole of that book may be a translation from Greek. It will have been noticed, however, that three of the authorities quoted above are Latin writers, and, in particular, the reference supplied by the MSS. of Lactantius may very fairly be taken as

INTRODUCTION.

indicating that an old Latin version existed at one time. This is, on other accounts, probable enough : it seems likely from Priscillian's tracts, the Gelasian Decree and other lists, that very obscure apocryphal books were well known in the West. No one would have suspected the existence of a Latin Book of Jubilees or Assumption of Moses; yet the Milan palimpsest established their existence. We are not aware that a trace of any other version—Ethiopic, Syriac or Armenian—has ever been pointed out.

§ iii. *The MSS.*

There are at present four MSS. of the Psalms of Solomon known to exist, and of one, which is lost, we possess a printed edition. Two of these MSS. were first noticed by Dr Oscar von Gebhardt, and one by that excellent palaeographer, the late M. Charles Graux. The present edition is the first in which all five authorities have been used.

We proceed to describe the MSS.

1. A. Augustanus. This MS., from which the Psalms were first printed by J. L. de la Cerda, was in his time preserved in the Public Library at Augsburg. We first hear of it in a letter from Andreas Schott to Johannes Meursius written in 1615 (*Meursii opera, ed. J. Lamy*, XI. p. 249). Schott says: 'Hoeschelius Graece pollicetur editurum se Cyrilli Alexandrini adversus Julianum παραβάτην libros; nactum se quoque Salomonis exemplar vetustissimum Constantinopoli adlatum, in quo psalmi xviii Salomonis, hactenus ἀνέκδοτοι et invisi.' Cerda, in his prefatory note to the Psalms, does not tell us even so much as this about the MS. He says: 'Misit adhuc Reuerentissimus Pater Andreas Schottus Societatis nostrae hos Psalmos Salomonis recens in membranis antiquissimis Bibliothecae Augustanae repertos, Graece solum manu scriptos.' Fabricius says that Cerda professes only to have received a transcript of the MS., but the latter's notes led one to believe that Schott sent him the MS. itself (see p. xiii.). No one has ever seen it since, though Hilgenfeld and Geiger both made enquiries after it. From these extremely meagre accounts we gather that the MS. was a parchment one, of considerable age (the 'vetustissimus' can hardly be pressed), and that it contained some of the other Sapiential books (Schott speaks of it as 'Salomonis exemplar'): from Cerda's notes we gather further that it was difficult to read or damaged in some places; 'obscure scriptum ut legere nequirem' and similar expressions occur with some frequency.

If Cerda's reprint is to be trusted, the Augsburg MS. cannot be identified with any of those now known. But on this matter see below.

2. V. Vindobonensis. This MS., which was first used by Hilgenfeld for the text of the Psalms, is mentioned first by Petrus Lambecius in his *Commentarius de Bibl. Caes. Vindob.* III. p. 20; next by Nessel in his catalogue, p. 31. Fabricius (p. 973) notices its existence. Hilgenfeld obtained a collation and description of it from Jos. Haupt (*Mess. Jud.* p. xiii.).

It is numbered as Cod. Gr. Theol. 7 (11 in Nessel), a folio measuring $13\frac{1}{2}$ by $10\frac{1}{4}$ Vienna inches, of the xth century, written in double columns of 26 lines, $7\frac{1}{2}$ Vienna inches high, in one hand, written in semi-uncials. The ink has faded somewhat, *even* the rubricated titles and initials of the Psalms. The margins of the pages are prepared for Scholia.

The contents of the MS. are as follows:

Job,	with a catena	f. 1.
Proverbs	,, ,,	34.
Ecclesiastes	,, ,,	61.
Song of Solomon	,, ,,	77.
Wisdom, without a catena		86.
Ψαλμοὶ Σολομῶντος		105 b.
Ecclesiasticus		118—166.

Twenty-two leaves are lost between ff. 33—34. The MS. was bought by Augier de Busbecq at Constantinople cir. 1570. Lambecius, in a marginal note, mentions Cerda's work, and recommends the collation of this copy.

We depend on Hilgenfeld's edition for our knowledge of this MS.

[Since the above was written, we have obtained a full collation of V made by Dr Rudolf Beer, which shows that Haupt's was most inaccurate, and materially changes our estimate of the MS.]

3. K. Havniensis. This MS., now preserved in the Royal Library at Copenhagen, was first noticed by M. Charles Graux, who, in the *Revue Critique* for 1877, p. 291—3, in a review of Dr Chr. Bruun's *Aarsberetningen og Meddelelser fra det Store Kongelige Bibliothek*, Pt iii. 1877, describes the MS. briefly and gives a few specimens of its readings. He subsequently gave a fuller description in his *Notices sommaires des MSS. grecs de la Grande Bibliothèque Royale de Copenhague.* Paris, 1879, pp. 1—4. From these sources we gather the following facts.

The MS. is no. 6 of the old Royal collection. It was bought at Venice in 1699 by Frederick Rostgaard, along with most of the other Greek MSS. at Copenhagen. In 1726, Count Danneskjold bought his

INTRODUCTION. xxix

collection, and in 1732 most of it passed into the Royal Library. This volume consists of quires 11—39 of a xth century MS. in folio, written in double columns, with scholia, in a very beautiful hand. It contains:

- Job, with a catena.
- Proverbs, ⎫
- Ecclesiastes, ⎬ with Scholia.
- Song of Songs, ⎭
- Wisdom, ⎫
- Psalms of Solomon, ⎬ without Scholia.
- Ecclesiasticus. ⎭

At fol. 84 is a very fine full-page painting representing Solomon enthroned. A facsimile of this may be seen in M. Bruun's work referred to above. Graux also gives two pages of the Psalms in facsimile. The liberality of the authorities at Copenhagen permitted this precious volume to be sent to the Cambridge University Library in the summer of 1888, and here Professor Ryle collated it for the purposes of this edition. To Dr Bruun in particular, for his great services to us in this matter, we beg to offer a sincere expression of our gratitude.

4. M. Mosquensis. This MS. was discovered by Dr Oscar von Gebhardt in 1879. The discovery is announced in an article by Dr Harnack in the *Theologische Litteratur-Zeitung* for 1877, p. 627. No description of the MS. is there given.

We owe our knowledge of this MS. to the very great kindness of the Archimandrite Wladimir who holds the position of Συνοδικὸς Σκευοφύλαξ καὶ Χαρτοφύλαξ, to whom we desire hereby to render our warmest thanks. On being asked to furnish us with a collation of the MS. he at once sent a transcript of the entire text, made by himself, and a description of the MS. which we here subjoin. Such signal kindness as this deserves a better recognition than we can give.

Mosquensis Sanctissimae Synodi Bibliothecae Graecae Codex N 147, membranaceus, sec. xiii. fol. 225 (longitudo 13¾ digitos, latitudo 11 d.), duabus et tribus columnis paginae scriptae sunt, celere charactere. Tituli librorum et litterae initiales minio scripti sunt. Mosquam hic Codex translatus est ex monasterio Iberorum in Monte Atho, ab Arsenio Suchanow anno Christi 1653. Huic Codici in principio adscriptum Ἀρσενίῳ ΗΓ τῶν Ἰβήρων. Continet (1) fol. 3—82, Βίβλος τοῦ Ἰώβ; habet 33 capita cum catena variorum patrum: Chrysostomi, Dion. Areopagitae, Basilii Magni, Greg. Naz., Olympiodori, Theod. Mops., Polychronii, Didymi, Apolinarii, Origenis, Juliani, Theoph. Alex., et Cyrilli, Severi Antioch., Methodii, et Evagrii. Initium catenae,

Ἡ χώρα ἡ Αὐσίτις, χώρα ἦν τῷ Ἡσαῦ. Finis texti in f. 82, οἱ δὲ ἐλθόντες πρὸς αὐτὸν φίλοι, Ἐλιφὰζ τῶν Ἡσαῦ υἱῶν, Θαιμανῶν βασιλεὺς, Βαλδὰδ ὁ Σαυχαίων τύραννος. Σωφὰρ ὁ Μιναίων βασιλεύς. Ultimum scholium Evagrii, τοῦ Ἐλιφὰζ ἦν υἱὸς Σωφὰρ καὶ Ἀμαλήκ, etc. (2) f. 83—125, Παροιμίαι Σολομῶντος. Init. catenae, Εἰ καὶ κατὰ τὸ ῥητὸν τὸ εὐθὲς οἱ τῶν Παροιμιῶν ἀποσώζουσι λόγοι. Nomina commentatorum: Apol., Did., Dionys., Cyr., et Marcus. (3) f. 126—142, ἐκκλησιαστής cum scholiis anon. quorum init. Εἰ ἐκκλησιαστὴς ὁ λαλῶν, ἐκκλησίας ἄξια τὰ λεγόμενα. (4) f. 142—150 Ἄσμα ἀσμάτων. Nomen auctoris et init. scholii amplius legi nequit, atramentum enim expalluit. (5) f. 151—168 Σοφία Σολομῶντος sine scholiis. (6) hic in f. 168—179 leguntur xviii Psalmi et Odae qui [ab] aliis tribuuntur Salomoni, sine titulis, sine divisione in capita et carmina, et sine scholiis. (7) f. 179—225 Σοφία Ἰησοῦ υἱοῦ Σιράχ, sine scholiis. Init. prologi, Πολλῶν καὶ μεγάλων. In fol. 224 Προσευχὴ Ἰησοῦ υἱοῦ Σιράχ. Init. ἐξομολογήσομαί σοι, κ.τ.λ.

5. P. Parisiensis. This MS. was also first noticed by Dr O. v. Gebhardt, and the discovery announced in Dr Harnack's article referred to above. In the case of this MS. also we have to acknowledge a debt of gratitude to a scholar who has been kind enough to devote time and thought to furnishing us with a full collation of the text. The Rev. Pierre Batiffol, well known as the discoverer of Codex Φ (Beratinus), and as the editor of the Nicene Canons, and of Études Patristiques, etc., has most generously furnished us with a collation of the MS. in question: and it is with the greatest pleasure that we place on record this instance of his courtesy, and offer him our sincerest acknowledgments. In September of this year (1890) Mr James was able to make a brief inspection of the MS. and to glean a few additional particulars of it.

The MS. is no. 2991 A in the National Library at Paris. It is a paper book written in 1419 in 'petit format,' of 495 leaves. The contents are very miscellaneous, but fall for the most part into well-defined groups.

I.

a. First comes Isocratis oratio ad Demonicum .... f. 2
                 Oratorum nomina, etc. .... 11 *b*
                 Aesopi fabulae aliquot 12
b. Next two Byzantine tracts.
                 Mich. Attaliotae promptuarium juris, imperfect... 14
                 Georg. Codini de officiis aulae CP 65
c. Then Letters of Basil to Gregory Naz. 135
                 Letters of Libanius and Basil 143
d. Niceph. Gregoras. two 'monodiae' and some letters 154

e. Speeches and excerpts from Josephus, including the Hippolytean fragment περὶ τοῦ παντός..................173

II.

f. Wisdom of Solomon 195
Psalms of Solomon ....224 *b*
Ecclesiasticus 244
g. Physiognomic signs of character ....320 *b*
h. Prayer by Matthew of Philadelphia ....324 *b*
i. The Emperor Basil's exhortations to his son 334
Gymnosophistarum responsiones ....360 *b*
Secundus the Pythagorean, his answer to Hadrian ....363 *b*
On the 8 deadly sins 366
Dionysii Catonis sententiae ....366 *b*
vii sapientium apophthegmata ....371 *b*
k. A group of chronological lists 372–381
l. A Byzantine miscellany of letters and verses 381 *b*–427
m. An ethical miscellany 427 *b*–447

III.

n. Satires and letters of Mazaris and Manuel Holobolus 448–495

Groups *f* to *m* are all in one and the same hand: the colophon on *f* 446 *b* states that the book was written at the expense τοῦ πανευγενεστάτου κυροῦ Ματθαίου Παλαιολόγου τοῦ Λασκάρι.

These are all the MSS. known at present. That more may be discovered, even in European libraries, is by no means an impossibility.

We have now to investigate the relations of these authorities to one another. The most practical way of doing this will be to tabulate the readings peculiar to each. Two points—the numeration and titles of the Psalms,—we reserve for a subsequent period.

The following are the principal readings peculiar to A (excluding probable misprints in Cerda's book).

i. 8. ἁμαρτίαι for ἀνομίαι, very likely repeated by Cerda from the line before. On ii. 4 see notes.
iv. 4. om. οἱ.
v. 15. δετερώσῃ for δευτ., but ? misread.
vi. 5. σαλῶν for σάλων.
viii. 4. πόλει for πόλιν. 38. om. οὐκ.
ix. 2. ᾗ for ᾗς. 16. om. καὶ ἡμεῖς—οἴκτειρον.
xi. 9. om. ἐν ὀνόματι—'Ισραήλ.
xii. 4. om. χείλη—φοβουμένων.
xiii. 5. καταρροφὴ for καταστροφή, but probably Cerda read this wrong.

J. P.

xxxii   INTRODUCTION.

xv. 10. om. τῆs.   11. om. αὐτῶν.
xvii. 12. τὰ for οἷs.   31. ἔθνη καὶ λαοὺs for λ. κ. ἔ.   32. om. τὸν κύριον.
xviii. 5. ἀμαρθίαs for ἀμαθίαs, ? mistake of Cerda's.

Another class of peculiar readings we regard as most probably misreadings of Cerda's.

ii. 15. αὖθαι.
iii. 2. ψάλλατε for ψάλατε.
iv. 2. σημειῶσαι for -ώσει.   19. κεῖνοs (?) for κενόs. ἐμπλῆσαι for -ει.   21. ἀπολημρίων for ὑπὸ θηρίων.
v. 1. αἰνέτω for -οs.   11. χιλόηs for χλόηs.   16. φύσται for φείσεται.
vi. 9. εὐλογήτω for -όs.
viii. 13. ἐν φέδρῳ for ἀφέδρῳ.   16. κρατερῶs for -αιῶs.   40. ἀνετὸs for αἰνετόs.
ix. 6. καὶ οὐ for κ. ποῦ.   7. ἔρνα ἡμ. ἐν εὐλογῇ.   12. ὁμολογήσει for ἐξομ.
16. σοῦ...ἀποστήσειs for σοι...ἀποστήσῃs.
xi. 6. δρομοὶ for δρυμοί.
xiii. 1. ἐσπέσασε for ἐσκέπ. or ἐπήσπ.
xvii. 9. ἡριτῶν for ἡμῶν.   23. εἶδεs for οἶδεs or -αs.   27. ἀπελλῇ.
xviii. 12. κυρείᾳ for πορείᾳ.

There is a 3rd class of obvious misprints which are very numerous. We will instance a few.

i. 6. ἀγατοῖs.
v. 7. ἐπικαλασόμεθα.   15. ανἔκ.
viii. 23. ὀερουσαλήμ, etc.
ix. 17. ἠρέτισε for -ω or -αs ('elegisti').

Eight out of seventeen readings in the first class consist in omissions, and consequently there is a possibility that Cerda, who does not seem to have spent a very long time over his work, may be responsible for them. It does not seem to us that he was at all a skilled palaeographer, and certainly he did not keep his printer at all well in hand: so that a certain doubt hangs over almost every reading *peculiar* to A. In a note on vi. 7 Cerda says he has made several tacit corrections: 'restitui...ut et alia levia quae omitto.'

Next, of readings peculiar to V. The following are given by Hilg.

ii. 3. δώρῳ sic [really δῶρα].   4. ἠτιμένθη [ἠτιμ͂θη as K=ἠτιμώθη].
v. 16. τὸ δεὶ for τὸ δὲ. [The MS. has δὲ.]
x. 9. εὐφροσύνην for σωφρ. [The MS. has σωφρ.]
xiii. 1. ἐπήσπασε for ἐσπέσασε or ἐσκεπ (?). [The MS. has ἐσκέπασε.]
xvii. 9. γένοs for -ουs. [The MS. has γένουs.]

It will be seen that every one of these is discredited by the new collation.

See further the additional note.

The readings in which K stands alone amount to no more than two,

xi. 9. om. τὸ ἔλεοs.   xvii. 9. γένοs.

and we think that these may be oversights in collation.

INTRODUCTION.

Readings peculiar to P.
iv. 17. ἀπορίαις for the 2nd ἀπορίᾳ.
viii. 34. ἐλαίου for ἐλέου (an itacism).
xi. 6. ἐσκίρτησαν for ἐσκίασαν.
xii. 2. ἄλλῳ for ἅλῳ.
xvi. 1. καταφορᾷ for καταφθορᾷ. 12. ἰσχύσαι for ἐνισχῦσαι.
xvii. 35. δίκαιος καὶ διδακτός ins. καί. 40. αὔξει for ἄξει.

Readings peculiar to M.
ii. 4. ἐνέδωκεν. 5. αὐτῆς for αὐτοῦ. 21. σχινίον (itacism).
iii. 7. παρὰ θεὸν σωτῆρος (mistake).
viii. 13. ἀφαίδρω (itacism). 24. ἐγέννησεν (error).
xiv. 3. ἀνθρώπου for οὐρανοῦ. ? ουνου misread.
xvi. 9. φόβῳ for τόπῳ.
xvii. 3, 4. om. μετ' ἐλέου καὶ ἡ βασ: τοῦ θεοῦ ἡμ: εἰς τ. αἰῶνα (homoeoteleuton).
34. φέροντας? (obscurely written in the copy).

The above lists will be found, we believe, to contain all the important readings (diversities in titles and numerations excepted) which are peculiar to each MS. The following lists will show what *combinations* of MSS. are most common.

First we will take the group AV. They agree in the following readings:
iii. 11. om. μητρός.
v. 7. εἷς for εἶ.
ix. 17. om. παρά.
x. 1. ἐλέγχῳ for ἐλεγμῷ.

Other groups of two into which A enters:
A, K. ii. 25. ἔπαιξαν for ἐνέπαιξαν.
xvii. 30. καταμετρίσει for καταμερ.
A, P. ii. 41. ἐνωπ. τῶν δούλων (P ex silentio). xvii. 5. βασιλείαν.
A, M. xvii. 26. ἁμαρτωλῶν for -ους.

Groups of two into which V enters.
V, K. xvii. 23. οἶδες for -ας. 27. ἀπειλῇ.
V, P. nil.
V, M. xiv. 1. ἐννόμῳ.

Groups of two into which K enters.
A, K, V, K, see above. K, P, K, M, nil.

Groups of two into which P enters.
A, P, V, P, K, P, see above.
P, M. ii. 20. The lines of the verse are transposed. 24. ἐπαγωγῇ.
v. 1. τὸ ὄνομά σου (for dative).
xi. 8. ἀγαθά for -όν.
xii. 4. ἀπὸ κακῶν for ἀκάκ.
xvii. 23. οἶδας not εἶδες or οἶδες. 27. omit ἐν ἀπειλῇ—αὐτοῦ.

As a result of this investigation certain facts come forward prominently at once.

c 2

1. That A, V are very closely connected.
2. That K, P, M *usually* agree against them.
3. That P, M are very closely connected.

In other words, we arrive at a provisional genealogy of this form

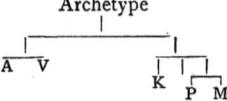

Can we define the relationships more precisely than this? A theory has occurred to us which we are on the whole not inclined to accept, but which is worth stating, because the statement of the pros and cons of it may save others from the trouble of formulating it in the future. It is that A and V are one and the same MS. From Augsburg to Vienna is no very far cry, though we are not at present able to trace any transference of MSS. from one to the other. But that is a minor point. What is important in favour of the idea is (α) the character of A's peculiar readings, (β) the paucity of V's peculiar readings, (γ) the number and character of those in which A and V agree.

As to (α) it has already been remarked that by far the most important of those given above consist in omissions, and we repeat the suggestion made there, that Cerda does not inspire sufficient confidence as an editor, to free us from the suspicion that he is to blame for these omissions.

As to (β) we have only given five readings peculiar to V, and one of them, which if correctly given would close the question, is inferred *ex silentio*. There are three readings of A's which if confirmed would break the theory down at once. σαλῶν (specially noticed by Cerda), καταμετρίσει and ἁμαρτωλῶν (xvii. 26). Of the first of these we can say nothing in face of Cerda's statement, but of the others it may be said that τρ is very easily read for ρ in some hands, and that ἁμαρτωλῶν may represent a wrongly expanded abbreviation.

In every one of the other cases we might suspect a misreading.

But there is another branch of evidence not yet alluded to, which is less easily set aside, namely, the titles and numbering of the Psalms. The following table gives a conspectus of the MS. evidence on this point.

Ps. i. A, ψαλμὸς τῷ Σ. αʹ.
V ⎫
K ⎬ omit.
P ⎭
M omits all numbers and titles, save in the case of Ps. iii.

ii. A, ψ. τῷ Σ. περὶ Ἱερουσαλὴμ βʹ.
V K have the numeral on the left, rather higher up.

INTRODUCTION. xxxv

iii.   A, ψ. τῷ Σ. περὶ δικαίων γ'.
       V K P omit γ'.
       M has the title but omits γ'.

iv.   A P, ψ. τῷ Σ. τοῖς ἀνθρωπαρέσκοις δ'.
       V P the same, but Γ' for δ'.
       K, Γ̄ ψ. τ. Σ.

v.   A, ψ. τ. Σ. ε'.
       V K P, Δ̄ ψ. Σ.

vi.   A, ψ. ἐν ἐλπίδι τῷ Σ. ϛ'
       V K P, Ε' ἐν ἐλπ. τῷ Σ.

vii.   A, ψ. τ. Σ. ἐπιστροφῆς ζ'.
       V K P, ϛ' τῷ Σ. ἐπιστρ.

viii. A, ψ. τ. Σ. εἰς νίκας η'.
       V K P, Z̄ Z' τῷ Σ. εἰς νῖκος.

ix.   A, ψ. τ. Σ. εἰς ἔλεγχον θ'.
       V K P, Θ̄ τ. Σ. εἰς ἐλ.

x.   A, ὕμνος τῷ Σ. ι'.
       V K prefix ι'.
       P has the same as A.

xi.   A, τῷ Σ. εἰς προσδοκίαν ια'. (Fabr. inserts ψαλμός.)
       V K P prefix ΙΑ'.

xii.   A P, τῷ Σ. ἐν γλώσσῃ παρανόμων ιβ'. (Fabr. adds ψαλμός.)
       V K prefix ιβ'.

xiii. A, ψ. τ. Σ. παράκλησις τῶν δικαίων ιγ'.
       V K P, ΙΓ̄ τῷ Σ. ψ. etc.

xiv.   A, ὕμνος τῷ Σ. ιδ'. A.
       V K P, ΙΔ̄ ὕμνος τῷ Σ.

xv.   A P, ψ. τ. Σ. μετ' ᾠδῆς ιε'.
       V K prefix ιε'.

xvi.   A, ψ. τ. Σ. εἰς ἀντίληψιν ιϛ'.
       V K P prefix ιϛ'.

xvii. A, ψ. τ. Σ. μετ' ᾠδῆς τῷ βασιλεῖ ιζ'.
       V K P as xvi.

xviii. A P, ψ. τ. Σ. ἐπὶ τοῦ χριστοῦ κυρίου ιη'.
       V K as xv.

Now from this table certain curious points arise. First as to titles. Psalm i. has no title but in A. Ps. iii. is the only one to which M gives a title at all.

Next as to numeration. V, K and P agree in numbering certain Psalms wrongly, thus. They omit the number of Ps. iii., and call Ps. iv., iii. instead. Then, according to them, Ps. v. = iv., Ps. vi. = v., Ps. vii. = vi., Ps. viii. = vii. They omit the number viii. altogether, and give Ps. ix. its correct number. The only other difference is that they consistently prefix the number to the title, instead of affixing it. In this last matter the scribe of P is influenced by the breadth of his margin.

We are inclined to attribute a considerable number of these differences to Cerda's editorship. When we see Fabricius consistently altering the position of the numeral and reading ψ. τ. Σ. β´ περὶ Ἰερουσαλήμ and so on, and twice inserting a ψαλμός which he did not find in Cerda, we see how little editors of two centuries back thought of alterations which we now consider inexcusable. And it is, we think, most likely that Cerda took great liberties in this particular. To begin with, he calls the collection by a name which no other MS. or authority is known to give, Ψαλτήριον (instead of Ψαλμοὶ) Σολομῶντος. This name he may very well have invented, as well as the title of the 1st Psalm, which is as obvious as it could well be. It is also most probable that, if A had the wrong numbering just noticed in V and K, Cerda would have corrected it without saying anything about it, and that he would have altered the position of the numerals. Again, it is by no means out of the question that he should have sometimes inserted Ψαλμός, where V and K omit it (as in vi. and viii.), and sometimes omitted to insert it (as in xi. and xii.). In Ps. viii. again, νίκας of A is very likely to be a misreading for νῖκος of VK.

The above paragraphs were written before we had found means to obtain a fresh collation of V, or indeed, had had reason to believe that such a thing was really needed. Had we procured it earlier, it is doubtful whether we should have laid such stress on the possibility of identifying A with V. Readings that had before seemed striking evidences of affinity (e.g. the omission of οὐρανοῦ in xiv. 3, and of ἕως in xviii. 13, and such coincidences as ἀληθείᾳ in xvii. 20) now prove to be simply mistakes in Haupt's collation: we had collected from Hilgenfeld's notes seventeen such instances of agreement between A and V against the other MSS.; and of these seventeen, thirteen are entirely set aside by the new evidence. In spite of this we have preferred to let the discussion stand. The tabulation of the titles is complete, and may prove useful; and the whole section, if it serves no other purpose, may at least prove an effective warning against the unquestioning employment of any old collation of a MS.

Moreover, it can hardly be said that the identity of A and V is absolutely out of the question even now. It might be argued, plausibly enough, that if Haupt in 1868 could commit such enormities, the probability that Cerda in 1626 may have done still worse, is increased. But as a whole, the case for the identity is considerably weakened, and the net result of the investigation has been to deepen our distrust in the *editio princeps*, and to bring all our authorities into closer connection with each other than we had before thought possible.

For, in spite of the subdivisions into which our five MSS. fall, they undoubtedly belong to one and the same family. This, we think, necessarily follows from the fact that they all contain the book in the same connection, i.e. they give it as an appendix to, or a component part of, the Solomonic writings contained in the LXX. Of this fact we are certain in four cases, and in each of these the position of the book is the same—between Wisdom and Ecclesiasticus—while in the fifth case (that of A) we know that other Solomonic writings were contained in the MS. It seems probable, then, that the Alexandrine MS. followed a tradition different from any of ours, for it placed the Psalm at the end of the sacred writings, as an appendix to the whole. There is no such difference, we believe, between our MSS., as would not be amply accounted for by the intervention of a few steps between the archetype and their immediate progenitors. Beyond the solitary indication afforded by the subscription of P in which λ' is expanded into τριάκοντα, there is nothing to show definitely that any one of them was copied from an uncial MS., and of course even this trace does not prove an immediate descent from an uncial ancestor.

The similarity of P to M might suggest the idea that P was a copy of M. But this is at once negatived by the absence of titles in M and by the fact that in xvii. 3, 4 M omits words which P inserts.

On the whole we are inclined to say that K is the best of our MSS. It is as old as any, and presents a very neutral text, though not free from corruption. On the whole we cannot feel ourselves justified in constructing any more precise genealogy of the MSS. than that given above, though the error in numeration common to V, K, and P, tends very considerably to closen the connection between the two main subdivisions of our authorities.

The scanty notes of provenance which we possess are not such as to be very helpful. A, V, and P (?), came from Constantinople. K was bought at Venice. M came from Iviron on Athos.

§ iv. *Date and Authorship of the Psalms.*

At what date were the Psalms composed? Internal evidence enables us to give the answer. We find in certain Psalms clear allusions to contemporary and recent historical events of momentous importance to the Jewish nation. If these can be identified, we are in a position at any rate approximately to determine the period at which the book was written; and the knowledge of their date, within certain limits, will be the key to various allusions descriptive of the internal condition of the Jewish community.

The historical events, to which we have referred, form the groundwork of Pss. i., ii., viii., xvii. 1—22; and indirect allusions to the same group of events may possibly be found in Pss. v., vii., ix., xv. One aspect of the social condition of the people is presented in Pss. iv. and xii.: Pss. xi., xvii. 23—end, xviii. give expression to the Messianic expectation: Pss. iii., vi., xiv., xvi. do not possess any distinctive colouring.

The following is the picture of contemporary events which we obtain from Pss. i., ii., viii., xvii.

The Jews are enjoying prosperity; they have grown greatly in numbers and fame (i. 3, 4); they are satisfied that God is thus blessing their upright and pious conduct (i. 2, viii. 7). They are however deceived. For suddenly there is an alarm of war (i. 2, viii. 1); a rumour comes of the advance of a hostile host, which threatens Jerusalem (viii. 2—4). The Psalmist now discovers the hollowness of his countrymen's piety, and sees in the approaching catastrophe a just judgment. The hostile army is led by a stranger, who comes from the uttermost parts of the earth; he is a mighty warrior, and, as the representative of the heathen foe, he is designated at different times 'the sinner,' 'the lawless,' 'the dragon,' 'the adversary' (cf. ii. 1 and 29, viii. 16, xvii. 9, 13, 15). He prepares war; but the rulers of Jerusalem go forth to meet him, they throw open the approaches to the city, and welcome him with acclamations; he enters and takes possession (viii. 17—20). From some quarter however resistance is offered; the invader with his battering-ram throws down strong walls, seizes the fortifications; Gentiles enter the sacred precincts of the Temple, and pollute the Altar with their presence (ii. 1, 2, viii. 21). A sanguinary vengeance is taken; a massacre takes place in which blood flows like water in Jerusalem (ii. 25—28, viii. 23, xvii. 13). Large numbers are sent away as exiles (viii. 24); they are taken to live the life of prisoners among the Gentiles (ii. 6, 13, 14); their destination is 'the bounds of the west' (ἕως ἐπὶ δυσμῶν), and even the rulers of the land are not spared, they are carried off to be the object of contumely and insult (xvii. 14). The conqueror in his pride and arrogance is guilty of acts of heathenish profanity in Jerusalem (viii. 15, 16, cf. ii. 29); his ambition has no limits, he does not realise that he is but a mortal man (ii. 32—33); God sends retribution; he is assassinated in Egypt, his body lies tossing on the waves, there is no one to bury him (ii. 30).

INTRODUCTION.

Such are the main features of the crisis in Jewish affairs, to which our Psalms allude. Who then is the foreigner, from the ends of the earth, who menaces Judæa, who, having been welcomed within Jerusalem, is nevertheless compelled to batter down walls with his siege-train, who massacres many citizens, and carries them off to 'the bounds of the west,' who is guilty of impious audacity, and receives a heaven-sent retribution, meeting an inglorious death on the shores of Egypt?

We will pass in review the names of the most eminent of Jerusalem's conquerors, and consider how far this description is applicable to them.

(1) The name of Titus need hardly come under serious discussion. The death of Titus, over which the Jews exulted as a heaven-sent retribution for the destruction of Jerusalem, bears no resemblance to the description in Ps. S. ii. 30. The welcome accorded to the invader in viii. 18—20 has no counterpart in the narrative of the great Jewish revolt against the Romans. Our Psalms moreover most certainly presuppose the survival of the city, after the invasion of the foreigner. It has been polluted by the Gentile (ii. 2, viii. 25, xvii. 25), but not destroyed. Some degree of mercy has been shown; the people have not been utterly consumed (ii. 26, xvii. 11).

(2) The name of Antiochus Epiphanes has with better show of reason received considerable support. His relations with the Jews introduce several points of similarity to the picture described above. But the more closely we carry the inspection, the less probable does this identification appear. The description of the invader 'as one who came from the uttermost parts of the earth' (τὸν ἀπ' ἐσχάτου τῆς γῆς, viii. 16), though possibly only an imitation of the old prophetical style, is scarcely appropriate to the monarch of the adjoining kingdom of Syria. It is true he oppressed the Jews and carried on numerous wars, but the epithet of 'the mighty striker' (τὸν παίοντα κραταιῶς) would be more suited to a warrior whose success in arms had been less chequered or on a larger scale. We know that at the beginning of his reign there was a strong Hellenizing party in Jerusalem; but we do not find that Antiochus ever received such a welcome as is described in viii. 18—20. On the contrary, he is said on two occasions to have been obliged to attack Jerusalem, and yet the resistance which he encountered was never obstinate enough to compel resort to such extreme measures as the battering-ram (ii. 1). The defilement of the altars and the pollution of the Temple (ii. 2—5, viii. 25, 26, xvii. 16) suggest the temporary dishonour, not the overthrow of the Temple and the complete cessation of the Temple worship, which signalized Antiochus' capture of Jeru-

salem. Granting that he may have carried away many Jewish prisoners, the statement that they were sent to 'the bounds of the west' would be quite inappropriate to the captives of the Syrian king. Lastly, although the conclusion of Ps. ii. might represent a Jew's exultation at the news of Antiochus' death, the passage in ii. 30, ἐκκεκεντημένον... Αἰγύπτου is quite sufficient to show that the Syrian monarch is not intended. Surely too a Jew, in any lyrical description of Antiochus Epiphanes, would have used the opportunities afforded by Pss. S. ii., iv., xvii. to denounce the oppressor of his nation in a far less measured strain.

(3) The name of Herod the Great is very naturally suggested by the description of the invader as a man who was a 'stranger to our race' (ἄνθρωπον ἀλλότριον γένους ἡμῶν, xvii. 9). We know too that he and Sosius combined to lay siege to Jerusalem, and that the former signalized the beginning of his reign by the cruel slaughter of the leading members of the Sanhedrin. But we should not expect that an Idumean by birth, even if he had as a youth been prisoner in Rome, would be called 'one that came from the uttermost parts of the earth'; the epithet of 'the mighty striker' would not be very applicable in Herod's case, who, with all his force and vigour, obtained greater triumphs in the field of diplomacy than in that of battle. Herod it is true was an alien by race, but he was most careful to conciliate the religious prejudices of the Jews, and the charge of idolatry and insolent infamy in xvii. 15, 16 is not what we should expect to find in a description of his deeds. Herod permanently resided in or near Jerusalem itself; the description in Pss. S. ii., iv., xvii. gives the impression only of a temporary occupation by heathen troops. We never find that Herod's arrival was welcomed by the leaders of the people (viii. 18 sqq.), and however relentless he may have been in the pursuit of a cruel policy— sufficiently so to justify such a description as viii. 23 sqq.—yet it could never, we think, be said of him that he sent away captives to 'the west' (xvii. 14), or that he made slaves of the children of Jerusalem (ii. 5). The last days of Herod have a tragic and terrible history; but there is nothing in them at all resembling the description of the conqueror's doom on the shores of Egypt (ii. 30).

(4) We have reserved to the last the name of Pompey. In his case we find the most striking resemblances to the historical picture presented by our Psalms. He comes from Rome, 'from the uttermost parts of the earth' (viii. 16). He as the greatest general of the day, who had just overthrown Mithridates, is 'the mighty striker' (τὸν παίοντα κραταιῶς, viii. 16). The haughtiness and ambition of the great Roman

correspond with the description of ii. 33 (εἶπεν· ἐγὼ κύριος γῆς καὶ θαλάσσης ἔσομαι). Pompey arrived in Syria not long after the Civil War between Hyrcanus II. and his brother Aristobulus II. had broken out. Hyrcanus was assisted by Aretas the Nabatæan king. This civil conflict which followed the peaceful and prosperous reign of Alexandra is possibly intended by the allusion to the sudden outbreak of war after a period of tranquillity (i. 1, viii. 1). Pompey was with his army at Damascus, when he received overtures from both these rivals and from a third party consisting of the supporters of a Theocratic policy. Pompey's march through Palestine to Jericho was unopposed; the chief fortresses were surrendered to him without a blow. In Jerusalem Hyrcanus' party prevailed; the gates of the city were thrown open; the Roman soldiers entered unopposed (cf. viii. 18—20). But the supporters of Aristobulus were determined to resist: they established themselves in the Temple and refused to capitulate. An obstinate conflict ensued. The strength of the Temple fortifications was immense; Pompey was compelled to invest it by a regular siege: his engines and battering-rams were brought from Tyre, and after three months a breach was effected (ii. 1), and an assault made: the Temple was taken and a bloody massacre ensued (viii. 23). It was computed that 12000 Jews lost their lives in this first desperate conflict against the Romans. Aristobulus himself and certain members of his family were sent to Rome (ἕως ἐπὶ δυσμῶν), to adorn the triumph of Pompey (εἰς ἐμπαιγμὸν, xvii. 14). Hyrcanus was spared, and reinstated in the High Priesthood. Pompey acted with clemency and consideration (cf. ii. 26, xvii. 11): he restored the worship of the Temple, and did not touch its treasury; but by entering the Holy of Holies he was guilty of an unpardonable act of profanation. In strict correspondence with this description of Pompey's behaviour, we find that the Psalmist, who does not denounce the invader in nearly such unmeasured terms as he expends upon his own countrymen, refers to certain profane and insolent acts, perpetrated by the conqueror, in his ignorance of the Jewish God (xvii. 15). For some such profanation the doom described in ii. 30—35 befell the invader as a divine retribution; and it is impossible not to recognise in the picture of the stabbed and dishonoured corpse on the borders of Egypt a description of Pompey's treacherous assassination.

In this identification two points demand further consideration. (1) It may be objected that the penetration into the Holy of Holies, which the Jews so bitterly resented, would have been mentioned more definitely. But it must be remembered that, if in this matter Pompey displayed contempt for the religious scruples of the Jews, in other respects he had shown consideration and kindness. Moreover we should not expect to find in a liturgical Psalm any detailed reference to an act so abhorrent to the pious Jew, that its Divine permission seemed an inexplicable mystery. In these Psalms Pompey is referred to as the scourge of Jewish iniquity; his profane acts are those of ignorance (xvii. 16, 17), and, although the detailed description of his doom is best understood in the light of this crowning act of profanity, the purpose of the Psalms is to describe not the impiety of the captor, but the heaven-sent disasters of Jerusalem as a judicial visitation for sin.

(2) It may be objected that the passages describing wholesale slaughter (viii. 23, xvii. 13) and large numbers of captives (ii. 6, viii. 24, xvii. 14) give a darker page of history than we should be justified, by Josephus' account, in attaching to Pompey's capture of Jerusalem. But Josephus wrote a century and a half after these events took place; and it is difficult to realise from his concise and simple narrative, that he is telling us of the loss of 12,000 Jewish lives in three months fighting over the walls of the Temple. The number of Jewish captives conveyed to Rome by Pompey laid the foundation of the large Jewish community of which Philo speaks a few decades later (*De Leg. ad Caium*, § 23). These disasters are insignificant by comparison with those which Josephus himself witnessed. But to the Jew, who wrote our Psalms, with the slaughter of so many countrymen, the dishonourable captivity of many others, and the utter overthrow of national independence fresh in his memory, it was impossible not to paint in darkest tints the crisis through which the country had passed.

That Pompey's invasion of Judæa is the historical event to which this group of Psalms refers, may possibly be indicated by two further pieces of evidence. (1) In xvii. 22 we have the mention of a Jewish king (ὁ βασιλεύς). Now the title of king, which was first assumed in the Asmonean dynasty by Aristobulus (105—104) and appears on the coins of his brother Alexander Jannæus (104—78), was dropped after Pompey's capture of Jerusalem. Pompey restored to Hyrcanus the High Priesthood but not the royal power: Hyrcanus is called 'the High Priest and Ethnarch of the Jews' (Joseph. *Ant.* XIV. xii. 3). In later years Herod the Great received the kingdom of Judæa from Mark Antony (Jos. *Ant.* XIV. xiv. 4—6); but if Josephus may be trusted, the Jews never regarded him as a true king, 'the royal authority, which was a dignity formerly bestowed on those that were high priests by right of their birth, became the property of common men (δημοτικῶν ἀνδρῶν),' Jos. *Ant.* XIV. iv. 5. Now the title ὁ βασιλεύς in xvii. 22 is clearly applied to a native prince and therefore to some one quite distinct from 'the stranger' (ὁ ἀλλότριος) of xvii. 9. Accordingly it cannot be used either of Herod or of Antiochus Epiphanes; while if 'the stranger' be, as we contend, Pompey, then the mention of Hyrcanus II. or Aristobulus II., the rival Asmonean princes of the blood royal, by the title of 'the king' would be quite appropriate in the writing of a contemporary Jew.

(2) The allusions in our Psalms to drought and famine (ii. 10, v., xvii. 21) occurring at or near the time of the invasion of Judæa are not sufficiently definite to admit of any very certain identification. It is interesting however to find that in a passage where Josephus is speaking of the outbreak of hostilities between Hyrcanus and Aristobulus, he mentions a holy man named Onias, whose prayers were said to have prevailed with God to cause a certain drought to cease (Jos. *Ant.* XIV. ii. 1). In the very next chapter of his history, he describes how God punished the impiety of the Jews by sending 'a strong and vehement storm of wind' that destroyed the crops of the whole country, till a measure of wheat was bought for eleven drachmæ (Jos. *Ant.* XIV. ii.).

If we may assume that Pompey's capture of Jerusalem is the historical event to which Pss. S. i., ii., viii., xvii. refer, we may approximately determine the limits of date within which our Psalms were composed. There is nothing in the style or contents of the other Psalms to separate them in respect of date of composition from those which are definitely historical in colouring. We have no hesitation in assuming that the whole collection springs from the literary activity, if not of a single writer, at any rate of a single generation. Judging from the detailed character of the allusions, the historical Psalms must have been composed not very long after the events which they describe. The impressions are still fresh in the Psalmist's mind.

Wellhausen's supposition that Ps. S. iv. expressed the exasperation of the Pharisees against Alexander Jannæus is based on a misconception of iv. 11 (see note). The earliest direct allusions in the collection are to be found in Pss. S. i. and viii. which describe the outbreak of the war and the invasion of Pompey (B.C. 63). The latest event to which reference is certainly made is Pompey's death which took place in B.C. 48. It is we think conceivable that the tone of exultation which succeeds the description of Pompey's fate (ii. 36—41), the strain of joy which pervades Ps. S. x., and the confident expectation of the restoration from the Dispersion to be observed in Ps. S. xi. and xvii., may be explained by the enthusiasm, with which the Jews would hail the success of Julius Cæsar. From his hand they received especial favours and privileges, and presumably they hoped to obtain from him a yet more complete measure of freedom. This however belongs to the region of conjecture. We find no allusion either to Cæsar's death or to the ascendancy of Herod the Great.

We are of opinion that Pss. S. iv. and xii. are among the earliest in the collection. For, whereas in Pss. S. i., viii., xiii., xvii. 'the sinners' are already punished by the disasters of the Pompeian invasion, in Pss. S. iv. and xii. 'the sinners' are only denounced with the utmost hatred, while the visitation by 'the Gentiles' is not mentioned, and the interference of a foreigner with Jewish affairs is apparently not foreseen.

In assigning the years B.C. 70 and B.C. 40 as the extreme limits of date within which our Psalms were written, we keep securely within the bounds of probability.

§ v. *Jewish Parties; and the Religious Thought of the Psalms of Solomon.*

This period of thirty years (70—40 B.C.) witnessed the last scenes of the prolonged struggle between the two great parties in Palestine, the Pharisees and the Sadducees. With the downfall of the Asmonean dynasty and the irresistible assertion of Roman rule, the conflict between the two factions began insensibly to be withdrawn from the arena of politics. But the feeling throughout the twenty years that elapsed between Pompey's capture of Jerusalem and Cæsar's death was at all times bitter. We should naturally expect that Palestinian Psalms of this period would throw light upon the condition of Jewish society or would at any rate reveal to which side in this intestinal contest the writer or writers inclined. Nor are we altogether disappointed, although we might have hoped for more. The Psalms reflect something of the intensity of the current animosities of the time. They leave the reader in no doubt to which party they belong. We shall have no difficulty in establishing the general grounds on which we give to the 'Psalms of Solomon' the significant title of 'Psalms of the Pharisees.'

A brief digression is here necessary in order to remind the reader as to the origin of the differences between the Pharisees and the Sadducees. It will be remembered that at the outbreak of the persecution of Antiochus Epiphanes there were two sections of the Jewish community bitterly opposed to one another. On the one side stood the Hellenizing party, including many of the aristocracy and led by the High Priest himself, prepared for the sake of political advantage or private gain to make any sacrifice of national religion or to adopt any practice from among pagan superstitions. On the opposite extreme stood the Asideans, the fanatical followers of the Jewish law, devoted to the principle of theocratic Judaism, prepared to suffer any hardship and to endure any loss rather than abandon a syllable of the sacred heritage. The fervour of the Maccabean revolt swept away the Hellenizers. The Asideans were strengthened by the successes of the patriots. The cause of Theocracy triumphed. But the spirit which had given rise to the Hellenizing of the former generation was still at work; it was fostered by the military successes of the Jewish captains and by the growth of Jewish prosperity. The Asmonean princes, to whose family the people had given the High Priesthood, upheld the sanctity of the law and the honour of the race. But the stricter Jews took umbrage nominally at the secularizing of the nation by enterprises undertaken not for the defence of religion, but for the gain of political liberty; they cavilled at the right of the Asmonean princes to hold the High Priesthood; they murmured at the erection of an earthly kingdom. The fanaticism of these men who, as those who separated themselves from all impurity, were called Pharisees or 'Separatists,' gradually drove the Asmonean princes, their natural champions, to seek the support of the old aristocracy, who had no sympathy with the new enthusiasm. Among the latter were the leading Priests who claimed to be the true sons of Zadok (Sadducees), conservative of the letter of the Mosaic law, but paying little heed to the teaching of the Scribes either upon future retribution or upon the countless methods of purification multiplied by tradition.

For some years before his death Johannes Hyrcanus († 105) had utterly broken with the Pharisees. During the reign of his son Alexander Jannæus the opposition between the two parties reached a climax in the great Civil War which raged for six years (*circ.* 86—80). The power and influence of the Pharisees increased in proportion as the Asmonean ruler seemed to abandon the religious spirit of his great ancestors. A High Priest whose whole life was given to military adventure seemed to degrade the religion of his nation. The triumph of Alexander Jannæus and his Sadducee supporters, followed by the wholesale slaughter and banishment of Pharisee foes, was powerless to stem the current of popular feeling. When Alexandra succeeded to her husband's throne in B.C. 78, she could only maintain her position by the reversal of the previous policy and the recall of the exiles. Her reign was prosperous and peaceful; by the Pharisees it was regarded as a golden period (*Taanith* 23a). The Sadducees however felt themselves displaced from their rightful position. Their nobles, with the young prince Aristobulus at their head, began to demand a larger control in the administration of the kingdom. Already in the year of the queen's death, B.C. 69, they had succeeded in occupying some of the strongest fortresses. On Hyrcanus' succeeding to the throne, a determined move was made to regain a complete Saducean ascendancy. Aristobulus, in whom there lived again the spirit of Alexander Jannæus, was made king and High Priest in his brother's room. It looked as if the day of persecution and exile for the Pharisees had returned, when Antipater the Idumean induced Aretas king of Nabatæa to espouse the cause of Hyrcanus. War broke out between the two brothers; Scaurus, Pompey's lieutenant, who appeared in Syria in B.C. 65, favoured the cause of Aristobulus. But Pompey himself, on arriving in the spring of B.C. 63, was met not only by Aristobulus and Hyrcanus, but also by an influential gathering of the Pharisees who protested against the rule of an earthly king. The deposition and capture of Aristobulus was the death-blow of the Asmonean dynasty and of the Saducean political ascendancy. The Saducean aristocracy suffered heavily in the capture of the Temple. The animosity between them and the Pharisees did not diminish. In social and religious matters it continued to burn fiercely. The Sadducees were an aristocratic clique, at the head of which stood the High Priest; the Pharisees impersonated the religious fervour of the masses, guided and directed by the teaching of the Scribes. The Sadducees were tenacious of the Mosaic law, and refused to accept the expansion which it received from the teaching of the Pharisees; they had no sympathy with the new development of religious thought respecting the resurrection, a world to come, or a future retribution. The Sadducees were ready to make the most of their connection with the outside world by political intrigue and commercial enterprise. The Pharisees on the other hand would have nothing to do with the Gentiles.

When we compare the statements contained in our Psalms with the picture of the internal condition of Judæa, we think there can be no doubt of their Pharisaic origin. The Psalmist who divides the whole community into 'righteous' (δίκαιοι), or 'saints' (ὅσιοι), and 'sinners' (ἁμαρτωλοί), or 'transgressors' (παράνομοι), seems to have in view the opposition between the Pharisees and the Sadducees.

That the Sadducees are designated as 'sinners,' appears from a variety of allusions.

(*a*) The Psalmist denounces the 'sinners' for having violently usurped and taken possession of the throne of David (xvii. 5, 8). This is an unmistakable reference to the Asmonean house. That the king himself is implicated in 'transgression' (xvii. 22) could only have been asserted by one who was hostile to the dynasty upheld by the Sadducees. The Psalmist includes in his condemnation the nobles and princes of the land (xvii. 21); his prayer that the Messiah may sweep away 'unjust rulers' (xvii. 24, 41) probably reflects his sentiments towards existing authority. The overthrow of the rulers (viii. 23, xvii. 14) who received 'the stranger' into their land is regarded as a divine judgment for their iniquities (viii. 15, xvii. 8).

(*b*) The complaint is made that these 'sinners' have taken violent possession of that to which they had no rightful claim, the reference evidently being to the High Priesthood (xvii. 6). In the absence of the true lineage, they had laid sacrilegious hands on the sacred heritage (viii. 12) from which the Messiah is to eject them (xvii. 26). In these allusions we cannot doubt that a Pharisee assails the Asmonean house for its retention of the High Priesthood.

(*c*) The Psalmist avers that those who discharge the sacred functions pollute the holy things and the offerings by their neglect of the true observances and by their ceremonial uncleanness (cf. i. 8, ii. 3, 5, vii. 2, viii. 13, 26, xvii. 51). It is notorious that the Sadducees were not so scrupulous as the Pharisees, and did not accept all the rules of purification required by the tradition of the Scribes. The Pharisaic origin of the Psalms would give especial point to the charges made against the Priests of the Sadducee faction in viii. 13.

(*d*) The Asmonean princes and Sadducee nobles were as a rule more ready than the rest of their countrymen to comply with foreign customs. This tendency may easily have received a damaging misinterpretation from their political foes. There may also have been too much foundation of truth in the rumours about foul rites and nameless horrors. 'The sinners' are accused in our Psalms of 'secret enormities' for which God has brought judgment upon the people (i. 7, ii. 18, iv. 5, viii. 9), and of surpassing the heathen in the wickedness accompanying their worship (i. 8, viii. 14, xvii. 17). Whether the accusations are true or not, they correspond on the one hand to the judgment, which the Pharisees would pass upon any acts of Sadducee connivance at Pagan rites, and on the other hand to the low moral life, which the last Asmonean kings tolerated at their court.

The tone of virulent denunciation in Pss. S. iv. and xii. must be attributed to some recent injury or affront. But the offenders clearly belong to the same class. They are men of influence, they are on the Council (iv. 1); they combine severity in judicial duties with immoralities in private life; they are full of cleverness, and by appeals to the law can justify their actions to the simple-minded (iv. 10, 25); they are full of deceit (iv. 12, 26, xii. 1—4); they live and consort with 'the saints' (iv. 7), but they are not to be trusted, they are all things to all men, mere menpleasers (iv. 10). Such language would well suit an indignant Pharisee's description of bitter foes, who in his opinion made an unscrupulous use of their high position in the land, only studying the law in order to delude the people, and ever seeking to ingratiate themselves with the Gentile.

Another element in the Psalmist's accusation against these foes is that, in order to compass their own ends of avarice and vice, they made desolate whole houses (iv. 11, 13, 15, 23, xii. 2, 4); they dispersed (iv. 13, 23) the inhabitants, and 'the saints' were scattered before them, they were banished and could no longer dwell in their own land (xvii. 18). We are forcibly reminded of the action taken by Alexander Jannæus and his Sadducee supporters in order to get rid of their Pharisee adversaries: perhaps a renewal of the same policy was threatened when the Sadducees attempted to regain their lost authority after the death of Alexandra.

That the Psalmist refers to the Sadducees is perhaps also to be inferred from the stress laid upon the pride and insolence of his foes, e.g. ii. 35, iv. 28, xvii. 26, 46. This would inevitably be an accusation of the popular against the aristocratic party.

Over against 'the sinners' and 'the transgressors' our Psalmist sets 'the righteous' (ii. 38, 39, iii. 3—5, 7, 8, 14, iv. 9, ix. 15, x. 3, xiii. 5—9, xv. 8, xvi. 15) and 'the saints' (iii. 10, iv. 7, viii. 40, ix. 6, x. 7, xii. 5, 8, xiii. 11, xv. 11, 'saints of God' viii. 28, 'saints of the Lord' xii. 8, xiii. 9, xiv. 2, 9): and it is obvious that if the Sadducees are intended by the one class, the only class which could thus be contrasted with them by a Jew in the middle of the last century B.C. would be the Pharisees. That this is the case appears at every turn. Thus, in contrast to the noble and wealthy families of the Sadducees, the Pharisees who do not follow after earthly riches are for the most part 'poor.' It is the poor whom God blesses (cf. v. 2, x. 7, xv. 2, xviii. 3). They are the true 'fearers of God' (ii. 37, iii. 16, v. 21, vi. 8, xii. 4, 8, xiii. 11, xv. 15). Their fear of God is not for any ulterior purpose of profit or worldly advantage, but in simplicity and singleness of heart ($\dot{\epsilon}\nu\ \dot{\alpha}\kappa\alpha\kappa\acute{\iota}\alpha$, iv. 26, cf. iv. 25, xii. 4). Their religion is not counterfeited for office or assumed for purposes of policy like that of 'the profane' and 'the menpleasers' (iv. 1); they love God 'in truth' ($\dot{\epsilon}\nu\ \dot{\alpha}\lambda\eta\theta\epsilon\acute{\iota}\alpha$, vi. 9, x. 4, xiv. 1).

In order to appreciate the Pharisaic colouring in the religious thought of these Psalms, we propose at this point to review briefly its most distinctive features.

(*a*) The conception of a Theocracy lay at the root both of the religion and of the politics of the Pharisees. Loyalty to this thought made them rebellious subjects of the Asmonean princes as well as devoted servants of the sacred law. The words 'The Lord is King' were the watchword which upheld the Pharisees in the face of Roman oppression (see ii. 34, 36, v. 21, 22, xvii. 1, 38, 51).

(*b*) (1) The sacred 'Torah' or Law, which the 'menpleasers' handled deceitfully (iv. 10), is God's witness upon earth (x. 5). True righteousness is fulfilled in the life that does not swerve from its ordinances (xiv. 1). The righteousness of our Psalms is conspicuously 'the righteousness of the Pharisees.' It is fulfilled in deeds (cf. ix. 7, 9, xvii. 21, xviii. 9), and especially in deeds which carried out the rules, or avoided the violation, of the ceremonial law (iii. 8—10, v. 20). The neglect of such rules was the contradiction of all righteousness (cf. i. 2, 3 with 8; viii. 7 with 13, 14. (2) 'The righteous' however do not differ from 'the sinners' only by the performance of mere external acts, but also by the spirit of true worship; and emphasis is laid upon the necessity of praise (iii. 1—3, v. 1, vi. 6, x. 6, 7, xi., xv. 3—5, xvi. 7, xix.), prayer (ii. 24, v. 7, vi. 1, 7, 8, vii. 7, viii. 37, xv. 1), and repentance (iii. 5, 6, ix. 11—15, xvi.). (3) Although we are not prepared to admit that συναγωγή is necessarily used in x. 8, xvii. 18 in its most limited sense, it is possible that these passages, along with such expressions as ἐν μέσῳ ἐπισταμένων τὰ κρίματά σου in v. 1 and παροικία in xvii. 19, may contain some allusion to the Synagogal institutions which were the strength of the Pharisaic organization.

(*c*) The attitude with which our Psalmist regards the subjugation of his country to the heathen is highly characteristic of a Theocratic Jew. He does not, as a Sadducee would have done, lament the extinction of the Jewish dynasty and the overthrow of hopes for Jewish independence or an earthly empire; nor does he denounce with any venomous hatred the foreign foe who had been the instrument of his country's calamity and disgrace. He regards these troubles and disasters as the necessary discipline (παιδεία) for the offences of his people; in the face of the humiliation and loss which his country had sustained, he justifies God's dealings with men (cf. ii. 16, vii. 3, viii. 7, 27, 31, x. 1—3, xiii. 6—8, xiv. 1, xvi. 11, xviii. 4). He asserts that God has permitted, nay, has ordained the visitation (ii. 1, 15, 24, viii. 15, xvii. 8).

The Psalmist by his praise of patience and resignation distinguishes himself no less from the political fanatics of his own party, who, afterwards known as the Zealots, hastened the final downfall of the nation (ii. 40, x. 2, xiv. 1, xvi. 15). Not that the Pharisee abandoned all hopes for the restoration of his people. That he did not resign himself to apathetic despair is abundantly clear from the great strain of Messianic hope in xi., xvii., xviii. But in Ps. S. xvii. it is very noticeable that the agent of Israel's restoration is the Messiah himself, unaided by earthly weapons. The loyal supporter of the Theocracy is ready to wait until the time comes when God shall fulfil His promise (vii. 9, xvii. 23, xviii. 6).

It is true that at the approach of the invader, who executed the Divine judgment, 'the righteous' no less than 'the sinners' were thrown into consternation (viii. 5, 6, xiii. 4 ὁ εὐσεβὴς (?)). But it was upon 'the sinners' that the heaviest calamities fell; 'the righteous' were protected from harm (xiii. 2, 5, xv. 6, 8). The prayer of 'the righteous' was heard (xv. 1, cf. vi. 8); and the intercession of the true Israel is represented as averting the annihilation of the race (ii. 26—30).

(*d*) In the matter of Divine Providence and man's free will the religious teaching of our Psalms is unmistakably on the side of the Pharisees. According to the somewhat questionable assertion of Josephus, the Sadducees of his time maintained the absolute freedom of man's will, and denied the possibility of Divine cooperation or interposition in things human; the Pharisees, on the other hand, while admitting the freedom of man's power of choice, recognised the operation of Providence in all human affairs (Jos. *Bell. Jud.* II. viii. 14). It would be impossible to state the Pharisee position more accurately than it appears in Ps. S. ix. 7, 8 (ὁ θεὸς, τὰ ἔργα ἡμῶν ἐν ἐκλογῇ καὶ ἐξουσίᾳ τῆς ψυχῆς ἡμῶν τοῦ ποιῆσαι δικαιοσύνην καὶ ἀδικίαν ἐν ἔργοις χειρῶν ἡμῶν· καὶ ἐν τῇ δικαιοσύνῃ σου ἐπισκέπτῃ υἱοὺς ἀνθρώπων). Man's complete dependence upon his Maker in all things is asserted under the striking image of Ps. v. 4—6, with which our Lord Himself seems to suppose His hearers to be familiar (cf. Matt. xii. 29; Mark iii. 27; Luke xi. 21, 22).

The whole universe is the sphere of Divine operation. God's mercy is over all the earth (v. 17, xvii. 38, xviii. 3), and His justice extends to every part of the world (viii. 29, ix. 4). The thought of Divine justice is constantly brought before us, primarily no doubt with the object of reconciling the devout Jews to acquiesce in the calamities of the time, but also by way of contrast to the tyranny and injustice of the time (cf. ii. 12, 16, 19, 37, iv. 28, viii. 7, 32, x. 6).

But the universality of Divine mercy and justice in no way affects the peculiar relations of Israel with Jehovah. He is the God of Israel

(iv. 1, xi. 2, xii. 6, xviii. 6; cf. viii. 37, ix. 16) and the God of Jacob (xvi. 3). Israel is His portion and heritage (xiv. 3). 'The seed of Abraham' was chosen above all the nations, the Divine name set upon it, the holy covenant established with the patriarchs (ix. 17—20). God's love and mercy are always towards Israel (v. 21, vii. 8, xviii. 2—4). Israel is His servant (xii. 7, xvii. 23), for whom He hath promised blessings (xi. 8; cf. xvii. 50). Jerusalem is the holy city (viii. 4).

But it may be doubted whether the Psalmist includes under Israel all the children of Israel. To the Psalmist the true Israel is the ideal Israel, 'the flock of the Lord' (xvii. 45). It excludes those that dwell with the saints in hypocrisy (iv. 7). From them God will deliver the true Israel (iv. 27, xvii. 51). The true Israel will consist of those that 'call upon Him in patience' (ii. 40), 'that fear Him and love Him in sincerity' (iv. 29, x. 4, xiii. 11), 'the saints of God' (viii. 28).

(*e*) The doctrine of Retribution, which the Sadducees rejected, but which was regarded as a cardinal doctrine of the Pharisees, is strongly asserted (ii. 7, 17, 30—32, 37, 39, ix. 9, xiii. 5, xv. 14, xvii. 10).

Our Psalms, it seems clear to us, do not limit the principle of retribution to the present stage of life. There is to be a day of judgement, when the Lord will 'visit' the earth with judgement (iii. 14, xv. 14); a day of mercy and 'election' for the righteous (iii. 14, xiv. 6, xviii. 6), but of destruction for sinners (xv. 13). We find also stated very simply the Jewish teaching upon the Resurrection, which the Pharisees held and the Sadducees denied. 'The righteous' will at the time of 'the visitation of God' rise again, whether in the body or not is not told us; they will rise into 'life eternal' (iii. 16, xiii. 9); they will enter into 'eternal joy' (x. 9); happiness will be their inheritance (xiv. 7, xv. 15); they will inherit 'the promises of the Lord' (xii. 8). These are expressions whose meaning cannot be exhausted by the thought of the prolongation of life or of the continuance of prosperity on earth. 'Eternal life' is introduced as a justification for Divine righteousness: the calamities of the righteous receive an explanation in the doctrine of 'the coming age' (העולם הבא).

On the other hand, the future condition of the wicked is stated in terms which leave the reader in doubt whether a doctrine of annihilation is intended. 'The destruction of the sinner is for ever' (iii. 13; cf. ix. 9, xii. 8, xiii. 10). Religious opinion on this subject was probably not yet fully formed. Perhaps we should be right in concluding that our Psalmist denied 'a resurrection to life' in the case of the wicked, although he did not call in question the continuity of their personal existence. Hence, when the righteous shall be remembered with mercy, the sinners will be forgotten (iii. 13, xiv. 10), their memorial will no longer be found (xiii. 10); but if their destruction is to be for ever (iii. 13), their inheritance is to be Sheol, an unending portion of darkness and destruction (xiv. 6, xv. 11).

(*f*) Angels. It is due perhaps chiefly to the simplicity of thought in our Psalms, that the doctrine of angels is only once with certainty referred to (xvii. 49 ὡς λόγοι ἁγίων). The belief that the heavenly bodies were under the control of angelic beings is possibly hinted at in xviii. 12—14 (xix. 2—4).

(*g*) The Messiah. The finely conceived and fully detailed description of the Messiah and His Kingdom contained in Pss. S. xvii. 23—end, xviii. 1—9 has naturally excited greater attention than any other part of our book. It is in fact as important a piece of Messianic literature as any later Jewish books have to show. It may be taken, we believe, as presenting more accurately than any other document a statement of the popular Pharisaic expectation regarding the Messiah, shortly before the time when our Lord Jesus, the Christ, appeared. This fact alone should have led to its being widely known and carefully examined by students of the Gospels: but in common with the rest of the book it has suffered unmerited neglect. Nieremberg is the first scholar who called particular attention to it, and in his book, *De Origine S. Scripturae* (1641), IX. 39 (p. 341), he prints a Latin version of Ps. S. xvii. 23—end. But we cannot find that after him any writer has made use of this passage before Bengel.

§ vi. *The Idea of the Messiah in the Psalms of Solomon.*

We propose here to consider

(i) the main outline of the picture of the Messiah and His times, as represented in our Psalms;

(ii) certain distinctive characteristics of the Messiah here described;

(iii) the special significance of this representation of the Messiah (*a*) in the history of the doctrine, (*b*) in the history of the Jewish people.

(i) The main outline of the picture of the Messiah and His times.

(*a*) *The time of His coming.* The time of the Messiah's coming is known to God only (xvii. 23, 47). But from the fact that the Psalmist's prayer for the coming of the Messiah follows immediately upon the description of the triumph of the Romans, the downfall of the Asmonean dynasty, and the calamities of the people, we may infer that, in the ex-

INTRODUCTION.   liii

pectation of the writer, the Messiah's coming was likely to be preceded by great disasters.

(*b*) *His origin.* He is to be raised up by God Himself (xvii. 23, 47, xviii. 6). He is to be a descendant of David (xvii. 23).

(*c*) *His Mission* is of a twofold character, destructive and restorative, expressed in the word 'purification' (xvii. 25, xviii. 6).

It is *destructive*. He is summoned to overthrow the supremacy of the Gentiles (ἔθνη), to destroy them utterly from out of Jerusalem and from out of the borders of Israel (xvii. 25, 27, 31); He is summoned also to break up the power of 'unjust rulers' (xvii. 24) and to drive out from the heritage of God 'the proud sinners,' who had obtained unlawful possession (xvii. 26, 27, 41, 51; cf. with 6—8).

By 'the Gentiles,' allusion is made to the Romans: by 'the sinners,' to the Sadducees.

It is *restorative*. (α) The kingdom of the Messiah is to be set up in the room of the Gentiles and the sinners, and to be established over Israel (xvii. 23, 35, 36, 47). (β) He is to gather together again the dispersed tribes of Israel (xvii. 28, 30, 34, 46, 48, 50). (γ) He is to make Jerusalem his capital, and to restore the glory of her Temple worship (xvii. 33—35). (δ) He is to make the Gentiles subject to him; they shall bring tribute to him, and shall be converted to the true faith (xvii. 31, 32, 34).

(*d*) *The character of his rule*, spiritual, holy, wise and just.

It is *spiritual*. The Messiah king is not an aggressive conqueror by force of arms. His administration does not rest upon physical power (xvii. 37). His trust is not in the ordinary safeguards of a throne, but in Jehovah (xvii. 38).

It is *holy*. Holiness and purity are the instruments of his power (xviii. 33, 36, 46). His purity from sin is the measure of his authority (xvii. 41). He does not tolerate the presence of iniquity (xvii. 28): all his subjects will be 'sons of God' (xvii. 30), all will be holy (xvii. 36).

It is *wise*. With wisdom he is to begin his work of purification (xvii. 25), and with wisdom he is to judge the peoples (xvii. 31). God endows him with the Holy Spirit and makes him mighty in wisdom and understanding (xvii. 42, xviii. 8).

It is *just*. Upon this quality, inseparable from that of wisdom (xvii. 31), great stress is laid. Justice will attend his work of destruction (xvii. 25) and his task of ruling (xvii. 28, 29, 31). Justice will temper his might (xvii. 42, xviii. 8), and under his rule no oppression shall take place (xvii. 46). His utterance will be mighty to overthrow (xvii.

27, 39); but his words will be purer than the gold, and when he administers judgement they will be as 'the words of angels' (xvii. 48, 49).

(ii) Certain distinctive characteristics of the treatment of the Messiah in the Psalms of Solomon.

(*a*) The title 'Christ,' 'Anointed One' (Χριστὸς, מָשִׁיחַ) is here perhaps used for the first time in literature of the expected Deliverer of Israel. 'It is not a characteristic title of the promised Saviour in the O. T. It is not even specifically applied to Him, unless perhaps in Dan. ix. 25 f., a passage of which the interpretation is very doubtful' (Westcott, *Ep. of St John*, p. 189). Three times over this name, destined to play so unique a part, occurs (xvii. 36, xviii. 6, 8) in our book. Repeatedly as the word has occurred before in other writings, it has always had reference to actual monarchs then reigning, never to an ideal monarch who was to come.

(*b*) The Messiah of these Psalms is to be 'the son of David.' The significance of this must not be overlooked. We return to the conception of the Prophets. Haggai had been the last to point to the lineage of David (ii. 21—23). Zechariah had emphasized the priestly side of the Messianic hope (vi. 11—13). In the time of the Maccabees it centres in a 'faithful prophet' (1 Macc. xiv. 41; cf. iv. 46); and it is not David but Jeremiah who appears in a dream to Judas Maccabeus (2 Macc. xv. 12—16). In Ecclesiasticus again (xlviii. 10, 11) it is Elijah the prophet who is to 'establish the tribes of Jacob.' The Messianic vocation of the house of David, which since the Captivity had fallen into the background, and under the glorious reign of the first Asmonean princes had almost been lost to view, reappears in these Pharisaic Psalms.

(*c*) The Messiah is a vassal-king, not Supreme Sovereign. He is only God's vicegerent upon earth. Jehovah is 'his God' (xvii. 28, 41, xviii. 8); and Jehovah is his king (xvii. 38); his reign will be a blessing to the people of Jehovah (xvii. 40); he tends not his own, but Jehovah's flock (xvii. 45). The Messianic kingdom is not a pure theocracy: for, although God is at the head of the nation, there is a visible earthly king, who is strong because his hope is in God (xvii. 43).

(*d*) The Messiah unites the offices of king and priest. There is no reference to the priestly order in the description of the Messianic kingdom. This omission is of similar significance with the assertion of 'the Davidic lineage.' The son of David is the anointed one, consecrated to the work of purification and to the dispensation of unswerving justice. In this silence with regard to the priestly order, in this emphasis on Messianic justice, can we not read the indignation of the Pharisee oppressed by corrupt Sadducee nobles, and watching with anguished soul the irregularities of a worldly priesthood?

(*e*) The Messiah of this Psalm is not divine. Divinely appointed, divinely raised up, endowed with divine gifts, he is; but he is nothing more than man. Neither of supernatural birth, nor of pre-existence in the bosom of God or among the angels of God, do we find any trace. If he is called Lord (?xvii. 36), the word is only used of him as it might be of an earthly lord. However high the conception of his moral character and spiritual qualifications, he is man, and man only.

(*f*) To what figure in the history of Israel does he most nearly correspond? We answer, to that of Solomon. Was he not 'a son of David,' the extender of the boundaries of the kingdom, the restorer and beautifier of the worship of Jehovah, a receiver of tribute from foreign monarchs, who came to see his glory, and distinguished above all other princes for wisdom and justice? In all these particulars we see a resemblance between Solomon and the Messiah of our xviith Psalm. And contrasts are not wanting. Solomon *did* sin in multiplying silver and gold, horses, chariots and ships. That is exactly what the Messiah will not do. Solomon was not καθαρὸς ἀπὸ ἁμαρτίας: Solomon, as we see from the complaints to Rehoboam, was not guiltless of oppression. The Messiah will be pure of sin, and will suffer neither pride nor oppression.

Now in the earlier Jewish literature, the name of Solomon had been connected with Messianic aspirations. The lxxiind Psalm is called a Psalm εἰς Σαλόμων, and in it we have one of the most striking parallels to our Psalm. If that description of an idealised Solomon came to be attributed to the king himself, as it did, it is conceivable (and more than that we are not prepared to claim) that the ascription of the present collection to Solomon arose from the similarity of the leading Psalm to one that was already known as a Psalm of Solomon or was at least associated with his name.

(*g*) The description of the Messiah contains several passages drawn from the Old Testament, e.g.

xvii. 26 is based upon Psalm ii.
,, 34 ,, ,, 1 Kings x., Ps. lxxii. 10, Is. lxvi. 18—20.
,, 39 ,, ,, Is. xi. 4.
,, 42 ,, ,, Is. xlii. 6.

(iii) The special significance of this representation of the Messiah (*a*) in the history of the Doctrine, (*b*) in the history of the Jewish people. (See especially Prof. Robertson Smith's Article 'Messiah' in the *Encyclopædia Britannica*.)

(a) The picture of the Messiah in our xviith Psalm marks the most notable advance in the conception of the Messianic expectation. Here for the first time in *Palestinian* literature, the idea of a *personal* Messiah is unequivocally stated. The passage in Daniel (ch. vii.) which offers a possible exception is of much disputed interpretation, and the only other Palestinian writing of a date anterior to our Psalms that makes any reference to a personal Messiah [i.e. the First Book of Enoch (ch. xc. 37, 38), a document written perhaps about 120 B.C.], employs in its description the vague mystic style of apocalyptic language, 'And I saw till all their generations were changed, and they all became white bullocks, and the first one of them [was the word and that word] was a great animal, and had on its head large and black horns.'

On the other hand the literature of *Alexandrine* Judaism presents in a Sibylline Fragment (*Orac. Sibyll.* iii. 652 etc.), composed probably in the last quarter of the 2nd cent. B.C., a remarkable picture of the Messianic king:

καὶ τότ' ἀπ' ἠελίοιο θεὸς πέμψει βασιλῆα
ὃς πᾶσαν γαῖαν παύσει πολέμοιο κακοῖο·
οὓς μὲν ἄρα κτείνας οἷς δ' ὅρκια πιστὰ τελέσσας.
οὐδέ γε ταῖς ἰδίαις βουλαῖς τάδε πάντα ποιήσει,
ἀλλὰ θεοῦ μεγάλοιο πιθήσας δόγμασιν ἐσθλοῖς......

Here the king sent by God, possessing universal power, bringing peace, executing judgement, fulfilling the promises, subject to the Almighty, is in many respects a remarkable parallel to the representation in the Psalms of Solomon. But it is noticeable that later on in the same fragment the description of the Messianic kingdom takes no account of a personal ruler (766—783).

καὶ τότε δ' ἐξεγερεῖ βασιλήϊον εἰς αἰῶνας
πάντας ἐπ' ἀνθρώπους......
αὕτη γὰρ μεγάλοιο θεοῦ κρίσις ἠδὲ καὶ ἀρχή.

In our xviith Psalm the description of the expected Saviour is in striking contrast to the previous vague generalities of a glorious kingdom. The word 'Messiah,' which had hitherto been given to reigning earthly types, is appropriated to the personal ideal. The Davidic descent is revived from the writings of the people's Scriptures; and the longing for 'great David's greater son,' which has no place in Daniel, in Enoch, or the Assumption of Moses, perhaps first received from our Psalms the impulse, which in the next generation caused Davidic descent to be regarded as an essential element of any Messianic claim (cf. Matt. ii. 5, 6, xxii. 42).

Second only in importance to this added definiteness in the conception of the Messiah's person must rank the spiritual force and moral beauty which are here assigned to him. The sin and violence of the recent Asmonean rule had perhaps aroused in the mind of the Pharisee Psalmist the hope for a sinless ruler, whose weapons would be spiritual and whose moral force would be irresistible.

In this representation of the human Messiah, perfect in holiness and taught of God, free from sin and wielding only the weapons of spiritual power, we find ourselves brought more nearly than in any other extant pre-Christian writing to the idealization of 'the Christ' who was born into the world not half a century later than the time at which these Psalms were written.

(*b*) Its significance in the history of the Jewish people. The vividness and completeness of this Messianic picture are of deep historical significance. It marks the revolution which had passed over *Pharisaic* thought since the time, not a century before, when Israel's mission in the world was identified only with the fulfilment and dissemination of 'the Law,' when the whole duty of 'the righteous' seemed to be to fear God, to obey the Scribes and to live apart from the politics of the nations, when patriotism was satisfied by vague generalities respecting Israel's future greatness.

A complete change of view is presented in our Psalm; and we cannot doubt that this was brought about by the political events of the century which preceded the invasion of Pompey. The heroic deeds of Judas Maccabeus and his brothers had rekindled the ardour of the people for a Jewish dynasty and a Jewish kingdom; and the Pharisaic supporters of a Theocracy were powerless, so long as their teaching showed no sympathy with this patriotic enthusiasm. On the other hand, the deterioration in the character of the later Asmonean princes, their violence and cruelty, alienated the affections of the people: it was hopeless to look for Israel's restoration from a dynasty sunk in selfishness and cruelty. It is at this crisis that the Pharisaic idea of a Messiah king, of the house of David, combines the recognition of the failure of the Asmonean house with the popular enthusiasm for a Jewish monarchy. The Davidic Messiah is to overthrow the yoke of the Gentiles, he is to disperse the Sadducean nobles, he is to establish the universal kingdom of Israel upon the eternal foundations of a wise and just administration.

Such a treatment of the Messianic hope must have brought the Pharisees an immense accession of moral influence over the people at large. It appealed to the patriotic feelings of those who had no power to appreciate the abstract beauty of the old legalism. By its hope for a 'son of David,' it proclaimed the downfall of the Levitical Asmonean house. By its ideal reign of 'wisdom and righteousness,' it asserted the fundamental Pharisaic position that the Law was supreme. It united the craving for a Jewish king with the theocratic interpretation of Israel's mission to the world; it expressed the highest aspirations of the pious Jew, and satisfied the sense of partisan malignity against the Sadducee.

In the religious history of the nation, the Messianic representation of our xviith Psalm thus marks the stage, at which Pharisaic thought passed beyond the narrow limits of its earlier teaching, and availed itself of the popular aspiration for an earthly kingdom. The splendid vision of a Davidic Messiah, contrasting naturally with the degradation of the Asmonean line, became the source of a religious enthusiasm, which corresponded to the teaching of the Israelite prophets, but which entailed upon the theocratic party no policy beyond the exercise of patience, till God should raise up the king, and until then the minute observance of His law (cf. Pirqe Aboth i. 11. Shemaiah said, Love work; and hate lordship; and make not thyself known to the government). This hope became incorporated with the life of the Jews. And while the mass of the Pharisees contentedly awaited, in the discharge of their religious duties, the coming of the king, the more fiery and ill-regulated spirits of the patriots saw in every Theudas the personification of their expectations, and sought to interpret their own hopes in that succession of outbreaks, which culminated in the national overthrow of Barcochab's revolution.

§ vii. *Place of Writing, Authorship, Purpose, Style, Title, of the Psalms of Solomon.*

(a) *Where written?* The prominence given to Jerusalem makes it probable that our Psalms were composed by a Jew (or Jews) residing in the capital. 'The Holy City,' or 'The City of the Sanctuary' (viii. 4), is in the Psalmist's estimation the centre of the universe. The interest of the great events described in Pss. ii. viii. and xvii. is bound up with the unique position of the Jewish capital. The song of triumph (Ps. xi.) is to be proclaimed in Jerusalem: the city itself is addressed, she is bidden to go up and view the restoration of her children, and to put on festal attire; for the blessing of the Lord will rest on Jerusalem (xi. 3, 8, 9). It is with Jerusalem that the work of the purification by the Messianic 'son of David' will commence (xvii.

25): it is to Jerusalem that the nations of the earth will gather to see his glory (xvii. 33). The allusion to the 'profane' ones, members of 'the Council' (iv. 1), and the description of their vices and crimes in Ps. iv. 2—15, xii., are best understood of men whose life was spent in a city. Similarly the temptations to immorality referred to in Ps. xvi. will naturally be associated with the condition of things in an urban population.

(*b*) *By whom written?* The result of our enquiries has been to show that our book had its origin in the Pharisaic Judaism of Jerusalem in the middle of the last century, B.C. Whether we have the work of more than one writer it is impossible to determine. The difference of style to be noted, e.g. in ix.—xv., is largely to be accounted for by the difference of subject-matter, and at any rate is not sufficiently marked to supply any certain criterion.

The conjecture has suggested itself to us at various points in our investigation of the book, that the Pharisee writer or writers belonged to the order of the priesthood. It would be impossible to draw any line which could distinguish the sympathies of a Pharisee priest from those of a Pharisee patriotic layman. And we do not pretend to claim that the evidence upon which the conjecture rests is of a very convincing nature. But our theory invests the Psalms with an additional human interest, and we confess that our general impression in its favour has grown and not diminished with the progress of our work*.

It is based upon (*a*) the prominence given to ceremonial pollution (e.g. i. 8, ii. 2, 3, viii. 12, 13, 26) and purification (e.g. iii. 8—10, xvii. 25, 33); (*b*) the frequent use of thought and language borrowed from the priestly writings of Leviticus and Ezekiel; (*c*) the tone of jealousy with which it is implied that the Temple had passed into hands that had no legal right to it, and that the Psalmist would identify himself with those from whom its control had been forcibly wrested (e.g. vii. 2, xvii. 6, 7).

(*c*) *The purpose of the collection.* Judging from the character and contents of the more important Psalms, we can hardly doubt that their object is, in a great measure, polemical; they are intended to deliver the solemn protest of devout Pharisaism against the corrupting influence upon the nation of the surviving members of the Asmonean party.

To the distinctively political Psalms were added those of a more general character; and it is possible that the whole collection was in-

---

* It may be a fanciful thought, but no description could better represent our conception of the writer of these Psalms than the picture of Symeon in Luke ii. 25 (καὶ ἰδοὺ ἄνθρωπος ἦν ἐν Ἰερουσαλὴμ ᾧ ὄνομα Συμεών, καὶ ὁ ἄνθρωπος οὗτος δίκαιος καὶ εὐλαβής, προσδεχόμενος παράκλησιν τοῦ Ἰσραήλ), who must have been a man in the prime of life when they were written.

tended for public or even for liturgical use. The occurrence of 'Selah' (διάψαλμα) in xvii. 31, xviii. 10, if originally part of the text, and not introduced out of mere imitation of the Canonical Psalter, would go to support this view. Similarly if the titles of Pss. viii. x. xiv. are genuine, they would indicate that these Psalms at least were originally designed for adaptation to music.

(*d*) *Style and character.* The general character of these Psalms is extremely simple and straightforward. They are in a great measure based in tone and thought upon the Old Testament Scriptures, and this is shown even more in the adaptation of words and phrases than in the citation of passages. Written obviously in imitation of the Canonical Psalms, the collection preserves throughout the strictly Psalmic type of composition. Each Psalm is composed upon a clearly defined plan and forms a separate unity. By their simplicity both in thought and structure, they were well adapted for popular use.

In Palestinian literature they occupy in style, as in date of composition, a midway position between the familiar discourse of gnomic philosophy in Ecclesiasticus, and the more imaginative but diffuse and wearisome composition of the Apocalyptic writers, e.g. Enoch, 2 Esdras, Apoc. of Baruch.

We cannot claim any high standard of poetical merit for the majority of our Psalms. Generally speaking they are wanting both in originality and artistic beauty. But the passage describing Pompey's death is not without considerable lyrical force (ii. 24—35). Ps. viii. contains, in a short compass, a vigorous poetical sketch of the whole historical crisis of Pompey's invasion. In Ps. xvii. the Psalmist's conception of the Messiah is treated in a passage of sustained energy and loftiness of expression. The hatred and scorn which have dictated the denunciations of Ps. iv. produce a painfully vivid impression, to which the reposeful confidence of nature in the bounty of the Creator, described in Ps. v., offers an agreeable contrast.

The writings which, in our opinion, most nearly approach our Psalms in style and character, are the hymns preserved in the early chapters of St Luke's Gospel (i. 46—55, 67—79, ii. 10—14, 29—32), which in point of date of composition stand probably nearer to the Psalms of Solomon than any other portion of the New Testament.

(*e*) *The title 'Psalms of Solomon.'*

The origin of this title must remain in obscurity.

The opinion that they were the genuine writings of king Solomon was undoubtedly held at one time; but, except from the title, was absolutely devoid of evidence in its support. For Whiston's strange view, see p. xv.

INTRODUCTION.

The possibility must certainly be admitted that 'Solomon' may be the name of the author, an otherwise unknown Pharisee.

We entertain however no doubt that king Solomon is the Solomon intended, and that his name has been given pseudonymously. Now if we accept the pseudonymous character of the title, we have further to enquire whether the book received this title from the author, or from subsequent copyists or translators. According to the former alternative, we must class the collection with other pseudepigraphic writings of this period, e.g. the book of Enoch, the Wisdom of Solomon, etc., and assume that the writer hoped by the use of a revered name to secure a permanent position in literature for his work. Against this view it may be urged that, unlike the pseudepigraphic writings just mentioned, our Psalms contain no other certain allusion to their reputed author.

To us it appears most probable that copyists or translators are responsible for having ascribed the work to Solomonic authorship. For the selection of Solomon's name different reasons might be alleged. We have already mentioned (see p. lv.) that the picture of the Messianic king, the son of David, a man of peace, wisdom and might, might have given the title to the xviith Psalm, and have been transferred from this, the most important writing, to the whole collection. Other reasons based upon the contents of particular Psalms, are (1) the possible resemblance of certain passages (e.g. iv. 4—6, v. 15—20, vi. 1—3, ix. 5—9, xiv. 1—3, xvi. 7—15, xviii. 12—14) to the style of the book of Proverbs, and (2) the fact that the subject of Ps. xvi., a thanksgiving for pardon after a fall into grievous sensual sin, offered a sufficiently close parallel to the traditional close of Solomon's life.

But we are of opinion that Solomon's name was selected for reasons of a much less definite character. Given an anonymous collection of Jewish Psalms composed in imitation of the Canonical Psalter, it was desirable that they should be known by some definite name. The name of David was appropriated to the Canonical Psalter; the name of David's son, Solomon, would naturally suggest itself. Although Solomon's songs had been "a thousand and five" (1 Kings iv. 32), Canticles and two Psalms (lxxii. and cxxvii.) were all the Hebrew poetry that tradition had so far connected with Solomon's name. That the remainder of Solomon's writings might have included the present collection, would seem to an uncritical age, accustomed to the production of pseudepigraphic works, to constitute a very probable supposition. The prestige attaching to Solomon's name was so great, that no title would be more effective to secure the preservation of an otherwise obscure collection of Psalms; and the title did its work. To their name we owe the accident of their preservation. In the few extant MSS. which contain the Psalms of Solomon, they are found among the sapiential writings ascribed to king Solomon.

§ viii. *The Psalms of Solomon and Jewish Literature.*

The book occupies a unique position in the extant Jewish literature of the last century before the Christian era. The only other extant writings of Palestinian origin which belong to the same period are the Book of Enoch, fragments preserved in the Pirqe Aboth, and possibly the Book of Jubilees, representing apocalyptic, gnomic, and Midrashic elements respectively. With these it has no similarity in style or structure, although it is not without points of contact in its treatment of religious thought.

The Psalmic literature, with which we naturally class it, comprises (a) Ecclus. li., (b) Judith xvi. 2—17, (c) Tobit xiii., (d) Luke i. 47—55, 68—79; ii. 10—14, 30—32, to which some would add, (e) the so-called Maccabean Psalms xliv., lxxiv., lxxix., lxxxiii.

The Psalms in Ecclus. Judith and Tobit are possibly only incidentally introduced from other national collections of poetry, and bear some general resemblance to the characteristic features of our Psalter. But a closer resemblance is presented by the Songs contained in the opening chapters of St Luke's Gospel. Both in thought and in structure they seem to belong to the same class of literature as the Psalms of Solomon: and it is a matter not without interest and importance, that our Psalms, which stand closest of all extant Jewish religious poetry to the Christian era, are so conspicuously similar to the songs which are the earliest writings incorporated in the New Testament Scriptures.

We come next to consider the question, whether any traces are to be found in the Psalms of Solomon of the influence of other writings. It is scarcely an exaggeration to say that they are in a great measure constructed out of the language of the Old Testament. The books from which our Psalmist has most frequently borrowed are the Pentateuch, the Psalms, Isaiah and Ezekiel. His method is to appropriate a phrase or sentence of Scripture as preferable to one of his own coining because already sacred and familiar to his readers, and to fuse it with his own words, introducing some slight alteration or modification. No sign is given of a citation. At a time when all Jewish religious writing

INTRODUCTION.

was based upon Scripture, such acknowledgment would not be necessary: and in poetry it would not be expected.

Direct allusions are not as a rule made to events in the people's earlier history. The mention of the patriarch Abraham (ix. 17), of king David (xvii. 5), and of the Babylonian Captivity (ix. 1) is exceptional.

Allusions however of a more indirect nature are fairly numerous. Thus in i. 8 τὰ πρὸ αὐτῶν ἔθνη is a reference to the wickedness of the Canaanites; in ii. 24 there is an allusion to the staying of the plague in David's reign (2 Sam. xxiv. 16; 1 Chro. xxi. 15); in ii. 27 ἐν ζήλῳ the ferocity of the Romans is compared with the 'zeal' of Phinehas; in ii. 35 ἀνιστῶν...κοιμίζων we have an echo from the Song of Hannah (1 Sam. ii. 6—8); in vii. 3, 4 there is an allusion to David's prayer that he might fall into the hands of God rather than into the hands of his foes (2 Sam. xxiv. 14); in viii. 27, 28 and xiii. 4, 5 there seems to be a reference to Lot in Sodom; in xv. 6 we have an allusion to the Three Children; in xv. 7 to the overthrow of Korah, Dathan and Abiram, in xv. 9 to the mark set upon Cain; in xvi. 7 seqq. some have seen a reference to the fall of Solomon led away by 'strange wives'; in xvi. 11—15 we are reminded of the story of Job; in xvii. 5 seq. we are reminded of Nathan's declaration to David in 2 Sam. vii. 11—15; in xviii. 12 the creation of the 'heavenly bodies' in Gen. i. is referred to; in xviii. 4 the story of Joshua at Bethhoron (Jos. x. 12), or of Isaiah and the sun-dial of Ahaz (2 Kings xx. 11), or both together, are implied in the words, ἐπιταγῇ δούλων.

It is not, in our opinion, possible to prove that our Psalmist is influenced by Jewish literature not included in the Hebrew Canon of Scripture. The language and thought of Ecclesiasticus often illustrate our Psalms; actual correspondences of expression are found; but the agreement is generally to be explained by some passage of Scripture from which both writers have borrowed.

Ecclus. iii. 25 ὁ ἁμαρτωλὸς προσθήσει ἁμαρτίαν ἐφ' ἁμαρτίαις (v. 5, xxi. 1). Cf. Ps. S. iii. 7, 12.

,, ix. 8 ἀπόστρεψον ὀφθαλμὸν ἀπὸ γυναικὸς εὐμόρφου καὶ μὴ καταμάνθανε κάλλος ἀλλότριον· ἐν κάλλει γυναικὸς πολλοὶ ἐπλανήθησαν. Cf. Ps. S. xvi. 7, 8.

,, xvii. 14 καὶ μερὶς κυρίου Ἰσραήλ ἐστιν (xxiv. 12). Cf. Ps. S. xiv. 3.

,, xviii. 12 ἔλεος ἀνθρώπου ἐπὶ τὸν πλησίον αὐτοῦ, ἔλεος δὲ κυρίου ἐπὶ πᾶσαν σάρκα. Cf. Ps. S. v. 15—17.

,, xxxii. 12 κύριος κριτής ἐστι, καὶ οὐκ ἔστι παρ' αὐτῷ δόξα προσώπου. Cf. Ps. S. ii. 19.

J. P.

Ecclus. xxxvi. (xxxiii.) 17 λαὸν, κύριε, κεκλημένον ἐπ' ὀνόματί σου...οἰκτείρησον πόλιν ἁγιάσματός σου, Ἰερουσαλήμ, τόπον καταπαύματός σου. Cf. Ps. S. ix. 16—18.

„ xxxix. 29, 30 ...καὶ λιμὸς καὶ θάνατος,...θηρίων ὀδόντες...καὶ ῥομφαία ἐκδικοῦσα εἰς ὄλεθρον ἀσεβεῖς. Cf. Ps. S. xiii. 2, 3.

„ xl. 14 ἐν τῷ ἀνοῖξαι αὐτὸν χεῖρας εὐφρανθήσεται. Cf. Ps. S. v. 14.

„ xlv. 18 ἐπισυνέστησαν αὐτῷ ἀλλότριοι (= זרים for זדים). Cf. Ps. S. xvii. 6.

„ li. 6 ἤγγισεν ἕως θανάτου ἡ ψυχή μου, καὶ ἡ ζωή μου ἦν σύνεγγυς ᾅδου κάτω. Cf. Ps. S. xvi. 2.

This list might be considerably enlarged. But the instances already given will be sufficient to show the character of the resemblance.

The most ancient fragment contained in the Sibylline Oracles iii. 97 etc. (exc. 295—490) contains expressions, which will illustrate passages in our Psalms; but there is no probability in the view that the Sibyllines are actually quoted.

Orac. Sib. iii. 185   ...στήσουσί τε παῖδας
                        Αἰσχροῖς ἐν τεγέεσσι. Cf. Ps. S. ii. 13.

„ „ 316 Ῥομφαία γάρ σε διελεύσεται διὰ μέσσου,
        Σκορπισμὸς δέ τε καὶ θάνατος καὶ λιμὸς ἐφέξει.
                                        Cf. Ps. S. xv. 8.

„ „ 643 seq.   ἄταφοι δὲ ἅπαντες ἔσονται·
                Καὶ τῶν μὲν γῦπές τε καὶ ἄγρια θηρία γαίης
                Σαρκῶν δηλήσονται. Cf. Ps. S. iv. 21.

„ „ 652 seq. Καὶ τότ' ἀπ' ἠελίοιο θεὸς πέμψει βασιλῆα,...
                                    Cf. Ps. S. xvii. 23, seq.

„ „ 702 Υἱοὶ δ' αὖ μεγάλοιο θεοῦ περὶ ναὸν ἅπαντες
        Ἡσυχίως ζήσοντ'. Cf. Ps. S. xvii. 30.

„ „ 705 Αὐτὸς γὰρ σκεπάσειε μόνος μεγάλως τε παραστάς.
                                    Cf. Ps. S. xiii. 1.

„ „ 734 seq. Στεῖλον δὴ ἐπὶ τήνδε πόλιν τὸν λαὸν ἄβουλον...
                                    Cf. Ps. S. xi., xvii. 34.

„ „ 770 Καὶ νοῦν ἀθάνατον αἰώνιον εὐφροσύνην τε.
                                    Cf. Ps. S. x. 9.

„ „ 785 σοὶ δ' ἔσσεται ἀθάνατον φῶς. Cf. Ps. S. iii. 16.

The points of resemblance which have been noticed in the Book of Wisdom are of a similar character. (Respecting the instances, in which our Psalms have been alleged to borrow from the phraseology of 'Wisdom,' see below.)

INTRODUCTION. lxv

The earlier portions of the Book of Enoch present a remarkable parallel to the reference in Ps. S. xviii. 11 seq. to the ordered course of the heavenly bodies. Cf. chap. ii. 1 'the luminaries which are in the heavens do not depart from their paths, each one rises and sets in order, each in its time, and they do not depart from their laws,' and xxxvi. 3.

In the Jewish literature subsequent to the composition of our Psalms, we find no certain trace, except in Baruch v., of the influence of this work. (On the resemblance of Ps. S. xi. to Baruch v., see a full discussion p. lxxii. ff.)

On the other hand, there is hardly a single important Palestinian writing of the following century, which does not receive useful illustration from the language or religious teaching of the Psalms of Solomon.

1. The Parables in the Book of Enoch (cc. 37—71) were very probably written about B.C. 30. The general similarity of thought may be illustrated by

Enoch xli. 1 the deeds of men are weighed upon scales. Cf. Ps. S. v. 6.

„ xlix. 3 the spirit of wisdom, and the spirit of him who imparts understanding, and the spirit of doctrine and of power. Cf. Ps. S. xvii. 42, xviii. 8.

„ liii. 7 the just will rest from the oppression of sinners. Cf. Ps. S. ii. 39, xvii. 46.

„ lvi. 6 And they will ascend and step upon the land of their chosen, and the land of his chosen will be before them a threshing-floor and a path. Cf. Ps. S. ii. 2.

„ lviii. 3 the light of everlasting life. Cf. Ps. S. iii. 16.

„ lxii. 2 And the word of his mouth slew all the sinners and all the impious, and they were destroyed before his face. Cf. Ps. S. xvii. 27, 39, 41.

„ „ 8 the congregation of the holy. Cf. Ps. S. xvii. 18.

„ lxiii. 8 his judgement does not respect persons. Ps. S. ii. 19.

„ lxix. 27 he causes to disappear and to be destroyed the sinners from the face of the earth. Cf. Ps. S. xiii. 10, xv. 13.

2. The Book of Jubilees or 'the Little Genesis' (ed. Rönsch), written possibly about the time of the Christian era, has no very obvious points of resemblance with the contents of our book. The following instances show the general similarity of thought and language in the Jewish writing of that period:

Jub. xv. 14 non est super eum signum ut sit Deo sed exterminii et perditionis a terrâ. Cf. Ps. S. xv. 8, 10.

Jub. xvi. 29 laudans et confitens Deo suo secundum omnia in lætitia. Cf. Ps. S. xv. 3—5.

„ xxi. 4 quia Deus vivens est et sanctus et fidelis et justus et ex omnibus non est apud eum accipere personam. Cf. Ps. S. ii. 19.

„ xxiii. 22 et sanctificationem polluent in abominationibus pravitatis et immunditiis. Cf. Ps. S. i. 8, ii. 3, viii. 13.

„ „ 25 in die viæ judicii...et non erit illis omne nomen relictum super terram. Cf. Ps. S. xiii. 10, xv. 13.

„ „ 26 et si ascendetur usque ad cælum, inde deponetur. Cf. Ps. S. i. 5.

„ xxvii. 9 dirigentur omnes viæ ejus. Cf. Ps. S. vi. 3.

„ xxxi. 20, 21 Et Judæ dixit Dabit tibi Deus fortitudinem et virtutem, ut tu conculces omnes odientes te: princeps eris tu, et unus filiorum tuorum...erit alienus et optinens universam terram et regiones; hunc timebunt populi a facie tua et conturbabuntur universæ gentes. Cf. Ps. S. xvii. 38, 42.

3. The writings of the New Testament receive from our Psalms helpful illustration in certain particulars.

(*a*) 'The Songs' embodied in Luke i. ii.

(*b*) The expected Messiah is a son of David (e.g. Matt. ii., xxi. 9, xxii. 42—45; Joh. vii. 42; Rom. i. 3; 2 Tim. ii. 8; Rev. v. 5, xxii. 16). Cf. Ps. S. xvii.

(*c*) The description of 'the righteousness of the Scribes and Pharisees' (e.g. Matt. vi. 1—18). Cf. Ps. S. iii.

(*d*) The metaphor of 'the strong man' (Mark iii. 27). Cf. Ps. S. v. 4.

(*e*) The comparison of Divine and human kindness (Luke xi. 5—8). Cf. Ps. S. v. 15, 16.

(*f*) Certain phrases e.g. ἐκλογή 'Divine choice' Rom. ix. 11 etc., cf. Ps. S. ix. 7; κληρονομεῖν ἐπαγγελίας κυρίου Heb. xii. 12, cf. Ps. S. xii. 8; τὸ ποιμνίον κυρίου (= θεοῦ 1 Pet. v. 2), cf. Ps. S. xvii. 45; ἀνίστασθαι εἰς ζωὴν αἰώνιον (John v. 29 εἰς ἀνάστασιν ζωῆς), cf. Ps. S. iii. 16.

4. The Apocalyptic work, known as the 4th Book of Esdras, and dating from the close of the 1st cent. A.D., has been considered by Hilgenfeld and Geiger to show signs of having borrowed from, or at least of being acquainted with, the Psalms of Solomon. We give here the passages, which are alleged to show signs of this correspondence.

(*a*) 4 Esdr. iii. 8 'et tu non prohibuisti eos.' Cf. Ps. S. ii. 1 καὶ

INTRODUCTION. lxvii

οὐκ ἐκώλυσας. The words in 4 Esdr. are not found in the Latin, Ethiopic or Armenian versions; they appear in the Syriac and Arabic, where they are used with reference to the fact that the Lord did not restrain the wickedness of the Antediluvians. In Ps. S. the Psalmist is speaking of the heathen, whom the Lord did not prevent from attacking the Holy City.

(*b*) 4 Esdr. iv. 25 'Sed quid faciet nomini suo, qui invocatus est super nos?' and ix. 22 'et nomen quod nominatum est super nos pene profanatum est.' Cf. Ps. S. ix. 18 ἔθου τὸ ὄνομά σου ἐφ' ἡμᾶς, κύριε. Both passages have in common the thought which is based upon the Old Testament Scriptures, that the Lord had set His name upon His people. Cf. 2 Chron. vii. 14.

(*c*) 4 Esdr. vi. 24 et venæ fontium stabunt et non decurrent in tribus horis. Cf. Ps. S. xvii. 21 πηγαὶ συνεσχέθησαν αἰώνιοι ἐξ ἀβύσσων ἀπ' ὀρέων ὑψηλῶν. The stopping of the fountains of the earth is in 4 Esd. one of the portents preceding the coming of the Messiah; in Ps. S. the fact is also narrated, perhaps as a sign that the Messianic times had begun.

(*d*) 4 Esdr. vi. 58 nos autem populus tuus quem vocasti primogenitum unigenitum æmulatorem carissimum. Cf. Ps. S. xviii. 4 ἡ παιδεία σου ἐφ' ἡμᾶς ὡς υἱὸν πρωτότοκον μονογενῆ. The passage in Ps. S. is based upon Deut. viii. 5, and the words πρωτότοκον μονογενῆ may very probably be a duplicate rendering of one word in the original. The context in 4 Esdr. is of a different character; the combination of 'primogenitum, unigenitum,' which is possibly a similar instance of the same duplicate rendering, may conceivably be borrowed from our Psalmist.

(*e*) The description of the Messiah in 4 Esdras has some points of resemblance to that in Ps. S.

(1) The name 'Christ': 4 Esd. vii. 28 filius meus Christus. xii. 32 hic est Unctus. Cf. Ps. S. xvii. 36, xviii. 6, 8.

(2) The work of the Christ: 4 Esdr. xii. 32, 33 secundum impietates ipsorum arguet illos et incutiet coram ipsis spretiones eorum; statuet enim eos in judicium vivos et erit cum arguerit eos tunc corripiet eos. Cf. Ps. S. xvii. 27 καὶ ἐλέγξαι ἁμαρτωλοὺς ἐν λόγῳ καρδίας αὐτῶν, 31 κρινεῖ λαοὺς καὶ ἔθνη.

(3) The weapons of the Christ not earthly: 4 Esd. xiii. 9 non levavit manum suam neque frameam tenebat neque aliquod vas bellicosum...emisit de ore suo sicut flatum ignis...et succendit omnes... 37 ipse autem filius meus arguet quæ advenerunt gentes impietates eorum... et perdet eos sine labore per legem quæ igni assimilata est. Cf. Ps. S. xvii. 37 οὐ γὰρ ἐλπιεῖ ἐπὶ ἵππον καὶ ἀναβάτην καὶ τόξον. It will be observed

that 4 Esdras brings out in much closer detail the judicial functions of the Messiah than does our Psalmist: but that both lay stress on the pacific character of the Messiah, the xviith of our Psalms asserting the sinlessness of the King as the spiritual substitute for material power, 4 Esdras describing the overthrow of foes by the fire of the Divine law.

(*f*) The restoration of the tribes, 4 Esd. xiii. 39 et quoniam vidisti eum colligentem ad se aliam multitudinem pacificam, hæ sunt tribus, quæ captivæ factæ sunt etc. Cf. Ps. S. viii. 34 συνάγαγε τὴν διασπορὰν Ἰσραὴλ κ.τ.λ., xi. 3 καὶ ἴδε τὰ τέκνα σου κ.τ.λ., xvii. 50 ἐν συναγωγῇ φυλῶν. The passage in 4 Esdras refers especially to the 10 Tribes; the passages in Ps. S. refer to the Dispersion generally. But undoubtedly in both books the Restoration of the Tribes belongs to the Messianic thought.

We are not disposed to admit that the similarity in these passages is sufficiently close to justify the theory that Esdras has borrowed from the Psalms of Solomon. In the treatment of the Messianic idea, where the similarity is perhaps more definite, the resemblance springs from general agreement in the religious thought rather than from any special obligation of one writing to another. In the other instances the thought in which the two documents agree is not of a sufficiently striking character to render the hypothesis probable.

Other passages may be pointed out, where our Psalms illustrate 4 Esdras in phrase or thought, without any trace of closer dependence.
4 Esdr. iii. 12 impietatem facere plus quam priores. Cf. Ps. S. i. 8.
,, ,, 27 tradidisti civitatem tuam in manibus inimicorum tuorum, x. 23. Cf. Ps. S. ii. 7.
,, iv. 23 quem populum dilexisti. Cf. Ps. S. ix. 16.
,, v. 28 unicum tuum. Cf. Ps. S. xviii. 4.
,, ,, 30 et si odiens odisti populum tuum, tuis manibus debet castigari. Cf. Ps. S. vii. 3.
,, vii. 17 quoniam justi hæreditabunt hæc, impii autem peribunt. Cf. Ps. S. xii. 8.
,, viii. 5 venis (anima mea) sine voluntate tua et abis cum non vis; non enim data est tibi potestas nisi solummodo in vita temporis exigui. Cf. Ps. S. ix. 7.
,, ,, 52 apertus est paradisus, plantata est arbor vitæ. Cf. Ps. S. xiv. 2.
,, x. 22 sancta nostra contaminata sunt...et liberi nostri contumeliam passi sunt. Cf. Ps. S. ii. 3, 13.
,, ,, 50 pulchritudinis decoris ejus. Cf. Ps. S. ii. 5.
5 Esdr. ii. 28 zelabunt gentes et nihil adversus te poterunt. Cf. Ps. S. vii. 6.

5 Esdr. xv. 5 mala...gladium et famem et mortem et interitum. Cf. Ps. S. xiii. 2.

,, xvi. 6 ignem in stipula. Cf. Ps. S. xii. 2.

,, ,, 62 super vertices montium lacus ad emittendum flumina ab eminenti ut potaret terra. Cf. Ps. S. xvii. 21.

5. The Apocalypse of Baruch, composed at about the same date as 4 Esdras, has similar points of resemblance with our book. Thus the personal Messiah is mentioned by name (xxix. 2, xxx. etc.), and there is brief allusion to his judicial and punitive work.

> xl. 1 Messias meus arguet eum (ducem) de omnibus impietatibus suis. lxxii. 2 veniet tempus Messiæ mei et advocabit omnes gentes, et ex iis vivificabit et ex iis interficiet.

The frequent mention of the people's calamities as 'castigatio' ($=\pi\alpha\iota\delta\epsilon\iota\alpha$) introduces a thought very prominent in our Psalms.

In numerous passages we find expressions, which may be illustrated in an interesting way by the Pss. S.

Apoc. Bar. ix. 1 purum cor a peccatis. Cf. Ps. S. xvii. 41.

,, ,, x. 11 vos cœli retinete rorem vestrum neque aperiatis thesauros fluviæ. xxviii. 5, lxii. 4. Cf. Ps. S. xvii. 21.

,, ,, xx. 3 in penetralibus mentis tuæ. Cf. Ps. S. xiv. 5.

,, ,, xli. 3 jugum legis tuæ. Cf. Ps. S. vii. 8.

,, ,, xliv. 4 justus est ille cui servimus neque accipit personas fictor noster. Cf. Ps. S. ii. 19.

,, ,, xlviii. 9 sapientes facis orbes cœlestes ut ministrent in ordinibus suis. Cf. Ps. S. xviii. 12—14 (xix. 2—4).

,, ,, — 15 dono tuo venimus in mundum. Cf. Ps. S. v. 5.

,, ,, li. 11 pulchritudo majestatis (lxxxii. 7, lxxxiii. 12). Cf. Ps. S. ii. 5.

,, ,, lx. 1 permistio contaminationis eorum. Cf. Ps. S. ii. 15.

,, ,, lxviii. 2 decidet populus tuus in calamitatem ut periclitentur ut pereant omnes simul. Cf. Ps. S. ii. 24.

,, ,, lxxviii. 2 ut justificaretis judicium ejus. Cf. Ps. S. iii. 3, viii. 27.

,, ,, — 7 misericordia multa colligeret denuo omnes qui dispersi sunt. Cf. Ps. S. viii. 34.

,, ,, lxxix. 2 sed neque castigavit nos sicut digni eramus. Cf. Ps. S. ix. 15, xiii. 8.

,, ,, lxxxv. 7 adhuc in spiritu sumus et potestate libertatis nostræ. Cf. Ps. S. ix. 7.

,, ,, — 9 ut assumamus non ut assumamur. Cf. Ps. S. iv. 20.

6. The 'Assumptio Mosis,' belonging to the same class of literature, may also be illustrated from the Psalms of Solomon, although there is no appearance of actual borrowing from the latter work.

Assumpt. Mos. iii. 5 justus et sanctus Dominus, quia enim vos peccastis et nos pariter abducti sumus vobiscum. Cf. Ps. S. x. 16.

„   „   iv. 2 voluisti plebem hanc esse tibi plebem exceptam, tunc voluisti invocari eorum deus secus testamentum quod fecisti cum patribus suis. Cf. Ps. S. ix. 16—19.

„   „   v. 1 participes scelerum. Cf. Ps. S. xiv. 4.

„   „   — 3 contaminabunt inquinationibus domum servitutis suae...4 altarium inquinabunt...dedecoris muneribus quae imponent Domino qui non sunt sacerdotes sed servi de servis nati. Cf. Ps. S. viii. 12, xvii. 6.

„   „   — 6 impii judices. Cf. Ps. S. xvii. 22.

„   „   vi. 8 et occidentis rex potens qui expugnabit eos. Cf. Ps. S. viii. 16.

„   „   vii. 4 homines dolosi, sibi placentes, exterminatores, queruli et fallaces, celantes se.

„   „   — 9 et manus eorum et dentes immunda tractabunt, et os eorum loquetur ingentia et superdicent Noli tu me tangere ne inquines me. Cf. Ps. S. iv. xii.

„   „   x. 6 fontes aquarum deficient. Cf. Ps. S. xvii. 21.

„   „   — 9 faciet te haerere caelo stellarum. Cf. Ps. S. i. 5.

„   „   xi. 12 tanquam pater unicum filium. Cf Ps S xiii. 8.

7. The 'Testamenta xii. Patriarcharum,' which are perhaps to be assigned in their present form to the beginning of the 2nd cent. A.D., have not much in common with the Psalms of Solomon. The Messianic thought is much more advanced: the Messiah is Divine as well as Human; his priestly functions are more conspicuous than his regal. The sinlessness of the Messiah, which is so strongly emphasized in our xviith Psalm, receives here also especial recognition, e.g. Lev. ιγ΄. ἐπὶ τῆς ἱερωσύνης αὐτοῦ ἐκλείψει πᾶσα ἁμαρτία. Jud. κδ΄. πᾶσα ἁμαρτία οὐχ εὑρεθήσεται ἐν αὐτῷ.

The following are instances of general correspondence in thought and phraseology.

Reub. δ΄. μὴ οὖν προσέχετε κάλλος γυναικῶν. Iud. ιγ΄. μηδὲ ἐμβλέπειν εἰς κάλλος γυναικῶν. Cf. Ps. S. xvi. 8.

Sim. γ΄. ἐκάκωσα ἐν νηστείᾳ τὴν ψυχήν μου. Cf. Ps. S. iii. 9.

INTRODUCTION. lxxi

ζ'. ἀναστήσει γὰρ κύριος ἐκ τοῦ Λευὶ ὡς ἀρχιερέα καὶ ἐκ τοῦ Ἰούδα ὡς βασιλέα θεὸν καὶ ἄνθρωπον. Cf. Ps. S. xvii. 23.

Lev. γ'. εἰς ἡμέραν προστάγματος κυρίου ἐν τῇ δικαιοκρισίᾳ τοῦ θεοῦ. Cf. Ps. S. xv. 13.

ιζ'. ἥξουσιν οἱ ἱερεῖς...μάχιμοι φιλάργυροι ὑπερήφανοι, ἄνομοι, ἀσελγεῖς. Cf. Ps. S. xii., xvii. 6—8, 22.

Jud. κα'. ἔσονται ὡς καταιγίδες ψευδοπροφῆται. Ps. S. xvii. 13 (MSS.).

κβ'. τοῦ θεοῦ τῆς δικαιοσύνης. Cf. Ps. S. viii. 32.

κγ'. λιμὸν καὶ λοιμὸν θάνατον καὶ ῥομφαίαν. Cf. Ps. S. xiii. 2, xv. 8.

Zabul. γ'. (ἐν ὑποδήμασιν) καταπατήσει καταπατήσωμεν. Cp. Ps. S. ii. 2.

Nepht. β'. σταθμῷ γὰρ καὶ μέτρῳ καὶ κανόνι πᾶσα κτίσις ὑψίστου. Ps. S. v. 6.

ibid. ὡς ἡ ἰσχὺς αὐτοῦ, οὕτω καὶ τὸ ἔργον αὐτοῦ.

ibid. ὡς ἡ προαίρεσις αὐτοῦ, οὕτω καὶ ἡ πρᾶξις αὐτοῦ. Cf. Ps. S. xvii. 2.

γ'. ἥλιος καὶ σελήνη καὶ ἀστέρες οὐκ ἀλλοιοῦσι τάξιν αὐτῶν. Ps. S. xviii. 12.

Asher α'. ἐὰν οὖν ἡ ψυχὴ θέλῃ ἐν καλῷ, πᾶσα πρᾶξις αὐτῆς ἐστιν ἐν δικαιοσύνῃ...ἐὰν δὲ ἐν πονηρῷ κλίνῃ τὸ διαβούλιον, πᾶσα πρᾶξις αὐτῆς ἐστιν ἐν πονηρίᾳ. Cf. Ps. S. ix. 7.

ζ'. ὡς ὕδωρ ἄχρηστον. Cf. Ps. S. viii. 23.

ibid. ἡ γῆ ὑμῶν ἐρημωθήσεται. Ps. S. xvii. 13.

Joseph. β'. πρὸς γυναῖκα ἀναιδῆ ἐπειγούσαν παρανομεῖν μετ' αὐτῆς. Cf. Ps. S. xvi. 8.

ζ'. καὶ ἀπολέσει τὸ μνημόσυνόν σου ἀπὸ τῆς γῆς. Cf. Ps. S. xiii. 10.

Ben. α'. καὶ θεὸς ἐσκέπασεν αὐτόν. Cf. Ps. S. xiii. 1.

ε'. ἐὰν ἦτε ἀγαθοποιοῦντες καὶ τὰ ἀκάθαρτα πνεύματα φεύξεται ἀφ' ὑμῶν καὶ αὐτὰ τὰ θήρια φεύξεται ἀφ' ὑμῶν φοβηθέντες. Cf. Ps. S. xv. 9.

8. The collection of ancient Rabbinic sayings preserved in the Pirqe Aboth contains probably materials as old as the Psalms of Solomon.

The following extracts derive especial interest from comparison with passages in our book.

Pirqe Aboth i. 3. Antigonus of Soko...used to say, Be not as slaves that minister to the lord with a view to receive recompense; but be as slaves that minister to the lord without a view to receive recompense; and let the fear of heaven be upon you. Cf. Ps. S. iv. 26 μακάριοι οἱ φοβούμενοι τὸν κύριον ἐν ἀκακίᾳ αὐτῶν.

Pirqe Aboth i. 17. Shammai said…'And receive every man with a pleasant expression of countenance' (iii. 18). Cf. Ps. S. v. 6 ἐν ἱλαρότητι. xvi. 12 μετὰ ἱλαρότητος.

— iii. 8. The yoke of Torah. Cf. Ps. S. vii. 8 ἡμεῖς ὑπὸ ζυγόν σου τὸν αἰῶνα.

— iii. 10. R. Lázar…said, Give Him of what is His, for thou and thine are His. Cf. Ps. S. v. 5.

— 22. Beloved are Israel that they are called children of God. Cf. Ps. S. xvii. 30 γνώσεται γὰρ αὐτοὺς ὅτι πάντες υἱοὶ θεοῦ αὐτῶν εἰσι.

— 24. Everything is foreseen; and free will is given. And the world is judged by grace; and everything is according to work. Cf. Ps. S. ix. 7—15.

— iv. 3. Who is rich? He that is contented with his lot. Cf. Ps. S. v. 18—20, xvi. 12.

— 31. And He is about to judge with whom there is no iniquity, nor forgetfulness, nor respect of persons, nor taking of a bribe, for all is His, and know that all is according to plan. Cf. Ps. S. ii. 19, viii. 27.

— v. 11—14. Seven kinds of punishments: dearth from drought, dearth from tumult, deadly dearth, pestilence, the sword, noisome beasts, captivity. Cf. Ps. S. xiii. 2, 3, xv. 8.

9. There is one book and only one of which we can say with certainty that it is connected with the Psalms of Solomon. No one who has read the Book of Baruch with attention can have failed to notice the similarity of its concluding verses (iv. 36—v. 9) to the xith Psalm of our collection. A glance at the two documents will suffice to show that they cannot possibly be independent of one another; and attention has been called to the fact by several of those who have edited each book. Geiger seems to have been the first: he, as we should be inclined to expect, regards Baruch as the earlier of the two. Schürer (*Gesch. Jüd. Volkes*, II. 591, 724) looks upon it as the later, while Kneucker (*Das Buch Baruch*, p. 43, etc.) thinks that the two writers borrowed independently from the LXX., and considers that this hypothesis, coupled with the similarity of the circumstances in which they lived, will sufficiently account for the resemblance. We have already intimated that such a view is in our opinion untenable: and we have now to examine the extent and character of the parallelisms, with the view of ascertaining what is the most reliable hypothesis.

INTRODUCTION. lxxiii

The most striking resemblances to Baruch occur in xi. 3—8, and will be easily seen from a glance at the text. In view of Kneucker's theory, stated above, and by way of clearing the ground, we will next set down those passages of the LXX. to which reference appears to be made in both documents.

xi. 3 στῆθι—ὑψηλοῦ.

Is. xl. 9 ἐπ᾽ ὄρος ὑψηλὸν ἀνάβηθι, ὁ εὐαγγελιζόμενος Σιών.
καὶ ἴδε—κυρίου. ἀπὸ βορρᾶ.

Is. xliii. 5—6 ἀπὸ ἀνατολῶν ἄξω τὸ σπέρμα σου, καὶ ἀπὸ δυσμῶν συνάξω σε. ἐρῶ τῷ βορρᾷ Ἄγε...τοὺς υἱούς μου ἀπὸ τῆς πόρρωθεν.

„ xlix. 12 ἰδοὺ...οὗτοι ἀπὸ βορρᾶ.

Jer. xiii. 20 ἀνάλαβε τοὺς ὀφθαλμούς σου Ἰερουσαλήμ, καὶ ἴδε τοὺς ἐρχομένους ἀπὸ βορρᾶ.

„ xxxi. (LXX. xxxviii.) 8 ἰδοὺ ἐγὼ ἄγω αὐτοὺς ἀπὸ βορρᾶ καὶ συνάξω αὐτοὺς ἀπ᾽ ἐσχάτου τῆς γῆς.

Ps. cvi. (cvii.) 3 συνήγαγεν αὐτοὺς ἀπὸ ἀνατολῶν καὶ δυσμῶν καὶ βορρᾶ καὶ θαλάσσης.

4. ἐκ νήσων.

Is. xlix. 22 εἰς τὰς νήσους ἀρῶ τὸ σύσσημόν μου, καὶ ἄξουσι τοὺς υἱούς σου.
Jer. xxxi. (xxxviii.) 10 ἀναγγείλατε εἰς νήσους τὰς μακρόθεν.

5. ὄρη ὑψηλά.

Is. xl. 4 πᾶν ὄρος καὶ βουνὸς ταπεινωθήσεται.

„ 11 θήσω πᾶν ὄρος εἰς ὁδόν...αὐτοῖς.

6. οἱ βουνοί.

Is. lv. 12 ἐν γὰρ εὐφροσύνῃ (cf. v. 4) ἐξελεύσεσθε...τὰ γὰρ ὄρη καὶ οἱ βουνοὶ ἐξαλοῦνται...καὶ πάντα τὰ ξύλα τοῦ ἀγροῦ ἐπικροτήσει.

7. πᾶν ξύλον.

Is. lv. 12 ἀντὶ τῆς στοιβῆς ἀναβήσεται κυπάρισσος.

ἵνα παρέλθῃ.

Ex. xv. 16 ἕως ἂν παρέλθῃ ὁ λαός σου οὗτος.

8. ἔνδυσαι Ἰερουσαλήμ.

Is. lii. 1 ἔνδυσαι τὴν ἰσχύν σου, Σιών, καὶ σὺ ἔνδυσαι τὴν δόξαν σου, Ἰερουσαλήμ.

ὅτι ἐλάλησεν.

Ps. lxxxiv. (lxxxv.) 8 λαλήσει εἰρήνην ἐπὶ τὸν λαὸν αὐτοῦ.

Against these parallels let us set the verbal similarities which we find in Baruch.

Bar. v. Ἰερουσαλήμ...στῆθι ἐπὶ τοῦ ὑψηλοῦ.
καὶ ἴδε συνηγμένα τὰ τέκνα σου ἀπὸ ἡλίου δυσμῶν ἕως ἀνατολῶν.

ἴδε τὴν εὐφροσύνην τὴν παρὰ τοῦ θεοῦ σοι ἐρχομένην...
ἔρχονται οἱ υἱοί σου...ἔρχονται συνηγμένοι ἀπὸ ἀνατολῶν ἕως
δυσμῶν...χαίροντες τῇ τοῦ θεοῦ δόξῃ.
ταπεινοῦται πᾶν ὄρος ὑψηλὸν...εἰς ὁμαλισμὸν, ἵνα βαδίσῃ
Ἰσραὴλ...τῇ τοῦ θεοῦ δόξῃ.
ἐσκίασαν δὲ καὶ οἱ δρυμοὶ καὶ πᾶν ξύλον εὐωδίας.
μετ' εὐφροσύνης.
Ἰερουσαλήμ...ἔνδυσαι τὴν εὐπρέπειαν τῆς παρὰ τοῦ θεοῦ δόξης.

There can be little room for doubt as to which list contains the more striking coincidences. We have, naturally, no wish to deny that the *ultimate* source of our documents is to be sought in such passages as those quoted from the LXX. But we do assert that it is unnatural to suppose that we have two independent copyists to reckon with: and if this be granted, as we think it must, the question necessarily arises— which is the original of the two, and which the adaptation? It is a question of considerable importance, inasmuch as it affects the date of both books. We are already in possession of the views held by various writers as to the date of the Psalms of Solomon, and we have seen that no critic of note places them later than the 1st century B.C. It will therefore be only necessary to state the views held by some good modern critics as to the date of the Book of Baruch.

1. Ewald, who, in common with most writers, divides the book into two parts (i.—iii. 8, and iii. 9—end), places Part I. in the last period of the Persian rule, and abstains from assigning a date to Part II., of which he merely says that it is later.

2. Fritzsche places the book in the late Maccabean period.

3. Kneucker puts the book in its present form after the destruction of Jerusalem by Titus: but, as we have seen, denies the direct connection with the Psalms of Solomon.

4. Schürer relies on such a connection for assigning a late date to Baruch.

With this last estimate we ourselves decidedly agree: and our reasons, stated *in extenso*, are as follows.

1. The Psalm is concise, well ordered, and logically developed. Baruch spreads the same amount of matter over a space just twice as large, and, besides, repeats himself. Thus, in iv. 37, v. 5 ἰδοὺ ἔρχονται, ἔρχονται συνηγμένοι ἀπὸ ἀνατολῶν, we have repetitions of identical words with only slight variations.

Again v. 2 is an expansion of v. 1, for Jerusalem is told to put off her mourning and to put *on*, not only her beauty, but the διπλοΐς and μίτρα of glory (cf. Ps. S. ii. 22).

Further v. 5 ἀνάστηθι...καὶ στῆθι has all the air of an expansion of the simple στῆθι of Ps. S.

v. 7 should be particularly noticed in this connection. It is far less vivid than xi. 5, 6. Baruch does not tell that God actually did or will lower the hills, but that he has *appointed* to do so: and the simple βουνοὶ is replaced by the more pretentious expression θῖνες ἀέν ναοι and supplemented by φάραγγες (from Is. xl.); while the common word παρέλθῃ gives way in Baruch to the more literary βαδίσῃ.

In v. 8, again, it is difficult to resist the conviction that we are reading a paraphrase of the more direct words of the Psalm. The phrase πᾶν ξύλον εὐωδίας, which is common to both writers, has an appropriate function in Ps. S. God makes sweet plants spring up at the approach of the people. In Baruch it forms an appendix to the δρυμοί, woods and sweet plants overshadow Israel: and there is a relic of the Psalmist's ἀνέτειλεν in the προστάγματι τοῦ θεοῦ of Baruch.

Further, besides being the more diffuse, Baruch is less well knit together than Ps. S. The argument of his prophecy runs thus.

iv. 36—7. Jerusalem is to look about and see her children's return.
v. 1—4. She is to deck herself with glory, for God will glorify her for ever.
5, 6. She is to get up on high (for the second time) and look about to see her children return—not as they had gone out from her.
7—9. Their progress is described, and the whole ends abruptly.

The Psalmist's order is logical. First, the news is announced: then Jerusalem, on receipt of it, is to get up on high and see her children returning. Their return is described, and then, in order to receive them, Jerusalem is bidden to deck herself gloriously, and the whole is rounded off with a prayer for the speedy realisation of these hopes. Is it likely, or even conceivable, that a concise coherent whole of this kind should have been made out of a diffuse disconnected passage without distinct beginning or end? Does not the Psalmist approach far more nearly than Baruch to the old Prophetic sources in respect of simplicity and directness? and is he not therefore, according to all recognised rules of development, the predecessor of Baruch?

Two considerations should be added. One, that the tendency to amplify is on the whole commoner than the tendency to contract, in documents of the poetical (as opposed to the narrative) class. The

other, that the Book of Baruch is throughout somewhat of a mosaic. The posteriority of the prayer of the exiles (i. 15—iv. 8) to the prayer in Dan. ix., and its dependence on the latter, are generally acknowledged. This is a matter deserving of a passing notice, notwithstanding the large probability that the two halves of the book come from different authors.

Other resemblances between Ps. S. and Baruch have been noticed. Kneucker (p. 43 n.) gives the following list of parallel passages:

(1) B. iv. 10, 12; Ps. S. ii. 6, 7, ix. 1, referring to the Captivity.
(2) B. iv. 6, 7; Ps. S. iv. 25, παροργίσαι, παροξῦναι.
(3) B. iv. 15, 16; Ps. S. ii. 8, viii. 16, 24. Foreign captors.
(4) B. iv. 20; Ps. S. ii. 21, 22. Jerusalem clothed in sackcloth.
(5) B. iv. 26; Ps. S. viii. 19. ὁδοὶ τραχεῖαι.
(6) B. iii. 33, 34; Ps. S. xviii. 11—13. God's ordering of the heavenly bodies.

Perhaps the following additional resemblances of thought and diction may be worth noting. In Part II. we have;

(1) B. iii. 13 τὸν αἰῶνα without εἰς (also iii. 3). Ps. S. vii. 8.
(2) iii. 9 ἐντολὰς ζωῆς, iv. 1 εἰς ζωήν. Ps. S. xiv. 1 νόμῳ ᾧ ἐνετείλατο ἡμῖν εἰς ζωὴν ἡμῶν.
(3) iii. 10 γῇ ἀλλοτρίᾳ. Ps. S. ix. 1.
(4) iii. 19, 24 use of τόπος. Ps. S. xvi. 9 MSS.
(5) iii. 36 Ἰακὼβ παῖς Ἰσραὴλ ἠγαπημένος. Ps. S. ix. 16, xii. 7, xvii. 23.
(6) iv. 1 νόμος ὁ ὑπάρχων εἰς τὸν αἰῶνα (also iii. 35). Ps. S. x. 5.
(7) iv. 3 ἔθνος ἀλλότριον. Ps. S. ii. 2.
(8) iv. 6 οὐκ εἰς ἀπώλειαν. Ps. S. vii. 4.
(9) iv. 12, 31 ἐπιχαίρειν. Ps. S. xiii. 7.
(10) iv. 17 τί δυνατή. Ps. S. xv. 4.
(11) iv. 22, 23, 24, 29, v. 9 ἐλεημοσύνη σωτηρία εὐφροσύνη. Ps. S. ix. 20, x. 9.

In Part I.

(1) i. 14 ἐξαγορεῦσαι. Ps. S. ix. 12 ἐξηγορία.
(2) i. 15 τῷ Κυρίῳ...δικαιοσύνη. Ps. S. ii. 16, etc.
(3) ii. 4. Ps. S. ii. 6.
(4) ii. 15. Ps. S. ii. 12, vii. 5, 8, viii. 8, ix. 18, etc.
(5) ii. 27, ἐπιείκεια of God. Ps. S. v. 14.

Should this attempt to prove that Baruch (Part II.) is posterior to the Psalms of Solomon be accounted a successful one, it will follow that a considerable step has been taken towards fixing a *terminus ad quem* for the latter book, and also towards determining the character and date of the former. For in that case, Baruch II. can have had no Hebrew original—it being next door to impossible that an adapter and a translator of the same Hebrew Psalm should have hit upon the same Greek words to render the text before them.

But, if so much be true, we are led on to ask, what date can we assign to Baruch in its present form? and the obvious answer seems to be, that if Part I. be a distinct composition, it must have been re-edited along with Part II. at a time when the Psalms of Solomon had been already translated into Greek and had attained some degree of popularity. We regard it as certain that the Psalms are posterior to the Pompeian invasion, and we are consequently forced to the conclusion that the only time appropriate to such a re-edition of Baruch as is here postulated, is the period after the destruction of Jerusalem by Titus, when such consolatory and hortatory matter as Baruch supplies would be most needed and most welcome.

It follows that the Psalms of Solomon had been turned into Greek some considerable time before A.D. 70, and they assume new importance, as monuments of Hellenistic Greek of the first century, and as most likely anterior in date to the whole New Testament literature.

The converse of the hypothesis, the view, namely, that the Psalmist copied Baruch, lands us in at least one very considerable difficulty. We are forced to allow—in clean contradiction to all our previous investigation—that the xith Psalm—and with it almost necessarily the rest of the collection—had no Hebrew original. To those who are not convinced by our arguments on this head, the view may seem a tenable one; but even these would, we believe, be forced by the perusal of the documents in question to admit that Baruch II. bears throughout the character of a composition originally Greek, and not of a translation from the Hebrew, the language in which these Psalms were written.

§ ix. *The Probability of a Hebrew Original.*

If we are right in ascribing the authorship of these Psalms to a Pharisee (or Pharisees) residing in Jerusalem, the hypothesis of a Hebrew original will naturally suggest itself for two reasons.

(1) The strict Pharisees took a patriotic pride in maintaining the Palestinian dialect and in resisting the encroachments of the Greek language: we should not expect a collection of Pharisee Psalms, breathing hostility to the Sadducee "menpleasers" (Ps. S. iv.), to have been issued in the Græco-Judaic dialect of the Dispersion.

(2) It is a reasonable assumption that Jewish Psalms, modelled on

the pattern of the national Psalter, and possibly intended for liturgical use, would have been composed neither in the Judæo-Greek nor in the colloquial Aramaic dialects, but in the Hebrew; since the Hebrew language, by reason of its association with the Jewish Scriptures and the Temple services, never ceased to be regarded as the language of Jewish worship.

There is therefore an antecedent probability that our present Greek text is a translation from the Hebrew; and in our opinion a close investigation of language tends to confirm this supposition. The reasons, which we propose at this point to state in favour of a Hebrew original, are not all of an equally convincing nature. But, when taken in combination, they are sufficient to establish a strong case for the conclusion, at which we have been able to arrive without much hesitation.

At the time when the Psalms of Solomon were written, all Judæo-Greek writings reflected the influence of Hebrew or Aramaic upon Greek vocabulary and syntax, and in a greater or less degree gave proof of the commanding position occupied by the Alexandrine version. It is therefore often a matter requiring very careful and minute investigation, whether we have to deal with an original Greek work written by a Jew, or with a Greek Version of a Hebrew work. In both cases the presence of Hebraisms will be observed. A more comprehensive and complex test must be applied, if we are to arrive at conclusive results; but it is obvious that the more skilful the translator was, the more difficult is the task for us to distinguish between a translation from the Hebrew or Aramaic and a work originally written in Greek.

Under the following heads we have attempted to group together the principal grounds for the hypothesis of a Hebrew original.

1. There are certain obscure passages in our book, in which no conjectural emendation of the Greek text has as yet been successful, or seems likely to succeed. It is almost incredible that they can be the Psalmist's original composition. The supposition that their obscurity has arisen from the defectiveness either of the translation or of the Hebrew text, upon which the translation was based, accounts satisfactorily for the appearance of the Greek. Thus, to select the most signal instance, xii. 1—4, it appears to us inconceivable that a Greek writer, for the most part so simple and intelligible in style as he appears to be in our Psalms, should here have written such desperately confused and bewildering sentences. On the supposition of a Hebrew original, these obscurities may be explained, either on the ground of the translator's inability to cope with the difficulties of the Hebrew, or on the ground of his having before him a Hebrew text, which was at this point corrupt or

defective. It is no sufficient answer to plead that the obscurity of this passage characterizes the style of only the composer of this one Psalm. For (1) the remainder of the Psalm (5—8) is comparatively simple and straightforward, and (2) analogous, though not quite such puzzling, obscurities are to be found elsewhere in our book, and in our opinion are capable of receiving a similar explanation, e.g. ii. 13—15, iv. 9—12, v. 15, vii. 8, xv. 9, xvii. 2.

2. The attempt to apply this solution may be open to the charge of a perverse ingenuity, but in some of the following examples, it appears to us, the obscurity of the Greek may reasonably be assigned to a mis-apprehension of the Hebrew or to errors in the Hebrew text.

A. Possible errors of translation, e.g.

i. 4 διέλθοι = יָבוֹא for διῆλθε or διελήλυθε. ii. 29 τοῦ εἰπεῖν (?) = לְדַבֵּר 'to destroy' (Geiger). iii. 8 ἐν παραπτώματι: should stand in the next clause with ἐξιλάσατο to balance ταπεινώσει ἐν νηστείᾳ, the Hebrew word being the same for 'guilt' and 'guilt-offering.' iv. 13 ἕως ἐνίκησε = עַד־לָנֶצַח. iv. 19 ἀπὸ παντὸς οὗ ἐμπλήσει ψυχὴν αὐτοῦ; a misrendering of the relative. iv. 23 οἴκους πολλοὺς ἀνθρώπων: an error for οἴκους πολλῶν ἀνθρώπων. vii. 2 ὅτι = כִּי, where כִּי was used adversatively. viii. 3 ποῦ ἄρα. (Wellhausen): the interrogative wrongly here used to translate אֵפוֹא instead of 'assuredly.' xiii. 2 θανάτου ἁμαρτωλῶν. θανάτου = דֶּבֶר parallel to λιμοῦ: ἁμαρτωλῶν should have been in the nom. at head of next clause. xvii. 6 οἷς for ἅ...αὐτοῖς = אֲשֶׁר...לָהֶם. xvii. 9 ἐπαναστῆναι (?) for ἐπαναστῆσαι. xvii. 14 καὶ τοὺς ἄρχοντας...εἰς ἐμπαιγμὸν for καὶ οἱ ἄρχοντες...ἦσαν εἰς ἐμπαιγμόν. xviii. 8 ἐν σοφίᾳ πνεύματος for ἐν πνεύματι σοφίας. xviii. 9, 10 πάντας αὐτοὺς.. γενεὰ ἀγαθὴ for γενεὰν ἀγαθήν.

B. Possible errors arising from misapprehension of the vowels in 'unpointed' Hebrew.

ii. 26 καὶ συντελεσθήσονται, וְיִכְלוּ for וִיכַלּוּ. 30 ὑπὲρ ἐλάχιστον, מִצְעִיר for מִצְעָר. iii. 16 ἔτι, עוֹד for עַר, cf. ix. 20, xi. 8, xvii. 51. viii. 3 κρινεῖ αὐτὸν for ἡμᾶς, יִשְׁפְּטֵנוּ for יִשְׁפְּטֵנוּ. viii. 11 περὶ τούτων, אֵלֶּה for אָלָה. xiii. 8 νουθετήσει δίκαιον: no subject : יִסֵּר for יָסֵר. xvii. 36 χριστὸς κύριος, מָשִׁיחַ יְהֹוָה for מְשִׁיחַ יְהֹוָה. 48 ἐν συναγωγαῖς, בַּעֲדוֹת for בְּעֵרוּת.

C. Possible errors arising from confusion of Hebrew consonants or a defective Hebrew Text.

ii. 29 τοῦ εἰπεῖν, לֵאמֹר for לְהָמִיר = לָמִיר 'to change' (Wellhausen). iii. 2 ψάλατε: ו for י, זַמְּרוּ instead of יַמְּרוּ. iii. 3 γρηγόρησον...γρηγόρησιν, confusion between the roots עור and רוע. v. 15 ἐν φίλῳ καὶ ἡ αὔριον:

J. P.   f

היום σήμερον dropped out before ומחר (?). v. 16 οὐ φείσεται ἐν δόματι, יחום for יחסר. viii. 17 ἔκρινε, ידי for יכין. xiii. 7 ἐν περιστολῇ, בְּמַטָּה for בְּמַטֶּה. xvii. 14 ἐν ὀργῇ κάλλους αὐτοῦ, יפי for אפיו.

3. It is generally symptomatic of a translation from Hebrew, that the structure of sentences is very simple and that there is a conspicuous absence of particles etc. expressive of finer shades of meaning. This we find in the Psalms of Solomon.

A. Clauses apparently grammatically dependent on one another are treated coordinately, e.g. iv. 8, 9 ἀνακαλύψαι...καὶ δικαιώσαιεν οἱ ὅσιοι. vii. 7 καὶ...ἐπικαλεσώμεθα καὶ...ἐπακούσῃ. ix. 18 καὶ ἔθου τὸ ὄνομα...καὶ...καταπαύσῃ. xviii. 2 οἱ ὀφθαλμοὶ ἐπιβλέποντες καὶ...οὐχ ὑστερήσει.

B. The only conjunction used with frequency is καί. We find also γάρ, and less often ἀλλά. The particle δέ is only used some eight times (iii. 16; v. 16; xiii. 10, 11; xiv. 7; xv. 15; xvi. 19; xvii. 3). The particle δή occurs once, viii. 30, and ἄρα once, viii. 3. Other particles, e.g. οὖν, γε, μέντοι, μὲν...δέ, πλήν, are not found.

Of the conjunctions denoting a cause ὅτι is used constantly, and ἀνθ' ὧν occurs in ii. 3, 15, 39. Temporal conjunctions occur very rarely (e.g. ὅταν iii. 14; xv. 7, 14), ἐν τῷ with the Inf. being used instead. A purpose is expressed by ἵνα, but not often (e.g. ii. 18; v. 8; vii. 1; viii. 36; ix. 3, 16; xi. 7; xiii. 7), the construction of τοῦ with the Infin. or Epexegetical Infin. being preferred. ὅπως does not occur, nor the construction of εἰς τό with the Inf.

The conditional clause is expressed by ἐάν, e.g. ii. 26; v. 5, 9, 10, 12, 15, 19; vii. 4; xvi. 11, 13), and once by εἰ (xviii. 14). We do not find ἄν used once; and the consequently defective method of expressing an apodosis is illustrated by ii. 26.

4. If we may judge from the example of the LXX. version of the Old Testament, one marked characteristic of a Greek translation from a Hebrew book is the inability to render the meaning of the Hebrew tenses; the uncertainty how to translate the Imperf. being especially fruitful of confusion.

In our Psalms we notice (A) strange interchange of tenses, (B) possible traces of the difficulty caused by the Hebrew Impf.

A. The interchange of tenses, without any marked change implied in the action of the verb.

(1) Pres. Aor. and Fut., e.g. iii. 8—10 ἐπισκέπτεται...ἐξιλάσατο... ταπεινώσει. xiii. 4—7 ἐταράχθη...ἅψεται...παιδεύεται.

INTRODUCTION. lxxxi

(2) Aor. and Fut., e.g. ii. 12 ἐποίησε...καὶ γνώσεται (? וַיֵּדַע). xvii. 8—13 ἠρήμωσαν...καταβαλεῖς...ἐλεήσει...ἐξηρεύνησε.

(3) Aor. and Pres., e.g. iv. 15 ἐπλήσθη...ἐμπίπλαται. vi. 8 εἰσήκουσε...ἐπιτελεῖ. xi. 4 ἔρχονται...συνήγαγεν.

B. Possible traces of the Hebr. Impf. are to be seen in

(1) the Fut. Indic. employed very frequently to represent a present or continuous state, e.g. ii. 19 ὁ θεὸς οὐ θαυμάσει πρόσωπον. iii. 4 οὐκ ὀλιγωρήσει δίκαιος. iv. 6 ὁ κύριος ῥύσεται. v. 12 πρόσωπα ἀροῦσι. v. 14 σὺ ἐπακούσῃ. ix. 5 οὐ κρυβήσεται ἀπὸ τῆς γνώσεώς σου. x. 3 ὀρθώσει (ὁ κύριος). xiii. 8, 9 νουθετήσει...φείσεται κύριος. xvii. 1 καυχήσεται ἡ ψυχὴ ἡμῶν. xviii. 3 τὰ ὦτά σου ἐπακούσει.

(2) the occasional use of an apparently inappropriate Optative, where, on the supposition of its rendering the Hebrew Impf., a good explanation is offered : i. 4 διέλθοι for διῆλθεν. iv. 9 καὶ δικαιώσαιεν for καὶ δικαιώσουσι, in the sense of ἵνα δικαιῶσι. v. 15 θαυμάσειας for θαυμάζοις ἄν. xvii. 10 εὑρεθείη between ἀποδώσεις and ἐλεήσει, where we should expect εὑρεθήσεται. 51 ταχύναι is parallel with ῥύσεται. xvii. 26 ἐξῶσαι, ὀλοθρεῦσαι etc., if Optatives, should possibly have been Futures, as συνάξει, ἀφήσει in vv. 28, 29. (Cf. iv. 28 ἐξάραι ὁ θεός.)

5. Familiar features of translation from the Hebrew in the LXX. version are (1) 'duplicate renderings' of the same word or phrase, (2) words added by the translator to make the meaning of his rendering clearer.

(1) The following list seems to indicate the presence of duplicate renderings:

vi. 4 ὁράσεων πονηρῶν ἐνυπνίων. viii. 12 κληρονόμου λυτρουμένου. ix. 12 ἐν ἐξομολογήσει ἐν ἐξηγορίαις. xi. 1 ἐν σάλπιγγι σημασίας ἁγίων. xvi. 8 ἀνωφελοῦς ἁμαρτίας. xvii. 14 ἕως ἐπί. 17 ἐθνῶν συμμίκτων. 37 συνάξει ἐλπίδας. 48 χρυσίον τίμιον τὸ πρῶτον. xviii. 4 πρωτότοκον μονογενῆ. xviii. 5 ἀπὸ ἀμαθίας ἐν ἀγνοίᾳ.

(2) The following genitives seem to be added for the purpose of defining or explaining the substantive which they qualify, without however adding to the meaning :

iii. 11 ὠδῖνας μητρός. iv. 20 μονώσει ἀτεκνίας. v. 18 συμμετρίᾳ αὐταρκεσίας. xvi. 1 καταφορᾷ ὕπνου. xvi. 4 κέντρον ἵππου. xvii. 9 ἀλλότριον γένους ἡμῶν.

6. The LXX. frequently differs from the Hebrew "in respect of the number of a verb" (see Driver, *Notes on the Heb. Text of the Books of Samuel*, p. lxiii.).

lxxxii *INTRODUCTION.*

The following instances in our Psalms may possibly exemplify the same variation, e.g. ii. 14 παρεδειγμάτισαν (?) for παρεδειγμάτισεν. iii. 2 ψάλατε between εὐλογεῖς and ψάλλε. viii. 18 ἡ ὁδός σου, δεῦτε καὶ εἰσέλθετε. xvii. 13 (ὁ ἄνεμος) ἠφάνισαν.

7. Possible literal reproduction of Hebrew. Under this head must be classed many Hebraisms, which we should expect to find in any Judæo-Greek writing. But while their presence does not prove that the Greek is a translation, their absence would be conclusive against it.

A. 1. Substantives, which are the conventional equivalents of certain Hebrew words: of this large class we need only give a few examples, e.g.

ii. 32 τὸ ὕστερον (אחרית). iii. 7 ἀλήθεια (אמונה). iv. 1 βέβηλος (חנף). iv. 27 σκάνδαλον (מכשול). viii. tit. εἰς νῖκος (למנצח). ix. 6 αἱ δικαιοσύναι (צדקות). ix. 20 ἐλεημοσύνη (צדקה). xii. 7 παῖς (עבד). xv. 8 θάνατος (דבר). xvi. 1 καταφορά (תרדמה). xvi. 11 ὀλιγοψυχία (קצר רוח). xvii. 31, xviii. 10 διάψαλμα (סלה). xvii. 36 Χριστός (משיח). 37 ἀναβάτης (רכב).

2. The Hebrew use of substantives to express ideas for which an adjective would naturally be used in Greek:

ii. 20 θρόνου δόξης. ii. 21 ἐνδύματος εὐπρεπείας. iv. 15 λόγοις ἀναπτερώσεως. viii. 4 πόλει ἁγιάσματος. viii. 15 πνεῦμα πλανήσεως. xi. 7 ξύλον εὐωδίας. xiii. 8 υἱὸν ἀγαπήσεως. xiv. 4 μικρότητι σαπρίας. xvii. 8 ὑπερηφανίᾳ ἀλαλάγματος. xviii. 6 ἡμέραν ἐκλογῆς. Other genitives recalling the Hebraic idiom are iv. 18 ἔργον χειρὸς (vi. 3; ix. 7; xviii. 1). viii. 28 οἱ ὅσιοι τοῦ θεοῦ. xii. 3 δένδρα εὐφροσύνης. xiv. 14 τὰ ξύλα τῆς ζωῆς. xv. 5 καρπὸς χείλεων. xvi. 2 πύλαι ᾅδου. xvii. 17 οἱ υἱοὶ τῆς διαθήκης. xviii. 13 καιροὺς ὡρῶν.

3. The plural number in the following words is possibly an imitation of the Hebrew which they translate:

i. 7 ἐν ἀποκρύφοις (בְּמִסְתָּרִים). iii. 11 ὠδῖνας (חֲבָלִים). viii. 9 ἐν καταγαίοις (בְּתַחְתִּיּוֹת אָרֶץ). ix. 13 τοῖς προσώποις ἡμῶν (לְפָנֵינוּ). xvii. 19 ἐν ἐρήμοις (בָּחֳרָבוֹת). xviii. 11 ἐν ὑψίστοις (בִּמְרוֹמִים).

B. Verbs.

Besides the peculiarity noticed above in the use of the tenses we may observe the following possible traces of a Hebrew original.

1. The Hebrew idiom of expressing the dependence of one verb upon another by putting the second verb in the Infin.: ii. 24 ἱκάνωσον τοῦ βαρύνεσθαι χεῖρά σου. v. 6 προσθήσει τοῦ πλεονάσαι. vii. 4 ὀργισθήσῃ τοῦ συντελέσαι.

INTRODUCTION. lxxxiii

2. An epexegetic use of the Inf., the verb not standing in any close grammatical connection with the previous clause, e.g. ii. 28 ἐκχέαι. ii. 40 ποιῆσαι...παρεστάναι. iv. 11 διαλῦσαι. iv. 15 ὀλοθρεῦσαι. v. 11 ἑτοιμάσαι. v. 14 εὐφρᾶναι. x. 1 καθαρισθῆναι. xv. 7 ὀλοθρεῦσαι. xvii. 19 σωθῆναι. xvii. 27 φυγεῖν. xvii. 34 ἔρχεσθαι. xvii. 41 ἐλέγξαι. xvii. 50 ἰδεῖν (xviii. 7).

3. The intensive use of the Hebr. Infin. Abs. may possibly account for i. 8 ἐβεβήλωσαν...ἐν βεβηλώσει. ix. 19 ἐν διαθήκῃ διέθου. xvii. 7 ἐδόξασαν ἐν δόξῃ.

4. The Aor. Indic. possibly reproduces the use of the Hebr. Perf. to represent an action begun in the past and continued in the present, (cf. odi, memini, novi), e.g. i. 2 ἐπλήσθην. vii. 9 ἐπηγγείλω. viii. 37 ἠλπίσαμεν. ix. 16 (xiv. 4) ἠγάπησαν. x. 1 ἐμνήσθη (xiv. 5). xiv. 1 ἐνετείλατο (xix. 2).

5. The 3rd Plur. in ἐπιθῶνται (ix. 16), which has no subject expressed, may reproduce the Hebr. impersonal use.

C. The Prepositions.

ἀπό. 1. The Hebrew construction of מִן and לְ gives the best explanation of xvii. 21 ἀπὸ ἄρχοντος αὐτῶν καὶ λαοῦ ἐλαχίστου. xviii. 13 ἀφ᾽ ἧς ἡμέρας...καὶ ἕως αἰῶνος. Similarly xviii. 12 ἀφ᾽ ἡμερῶν εἰς ἡμέρας is a reproduction of מִיָּמִים יָמִימָה.

2. In viii. 13 ἀπὸ πάσης ἀκαθαρσίας the preposition, in the sense of "immediately after," possibly translates מִן.

3. The use of ἀπό in iv. 19 ἐλλιπής...ἀπό, v. 5 λήψεται ἀπό, xvi. 8 τὸ συγκείμενον ἀπό, xvii. 13 ἠρήμωσεν ἀπό, xvii. 15 ἀλλοτρία ἀπό, xvii. 41 καθαρὸς ἀπό, can be paralleled in Judæo-Greek writings, but, if our Psalms are a translation, will naturally be explained as the rendering of מִן.

4. ἀπό in the sense of 'because of' = מִן. ii. 39 ἀπὸ ταπεινώσεως. vi. 4 ἀπὸ ὁράσεων. viii. 5 ἀπὸ ἀκοῆς. xv. 6 ἀπὸ κακοῦ; 'from before,' מִפְּנֵי. viii. 9 ἀπὸ εἰσόδου αὐτῶν. xii. 4 ἀπὸ φοβουμένων κύριον. xv. 9 ἀπὸ ὁσίων.

εἰς. 1. Of time at which an event takes place, as an equivalent of לְ: vii. 9. xviii. 6 εἰς ἡμέραν. xvii. 23 εἰς τὸν καιρόν. xviii. 11 εἰς καιρούς.

2. Of the extreme point attained: iv. 20 εἰς ἀνάληψιν (?) = עַד פְּטִירָה. v. 20 εἰς πλησμονήν = לָשֹׂבַע. viii. 15 εἰς μέθην = לְשִׁכָּרוֹן. xvi. 2 εἰς θάνατον = עַד מוּת.

3. Of the purpose: v. 7. xvi. 1 εἰς βοήθειαν (לְעֶזֶר). xiv. 1

εἰς ζωὴν ἡμῶν. xv. 8 εἰς σωτηρίαν. xvi. 11 εἰς ἐπιστροφήν. xvii. 14 εἰς ἐμπαιγμόν.

ἐν. 1. In iv. 15, 24 ἐν πᾶσι τούτοις may very possibly render the phrase בְּכָל־זֹאת.

2. ἐν is by far the commonest preposition used in this book (see Index); it is frequently used for the instrument, like בְּ, e.g. ii. 1 ἐν κριῷ. iii. 9 ἐν νηστείᾳ. x. 1 ἐν μάστιγι. (xi. 1. xiii. 9. xvii. 27, 41.)

Other prepositions, e.g. ὑπὲρ and παρὰ with the acc. for the comparative (= מִן). Cf. i. 8. ii. 30. v. 6. viii. 14. ix. 17. xvii. 48. ἀπὸ προσώπου (= מִפְּנֵי) iv. 9. xii. 8. xv. 7. xvii. 27. ἐν χειρὶ (בְּיַד) xvi. 14. ἐν ὀφθαλμοῖς (בְּעֵינֵי) xvii. 19. ἐνώπιον i. 2. ii. 41, etc. κατέναντι ii. 13. ἀπέναντι ii. 14. xvii. 5.

D. The Negative. The Hebraic idiom is reproduced in ii. 11 οὐ...πᾶς ἄνθρωπος. ix. 5 οὐ...πᾶς (xvii. 29). ix. 18 οὐ...εἰς τὸν αἰῶνα (xv. 6). xiii. 5 οὐχ...ἐκ πάντων τούτων οὐδέν. xiv. 3 οὐκ...πάσας τὰς ἡμέρας. xvii. 45 οὐκ...ἐν τούτοις. xviii. 2 οὐχ...ἐξ αὐτῶν.

E. Miscellaneous.

1. The αὐτὸς in xvii. 1 σὺ αὐτὸς βασιλεὺς (38, 51) probably reproduces the idiomatic use of הוּא.

2. The phrase πάντας αὐτοὺς in xvii. 46, xviii. 9 suggests כֻּלָּם.

3. κηρύξατε...φωνὴν (xi. 2): the accus. is probably due to the literal reproduction of הַעֲבִיר קוֹל.

4. In viii. 30 ἰδοὺ δή, where we find δή for the only time, the Greek probably translates רְאֵה נָא, since נָא is in the LXX. very generally rendered by δή.

5. The absence of the article before the substantive in ii. 33 ἐν ἰσχύι αὐτοῦ τῇ μεγάλῃ (בְּעָזּוֹ הַגָּדוֹל). xviii. 7 γενεᾷ τῇ ἐρχομένῃ (לַדּוֹר הַבָּא), though admitting of frequent illustration from Greek writers, is explained very exactly by the Hebrew.

6. The use of such expressions as σφόδρα (ii. 17), δεηθῆναι προσώπου (ii. 21, v. 7), οὐχ οὕτως (xiv. 4), κάτω (xv. 11), ὡς καὶ τὸ ἀπ' ἀρχῆς (xvii. 34) is best understood by comparison with the Hebrew equivalent.

The results of this enquiry are, in our opinion, of a nature to make it in the highest degree probable that the book was first written in Hebrew. This is the view held by the majority of modern scholars who have investigated the subject; e.g. Geiger, Wellhausen, Schürer.

Hilgenfeld (*Messias Iudaeor*. Prolegg. xvi., xvii.), however, defends the originality of the Greek text. In support of his opinion ("primitus græce scriptos esse censeo hos psalmos") he cites ii. 36 τὴν ὑπ' οὐρανόν.

INTRODUCTION. lxxxv

v. 3 μὴ παρασιωπήσῃς ἀπ' ἐμοῦ. vii. 1 οἱ μισήσαντες ἡμᾶς δωρεάν. viii. 15 ἐπότισεν αὐτοὺς ποτήριον οἴνου ἀκράτου εἰς μέθην. viii. 39. xv. 14 εἰς τὸν αἰῶνα χρόνον. xvi. 8 παντὸς ὑποκειμένου ἀπὸ ἁμαρτίας ἀνωφελοῦς. xvi. 14 ἐν χειρὶ σαπρίας αὐτῆς. xvii. 7 ἀντὶ ὕψους αὐτῶν. xvii. 7 ἐν μέσῳ ἐθνῶν συμμίκτων. xvii. 31. xviii. 10 διάψαλμα. It will be seen in the notes attached to our text that the greater number of these phrases are based on the language of the LXX. version. This however is a fact which in no way militates against the theory of a translation. A translator, well acquainted with the LXX. version, and translating Hebrew Psalms largely based upon the Jewish Scriptures, would naturally avail himself of the renderings which had become generally recognised. There is nothing in the Greek to make us regard the translator as a very gifted or independent scholar. And, this being so, we may suppose that he would make use of his acquaintance with the LXX. version, wherever an opportunity presented itself. Hilgenfeld's list is for the most part evidence, not of a Greek original, but of acquaintance with LXX. renderings.

Even less conclusive is his other line of argument, according to which he claims that our book must have been written in Greek, because it contains traces of the influence of the book of Wisdom. Here again, we might reply that a translator might employ Greek phrases coinciding with, and even based upon, the language of a well-known contemporary work. But even this simple hypothesis is seen to be unnecessary, when we discover on what very precarious grounds Hilgenfeld has asserted the indebtedness of our book to the book of Wisdom. The passages which he compares are seven in number; a few words in each case will explain the real character of their resemblance.

(a) Wisd. i. 11 φυλάξασθε τοίνυν γογγυσμὸν ἀνωφελῆ. Cf. Ps. S. xvi. 8 ἀπὸ ἁμαρτίας ἀνωφελοῦς. Between the subject-matter of these two passages there is no sort of resemblance. The adjective ἀνωφελής, common to both of them, is a straightforward word, which was afterwards frequently used in the versions of the O. T.

(b) Wisd. i. 16 συνθήκην ἔθεντο πρὸς αὐτόν. Cf. Ps. S. viii. 11 συνέθεντο αὐτοῖς συνθήκας μετὰ ὅρκου. There is no resemblance in the subject-matter; the similarity of the phrase employed loses all force as evidence of the dependence of one writing upon the other, when we note that in the one case we have συνθήκην, in the other συνθήκας; in the one θέσθαι, in the other συνθέσθαι; in the one πρὸς with the acc., in the other the dative without a preposition.

(c) Wisd. v. 17 ὅτι τῇ δεξιᾷ σκεπάσει αὐτοὺς καὶ τῷ βραχίονι ὑπερασπιεῖ αὐτῶν. xix. 8 οἱ τῇ σῇ σκεπαζόμενοι χειρί. Cf. Ps. S. xiii. 1, 2 δεξιὰ κυρίου ἐσκέπασέ με, δεξιὰ κυρίου ἐφείσατο ἡμῶν, ὁ βραχίων κυρίου ἔσωσε ἡμᾶς. There is a general resemblance of thought and language; but both passages are such as very naturally expand the thought of the Canonical Psalms, e.g. Ps. xcviii. 1, cxviii. 16. The use of the words δεξιά, σκεπάζειν, βραχίων is clearly based on such passages of Scripture; and their occurrence in a similar context in Wisd. and Ps. S. hardly calls for further remark.

(d) Wisd. v. 24 ἐρημώσει πᾶσαν τὴν γῆν ἀνομία. Cf. Ps. S. xvii. 13 ἠρήμωσεν ὁ ἄνομος τὴν γῆν αὐτῶν. The resemblance turns upon the correctness of the conjectural reading ἄνομος. In any case the sentence in the book of Wisdom is very general; that in our xviith Psalm is very definite. Without denying the possibility that the form of the Greek in Ps. S. xvii. 13 may reflect the influence of Wisd. v. 23, it appears to us more probable that the resemblance is purely accidental, the words ἐρημόω and ἄνομος (ἀνομία) being of such frequent use. But see note, accepting ἄνεμος in xvii. 13.

(e) Wisd. vi. 26 εὐστάθεια δήμου. Cf. Ps. S. iv. 11 ἀνὴρ ἐν εὐσταθείᾳ. vi. 17 ἐν εὐσταθείᾳ καρδίας. The substantive εὐστάθεια is not very common; but it is a good word and of regular formation. It occurs in both passages in our Pss. with appropriate meaning; and there is no ground for supposing that its occurrence is due to the influence of a passage in Wisdom.

(f) Wisd. xi. 21 πάντα μέτρῳ καὶ ἀριθμῷ καὶ σταθμῷ διέταξας. Cf. Ps. S. v. 6 ὅτι ἄνθρωπος καὶ ἡ μερὶς αὐτοῦ παρὰ σοὶ ἐν σταθμῷ. The two passages are quite distinct in meaning; and the word σταθμῷ, which in the passage from Wisdom is used in the abstract sense of 'weight,' as a parallel to 'measure' or 'number,' occurs in the passage from our book in the sense of that which tests the weight, 'balances' or 'scales.'

(g) Wisd. xv. 2 ὅτι σοὶ λελογίσμεθα. Cf. Ps. S. ix. 16 ὅτι σοί ἐσμεν. The similarity here in the words ὅτι σοὶ is not so striking as the difference between λελογίσμεθα and ἐσμέν. It is strange that any one should refer the words from our Psalter to the book of Wisdom, when passages in the O. T., e.g. Ex. xxxiv. 9 καὶ ἐσόμεθά σοι, are so obviously their source.

The reader will be able to judge for himself how far these passages support Hilgenfeld's contention, that the text of our Psalms shows the influence of the book of Wisdom. We are inclined to say that a much closer verbal correspondence would have to be made out, in order to prove that the vocabulary of one book has affected that of another.

INTRODUCTION. lxxxvii

But even if we were prepared to concede this point, which we are far from doing, Hilgenfeld's argument would only prove that the diction of the book of Wisdom has left its traces upon our Psalter. It is needless to say that this is as likely to happen in a Greek *translation* from the Hebrew as in an original Greek work by an Alexandrian Jew, such as Hilgenfeld supposes the author to be.

In conclusion, in our opinion, the probability, that the Greek is a translation from the Hebrew, is not affected by Hilgenfeld's appeal to the alleged parallels in the book of Wisdom.

§ x. *The Character of the Greek Translation.*

Hilgenfeld's verdict, that, if a translation at all, it is an excellent one (ceterum si græce versi essent Salomonis psalmi, optime versi essent), needs some qualification. Although, as a general rule, the meaning of each sentence is simple and clear, there are numerous instances, of which we have already given examples, where the obscurity is very considerable. In addition to those mentioned above, we may here refer to

i. 6 καὶ οὐκ ἤνεγκαν. ii. 6 ἐν σφραγῖδι...ἔθνεσιν. iv. 15 ἐπλήσθη ἐν παρανομίᾳ ἐν αὐτῇ. x. 5 ἡ μαρτυρία...ἐπισκοπῇ. xiv. 4 οἳ ἠγάπησαν ἡμέραν...ἐν μικρότητι σαπρίας. xvii. 38 ἐλπὶς τοῦ δυνατοῦ ἐλπίδι θεοῦ.

As we have no other version with which to compare it, it is not possible to determine its real merits as a translation. Its apparent excellence may be due only to the freedom with which the translation has been executed.

The *Index Græcitatis*, appended to this volume, will sufficiently illustrate the characteristics of the not very copious vocabulary employed by the translator. The following words seem only to occur in our book: ἄναξις (xviii. 6), ἀναπτέρωσις (iv. 15), αὐταρκεσία (v. 18), μήνισις (ii. 25).

We do not find elsewhere any precise parallel to the strange usage of ἀνάληψις (iv. 20), ἐπίσημον (ii. 26), περιστολή (xiii. 7), σημείωσις (iv. 2) in these Psalms.

We give here some lists as samples of the principal words of interest to be found in the Psalms of Solomon.

Substantives.

ἄβυσσος (xvii. 21), ἀγάπησις (xiii. 8), ἁγιασμός (xvii. 33), ᾅδης (xiv. 6. xv. 11), ἀκρασία (iv. 3), ἀλάλαγμα (xvii. 8), ἀλλοτριότης (xvii.

15), ἀμαθία (xviii. 5), ἀνάμιξις (ii. 15), ἀναβάτης (xvii. 37), ἀνατολή (v. 11), ἀντιλήπτωρ (xvi. 4), ἀντίληψις (vii. 9), ἀπαρχή (xv. 5), ἀποικεσία (ix. 1), ἅρπαγμα (ii. 28), ἀτεκνία (iv. 20), ἄφεδρος (viii. 13), βεβήλωσις (i. 8. viii. 24), γογγυσμός (v. 15. xvi. 11), γρηγόρησις (iii. 2. xvi. 4), διασπορά (viii. 34. ix. 2), διαστολή (iv. 4), διαστροφή (xii. 2), δοκιμασία (xvi. 14), ἐκλογή (ix. 7. xviii. 6), ἔλεγχος (x. 1), ἐλεημοσύνη (ix. 20. xv. 15), ἔλεος (trans.) (ii. 8. xiv. 6), ἐξηγορία (ix. 12), ἐξομολόγησις (iii. 3. ix. 12), ἐπαγγελία (xii. 8), ἐπαγωγή (ii. 24), ἐπιστροφή (ix. 19. xvi. 11), ἐπιταγή (xviii. 14), εὐλογία (xvii. 43. xviii. 6), εὐστάθεια (iv. 11. vi. 7), εὐωδία (xi. 7), ἱλαρότης (iv. 6. xvi. 12), καταιγίς (viii. 2), καταπάτησις (ii. 20), καταστροφή (xiii. 5, 6), καταφορά (xvi. 1), καταφυγή (v. 2), μαρτυρία (x. 5), μεταμέλεια (ix. 15), μετοχή (xiv. 4), μικρότης (xiv. 4), ὀλιγοψυχία (xvi. 11), ὁμαλισμός (xi. 5), ὄργανον (xv. 5), ὀρφανία (iv. 13), ὁσιότης (xvii. 46), παράδεισος (xiv. 2), παραλογισμός (iv. 12, 25), παροικία (xii. 3. xvii. 19), πάροικος (xvii. 31), πλάνησις (viii. 15), πλησμονή (v. 20), ποικιλία (iv. 3), πορεία (xviii. 12), πρεσβύτης (ii. 8. xvii. 13), πυργόβαρις (viii. 21), ῥομφαία (xiii. 2), σαλός (vi. 5), σημασία (xi. 1), σκάνδαλον (iv. 27), σκορπισμός (xvii. 20), συμμετρία (v. 18), συναγωγή (x. 8. xvii. 18, 50), συνάλλαγμα (iv. 4), συνέδριον (iv. 1), συνταγή (iv. 5), ταμιεῖον (xiv. 5), ταπείνωσις (ii. 39), ὑπερασπιστής (vii. 6), ὑπόκρισις (iv. 7), ὑπομονή (ii. 40), ὑπόστασις (xv. 7. xvii. 26), φυρμός (ii. 15), φωστήρ (xviii. 12), χριστός (xvii. 36. xviii. 6, 8).

Adjectives.

αἰώνιος (x. 5, 9), ἄκακος (iv. 6, etc.), ἀλλογενής (xvii. 31), ἄλογος (xvi. 10), ἀνωφελής (xvi. 8), ἀσεβής (xiii. 4), βέβηλος (ii. 14. iv. 1. viii. 13), διδακτός (xvii. 35), ἐλλιπής (iv. 19), ἔμπειρος (xv. 9), ἔνοχος (iv. 3), ἐπιεικής (v. 14), ἐπίσημος (xvii. 32), ἡσύχιος (xii. 6), κατάγαιος (viii. 9), κρύφιος (viii. 9), μέτριος (v. 20), μονογενής (xviii. 4), περισσός (iv. 2), πρωτότοκος (xiii. 8. xviii. 4), σκληρός (iv. 2), συμμικτός (xvii. 17), ψίθυρος (xii. 1).

Verbs.

ἁγιάζω (xvii. 28, 48, 49), αἱρετίζω (ix. 17), ἀνακαλύπτω (ii. 18. viii. 8), ἀναλογίζομαι (viii. 7), ἀποβλέπω (iii. 5), ἀποσκηνόω (vii. 1), ἀποσκοπεύω (iii. 6), αὐλίζομαι (iii. 7), βαρυθυμέω (ii. 10), βδελύσσομαι (ii. 10), βεβηλόω (i. 8), δευτερόω (v. 15), διακρίνω (xvii. 48), διαστέλλω (ii. 38), διαφέρω (xvi. 3), δικαιόω (iii. 3, 5, etc.), ἐκκεντέω (ii. 30), ἐκτίλλω (xiv. 3), ἐνισχύω (xvi. 12), ἐξαλείφω (xiii. 9), ἐξαμαρτάνω (v. 19), ἐξασθενέω (xvii. 34), ἐξερευνάω (xvii. 11), ἐξερημόω (xv. 13), ἐξιλάσκομαι (iii. 9), ἐξουθενέω (ii. 5), ἐξυβρίζω (i. 6), ἐπικρατέω (xvi. 7. xvii. 17), ἐρημόω (iv. 13. xvii. 13), εὐαγγελίζομαι (xi. 2), εὐθηνέω (i. 3), εὐθύνω (ix. 15), εὐοδόω (ii. 4), θησαυρίζω (ix. 9), καταδυναστεύω (xvii. 46), καταπαύω (ix. 18),

INTRODUCTION. lxxxix

καταμερίζω (xvii. 30), κατασκηνόω (vii. 5), κηρύσσω (xi. 2), κληρονομέω (xii. 8. xiv. 7), κυκλόω (x. 1), νύσσω (xvi. 4), νυστάζω (xvi. 1), ὀλιγωρέω (iii. 4), ὀλισθάνω (xvi. 1), ὀλοθρεύω (xv. 7), ὁμαλίζω (viii. 19), παραδειγματίζω (ii. 14), παρανομέω (xvi. 8), παρασιωπάω (v. 3), περιστέλλω (xvi. 10), ποιμαίνω (xvii. 45), προσκόπτω (iii. 5, 11), πυρόω (xvii. 48), σκανδαλίζω (xvi. 7), σκεπάζω (xiii. 1), σκιάζω (xi. 6), σκορπίζω (iv. 21. xii. 4), στεφανόω (viii. 19), στηρίζω (xvi. 12), συμπαραλαμβάνω (xiii. 4), συμφύρω (viii. 10), ὑπερπλεονάζω (v. 19), ὑποκρίνομαι (iv. 25), χρηστεύομαι (ix. 11).

Adverbs.

ἅμα (xvii. 13), ἅπαξ (xii. 8), διαπαντός (ii. 50 etc.), εἰσάπαξ (ii. 8. xi. 3) = ἅμα, ἐνταῦθα (iv. 15), ἐξάπινα (i. 2), μακράν (ii. 4. xvi. 10), σύνεγγυς (xvi. 2).

Some of the chief characteristics in the use of the *Prepositions* have already (pp. lxxxiii. lxxxiv.) been considered. The following also deserve notice.

1. The preposition ἐν is almost as frequently used as all the other prepositions reckoned together. (*See Index.*)

(*a*) It is often used instrumentally: e.g. iii. 9. xiv. 9. xvii. 27, 41. xviii. 14.

(*b*) It is characteristic of this book to use ἐν with a substantive almost in the place of an adjective: e.g. iv. 11 ἀνδρὸς ἐν εὐσταθείᾳ = ἀνδρὸς εὐσταθοῦντος. vi. 8 παντὸς ἐν φόβῳ θεοῦ = παντὸς φοβουμένου θεόν. viii. 28 ἀρνία ἐν ἀκακίᾳ = ἀρνία ἄκακα. ix. 15 ἁμαρτάνοντας ἐν μεταμελείᾳ = μεταμελομένους ἁμαρτωλούς. xviii. 3 πτωχοῦ ἐν ἐλπίδι = πτωχοῦ ἐλπίζοντος.

(*c*) ἐν with an abstract substantive is frequently found at the end of a sentence, especially in the earlier portion of the book, e.g. i. 8 ἐν βεβηλώσει. ii. 2 ἐν ὑπερηφανίᾳ. ii. 20 ἐν καταπατήσει. ii. 29, 32. iv. 18, 22 ἐν ἀτιμίᾳ. ii. 40 ἐν ὑπομονῇ.

2. The use of the prepositions is not very regular.

ἐπί. iii. 7 οὐκ αὐλίζεται ἐν οἴκῳ τοῦ δικαίου ἁμαρτία ἐφ' ἁμαρτίαν. xvii. 14 ἕως ἐπὶ δυσμῶν. xvii. 18 τὸ σημεῖον τοῦ θεοῦ ἐπὶ δικαίους. xvii. 4, 12, 23, 35 (cf. ii. 34).

ἀπό. viii. 19 ὡμάλισαν ὁδοὺς τραχείας ἀπὸ εἰσόδου αὐτῶν. xii. 4 σκορπισθείη ὀστᾶ ψιθύρων ἀπὸ φοβουμένων κύριον. xii. 5 γλῶσσα ψιθυρὸς ἀπόλοιτο ἀπὸ ὁσίων. xvi. 8 πᾶν τὸ συγκείμενον ἀπὸ ἁμαρτίας.

πρός. vi. 18 ἐλπίζειν πρός.

μετά is used (but never σύν). See *Index of Prepositions.* It is also found almost in the sense of the copula, e.g. xvii. 40 ἐν σοφίᾳ μετ' εὐφροσύνης. 42 ἐν βουλῇ συνέσεως μετ' ἰσχύος καὶ δικαιοσύνης.

§ xi. *The Date of the Greek Translation.*

I. It will be seen from pp. lxxii.—lxxvii. that, in our opinion, the Greek version of Psalm S. xi. was the original from which Baruch v. was expanded. Now Baruch v. is quoted at length by Irenæus; and must have been known and read for some considerable time previously. The date, therefore, at which the latter portion of Baruch was composed and added to the former portion, could hardly have been later than the close of the First Century A.D.

Assuming then that Baruch v. is based upon Ps. S. xi., it is reasonable to suppose that the Greek version of Ps. S. xi. was current for some time before it was made use of for such a purpose. On this hypothetical train of reasoning the translation is not later than the middle of the First Century A.D.

II. There is no trace in the Greek of Christian influence at work, nor, in our opinion, of Christian glosses. The mention of the χριστὸς κύριος does not necessarily imply a reference to Christian thought (see note on xvii. 36), nor do the words ἐν ἀνάξει χριστοῦ αὐτοῦ contain any allusion to a belief in the Second Advent. (See note on xviii. 6.)

Indeed we regard it as inconceivable, if the text had been tampered with in the interest of Christian doctrine, that the Divinity of the Messiah should not have been asserted, and that no reference should have been made to the Death or Resurrection of our Lord in the xviith and xviiith Pss.

III. It is possible that the use of certain words in the Greek may further help us to determine the date of the translation.

iv. 7 ἐν ὑποκρίσει. This word ὑπόκρισις, occurring in the LXX. only in 2 Macc. vi. 25, becomes frequent in N. T.

iv. 20 εἰς ἀνάληψιν. It is unlikely that this word would have been used of a wicked man's (evil) end, if the translator had been familiar with the technical meaning of 'Assumptio,' which ἀνάληψις obtained apparently in the course of the First Century A.D.

ix. 7. ἐν ἐκλογῇ. The word, which does not occur in the LXX., may possibly be used in the sense of 'Divine Election,' which is found in St Paul's Epistles.

ix. 11 χρηστεύσῃ. The word χρηστεύομαι, which does not occur in the LXX., is found in 1 Cor. xiii. 2.

x. 5. μαρτυρία. This word is rare in the LXX., μαρτύριον being preferred; in the N. T. μαρτυρία is more often found than μαρτύριον.

INTRODUCTION.

xii. 8 ἐπαγγελίας. This word in the Plur. with a reference to the Messianic promises contained in the O. T. Scriptures does not occur in the LXX., but is frequently used in the N. T.

xvi. 1 καταφορά in the sense of 'deep sleep' is found perhaps here for the first time in Judæo-Greek. It is Aquila's rendering for תרדמה, Gen. ii. 21.

xvii. 19 παροικία. Used in the concrete for a community of sojourners, the word perhaps occurs here for the first time.

xvii. 36 (xviii. 6, 8). Χριστὸς occurs here for the first time as a title to represent the Personal Deliverer for whom the Jews hoped.

The evidence is very meagre. The presumption however is strongly in favour of the translation having been made between 40 B.C. and 40 A.D. We are inclined ourselves to assign it to the last decade of the 1st cent. B.C.

It is therefore interesting to observe the similarity in phraseology between our Psalms and 'the Songs' in Luke i., ii.

a. The Magnificat.

Luke i. 47 ἐπὶ τῷ θεῷ τῷ σωτῆρί μου. Cf. Ps. S. iii. 7. viii. 39. xvi. 27. xvii. 2.

,, 48 ἐπέβλεψεν ἐπὶ. Cf. Ps. S. xviii. 2. τὴν ταπείνωσιν. Cf. Ps. S. ii. 39. τῆς δούλης αὐτοῦ. Cf. Ps. S. ii. 41. x. 4.

,, 49 ἐποίησέν μοι μεγάλα ὁ δυνατός. Cf. Ps. S. ii. 33. ἅγιον τὸ ὄνομα αὐτοῦ. Cf. Ps. S. vi. 2, 6, 7. viii. 31. xv. 3.

,, 50 τὸ ἔλεος αὐτοῦ κ.τ.λ. Cf. Ps. S. x. 4. xiii. 11.

,, 51 ἐν βραχίονι. Ps. S. xiii. 1, 2. διανοίᾳ καρδίας αὐτῶν. Ps. S. xvii. 27. ὑπερηφάνους. Ps. S. iv. 26. xvii. 8, 26.

,, 52 καθεῖλεν κ.τ.λ. Ps. S. ii. 35. xvii. 8.

,, 53 πεινῶντας ἐνέπλησεν κ.τ.λ. Ps. S. v. 10—12. x. 7. κενούς. Ps. S. iv. 19.

,, 54 ἀντελάβετο. Ps. S. vii. 9. xvi. 3—5. Ἰσραὴλ παιδός σου. Ps. S. xii. 7. xvii. 23. μνησθῆναι ἐλέους. Epex. Inf. Ps. S. x. 4.

,, 55 καθὼς...πατέρας ἡμῶν. Ps. S. ix. 19. xi. 8. τῷ Ἀβραὰμ κ. τῷ σπέρματι αὐτοῦ. Ps. S. ix. 17. xviii. 4.

b. The Benedictus.

Luke i. 68 εὐλογητὸς κύριος. Ps. S. vi. 9. ὁ θεὸς τοῦ Ἰσραήλ.

xcii *INTRODUCTION.*

     Ps. S. iv. 1. xi. 2. xviii. 6. ἐπεσκέψατο. Ps. S.
     iii. 14. ἐποίησεν λύτρωσιν. Ps. S. viii. 12, 36.
     ix. 1.
Luke i. 69 σωτηρία. Ps. S. x. 9. xii. 7. ἐν οἴκῳ Δαυείδ. Ps. S.
    xvii. 8, 23.
 ,, 70 καθὼς ἐλάλησεν. Ps. S. xi. 8. ἐξ ἐχθρῶν ἡμῶν. Ps. S.
    xvii. 51. τῶν μισούντων ἡμᾶς. Ps. S. vii. 1.
 ,, 72 ποιῆσαι...μνησθῆναι. Epex. Inf. ποιεῖν ἔλεος Ps. S.
    vi. 9. διαθήκης ἁγίας αὐτοῦ. Ps. S. vi. 9. ix.
    19.
 ,, 74 ἐκ χειρὸς ἐχθρῶν ῥυσθέντας. Ps. S. iv. 27. xiii. 3.
    xvii. 51.
 ,, 75 ἐν ὁσιότητι καὶ δικαιοσύνῃ. Ps. S. x. 6 (xvii. 46).
    λατρεύειν...ἐνώπιον αὐτοῦ. Ps. S. ii. 40.
 ,, 77 ἐν ἀφέσει ἁμαρτιῶν. Ps. S. ix. 14.
 ,, 78 ἐξ ὕψους. Ps. S. xvii. 7.
 ,, 79 ἐπιφᾶναι κ.τ.λ. Ps. S. iii. 16. Epex. Inf. κατευθῦναι
    Ps. S. vi. 3. vii. 9. xvi. 9. xviii. 9.

(*c*) The Angelic Hymn.

Luke ii. 10. εὐαγγελίζομαι. Ps. S. xi. 1.
 ,, 11. Χριστὸς Κύριος. Ps. S. xvii. 36. Δαυείδ, *ut supra.*
 ,, 14. δόξα ἐν ὑψίστοις θεῷ. Ps. S. xviii. 11. εὐδοκίας. Ps. S.
    viii. 39.

(*d*) The Nunc Dimittis.

Luke ii. 30 τὸ σωτήριόν σου. Ps. S. x. 9.
 ,, 32 φῶς εἰς ἀποκάλυψιν ἐθνῶν. Ps. S. xvii. 32. δόξαν λαοῦ
    αὐτοῦ Ἰσραηλ. Ps. S. xvii. 34, 35.

Additional Note on Cod. V.

  This note contains the results of Dr Rudolf Beer's collation of the Vienna MS. On the merits of the former collation we have said something on p. xxxvi. of the Introduction. The list of readings that follows will be more eloquent than anything we could add here.

Ps. i. V gives the number Α′ but omits the title.
   5. εἶπαν apparently corrected to εἶπον.

Ps. ii. 3. δῶρα not δώρῳ.
  4. εὐώδωκεν (contracted) αὐτοῖς, not εὐώδω ἡ αὐτοῖς.
  5. ἠτιμώθη (contracted) not ἠτιμένθη.
  9. εἰς ἅπαξ.
  20. The clauses are transposed, as in P. κατέσπ.—δόξης follows καταπατήσει.
  25. μηνήσεως, not -ισ-.
  30. ἐκκεκεντημένον, not -ου.
iii. 1. Ἵνα τί (also iv. 1).
  8. ἐξάραι.
  12. προσέθηκαν, not -εν.
iv. 13. οὐ ἀνέστη.
  21. σκορπισθείησαν, not -θησαν.
v. 16. τὸ δὲ, not δεῖ.
vi. 3. adds ὑπὸ κυρίου θεοῦ αὐτοῦ.
vii. 4. σὺ ἐντελῇ, not σὺν ἐντολῇ.
  8. οἰκτειρήσεις, not -τηρ-.
viii. 18. ἐπευκτὴ, not -αυ-.
  32. σὺ ὁ θεός.
  39. σαλευθησόμεθα, not -ώ-.
ix. 3. ἡμῶν, not αὐτῶν (a mistake of Hilg.).
  6, 7. σου ὁ θεός: τα κ.τ.λ.
  20. ἐπὶ οἶκον, om. τὸν.
x. 1. πληθύναι, not -ῆναι.
  6. ὅσιος ὁ κύριος.
  9. σωφροσύνην, not εὐφρ-.
xi. 3. εἰς ἅπαξ.
  9. ποιήσαι, not -ῆσαι.
xii. 4. ὀστᾶ.
xiii. 1. ἐσκέπασε, not ἐπήσπασε.
xiv. 1. ἐν νόμῳ.
  3. add τοῦ οὐρανοῦ with KP(M).
xvi. 2. ἐξεχύθη, not -ώθη.
  5. ἐλογίσω, not ἐλλ-.
  12. ἐνισχύσαι.
    B a
  13. ἐν πενία παιδείαν *sic*
xvii. 9. γένους, not -ος.
  20. τὴν γῆν, not τῆς γῆς.
  22. ἀπειθείᾳ, not ἀληθείᾳ.
  47. ἀναστῆσαι, not -ή-.

Ps. xviii. 9.   κατευθῦναι.
              καταστῆσαι, not -ή-.
       13.   καὶ ἕως αἰῶνος.

We have to apologise to our readers for the somewhat clumsy arrangement we have adopted. It is due to the fact that several sheets had been already passed for the press, and we were unwilling to introduce further alterations into them. The list is intended, therefore, to serve in some sort as a table of Errata.

ΨΑΛΜΟΙ ΣΑΛΟΜΩΝΤΟΣ.

α̅. ψαλμὸς τῷ cαλομών.

I. Ἐβόησα πρὸς κύριον ἐν τῷ θλίβεσθαί με εἰς τέλος,
πρὸς τὸν θεὸν ἐν τῷ ἐπιθέσθαι ἁμαρτωλούς.

1 Inscriptio Cod. A, Ψαλμὸς τῷ Σαλομὼν α΄, abest a V, K, P, M.

Ps. I. *Argument.* The False Security.
1, 2 a. Zion's Prayer, when assailed by 'sinners' and threatened with war.
2 b—5. Zion's Confidence. She was confident that her prayer would be heard, because she was 'righteous'; and of her 'righteousness' she thought she had a pledge in her material prosperity, and in the multitude and wealth of her sons.
6—8. Zion's disappointment. But her confidence has proved to have been misplaced: her children have abused the blessings of prosperity by 'secret' sin, and especially by violation of 'the holy things.'
The Psalm here breaks off. The reader is left to supply the conclusion, viz. that Zion, having forfeited her righteousness, could no longer hope for a favourable answer to her prayer for help.
That the Psalmist impersonates Zion or the true Israel seems to be clear from ver. 3 ἐν τῷ εὐθηνῆσαί με καὶ πολὺν γενέσθαι ἐν τέκνοις.
The allusions contained in the Psalm are therefore to matters of national interest.
The circumstances under which the Psalm was written must depend upon the explanation given of vv. 1, 2 a, 7, 8 (see notes, esp. on ver. 1). But the close correspondence both in thought and language with Ps. S. viii. 1—14 is in our opinion convincing proof that the two Psalms refer to the same historical incidents, and suggests the probability of their having been written by the same author. (See Introd. to Ps. viii.)

1 The absence of the heading 'A Psalm of Solomon' in four out of the five MSS. is probably due to the fact that the general title 'Psalms of Solomon' rendered it unnecessary to preface the opening Psalm with an inscription to the same effect. The first canonical Psalm, similarly, has no heading. It is also a question how far any of the titles of our Solomonic collection are genuine.

Ἐβόησα…ἐν τῷ θλίβεσθαί με. The language of this clause seems to be based on 2 Sam. xxii. 7; Ps. xvii. (xviii.) 7, but there is no exact reproduction of the LXX. The words πρὸς—με, however, occur literally in Ps. cxix. (cxx.) 1.

ἐν τῷ θλίβεσθαί με = בַּצַּר־לִי, cf. Heb. Ps. iv. 2, lxv. (lxvi.) 14, cv. (cvi.) 44, cvi. (cvii.) 6, 19, 28; Isai. xxv. 4; Hos. v. 15.

εἰς τέλος, i.e. 'utterly,' 'completely.' The translation of נֶצַח and לָנֶצַח by εἰς τέλος is very common in the LXX. [e.g. Ps. ix. 32 (x. 11), xii. (xiii.) 2, xliii. (xliv.) 24, xlviii. (xlix.) 10, lxvii. (lxviii.) 17, lxxiii. (lxxiv.) 1, 10, 19, lxxviii. (lxxix.) 5, lxxxviii. (lxxxix.) 47, cii. (ciii.) 9] with the meaning of 'in æternum'; this is also the meaning of the other rendering εἰς νῖκος (e.g. Jer. iii. 5). The rendering 'perfectly,' 'completely,' which has sometimes been defended, is improbable even in such a passage as Ps. xiii. 1, and is unsupported by the analogy of the other instances where the word occurs.

Accordingly in this passage where the

PSALM I.

A Psalm of Solomon.

1 I cried unto the LORD in my sore distress, *even* unto God when sinners assailed.

---

sense 'for ever' is unsuitable, εἰς τέλος will not represent לָנֶצַח. The suggestion that εἰς τέλος is out of its place and should be compared with εἰς τὸ τέλος in the Inscription of Ps. liv. (lv.) (where the LXX. blundered over למנצח 'For the Chief Musician'), deserves to be mentioned. But the phrase probably interprets some intensive, such as לכלה (2 Chron. xii. 12), or עד לכלה (2 Chron. xxxi. 1), both of which are rendered by εἰς τέλος in the LXX. Cf. 1 Thess. ii. 16 ἔφθασεν...ἡ ὀργὴ εἰς τέλος.

ἐπιθέσθαι. A word of frequent occurrence in these Psalms. Cf. vii. 1, ix. 16, xvii. 6.

ἁμαρτωλούς. This adjective, occurring 32 times in these Psalms, is used with especial significance. It may be noticed that it is not found in Pss. v.—xi., xviii. The ἁμαρτωλοί are especially distinguished from the δίκαιοι (e.g. ii. 38, iii. 13, 14, iv. 9, xiii. 5, 6, 7, 10), οἱ φοβούμενοι τὸν κύριον (iii. 16, iv. 26, xv. 14, 15), and ὅσιοι (xii. 8, xiv. 2, 4). By this term the Psalmist probably refers to the Sadducees. In the days of the Maccabean Rebellion it had been used of Hellenising Jews, 1 Macc. ii. 48.

In view of its special application in our book, the reference in the present passage to 'sinners' must be understood to denote the irreligious (i.e. Sadducaic) Jews, and not the Romans or the heathen.

Wellhausen sees in these verses an epitome of a whole century of Jewish history; the 'sinners' are the heathen, and the allusion is to the persecution of Antiochus Epiphanes; the 'war' is the Maccabean rebellion; this led to the temporary independence of the Jews, extended their material power, and established the glory of the Asmonean house: their prosperity is only external: Zion sees, only too late, the sin that underlies the increase of power, and predicts the doom of those who do not shrink from profaning the most sacred things.

Perhaps no convincing test can be applied to this hypothesis, but is not the general impression conveyed by the Psalm that of one special crisis, not of a long development? The other Psalms in this collection give no support to Wellhausen's view. So far as they are historical, they express the emotions consequent upon the recent occurrence of important events. To summarize in a Psalm the survey of a century's history implies a philosophical attitude natural enough in modern times, but foreign to the simplicity of thought of our Psalmist.

We have already mentioned that a comparison of Ps. i. with Ps. viii. 1—14 shows a striking identity of situation (see note on viii. 7). In that Psalm Pompey's entry into Jerusalem is unmistakably described, and the historical allusions of the present Psalm may be assigned to the same period.

4 ΨΑΛΜΟΙ ΣΑΛΟΜΩΝΤΟΣ [I. 2

² ἐξάπινα ἠκούσθη κραυγή πολέμου ἐνώπιόν μου·
ἐπακούσεταί μου, ὅτι ἐπλήσθην δικαιοσύνης.
³ ἐλογισάμην ἐν καρδίᾳ μου ὅτι ἐπλήσθην δικαιοσύνης,
ἐν τῷ εὐθηνῆσαί με καὶ πολὺν γενέσθαι ἐν τέκνοις.
⁴ ὁ πλοῦτος αὐτῶν διέλθοι εἰς πᾶσαν τὴν γῆν,
καὶ ἡ δόξα αὐτῶν ἕως ἐσχάτου τῆς γῆς.
⁵ ὑψώθησαν ἕως τῶν ἄστρων,
εἶπαν· οὐ μὴ πέσωσιν.
⁶ καὶ ἐξύβρισαν ἐν τοῖς ἀγαθοῖς αὐτῶν,
καὶ οὐκ ἤνεγκαν·
⁷ αἱ ἁμαρτίαι αὐτῶν ἐν ἀποκρύφοις,
κἀγὼ οὐκ ᾔδειν·

2 Conj. M. Schmidt. ap. Hilg.² εἶπα 'Ακούσεται.   **4** Fabr.conj. διῆλθε.
5 εἶπαν Codd. A, V, K, M.   εἶπον P, Hilg. conj. (Fritzsch. Pick.). Fabr. conj. ὅτι post εἶπαν. πέσωσι P, M.   **6** Cerda ἀγατοῖς.

2 κραυγὴ πολέμου. This expression recalls the תְּרוּעַת מִלְחָמָה of Jer. iv. 19, xlix. 2 Heb. Cf. also viii. 1.

The sudden outbreak of war here referred to should probably be identified with the conflict between Aristobulus and Hyrcanus which arose on the death of Alexandra (69), or with the hostilities commenced by Aristobulus against Pompey, while the latter was marching upon Jerusalem (63). See Introd.

ἐπακούσεται. It is noticeable that in 2 Sam. xxii. 7 וַיִּשְׁמַע is rendered by ἐπακούσεται, where the LXX. give a wrong rendering of the tenses. Our translator possibly borrows from the LXX. of that passage. But here we should in any case probably rightly render it by the future, since the clause is to be regarded as a soliloquy following upon the entreaty. Schmidt's conjecture εἶτα ἀκούσεται is ingenious and gives the full sense of the passage. Against it however is to be set the fact that the 1st Per. Sing. in Ps. S. viii. 3 is εἶπον not εἶπα.

δικαιοσύνης. Cf. Ps. xvii. (xviii.) 21 καὶ ἀνταποδώσει μοι κύριος κατὰ τὴν δικαιοσύνην μου and 2 Sam. xxii. 21. The character of the 'righteousness' here spoken of will be best understood from the description of the 'righteous man,' e.g. in Psalm iii.

3 ἐλογισάμην ἐν καρδίᾳ. Cf. Ps. cxxxix. (cxl.) 2, where however the words occur in a different sense.

εὐθηνῆσαι. This word is not very frequently used. It is found in the LXX. to represent a *fruitful* vine [Ps. cxxvii. (cxxviii.) 3], where it translates פֹּרִיָּה. In Job xxi. 9, οἱ οἶκοι αὐτῶν εὐθηνοῦσι, the original is שָׁלוֹם; in Job xxi. 23, ὅλος δὲ εὐπαθῶν καὶ εὐθηνῶν, it is שַׁלְאֲנָן, and in Ps. lxxii. (lxxiii.) 12, οὗτοι οἱ ἁμαρτωλοὶ καὶ εὐθηνοῦντες, it is שַׁלְוֵי; in Jer. xii. 1 εὐθήνησαν=שָׁלוּ, Lam. i. 5 εὐθηνοῦσαν=שָׁלוּ.

See also Zech. vii. 7 εὐθηνοῦσα=שְׁלֵוָה and Ps. xxix. (xxx.) 7 ἐν τῇ εὐθηνίᾳ μου= בְּשַׁלְוִי. From these instances it is seen that the word was used to represent the notion of material prosperity and quiet security.

πολὺν γενέσθαι ἐν τέκνοις. The blessing of many children was, according to the promises of the Law, a reward for true obedience. Cf. Ex. xxiii. 25, 26; Dt. vii. 13.

4 αὐτῶν: referring to τέκνοις. Geiger wrongly understands it of ἁμαρτωλοί (ver. 1). For the combination of δόξα and πλοῦτος he quotes Ps. cxi. (cxii.) 3 δόξα (הוֹן) καὶ πλοῦτος (עֹשֶׁר) ἐν τῷ οἴκῳ (τοῦ φοβουμένου τὸν κύριον).

The general tone of the passage seems to be caught from Ps. lxxii. (lxxiii.) 9—12.

διέλθοι. The Optative is a misrendering of the frequentative Imperfect in the Hebrew. Cf. xvii. 10. Both this

2 Suddenly the alarm of war was heard before me. *I said*, He will hearken unto me, for I am full of righteousness.

3 I considered in my heart, that I was full of righteousness, because I was prosperous and had become plenteous in children.

4 Their riches were gone¹ forth into all the world, and their glory unto the ends of the earth. ¹ Gr. *May their riches go*

5 They were lifted up to the stars; they said, We² shall never fall. ² Gr. *They*

6 But they waxed haughty in their prosperity, and were not able to endure.

7 Their sins were in secret; and I knew *it* not.

---

and the following verse describe the great prosperity of the Jewish people. It is possible that the Psalmist is referring to the period of tranquillity in the reign of Alexandra (78—69), which was followed by the Civil War and the intervention of Rome.

Geiger, who renders the tense by the Future, is mistaken in referring the verse to the violent dispersion of the wealth of the Maccabean Princes by Pompey and their being led in captivity to Rome (ἕως ἐσχάτου τῆς γῆς). This view seems to be shared by Hilgenfeld who adduces this verse, along with xvii. 6, to show how the writer has imitated the Wisdom of Solomon, 'is enim (i. 3 sq.) in Salomonis persona *filiorum fata luget*.' See Introd.

But the fact that this verse is followed by ὑψώθησαν ἕως τῶν ἄστρων should be sufficient to make it impossible that anything calamitous could be intended in the mention of the wide dispersion of Jewish wealth. It is the extent of their commercial undertakings and the fame of their riches, which are alluded to. Διέλθοι would, besides, be a curiously inappropriate word to describe a violent dispersion of wealth.

5 ἕως τῶν ἄστρων. In the O. T. this metaphor is only elsewhere found in Jer. li. (xxviii.) 9 ἐξῆρεν ἕως τῶν ἄστρων, where ἄστρων renders שְׁחָקִים 'skies.' We may compare Isai. xiv. 13 'I will exalt my throne above the stars of God' (LXX. ἐπάνω τῶν ἀστέρων τοῦ οὐρανοῦ θήσω τὸν θρόνον μου).

εἶπαν. Hilgenfeld's emendation εἶπον (1st Pers. Sing.) was intended to get rid of the grammatical difficulty in οὐ μὴ πέσωσιν, by making the words a soliloquy of the Psalmist. It has apparently the support of the Parisian MS. But the Plural gives a good sense: 'In their exaltation they uttered their boastful cry, that they should never fall,' and receives an apposite illustration from the καὶ εἶπαν in Ps. lxxii. (lxxiii.) 11. The use of the 3rd Plur. οὐ μὴ πέσωσι, by attraction for οὐ μὴ πέσωμεν, presents a little difficulty. But it is probably to be accounted for as a very literal rendering of the Hebrew. Compare for the construction Ps. ix. 21. For the thought of the verse compare Ps. xxix. (xxx.) 7.

6 ἐξύβρισαν. See Gen. xlix. 4; Ezek. xlvii. 5; 2 Macc. i. 28.

οὐκ ἤνεγκαν. The most probable explanation of this expression is to be obtained from a comparison with Jer. xx. 9 'I am weary with forbearing, and I cannot contain' (καὶ οὐ δύναμαι φέρειν = לֹא אוּכַל)׃ cf. also Job xxxi. 23; Jer. ii. 13, x. 10; Joel ii. 11.

They could not keep their ambition under control; their arrogance knew no bounds. The Psalmist is referring to the wealthy Sadducees.

Fabricius' explanation 'decimas, primitias, sacrificia offerre omiserunt' has nothing to recommend it; but no doubt gave rise to Whiston's 'have brought no oblation.'

7 ἐν ἀποκρύφοις. As in Ps. ix. 30 (x. 9), xvi. (xvii.) 12, lxiii. (lxiv.) 5; Ezek. viii. 12. On the 'secrecy' of the sins against which the Psalmist speaks, see also iv. 45, viii. 9. From these passages it is evident that the allusion is to the immoralities, which the Jewish aristocracy practised in defiance of the Law.

⁸ αἱ ἀνομίαι αὐτῶν ὑπὲρ τὰ πρὸ αὐτῶν ἔθνη,
ἐβεβήλωσαν τὰ ἅγια κυρίου ἐν βεβηλώσει.

8 ἀνομίαι V, K, P, M.   ἁμαρτίαι A (Cerd., Fabr.).

B. ψαλμὸς τῷ σαλομὼν περὶ Ἱερουσαλήμ.

II. Ἐν τῷ ὑπερηφανεύεσθαι τὸν ἁμαρτωλὸν, ἐν κριῷ κατέβαλε τείχη ὀχυρά,
καὶ οὐκ ἐκώλυσας.

Inscriptio Ψαλμὸς τῷ Σαλομὼν περὶ Ἰερουσαλὴμ β' A et, ut vid., P, a sinistrâ parte B̄ superscriptum in Codd. V et K (Ψαλμὸς τῷ Σαλομὼν β' περὶ Ἰερουσαλὴμ Fabr.): deest in M.

---

8 τὰ πρὸ αὐτῶν ἔθνη. This expression, if taken in close connection with the previous verse, might lead us to suppose that the *primitive inhabitants* here mentioned were the dwellers in Sodom (Gen. xix.), whose wickedness is surpassed by the sins done 'in secret,' the sensualities introduced into Palestine by the spread of heathen rites. Comp. iv. 4, 5, viii. 9, 10, 14.

On the other hand, if the expression be understood generally, we should compare Lev. xviii. 27, 28; 2 Kings xxi. 9; 2 Chr. xxxiii. 9. These passages offer the most natural illustration of our verse, and in particular the LXX. of Lev. xviii. 27, 28 presents a close parallel, πάντα γὰρ τὰ βδελύγματα ταῦτα ἐποίησαν οἱ ἄνθρωποι τῆς γῆς, οἱ ὄντες πρότερον ὑμῶν, καὶ ἐμιάνθη ἡ γῆ. καὶ ἵνα μὴ προσοχθίσῃ ὑμῖν ἡ γῆ ἐν τῷ μιαίνειν ὑμᾶς αὐτήν, ὃν τρόπον προσώχθισε τοῖς ἔθνεσι τοῖς πρὸ ὑμῶν.

ἐβεβήλωσαν...ἐν βεβηλώσει. For this construction compare ix. 19. It probably represents the intensive use of the Inf. Absol. with the Finite Verb in the Hebrew.

τὰ ἅγια κυρίου. Cf. ii. 3, viii. 12, xviii. 51.

The phrase βεβηλοῦν τὰ ἅγια κυρίου occurs frequently in the LXX. (e.g. Lev. xix. 8, xxii. 15; Num. xviii. 32; Ps. lxxxviii. (lxxxix.) 40; Ezek. xxii. 26, xxiv. 21, etc.; Zeph. iii. 4; Mal. ii. 11; 1 Macc. iii. 51).

The words of Lev. xix. 8, where the LXX. rendering is ὁ δὲ ἔσθων αὐτὸ ἁμαρτίαν λήψεται ὅτι τὰ ἅγια κυρίου ἐβεβήλωσε, will best explain this concluding sentence of the Psalm. The correspondence of the language is so close that in all probability it has been borrowed by our translator, and therefore should supply the true interpretation of τὰ ἅγια κυρίου. These words might be taken to mean 'the sanctuary of the LORD,' for which they commonly stand in the LXX.; and this translation is followed by Geiger ('*das Heiligthum*') and Pick ('*the Sanctuary*'). But both in this verse and in ii. 3 the Psalmist is alluding especially to the profane and irreverent action of the Jews, and of their Priests in particular, in the ritual of the sacrifices, as, for example, by approaching the altar when ceremonially unclean, a form of profanation singled out for especial opprobrium in viii. 13, 14. The violation of the Mosaic law under this head represented to the true Pharisee the extreme of impiety, which God would surely not suffer to go unpunished.

Ps. II. *Argument.*

A. Jerusalem's overthrow (1—15).

(i) The Temple defiled by the Gentiles in return for the profaneness of the 'sons of Jerusalem' (1—5).

(ii) The inhabitants of Jerusalem captives in return for their unparalleled wickedness (6—12).

(iii) Their wickedness returns on their own heads (13—15).

B. God's judgement justified (16—23).

(i) He is righteous in visiting the people for their sin (16—19).

(ii) in humiliating the chosen city (20—23).

C. The Intercession of the holy (24—29).

(i) Let not Israel be wholly consumed (24—26).

II. 1] ΨΑΛΜΟΙ ΣΑΛΟΜΩΝΤΟΣ. 7

8 Their transgressions were greater than *those of* the heathen that were before them ;
9 The holy things of the LORD they *had* utterly polluted.

PSALM II.

A Psalm of Solomon concerning Jerusalem.

1 When the sinful man waxed proud, he cast down fenced walls with a battering-ram, and thou didst not prevent *him*.

(ii) Let vengeance overtake the oppressors who overthrow Jerusalem with savagery, not judicially (27—29).
D. The Divine Answer (30—35).
(i) The death and dishonour of the Oppressor (30, 31).
(ii) The doom of the would-be king for arrogance and blindness (32—35).
E. The call to recognise the true King (36—40).
(i) The great King (36).
(ii) His mercy and justice (37).
(iii) His lovingkindness (38—40).
F. Doxology (41).

The speaker, who refers to himself only in vv. 24 and 30, does not identify himself with Jerusalem or Zion. The point of view is therefore different from that of the preceding Psalm. The Psalmist is the spokesman of the theocratic party referred to in vv. 37, 38, 40, 41, as those 'that fear the Lord with understanding,' 'the righteous,' 'that call upon Him in patience,' 'His servants.'

The allusions in this Psalm to historical events are of very great importance. Their identification supplies not only a clue to the date of the composition of this particular Psalm, but also a 'terminus ad quem' for the date of the whole collection.

(*a*) Jerusalem has been at the mercy of invaders, her walls have been battered down, the sacred altar has been profaned (vv. 1, 2). Jews have been enslaved by their oppressors (6, 7).

This agrees with the occupation of Jerusalem by Pompey, with his siege of the Temple which lasted for three months, and its final capture, followed by the massacre of Aristobulus' supporters, and by his removal along with other Jews of distinction into captivity at Rome.

(*b*) The 'sinful man' (ver. 1), 'the dragon' (29), whose purpose had been to rule the world, who had set his 'greatness' against that of God (33), is pierced and slain in Egypt (30), his body lies neglected, unburied, on the waves (30, 31).

This description agrees closely with the fate of Pompey. He made a bid for supreme power against Cæsar; he was surnamed 'the Great.' He was treacherously assassinated on the shores of Egypt (Sept. 28, 48 B.C.).

(*c*) The overthrow of the Oppressor heralds the triumph of the lowly (ver. 35).

It is worth observing that while, as appears from this Psalm, the Jews regarded Pompey as a tyrant, they glorified Cæsar on account of his clemency and consideration towards their own race. The concluding burst of triumph in our Psalm very probably indicates the satisfaction of the patriot Jews at the complete success of Cæsar's arms. After arranging matters in Egypt and overthrowing Pharnaces, king of Pontus, with extraordinary suddenness, he returned to Syria, and in July of 47 was in Antioch, making provision for the good government of the province of Syria and dispensing favours to the states who had supported him during his recent campaigns. The special privileges which he awarded to the Jews are recorded in Jos. *Ant.* XIV. x. 1—10.

It is to this period of the Dictator's favour that we are inclined to assign the composition of this Psalm.

The Inscription 'concerning Jerusalem' is of such a general nature that it is hardly likely to be original. The mention of the 'walls' in ver. 1, and the frequent occurrence of the name of the city throughout the Psalm (vv. 3, 13, 14, 20, 24), are quite sufficient to account for the title having been added. Jerusalem however is personified throughout. There is no reference to 'πόλις'; even the 'walls' of ver. 1 are not the city walls.

1 Ἐν τῷ ὑπερηφανεύεσθαι τὸν ἁμαρτωλόν. This opening clause is taken from Ps. ix. 23 (x. 2).

8   ΨΑΛΜΟΙ ΣΑΛΟΜΩΝΤΟΣ.   [II. 2

²ἀνέβησαν ἐπὶ τὸ θυσιαστήριόν σου ἔθνη ἀλλότρια,
κατεπάτουν ἐν ὑποδήμασιν αὐτῶν ἐν ὑπερηφανίᾳ.

2 ἔθη Cerda, sed interpr. 'gentes.'

Pompey, as the representative of the foreign power that had reduced Zion to servitude, is the personification of sin, *the* sinner. Thus while ἁμαρτωλοί may indicate all whether Jews or Gentiles, who do not 'fear God,' this estrangement from God is concentrated in the man, who has been the instrument of Jerusalem's humiliation.

The reader will be reminded of the reference to the representative of the Roman Empire in 2 Thess. (ii. 3, 4 ὁ ἄνθρωπος τῆς ἀνομίας, ὁ υἱὸς τῆς ἀπωλείας, and 8, ὁ ἄνομος). There were obvious reasons why such allusions should be made in guarded terms.

For other probable references to Pompey beside those contained in the present Psalm, compare viii. 16 τὸν ἀπ' ἐσχάτου τῆς γῆς, τὸν παίοντα κραταιῶς κ.τ.λ. and xvii. 13 ἠρήμωσεν ὁ ἄνομος (?) τὴν γῆν ἡμῶν.

τείχη ὀχυρά. Cf. LXX. in Dt. xxviii. 52.

The allusion here is in all probability to the siege of the Temple by Pompey. He had occupied the city of Jerusalem without opposition. But the Temple with precipitous sides on S. and E., with a ravine on the W., strengthened at every point by massive fortifications, was manned by the adherents of Aristobulus, who offered a stubborn resistance. Pompey was compelled to lay regular siege to the Temple. Josephus expressly mentions that Pompey sent for his siege-train from Tyre (προσβαλὼν μηχανὰς καὶ ὄργανα ἐκ Τύρου κομισθέντα ἐπιστήσας κατήρασσε τὸ ἱερὸν τοῖς πετροβόλοις), *Ant.* XIV. iv. 2. In order to bring his siege-train into play upon the Temple walls, it was necessary to fill up the great dyke which protected the N., the only vulnerable side of the Temple fortifications. This dyke is described by Warren in *Underground Jerusalem* (London, 1876), pages 65, 66, 72. Strabo speaks of it as cut out of the rock, 60 feet deep, 250 wide (xvi. 2).

The allusion to the battering-ram (ἐν κριῷ) becomes a truthful touch. It recalled a memorable scene—the Roman soldiers for the first time in Jerusalem, and plying their 'aries' against the massive masonry of the Holy Temple.

The capture of the Temple was only effected after a three months' heroic defence; a breach was made in the walls apparently by the destruction of its largest tower; and it was the battering-ram mentioned by the Psalmist that accomplished for the Romans the fatal work against the ὀχυρὰ τείχη. The Roman soldiers led by a son of Sulla the Dictator poured in through the breach, and a general massacre ensued. ἐπεὶ δὲ τοῦ μηχανήματος προσαχθέντος σεισθεὶς ὁ μέγιστος τῶν πύργων κατηνέχθη, καὶ παρέρρηξέ τι χωρίον, εἰσεχέοντο μὲν οἱ πολέμιοι, πρῶτος δὲ αὐτῶν Κορνήλιος Φαῦστος Σύλλα παῖς σὺν τοῖς ἑαυτοῦ στρατιώταις ἐπέβη τοῦ τείχους…φόνου δὲ ἦν πάντα ἀνάπλεω. *Ant.* XIV. iv. 4. The 'battering-ram' appears in Assyrian sculptures, and is mentioned in Ezek. iv. 2, xxi. 22, where the Hebrew כָּרִים 'rams' clearly indicate the same weapons as the κριοί and 'arietes' of the Greeks and Romans. The LXX. however does not reproduce the word in these passages; and apparently only employs κριός to denote an engine of war in 2 Macc. xii. 15. The name seems to appear in classical literature first in Xenophon's *Cyropaedeia* (VII. iv. 1), but the thing is indicated plainly enough as in use at the siege of Plataea, Thuc. II. 76. Vitruvius (x. xiii. 19) describes the various stages of its development, and Josephus, *Bell. Jud.* III. vii. 19. There is a good representation of the machine in use on the Column of Trajan.

The accounts of the capture of Jerusalem by Antiochus Epiphanes (which Ewald considers to be here referred to) have nothing corresponding to the historical reminiscence contained in ἐν κριῷ κατέβαλε. (1) Josephus states that Antiochus obtained possession of the city on the first occasion (169) ἀμαχητί, and on the second (167) ἀπάτῃ. (2) The description in 1 Macc. i. 20, 29—31, 2 Macc. v. 11 does not exclude the idea of a regular assault and defence; but certainly implies that the Syrian conqueror met with little serious resistance.

οὐκ ἐκώλυσας. The Psalmist in this

II. 2] ΨΑΛΜΟΙ ΣΑΛΟΜΩΝΤΟΣ. 9

2 The heathen[1] went up against thine altar, they trampled it down, *yea*, with their sandals in their pride,

[1] Gr. *Strange peoples*

---

and the following verse addresses the Almighty, but adopts the form of narrative in vv. 3, 4, 5.

Josephus expressly states that the success of the Romans in the siege of the Temple was largely due to the progress they were able to make on the Sabbathdays, when the beleaguered Jews in strict conformity with their tradition discontinued their works of defence.

But even such piety was unrewarded; and the Lord 'hindered not' the success of the Gentiles.

For Hilgenfeld's theory that this verse is quoted in 4 Esdr. iii. 8 (*Vers. Arab.*), see Introd.

The thought of this clause is expressed in 4 Esdr. iii. 29—31 'et excessit cor meum, quoniam vidi, quomodo sustines eos peccantes et pepercisti impie agentibus et perdidisti populum tuum et conservasti inimicos tuos et non significasti nihil nemini, quomodo debeat derelinqui via hæc. Numquid meliora fecit Babylon quam Sion?' It was a very natural question to arise in the mind of the pious Jew. How was it that, however sinful and rebellious the sons of Jerusalem might be, God had suffered the yet more sinful Gentiles to trample her down?

See also *Apoc. Bar.* xi. 2, 3 'nunc vero ecce dolor infinitus, et gemitus sine mensura, quia tu (Babylon) ecce prosperata es, et Sion desolata. Quisnam erit judex de istis? aut cuinam conqueremur de iis quæ acciderunt nobis? O Domine, *quomodo sustinuisti?*

2 ἀνέβησαν ἐπὶ τὸ θυσιαστήριόν σου ἔθνη ἀλλότρια. The language in this and the following verse is an echo of Ps. lxxviii. (lxxix.) 1 and Lam. i. 10.

At the capture of the Temple the Roman soldiers bursting in cut down the priests, who continued to occupy themselves at the altar in their sacrificial duties to the very last. The scene is vividly given by Josephus, *Antiq. Jud.* XIV. iv. 3 οἱ πολέμιοι μὲν εἰσπεσόντες ἔσφαττον τοὺς ἐν τῷ ἱερῷ· οἱ δὲ πρὸς ταῖς θυσίαις οὐδὲν ἧττον ἱερουργοῦντες διετέλουν, οὔτε ὑπὸ τοῦ φόβου τοῦ περὶ τῆς ψυχῆς οὔτε ὑπὸ τοῦ πλήθους τῶν ἤδη φονευομένων, ἀναγκασθέντες ἀποδρᾶναι, πᾶν δὲ ὅ τι δέοι παθεῖν τοῦτο παρ' αὐτοῖς ὑπομεῖναι τοῖς βωμοῖς κρεῖττον εἶναι νομίζοντες ἢ παρελθεῖν τι τῶν νομίμων.

But the event which impressed itself most deeply upon the mind of the Jews was the entry of Pompey and his companions not only into the sacred precincts reserved for the priests, but even into the Holy of Holies, which none but the High Priest might enter, and then but once a year after special and solemn ceremonial acts of purification. This disregard of their deepest religious sentiments was never forgiven by the Jews. At the same time Pompey does not seem to have stopped the worship or rifled the treasures of the Temple. Cicero *pro Flacco* 67 'Cn. Pompeius captis Hierosolymis victor ex illo fano nihil attigit.' It is noteworthy that the Psalmist makes no particular reference to this violation of the Holy of Holies, but the fact does not militate against the hypothesis of a Pompeian date. If anything, it serves to show that the fear of Rome was so strong that any more detailed allusions were felt to be dangerous.

Tac. *Hist.* v. 9 Romanorum primus Cn. Pompeius Judæos domuit, templumque jure victoriæ ingressus est, inde vulgatum nulla intus deûm effigie vacuam sedem et inania arcana. Muri Hierosolymorum diruti, delubrum mansit.

Josephus (*Antiq. Jud.* XIV. iv. 4) παρηνομήθη δὲ οὐ μικρὰ περὶ τὸν ναόν, ἄβατόν τε ὄντα ἐν τῷ πρὶν χρόνῳ καὶ ἀόρατον· παρῆλθε γὰρ εἰς τὸ ἐντὸς ὁ Πομπήϊος καὶ τῶν περὶ αὐτὸν οὐκ ὀλίγοι, καὶ εἶδον ὅσα μὴ θεμιτὸν ἦν τοῖς ἄλλοις ἀνθρώποις ἢ μόνοις τοῖς ἀρχιερεῦσιν. Ὄντων δὲ τραπέζης τε χρυσῆς καὶ λυχνίας ἱερᾶς καὶ σπονδείων καὶ πλήθους ἀρωμάτων, χωρὶς δὲ τούτων ἐν τοῖς θησαυροῖς ἱερῶν χρημάτων εἰς δύο χιλιάδας ταλάντων, οὐδενὸς ἥψατο δι' εὐσέβειαν, ἀλλὰ καὶ ἐν τούτῳ τῆς περὶ αὐτὸν ἀξίως ἔπραξεν ἀρετῆς. Τῇ τε ὑστεραίᾳ καθαίρειν παραγγείλας τὸ ἱερὸν τοῖς ναοπόλοις καὶ τὰ νόμιμα ἐπιφέρειν τῷ θεῷ τὴν ἱερωσύνην ἀπέδωκεν Ὑρκανῷ κ.τ.λ.

θυσιαστήριον. This and not βωμός is the word preferred in the LXX. to translate the altar (מזבח) of God. We find βωμός used frequently of 'high places,' perhaps from the similarity of sound with 'bāmôth' [see Isai. xv. 2, xvi. 12; Jer. vii. 30, xxxii. (Gr. xxxix.) 35, xlviii. (Gr. xxxi.) 35; Hos. x. 8; Am. vii. 9], and

³ ἀνθ' ὧν οἱ υἱοὶ Ἰερουσαλὴμ ἐμίανα τὰ ἅγια κυρίου,
ἐβεβήλουν τὰ δῶρα τοῦ θεοῦ ἐν ἀνομίαις·
⁴ ἕνεκεν τούτων εἶπεν· ἀπορρίψατε αὐτὰ μακρὰν ἀπ' ἐμοῦ·

3 δώρῳ V.

of heathen altars (Ex. xxxiv. 13; Num. xxiii. 1, 2, 4, &c.; Dt. vii. 5, xii. 3; 2 Chron. xxxi. 1; Is. xvii. 8, xxvii. 9; Jer. xi. 13). The word is also used of the disputed altar in Jos. xxii. Exceptions are Ecclus. l. 12, 14; 2 Macc. ii. 19, xiii. 8, where the altar at Jerusalem is called βωμός.
In 1 Maccabees βωμός (i. 59, ii. 23, 24, 25, 45, v. 68) is always used of a heathen altar. The distinction appears in a striking manner in 1 Macc. i. 59 'they did sacrifice upon the idol altar which was upon the altar of God' (θυσιάζοντες ἐπὶ τὸν βωμὸν ὃς ἦν ἐπὶ τοῦ θυσιαστηρίου). With this agrees the usage of the N.T.

ἔθνη ἀλλότρια. This phrase in the LXX. occurs, we believe, only in Ecclus. (xxxvi. 2, xxxix. 5, xlix. 6). The very similar expression ἀλλότριοι λαοί is found in Isai. i. 7, as the rendering of זָרִים, which was probably the word used in the original of the present passage.
κατεπάτουν. The change of tense from aor. to impf. should be observed here and in ver. 3.
The clause is identical in meaning with ver. 20 ὠνείδισαν γὰρ ἔθνη Ἰερουσαλὴμ ἐν καταπατήσει, where the verb and substantive change places. The verb καταπατεῖν may be illustrated by Is. lxiii. 18; Dan. viii. 13; 1 Macc. iii. 46, 52, iv. 60; 3 Macc. ii. 18. The expansion of the image by the words ἐν ὑποδήμασιν does not appear to have any parallel in the O.T. The 'locus classicus' in the O.T. showing that to remove the shoes on approaching a sanctuary was necessary is Ex. iii. 5; cf. Test. Zab. § 3.
For 'the trampling under foot', compare Apoc. Bar. xiii. 11 'nunc autem vos, populi et gentes, debitores estis, quia toto hoc tempore conculcastis terram &c.'
ἐν ὑπερηφανίᾳ. Cf. xvii. 15. It is very characteristic of the style of our Greek translator to close a clause with the preposition ἐν and an abstract subst. Cf. in this Psalm vv. 3, 20, 29, 32, 35, 37, 40.
3 οἱ υἱοὶ Ἰερουσαλήμ. For this expression, which occurs also in ver. 20, we

hardly find any parallel in the O.T. except Joel iii. 6 'the children also of Judah and the children of Jerusalem have ye sold unto the sons of the Grecians.' (LXX. τοὺς υἱοὺς Ἰερουσαλήμ.)
On the 'daughters of Jerusalem' see note on v. 14.
ἐμίαναν τὰ ἅγια κυρίου. In this and the following clause the language is based upon passages in Leviticus and Ezekiel. The Greek of this clause closely resembles the LXX. version in Ezek. v. 11 ζῶ ἐγὼ λέγει κύριος ἦ μὴν ἀνθ' ὧν τὰ ἅγιά μου ἐμίανας ἐν πᾶσι τοῖς βδελύγμασί σου, κἀγὼ ἀπώσομαί σε, xxiii. 38 ἕως καὶ ταῦτα ἐποίησάν μοι, τὰ ἅγιά μου ἐμίαναν, καὶ τὰ σάββατά μου ἐβεβήλουν. In both passages the term τὰ ἅγιά μου translates מִקְדָּשִׁי 'my sanctuary.' In the present passage we are of opinion that, as in i. 8, τὰ ἅγια κυρίου refers not to the Temple buildings but to the sacrifices and worship. Our reasons are (1) ver. 3 gives the explanation (ἀνθ' ὧν) of the dishonour to the 'altar' described in ver. 2: (2) the term is here employed as a parallel to τὰ δῶρα τοῦ θεοῦ: (3) it is the expression used by the LXX. to render the technical Levitical phrase 'the holy thing of the LORD' (קֹדֶשׁ יְהֹוָה) applied to sacrificial offerings, e.g. Lev. xix. 8 ὁ δὲ ἔσθων αὐτό, ἁμαρτίαν λήψεται, ὅτι τὰ ἅγια κυρίου ἐβεβήλωσε.
τὰ δῶρα τοῦ θεοῦ. This expression is used by the LXX. version to render 'the bread of God' (לֶחֶם אֱלֹהִים) in Levit. xxi. 6 ἅγιοι ἔσονται τῷ θεῷ αὐτῶν, καὶ οὐ βεβηλώσουσι τὸ ὄνομα τοῦ θεοῦ αὐτῶν· τὰς γὰρ θυσίας κυρίου δῶρα τοῦ θεοῦ αὐτῶν αὐτοὶ προσφέρουσι, καὶ ἔσονται ἅγιοι, and vv. 8, 17, 21—23, xxii. 25.
Both clauses therefore appear to be based upon the Levitical laws relating to the priests. It is natural to conclude that the Psalmist, though speaking of 'the sons of Jerusalem,' is pointedly referring to the malpractices and laxities of the priests. And it is to be remembered that the Sadducees were very numerous among the Priests, since the High-

II. 4] ΨΑΛΜΟΙ ΣΑΛΟΜΩΝΤΟΣ. 11

3 Because the sons of Jerusalem defiled the holy things of
the LORD, *and* polluted the gifts of God with iniquities,
4 For this cause said he: 'Cast ye them[2] afar off from me.'

[2] i.e. *the gifts*

Priest and his family stood at the head of the Sadducean party.

4 ἀποῤῥίψατε. Cf. Sym. Ps. lxxvii. (lxxviii.) 60 καὶ ἀπέρριψε τὴν σκήνωσιν τὴν Σηλώμ, Sym. Is. ii. 6 ἀπέρριψας. Aq. Jer. xiv. 19 μὴ ἀποῤῥίπτων ἀπέρριψας τὴν Ἰουδαίαν.

ἀποῤῥίψατε αὐτά. The neuter Plur. Pron. refers back to τὰ ἅγια κυρίου and τὰ δῶρα τοῦ θεοῦ in ver. 3. Geiger considers it a translator's error, and is of opinion that αὐτοὺς would more aptly have represented an original הַשְׁלִיכוּם. This is not impossible, and receives some support from the similar words in Jer. vii. 15 καὶ ἀποῤῥίψω ὑμᾶς ἀπὸ προσώπου μου.

οὐκ εὐώδωκεν αὐτοῖς. The reading οὐκ εὐώδωκεν αὐτοῖς is found in the Paris MS., and is supported by the Moscow MS. οὐκ εὐέδωκεν (sic) αὐτοῖς, as well as by the Copenhagen MS. οὐκ εὐώδωκεν ἡ αὐτοῖς (where however -κ̄ (=-κεν) was possibly added as a correction, and the presence of ἡ is either due to a clerical error or to the influence of the same MS. from which V is derived).

The other two MSS. (Augsburg and Vienna) favour the reading οὐκ εὐώδω-... αὐτοῖς. The Vienna MS. gives οὐκ εὐώδω ἡ αὐτοῖς, where the η perhaps reproduces the appearance of an illegible -κεν in the parent MS. (so Graux). The testimony of the Augsburg MS. needs to be carefully stated. The words in Cerda's edition stand thus: οὐκ εὐώδωδει εὐωδίᾳ ἡ αὐτοῖς τὸ κάλλος τῆς δόξης αὐτοῦ. Cerda however in his note says: 'perperam scripta haec in graeco ut legere nequirem, suspicor scriptum οὐκ εὐωδώδει εὐωδίᾳ.' It seems then that on the analogy of the other MSS. the reading of A must almost certainly have contained the common element οὐκ εὐωδω...ἡ; and possibly there may have been an erasure or flaw in the MS. which made the letters illegible. In any case it is an error to cite (as Fritzsche and Pick) -δει εὐωδίᾳ as a MS. reading.

Geiger's conjecture οὐκ εὐωδώθη αὐτοῖς appears to us very improbable. It introduces the impersonal construction of the Passive with the Dat. of the Pronoun which would be without parallel in the LXX. use of εὐοδόω. Cf. 2 Chron. xxxii. 30 εὐοδώθη Ἐζεκίας. 1 Macc. iii. 6 εὐοδώθη σωτηρία. xvi. 2 καὶ εὐοδώθη ἐν ταῖς χερσὶν ἡμῶν.

Hilgenfeld's conjecture οὐκ εὐδοκῶ ἐν αὐτοῖς is much more plausible. It gives a very simple and satisfactory sense. But (1) it diverges from the MSS. at the very syllable (ευωδ-) where they are unanimous: (2) it conflicts further with the evidence of the MSS., which connect these words with τὸ κάλλος τῆς δόξης αὐτοῦ and make them a continuation of the Divine utterance: (3) by substituting an easy text for an obscure one, it fails to account for the 'genesis' of the textual error.

If we adopted Hilgenfeld's conjecture, an exact parallel in thought and word would be found in Jer. xiv. 12 ἐὰν προσενέγκωσιν ὁλοκαυτώματα καὶ θυσίας οὐκ εὐδοκήσω ἐν αὐτοῖς. If in the face of the MSS. it were justifiable to separate these words from τὸ κάλλος τῆς δόξης αὐτοῦ, we should be inclined to suggest οὐκ εὐώδωκα (ἐν) αὐτοῖς 'I have not prospered them.'

The chief objection to the reading of the text οὐκ εὐώδωκεν αὐτοῖς τὸ κάλλος τῆς δόξης αὐτοῦ, lies in the Perf. tense following εἶπεν. An objection however, based on the use of the tenses in a translation from the Hebrew, is not a very serious obstacle, when we call to mind the capricious manner in which Hebrew tenses are rendered in the LXX. A very probable conjecture, however, ΟΥΚ ΕΓΩΛΩϹΕΝ ΑΥΤΟΙϹ, would obviate even this difficulty, and preserve the reading of the MSS. οὐκ εὐώδω...αὐτοῖς.

The origin of the textual confusion may be attributed either to a flaw in the parent copy, or to an error on the part of a scribe, who, not perceiving that τὸ κάλλος was the subject of εὐώδωκεν (-σεν), endeavoured to emend the passage.

5 τὸ κάλλος τῆς δόξης αὐτοῦ. Cf. ver. 20 κατέσπασε τὸ κάλλος αὐτῆς ἀπὸ θρόνου δόξης. The beauty of the Temple and the glory of its worship are intended.

αὐτοῦ. Fritzsche changes to αὐτῶν, referring the word to the offerings and gifts. The change is not necessary even

12   ΨΑΛΜΟΙ ΣΑΛΟΜΩΝΤΟΣ.   [II. 4

οὐκ εὐώδωκεν αὐτοῖς ⁵τὸ κάλλος τῆς δόξης αὐτοῦ·
ἐξουθενήθη ἐνώπιον τοῦ θεοῦ, ἠτιμώθη εἰς τέλος.

⁶Οἱ υἱοὶ καὶ αἱ θυγατέρες ἐν αἰχμαλωσίᾳ πονηρᾷ,
ἐν σφραγῖδι ὁ τράχηλος αὐτῶν, ἐν ἐπισήμῳ ἐν τοῖς ἔθνεσι.
⁷κατὰ τὰς ἁμαρτίας αὐτῶν ἐποίησεν αὐτοῖς·
ὅτι ἐγκατέλιπεν αὐτοὺς εἰς χεῖρας κατισχυόντων,
⁸ἀπέστρεψε γὰρ πρόσωπον αὐτοῦ ἀπὸ ἐλέου αὐτῶν,
νέον καὶ πρεσβύτην καὶ τέκνα αὐτῶν εἰσάπαξ·

4 οὐκ εὐώδω ἡ αὐτοῖς (A) V: οὐκ εὐώδωκεν ἡ αὐτοῖς τὸ κάλλος τῆς δόξης αὐτοῦ K (-κεν? corr.) et P (om. ἡ): οὐκ εὐέδωκεν αὐτοῖς τὸ κάλλος τῆς δόξης αὐτῆς M. Conj.: Cerda οὐκ εὐωδώδει εὐωδίᾳ ἡ αὐτοῖς: Fabr. οὐκ εὐωδώθη εὐοδίᾳ ἐν αὐτοῖς: Hilgenf. οὐκ εὐδοκῶ ἐν αὐτοῖς (ita Fritzsch. Pick.): Geig. οὐκ εὐωδώθη αὐτοῖς.
5 αὐτοῦ A, V, K, P: αὐτῆς M. Fritzsch. conj. αὐτῶν (ita Pick.). ἠτιμώθη A, K, P, M: ἠτιμενθη V: ἠτιμήθη conj. Hilg. (ita Geig.).
8 ἐλέους A, ἐλέου V, K, P, M: εἰς ἄπαξ A, K, εἰσάπαξ V, (P), M.

---

in his text, where τὸ κάλλος...αὐτῶν stands in the same clause with ἐξουθενήθη.

ἐνώπιον τοῦ θεοῦ. Cf. 'none shall appear *before me* empty,' οὐκ ὀφθήσῃ ἐνώπιόν μου κενός, Ex. xxiii. 15; Dt. xvi. 10. See note on ver. 40.

εἰς τέλος. See note on i. 1.

6 Οἱ υἱοὶ καὶ αἱ θυγατέρες, i.e. the children of Jerusalem. Cf. vv. 3, 13, 14.

ἐν αἰχμαλωσίᾳ πονηρᾷ. The adjective πονηρός is here used in the sense of 'grievous,' 'sore.'

Compare iii. 13 πονηρὸν τὸ πτῶμα αὐτοῦ.

ἐν σφραγῖδι ὁ τράχηλος αὐτῶν, ἐν ἐπισήμῳ ἐν τοῖς ἔθνεσι. This passage is one of great obscurity. The general sense however is clear. The words expand in detail the 'sore captivity.' 'The sons and daughters' of Jerusalem are subjected to the usual indignities perpetrated on slaves.

The expression ἐν σφραγῖδι ὁ τράχηλος αὐτῶν does not seem to have any parallel. We should rather have expected some such expression as ἐν κλοιῷ, ἐν ζυγῷ or ἐν κύφωνι.

We interpret the passage on the assumption that both phrases, ἐν σφραγῖδι and ἐν ἐπισήμῳ, refer to badges of slavery impressed by branding and tattooing upon the necks of slaves.

ἐν σφραγῖδι. The 'seal' of the master was impressed upon the neck of the slave. For this explanation we cannot adduce any support from other literature. But we have the fact that many slave-collars have been found on Roman sites, inscribed with the master's name and some such addition as 'Tene me, quia fugio'; and further we have copious references to the branding of slaves' foreheads and hands (e.g. Mart. XII. 61, Frons hæc stigmate non meo notanda est. Petron. 107, implevit Eumolpus frontes utriusque ingentibus litteris, et notum fugitivorum epigramma per totam faciem liberali manu duxit: cf. Wetstein's note on Gal. vi. 17).

Here the τράχηλος is either used poetically for the slave's collar, or, as seems to us preferable, it implies that the flesh of the slave's neck was marked with the master's badge by a process of tattooing.

ἐν ἐπισήμῳ. It has been customary to render this expression as if it meant 'publicly,' 'in the sight of the world,' a sense in which the words occur in xvii. 32. Such a translation assumes that the adjective is here used adverbially like ἐν φανερῷ, ἐν κρυπτῷ. (For the use of the adj. with τόπος see 1 Macc. xii. 37, xiv. 48, and comp. Sym. Ps. iv. 7 ἐπίσημον ποίησον = נְסָה.)

The substantive however ἐπίσημον, which is used for a 'badge' (e.g. the flag of a ship, the device of a coin), seems to give here a better meaning than the adjective. Hesychius (s.v.) states that it was used of the 'brand' applied to slaves. Its use in that sense appears most appropriate to the present passage; it is then equivalent to ἐν στίγματι, and developes the picture presented under ἐν σφραγῖδι. For the practice of branding

II. 8] ΨΑΛΜΟΙ ΣΑΛΟΜΩΝΤΟΣ. 13

5 The beauty of his glory did not prosper them[3]; it was set at nought before God, it was utterly dishonoured.

6 Her sons and her daughters were in grievous captivity; their neck *was marked* with a seal, with the brand *of slavery*[4] among the Gentiles.

7 According to their sins he dealt with them, for he gave them up into the hands of oppressors,

8 —yea, he turned away his face from showing them mercy— *he gave them up, I say*, the young man and the old man and their children together,

[3] Text doubtful. Another reading: *He caused them not to prosper. The beauty of his glory was set* &c.

[4] Or, *they were a gazing-stock*

---

slaves see 3 Macc. ii. 29, and Bp Lightfoot's note on the στίγματα of Gal. vi. 17.

Geiger's translation 'Ihr Nacken ist belastet unter den Heiden' is due to his supposition that the collocation of σφραγίς and ἐπίσημος is in some way due to Job xiv. 17 ἐσφράγισας δέ μου τὰς ἀνομίας ἐν βαλαντίῳ ἐπεσημήνω δὲ εἴ τι ἄκων παρέβην.

Wellhausen renders 'im Ring ihr Hals, als Schaustück unter den Heiden,' which is reproduced by Pick 'Their neck in the ring, in the sight of the heathen.' But σφραγίς means a 'seal,' whether that which gives the impression or the impression itself; we question whether it can be used as a synonym for δακτύλιος except with the sense of 'a signet,' and even if it could be, its association, in the sense of 'a ring,' with ὁ τράχηλος αὐτῶν is quite out of the question.

Add here three references all of which bear on the subject.

1. iv. Esdr. x. 23. Signaculum (σφραγίς) Sion quoniam resignata est de gloria sua nunc et tradita est in manibus eorum qui nos oderunt.

2. Acta S. Maximiliani ap. Ruinart, p. 340 (referred to by Hilg.²). Accipe signaculum ... non licet mihi plumbum collo portare.

3. Sib. Or. viii. 244. Of the Cross. Σῆμα δέ τοι τότε πᾶσι βροτοῖς σφρηγὶς ἐπίσημος. This last passage is important. It unites the two crucial words and brings out the sense of a brand, with an obvious allusion to Ezek. ix.

7 κατὰ τὰς ἁμαρτίας αὐτῶν. The thought of retribution is especially prominent in this Psalm, see 13—15, 17, 28, 39. Cf. Ps. cii. (ciii.) 10 οὐ κατὰ τὰς ἁμαρτίας ἡμῶν ἐποίησεν ἡμῖν.

ἐγκατέλιπεν εἰς χεῖρας. Cf. Ps. xxxvi. (xxxvii.) 33 ὁ δὲ κύριος οὐ μὴ ἐγκαταλίπῃ αὐτὸν εἰς τὰς χεῖρας αὐτοῦ.

κατισχυόντων. 'Oppressors' or 'tyrants.' For this use of the Participle as a substantive cf. Wisd. x. 11 ἐν πλεονεξίᾳ κατισχυόντων. In 1 Chron. xi. 10 it is applied to David's mighty men 'who showed themselves strong with him.'

8 ἀπέστρεψε γὰρ πρόσωπον αὐτοῦ. This clause explains how the Lord had deserted his people. The phrase ἀποστρέφειν πρόσωπον is the rendering in the LXX. for הִסְתִּיר פָּנֶי, or 'hide the face,' so common in the O. T., e.g. Dt. xxxi. 17; Ps. ix. 32 (x. 11). On another use of ἀποστρέφω see v. 9.

ἀπὸ ἐλέους αὐτῶν. In the LXX. the phrase ἀποστρέφειν πρόσωπον is almost uniformly found with ἀπό and the gen. of the person, from whom the face is averted. Here, as often in this collection of Psalms, the simple usage receives a slight modification. Instead of the recipient it is the act of mercy from which the Divine countenance is as it were averted. Instead of ἀπ' αὐτῶν we have ἀπ' ἐλέους αὐτῶν in the sense of τοῦ μὴ ἐλεῆσαι αὐτούς.

For this transitive use of ἔλεος see xiv. 6 ἐν ἡμέρᾳ ἐλέου δικαίων, and it is hard to find another parallel. Perhaps the nearest is to be found in Jer. xlix. (Heb. xlii.) 2 πεσέτω δὴ τὸ ἔλεος ἡμῶν κατὰ πρόσωπόν σου.

νέον κ.τ.λ. The accusatives here may be explained *either* as the object of ἐγκατέλιπεν in ver. 7, and therefore in apposition to αὐτοὺς, ἀπέστρεψε γὰρ...αὐτῶν being regarded as parenthetical, *or*, as the objects of the compassion expressed in ἐλέου in sense of ἐλεῆσαι.

For the clause itself compare xviii. 13 ἠφάνισεν νέον καὶ πρεσβύτην καὶ τέκνα αὐτῶν ἅμα. See Ezek. ix. 6. νέος for νεανίσκος is not common. Cf. Sym. Ps. xxxvii. (xxxvi.) 25 νέος ἐγενόμην (נַעַר

ΨΑΛΜΟΙ ΣΑΛΟΜΩΝΤΟΣ. [II. 9

⁹ ὅτι πονηρὰ ἐποίησαν εἰςάπαξ τοῦ μὴ ἀκούειν.
¹⁰ καὶ ὁ οὐρανὸς ἐβαρυθύμησε,
καὶ ἡ γῆ ἐβδελύξατο αὐτούς·
¹¹ ὅτι οὐκ ἐποίησε πᾶς ἄνθρωπος ἐπ' αὐτῆς ὅσα ἐποίησαν,
¹² καὶ γνώσεται ἡ γῆ τὰ κρίματά σου πάντα τὰ δίκαια, [ὁ
θεός.]

¹³ Ὁ θεὸς ἔστησεν τοὺς υἱοὺς Ἰερουσαλὴμ εἰς ἐμπαιγμὸν
ἀντὶ πορνῶν ἐν αὐτῇ·
πᾶς ὁ παραπορευόμενος εἰϲεπορεγετο κατεναντι τογ Ηλίογ·
ἐνέπαιζον ταῖς ἀνομίαις αὐτῶν.

9 εἰς ἅπαξ A, K, εἰσάπαξ V, (P).
12 τὰ δίκαια ὁ θεός· (interpung. ita A? V, K, P, Cerd. Fabr. Geig.): τὰ δίκαια.
ὁ θεὸς M, Hilg. Fritzsch. Pick.
13 ἔστησεν A, V, K, M, ἔστησε P. εἰς ἐμπαιγμὸν ἀντὶ πορνῶν ἐν αὐτῇ· πᾶς κ.τ.λ.
A, K, P, M, Fabr. Geig.: εἰς ἐμπαιγμὸν. ἀντὶ πορνῶν ἐν αὐτῇ κ.τ.λ. V, Hilg. Fritzsch.
Pick.: conjec. Lagarde ἀντὶ πορνώνος αὕτη, πᾶς κ.τ.λ.:
πᾶς ὁ παραπορευόμενος εἰσεπορεύετο κατέναντι τοῦ ἡλίου A, K, P, M, Fabr. Geig.: πᾶς
ὁ......εἰσεπορεύετο. κατέναντι τοῦ ἡλίου ἐνέπαιζον V, Hilg. Fritzsch. Pick.: conjec. Fabr.
παραπορνευόμενος. ἐνέπαιζον, Cerda ἐνέπαιτου, sed interpr. 'illudebant.'
ταῖς ἀνομ. αὐτῶν. καθὰ ἐποίουν αὐτοί, ἐπέναντι (sic) τοῦ ἡλίου παρεδιγ. κ.τ.λ. A,
Fabr. Geig.: ταῖς ἀνομ. αὐτῶν, καθὰ ἐποίουν αὐτοὶ ἀπέναντι τοῦ ἡλίου, παρεδ. κ.τ.λ. V, M,
Hilg. Fritzsch. Pick.: ταῖς ἀνομ. αὐτῶν, καθὰ ἐποίουν αὐτοὶ· ἀπέναντι τοῦ ἡλ. παρεδ.
κ.τ.λ. K, P: conjec. Hilg. κακὰ pro καθὰ. Lagarde, καθὰ......παρεδειγμάτισεν.

(הָיִיתִי). Prov. xx. 11 ἐπιγνωρισθήσεται
νέος (נַעַר). For πρεσβύτης compare
Philem. 9 τοιοῦτος ὢν ὡς Παῦλος πρεσβύτης, Lam. ii. 21 ἐκοιμήθησαν εἰς τὴν
ἔξοδον παιδάριον καὶ πρεσβύτης· παρθένοι
μου καὶ νεανίσκοι μου ἐπορεύθησαν ἐν αἰχμαλωσίᾳ.
εἰσάπαξ in this book translates יַחַד
'together,' cf. ver. 9. It is used in this
sense in Dan. ii. 35 τότε ἐλεπτύνθησαν
εἰσάπαξ (כַּחֲדָה) τὸ ὄστρακον, ὁ σίδηρος, ὁ
χαλκὸς, ὁ ἄργυρος, ὁ χρυσός.
10 Cf. xvii. 21.
ὁ οὐρανὸς ἐβαρυθύμησε. Cf. Jer. ii. 9
ἐξέστη ὁ οὐρανὸς ἐπὶ τούτῳ κ.τ.λ.
ἡ γῆ ἐβδελύξατο. The words are an
allusion to the passage in Lev. xviii. 24—
30, where 'abominations' (βδελύγματα)
are denounced. Compare especially ver.
25 'the land itself vomiteth out her inhabitants,' and 28 'that the land spue
not you out also, when ye defile it, as it
spued out the nations that were before
you,' where the LXX. rendering of 'spue'
(קוֹא) is προσοχθίζω. The substance of

the passage is in the writer's mind, but
the translator has not used the LXX.
rendering of it.
11 οὐ...πᾶς ἄνθρωπος. A common
Hebraism. Cf. vii. 6, ix. 5, xvii. 29.
ἐπ' αὐτῆς. Cf. i. 8, viii. 14.
12 γνώσεται. The future with καὶ
is possibly the rendering of the Hebrew
Impf. and Vau conversive = ἔγνω viii. 8.
τὰ κρίματά σου πάντα τὰ δίκαια, cf.
viii. 8.
A probable error in the text of the MSS.
is the omission of ὁ θεὸς at the end of
ver. 12, or at the beginning of ver. 13.
The words τὰ κρίματά σου evidently
point to the presence of a vocative; ὁ
θεὸς however is equally required at the
opening of ver. 13. We are of opinion
that ὁ θεὸς at the end of this verse slipped
out in an early MS. before the ὁ θεὸς
of the next. ὁ θεὸς closes ver. 12 in the
Copenhagen and Paris MSS., but stands
at the head of ver. 13 in the Vienna
Augsburg Moscow MS.
13 This passage offers one of the
chief difficulties to be found in the whole

II. 13]   ΨΑΛΜΟΙ ΣΑΛΟΜΩΝΤΟΣ.   15

9 Because they wrought evil together, to the intent that they should not hearken *unto him:*

10 And the heaven was grieved at them, and the earth abhorred them.

11 For none had done upon it all the things that they had done;

12 And the earth shall know all thy righteous judgements.

13 God set forth the sons of Jerusalem in derision that they should be as harlots in her midst; every one that passed by went in unto *them* before the sun, they made a mock of their transgressions.

---

book. The doubts felt as to the correct punctuation and arrangement of the clauses may be gathered from the Apparatus Criticus. The punctuation which we have followed (i) has good MS. authority, (ii) seems best to suit the original stichometric arrangement, (iii) furnishes the means of a fairly adequate translation.

τοὺς υἱοὺς Ἱερουσαλήμ. See on ver. 3.

εἰς ἐμπαιγμόν. Comp. xvii. 14. The language seems to recall Ezek. xxii. 4 διατοῦτο δέδωκά σε εἰς ὀνειδισμὸν τοῖς ἔθνεσι καὶ εἰς ἐμπαιγμὸν πάσαις ταῖς χώραις. Cf. Apoc. Bar. xlviii. 35 'et convertetur honor in ignominiam, et humiliabitur robur in contemptum.'

ἀντὶ πορνῶν ἐν αὐτῇ. (1) It is possible to suppose that, under a repulsive metaphor, the Psalmist represents the Jews as an object of contempt because they had prostituted their theocratic honour for commercial gain. The passage then will have points of resemblance to Hosea i., ii. (2) But the more literal interpretation of the passage is rendered only too probable by the similar invectives in Ps. S. viii. 9—14. The meaning then is that 'the sons of Jerusalem' were so sunk in shamelessness as to minister to the vile licentiousness of the Gentiles within the walls of the Holy City (ἐν αὐτῇ).

The expression ἀντὶ πορνῶν ἐν αὐτῇ is very awkward. It is just possible that the awkwardness is due to the translator's having faithfully rendered a corrupt Hebrew text, which did not offer any good meaning. If we may assume that the translator is rendering תַּחַת זְנוּתֶיהָ 'in the place of her harlots,' a slight alteration of vowels and the repetition of the final letter of תַּחַת, would give a reading תַּחַת תַּזְנוּתֶיהָ 'in return for her whoredoms' (cf. Ezek. xxiii. 14, 18), which would offer a very good and probable sense, and would explain the peculiarity of the Greek by the supposition of the loss of a single Hebrew letter (i.e. ת for תח). If conjectural emendation be necessary, this is undoubtedly preferable to Lagarde's ἀντὶ πορνῶνος αὕτη, i.e. 'She (Jerusalem) is in the place of a brothel.' The word which he suggests is destitute of LXX. analogy, and the idea is radically false to the spirit of Hebrew poetry.

πᾶς ὁ παραπορευόμενος εἰσεπορεύετο. The Imperf. of frequency. That the participle may be taken with ἐν αὐτῇ is rendered possible by such a passage as Theod. Isai. xxxiv. 10 οὐκ ἔστιν ὁ παραπορευόμενος ἐν αὐτῇ (אֵין עֹבֵר בָּהּ) κατέναντι τοῦ ἡλίου. Cf. viii. 8.

The open shame of the Jews is metaphorically expressed in language which recalls Num. xxv. 4, and the ἐναντίον τοῦ ἡλίου, ἀπέναντι τοῦ ἡλίου, of 2 Sam. xii. 11, 12.

ἐνέπαιζον ταῖς ἀνομίαις αὐτῶν. The subject is 'the Gentiles'; αὐτῶν refers to the Jews. The iniquities of Jerusalem did not really strengthen her position, but only exposed her to the contempt of the heathen.

For ἐμπαίζω cf. Gen. xxxix. 14, 17. Pick's rendering: 'Because of the prostitutes therein every passer-by enters, Before the sun they flaunted their wickedness,' makes ἀντί = διά.

16   ΨΑΛΜΟΙ ΣΑΛΟΜΩΝΤΟΣ.   [II. 14

¹⁴ καθὰ ἐποίουν αὐτοί, ἀπέναντι τοῦ ἡλίου παρεδειγμάτισαν ἀδικίας αὐτῶν.
καὶ θυγατέρες Ἰερουσαλὴμ βέβηλοι κατὰ τὸ κρίμα σου,
¹⁵ ἀνθ᾽ ὧν αὐταὶ ἐμίαινον ἑαυτὰς ἐν φυρμῷ ἀναμίξεως.
τὴν κοιλίαν μου καὶ τὰ σπλάγχνα μου πονῶ ἐπὶ τούτοις.

¹⁶ Ἐγὼ δικαιώσω σε, ὁ θεός, ἐν εὐθύτητι καρδίας,
ὅτι ἐν τοῖς κρίμασί σου ἡ δικαιοσύνη σου, ὁ θεός·
¹⁷ ὅτι ἀπέδωκας τοῖς ἁμαρτωλοῖς κατὰ τὰ ἔργα αὐτῶν,
κατὰ τὰς ἁμαρτίας αὐτῶν τὰς πονηρὰς σφόδρα.
¹⁸ ἀνεκάλυψας τὰς ἁμαρτίας αὐτῶν, ἵνα φανῇ τὸ κρίμα σου·
¹⁹ ἐξήλειψας τὸ μνημόσυνον αὐτῶν ἀπὸ τῆς γῆς.
ὁ θεὸς κριτὴς δίκαιος καὶ οὐ θαυμάσει πρόσωπον.

15 αὗται V, K, P (αὗθαι A), Fabr. Geig., αὐταί M, Hilg. Fritzsch. Pick.
17 κατὰ ἔργα Fabr. errore.
19 θεὸς (om. ὁ) M.

---

14 καθὰ ἐποίουν αὐτοί...παρεδειγμάτισαν...αὐτῶν. It is important to distinguish the subject of the two verbs. According as the Jews (αὐτοί) were wont to do, even so by way of retribution the Gentiles exposed to the world the iniquities of the Jews.

ἀπέναντι. The same word is used by the LXX. in 2 Sam. xii. 12.

παρεδειγμάτισαν. We were at first tempted to suggest the reading παρεδειγμάτισεν, which Lagarde had already conjectured; the subject then being ὁ θεὸς understood, and the verb corresponding to ἔστησεν...εἰς ἐμπαιγμόν. But as κρίμα σου follows in the next line, there would be an obvious objection to the use of the 3rd Pers. Sing. The meaning too is really the same. The Gentiles are carrying out the Divine judgement in 'making an open show' of Jewish iniquities.

For παραδειγματίζω cf. Matt. i. 19. The language and context again recall Ezek. xxii., which in ver. 2 has the words καὶ παράδειξον αὐτῇ πάσας τὰς ἀνομίας αὐτῆς.

θυγατέρες Ἰερουσαλήμ, corresponding to τοὺς υἱοὺς Ἰερουσαλὴμ in ver. 13. The expression 'daughter of Jerusalem' as impersonating the Holy City is not uncommon, e.g. Is. xxxvii. 22; Lam. ii. 13, 15; Mic. iv. 8; Zeph. iii. 14; Zech. ix. 9. But 'daughters of Jerusalem' are very rarely spoken of. The term is a characteristic feature in Canticles (e.g. i. 5, ii. 7, iii. 5, 10, v. 8, 16, vi. 4, viii. 4). But it does not seem to occur in the prophets nor elsewhere in Hebrew poetry; 'the daughters of Judah' (Ps. xcvii. 8), 'the daughters of thy people' (Ezek. xiii. 17), 'the virgins of Jerusalem' (Lam. ii. 10), are the nearest approach to it. 'The daughters of Samaria and Sodom' in Ezek. xvi. are metaphorically spoken of. The humiliation of 'the daughters of Jerusalem,' and the rarity of the phrase, give a special interest to the obvious comparison with our Lord's words in Luke xxiii. 28, warning them of an impending calamity surpassing all previous ones.

βέβηλοι. Pick's rendering 'profane' gives a wrong idea. κατὰ τὸ κρίμα σου gives the hint as to the true significance of the retribution for licentiousness.

15 ἀνθ᾽ ὧν. Cf. vv. 3, 15.

ἐν φυρμῷ ἀναμίξεως. Literally 'in the confusion of mingling.' This might be understood to refer (1) either to idolatry, following the strong metaphor of the prophets Hosea and Ezekiel (xxiii.), (2) or to the sin of mixed marriages, (3) or to gross forms of impurity. (1) As the subject of idolatry does not occupy the attention of our Psalmist, our choice lies between the last two. In favour of (2) we may compare 2 Macc. xiv. 3 μεμολυμμένος ἐν τοῖς τῆς ἐπιμιξίας χρόνοις. This evil assumed critical proportions in the days of Nehemiah, and in

ΨΑΛΜΟΙ ΣΑΛΟΜΩΝΤΟΣ.

14 According as they were wont to do, even so did *the Gentiles*[5] make an open show of their iniquities before the sun; and the daughters of Jerusalem were polluted according to thy judgement, 15 because they had defiled themselves in unclean intercourse.
My belly and my bowels pain me because of these things.

[5] Another reading: *he* Gr. *they* i.e. *the Gentiles*

16 I will justify thee, O God, in uprightness of heart; for in thy judgements is thy righteousness, O God.
17 For thou didst recompense sinners according to their works, according to their sins that were wicked exceedingly.
18 Thou didst lay bare their sins, to the end that thy judgement might appear.
19 Thou didst blot out their memorial from off the earth. God is a righteous judge and respecteth[6] no man's person.

[6] Gr. *will wonder at*

---

the time of the Maccabean revolution excited the grave apprehensions of the stricter Jews. But in our book, with the exception of this single doubtful allusion, this source of evil does not seem to have been especially present to the mind of the Psalmist. (3) On the other hand the spread of foul and nameless impurities accompanying the influence of the outer world upon Palestine caused him great apprehension, and he refers to them repeatedly, e.g. i. 7, iv. 4, viii. 10, xvi. 7, 8. It is also noticeable that the passage in Leviticus (xviii. 23, 24), to which upon this supposition the writer refers, combines like the present clause the two ideas of 'pollution' and 'confusion.' This explanation may be very appositely illustrated by a passage in Apoc. Baruch ch. lx. 'flagitia mysteriorum eorum et *permistio contaminationis* eorum,' where we may conjecture φυρμὸς ἀναμίξεως was very probably used in the Greek. See later on, viii. 10 (συμφύρω).

τὴν κοιλίαν μου καὶ τὰ σπλάγχνα μου. For these expressions compare Isai. xvi. 11; Jer. iv. 19; Lam. i. 20. Aq. Jer. xxxi. (xxviii.) 20 ἔτι διὰ τοῦτο ἤχησεν ἡ κοιλία μου αὐτῷ. Sym. ἐταράχθη τὰ ἐντός μου.

16 Ἐγὼ δικαιώσω σε, ὁ θεός. This thought that the 'pious' should 'justify God' occurs frequently in these Psalms (cf. iii. 5, iv. 9, viii. 7, 27, 31, ix. 3). The nearest approach to it in the O. T. is Ps. li. 4 'that thou mayest be justified when thou speakest.' Lam. i. 18. We find it also in Luke vii. 29 'the publicans justified God' (οἱ τελῶναι ἐδικαίωσαν τὸν θεόν).

εὐθύτητι καρδίας. Compare for this phrase and the substance of the verse Ps. cxviii. (cxix.) 7 ἐξομολογήσομαί σοι ἐν εὐθύτητι καρδίας ἐν τῷ μεμαθηκέναι με τὰ κρίματα τῆς δικαιοσύνης σου.

17 ἀπέδωκας κ.τ.λ. For this emphatic description of retribution compare Ps. xxvii. (xxviii.) 4 δὸς αὐτοῖς κατὰ τὰ ἔργα αὐτῶν καὶ κατὰ τὴν πονηρίαν τῶν ἐπιτηδευμάτων αὐτῶν· κατὰ τὰ ἔργα τῶν χειρῶν δὸς αὐτοῖς, ἀπόδος τὸ ἀνταπόδομα αὐτῶν αὐτοῖς, lxi. (lxii.) 12 ἀποδώσεις ἑκάστῳ κατὰ τὰ ἔργα αὐτοῦ.

τοῖς ἁμαρτωλοῖς. The reference here is clearly not to the soldiers of Pompey (ver. 1), but to the sinful members of the Jewish community. See note on i. 1.

τὰς πονηρὰς σφόδρα. This use of σφόδρα is due to the literal reproduction of מְאֹד. Compare Ezek. ix. 9 καὶ εἶπε πρός με ἀδικία τοῦ οἴκου Ἰσραὴλ καὶ Ἰούδα μεμεγάλυνται σφόδρα σφόδρα.

18 ἀνεκάλυψας. The exposure of Jewish iniquity described vv. 13—15 had as its purpose the explanation of the Divine visitation. For the use of this thought and phrase cf. viii. 8 ἀνεκάλυψεν ὁ θεὸς τὰς ἁμαρτίας αὐτῶν ἐναντίον τοῦ ἡλίου; Job xx. 27 ἀνακαλύψαι δὲ αὐτοῦ ὁ οὐρανὸς τὰς ἀνομίας; Hos. vii. 1 ἐν τῷ ἰάσασθαί με τὸν Ἰσραὴλ καὶ ἀποκαλυφθήσεται ἡ ἀδικία Ἐφραίμ.

19 ἐξήλειψας τὸ μνημόσυνον αὐτῶν. Cf. iii. 10 οὐχ εὑρεθήσεται μνημόσυνον αὐτῶν ἔτι. The phrase is based upon Ex. xvii. 14 'I will utterly blot out (A.V. put out) the remembrance of Amalek' (ἀλοιφῇ ἐξαλείψω τὸ μνημόσυνον Ἀμαλήκ).

²⁰ κατέσπασε τὸ κάλλος αὐτῆς ἀπὸ θρόνου δόξης,
ὠνείδισαν γὰρ ἔθνη Ἱερουσαλὴμ ἐν καταπατήσει.
²¹ περιεζώσατο cάκκον ἀντὶ ἐνδύματος εὐπρεπείας,
cχοινίον περὶ τὴν κεφαλὴν αὐτῆς ἀντὶ στεφάνου,
²² περιείλετο μίτραν δόξης, ἣν περιέθηκεν αὐτῇ ὁ θεός·
²³ ἐν ἀτιμίᾳ τὸ κάλλος αὐτῆς ἀπερρίφη ἐπὶ τὴν γῆν.

²⁴ Καὶ ἐγὼ εἶδον καὶ ἐδεήθην τοῦ προςώπου κυρίου καὶ
εἶπον·
ἱκάνωσον, κύριε, τοῦ βαρύνεσθαι χεῖρά σου ἐπὶ Ἱερουσαλὴμ
ἐν ἐπαγωγῇ ἐθνῶν,

20 κατέσπασε......δόξης P, M ponunt post ἐν καταπατήσει.
23 ἀπερρίφη ἐπὶ τὴν γῆν, καὶ ἐγὼ εἶδον A: conjec. Lagarde ἀπερρίφη ἐπὶ τὴν γῆν καί.
24 ἀπαγωγῇ A, V, K (ἡ), ἐπαγωγῇ P (?), M, Hilg. (conj.).

And the same words are found in close proximity Ps. cviii. (cix.) 14, 15 ἡ ἁμαρτία τῆς μητρὸς αὐτοῦ μὴ ἐξαλειφθείη...καὶ ἐξολοθρευθείη ἐκ γῆς τὸ μνημόσυνον αὐτῶν. Cf. Deut. xxv. 6 οὐκ ἐξαλειφθήσεται τὸ ὄνομα αὐτοῦ ἐξ Ἰσραήλ.

ὁ θεός. An abrupt change from the second person.

ὁ θεὸς κριτὴς δίκαιος. Ps. vii. 11. Cf. Gen. xviii. 25.

οὐ θαυμάσει πρόσωπον, i.e. is no respecter of persons, as Acts x. 34 οὐκ ἔστι προσωπολήπτης ὁ θεός. The usual rendering of the Hebrew phrase by πρόσωπον λαμβάνειν is here varied as in Gen. xix. 21 ἰδοὺ ἐθαύμασά σου τὸ πρόσωπον; Lev. xix. 15 οὐ ποιήσετε ἄδικον ἐν κρίσει· οὐ λήψη πρόσωπον πτωχοῦ, οὐδὲ μὴ θαυμάσῃς πρόσωπον δυνάστου; Deut. x. 17 ὁ θεὸς—ὅστις οὐ θαυμάζει πρόσωπον; Prov. xviii. 5; 2 Chr. xix. 7; Jude 16. Cf. Wisd. vi. 8 οὐ γὰρ ὑποστελεῖται πρόσωπον ὁ πάντων δεσπότης. The impartiality of the Divine judgement is perhaps here emphasized with a side thrust at the High Priest's court of justice.

20 κατέσπασε τὸ κάλλος αὐτῆς ἀπὸ θρόνου δόξης. This clause stands in two MSS., P and M, after καταπατήσει. But the arrangement of the other MSS. appears to us the more correct one. For (1) such a clause with a γὰρ would not be natural after ὁ θεός...πρόσωπον. (2) The more prosaic clause ὠνείδισαν... καταπατήσει seems to follow as an explanation of the more poetical but less explicit sentence κατέσπασε...δόξης: such an arrangement agrees with the parallelism of the clauses often to be observed in these Psalms, cf. iv. 2, v. 6. (3) According to the Parisian MS. κατέσπασε and περιεζώσατο would stand in adjoining clauses, the one referring to ὁ θεός, the other to Ἱερουσαλήμ, but each separated by a clause from its true subject.

The clause, which is practically equivalent in meaning to ver. 23, reproduces the thought of Ps. lxxxviii. (lxxxix.) 45 τὸν θρόνον αὐτοῦ εἰς τὴν γῆν κατέρραξας. But the exact meaning of the line is not very obvious on account of the word αὐτῆς, which anticipates the mention of Jerusalem in the next line. The sentence 'he tore her beauty from the throne of glory' contains no very definite meaning beyond that of a queen's humiliation generally. It must not be understood as equivalent to 'he tore her beauteous form from the throne of glory,' for it is not implied that Zion is removed from her throne, but only that she is humiliated while occupying it. It is best to regard the clause as an anticipation of ver. 23 and to understand by τὸ κάλλος the outward splendour of the Zion Queen's magnificence.

Something is to be said in favour of Geiger's view that αὐτῆς is an error of the translator, who having before him הֲדָרָהּ read הֲדָרָהּ τὸ κάλλος αὐτῆς instead of הֲדָרָה κάλλος (Ps. xxix. 2; Prov. xiv. 28).

The best explanation of θρόνος δόξης is given by Jer. xvii. 12 θρόνος δόξης ὑψωμένος ἁγίασμα ἡμῶν. The phrase

ΨΑΛΜΟΙ ΣΑΛΟΜΩΝΤΟΣ.

20 He cast down her beauty from the throne of glory, for the Gentiles brought reproach upon Jerusalem by treading *her* under foot.

21 She girded herself with sackcloth instead of fair raiment; *she put* a rope about her head instead of a crown;

22 She put off the diadem of glory, which God had set upon her;

23 Her beauty was cast aside in dishonour upon the ground.

24 And I beheld and I intreated the face of the LORD and said; 'Enough, O LORD; let not thy hand be any more heavy[7] upon Jerusalem, in bringing the Gentiles upon *her*.

[7] Lit. *Make sufficient... that thy hand should be heavy*

occurs also in Jer. xiv. 21 'do not disgrace the throne of thy glory.' Cf. 1 Sam. ii. 8; Is. xxii. 23. The beauty of the queen's throne is gone. She herself puts off her glorious attire (ver. 21).

ὠνείδισαν with ἔθνη. Cf. Ps. lxxxv. (lxxxvi.) 9 πάντα τὰ ἔθνη...ἥξουσιν καὶ προσκυνήσουσιν ἐνώπιόν σου, κύριε, καὶ δοξάσουσιν τὸ ὄνομά σου.

ἐν καταπατήσει. Cf. 2 Kings xiii. 7 ἔθεντο αὐτοὺς ὡς χοῦν εἰς καταπάτησιν (R.V. in threshing *or* to trample upon). For καταπατεῖν see Ps. lvi. (lvii.) 3 ἔδωκεν εἰς ὄνειδος τοὺς καταπατοῦντάς με; Ezek. xxxvi. 4 ἐγένοντο εἰς προνομὴν καὶ εἰς καταπάτημα τοῖς καταλειφθεῖσιν ἔθνεσι περικύκλῳ. Cf. Jer. xii. 10.

21 περιεζώσατο. The subject is here changed. Jerusalem in her humiliation lays aside her queenly attire, and puts on the symbols of mourning. See Isai. iii. 24 &c. ἀντὶ ζώνης σχοινίῳ ζώσῃ καὶ ἀντὶ τοῦ κόσμου τῆς κεφαλῆς τοῦ χρυσίου φαλάκρωμα ἕξεις διὰ τὰ ἔργα σου· καὶ ἀντὶ τοῦ χιτῶνος τοῦ μεσοπορφύρου περιζώσῃ σάκκον. The words περιζώννυμι, σάκκος, σχοινίον are similarly found together in 1 Kings xxi. 31 καὶ περιεζώσαντο σάκκους ἐπὶ τὰς ὀσφύας αὐτῶν καὶ ἔθεσαν σχοινία ἐπὶ τὰς κεφαλὰς αὐτῶν.

σάκκον. Cf. Is. iii. 24, xv. 3; Lam. ii. 10. Aseneth x. ἔλαβε σάκκον καὶ περιεζώσατο τὴν ὀσφὺν αὐτῆς, ἐξέλυσε δὲ καὶ τὸ ἐμπλόκιον τοῦ τριχώματος αὐτῆς.

ἀντὶ ἐνδύματος εὐπρεπείας. Perhaps the allusion here is to Isai. lii. 1 'put on thy beautiful garments O Jerusalem, the holy city.'

εὐπρέπεια. Cf. xi. 8, xvii. 47.

The phraseology of our passage closely resembles Baruch v. 1; 2 ἔκδυσαι Ἰερουσαλὴμ τὴν στολὴν τοῦ πένθους...καὶ ἔνδυσαι τὴν εὐπρέπειαν τῆς παρὰ τοῦ θεοῦ δόξης εἰς τὸν αἰῶνα. περιβαλοῦ τὴν διπλοΐδα τῆς παρὰ τοῦ θεοῦ δικαιοσύνης, ἐπίθου τὴν μίτραν ἐπὶ τὴν κεφαλήν σου τῆς δόξης τοῦ αἰωνίου.

σχοινίον...ἀντὶ στεφάνου. See 1 Kings xxi. 32; Is. iii. 24. For στέφανος cf. Lam. v. 16 ἔπεσεν ὁ στέφανος ἡμῶν τῆς κεφαλῆς.

22 περιείλετο. Ex. xxxiii. 6 καὶ περιείλαντο (הִתְנַצְּלוּ) οἱ υἱοὶ Ἰσραὴλ τὸν κόσμον αὐτῶν; Jon. iii. 6 καὶ περιείλατο (הֶעֱבִיר) τὴν στολὴν αὐτοῦ ἀφ' ἑαυτοῦ καὶ περιεβάλετο σάκκον; Bar. iv. 34 καὶ περιελῶ αὐτῆς τὸ ἀγαλλίαμα τῆς πολυοχλίας.

μίτραν...περιέθηκεν, cf. Isai. lxi. 10 ὡς νυμφίῳ περιέθηκέ μου μίτραν.

The same imagery appears in Ezek. xxvi. 16 καὶ ἀφελοῦνται τὰς μίτρας ἀπὸ τῶν κεφαλῶν αὐτῶν, where the Hebrew gives a different sense.

Aseneth (x.) wears a διάδημα and κίδαρις.

23 ἐν ἀτιμίᾳ. A frequent expression in these Psalms, see ver. 29, 32, 35.

ἀπερρίφη ἐπὶ τὴν γῆν. For this picture combining rejection and dishonour compare Ps. lxxxviii. (lxxxix.) 39 'Thou hast profaned his crown *even* to the ground (ἐβεβήλωσας εἰς τὴν γῆν τὸ ἁγίασμα αὐτοῦ), Lam. ii. 1 'He hath cast down from heaven unto earth the beauty of Israel' (κατέρριψεν ἐξ οὐρανοῦ εἰς γῆν δόξασμα Ἰσραήλ).

24 Καὶ ἐγὼ εἶδον καὶ. The Psalmist is referring to the vision of Zion humiliated and disgraced, which had risen before his eyes. Cf. viii. 1, 3, 4.

ἐδεήθην τοῦ προσώπου κυρίου. Cf. vi. 7.

For this rendering of the Hebrew idiom (חִלָּה פָנִים) compare 1 Sam. xiii. 12 καὶ τοῦ προσώπου τοῦ κυρίου οὐκ ἐδε-

20 ΨΑΛΜΟΙ ΣΑΛΟΜΩΝΤΟΣ. [II. 25

²⁵ ὅτι ἐνέπαιξαν καὶ οὐκ ἐφείσαντο ἐν ὀργῇ καὶ θυμῷ μετὰ μηνίσεως,
²⁶ καὶ συντελεσθήσονται, ἐὰν μὴ σύ, κύριε, ἐπιτιμήσῃς αὐτοῖς ἐν ὀργῇ σου·
²⁷ ὅτι οὐκ ἐν ζήλῳ ἐποίησαν, ἀλλὰ ἐν ἐπιθυμίᾳ ψυχῆς,
²⁸ ἐκχέαι τὴν ὀργὴν αὐτῶν εἰς ἡμᾶς ἐν ἁρπάγματι.
μὴ χρονίσῃς, ὁ θεός, τοῦ ἀποδοῦναι αὐτοῖς εἰς κεφαλάς,

25 ἔπαιξαν A, K, ἐνέπαιξαν V, P, M. μηνίσεως A, V, μηνήσεως K, P, M.
26 Conj. Hilg. καὶ οὐ συντ., Fr. συντελεσθησόμεθα.

ἤθην; Dan. ix. 13 καὶ οὐκ ἐδεήθημεν τοῦ προσώπου κυρίου τοῦ θεοῦ ἡμῶν; 1 Kings xiii. 6; Jer. xxvi. 19 (=xxxiii. 19 LXX.).

ἱκάνωσον...τοῦ κ.τ.λ. For this form of the idiom there is no very obvious parallel. But the words represent the Hebrew rendered in the LXX. by ἱκανούσθω σοι (Deut. iii. 26; 1 Chron. xxi. 15), cf. Num. xvi. 3, ἐχέτω ὑμῖν (רַב־לָכֶם), Sym. ἀρκείτω; Deut. i. 6 ἱκανούσθω ὑμῖν.

The passage in 2 Sam. xxiv. 16, 1 Chron. xxi. 15 presents the root idea of the sentence. There is however this characteristic difference, that whereas in the O.T. narrative the mercy of God stays the hand of the destroying Angel, here the 'pious' Jew, interceding directly with the Almighty, pleads that sufficient punishment has been meted out.

τοῦ βαρύνεσθαι χεῖρά σου. Cf. v. 8. For this phrase, which literally renders the Hebrew idiom, compare Judg. i. 35 ἐβαρύνθη ἡ χεὶρ οἴκου Ἰωσὴφ ἐπὶ τὸν Ἀμορραῖον; 1 Sam. v. 6 ἐβαρύνθη ἡ χεὶρ κυρίου ἐπὶ Ἄζωτον; Ps. xxxi. (xxxii.) 4 ὅτι ἡμέρας καὶ νυκτὸς ἐβαρύνθη ἐπ᾽ ἐμὲ ἡ χείρ σου. From these passages it is evident that βαρύνεσθαι is here used in the Passive and not in the Middle Voice, and that Ἰερουσαλήμ is in the accusative.

ἐν ἐπαγωγῇ ἐθνῶν. ἐπαγωγῇ is the reading of the Paris and Moscow MSS.; ἀπαγωγῇ that of the other MSS. ἀπαγωγῇ however fails to give any appropriate sense. The only meaning which ἐν ἀπαγωγῇ ἐθνῶν could bear here would be 'by the Gentiles carrying off (her inhabitants) into captivity.' But from the following sentence ὅτι...μηνίσεως which serves to explain the words, it appears that actual outrages perpetrated in Jerusalem must be intended; moreover βαρύνεσθαι χεῖρά σου ἐπὶ Ἰερουσαλήμ would not be sufficiently explained by limiting its application to the removal of a portion of the inhabitants by the Romans.

The internal evidence is therefore strongly in favour of ἐν ἐπαγωγῇ ἐθνῶν, which gives a good and natural sense. The word ἐπαγωγή acquired a special meaning of 'visitation,' in the sense of that which is 'brought upon a people or individuals by God on account of their sin.' Cf. Deut. xxxii. 36 εἶδε γὰρ παραλελυμένους αὐτοὺς καὶ ἐκλελοιπότας ἐν ἐπαγωγῇ. Prov. xxvii. 10 (Theodot.) ἐν ἡμέρᾳ ἐπαγωγῆς (σου) = אֵידְךָ. Ecclus. ii. 2 καὶ μὴ σπεύσῃς ἐν καιρῷ ἐπαγωγῆς, iii. 28, v. 8, x. 13, xxiii. 11, xxv. 14, xl. 9; and probably also Isai. xiv. 17 τοὺς ἐν ἐπαγωγῇ (אֲסִירָיו, captivos ejus) οὐκ ἔλυσεν. We might therefore translate the present words 'by the visitation (consisting) of the Gentiles.' But probably the simplest rendering is here the best. Cf. Lev. xxvi. 25 καὶ ἐπάξω ἐφ᾽ ὑμᾶς μάχαιραν ἐκδικοῦσαν δίκην διαθήκης; Baruch iv. 15 ἐπήγαγε γὰρ ἐπ᾽ αὐτοὺς ἔθνος μακρόθεν.

25 ἐνέπαιξαν, and not ἔπαιξαν, is required by the context. The meaning is evidently mockery with ill usage, as in 1 Sam. vi. 6 οὐχὶ ὅτε ἐνέπαιξεν αὐτοῖς, xxxi. 4; 1 Chron. x. 4 where the Hebrew is הִתְעַלֵּל. Compare 1 Macc. ix. 26 καὶ ἦγον αὐτοὺς πρὸς Βακχίδην· καὶ ἐξεδίκει ἐν αὐτοῖς καὶ ἐνέπαιξεν αὐτοῖς; 2 Macc. viii. 17 τὸν τῆς ἐμπεπαιγμένης πόλεως αἰκισμόν.

μετὰ μηνίσεως. The reading μηνήσεως is a mere itacism. The word μῆνις does not seem to occur in the O.T., the passages quoted by Tromm in Isai. xiii. 9, xvi. 6 not giving it in the best text. The verb μηνίω in Lev. xix. 18; Ps. cii. (ciii.) 9; Jer. iii. 12 translates the Hebrew expression 'to keep anger.'

II. 28]   ΨΑΛΜΟΙ ΣΑΛΟΜΩΝΤΟΣ.   21

25 For they mocked, and spared *her* not in their wrath and anger and vengeance.
26 And they[8] will be utterly consumed, unless thou, O LORD, rebuke them in thy wrath,   [8] i.e. Israel
27 For they[9] have done *it* not in zeal, but in the lust of their soul,   [9] i.e. the Gentiles
28 That they might pour out their anger against us in rapine. Delay not, O God, to recompense *it* upon their heads,

---

In Ecclesiasticus we find in xxvii. 30 μῆνις καὶ ὀργὴ καὶ ταῦτά ἐστι βδελύγματα, xxviii. 5 αὐτὸς σὰρξ ὢν διατηρεῖ μῆνιν, xl. 5 θυμὸς καὶ ζῆλος καὶ ταραχὴ καὶ σάλος καὶ φόβος θανάτου καὶ μήνιμα (vulgo μηνίαμα) καὶ ἔρις. The verb μηνίω also occurs in x. 6, xxviii. 7.

26 καὶ συντελεσθήσονται. Observe the change of subject. So merciless are the Gentiles, that the Jews will be utterly consumed, unless the LORD rebuke them (the Gentiles). Hilgenfeld by introducing οὐ before συντελεσθήσονται imports into the passage a wholly uncalled for change in a simple sentence. Fritzsche says 'videtur scribendum συντελεσθησόμεθα, cf. vs. 28.' But the 3rd Pers. Plur. can without any violence to grammar be referred to the inhabitants of Jerusalem, implied in the mention of the city in ver. 25. We believe that the translation given above fully expresses the meaning of the Greek words. It is not however improbable that συντελεσθήσονται is a translator's blunder. The Hebrew letters ויכלו are capable of being rendered in different ways according to the punctuation, either passively (וְיִכָלוּ = συντελεσθήσονται) as in Isai. i. 28; Ezek. v. 12, and very frequently; or transitively (וְיִכַלוּ) or וְיִכַלּוּ καὶ συντελέσουσιν) as in Ps. cxviii. (cxix.) 87. We may conjecture that the translator here rendered the letters on the supposition that they represented the more frequent intransitive form, which would naturally be reproduced by συντελεσθήσονται. If, as we are disposed to think, the meaning of the original was 'And they will consume *or* make a full end,' the more correct translation would have been καὶ συντελέσουσι.

ἐπιτιμήσῃς. Cf. Ps. ix. 5 ἐπετίμησας ἔθνεσι καὶ ἀπώλετο ὁ ἀσεβής, cxviii. (cxix.) 21 ἐπετίμησας ὑπερηφάνοις, where the Divine rebuke (גָּעַר) conveys the notion of complete overthrow.

27 ὅτι οὐκ ἐν ζήλῳ κ.τ.λ. The Pharisee interceding for Zion pleads that the Gentile oppressors exceeded the bounds of judicial visitation. The work of punishment had been carried out not 'in zeal' for the Lord of righteousness, but in the 'lust of their soul,' with savagery and wanton rapine. The words ἐν ζήλῳ require explanation (cf. iv. 2). The 'jealousy' or 'zeal' (קִנְאָה, ζῆλος) of the LORD is frequently spoken of in the O.T. as excited or directed in wrath against faithlessness and wrong-doing (cf. Ezek. v. 13, xvi. 38, 42, xxxviii. 19 &c.). In our verse it is implied that the Gentiles were used as the unconscious instruments of Divine 'zeal' against Zion, but had gone beyond the limits of their mission. The true type in the history of Israel of righteous zeal was Phinehas. Cf. Num. xxv. 10, 11 'And the LORD spake unto Moses saying, Phinehas, the son of Eleazar, the son of Aaron the priest, hath turned my wrath away from the children of Israel, in that he was jealous with my jealousy (LXX. ἐν τῷ ζηλῶσαί μου τὸν ζῆλον) among them so that I consumed not the children of Israel in my jealousy.' The Gentiles, however, though executing the Divine punishment, had not been 'jealous with Divine jealousy.'

ἐν ἐπιθυμίᾳ ψυχῆς. Cf. Ps. ix. 23 (x. 3) ἐπαινεῖται ὁ ἁμαρτωλὸς ἐν ταῖς ἐπιθυμίαις τῆς ψυχῆς αὐτοῦ; Jer. ii. 24 ἐν ἐπιθυμίαις ψυχῆς αὐτῆς ἐπνευματοφορεῖτο. For the thought here conveyed compare Zech. i. 15 'And I am very sore displeased with the nations that are at ease: for I was but a little displeased, and they helped forward the affliction.' Isaiah's denunciation of Sennacherib for forgetting that in his successes he was only God's instrument of punishment is very similar, 2 Kings xxi. 23—25.

28 ἐκχέαι τὴν ὀργὴν αὐτῶν. For this phrase compare Ps. lxviii. (lxix.)

ΨΑΛΜΟΙ ΣΑΛΟΜΩΝΤΟΣ. [II. 29

²⁹ τοῦ εἰπεῖν τὴν ὑπερηφανίαν τοῦ δράκοντος ἐν ἀτιμίᾳ.

³⁰ Καὶ οὐκ ἐχρόνισα ἕως ἔδειξέ μοι ὁ θεὸς
τὴν ὕβριν αὐτοῦ ἐκκεκεντημένον ἐπὶ τῶν ὀρέων Αἰγύπτου,
ὑπὲρ ἐλάχιστον† ἐξουδενωμένον ἐπὶ γῆς καὶ θαλάσσης,

29. τοῦ εἰπεῖν codd. Fabr. Geig.: conj. Fabr. ἰδεῖν, Hilg. εἴκειν, Hilg.² (Pick.) τρέπειν.
30 ἐχρόνισα codd. Hilg. (text.), Cerda interpr. *distulit* (Hilg. Geig. Fritzsch. Pick.). ἐκκεκεντημένον A, V, K, M, P, Fabr. Geig.: Hilg. conj. ἐκκεκεντημένην, ita Fritzsch. Pick. ὑπὲρ codd.: ὑπ' conj. Hilg. Fritzsch. Pick. ὀρέων codd. et edd., conj. Hilg.² ὁρίων (Pick.). ἐλαχίστου codd. et edd., nos ἐλάχιστον.

---

25 ἔκχεον ἐπ' αὐτοὺς τὴν ὀργήν σου; Jer. x. 25 ἔκχεον τὸν θυμόν σου ἐπὶ ἔθνη κ.τ.λ.; Ezek. vii. 8 ἐκχεῶ τὴν ὀργήν μου ἐπὶ σέ.

ἐν ἁρπάγματι. Cf. Ps. lxi. (lxii.) 11 καὶ ἐπὶ ἁρπάγματα (גזל) μὴ ἐπιποθεῖτε.
In this respect Pompey stood out as an honourable exception to the general conduct of Roman conquerors in the East. He is said to have left the treasures of the Temple untouched. His lieutenants were not accustomed to imitate his forbearance. Gabinius, who was one of Pompey's strongest adherents, earned an evil notoriety for his excessive extortions during his two years' Proconsulship in Syria 57—55, cf. Cicero Pro Sest. 43, Gabinium haurire quotidie ex paratissimis atque opulentissimis Syriae gazis innumerabile pondus auri, bellum inferre quiescentibus, ut eorum veteres illibatasque divitias in profundissimum libidinum suarum gurgitem profundat. De Prov. Cons. 4; Dio Cass. XXXIX. 55, 56.
Gabinius was afterwards put upon his trial for his conduct in Syria, and though defended by Cicero was found guilty and banished (Dio Cass. XXXIX. 59—63).

μὴ χρονίσῃς. The verse is wrongly divided. These words addressed in prayer to God are found in Ps. xxxix. (xl.) 18, lxix. (lxx.) 7, Dan. ix. 19.

χρονίζω is found with τοῦ and the Inf. Gen. xxxiv. 19 and Eccles. v. 3 μὴ χρονίσῃς τοῦ ἀποδοῦναι αὐτήν: with the Inf. Deut. xxiii. 22 οὐ χρονιεῖς ἀποδοῦναι αὐτήν, Ex. xxxii. 1 κεχρόνικε Μωϋσῆς καταβῆναι.

ἀποδοῦναι...εἰς κεφαλὰς. This rendering of a common Hebrew phrase may best be illustrated by a passage in which there is a considerable resemblance in the language with the present context. Ezek. xxii. 31 καὶ ἐξέχεα ἐπ' αὐτὴν θυμόν μου ἐν πυρὶ ὀργῆς μου τοῦ συντελέσαι· τὰς ὁδοὺς αὐτῶν εἰς κεφαλὰς αὐτῶν δέδωκα. Cf. 2 Chr. vi. 23.

29 τοῦ εἰπεῖν. This, the reading of all the MSS., apparently gives no intelligible meaning; compare Cerda's rendering 'ut dicant superbiam draconis in ignominia.'
The ingenuity of successive editors has been taxed to supply a suitable conjecture. Fabricius proposed ἰδεῖν 'ut videant,' which would give a very tame conclusion to τοῦ ἀποδοῦναι εἰς κεφαλάς. The same may be said of Hilgenfeld's more ingenious εἴκειν, which appears to us a very unlikely word to occur here, and is only found, according to Tromm, in the LXX., Wisd. xviii. 25.
τρέπειν, suggested by Hilgenfeld² and adopted by Pick and Wellhausen, which in the LXX. is nearly always (except Ex. xvii. 13) found in the Middle or Passive (cf. Judith xv. 2 τραπῆναι εἰς φυγήν; 2 Macc. iii. 24 εἰς ἔκλυσιν καὶ δειλίαν τραπῆναι), would hardly have been used in the Greek of this period in the sense of στρέφω or ἀλλάσσω (cf. Wellh. p. 133).
The difficulty however receives a simple and satisfactory explanation on the supposition of a translator's error. (i) The Hebrew לדבר would very naturally be rendered by τοῦ εἰπεῖν: but according to a late usage of the language, the verb דָּבַר was used for 'to destroy,' 'to overthrow' (cf. the substantive דֶּבֶר 'destruction,' 'plague'). Thus we find in 2 Chron. xxii. 10 'she arose and destroyed (Heb. וַתְּדַבֵּר, LXX. καὶ ἀπώλεσε) all the seed royal,' where the parallel passage in 2 Kings xi. 1 has וַתְּאַבֵּד. Upon the strength of this analogy we might assume that לְדַבֵּר should have been rendered τοῦ ἀπολέσαι in the sense of לְאַבֵּד instead of by τοῦ εἰπεῖν.

29 To turn[10] the pride of the dragon to dishonour.'

30 And I delayed not until[11] God showed to me that insolent one[12], lying pierced upon the high-places[13] of Egypt, made of less account than him that is least on earth and sea;

[10] Or, To destroy... in dishonour Gr. To say
[11] Perh. had not yet ceased when
[12] Gr. his insolence
[13] Gr. mountains Another reading: borders

This explanation, suggested first by Geiger, seems to us very probable. The chief objection to this theory is the rarity of the verb in this sense. And it is of course a possible explanation that, while τοῦ εἰπεῖν literally rendered the לדבר of the translator's text,. the לדבר itself might have been an early corruption for לאבד. But of the two we prefer the explanation which ascribes the difficulty to the translator's error to that which has to presuppose an earlier corruption of the Hebrew text.

(ii) But a still more ingenious conjecture on the same lines is put forward by Wellhausen. He assumes that τοῦ εἰπεῖν represents לאמר in the Hebrew, and in לאמר he discerns a late Hebrew form for לְהָמִיר = לָמִיר 'to change.' This very word occurs in Hos. iv. 7 כְּבוֹדָם בְּקָלוֹן אָמִיר 'I will change their glory into shame,' where the similarity of thought to the present clause is very striking; indeed, if the conjecture is correct, it is hard to resist the impression that the prophet's words are here reproduced by our Psalmist.

Between the conjectures of Geiger and Wellhausen it is not easy to decide. The rarity of דבר in the sense of 'destroy' militates against Geiger's view; the late form of a common word weakens Wellhausen's case. We incline to favour the latter critic, partly on the ground that τοῦ εἰπεῖν probably represents לֶאֱמֹר more naturally than לְדַבֵּר, partly on the ground of the appropriate illustration of our passage by Hos. iv. 7. But we think that the 'genesis' of the error was different from that which Wellhausen proposes: לָמִיר might have been read for לְהָמִיר, and by the common change of י to ו a reading לָמוּר arose, which gave rise to the rendering τοῦ εἰπεῖν.

In either case the theory of a Hebrew original successfully explains the otherwise unintelligible words of the Greek text.

ὑπερηφανίαν. Cf. vv. 1, 2.

δράκοντος. It is evident that ἡ ὑπερηφανία τοῦ δράκοντος of this line is further described in the next verse as ἡ ὕβρις αὐτοῦ; and the details of the subsequent passage combine to make the identification of the δράκων with Pompey almost certain. The imagery of the 'dragon' or 'leviathan' in the O.T. is applied especially to Egypt. Cf. Ps. lxxiii. (lxxiv.) 14 σὺ συνέτριψας τὰς κεφαλὰς τοῦ δράκοντος (לִוְיָתָן); Ezek. xxix. 3 ἰδοὺ ἐγὼ ἐπὶ σὲ Φαραώ, βασιλεῦ Αἰγύπτου, τὸν δράκοντα (הַתַּנִּים) τὸν μέγαν τὸν ἐγκαθήμενον ἐν μέσῳ ποταμῶν αὐτοῦ, xxxii. 2 λέοντι ἐθνῶν ὡμοιώθης σὺ καὶ ὡς δράκων (כַּתַּנִּים) ὁ ἐν τῇ θαλάσσῃ. But this is no sufficient reason for making the present allusion apply to Antiochus Epiphanes, as Ewald does.

The metaphor is also used of Nebuchadnezzar in Jer. li. 34 Heb. (=xxviii. 34 in LXX.) Ναβουχοδονόσορ βασιλεὺς Βαβυλῶνος κατέπιέ με, ὡς δράκων (כַּתַּנִּין) ἔπλησε τὴν κοιλίαν αὐτοῦ.

According to the Apocalyptic method of transferring to Rome the imagery of Babylon, the application of 'the dragon' to Pompey, who was the impersonation of Roman power, as Nebuchadnezzar had been of Babylonian, is perfectly natural in the present passage.

30 Καὶ οὐκ ἐχρόνισα ἕως ἔδειξέ μοι ὁ θεός. The sense is obvious. 'And I had not to wait long; very soon God showed me, etc.'

ἐχρόνισα, read by all the MSS., has occasioned editors much difficulty. Cerda following the Aug. MS. read ἐχρόνισα but translated 'distulit.' Hilgenfeld introduced ἐχρόνισεν into his text, and has been followed by Fritzsche, Geiger, and Pick. The difficulty of translation however is not to be removed by this expedient, as may be shown by the renderings. Geiger 'Und alsbald zeigte mir Gott seine Schmach,' Pick 'And very soon God showed me &c.,' Wellhausen 'Nicht lange, da zeigte mir Gott,' in none of which is there any attempt to render ἐχρόνισεν literally.

³¹ τὸ σῶμα αὐτοῦ διεφθαρμένον ἐπὶ κυμάτων ἐν ὕβρει πολλῇ,
καὶ ογκ ἦν ὁ θάπτων·

Against ἐχρόνισεν, besides the absence of MS. support, we find the following objections: (1) the position of ὁ θεός next to ἔδειξε shows that, whatever the original may have contained, the translator considered ὁ θεός to be the subject of ἔδειξε especially; had ἐχρόνισεν been the reading, we should certainly have expected οὐκ ἐχρόνισεν ὁ θεός. (2) The construction οὐκ ἐχρόνισεν ἕως ἔδειξε, when literally rendered 'he tarried not until he had shown,' makes nonsense; and so far as χρονίζω is concerned there is nothing in LXX. or N.T. to show that οὐκ ἐχρόνισεν ἕως ἔδειξε could be used for οὐκ ἐχρόνισε δεῖξαι or τοῦ δεῖξαι. (3) The apparent correspondence of ἐχρόνισεν with μὴ χρονίσῃς of ver. 28 has influenced the editors. But surely it cannot be relied on; for (a) the construction is altered from τοῦ with Inf. to ἕως with Indic. and (b) the solemn prayer 'Delay not to revenge us, O God' would obtain a strangely prosaic anticlimax in the statement that 'God delayed not to show the Psalmist a vision of revenge.'

If we accept the text ἐχρόνισα, the sense of the passage is that of Dan. ix. 21 'Yea whiles I was speaking in prayer, the man Gabriel...touched me.' The reply came at once or after a very short interval.

We conjecture that the true explanation is to be derived from the abrupt ending of the prayer in ver. 29, and that οὐκ ἐχρόνισα ἕως is a mistranslation of a Hebrew idiomatic expression for 'before I had ceased,' 'I had not yet ceased when' (עַד לֹא אָדֹם ו״), or 'I had added no more when' (וְלֹא אַאֲרִיךְ ו״).

τὴν ὕβριν αὐτοῦ. This word, here applied to Pompey, is found often in the LXX. as the rendering of גָּאוֹן both in a good and a bad sense, cf. Nah. ii. 2 'the *excellency* of Jacob, as the *excellency* of Israel,' Ezek. xxxii. 12 'the *pride* of Egypt,' Zech. x. 11 'the *pride* of Assyria.' The feature of its use in this passage is its application to the man who had profaned by his presence the Holy of Holies and afterwards contested with Cæsar the supreme authority of the Roman world.

ἐκκεκεντημένον. Hilgenfeld's emendation ἐκκεκεντημένην intended to improve the grammar of the passage is quite unnecessary. The Accus. Masc. is an instance of the common irregular construction κατὰ σύνεσιν, as if τὴν ὕβριν αὐτοῦ had been τὸν ὑβριστήν.

The use of the word ἐκκεκεντημένος recalls the LXX. version of the passage upon which the present description is probably based. Isai. xiv. 19 σὺ δὲ ῥιφήσῃ ἐν τοῖς ὄρεσιν, ὡς νεκρὸς ἐβδελυγμένος, μετὰ πολλῶν τεθνηκότων ἐκκεκεντημένων μαχαίραις κ.τ.λ. It is the word used twice by St John in quoting Zechariah; Joh. xix. 37; Apoc. i. 7.

ἐπὶ τῶν ὀρέων Αἰγύπτου. For this expression a very obvious emendation ἐπὶ τῶν ὁρίων Αἰγύπτου 'upon the borders of Egypt' (cf. τὰ ὅρια Αἰγύπτου, Ex. x. 14; 1 Kings iv. 21 A) is suggested by Hilgenfeld[2] and adopted by Wellhausen 'an der Grenze Aegyptens.' Pick, who translates 'on the mountains of Egypt,' adds the mysterious note, "'τῶν ὀρέων' in the codd., perhaps that the reading was ὁρίων 'shores,'" where we are unable to understand the meaning of 'perhaps that,' and Pick himself fails to distinguish between 'shores' and 'coasts.'

The strongest argument for this emendation is supplied by Ezek. xi. 10 ἐν ῥομφαίᾳ πεσεῖσθε, ἐπὶ τῶν ὀρέων τοῦ Ἰσραὴλ (עַל גְּבוּל יִשְׂרָאֵל) κρινῶ ὑμᾶς, in which verse some copies of the LXX. read ὁρίων. Our translator has possibly followed this passage in the LXX. But does not this emendation substitute the language of prose for that of poetry? 'The borders of Egypt' seems to us so prosaic as only to be justifiable here as a quotation from Ezek. xi. 10.

We prefer to think that the reading of the MSS. represents the true Greek text with a special reference to Isai. xiv. 19 (see above). We do not expect accuracy from the poetical flight of a Jew writing probably in Jerusalem. The Psalmist may well have based his language upon the old Hebrew elegy beginning with the words 'Thy glory, O Israel, is slain upon thy high places' (2 Sam. i. 19), and it is quite possible that the words of the original may have been עַל בָּמוֹתַי מָצוֹר

31 *Even* his dead body *lying* corrupted upon the waves in great contempt: and there was none to bury *him*;

Although we accept the Greek text ὀρέων, we do not exclude the probability that the Greek translator may here have blundered or have had to do with a defective Hebrew text. The most natural conjecture would be to read עַל יְאֹרֵי מִצְרָיִם (cf. Isai. vii. 18; 2 Kings xix. 24) 'by or upon the rivers of Egypt' instead of עַל הָרֵי מִצְרָיִם.

The desire to find a perfectly literal application of ἐπὶ τῶν ὀρέων Αἰγύπτου may be satisfied by the statement of Dion Cassius that Pompey fell by the 'Cassian mountain.' XLII. 5 Πομπήιος μὲν δὴ κράτιστος πρότερον Ῥωμαίων νομισθείς, ὥστε καὶ Ἀγαμέμνονα αὐτὸν ἐπικαλεῖσθαι, τότε, καθάπερ τις καὶ αὐτῶν τῶν Αἰγυπτίων ἔσχατος, πρός τε τῷ Κασσίῳ ὄρει καὶ ἐν τῇ ἡμέρᾳ ἐν ᾗ ποτε τά τε τοῦ Μιθριδάτου καὶ τὰ τῶν καταποντιστῶν ἐπινίκια ἤγαγεν, ἐσφάγη.

ὑπὲρ ἐλαχίστου ἐξουδενωμένον. Hilgenfeld's ὑπ' ἐλαχίστου, adopted by Pick, gives the sense 'despised by him that is least.' A better emendation would be ἐλάχιστον for ἐλαχίστου (= נִבְזֶה מִצָּעִיר) in the sense of 'more contemned than one that is least among the people.' The use of ὑπέρ with the acc. as a comparative is very common, and instances in this book are frequent, e.g. i. 8, iv. 2, viii. 14.

The ὑπέρ (מִן) appears to us to represent the accidental repetition of the final 'm' of 'Mizraim' (Egypt), and ἐλαχίστου ἐξουδενωμένον may repeat the words of Ps. cxviii. (cxix.) 141 צָעִיר...וְנִבְזֶה 'I am small and despised' (LXX. νεώτερος...καὶ ἐξουδενωμένος), cf. Sym. Isai. liii. 3 ἐξουδενωμένος καὶ ἐλάχιστος ἀνδρῶν.

Wellhausen's 'verschmäht, verachtet,' seems to suggest two participles.

31 τὸ σῶμα αὐτοῦ διεφθαρμένον ἐπὶ κυμάτων κ.τ.λ. Cerda, who thought Nebuchadnezzar is spoken of, understood ἐπὶ κυμάτων metaphorically.

Ewald, who thought Antiochus Epiphanes was referred to, was obliged to explain the passage as a Jew's prayer for the doom of Antiochus.

But the language is neither that of metaphor nor of denunciation; and it describes circumstances which seem to suit the end of Pompey better than that of any other of the oppressors of the Jewish race. We know that Pompey after the defeat at Pharsalia sought refuge in Egypt. The king of Egypt went down to the shore to receive him. Pompey left his ship in a boat, and was rowed to land. He was just rising from his seat in order to step on land, when 'he was stabbed in the back by Septimius, who had formerly been one of his centurions and was now in the service of the Egyptian monarch.... His head was cut off and his body, which was thrown out naked on the shore, was left exposed to all who were desirous of such a sight. His freedman Philip, having waited till public curiosity was satisfied, washed the body with seawater, and wrapped it in one of his own garments, because he had nothing else at hand. The next thing was to look out for wood for the funeral-pile; and casting his eyes over the shore, he spied the old remains of a fishing-boat; which, though not large, would make a sufficient pile for a poor naked mutilated body.' (Plutarch.) One old Roman soldier was the only other mourner at this funeral ceremony.

Pompey's head was displayed before Cæsar upon the conqueror's arrival in Egypt shortly afterwards.

Wellhausen's rendering 'zerschmettert von den Wogen' indicates the view that the Greek translator had given a wrong turn to the Hebrew preposition בְּ, and that the original would be more correctly translated 'by' than 'upon.'

οὐκ ἦν ὁ θάπτων. In Pompey's case these words can almost be understood literally. The contrast between the funeral pile of a few spars from an old boat hastily erected by a solitary servant and the magnificent ceremonial attending the obsequies of a great and wealthy Roman naturally seized upon the imagination of the Jewish poet.

That a body should be denied the decencies of burial, was always regarded as the height of ignominy. Cf. Ps. lxxviii. (lxxix.) 3 καὶ οὐκ ἦν ὁ θάπτων; 2 Kings ix. 10 καὶ τὴν Ἰεζεβὲλ καταφάγονται οἱ κύνες...καὶ οὐκ ἔστιν ὁ θάπτων; Jer. xxii. 19 of king Jehoiakim.

ΨΑΛΜΟΙ ΣΑΛΟΜΩΝΤΟΣ. [II. 32

³² ὅτι ἐξουδένωσεν αὐτὸν ἐν ἀτιμίᾳ.
οὐκ ἐλογίσατο ὅτι ἄνθρωπός ἐστι,
καὶ τὸ ὕστερον οὐκ ἐλογίσατο.
³³ εἶπεν· ἐγὼ κύριος γῆς καὶ θαλάσσης ἔσομαι,
καὶ οὐκ ἐπέγνω ὅτι ὁ θεὸς μέγας,
κραταιὸς ἐν ἰσχύϊ αὐτοῦ τῇ μεγάλῃ.
³⁴ αὐτὸς βασιλεὺς ἐπὶ τῶν οὐρανῶν
καὶ κρίνων βασιλεῖς καὶ ἀρχὰς,
³⁵ ἀνιστῶν ἐμὲ εἰς δόξαν
καὶ κοιμίζων ὑπερηφάνους εἰς ἀπώλειαν αἰώνιον ἐν ἀτιμίᾳ,
ὅτι οὐκ ἔγνωσαν αὐτόν.

³⁶ Καὶ νῦν ἴδετε, οἱ μεγιστᾶνες τῆς γῆς, τὸ κρίμα κυρίου,
ὅτι μέγας βασιλεὺς καὶ δίκαιος κρίνων τὴν ὑπ' οὐρανόν.

32 οὐκ ἐλογίσατο· ὅτι ἄνθρ. ἐστι etc. Cerda, txt. non interpr.
33 εἶκεν (Α?), sed *dixit* Cerda. τῇ μεγάλῃ A, V, P, M, μεγάλη K (?), Fabr.
35 κοιμίζων codd.: conj. Hilg. κομίζων, ita Fritzsch. Pick.

32 ἐξουδένωσεν αὐτόν. We take ὁ θεὸς (ver. 30) to be the subject of the verb, and αὐτὸν to be Pompey. Pick on the other hand renders 'Because he had dishonoured Him.' This, though of course possible, does not seem to us probable: (1) αὐτὸν should refer to the same person as αὐτοῦ in ver. 30, 31; (2) the expression ἐξουδένωσεν...ἀτιμίᾳ points back to ver. 29; it describes God's infliction of the dishonour for which the Psalmist prayed: (3) the words are more applicable to the humiliation of man by Divine visitation than to the contemptuous defiance of God by a man.

οὐκ ἐλογίσατο ὅτι ἄνθρωπός ἐστι. Cf. Ezek. xxviii. 1, 2 'The word of the LORD came again unto me, saying, Son of man, say unto the prince of Tyre, Thus saith the LORD GOD: Because thine heart is lifted up, and thou hast said, I am a god, I sit in the seat of God, in the midst of the seas; yet thou art man, and not God, though thou didst set thine heart as the heart of God, etc.' Cf. 2 Thess. ii. 4.

καὶ τὸ ὕστερον οὐκ ἐλογίσατο. These words expand the previous clause: 'he considered not that he was a man, he considered not that he had to die.' Cf. Isai. xlvii. 7 'And thou saidst, I shall be a lady for ever; so that thou didst not lay these things to thy heart, neither didst remember the latter end thereof' (LXX. οὐδὲ ἐμνήσθης τὰ ἔσχατα). Lam. i. 9 'She remembered not her latter end' (LXX. οὐκ ἐμνήσθη ἔσχατα αὐτῆς).

33 ἐγὼ κύριος...ἔσομαι. Geiger points out that it is not stated that he was 'lord of heaven and earth,' but that this was his ambition. Pompey's aims were never realized. But, considering the uncertainty of the tenses representing the Hebrew imperfect, this point must not be pressed. For the spirit of arrogance described in this verse cf. Ezek. xxix. 3 'Thus saith the LORD GOD, Behold, I am against thee, Pharaoh, king of Egypt,...which hath said, My river is mine own, and I have made it for myself.'

καὶ οὐκ ἐπέγνω. ἐπιγινώσκω is a word that occurs with especial frequency in the LXX. version of Ezekiel, and the reader will have observed how often the Psalmist uses the language of that Prophet.

ὅτι ὁ θεὸς μέγας. It is a suggestion worthy to be considered that in these words there is an allusion to Pompey's 'soubriquet' of 'Magnus.' It is God alone, says the Jewish Psalmist, who is 'Great.' Cf. Deut. x. 17 'For the LORD your God, he is God of gods, and Lord of lords, the great God, the mighty,' Psalm xciv. (xcv.) 3 'For the LORD is a great God.'

κραταιὸς ἐν ἰσχύϊ αὐτοῦ τῇ μεγάλῃ. These words echo a familiar formula, e.g. Deut. ix. 29 οὓς ἐξήγαγες ἐκ γῆς Αἰγύπτου

II. 36] ΨΑΛΜΟΙ ΣΑΛΟΜΩΝΤΟΣ. 27

32 for he[14] set him at nought in dishonour.   [14] i.e. *God*
He considered not that he was a man, and his latter end he did not consider.

33 He said: I will be lord of earth and sea; and perceived not that it is God who is great, powerful in the greatness of his strength.

34 He is king over the heavens and judgeth kings and rulers.

35 It is he that lifteth me up unto glory, and layeth low the proud in eternal destruction in dishonour, because they knew him not.

36 And now behold, ye princes of the earth[15], the judgement of the LORD, that[16] he is a great and righteous king, judging the whole earth.

[15] Or, *the land*
[16] Or, *for*

ἐν τῇ ἰσχύϊ σου τῇ μεγάλῃ καὶ ἐν τῇ χειρί σου τῇ κραταιᾷ καὶ ἐν τῷ βραχίονί σου τῷ ὑψηλῷ, Jer. xxvii. (=LXX. xxxiv.) 5 ὅτι ἐγὼ ἐποίησα τὴν γῆν ἐν τῇ ἰσχύϊ μου τῇ μεγάλῃ. Cf. xxxii. (=LXX. xxxix.) 17.

34 αὐτὸς βασιλεὺς ἐπὶ τῶν οὐρανῶν. Cf. Ps. xi. 4 'The LORD'S throne is in heaven'; ciii. 19 'The LORD hath established his throne in the heavens.'

35 ἀνιστῶν ἐμὲ εἰς δόξαν. The resumption of the 1st person is here noticeable. It would be natural to see in the words an allusion to the temporal triumph of the Pharisaic party as the result of recent political events. But inasmuch as εἰς δόξαν corresponds to εἰς ἀπώλειαν αἰώνιον, the whole verse is best understood as standing in immediate connection with the reference to Divine judgement mentioned in ver. 34. From this judgement of God, the 'pious' Pharisee looks for 'resurrection unto glory'; but he predicts for the 'proud,' i.e. the Sadducees and their foreign allies, destruction with 'shame and everlasting contempt' (Dan. xii. 2).

On the subject of the resurrection see note on iii. 16. The use of ἐμὲ, the impersonation of the true Israel, is to be noted in favour of the view that ἀνιστῶν ...εἰς δόξαν refers to something more than the restoration to secular glory.

ἀνιστῶν. The language of this verse reminds us of Hannah's song; see espec. 1 Sam. ii. 8, where occur the words ἀνιστᾷ ἀπὸ γῆς πένητα.

κομίζων. A striking word to use in the sense of 'bringing down,' 'laying low,' which is plainly the meaning required here. The strangeness of the expression has caused Hilgenfeld to substitute κομίζων. But for κομίζειν τινὰ εἰς ἀπώλειαν it would be hard to find any authority: the passage in Ezr. vi. 5 καὶ ἐκόμισεν (τὰ σκεύη) εἰς Βαβυλῶνα is scarcely sufficient to warrant its introduction in a metaphorical sense here: two other passages, 1 Esd. iv. 5, ix. 40, employ the word in its literal signification, but elsewhere it seems in the LXX. to be used in the Middle Voice.

There is no need to introduce in the face of the MSS. an insipid prose word as a substitute for a vigorous metaphor. κομίζειν occurs in a hostile sense in 2 Sam. viii. 2 'And he smote Moab, and measured them with the line, making them to lie down on the ground' (κοιμίσας αὐτοὺς ἐπὶ τὴν γῆν), where it renders השכיב. In its literal sense κομίζειν occurs 1 Kings iii. 20, 2 Kings iv. 21, 32 as a translation of השכיב: it is also found in Gen. xxiv. 11; Jud. xvi. 29; Nah. iii. 18.

ὑπερηφάνους. This does not refer to the Romans whose ὑπερηφανία is spoken of in vv. 1, 2, but to the Sadducaic princes and their party; cf. i. 6 ἐξύβρισαν ἐν τοῖς ἀγαθοῖς αὐτῶν, xvii. 26.

ἀπώλειαν αἰώνιον. Cf. on iii. 13, xiii. 10, xiv. 6.

ὅτι οὐκ ἔγνωσαν αὐτόν. Cf. 1 Cor. xv. 34 ἀγνωσίαν γὰρ θεοῦ τινες ἔχουσι.

36 Καὶ νῦν. Cf. ix. 16.

οἱ μεγιστᾶνες τῆς γῆς. Who are the persons thus addressed? They stand in distinction from the οἱ φοβούμενοι τὸν κύριον ἐν ἐπιστήμῃ. They may be the princes and leading men of Palestine. But we are inclined to think that the victorious party of Cæsar are meant.

τὴν ὑπ' οὐρανὸν, i.e. τὴν γῆν. A com-

28   ΨΑΛΜΟΙ ΣΑΛΟΜΩΝΤΟΣ.   [II. 37

³⁷ εὐλογεῖτε τὸν θεόν, οἱ φοβούμενοι τὸν κύριον ἐν ἐπιστήμῃ,
ὅτι τὸ ἔλεος κυρίου ἐπὶ τοὺς φοβουμένους αὐτὸν μετὰ κρίματος,
³⁸ τοῦ διαστεῖλαι ἀνὰ μέcον δικαίου καὶ ἁμαρτωλοῦ,
ἀποδοῦναι ἁμαρτωλοῖς εἰς τὸν αἰῶνα κατὰ τὰ ἔργα αὐτῶν,
³⁹ καὶ ἐλεῆσαι δίκαιον ἀπὸ ταπεινώσεως ἁμαρτωλοῦ,
καὶ ἀποδοῦναι ἁμαρτωλῷ ἀνθ' ὧν ἐποίησε δικαίῳ·
⁴⁰ ὅτι χρηστὸς ὁ κύριος τοῖς ἐπικαλουμένοις αὐτὸν ἐν ὑπομονῇ,
ποιῆσαι κατὰ τὸ ἔλεος αὐτοῦ τοῖς μετ' αὐτοῦ,
παρεστάναι διὰ παντὸς ἐνώπιον αὐτοῦ ἐν ἰσχύϊ.
⁴¹ εὐλογητὸς κύριος εἰς τὸν αἰῶνα ἐνώπιον τῶν δούλων αὐτοῦ.

γ. ψαλμὸς τῷ Cαλομὼν περὶ δικαίων.

III. Ἱνατί ὑπνοῖς, ψυχή, καὶ οὐκ εὐλογεῖς τὸν κύριον;

38 ἀνάμεσον A, K, P, ἀνὰ μέσον V, M.
40 ποιῆσαι A, V, M, Fabr. Geig., ποιήσαι K, P, Hilg. Fritzsch. Pick.
41 τῶν δούλων A, P, Fabr. Fritzsch. Pick. τῶν om. V, K, M, Hilg. Geig. Cerda om. ἐνώπιον, sed interpr. *coram*.
Inscriptio: Ψαλμὸς τῷ Σαλομὼν περὶ δικαίων γ' A, K et, ut videtur, P (K omittit γ'). V, M om. Inscript.

mon expression in the LXX. version of Job. Compare also Bar. v. 3 ὁ γὰρ θεὸς δείξει τῇ ὑπ' οὐρανὸν πάσῃ τὴν σὴν λαμπρότητα.
In Prov. viii. 28 τῆς ὑπ' οὐρανόν renders תְּהוֹם 'the abyss.'

37 οἱ φοβούμενοι τὸν κύριον ἐν ἐπιστήμῃ. By the expression οἱ φοβούμενοι τὸν κύριον the Psalmist seems to indicate the 'pious' Pharisees, whose object it was to maintain the purity of theocratic principles; cf. iii. 16, v. 21, xiii. 11.

For the addition of ἐν ἐπιστήμῃ compare the other qualifying phrases, e.g. ver. 40 ἐν ὑπομονῇ, iv. 26 ἐν ἀκακίᾳ, vi. 9, x. 4 ἐν ἀληθείᾳ, by which the Psalmist distinguishes the true fear and love of God that characterized the Pharisee from the mere religious pretence of the opposite faction.

Geiger suggests that ἐν ἐπιστήμῃ represents the musical word 'Maschil' (בְּמַשְׂכִּיל) and compares Ps. xlvii. 8 'sing ye praises with *understanding*' (marg. Or *in a skilful psalm* Heb. Maschil), where the LXX. has ψάλατε συνετῶς. But (*a*) the phrase 'with a skilful Psalm,' appropriate in connection with 'singing,' is less so in connection with 'blessing.' (*b*) Again,

the word in the Greek is certainly to be connected with οἱ φοβούμενοι, not with εὐλογεῖτε, and the qualification 'with understanding' added to 'the fear of the LORD' had, as we suggest, a special significance. (*c*) It should also be noticed that 'Maschil,' with the exception of the passage quoted above, only appears in the musical sense in the titles of Psalms (i.e. xxxii. xlii, xliv. xlv. lii.—lv. lxxiv. lxxviii. lxxxviii. lxxxix. cxlii.).

ὅτι τὸ ἔλεος...μετὰ κρίματος. A sentiment which reappears in a variety of forms throughout these Psalms. Cf. Ps. ciii. 17, 'But the mercy of the LORD is from everlasting to everlasting upon them that fear him, and his righteousness unto children's children.'

38 τοῦ διαστεῖλαι. Cf. Ezek. xxii. 26 ἀνάμεσον ἁγίου καὶ βεβήλου οὐ διέστελλον, καὶ ἀνάμεσον ἀκαθάρτου καὶ τοῦ καθαροῦ οὐ διέστελλον; and see on iv. 4.

The discrimination between the 'righteous' and the 'sinner' is impossible under present conditions. It is spoken of as that which shall take place in the day of the LORD, Mal. iii. 18 'Then shall ye return and discern between the righteous and the wicked, between him that serveth God and him that serveth him not.'

ΨΑΛΜΟΙ ΣΑΛΟΜΩΝΤΟΣ.

37 Bless ye God, ye that fear the LORD with understanding; for the mercy of the LORD is with judgement upon them that fear him,

38 To separate between the righteous and the sinner, to recompense unto the sinners for ever according to their works,

39 And to show mercy unto the righteous because of their oppression by[17] the sinner, and to recompense unto the sinner in return for that which he hath done unto the righteous.

40 For the LORD is gracious unto them that call upon him in patience, to deal according to his mercy with them that are his[18], that they may stand continually in his presence in strength.

41 Blessed be the LORD for ever in the presence of his servants.

[17] Gr. *from the oppression of*
[18] Gr. *that are with him*

PSALM III.

Concerning the Righteous.

1 Why sleepest thou, O my soul, and blessest not the LORD?

The judgement belongs to God, Ezek. xxxiv. 17 'Behold I judge between cattle and cattle, as well the rams as the he-goats' (ἰδοὺ ἐγὼ διακρινῶ ἀνάμεσον προβάτου καὶ προβάτου, κριῶν καὶ τράγων), cf. Matt. xiii. 49, xxv. 32.

ἀποδοῦναι. See on ver. 17.

39 ἀπὸ ταπεινώσεως ἁμαρτωλοῦ, i.e. because of (lit. from before) the humiliation which the sinner inflicts upon the righteous. ἁμαρτωλοῦ is the Gen. of the subject, not of the object.

For ταπείνωσις compare Lam. i. 3 μετῳκίσθη Ἰουδαία ἀπὸ ταπεινώσεως αὐτῆς, where however αὐτῆς is the Gen. of the object.

The Psalmist probably refers to the oppression which the 'pious' Jews underwent at the hands of the Sadducee princes.

ἀποδοῦναι. The LORD recompensed humiliation upon the 'sinner,' cf. Ps. cxlvi. (cxlvii.) 6 ἀναλαμβάνων πραεῖς ὁ κύριος ταπεινῶν δὲ ἁμαρτωλοὺς ἕως τῆς γῆς.

ἀνθ' ὧν, cf. ver. 3, 15.

40 τοῖς ἐπικαλουμένοις αὐτόν. Cf. ix. 11. The expression is practically synonymous with οἱ φοβούμενοι ἐν ὑπομονῇ. The whole phrase combines Ps. cxliv. (cxlv.) 9 χρηστὸς κύριος τοῖς ὑπομένουσιν and 18 ἐγγὺς κύριος πᾶσιν τοῖς ἐπικαλουμένοις αὐτόν, πᾶσι τοῖς ἐπικαλουμένοις ἐν ἀληθείᾳ. The 'patience' of the pious Jew is perhaps contrasted with the violence of the zealot.

ποιῆσαι. We prefer the Inf., carrying out the idea of χρηστός, to the Opt.

κατὰ τὸ ἔλεος αὐτοῦ τοῖς μετ' αὐτοῦ. The last words are very strange, and probably indicate some corruption in the text. We conjecture some confusion between 'immô' (with him) and 'ammô' (his people), עמו and עמו.

παρεστάναι ... ἐν ἰσχύϊ. The Inf. παρεστάναι we take to be dependent on ποιῆσαι. 'To stand before the LORD' (παρεστάναι ἔναντι κυρίου) is the privilege of the Levites (e.g. Deut. x. 8, xviii. 7) and, in the N.T., of the Israel of God, Rev. vii. 15.

41 The Doxology—εὐλογητὸς κύριος. Cf. Gen. ix. 26; Luke i. 68.

ἐνώπιον τῶν δούλων αὐτοῦ. i.e. Let His name and power be praised and held in honour wherever His servants are.

For the LORD's servants cf. Deut. xxxii. 36 ὅτι κρινεῖ κύριος τὸν λαὸν αὐτοῦ καὶ ἐπὶ τοῖς δούλοις αὐτοῦ παρακληθήσεται, Ps. cxxxiv. (cxxxv.) 1 αἰνεῖτε τὸ ὄνομα κυρίου, αἰνεῖτε δοῦλοι κυρίου. Here the servants of the LORD represent the 'pious' Jews with whose cause the Psalmist identifies himself. There is possibly a reference to the orthodox priests of the time.

Ps. III.—*Argument.*

1. The summons to cast away lethargy and to praise the LORD anew (1, 2).
2. The righteous ever praiseth the LORD: he acknowledgeth Divine justice,

ΨΑΛΜΟΙ ΣΑΛΟΜΩΝΤΟΣ. [III. 2

² ὕμνον καινὸν ψάλατε τῷ θεῷ τῷ αἰνετῷ.
ψάλλε καὶ γρηγόρησον ἐπὶ τὴν γρηγόρησιν αὐτοῦ·
ὅτι ἀγαθὸς ψαλμὸς τῷ θεῷ ἐξ ὅλης καρδίας.

³ Δίκαιοι μνημονεύουσι διὰ παντὸς τοῦ κυρίου
ἐν ἐξομολογήσει, καὶ †δικαιοῦσιν [ἐν αἰνέσει]† τὰ κρίματα
κυρίου.

2 ψάλατε V, K, P, Hilg. Fritzsch. Pick.: ψάλλατε A, M: ψάλλετε Fab.
3 κυρίου, ἐν ἐξομολογήσει καὶ δικαιώσει codd., Fab. Hilg. Fritzsch. Pick.: κυρίου ἐν ἐξομολογήσει, καὶ Geig. Wellh. (?). Txt. nos e conjectura.

when he is chastened : he is prepared for chastisement, when he falleth: his confidence is in God his Saviour. He endeavoureth to live void of offence; the sins of his household he seeketh to put away: for errors of ignorance he maketh trespass offering, he fasteth to make amends; and is cleansed, he and his house (3—10).

3. The sinner in trouble raileth and is profane: for him there is no hope or pity; his destruction is for ever.

The righteous shall rise again, unto eternal life (11—16).

This Psalm is of a more general character than the two preceding ones. The Psalmist does not introduce himself, nor is Zion personified. But the description of the 'righteous' and the 'sinner' gives in sharp contrast the Psalmist's view of the two opposing types of Judaism. Their true character is revealed under the discipline of Divine chastisement (vv. 4, 5, 11, 13, 14). Whether this chastisement is to be understood to mean the oppression of Judæa by the Romans, we have not sufficient evidence to determine.

In two respects the Psalm is of considerable interest and importance: (1) for its description of ideal Pharisaic righteousness 7—10, (2) for its allusions to the doctrine of the resurrection (13—16).

Inscription. It is to be observed that the Copenhagen MS. does not attach a number to the title of this Psalm, and the mistake in the numeration of the following Psalms is not corrected until Ps. ix. The title 'Concerning the Righteous' conveys no impression of originality.

1 Ἱνατί ὑπνοῖς. The words recall the very different supplication in Ps. xliii. (xliv.) 24 ἐξεγέρθητι· ἵνα τί ὑπνοῖς κύριε; Compare the opening verses of xvi.

For the address to the soul οὐκ εὐλογεῖς, cf. 'Bless the LORD, O my soul' (εὐλόγει ἡ ψυχή μου τὸν κύριον), Ps. cii. (ciii.) 1, 2, 22, ciii. (civ.) 1, 35.

2 ὕμνον καινὸν ψάλατε. It has been suggested (Geiger) that the Psalmist by these words is referring to some recent event that called for new and special thanksgiving; and that the subject-matter of the preceding Psalm, the death of Pompey, is the occasion for exultation on the part of those Jews, who welcomed in his fate the vindication of Zion's honour.

On the other hand the words are based on well-known O.T. phraseology, and the general tone of the Psalm is social and not political. Without excluding the possibility of the other view, it is more natural to regard the opening words as an instance of a common poetic artifice, an invitation to try a new theme for song,—the contrast between the 'righteous' and the 'sinner.' Again, the description of ἁμαρτωλὸς is a convincing proof to us that the thought of Pompey is not in the Psalmist's mind.

The Greek translator does not follow the words of the LXX., cf. Ps. xxxii. (xxxiii.) 3 ᾄσατε αὐτῷ ᾆσμα καινόν, καλῶς ψάλατε ἐν ἀλαλαγμῷ, xxxix. (xl.) 3 ᾆσμα καινόν, xcv. (xcvi.) 1, xcvi. (xcvii.) 1, cxlix. 1 ᾄσατε τῷ κυρίῳ ᾆσμα καινόν, cxliii. (cxliv.) 9 ᾠδὴν καινὴν ᾄσομαι; Isai. xlii. 10 ὑμνήσατε τῷ κυρίῳ ὕμνον καινόν.

The plural ψάλατε is strange, being preceded by the singular ὑπνοῖς and εὐλογεῖς, and followed by ψάλλε. (1) The transition to the Plural may be a poetical license, the Psalmist momentarily addressing himself to all οἱ φοβούμενοι (ver. 16) just as in vv. 3, 4, 7 he interchanges δίκαιος and δίκαιοι.

(2) Or, inasmuch as in six out of the seven passages where 'a new song' occurs in the O.T., the words are connected with an invitation in the 2nd Pers. Plur., the translator may very possibly have adopted the Plur. unconsciously from the familiar language of the Canonical Psalms.

III. 3] ΨΑΛΜΟΙ ΣΑΛΟΜΩΝΤΟΣ. 31

2 Sing[1] a new song unto God who is worthy to be praised.
Sing, yea shout unto him with a joyful noise[2],
for it is good to sing praises unto God with the whole heart.

3 The righteous ever make mention of the LORD with praise,
and justify the judgements of the LORD [with thanksgiving];

[1] Gr. *Sing ye*
[2] Gr. *keep watch for his watching*

(3) Or, as is very possible from the frequent interchange of ו and י, זַמְּרִי may have become זַמְרוּ, and the translator's ψάλατε have perpetuated the error.

τῷ αἰνετῷ...cf. viii. 29, αἰνετός = laudandus (מְהֻלָּל), as in 2 Sam. xxii. 4; Ps. xlvii. (xlviii.) 1.

γρηγόρησον ἐπὶ τὴν γρηγόρησιν αὐτοῦ. Compare xvi. 4 ἔνυξέ με ὡς κέντρον ἵππου ἐπὶ τὴν γρηγόρησιν αὐτοῦ.

These very obscure words almost defy translation. Cerda renders 'vigila ad vigiliam tuam (*Gr.* ejus)': Geiger, 'erwache zu seiner Wache': Pick, 'awake up to his watch.' But against these versions it is sufficient to observe that γρηγόρησις must be something quite distinct from φυλακή (cf. Hab. ii. 1 ἐπὶ τῆς φυλακῆς μου στήσομαι). Wellhausen gives more accurately 'erwache, da er erwacht ist,' i.e. 'be wakeful with respect to, towards or against His awaking,' a quite literal translation which gives the only intelligible meaning. The sense then is 'Arouse thyself from the slumber of apathy, O my soul: praise Him who never slumbers or sleeps; let the energy of thy praise respond to the unceasing operation of His blessings.' Cp. Ps. cviii. (cix.) 2 'Awake, psaltery and harp; I myself will awake right early.'

But we are unable to believe that the Greek can be a true rendering of the original. We surmise that the difficulty has sprung from a very probable error that arose either in the Hebrew text or in the translator's rendering of it, in consequence of a confusion between the two very similar Hebrew roots עוּר and רוּעַ, meaning respectively 'to arouse' and 'to shout.'

The translation which we give is based on the supposition that the original Hebrew text contained words formed from the root רוּעַ. It certainly furnishes a more vigorous as well as a more connected meaning to the verse. For according to the common text the verse runs 'Sing a new song; yea, sing and be wakeful; for it is good to sing lustily,' in which the last clause stands in no connection with the appeal for wakefulness. According to

our rendering the last clause is forcible and natural: 'Sing a new song; yea, sing and shout aloud; for it is good to sing lustily.' The 'shout' then corresponds to the words 'with the whole heart.'

The root רוּעַ 'to shout' occurs in the verse, the resemblance of which to the present passage has been already noticed, Ps. xxxiii. 3 'Sing unto him a new song; play skilfully with a loud noise' (בִּתְרוּעָה, LXX. ἐν ἀλαλαγμῷ). In Ps. lix. (lx.) 10 (cf. cviii. 10) 'Philistia, shout thou (הִתְרוֹעֲעִי) because of me,' the root was misunderstood by the LXX. ἐμοὶ ἀλλόφυλοι ὑπετάγησαν. In Ps. lxiv. (lxv.) 13 'they shout for joy (יִתְרוֹעֲעוּ), they also sing' (κεκράξονται, καὶ γὰρ ὑμνήσουσιν), we find the same thought as in the present verse.

The similarity of the two roots (עוּר and רוּעַ) will be best illustrated by comparing Ps. xxxiv. (xxxv.) 22 'Stir up thyself (הָעִירָה ἐξεγέρθητι) and awake to my judgement' with Ps. xlvi. (xlvii.) 2 'Shout (הָרִיעוּ) unto God with the voice of triumph' (ἀλαλάξατε τῷ θεῷ ἐν φωνῇ ἀγαλλιάσεως), lxv. (lxvi.) 1 'make a joyful noise' (הָרִיעוּ ἀλαλάξατε), lxxx. (lxxxi.) 1 'Sing aloud...make a joyful noise' (הָרִיעוּ ἀλαλάξατε); cf. xcv. 1, 2, xcviii. 4, c. 1.

On this supposition we conjecture that the original Hebrew had something like הָרִיעִי לוֹ תְּרוּעָה or הִתְרוֹעֲעִי לוֹ ἀλάλαξον αὐτῷ ἐν ἀλαλαγμῷ.

ὅτι ἀγαθὸς ψαλμὸς τῷ θεῷ ἐξ ὅλης καρδίας. The words are based on Ps. cxlvii. 1 'Praise ye the LORD; for it is good to sing praises unto our God'; but it is clear that the Greek rendering is not taken from the LXX. version αἰνεῖτε τὸν κύριον, ὅτι ἀγαθὸν ψαλμός· τῷ θεῷ ἡμῶν ἡδυνθείη αἴνεσις.

For ἐξ ὅλης καρδίας cf. Deut. vi. 5 ἀγαπήσεις κύριον τὸν θεόν σου ἐξ ὅλης τῆς διανοίας σου καὶ ἐξ ὅλης τῆς ψυχῆς σου καὶ ἐξ ὅλης τῆς δυνάμεώς σου. Ps. ix. 2 ἐξομολογήσομαί σοι, κύριε, ἐν ὅλῃ καρδίᾳ μου. Apoc. Bar. lxvi. 1 ex toto corde suo et ex tota anima sua.

3 Δίκαιοι. The 'righteous' alone know how to praise at all times, in chas-

⁴ οὐκ ὀλιγωρήϲει δίκαιοс παιδεγόμενοс ὑπὸ κγρίογ,
ἡ εὐδοκία αὐτοῦ διὰ παντὸς ἐναντίον κυρίου.
⁵ προσέκοψεν ὁ δίκαιος καὶ ἐδικαίωσε τὸν κύριον,
ἔπεσε καὶ ἀποβλέπει τί ποιήσει αὐτῷ ὁ θεός·
⁶ ἀποσκοπεύει, ὅθεν ἥξει σωτηρία αὐτοῦ.

---

tisement as well as joy. μνημονεύουσι 'remember,' as Ps. lxiii. 6 'when I remember thee upon my bed' (LXX. εἰ ἐμνημόνευόν σου, אִם־זְכַרְתִּיךָ), Tobit iv. 5 κυρίου τοῦ θεοῦ ἡμῶν μνημόνευε. The more common expression 'make mention of' (הִזְכִּיר), e.g. Ps. lxxi. 16; Isai. lxviii. 1, lxii. 6, is generally rendered in the LXX. by μιμνήσκομαι.

ἐν ἐξομολογήσει. Cf. Ps. xcv. 2 'Let us come before his presence with thanksgiving' (בְּתוֹדָה, LXX. ἐν ἐξομολογήσει): c. 3 'Enter into his gates with thanksgiving': cxlvii. 7 'Sing unto the LORD with thanksgiving.'

καὶ δικαιοῦσιν. The reading of the MSS. and of previous editions καὶ δικαιώσει seems to present insuperable objections.

Accepting the text of the MSS., editors have differed from one another on the question whether δικαιώσει should be rendered as a substantive or as a verb. (*a*) Those who believe it to be a substantive, punctuate at τοῦ κυρίου and begin a fresh clause with ἐν ἐξομολογήσει. Thus Cerda renders 'in confessione et justitia judicia illius'; and this punctuation is adopted by Fabricius, Hilgenfeld, Fritzsche and Pick. Pick's translation 'in giving thanks and justifying the judgments of the Lord' is literal, but cannot be pronounced free from ambiguity. Against this method of translating the words is to be set the difficulty respecting δικαιώσει. (1) The substantive δικαίωσις only occurs once, according to Tromm, in the LXX., Lev. xxiv. 22 δικαίωσις (מִשְׁפָּט) μία ἔσται τῷ προσηλύτῳ καὶ τῷ ἐγχωρίῳ, and once in Symmachus' Version of Ps. xxxiv. 26. It occurs twice in the N. T., in Rom. iv. 25, v. 18. (2) The only meaning which ἐν...δικαιώσει could here give would be 'in confession and in the declaration of their justice are the judgments of the LORD,' i.e. the righteous confess their guilt and acknowledge the justice of Divine punishment. But even if this explanation be accepted, it does not get over the awkwardness of such a clause, in its relation to the immediate context; while the rarity of the substantive δικαίωσις seems to us to make it necessary to resort to some other way of interpreting the passage.

(*b*) With δικαιώσει as a verb, a comma is placed at ἐξομολογήσει, and καὶ δικαιώσει begins a new clause. The objections are obvious: the Present tense and Plural number of μνημονεύουσι are followed in the immediately ensuing parallel clause by a Future and the Singular. But the change from the Plural to the Singular might be defended by e.g. ver. 2 or ver. 7, iv. 7—10; and the alteration from Present to Future offers no real obstacle, when we remember how irregularly the Tenses are treated in translation from the Hebrew. Geiger adopting this explanation renders 'und ihrer jeder preist des Herrn Entscheidungen gerecht,' and Wellhausen gives 'und erkennen seiner Gerichte Gerechtigkeit.'

We fully grant the possibility of this translation, 'The righteous ever remember the LORD with thanksgiving, yea each one justifies the judgements of the LORD.' But we prefer to conjecture that the similarity of the termination in ἐξομολογήσει—δικαιώσει has been the cause of confusion in the text. The change of δικαιώσει to δικαιοῦσι is a very possible restoration of the Greek text, the alteration involved being very slight, and recovering to the verb both the Present tense and the Plural number.

If further conjecture be not too venturesome, we would suggest that δικαιοῦσιν [ἐν αἰνέσει] may have been the original words, and that by an error of sight the scribe wrote δικαιουσει, which became corrected to δικαιώσει. In favour of this we would plead the parallelism of the clauses, which seem to require the mention of praise in both members of the verse. The words αἰνεῖν and αἴνεσις also

III. 6] ΨΑΛΜΟΙ ΣΑΛΟΜΩΝΤΟΣ. 33

4 The righteous man despiseth not the chastening[3] of the [3] Gr. *when he is chastened*
LORD; his good pleasure is continually before the LORD.
5 The righteous stumbleth and justifieth the LORD; he falleth
and looketh to see what God will do unto him;
6 He gazeth earnestly to see from whence cometh his help[4]. [4] Gr. *salvation*

---

are frequently found associated with ἐξομολογεῖσθαι and ἐξομολόγησις. Ps. xcix. (c.) 3 ἐξομολογεῖσθε αὐτῷ, αἰνεῖτε τὸ ὄνομα αὐτοῦ. 1 Chron. xvi. 4 καὶ ἐξομολογεῖσθαι καὶ αἰνεῖν τὸν κύριον. 2 Chron. xx. 22 ἐν τῷ ἄρξασθαι τῆς αἰνέσεως καὶ τῆς ἐξομολογήσεως. Ecclus. xxxix. 15 ἐξομολογήσασθε ἐν αἰνέσει αὐτοῦ. li. 1 ἐξομολογήσομαί σοι, κύριε, βασιλεῦ, καὶ αἰνέσω σε...ἐξομολογοῦμαι τῷ ὀνόματί σου. For δικαιοῦν τὰ κρίματα see note on ver. 5.

4 οὐκ ὀλιγωρήσει κ.τ.λ. The clause in the Greek is based on Prov. iii. 11 'My son, despise not the chastening of the LORD (υἱὲ μὴ ὀλιγώρει παιδείας κυρίου),' quoted also in Heb. xii. 5; but the resemblance of thought is even closer in Job v. 15 'Behold, happy is the man, whom God correcteth: therefore despise not thou the chastening of the Almighty.' ὀλιγωρεῖν in the LXX. seems only to occur in Prov. iii. 11 (נאץ). Wellhausen's rendering 'Der Gerechte verliert den Muth nicht,' seems to lose sight of this parallel, and would be better suited to ὀλιγοψυχεῖν in the sense of ἐγκακεῖν.

ἡ εὐδοκία αὐτοῦ διὰ παντὸς ἐναντίον Κυρίου. The general sense of these words is obvious, 'the righteous always finds favour with the LORD.' But their precise interpretation is not so easy; and the renderings of Cerda 'complacentia illius semper coram Deo,' of Geiger 'Stets ist seine Lust vor dem Ewigen,' and of Pick 'His pleasure is always before the Lord,' must be almost unintelligible. Wellhausen's translation 'denn er bleibt doch in Gnade bei dem Herrn' gives the true idea of the clause, without however reproducing the Greek.

There are two ways of explaining the clause. (1) ἡ εὐδοκία αὐτοῦ = 'the goodwill of God towards the righteous man,' i.e. 'the favour in which he stands.' This use of εὐδοκία can be illustrated by Luke ii. 14 ἐν ἀνθρώποις εὐδοκίας, i.e. among men to whom the Divine good pleasure and kindly favour was constantly shown.

So in this verse 'the Divine good-will and favour towards the righteous man' stands like his good angel ever beholding the presence of the Father which is in heaven.

(2) ἡ εὐδοκία αὐτοῦ = 'the righteous man's good will and pleasure'; which he places, as it were, at the service of God, ready to perform His command.

5 προσέκοψεν...ἔπεσε, 'stumbled and fell.' See Ps. xxvii. 2; Is. viii. 15; Dan. xi. 19.

It does not appear that the aor. refers to any actual incident; it merely emphasizes the suddenness of the transition from prosperity to trouble.

The words must not be understood of moral failure in the modern sense of the word 'fall.' They denote reverse of fortune or some great calamity, as in Prov. xxiv. 16, 17 'A righteous man falleth seven times, and riseth up again; but the wicked are overthrown by calamity. Rejoice not when thine enemy falleth, and let not thine heart be glad when he is overthrown.' Cf. Ps. xxxvii. 24 'Though he fall, he shall not be utterly cast down: for the LORD upholdeth him with his hand.' cxlv. 19 'The LORD upholdeth all that fall.'

ἐδικαίωσε. Cf. ii. 16, iv. 9, viii. 31. Cf. Apoc. Bar. 78 ut justificaretis judicium ejus.

ἀποβλέπει. For the thought cf. Ps. xxxiv. 5 'They looked unto him and were lightened: and their faces shall never be confounded.'

Observe ἀπό in a compound giving the sense of earnest concentration. Cf. Heb. xi. 26 ἀπέβλεπε, xii. 2 ἀφορῶντες.

6 ἀποσκοπεύει, 'watcheth or looketh forth to see.' Cf. Hab. ii. 1 ἀποσκοπεύει τοῦ ἰδεῖν τί λαλήσει: Lam. iv. 17 μάταια ἀποσκοπευόντων ἡμῶν. ἀπεσκοπεύσαμεν εἰς ἔθνος οὐ σῷζον: Judith x. 10 ἀπεσκόπευον δὲ αὐτὴν οἱ ἄνδρες τῆς πόλεως: Ps. v. 4 (Aquila).

ὅθεν ἥξει κ.τ.λ. Cf. Ps. cxxi. 1 'from whence cometh my help' (ὅθεν ἥξει ἡ βοήθειά μου).

J. P.

ΨΑΛΜΟΙ ΣΑΛΟΜΩΝΤΟΣ.   [III. 7

⁷ ⁷Ἀλήθεια τῶν δικαίων παρὰ θεοῦ ϲωτῆροϲ αὐτῶν,
οὐκ αὐλίζεται ἐν οἴκῳ τοῦ δικαίου ἁμαρτία ἐφ᾽ ἁμαρτίαν.
⁸ἐπισκέπτεται διὰ παντὸς τὸν οἶκον αὐτοῦ ὁ δίκαιος,
τοῦ ἐξᾶραι ἀδικίαν.
ἐν παραπτώματι αὐτοῦ ⁹ἐξιλάϲατο περὶ ἀγνοίαϲ
καὶ ἐν νηϲτείᾳ ταπεινώϲει τὴν ψυχὴν αὐτοῦ.

7 θεὸν (sic) M.
8 ἐξᾶραι P, M.   ἀδικίαν ἐν παραπτώματι, codd. et edd., nos ἀδικίαν.   ἐν π.
9 om. τὴν K, P, M.   ἐν νηστείᾳ καί codd. et edd., nos καὶ ἐν νηστ.

---

7 ἀλήθεια τῶν δικαίων παρὰ θεοῦ σωτῆρος αὐτῶν. Geiger renders 'Sicher sind die Gerechten in Gott,' which is adopted by Pick 'The righteous are safe in God.' But there is no reason for this interference with the Greek. 'The safety or security of the righteous is or springs from God' is the obvious meaning of the words; 'are safe in God' gives a collateral but perfectly distinct idea. ἀλήθεια is here used in the unusual sense, 'confidence' or 'security.' The clause, that is, sums up the preceding sentences. ἀλήθεια probably translates one aspect of *e'munah* (אמונה), a word generally occurring with the sense of 'faithfulness,' but also used for the 'strength,' 'confidence,' and 'firmness' arising from trust. Compare Ex. xvi. 21 'And his hands were steady' (literally 'for faithfulness' LXX. ἐστηριγμέναι). 2 Sam. xx. 19 'I am of them that are peaceable and faithful in Israel' (ἐγώ εἰμι εἰρηνικὰ τῶν στηριγμάτων Ἰσραήλ).

παρὰ θεοῦ σωτῆρος αὐτῶν. Cf. Ps. xxiii. 5 (xxiv.) οὗτος λήψεται...ἐλεημοσύνην παρὰ θεοῦ σωτῆρος αὐτοῦ: Ps. cvi. 21; Luke i. 47; 1 Tim. i. 1, ii. 3; Tit. i. 3, ii. 10, 13, iii. 4; 2 Pet. i. 1; Jud. 25. The title of 'Saviour,' here applied to 'God' in His dealings with 'the righteous,' is generally found in connexion with the mercies shown to the nation (e.g. xvii. 3). The true 'Israel' and the 'righteous' are one.

αὐλίζεται. This word is used sometimes of habitual habitation, as in Job xi. 14 ἀδικία δὲ ἐν διαίτῃ σου μὴ αὐλισθήτω, but more generally of 'lodging for the night' = 'pernoctare,' as a rendering of לין, e.g. Ps. xxv. 13 'His soul shall dwell (תָּלִין) at ease' (ἐν ἀγαθοῖς αὐλισθήσεται). Cf. Matt. xxi. 17; Luke xxi. 37.

ἁμαρτία ἐφ᾽ ἁμαρτίαν. These words seem to be based on Isai. xxx. 1 'that they may add sin to sin' (LXX. προσθεῖναι ἁμαρτίας ἐφ᾽ ἁμαρτίας), though less obviously than in ver. 12. Cf. Ecclus. v. 5 προσθεῖναι ἁμαρτίαν ἐφ᾽ ἁμαρτίαις. The idea is that of abundant sin, one following upon another in succession. The use of the accusative after ἐπί may be illustrated by Phil. ii. 27 ἵνα μὴ λύπην ἐπὶ λύπην σχῶ.

The Rabbins had a saying that 'one sin caused another' (עבירה גוררת עבירה. Tanchum. fol. 83. 2) quoted by Schöttgen (*Hor. Heb.* i. 518) in illustration of Rom. vi. 19 τῇ ἀνομίᾳ εἰς ἀνομίαν.

8 ἐπισκέπτεται. ἐπισκέπτομαι, generally used in this book with reference to Divine visitation either for purposes of punishment or deliverance, has here its primary sense of inquisitorial search.

The righteous man is here represented as carrying into practice the language of Ps. ci. 7 'He that worketh deceit shall not dwell within my house: He that speaketh falsehood shall not be established before mine eyes. Morning by morning will I destroy all the wicked of the land, etc.'

τοῦ ἐξᾶραι ἀδικίαν. The purpose of the ἐπίσκεψις. ἐξαίρω is used in the LXX. for the frequent phrase found in Deut. 'thou shalt put the evil away from among you' (xvii. 7, 12, xix. 9, xxi. 9, etc.).

ἐν παραπτώματι αὐτοῦ. These words are generally taken in immediate connexion with ἀδικίαν. But whether in that case αὐτοῦ refers to τὸν οἶκον or to ὁ δίκαιος does not appear certain. Geiger 'bei dessen Falle,' explains it 'of the transgression of the household'; Cerda 'in lapsu illius (suo),' Wellhausen 'bei seiner Uebertretung' and Pick 'in his fall,' explain it of the transgression of the righteous man.

The awkwardness and obscurity of the

III. 8]   ΨΑΛΜΟΙ ΣΑΛΟΜΩΝΤΟΣ.   35

7 The confidence[5] of the righteous *cometh* from God their Saviour.   [5] Gr. *truth*

There lodgeth not in the dwelling of the righteous sin upon sin.

8 The righteous man maketh inquisition continually in his own house to the end that he may put away iniquity;

With his trespass offering 9 he maketh atonement for that wherein he erreth unwittingly,

and with fasting he afflicteth his soul.

---

phrase here used at the end of the verse is due in our opinion to the translator having probably misapprehended the passage. By punctuating at ἀδικίαν instead of at αὐτοῦ, we suggest that the full meaning of the passage can be restored without alteration of the text beyond shifting the position of καί. (1) We believe that ἐν νηστείᾳ should be in close conjunction with ταπεινώσει (see Ps. xxxv. 13), and that ἐν νηστείᾳ ταπεινώσει corresponds to ἐν παραπτώματι ἐξιλάσατο. (2) The Hebrew words hattâth and ashâm are both employed to denote either *sin* and *guilt* or the *sin-offering* and *guilt-offering*, according to the context. (3) The translator, tripping over this ambiguity, has connected the word (?ashâm) in a meaningless manner with the previous clause τοῦ ἐξᾶραι ἀδικίαν: (4) instead of which he should have begun a fresh clause by ἐν πλημμελείᾳ 'by means of a guilt-offering he maketh atonement for, etc.'

The probability of this view is increased by the fact that ἐξιλάσκεσθαι περὶ ἀγνοίας is the technical term for 'to make atonement' for sins of ignorance in Lev. iv. v.; and the means of making such atonement was the sin-offering or guilt-offering, the names of which were subject to misunderstanding.

The technical term πλημμέλεια is not found in this book. On the other hand in Ezek. xxii. 4 ἐν τοῖς αἵμασιν αὐτῶν οἷς ἐξέχεας παραπέπτωκας, we find παραπίπτειν renders the root 'ashâm,' which possibly occurred here.

According to our rendering 'The righteous man' of the Psalmist is the strict Pharisee; who not merely purges sin from his household, but is careful (1) to obey the *written* law by making offerings for the sins of which he has been guilty through ignorance, and (2) to follow the *oral* tradition by observing the days of fasting.

9 ἐξιλάσατο. ἐξιλάσκομαι, a very common word rendering the Hebrew 'kippêr,' is almost exclusively used in Lev. and Num. of the atonement made by the priest. If we might conjecture from its use here that 'the righteous man' in this passage is 'the righteous priest' in distinction from the ungodly Sadducee priesthood, we should obtain a further detail in the picture presented by our Psalm.

περὶ ἀγνοίας. Cf. Lev. v. 18 'the priest shall make atonement for him concerning the thing wherein he erred unwittingly and knew it not, and he shall be forgiven. It is a guilt-offering.' (See also Lev. iv. 1, 13, 22; v. 15.) The LXX. version runs καὶ ἐξιλάσεται περὶ αὐτοῦ ὁ ἱερεὺς περὶ τῆς ἀγνοίας αὐτοῦ, ἧς ἠγνόησε, καὶ αὐτὸς οὐκ ᾔδει, καὶ ἀφεθήσεται αὐτῷ. ἐπλημμέλησε γὰρ πλημμελείᾳ.

The same expression is used by Aquila in Num. xv. 27; xxxv. 11, &c., where the LXX. uses ἀκουσίως to denote the offences committed unconsciously. In Ezek. xlii. 13; xliv. 29 τὰ περὶ ἀγνοίας is the LXX. rendering of 'ashâm' the guilt-offering.

The importance of this offering for sins committed in ignorance can only be appreciated, when we remember how difficult it was for a Jew to avoid contracting pollution in the discharge of his daily duties as a citizen. It was this irksomeness of the Jewish Law which dictated the fundamental maxim of the Scribes 'make a fence about the Law,' and caused St Peter to speak of it as a yoke 'which neither our fathers nor we were able to bear' (Acts xv. 10).

καὶ ἐν νηστείᾳ. The MSS. and Edd. ἐν νηστείᾳ, καί. For our reading and punctuation see preceding note. When ἐν παραπτώματι αὐτοῦ was given by the translator to the preceding verse, the parallelism of the present verse was destroyed.

¹⁰ καὶ ὁ κύριος καθαρίζει πάντα ἄνδρα ὅσιον καὶ τὸν οἶκον αὐτοῦ.

¹¹ Προσέκοψεν ἁμαρτωλός, καὶ καταρᾶται ζωὴν αὐτοῦ,
τὴν ἡμέραν γενέσεως αὐτοῦ καὶ ὠδῖνας μητρός.
¹² προσέθηκεν ἁμαρτίας ἐφ' ἁμαρτίας τῇ ζωῇ αὐτοῦ.
¹³ ἔπεσεν, ὅτι πονηρὸν τὸ πτῶμα αὐτοῦ, καὶ οὐκ ἀναστήσεται·
ἡ ἀπώλεια τοῦ ἁμαρτωλοῦ εἰς τὸν αἰῶνα.
¹⁴ καὶ οὐ μνησθήσεται, ὅταν ἐπισκέπτηται δικαίους.
¹⁵ αὕτη μερὶς τῶν ἁμαρτωλῶν εἰς τὸν αἰῶνα.
¹⁶ οἱ δὲ φοβούμενοι κύριον ἀναστήσονται εἰς ζωὴν αἰώνιον,
καὶ ἡ ζωὴ αὐτῶν ἐν φωτὶ κυρίου καὶ οὐκ ἐκλείψει ἔτι.

11 αὐτοῦ post ζωὴν codd.: om. Fab. μητρὸς K, P, M. om. A, V.
12 προσέθηκαν K, P.
13 οὐκ ἀναστήσεται ἡ ἀπώλ. M.
14 δίκαιος Cerda, sed interpr. 'iustos.'

ταπεινώσει τὴν ψυχὴν αὐτοῦ. For this phrase see Lev. xvi. 29, 31; xxiii. 29, 32; Isai. lviii. 5; Ecclus. ii. 17; Judith iv. 9, in all of which it is found in connexion with fasting. To connect ἐν νηστείᾳ with ταπεινοῦν τὴν ψυχὴν appears to us the most natural arrangement of the words: and it is difficult to resist the impression that our clause is based on Ps. xxxv. 13 'I afflicted my soul with fasting' (LXX. καὶ ἐταπείνουν ἐν νηστείᾳ τὴν ψυχήν μου): lxviii. 10 'When I wept and chastened my soul with fasting' (καὶ συνέκαμψα ἐν νηστείᾳ τὴν ψυχήν μου).

The tense of ταπεινώσει coming immediately after ἐξιλάσατο affords a good instance of the confusion arising from the translation of the Hebrew Impf., which denotes continuous action, as if it were a Future.

The affliction of the soul by fasting, standing as it does in parallelism with atonement for sins of ignorance, occupies here a prominent position in the description of the religious life of the righteous man; and corresponds with the prominence of fasting in the picture of Pharisaic externalism, which appears in the Gospel narrative, cf. Matt. vi. 6; Luke xviii. 12.

10 ὁ κύριος καθαρίζει. For the cleansing which follows upon the act of atonement, see the use of ἐξιλάσκομαι and καθαρίζω in Lev. xii. 8; xiv. 19, 53; Ezek. xliii. 26.

ὅσιον. This adjective is used in almost a technical sense, cf. viii. 28, 40; xii. 8; xiv. 2, 7 as a translation of 'chāsîd' 'pious.' The strictest and most theocratic Jews were intended by the 'pious' (chasidim). Hence arose the title of 'Asideans,' which was given at the time of the Maccabean revolt to the section of the people most fanatically devoted to the observances of the law (cf. 1 Macc. ii. 34—38).

"The *chasid* is of greater excellence than the *çaddiq* (δίκαιος). Cf. the gradation: 'Three things are said of nailparings. He who burns them is *chasid*; He who buries them is *çaddiq*; He who throws them away is *rāshā*'" (Niddah 17, a), Taylor's *Sayings of the Jewish Fathers*, p. 48, n. 24. It is interesting to observe that the epithet 'pious,' in the passage thus commented on by Taylor, is applied to one 'Jose the Priest': ὅσιος in the LXX. is used to designate the Levites in Deut. xxxiii. 8 καὶ τῷ Λευὶ εἶπε Δότε Λευὶ δήλους αὐτοῦ καὶ ἀλήθειαν αὐτοῦ τῷ ἀνδρὶ τῷ ὁσίῳ.

For another rendering of חֲסִידִים in the LXX. cf. Prov. ii. 6 εὐλαβούμενοι, for which cf. εὐλαβὴς Mic. vii. 2, and Luke ii. 25; Acts ii. 5; viii. 2 (xxii. 12).

καὶ τὸν οἶκον αὐτοῦ. Compare the description of the High Priest in Lev. xvi. 17, 'until he come out and have made atonement for himself, and for his household and for all the assembly of Israel.'

ΨΑΛΜΟΙ ΣΑΛΟΜΩΝΤΟΣ.

10 And the LORD purifieth every man that is holy and his house.

11 The sinner stumbleth and curseth his own life, the day of his birth and his mother's pangs.

12 While he liveth, he addeth sin to sin.

13 He falleth; verily grievous is his fall, and he shall not rise again: the destruction of the sinner is for ever.

14 And *the LORD* shall not have him in remembrance, when he visiteth the righteous.

15 This is the portion of sinners for evermore.

16 But they that fear the LORD shall rise again unto life eternal, and their life shall be in the light of the LORD, and it shall fail no more.

---

11 προσέκοψεν ἁμαρτωλός. Corresponding to ver. 5.

καταρᾶται ζωὴν αὐτοῦ, the converse of ἐδικαίωσε τὸν κύριον.

τὴν ἡμέραν γενέσεως. Cf. Job iii. 3 'Let the day perish wherein I was born,' and vv. 4—12; Jer. xx. 14, 15.

12 προσέθηκεν ἁμαρτίας ἐφ' ἁμαρτίας: based on Is. xxx. 1; cf. Ps. lxix. 27.

τῇ ζωῇ αὐτοῦ. The Psalmist amplifies with these words his extract from Isaiah. The words of the original probably meant 'the longer he lived.'

13 ἔπεσεν...πτῶμα. Cf. note on ver. 5.

πονηρόν, see note on ii. 6 ἐν αἰχμαλωσίᾳ πονηρᾷ.

καὶ οὐκ ἀναστήσεται. This expression emphasizes the irretrievable character of the disaster which overtakes 'the sinner.' Cf. Isai. xxiv. 20 'the transgression thereof shall be heavy upon it, and it shall fall, and *not rise again*'; xliii. 17 'the chariot and the horse, the army and the power; they lie down together, *they shall not rise.*'

It cannot be asserted that these words entail any reference to a belief in the resurrection. It is after this sentence that the view widens, and the eternal issues of life are considered.

ἡ ἀπώλεια τοῦ ἁμαρτωλοῦ εἰς τὸν αἰῶνα. Cf. ii. 35; xiii. 10; xiv. 6; xv. 14; xvii. 26. The contrast is given by the ζωὴ αἰώνιος of ver. 16. The meaning of εἰς τὸν αἰῶνα is surely that the doom of the wicked is not pronounced for this life only. This passage and the whole context contemplate the annihilation of the 'sinner.' For him there is no hope, no mercy, now or hereafter. The resurrection of the wicked, so briefly stated in Dan. xii. 2, 'and some to shame and everlasting contempt,' for a long time was not part of the Jewish doctrine of the resurrection. (Cf. 2 Macc. vii. 14 σοὶ μὲν γὰρ ἀνάστασις εἰς ζωὴν οὐκ ἔσται, where Antiochus Epiphanes is addressed.) Our Psalmist nowhere favours the view that any existence worthy of the name awaited the 'sinner.'

It appears to us that to interpret this and the two following lines as if they only referred to the material ruin of the ἁμαρτωλοί and the frustration of their schemes, disregards the force of εἰς τὸν αἰῶνα here and in ver. 15, and renders ζωὴ αἰώνιος in ver. 16 unintelligible.

14 οὐ μνησθήσεται, sc. ὁ θεός, which is also the subject to ἐπισκέπτηται.

ὅταν ἐπισκέπτηται δικαίους. The 'visitation,' which is generally mentioned under the aspect of punishment and vengeance, is here alluded to in its merciful light. Cf. Wisd. iii. 7 καὶ ἐν καιρῷ ἐπισκοπῆς αὐτῶν ἀναλάμψουσιν. Luke i. 68 εὐλογητὸς κύριος ὁ θεὸς τοῦ Ἰσραήλ, ὅτι ἐπεσκέψατο καὶ ἐποίησεν λύτρωσιν τῷ λαῷ αὐτοῦ.

The teaching of the verse is repeated in xiv. 6 διὰ τοῦτο ἡ κληρονομία αὐτῶν ᾅδης καὶ σκότος καὶ ἀπώλεια καὶ οὐχ εὑρεθήσονται ἐν ἡμέρᾳ ἐλέους δικαίων.

15 μερίς. Cf. Ps. xi. 6 'Fire and brimstone and burning wind shall be the portion of their cup' (ἡ μερὶς τοῦ ποτηρίου αὐτῶν).

εἰς τὸν αἰῶνα, 'for eternity,' cf. 13: not to be weakened down to 'misfortune shall continually be their portion.'

16 οἱ δὲ φοβούμενοι κύριον. See note on ii. 37. Under this head would be included the δίκαιοι of vv. 3, 4, 5, 7

ΨΑΛΜΟΙ ΣΑΛΟΜΩΝΤΟΣ.

δ. ψαλμὸс τῶι cαλομὼν τοῖс ἀνθρωπαρέсκοιс.

IV. Ἱνατί σὺ κάθησαι, βέβηλε, ἐν συνεδρίῳ,
καὶ ἡ καρδία σου μακρὰν ἀφέστηκεν ἀπὸ τοῦ κυρίου,
ἐν παρανομίαις παροργίζων τὸν θεὸν Ἰσραήλ;

Inscriptio: Ψαλμὸς τῷ Σαλομὼν τοῖς ἀνθρωπαρέσκοις δ' A, V, P: Γ´ ψαλμὸς τῷ Σαλόμων K: deest M. ἀνθρωπορέσκοις (sic) Cerda.
1 ἵνα τί σύ M.

and the ὅσιος of ver. 10. It appears to us impossible not to recognize in these words a reference to the doctrine especially connected with Pharisaic teaching.

ἀναστήσονται εἰς ζωὴν αἰώνιον. The belief in the resurrection unto eternal life had first been unequivocally stated in Dan. xii. 2, upon which passage the present words are probably based (Theodot. καὶ πολλοὶ τῶν καθευδόντων ἐν γῆς χώματι ἐξεγερθήσονται, οὗτοι εἰς ζωὴν αἰώνιον, καὶ οὗτοι εἰς ὀνειδισμὸν καὶ εἰς αἰσχύνην αἰώνιον). Compare 2 Macc. vii. 9 εἰς αἰώνιον ἀναβίωσιν ζωῆς ἀναστήσει. Matt. xxv. 46 καὶ ἀπελεύσονται οὗτοι εἰς κόλασιν αἰώνιον, οἱ δὲ δίκαιοι εἰς ζωὴν αἰώνιον. We cannot understand how, in the face of this verse, Kabisch (*das Vierte Buch Esra* p. 168) and Hitzig (*Gesch. d. Volkes Israel*, p. 502) should deny the author's belief in the resurrection, or call him a Sadducee. It is important to bear in mind that the 'eternal life' (ζωὴ αἰώνιος) so often referred to in the writings of the N.T., had, half a century before the Christian era, been accepted as part of a feature in Jewish religious thought.

The insistence on the doctrine of the resurrection is especially noticeable in a Psalm, in which the Pharisee contrasts the 'pious' Jew with the Sadducee who said there was no resurrection (Matt. xxii. 23; Acts xxiii. 6—8).

καὶ ἡ ζωὴ κ.τ.λ. To our mind this striking clause, so apposite in connexion with the thought of the resurrection, loses all force if the words ἀναστήσονται ...αἰώνιον and οὐκ ἐκλείψει ἔτι are to be taken as denoting material success.

ἡ ζωὴ αὐτῶν ἐν φωτὶ κυρίου. Cf. Job xxxiii. 29, 30 'Lo, all these things doth God work, twice, *yea* thrice, with a man, To bring back his soul from the pit, that he may be enlightened with the light of the living (or *life*)'; Is. ii. 5, 'Come and let us walk in the light of the LORD'; lx. 19, 'The LORD shall be unto thee an everlasting light.' Cf. Prov. xx. 27 φῶς κυρίου πνοὴ ἀνθρώπων.

The 'light of the LORD' suggests numerous parallels in the N.T. (1 Tim. vi. 15; Jas. i. 17; 1 Pet. ii. 9; 1 Joh. i. 5, 7; ii. 9, 10), and the association of 'the light' with 'the life' recalls a characteristic phrase of Johannine teaching (John i. 4, 5). The φῶς κυρίου stands in contrast to the σκότος ᾅδου, cf. xiv. 6.

οὐκ ἐκλείψει ἔτι. These words referred probably in the original to the φῶς κυρίου and are based on Is. lx. 19, 20, where ἐκλείπειν occurs in the LXX. For ἔτι compare Am. viii. 14 'and never rise up again' (καὶ οὐ μὴ ἀναστῶσιν ἔτι).

Ps. IV.—*Argument*.

(i) A denunciation of the typical profane person, a member of the nation's Council, but no true Israelite, outwardly a stern judge of others' sins, secretly a profligate of unbridled lust (1—6).

(ii) A prayer, that God would overthrow and expose the true character of these false professors of Israel's faith, passes off into a detailed description of the type of men-pleasers,—subtle and deceitful, but lascivious, savage, unscrupulous (7—11) and unsparing (12—15).

(iii) A curse, apparently twofold, is pronounced (*a*) against the individual of this type, in his daily life, personal projects, and household (16—20); (*b*) against the whole class of Jewish men-pleasers, that they may come to a violent end and their bodies lie unburied in dishonour; in requital for their cruelty and rapacity, for their forgetfulness of their God, and for their dissimulation towards the true Israelites (20—25).

(iv) 'They that fear God' shall be blessed: He will deliver them from the snares of the ungodly: He is just and mighty; He will overthrow the proud and show mercy to them that love Him (26—29).

Though not one of the most attractive, this Psalm is one of the most important in the whole collection. Breathing

PSALM IV.

A Psalm of Solomon against the Men-pleasers.

1 Wherefore sittest thou, O profane one, in the assembly, ¹when thy heart is far removed from the LORD, and provokest the God of Israel by thy transgressions?

¹ Gr. *and*

throughout a spirit of intense hatred, it paints the picture of the Pharisees' most bitter adversaries as viewed from the point of view of the 'pious' Pharisee. It is an attack upon the inner life of the Sadducaic faction conceived in all the malignity of the partisanship prevalent in Judæa during the first half of the last century B.C.

The writer, whose personality is only once (ἡμᾶς ver. 27) alluded to, identifies himself with them 'that fear the LORD in their innocency.' In this way he distinguishes his own party from those of his countrymen, who, though they equally claimed to fear the LORD, honoured Him with their lips while their heart was far from Him (ver. 1).

Thus the objects of his attack are Jews. They dwell with the Pharisees (ver. 7). They are of high rank; they sit on the nation's supreme Council (ver. 1); they dispense justice (vv. 2, 3); they expound law (ver. 10).

But in private life they are lax and immoral; in public they are cruel and implacable towards their own countrymen, making them houseless and spreading misery far and wide (vv. 23, 24).

The title by which he designates them is 'men-pleasers' (11—15), and in the opening words of the Psalm he addresses them collectively as 'profane' (ver. 1).

We have no doubt that the Psalmist is referring to the Sadducees. These in the eyes of the Pharisees were 'profane.' They numbered in their body the most influential priestly families, but were notoriously lax and neglectful in their observance of the Mosaic Law. Their sympathies lay with the politics rather than with the religion of their country; active diplomatists, but indifferent to the spirit of their faith, they seemed to the pious Pharisee to profane the mission of the chosen people by their secularity. These were the typical 'men-pleasers' who sacrificed the higher interests of the people to political alliances and schemes for aggrandisement. They were ready to break down the barriers of their religion in order to enjoy the favour of the powerful. Their religion was a mere lip-service. Their real devotion was given not to their God but to their dominant Asmonean house.

Wellhausen's conjecture that vv. 11—15 are a description of Alexander Jannæus, who for 26 years (104—78) reigned over the Jews and successfully overthrew the attacks of the Pharisaic party, was based on an interpretation of ver. 11 which we are unable to accept.

The intense bitterness of its tone indicates the temporary triumph of the Sadducees. Their punishment is the theme of a fervent prayer; but as no allusion is made to the judgment already, or likely to be, inflicted by God through the instrumentality of the heathen, we conclude that this Psalm was written before the advance of Pompey's army into Syria.

The barbarous and insolent behaviour of this Psalmist's foes in dispersing and banishing (13 and 23) their countrymen might be an allusion to the conduct of King Alexander Jannæus and his supporters, after their victory in 86 when they had quenched at a cost of some 50,000 lives the flames of hostile insurrection. But, as we are inclined to think more probable, it refers to the time at the close of Alexandra's reign, when the Sadducee party was being restored to favour and power. Aristobulus was determined to renew the policy of his father Alexander, The Pharisees saw their influence once more diminishing. They recalled the savagery, with which Alexander Jannæus celebrated his victory (Jos. *Ant.* XIII. 14, 2), and the wholesale banishment to which his foes were consigned. The Pharisees saw in Aristobulus a repetition of the father's policy.

For an instance of the cruelty of Alexander Jannæus we may cite the following terrible description from Jos. *Ant.* XIII. 14. 2 κατακλείσας δὲ τοὺς δυνατωτάτους αὐτῶν ἐν Βεθόμῃ πόλει ἐπολιόρκει· λαβὼν δὲ τὴν πόλιν καὶ γενόμενος ἐγκρατὴς αὐτῶν

40   ΨΑΛΜΟΙ ΣΑΛΟΜΩΝΤΟΣ.   [IV. 2

²περισσὸς ἐν λόγοις, περισσὸς ἐν σημειώσει ὑπὲρ πάντας,
ὁ σκληρὸς ἐν λόγοις κατακρίνων ἁμαρτωλοὺς ἐν κρίσει·

2 σημειώσει V, K, P, M (Fab. conjec.): σημειῶσαι A.

ἀπήγαγεν εἰς Ἱεροσόλυμα, καὶ πάντων ὠμότατον ἔργον ἔδρασεν. Ἑστιώμενος γὰρ ἐν ἀπόπτῳ μετὰ τῶν παλλακίδων ἀνασταυρῶσαι προσέταξεν αὐτῶν εἰς ὀκτακοσίους· τοὺς δὲ παῖδας αὐτῶν καὶ τὰς γυναῖκας ἔτι ζώντων παρὰ τὰς ἐκείνων ὄψεις ἐπέσφαττεν ......ὥστε διὰ τὴν τῆς ὠμότητος ὑπερβολὴν ἐπικληθῆναι αὐτὸν παρὰ τῶν Ἰουδαίων Θρακίδαν. Οἱ δὲ ἀντιστρατιῶται αὐτοῦ τὸ πλῆθος ὄντες περὶ ὀκτακισχιλίους φεύγουσι νυκτὸς καὶ παρ' ὃν ἔζη χρόνον Ἀλέξανδρος ἦσαν ἐν τῇ φυγῇ.

The story of the Elders and Susanna furnishes another obvious parallel to the Psalmist's description of the unjust judge. It is tempting to associate that famous legend with the incidents underlying the present Psalm.

The Psalmist denounces the insolence, immorality, and avarice for which the friends and supporters of a young prince like Aristobulus were probably notorious. The detailed reference to the shameless assaults upon the peace and purity of home life, seen in vv. 5, 6, 11, 12, 15, is best explained by some recent scandal in which the young nobles of the Sadducee houses had given deep offence to their countrymen.

The title 'Against the Men-pleasers' has in all probability been given to this Psalm by copyists. It is not likely to have been an original heading; but seems to be based upon the use in vv. 8, 10, 21 of a striking and uncommon name. ἀνθρωπάρεσκος occurs only once in the LXX. Ps. liii. (=LXX. lii.) 6 ὁ θεὸς διεσκόρπισεν ὀστᾶ ἀνθρωπαρέσκων, where the translators must have read חנה 'profane ones' instead of חנך 'him that encamped against thee.' In the N.T. we find it in the parallel passages Ephes. vi. 6 μὴ κατ' ὀφθαλμοδουλίαν ὡς ἀνθρωπάρεσκοι, Col. iii. 22 μὴ ἐν ὀφθαλμοδουλίαις ὡς ἀνθρωπάρεσκοι. The verb ἀνθρωπαρεσκεῖν occurs in Ignatius Rom. ii., the substantive ἀνθρωπαρέσκεια in Justin, *Apol.* I. 2.

1 'Ἱνατί σὺ κάθησαι, βέβηλε, ἐν συνεδρίῳ. This denunciation in the Second Person Singular is addressed to the body of the Sadducees collectively. The Psalmist seems to see before him the typical Sadducee, a man of high birth and great wealth, a member of the Sanhedrin, sitting in judgement upon his countrymen.

βέβηλε. For this use of the word compare Ezek. xxi. 25 καὶ σὺ βέβηλε ἄνομε, where the LXX. and A.V. 'profane' renders חלל (Aq. τραυματία, R.V. 'deadly-wounded') in the sense of חלל. It is generally used as in Ps. S. viii. 13 ὡς κρέα βέβηλα for *things* common or unclean in contrast to things sacred and dedicated, e.g. Lev. x. 10, Ezek. xxii. 26. We find it used of unhallowed and so profaning touch in 2 Macc. v. 16 ταῖς βεβήλοις χερσί. As applied to persons, it is found though less commonly in classical Greek, e.g. Plato, *Sympos.* 218 B καὶ εἴ τις ἄλλος ἐστὶ βέβηλος καὶ ἄγροικος, where it represents the vulgar man uninitiated into the graces of society.

The βέβηλος here is the man who, having to represent a holy people and to deal with holy things, is himself unholy: he is 'defiled' rather than 'defiling.'

It may be well to remember that the Pharisees regarded the High-Priesthood as having been wrongfully usurped by the 'unconsecrated' Asmonean princes. The leaders of the Sadducees were also defiled with the blood of massacred countrymen. Compare i. 8.

κάθησαι. Used of sitting in judgement, cf. Ex. xviii. 14 διατί σὺ κάθησαι μόνος, Acts xxiii. 3 καὶ σὺ κάθῃ κρίνων με κατὰ τὸν νόμον.

ἐν συνεδρίῳ. This refers to the Sanhedrin, the great administrative and judicial council of the nation, over which the High Priest presided. The Sadducees were here in our Psalmist's time in a majority, Acts v. 17; Jos. *Ant.* xx. 9, 1: they represented the nobility, the δυνατοί and ἄρχοντες. The word is used of the members of the Council collectively, cf. Matt. xxvi. 59 οἱ δὲ ἀρχιερεῖς καὶ τὸ συνέδριον ὅλον, Acts xxii. 30 τοὺς ἀρχιερεῖς καὶ πᾶν τὸ συνέδριον. Used in this sense we may compare with the present passage Acts vi. 15 πάντες οἱ καθεζόμενοι ἐν τῷ συνεδρίῳ (see also Matt. v. 22; Mark xiv. 55, xv. 1; Luke xxii. 66; John xi. 47;

IV. 2]   ΨΑΛΜΟΙ ΣΑΛΟΜΩΝΤΟΣ.   41

2 He surpasseth in words, yea in outward show he surpasseth all; he is austere in speech when he condemneth sinners in judgement:

Acts iv. 15, v. 21, vi. 12, xxiii. 1, xxiv. 20).
The words however may have a more general application. There was a 'bêth dîn' or 'court of judgement' in connexion with every synagogue throughout Judæa. There were local συνέδρια which decided petty cases, and administered justice in the district.
For the use of συνέδριον in the LXX. compare Prov. xxii. 10 ἔκβαλε ἐκ συνεδρίου λοιμόν...ὅταν γὰρ καθίσῃ ἐν συνεδρίῳ (=ודין) πάντας ἀτιμάζει (where the Greek differs widely from the Hebrew). It is possible, though not likely, that it is used here in this wider sense. At the time of the composition of this Psalm, there was undoubtedly a senate or γερουσία representing the nation, presided over by the High Priest, who was also the Asmonean Prince. Shortly afterwards (57—55) this National Council was broken up by Gabinius into five συνέδρια (Jos. Ant. XIV. 5, 4). But through the intervention of Julius Cæsar (47) the nation's Council seems to have been restored to Jerusalem, and we find Herod the Great defending himself as a young man before the Jewish συνέδριον at Jerusalem (Ant. XIV. 9, 3—5), after which time συνέδριον came to be the most common title.
Taking into account the political character of the present Psalm, it is probable that the allusion is to the National Council in the discharge of judicial functions. The word συνέδριον was very possibly not in use before the time of Gabinius as applied to the Council. But the translator lived at a time when the term had become generally accepted. (Cf. on the whole subject Schürer, Gesch. d. Jüd. Volkes I. pp. 146—8.)
καὶ ἡ καρδία σου μακρὰν ἀφέστηκεν ἀπὸ τοῦ κυρίου. A quotation from the well-known passage in Is. xxix. 13, cited by our LORD (Matt. xv. 6, 9). The Hebrew runs 'this people...have removed their heart far from me'; the LXX. version has ἡ δὲ καρδία ὑμῶν πόρρω ἀπέχει ἀπ' ἐμοῦ. The present clause agrees with the LXX. intransitive rendering; and as its language is quite independent of the Alexandrine version, it presumably translates a traditional Hebrew text, which must have had וְלִבּוֹ רָחַק (יִרְחַק) מִמֶּנִּי instead of וְלִבּוֹ רָחַק מִמֶּנִּי. This is an interesting early testimony in favour of the LXX. rendering against the Massoretic vocalization. For a similar passage compare Jer. ii. 5 ὅτι ἀπέστησαν ἀπ' ἐμοῦ.

παρανομίαις. Cf. viii. 9, xvii. 22.
παροργίζων τὸν θεὸν Ἰσραήλ. Cf. Isai. i. 4 παρωργίσατε τὸν ἅγιον τοῦ Ἰσραήλ; 1 Kings xvi. 2 τοῦ παροργίσαι με ἐν τοῖς ματαίοις αὐτῶν, Jer. vii. 18 καὶ ἔσπεισαν σπονδὰς θεοῖς ἀλλοτρίοις ἵνα παροργίσωσί με.

2 περισσὸς...ὑπὲρ πάντας. A peculiar phrase for which it would be hard to find an exact parallel. The meaning however is quite clear. The impious man is extravagant in virtuous language and assumed decorousness of manner.
For περισσὸς used in very different senses in the LXX. cf. 1 Kings xiv. 19 'And the rest of the Acts of Jeroboam' (καὶ περισσὸν ῥῆμα Ἰεροβοάμ), Eccles. vii. 17 'neither make thyself over-wise' (μηδὲ σοφίζου περισσά). In Daniel (Theodotion) we find 'excellent wisdom' (v. 13) and 'excellent spirit' rendered by 'περισσὴ σοφία' and περισσὸν πνεῦμα. It occurs in a depreciatory sense in 2 Macc. xii. 44 περισσὸν ἦν καὶ ληρῶδες ὑπὲρ νεκρῶν εὔχεσθαι. Cf. Edersheim on Ecclus. xxxiii. 29.

ἐν σημειώσει. A strange word to use in this connexion. It occurs once in the LXX. Ps. lix. 6 (Heb. lx. 4) ἔδωκας τοῖς φοβουμένοις σε σημείωσιν='thou hast given a banner (נֵס) to them that fear thee.' Meaning literally a 'distinctive mark,' it is here applied metaphorically to 'outward demeanour.'

ὁ σκληρός. Compare Gen. xlii. 7 ἐλάλησεν αὐτοῖς σκληρά, and so Isai. xix. 4 καὶ παραδώσω τὴν Αἴγυπτον εἰς χεῖρας ἀνθρώπων κυρίων σκληρῶν καὶ βασιλεῖς σκληροὶ κυριεύσουσιν αὐτῶν, Matt. xxv. 24 κύριε, ἔγνων σε ὅτι σκληρὸς εἶ ἄνθρωπος.

κατακρίνων. The Sadducees were proverbial for their severity in judgement, cf. Josephus, Ant. XX. 9, 1 περὶ τὰς κρίσεις ὠμοὶ παρὰ πάντας τοὺς Ἰουδαίους. On the other hand Josephus speaks of the leniency of the Pharisees (Ant. XIII. 10, 6) ἄλλως τε καὶ φύσει πρὸς τὰς κολάσεις ἐπιεικῶς ἔχουσιν οἱ Φαρισαῖοι.

42 ΨΑΛΜΟΙ ΣΑΛΟΜΩΝΤΟΣ. [IV. 3

³ καὶ ἡ χεὶρ αὐτοῦ ἐν πρώτοις ἐπ' αὐτὸν ὡς ἐν ζήλῳ,
καὶ αὐτὸς ἔνοχος ἐν ποικιλίᾳ ἁμαρτιῶν καὶ ἐν ἀκρασίαις.
⁴ οἱ ὀφθαλμοὶ αὐτοῦ ἐπὶ πᾶσαν γυναῖκα ἄνευ διαστολῆς,
ἡ γλῶσσα αὐτοῦ ψευδὴς ἐν συναλλάγματι μεθ' ὅρκου·
⁵ ἐν νυκτὶ καὶ ἐν ἀποκρύφοις ἁμαρτάνει ὡς οὐχ ὁρώμενος,
ἐν ὀφθαλμοῖς αὐτοῦ λαλεῖ πάσῃ γυναικὶ ἐν συνταγῇ κακίας·
⁶ ταχὺς εἰσόδῳ εἰς πᾶσαν οἰκίαν ἐν ἱλαρότητι ὡς ἄκακος.

⁷ Ἐξάραι ὁ θεὸς τοὺς ἐν ὑποκρίσει ζῶντας μετὰ ὁσίων,
ἐν φθορᾷ σαρκὸς αὐτοῦ καὶ πενίᾳ τὴν ζωὴν αὐτοῦ·

3 ἐπ' αὐτὸν A, V, K, P: ἐπ' αἴτιον M. conj. Hilg., Fritzsch., Pick.
4 οἱ V, K, P, M : om. A.
7 ὑποκρύσει (sic) Cerda.

3 **καὶ ἡ χεὶρ...ἐπ' αὐτόν.** The difficulty of this reading disappears when we see that it is adapted from the LXX. version of the Pentateuch. The law required the witness to be the first to throw the stone at the condemned prisoner; hence this profane one who was foremost in executing punishment was witness as well as judge. See Deut. xiii. 9 καὶ αἱ χεῖρές σου ἔσονται ἐπ' αὐτὸν ἐν πρώτοις ἀποκτεῖναι αὐτόν, xvii. 7 καὶ ἡ χεὶρ τῶν μαρτύρων ἔσται ἐπ' αὐτῷ ἐν πρώτοις θανατῶσαι αὐτόν. The translator evidently shaped his sentence by his recollection of the LXX. rendering of Deut. xiii. 9. ἐπ' αὐτόν thus receives a satisfactory explanation; the change from the plural ἁμαρτωλοὺς to the singular of the individual instance is quite in keeping with the style of our Psalms, cf. vv. 7, 8, 10, iii. 3, 5.
Hilgenfeld could hardly have realised the appositeness of this allusion when he conjectured ἐπ' αἴτιον. His conjecture has now the support of the Moscow MS., whose scribe introduced the same emendation.
ἔνοχος, 'guilty,' cf. Ex. xxii. 3; Lev. xx. 9. Deut. xix. 10 ἔνοχος αἵματι, Job xv. 5 ἔνοχος εἶ ῥήμασι στόματός σου.
ἐν ποικιλίᾳ ἁμαρτιῶν. Literally 'in respect of a varied tissue of sins.' ποικιλία in the LXX. occurs about five times, always in a literal sense, e.g. Ex. xxxv. 35 πᾶν ἔργον ἀρχιτεκτονίας ποικίλας.
ἐν ἀκρασίαις, i.e. in profligacy and sensuality. See on i. 7, 8, ii. 13. This word occurs in our Lord's denunciation of the hypocrisy of the Pharisees, Matt. xxiii. 25 οὐαὶ ὑμῖν, γραμματεῖς καὶ Φαρισαῖοι ὑποκριταί, ὅτι καθαρίζετε τὸ ἔξωθεν τοῦ ποτηρίου καὶ τῆς παροψίδος ἔσωθεν δὲ γέμουσιν ἐξ ἁρπαγῆς καὶ ἀκρασίας (extortion and excess).
Cf. 1 Cor. vii. 5 διὰ τὴν ἀκρασίαν ὑμῶν 'because of your incontinency.'
4 οἱ ὀφθαλμοὶ αὐτοῦ. Cf. Job xxxi. 1 διαθήκην ἐθέμην τοῖς ὀφθαλμοῖς μου καὶ οὐ μὴ συνήσω ἐπὶ παρθένον.
For the offence by look, cf. Prov. vi. 25, xxiii. 33; Ecclus. ix. 8, xxvi. 9; Matt. v. 28.
ἄνευ διαστολῆς, cf. Ex. viii. 23 δώσω διαστολὴν ἀνὰ μέσον τοῦ ἐμοῦ λαοῦ καὶ ἀνὰ μέσον τοῦ σοῦ λαοῦ. And see for διαστέλλω; Lev. xi. 47 διαστεῖλαι (לְהַבְדִּיל), xxii. 21. Dt. x. 8 διέστειλε (הִבְדִּיל). The usage of the word in Lev. v. 4; Num. xix. 2, xxx. 7, and Ps. lxv. (lxvi.) 14 (Sym.), cv. (cvi.) 33 (Sym.) is quite different.
For **συνάλλαγμα** cf. Isai. lviii. 6; 1 Macc. xiii. 42.
μεθ' ὅρκου, cf. Lev. v. 4 ὅσοι ἐὰν διαστείλῃ ὁ ἄνθρωπος μεθ' ὅρκου: Num. xxx. 11 ὁ ὁρισμὸς κατὰ τῆς ψυχῆς αὐτῆς μεθ' ὅρκου.
5 ἐν νυκτί, cf. Prov. vii. 9 בְּאִישׁוֹן לַיְלָה וַאֲפֵלָה. 4 Esdr. iii. 14 secrete noctu.
ἐν ἀποκρύφοις. See on i. 7.
ἐν ὀφθαλμοῖς αὐτοῦ λαλεῖ. Cf. Prov. vi. 13 'He winketh with his eyes, he speaketh with his feet, he maketh signs with his fingers' (=LXX. ὁ δ' αὐτὸς ἐννεύει ὀφθαλμῷ σημαίνει δὲ ποδὶ διδάσκει δὲ ἐννεύμασι δακτύλων) and x. 10.
συνταγῇ κακίας. For συνταγή compare Aquila in Ps. lxxiv. (Heb. lxxv.) 3 ὅταν λάβω συνταγὴν (מוֹעֵד). LXX. ὅταν λάβω καιρόν). Symmachus in Ps. lxxiii.

IV. 7] ΨΑΛΜΟΙ ΣΑΛΟΜΩΝΤΟΣ. 43

3 And his hand is first upon *the sinner*[2], as though he were full of zeal;

Yet he himself is guilty, because of all manner of wickedness, and because of incontinence.

4 His eyes are upon every woman without distinction; he speaketh lies with his tongue when he maketh contract with an oath;

5 In the night-season and in secret he sinneth, as if he were not seen; with his eyes talketh he to every woman, and maketh evil compact;

6 He is swift to enter every house with a merry countenance, as one of the innocent.

7 Let God destroy them that live in hypocrisy in the company of the saints,

yea, *destroy* the life of such an one, in the corruption of his flesh and in poverty[3].

[2] Gr. *him*. Cf. Dt. xiii. 9

[3] *his flesh with corruption, and with poverty his life*

(Heb. lxxiv.) 8 has ἐνεπύρισαν πάσας τὰς συνταγὰς τοῦ θεοῦ, where there is either a confusion with συναγωγὰς or a misrendering of מוֹעֲדֵי־אֵל. Aquila renders יָפַד by συνταγήν, Ezek. xxii. 9. See espec. xxiv. 44 τὰς γυναῖκας τῆς συνταγῆς (אֵשֶׁת הַיָּפָה).

6 ταχὺς εἰσόδῳ. The consciousness of an evil purpose does not make him ashamed.

For ταχὺς here cf. Ecclus. xxi. 22 ποὺς μωροῦ ταχὺς εἰς οἰκίαν.

ἐν ἱλαρότητι. Only once in the LXX. Prov. xviii. 22 ἔλαβε δὲ παρὰ κυρίου ἱλαρότητα. Cf. Rom. xii. 8 ὁ ἐλεῶν ἐν ἱλαρότητι. The thought of entry with a bright and cheerful look, disarming suspicion, occurs also in the LXX. of Job xxxiii. 26 εἰσελεύσεται προσώπῳ ἱλαρῷ σὺν ἐξηγορίᾳ.

ἄκακος. This word, used sometimes of the innocency of the simple, sometimes of the integrity of the virtuous, here occurs in a good sense, cf. Job ii. 3.

7 Ἐξάραι ὁ θεός...ἀνακαλύψαι ὁ θεός. Here as in many other places (e.g. xvii. 26 &c.) we are met by the question, in what mood and person are the verbs meant to be? Fritzsche punctuates as if ὁ θεὸς were the vocative, but in vv. 25 and 28, where the words recur, he leaves it to be understood that the 3rd Person is intended.

τοὺς ἐν ὑποκρίσει ζῶντας μετὰ ὁσίων. From these words it is clear that the Psalmist is denouncing his own countrymen. Outwardly the Sadducees were joined with the 'Chasidim' (cf. iii. 10) in national worship; but as they made use of it as a means of political ascendency, their religion was mere hypocrisy. A Pharisee who was also a priest, would have felt this most acutely.

ὑπόκρισις. In the LXX. this word occurs apparently only in 2 Macc. vi. 25 διὰ τὴν ἐμὴν ὑπόκρισιν. In Sym. Jer. xxiii. 15 ὑπόκρισις=חֲנֻפָּה. ὑποκριτὴς= חָנֵף in Job xxxiv. 30 βασιλεύων ἄνθρωπον ὑποκριτὴν ἀπὸ δυσκολίας λαοῦ, xxxvi. 13 καὶ ὑποκριταὶ καρδίᾳ τάξουσι θυμόν.

Cf. Aq. Sym. Theodot. Prov. xi. 9 ἐν στόματι ὑποκριτὴς (חָנֵף) διαφθείρει τὸν πλησίον αὐτοῦ. Is. xxxiii. 14 τοὺς ὑποκριτάς (חֲנֵפִים).

ἐν φθορᾷ σαρκὸς αὐτοῦ καὶ πενίᾳ τὴν ζωὴν αὐτοῦ. If the text is correct, the difficulty of the line is considerably diminished by observing that its peculiarities are repeated in the next verse. Thus (1) the Plural τοὺς...ζῶντας is followed by αὐτοῦ as in ver. 8 ἀνθρωπαρέσκων is followed by αὐτοῦ, (2) the word ζῶντας is reproduced in ζωήν, as in ver. 8 ἔργα occurs twice, (3) the order of the words ἐν φθορᾷ...καὶ πενίᾳ τὴν ζωὴν αὐτοῦ corresponds with ἐν καταγέλωτι καὶ μυκτηρισμῷ τὰ ἔργα αὐτοῦ.

On the other hand there is an obvious awkwardness in σαρκὸς αὐτοῦ preceding τὴν ζωὴν αὐτοῦ. The conjectural reading ἐν φθορᾷ σάρκας αὐτοῦ καὶ (ἐν) πενίᾳ τὴν ζωὴν αὐτοῦ is not without plausibility.

We suggest that the line in the original was more distinct from the preceding clause than the translator has made it.

⁸ ἀνακαλύψαι ὁ θεὸς τὰ ἔργα ἀνθρώπων ἀνθρωπαρέσκων,
ἐν καταγέλωτι καὶ μυκτηρισμῷ τὰ ἔργα αὐτοῦ·
⁹ καὶ δικαιώσαιεν οἱ ὅσιοι τὸ κρίμα τοῦ θεοῦ αὐτῶν
ἐν τῷ ἐξαίρεσθαι ἁμαρτωλοὺς ἀπὸ προσώπου δικαίου,
¹⁰ ἀνθρωπάρεσκον λαλοῦντα νόμον μετὰ δόλου.
¹¹ καὶ οἱ ὀφθαλμοὶ αὐτῶν ἐν οἴκῳ ἀνδρὸς ἐν εὐσταθείᾳ ὡς
  ὄφις,
διαλῦσαι σοφίαν, *λαλῶν* ἐν λόγοις παρανόμων·
¹² οἱ λόγοι αὐτοῦ παραλογισμοὶ εἰς πρᾶξιν ἐπιθυμίας ἀδίκου.

8 μυκτηρισμῷ V, K, P, M: μόκτηρισμεῖ ?A (Cerda).
11 εὐσταθίᾳ P.
  διαλύσαι A, K, P, Fab.   διαλῦσαι ?V, M, Hilg., Geig., Fritzsch., Pick.
  λαλῶν nos conj. codd. ἀλλήλων. conj. Hilg.² ἀγγέλων ita Wellh.

The Hebrew would then have run
'May God cut off them that live in hypocrisy...; may his flesh (be consumed) with corruption, and his life in poverty.'
On αὐτοῦ, Sing. after Plur., cf. on ver. 3.

8 ἀνακαλύψαι. Cf. ii. 18 ἀνεκάλυψας τὰς ἁμαρτίας αὐτῶν, Job xii. 7 τὰ δὲ ἔργα τοῦ θεοῦ ἀνακαλύπτειν. The more usual word is ἀποκαλύπτειν.

ἀνθρωπαρέσκων. See note on the Inscription. Clearly a synonym for τοὺς ἐν ὑποκρίσει ζῶντας. For as ἀνθρωπάρεσκος renders the reading חנף for יחן in Ps. liii. 6, and חנף is rendered ὑποκριτής in Job xxxiv. 30, xxxvi. 13, we may be sure that the two words ὑποκριτής and ἀνθρωπάρεσκος represent two aspects of one character, the dissimulation and the flattery.

ἐν καταγέλωτι καὶ μυκτηρισμῷ. Compare Ps. xliii. (xliv.) 14 ἔθου ἡμᾶς ὄνειδος τοῖς γείτοσιν ἡμῶν, μυκτηρισμὸν καὶ καταγέλωτα τοῖς κύκλῳ ἡμῶν.

9 δικαιώσαιεν. The optative here as in i. 4 is in all probability due to the translator's misapprehension of the Hebrew Tenses. The Hebrew Copula and the Imperfect would have been more accurately rendered καὶ (=ἵνα) δικαιώσουσι.
The verse is then seen to express not another wish, but the purpose of the prayer which has just been offered.
For δικαιοῦν τὸ κρίμα τοῦ θεοῦ, cf. iii. 3, 5.

10 λαλοῦντα νόμον μετὰ δόλου. To the Pharisee this was one of the chief grievances, that Sadducees, as members of the Sanhedrin or as Priests, interpreted the Torah, for which they had no true reverence.

δόλον, cf. 1 Pet. iii. 10 χείλη τοῦ μὴ λαλῆσαι δόλον.

11 καὶ οἱ ὀφθαλμοὶ αὐτῶν κ.τ.λ. This verse is by far the most obscure in the whole Psalm. The Greek as it stands is very nearly unintelligible. The MSS. do not help us. The chief difficulties are concerned with (a) ἐν οἴκῳ ἀνδρὸς: is the ἐν, like ἐπὶ in ver. 15, to be taken in a hostile sense? or is 'the house' the object of friendly regard? (b) ἐν εὐσταθείᾳ: are these words to be taken with οἱ ὀφθαλμοὶ αὐτῶν or with ἀνδρὸς? (c) to what does ὄφις refer, to ὀφθαλμοὶ or ἀνδρὸς? (d) what is the construction of διαλῦσαι? (e) the meaning of ἀλλήλων? Our rendering of this obscure passage requires a few words of explanation. In spite of its difficulties and the very different views which have been given of it, we feel fairly convinced of the correctness of the solution which we offer.

(a) οἱ ὀφθαλμοὶ αὐτῶν ἐν οἴκῳ. These words are used in a hostile sense. They mean practically the same as οἱ ὀφθαλμοὶ αὐτοῦ ἐπὶ οἶκον in ver. 15.
The change from the singular ἀνθρωπάρεσκον in ver. 10 to αὐτῶν here, and again to αὐτοῦ in ver. 12 need not surprise us after the changes of number in vv. 7, 8, 21 and often in this book.

(b) ἀνδρὸς ἐν εὐσταθείᾳ. These words are to be taken closely together. In accordance with the Psalmist's general style no particular emphasis rests on ἀνδρὸς: the words ἐν εὐσταθείᾳ might have been rendered by a participle εὐσταθοῦντος or an adjective εὐσταθοῦς, the construction here followed being the same as that found in vi. 8 προσευχὴν παντὸς ἐν φόβῳ, viii. 28 ἀρνία ἐν ἀκακίᾳ. The ἀνδρὸς ἐν

IV. 12]   ΨΑΛΜΟΙ ΣΑΛΟΜΩΝΤΟΣ.   45

8 Let God lay bare the deeds of men that are men-pleasers, yea the deeds of such an one in derision and scorn:
9 ⁴That the saints may justify the judgement of their God, when sinners are destroyed from before the face of the righteous,
10 even the men-pleaser when he uttereth law with deceit.
11 And their eyes are toward the house of a man that is prosperous like a serpent, to pervert wisdom, ⁵speaking with the words of transgressors:
12 His words are words of deceit to the intent that he may accomplish his ungodly desire;

⁴ Gr. *May the pious justify*
⁵ Gr. *of one another*

εὐσταθείᾳ is the man enjoying peaceful domestic security, ignorant of the subtle schemes against his home and happiness. (Cf. 2 Macc. xiv. 23 ἐγάμησεν, εὐστάθησεν.) On εὐστάθεια see note on vi. 7.

(c) **ὡς ὄφις**. The metaphor is taken from the temptation in the garden of Eden. The ruin of the house is compassed by the seduction of the good-wife, εἰς πρᾶξιν ἐπιθυμίας ἀδίκου (ver. 12). The ὡς ὄφις continues the description of the man-pleaser, but the clause is grammatically independent of the previous words.

(d) **διαλῦσαι σοφίαν**. The Inf. is loosely epexegetic of ὄφις, for τοῦ διαλῦσαι. For διαλύω = הָפֵר. Aq. Ps. lxxxiv. (lxxxv.). Sym. Jer. xxxi. (xxxviii:) 32.

(e) **ἀλλήλων**, the reading of the MSS., gives no satisfactory meaning. We conjecture λαλῶν, the corruption arising from the accidental repetition of the last two letters of σοφίαν: thus ΑΝΛΑΛΩΝ became ΑΛΛΑΛΩΝ = ΑΛΛΗΛΩΝ. The phrase 'speaking with the words of belial' explains the way in which 'the men-pleaser' overthrows wisdom, like the tempter of old. For λαλῶν ἐν λόγοις cf. 1 Cor. ii. 13 ἃ καὶ λαλοῦμεν οὐκ ἐν διδακτοῖς ἀνθρωπίνης σοφίας λόγοις.

We subjoin certain other renderings:
(1) Geiger's rendering 'Und ihre Augen sind der Schlange gleich in eines Jeden Hause zum Verderben, zu vernichten des Nächsten Weisheit,' assumes that ἀνδρὸς = אִישׁ corresponds to ἀλλήλων = רֵעֵהוּ, and that ἐν εὐσταθείᾳ = בְּנָכוֹן which the translator wrongly derived from כּוּן instead of from נכה.

(2) Wellhausen gives 'Deren Augen gerichtet sind auf das Haus eines Mannes, der es versteht wie die Schlange Gottesweisheit aufzulösen.' The chief features in this translation are, (a) that οἱ ὀφθαλμοὶ αὐτῶν ἐν οἴκῳ denote depen- dence upon, (b) that ἀνδρὸς refers to the head of the Asmonean house, (c) that ἐν εὐσταθείᾳ represents an adjective denoting skill or cunning (did the translator read נבון for נבון?), (d) that for ἀλλήλων he reads ἀγγέλων = אלהים, adopting a striking conjecture of M. Schmidt's. For Hilgenfeld's note here see Introduction. The total absence from our Psalms of the word ἄγγελος and of any reference, save one, to intermediate beings, makes us hesitate to adopt the suggestion here.

(3) Another possible rendering we mention here, 'And their eyes are toward (i.e. in a hostile sense) the house of a man with fixedness like a serpent to overthrow the wisdom of their neighbours.'

ἐν εὐσταθείᾳ ὡς ὄφις would represent the fixity of their purpose, under the image of the unblinking gaze of a serpent; ἀλλήλων is taken as an incorrect substitute for τῶν πλησίον.

With this rendering we presume we may associate Pick's 'And their eyes, in the house of a man in steadiness, are like the serpent to destroy.'

ἐν λόγοις παρανόμων. On παρανομία see ver. 1. The adjective παράνομος occurs also in this Psalm vv. 13, 21, 27. It is found in conjunction with πονηρὸς and ἁμαρτωλὸς in xii. 1, 4. Otherwise it is only found in this book in xii. 2, 3, 4, xvii. 27.

12 παραλογισμοί, cf. 25. In LXX. only 2 Macc. i. 13 παραλογισμῷ χρησαμένων τῶν περὶ τὴν Ναναίαν ἱερέων. The verb παραλογίζομαι is used for 'to deceive.' Lam. i. 29 αὐτοὶ δὲ παρελογίσαντό με. Gen. xxix. 25, Aq. Sym. Gen. xxxi. 7 παρελογίσατό με (הֵתֶל בִּי), Sym. Ps. xliii. (xliv.) 18 οὐδὲ παρελογισάμεθα (שִׁקַּרְנוּ) τὴν συνθήκην σου, Aq. Jer. ix. 5 (4) καὶ ἀνὴρ ἐν τῷ πλησίον αὐτοῦ παραλογίζονται (יְהָתֵלּוּ).

46   ΨΑΛΜΟΙ ΣΑΛΟΜΩΝΤΟΣ.   [IV. 13

¹³ οὐκ ἀνέστη ἕως ἐνίκησε σκορπίσαι ὡς ἐν ὀρφανίᾳ,
καὶ ἠρήμωσεν ἕνεκεν ἐπιθυμίας παρανόμου.
¹⁴ παρελογίσατο ἐν λόγοις, ὅτι οὐκ ἔστιν ὁρῶν καὶ κρίνων.
¹⁵ ἐπλήσθη ἐν παρανομίᾳ ἐν ταύτῃ.
καὶ οἱ ὀφθαλμοὶ αὐτοῦ ἐπὶ οἶκον ἕτερον ὀλοθρεῦσαι ἐν
        λόγοις ἀναπτερώσεως.
οὐκ ἐμπίπλαται ἡ ψυχὴ αὐτοῦ ἐν πᾶσι τούτοις.

¹⁶ Γένοιτο, κύριε, ἡ μερὶς αὐτοῦ ἐν ἀτιμίᾳ ἐνώπιόν σου,
ἡ ἔξοδος αὐτοῦ ἐν στεναγμοῖς,
καὶ ἡ εἴσοδος αὐτοῦ ἐν ἀρᾷ·
¹⁷ ἐν ὀδύναις καὶ ἐν πενίᾳ καὶ ἀπορίᾳ ἡ ζωὴ αὐτοῦ, κύριε,
ὁ ὕπνος αὐτοῦ ἐν ὀδύναις,
καὶ ἡ ἐξέγερσις αὐτοῦ ἐν ἀπορίαις.

13 ἀνέστη codd. Fab. Geig.   ἀπέστη Hilg., Fritzsch., Pick.
15 ἐν ταύτῃ codd.: conj. Hilg. ἐν αὐλῇ (ἐν κοίτῃ? ἐν διαίτῃ?). Hilg.², ἐνατῇ. Fritzsch. ἐνταῦθα, ita Pick.
    ἀναπτερώσεως codd. Hilg.²: ἐν λόγοις . ἀναπληρώσεως (ἀναπαύσεως) Hilg. ἐν λόγοις ἀναπλάσεως Fritzsch., Pick.
17 ἀπορίᾳ (pro ἀπορίαις) P, M.

---

13 οὐκ ἀνέστη ἕως ἐνίκησε. Geiger suggests that ἀνέστη is possibly the rendering of עמד in the sense of 'to stand still,' 'cease from action,' as in Jos. ix. 13; 2 Kings iv. 6; Jon. i. 15, where the LXX. render ἔστη. In Job iv. 16 ἀνέστην is the LXX. rendering of 'it stood still.'

If we could accept this explanation, no alteration of the text would be necessary. But Hilgenfeld's conjecture ἀπέστη seems most probable.

ἕως ἐνίκησε σκορπίσαι. Literally 'until he prevailed to scatter' or 'succeeded in scattering.' This construction with νικάω is not found in the LXX. or the N.T.

It appears to us most probable that ἕως ἐνίκησε is the rendering of לנצח 'for ever' which appears as εἰς νῖκος in 2 Sam. ii. 26; Job xxxvi. 7; Lam. v. 20; Amos viii. 7, and as εἰς τέλος frequently (see note on i. 1). The more correct rendering would have been εἰς τέλος ἕως ἐσκόρπισεν. For a similar error cf. Hab. iii. 19 τοῦ νικῆσαι.

σκορπίσαι, see ver. 21.
ὡς ἐν ὀρφανίᾳ. For this use of ὡς ἐν

cf. ver. 3.
The translator expresses the thought of bereavement, which is added to that of dispersion, by his favourite construction of ἐν with an abstract substantive. The allusion is to the dispersion and banishment of the leading Pharisees by the Asmonean house. See Argument to the Psalm.

For ὀρφανία cf. Is. xlvii. 8 οὐδὲ γνώσομαι ὀρφανίαν.

14 παρελογίσατο, cf. παραλογισμὸς in ver. 12.

ὅτι οὐκ ἔστιν ὁρῶν καὶ κρίνων. These words recall Ps. ix. 34 (x. 13) εἶπεν γὰρ ἐν καρδίᾳ αὐτοῦ οὐ ζητήσει: xciii. (xciv.) 7 καὶ εἶπαν οὐκ ὄψεται κύριος, οὐδὲ συνήσει ὁ θεὸς τοῦ Ἰακώβ. Ezek. viii. 12 οὐχ ὁρᾷ ὁ κύριος. We may compare our Lord's words in John viii. 50 ἔστιν ὁ ζητῶν καὶ κρίνων.

15 ἐπλήσθη ἐν παρανομίᾳ ἐν ταύτῃ. Hilgenfeld conjectures ἐν αὐλῇ, in his last edition, ἐνατῇ(!). Fritzsche ἐνταῦθα. Pick, who reads ἐνταῦθα, renders 'He is filled with iniquity besides'; but as he can hardly translate ἐνταῦθα by 'besides,' he seems to have adopted Fritzsche's text, but to have followed the translation of

IV. 17]   ΨΑΛΜΟΙ ΣΑΛΟΜΩΝΤΟΣ.   47

13 He never ceaseth to scatter and bereave⁶, and he maketh desolate for the sake of his wicked desire;   ⁶ Gr. *scatter as in bereavement*

14 He deceiveth with *his* words, saying, There is none that seeth and judgeth.

15 He is filled with transgression herein⁷;   ⁷ Gr. *obscure*
and his eyes are against his neighbour's house to destroy it with swelling words of flattery;
with all this is not his soul satisfied.

16 Let dishonour be his portion, O LORD, in Thy sight;
let his going out be with groaning and his coming in with a curse;

17 Let his life, O LORD, be *spent* in pain, in poverty and want:
let his sleep be in anguish and his awaking in perplexities.

---

another editor, perhaps Wellhausen's 'er ist voller Bosheit darnach noch.'

We do not see our way towards accepting any of the conjectural emendations.

ἐν ταύτῃ seems to imply the existence of some such word as בזאת 'in this (fem.).' We suggest three alternatives, (1) בזאת may mean 'in this matter,' cf. Ps. xxvii. 5. The sense then would be 'He is full of iniquity even in this, that his eyes are against his neighbour's house to destroy it.' (2) The possibility has suggested itself to us that the original had את־בן which by accidental transposition of letters became the almost unintelligible בזאת. The word בן denotes 'rapine' or 'spoil.' The sense would then have been 'through transgression he was filled with booty, and not only so, but his insatiable avarice made him perpetually cast about to procure the overthrow of fresh households.' (3) But very probably ἐν ταύτῃ has a personal reference, and obscurely hints at the wife of the ἀνδρὸς ἐν εὐσταθείᾳ mentioned in ver. 11. When 'the man-pleaser' is sated in iniquity with her, he turns to the ruin of another house.

ἐν λόγοις ἀναπτερώσεως. The MSS. agree in this reading; and there is no good reason to depart from it. The word ἀναπτέρωσις is very rare; but its meaning, which we obtain from the kindred forms of the word, is very apposite to our passage. Prov. vii. 11 ἀνεπτερωμένη δέ ἐστι καὶ ἄσωτος = 'She is clamorous (הֹמִיָּה) and wilful.' Cant. vi. 4 ἀπέ-

στρεψον ὀφθαλμούς σου ἀπεναντίον μου· ὅτι αὐτοὶ ἀνεπτέρωσάν με 'for they have overcome me' (הִרְהִיבֻנִי). Ecclus. xxxi. 1 καὶ ἐνύπνια ἀναπτεροῦσιν ἄφρονας. But the best illustration of its use is to be found in Aristoph. *Aves* 1436 &c., where the whole passage turns upon ἀναπτερόω in the sense of 'excite,' 'put wings to.'

οὐκ ἐμπίπλαται ἡ ψυχὴ αὐτοῦ ἐν πᾶσι τούτοις: cf. Prov. xiii. 25 ἐμπιπλᾷ τὴν ψυχὴν αὐτοῦ, Ezek. xvi. 28 καὶ οὐκ ἐνεπίπλω, v. 29 οὐδὲ ἐν τούτοις ἐνεπλήσθης, Eccles. vi. 3 καὶ ψυχὴ αὐτοῦ οὐ πλησθήσεται. For ἐμπίμπλαμαι cf. Prov. xxvii. 20 ᾅδης καὶ ἀπώλεια οὐκ ἐμπίμπλανται.

16 Γένοιτο...ἡ μερίς. For this curse compare especially Lev. xxvi.; Deut. xxviii. 16 &c.; see also Ps. lxix. 22—28, cix.

μερίς. Cf. iii. 15.

ἡ ἔξοδος...ἡ εἴσοδος. Cf. Deut. xxviii. 19 ἐπικατάρατος σὺ ἐν τῷ εἰσπορεύεσθαι σε καὶ ἐπικατάρατος σὺ ἐν τῷ ἐκπορεύεσθαί σε. For this summary of daily life compare Ps. cxx. (cxxi.) 8 κύριος φυλάξει τὴν εἴσοδόν σου καὶ τὴν ἔξοδόν σου. Is. xxxvii. 28.

ἐν στεναγμοῖς...ἐν ἀρᾷ. The Psalmist amplifies the Mosaic curse in greater detail.

Compare Ps. xxx. 10 (xxxi. 11) ὅτι ἐξέλιπεν ἐν ὀδύνῃ ἡ ζωή μου καὶ τὰ ἔτη μου ἐν στεναγμοῖς.

17 ὀδύναις...πενίᾳ...ἀπορίᾳ. Cf. Deut. xxviii. 20 ἀποστείλαι κύριος ἐπί σε τὴν ἔνδειαν καὶ τὴν ἐκλιμίαν, 22 πατάξαι σε κύριος ἐν ἀπορίᾳ. Lev. xxvi. 16, 26.

48 ΨΑΛΜΟΙ ΣΑΛΟΜΩΝΤΟΣ. [IV. 18

¹⁸ ἀφαιρεθείη ὕπνος ἀπὸ κροτάφων αὐτοῦ ἐν νυκτί,
ἀποπέσοι ἀπὸ παντὸς ἔργου χειρῶν αὐτοῦ ἐν ἀτιμίᾳ.
¹⁹ κενὸς χερσὶν αὐτοῦ εἰσέλθοι εἰς τὸν οἶκον αὐτοῦ,
καὶ ἐλλιπὴς ὁ οἶκος αὐτοῦ ἀπὸ παντὸς οὗ ἐμπλήσει ψυχὴν
αὐτοῦ.
²⁰ ἐν μονώσει ἀτεκνίας τὸ γῆρας αὐτοῦ εἰς ἀνάληψιν.
²¹ ϲκορπιϲθείηϲαν σάρκες ἀνθρωπαρέϲκων ὑπὸ θηρίων,
καὶ ὀϲτᾶ παρανόμων κατέναντι τοῦ ἡλίου ἐν ἀτιμίᾳ,

18 ἀποπέσει...χειρὸς P, M.
19 κενός. Obscure scriptum in A teste Cerda, 'ut κεῖνος potius legeretur.'
ἐμπλήσει K, P, M. ἐνπλήσει V: ἐμπλῆσαι A (non ἐμπλῆσαι).
21 σκορπισθείησαν K, P, M conj. Hilg.: σκορπίσθησαν A, V.
ὑπὸ θηρίων V, K, P, M : ἀπολ ηρίων A.

---

18 ἀφαιρεθείη ὕπνος. Cf. Prov. iv. 16 ἀφῄρηται ὕπνος αὐτῶν.
For the thought cf. Gen. xxxi. 40 καὶ ἀφίστατο ὁ ὕπνος μου ἀπὸ τῶν ὀφθαλμῶν μου. Esth. vi. 1 ὁ δὲ κύριος ἀπέστησε τὸν ὕπνον ἀπὸ τοῦ βασιλέως. 1 Macc. vi. 10 ἀφίσταται ὁ ὕπνος ἀπὸ τῶν ὀφθαλμῶν μου. Dan. ii. 1, vi. 18.

κροτάφων. Perhaps introduced from a recollection of Ps. cxxxi. (cxxxii.) 4 εἰ δώσω ὕπνον τοῖς ὀφθαλμοῖς μου καὶ τοῖς βλεφάροις μου νυσταγμὸν καὶ ἀνάπαυσιν τοῖς κροτάφοις μου.

ἀποπέσοι ἀπὸ παντὸς ἔργου. This may be rendered either 'let him fall by every work,' i.e. let every deed of his be his own ruin, or 'let him fall from every work,' i.e. let him fail and fall short in every project.

The latter, which seems to us the most probable rendering, expresses the same idea as Deut. xxviii. 20 'The LORD shall send upon thee cursing, discomfiture, and rebuke, in all that thou puttest thine hand unto for to do.'

The ambiguity is to be noticed in the use of the same verb in the passage, on which this clause is probably based, Ps. v. 11 ἀποπεσάτωσαν ἀπὸ τῶν διαβουλίων αὐτῶν. Cf. Ecclus. xiv. 2 μακάριος...ὃς οὐκ ἔπεσεν ἀπὸ τῆς ἐλπίδος αὐτοῦ.

19 κενὸς χερσὶν. For κενὸς in close connexion with ἀποπίπτειν cf. Ps. vii. 5 ἀποπέσοιμι ἄρα ἀπὸ τῶν ἐχθρῶν μου κενός. The curse is that of Lev. xxvi. 20 καὶ ἔσται εἰς κενὸν ἡ ἰσχὺς ὑμῶν.

ἐλλιπὴς...ἀπό. For this construction compare Eccles. vi. 2 καὶ οὐκ ἔστιν ὑστερῶν τῇ ψυχῇ αὐτοῦ ἀπὸ πάντων ὧν ἐπιθυμήσει.

παντὸς οὗ ἐμπλήσει ψυχὴν αὐτοῦ.

Literally 'everything with which he should satisfy his soul,' or, by a very harsh attraction of the relative, 'everything which should satisfy his soul.' The latter is possible if we may judge from the translator's rather similar mistranslation of the relative אֲשֶׁר in xvii. 6.

ψυχή representing נֶפֶשׁ is here, as often, used to denote the 'appetite.' Cf. Prov. xiii. 25 'But the belly of the wicked shall want'= ψυχαὶ δὲ ἀσεβῶν ἐνδεεῖς, and x. 3.

20 ἐν μονώσει ἀτεκνίας. We conjecture that the two words are a duplicate rendering of the same Hebrew word; or that in the original they were independent of one another, and that, instead of 'in the solitude of childlessness,' the ideas of widowed solitude and the loss of children were kept distinct. Cf. Isai. xlvii. 9 'These two things shall come to thee in one day, the loss of children and widowhood.'

εἰς ἀνάληψιν. This phrase occasions some difficulty. ἀνάληψις is not found in the LXX., and in the N.T. occurs only in Luke ix. 51 ἐν τῷ συμπληροῦσθαι τὰς ἡμέρας τῆς ἀναλήμψεως αὐτοῦ. In that passage it is generally assumed that 'the days...that he should be received up' must refer to the ascension; and confirmation of this view seems to be supplied by the use of ἀναλαμβάνω in 2 Kings ii. 11 καὶ ἀνελήμφθη Ἠλιοῦ...εἰς τὸν οὐρανόν. Mark xvi. 19 ἀνελήμφθη εἰς τὸν οὐρανόν. Ecclus. xlix. 14; Acts i. 2 ἄχρι ἧς ἡμέρας...ἀνελήμφθη and vv. 11, 22; 1 Tim. iii. 16 ἀνελήμφθη ἐν δόξῃ. Similarly ἀνάληψις came to be accepted as equivalent to 'Assumption' in connexion

ΨΑΛΜΟΙ ΣΑΛΟΜΩΝΤΟΣ.

18 Let sleep be withdrawn from his eyelids in the night-season;
let him miscarry with dishonour in every work of his hands;
19 Let him enter his house empty-handed;
and let his house lack everything wherewith he can satisfy his desire.
20 Let his old age be childless and solitary until the time of his being taken away[8].
21 Let the flesh of the men-pleasers be torn in pieces by the beasts of the field, and the bones of transgressors lie dishonoured in the sight of the sun.

[8] Or, *in order that (his family) may be taken away from the earth*

---

with Enoch, Moses, Abraham &c., and as the Greek rendering of the Rabbinic פטירה (=discessus).

It is evident however that this signification is a favourite one and implies a privilege conferred upon the blessed at the moment of dissolution.

Is it applicable to 'death' generally? Could it be used in the present instance of one who is the object of a curse? We are not aware of any instance, save that of Luke ix. 51, where it could carry the neutral significance which it seems to have here.

We are of opinion that ἀνάληψις is used here in a sense quite distinct from its later technical application. It more probably represents the translator's attempt to reproduce the Hebrew word נָשָׂא with its twofold meaning of 'to uplift' and 'to remove.'

The thought before the Psalmist was that of 'removal,' as in xiii. 10 ἁμαρτωλοὶ δὲ ἀρθήσονται εἰς ἀπώλειαν: the translator by taking the alternative meaning has given an inappropriate rendering, although he enables us to see the cause of his mistake.

The word is important from another point of view. It helps to determine the date and origin of the Greek translation. Neither a Jew nor a Christian, acquainted with the technical use of ἀνάληψις and ἀναλαμβάνω, would have employed the word in his translation.

It seems to be used here for the first time in extant Greek literature. And as it appears in the present passage in quite a different sense from that in which it was shortly afterwards technically employed, we are disposed to find in εἰς ἀνάληψιν an argument for the early date, i.e. the 1st cent. A.D., of this Greek translation.

Both in the Greek(?) versions of the Jewish writings cited below and in the writings of the N. T., the word has already received a special application to the 'Assumption of the Blessed,' which is quite out of place here.

The technical use of ἀνάληψις in the latter part of the 1st century A.D. may be gathered from the following passages: 4 Esd. vi. 26 et videbunt qui *recepti* sunt homines, qui mortem non gustaverunt a nativitate sua: viii. 20 (vid. App. Crit.): xiv. 49 et in eis raptus est Ezras et *assumptus* est in locum similium ejus. Testamenta XII. Patr. Lev. c. 18 ἕως ἀναλήψεως αὐτοῦ. Assumpt. Mosis x. 12 erunt enim a morte et receptione mea. Enoch cap. 70.

21 σκορπισθείησαν. The Augsburg and Vienna MSS. read σκορπίσθησαν. Hilgenfeld's conjecture of the Optative σκορπισθείησαν was required by the context, and is found to be confirmed by the Copenhagen, Paris and Moscow MSS.

On the change from the Singular to the Plural ἀνθρωπαρέσκων see vv. 7, 8; 9—12.

The words in the Greek were perhaps suggested by Ps. lii. (liii.) 5 ὅτι ὁ θεὸς διεσκόρπισεν ὀστᾶ ἀνθρωπαρέσκων, cxl. (cxli.) 7 διεσκορπίσθη τὰ ὀστᾶ ἡμῶν παρὰ τὸν ᾅδην, cf. lxxviii. (lxxix.) 2 τὰς σάρκας τῶν ὁσίων σου τοῖς θηρίοις τῆς γῆς.

The picture of a corpse lying unburied, a prey to the beasts of the field, is common in the O.T. as marking the extreme of ignominy and desertion. Cf. Dt. xxviii. 26; 1 Kings xiv. 11; Jer. vii. 33, viii. 1, 2, xv. 3; Ezek. vi. 5, xxix. 5, xxxix. 17.

See also the description in Ps. Sol. ii. 31.

J. P.

ΨΑΛΜΟΙ ΣΑΛΟΜΩΝΤΟΣ. [IV. 22

²² ἐκκόψειαν κόρακες ὀφθαλμοὺς ἀνθρώπων ὑποκρινομένων,
²³ ὅτι ἠρήμωσαν οἴκους πολλοὺς ἀνθρώπων ἐν ἀτιμίᾳ,
καὶ ἐσκόρπισαν ἐν ἐπιθυμίᾳ·
²⁴ καὶ οὐκ ἐμνήσθησαν θεοῦ,
καὶ οὐκ ἐφοβήθησαν τὸν θεὸν ἐν πᾶσι τούτοις·
²⁵ καὶ παρώργισαν τὸν θεὸν καὶ παρώξυναν,
ἐξᾶραι αὐτοὺς ἀπὸ τῆς γῆς,
ὅτι ψυχὰς ἀκάκων παραλογισμῷ ὑπεκρίνοντο.

²⁶ Μακάριοι οἱ φοβούμενοι τὸν κύριον ἐν ἀκακίᾳ αὐτῶν.
²⁷ ὁ κύριος ῥύσεται αὐτοὺς ἀπὸ ἀνθρώπων δολίων καὶ ἁμαρτωλῶν,
καὶ ῥύσεται ἡμᾶς ἀπὸ παντὸς σκανδάλου παρανόμου.
²⁸ ἐξάραι ὁ θεὸς τοὺς ποιοῦντας ἐν ὑπερηφανίᾳ πᾶσαν ἀδικίαν,
ὅτι κριτὴς μέγας καὶ κραταιὸς κύριος ὁ θεὸς ἡμῶν ἐν δικαιοσύνῃ.
²⁹ γένοιτο, κύριε, τὸ ἔλεός σου ἐπὶ πάντας τοὺς ἀγαπῶντάς σε.

24 ἐφοβήρησαν (sic) Cerda.
25 παρώξυναν ἐξᾶραι Μ (sine interpunct.).
27 ῥύσεται αὐτοὺς ἡμᾶς Α.
28, 29 κριτὴς μέγας ϗ κραταιός. (29) Κύριος ὁ θεὸς ἡμῶν ἐν δικαιοσύνῃ· ita Cerda.

---

22 ἐκκόψειαν. The idea is taken from Prov. xxx. 17 (=LXX. xxiv. 52), and the LXX. rendering has clearly influenced our translator ὀφθαλμὸν καταγελῶντα πατρὸς καὶ ἀτιμάζοντα γῆρας μητρὸς ἐκκόψαισαν αὐτὸν κόρακες...
ὑποκρινομένων. See note on ver. 7.
23 ἠρήμωσαν...ἐσκόρπισαν...ἐπιθυμίᾳ. See ver. 13, where these words have already occurred. The evil character of the Asmonean Prince is reproduced in the Sadducee nobles who depended on him.
πολλοὺς may be due to an error of copyists for πολλῶν, but is more probably an error on the part of the translator.
24 οὐκ ἐμνήσθησαν. Another indication (cf. ver. 7) that the Psalmist's opponents were Jews. Cf. Jud. viii. 34 καὶ οὐκ ἐμνήσθησαν οἱ υἱοὶ Ἰσραὴλ κυρίου τοῦ θεοῦ τοῦ ῥυσαμένου αὐτούς. Ps. lxxviii. 42, cvi. 13, 21.
ἐν πᾶσι τούτοις. Cf. ver. 15.
25 παρώργισαν. See ver. 1.
παρώξυναν. The two words are almost synonymous. παροξύνω, as a rendering of ‏נאץ‎, seems to have the thought of disrespectful conduct added to that of provocation. Cf. Num. xiv. 11 ἕως τίνος παροξύνει με ὁ λαὸς οὗτος; Dt. xxxi. 20 ἐπιστραφήσονται ἐπὶ θεοὺς ἀλλοτρίους καὶ λατρεύσουσιν αὐτοῖς καὶ παροξυνοῦσί με. Prov. i. 30 (Sym. Theod.).
ἐξᾶραι. It would be possible to accentuate this as the Aor. Opt. Act. ἐξάραι. The fact that the same word occurs in ver. 7 perhaps indicates its use here in the same sense, the denunciation closing with the same prayer with which it opened.
On the other hand the epexegetic infin. is more characteristic of this class of Greek. Cf. v. 11, 14.
ἀκάκων. See vv. 6 and 21. Unsuspecting Pharisees are clearly intended. The writer perhaps refers to occasions on which the Sadducees by a well-assumed attitude of devotion to the national religion had temporarily disarmed the opposition of the theocratic Jews. The ἄκακος of this verse would correspond rather to

22 Let ravens peck out the eyes of the men that work hypocrisy,

23 Because they have made desolate with dishonour many men's houses, and scattered *them* in their lust;

24 And remembered not God, nor feared God in all these things;

25 And provoked God to anger and vexed him; that he should cut them from off the earth, because with craftiness they beguiled the souls of the innocent.

26 Blessed are they that fear the LORD in their innocency:

27 The LORD will deliver them from deceitful and sinful men, and will deliver us from every snare of the ungodly.

28 Let God destroy them that work all iniquity with insolence, for a great and mighty judge *is* the LORD our God in righteousness.

29 Let thy mercy, O LORD, be upon all them that love thee.

---

the 'תְּפ (Prov. i. 4) than to דָם (Prov. x. 29).

ὑπεκρίνοντο. ὑποκρίνομαι is used in the sense of 'dissemble' in 2 Macc. v. 25, vi. 21, 24; Ecclus. i. 26. We are not aware of any other passage where it is found with an Accus. in the sense of 'deceive.'

26 οἱ φοβούμενοι τὸν κύριον ἐν ἀκακίᾳ αὐτῶν. See note on ii. 37 οἱ φοβούμενοι τὸν κύριον ἐν ἐπιστήμῃ.

ἀκακία (cf. ver. 6, viii. 28, xii. 4) is here the innocency of integrity. The Psalmist contrasts the sincere worship of the Pharisee with the religion of the Sadducees, which in the opinion of the theocratic Jews was used as a cloak for their ambitious policy.

We may compare Ps. xxvi. 6 'I will wash mine hands in innocency; so will I compass thine altar, O LORD,' ver. 11 'But as for me I will walk in mine integrity' (ἀκακίᾳ).

27 ἀνθρώπων δολίων καὶ ἁμαρτωλῶν. A description of the subtle character of the Sadducee leaders, based on Ps. xliii. 1 'O deliver me from the deceitful and unjust man' (ἀπὸ ἀνθρώπου ἀδίκου καὶ δολίου ῥῦσαί με). cxx. 2 'Deliver my soul, O LORD, from lying lips and from a deceitful tongue.'

ῥύσεται: the Fut. represents the Heb. Impf. denoting continuous action.

ἀπὸ παντὸς σκανδάλου παρανόμου, the snare or stumbling block laid by the ungodly man in the path of the righteous. Cf. Ps. cxli. 9 'Keep me from the snare which they have laid for me, and from the gins of the workers of iniquity' (φύλαξόν με ἀπὸ παγίδος ἧς συνεστήσαντό μοι καὶ ἀπὸ σκανδάλων τῶν ἐργαζομένων τὴν ἀνομίαν).

28 ἐξάραι. Cf. vv. 7, 9, 25. In this line it is very probable that ἐξάραι is 3rd Sing. Aor. Opt. by the translator's error for 3rd Sing. Fut. Ind., which would have corresponded with ῥύσεται. For the same error see xvii. 51.

The ὅτι in the next clause seems to follow an assertion rather than an entreaty.

ἐν ὑπερηφανίᾳ. The wickedness of the Sadducee was increased by the insolence and arrogance of the nobles who stood at the head of the party. The Psalmist seems to recall Ps. xxxi. 23 'The LORD preserveth the faithful, and plentifully rewardeth the proud doer' (LXX. τοῖς περισσῶς ποιοῦσιν ὑπερηφανίαν).

ὅτι κριτὴς μέγας. Pick's rendering 'Because a great judge and a mighty LORD is our God in righteousness' is a possible alternative. But it seems to us a mistake to divide κύριος ὁ θεὸς ἡμῶν. The Psalmist reverts to the thought of the opening verse, the impious man sitting in judgement in the council.

29 τοὺς ἀγαπῶντάς σε. Compare the Doxology in vi. 9.

The thought of love to God occurs in the passage referred to in ver. 28, Ps. xxxi. 23 'O love the LORD, all ye his saints.' Compare Dan. ix. 4 ὁ φυλάσσων ...τὸ ἔλεός σου τοῖς ἀγαπῶσι σε, and Ex. xx. 6; Dt. v. 10, vii. 9; Ps. v. 11.

ε. ψαλμὸc τῶι cαλομών.

V. Κύριε ὁ θεός, αἰνέσω τῷ ὀνόματί σου ἐν ἀγαλλιάσει,
ἐν μέσῳ ἐπισταμένων τὰ κρίματά σου τὰ δίκαια·
²ὅτι σὺ χρηστὸς καὶ ἐλεήμων εἶ, καταφυγὴ τοῦ πτωχοῦ.
³ἐν τῷ κεκραγέναι με πρὸc cὲ μὴ παραcιωπήcηc ἀπ' ἐμοῦ·

Inscriptio: ψαλμὸς τῷ Σαλομῶν. ε' A?: Δ̄ ψαλμὸς Σαλομῶν V, K: ψαλμὸς Σαλομῶν P?: deest M.
1 αἰνέτω A (Cerda, *laudetur*). τὸ ὄνομά σου P, M.

Ps. V. *Argument.*
1, 2. The Exordium. Praise for God's justice and mercy.
3—17. The Prayer.
(*a*) We pray to God in time of trouble.
4—6. (i) He gives freely: even a strong man gives without compulsion; how much more God without whom none is strong or rich.
7—10. (ii) He is our God: though he seem to refuse, we cannot desist from approaching him.
(*b*) In time of need and hunger our cry is to God.
11—14. (i) He feeds the birds and fishes; all that has life acknowledges him as the Giver; and in no less degree princes, nations, and even the beggars, receive provision from him.
(ii) He gives; but not as men give;
15—17. He gives continually, ungrudgingly, to all alike.
18—21. The answer has been given
18 (*a*) Blessed is he to whom God has given 'the golden mean' in material blessings;
19, 20 (*b*) for more than it leads to sin; but in it alone is fulness of righteousness possible.
21 (*c*) The subjects of his Kingdom are truly happy. Praise to the Divine King.
This Psalm is of a simpler character than the preceding four. It is not occupied with the religious or political condition of the people. The occasion of its composition seems to have been a drought, which threatened the country with a famine. The Psalmist, whether writing in his own name or as the representative of 'the true Israel,' prays for the removal of this calamity. His prayer is based on his perfect trust in the God of Israel, who is also the God of the whole Universe.

In ver. 18 the Psalmist seems to have received an answer or to be assured that the answer is coming. It is not great wealth, but the means of the subsistence 'in righteousness' which is God's best gift. Perhaps he tacitly contrasts here the wealth of the Sadducean princes with the poverty of the pious Jews. The happiness of those that fear God is the portion of 'the true Israel'; for they, he implies, set not their hopes on a terrestrial dynasty. God alone is their King.
The Psalm is one of considerable poetical merit. The language, it is true, is largely borrowed from the O.T. But the thought is simple and elevated, and the arrangement of the theme is artistic. The succession of striking ideas represented in 4—6, 11—13, 15—16, 18—20, makes us regard this Psalm as poetically the most original in the whole collection.
The Pharisaic origin of the composition appears in numerous details of the thought (see notes on vv. 6, 8, 19), but more especially in the reference to δικαιοσύνη (ver. 20) and to the kingdom and kingship of the Lord (vv. 21, 22).
Its date we have no sufficient means of estimating precisely. It is very probable that the scarcity alluded to should be identified with the drought and famine mentioned in ii. 9, xvii. 21. The allusion in the Psalm may be to the drought in B.C. 63, recorded by Josephus, *Ant.* XIV. 2.

1 Κύριε ὁ θεός. Cf. iv. 28.
αἰνέσω. That the Augsburg MS. read αἰνέτω is rendered clear from the fact that Cerda not only published it in his text (where it might easily have been mistaken for a printer's error), but translated it 'laudetur nomini tuo.' He evidently regarded αἰνέτω as an error for αἰνείσθω. Had he read αἰνέσω, he could

PSALM V.

A Psalm of Solomon.

1 O LORD God, I will praise thy name with rejoicing, in the midst of them that know thy righteous judgements :
2 For thou art gracious and merciful, a refuge for the needy.
3 When I cry unto thee, keep not thou silence from me.

---

hardly have avoided rendering it by 'laudabo.' Fabricius faithfully preserved the reading, which has not however been noticed in the Apparatus Criticus of the editions of Hilgenfeld, Geiger and Pick.

τῷ ὀνόματί σου. After αἰνεῖν the object is often found in the accus., always in the N.T. Compare the two passages most similar to the present, Ps. lxviii. (lxix.) 31 αἰνέσω τὸ ὄνομα τοῦ θεοῦ μετ' ᾠδῆς. lxxxiii. (lxxxiv.), cxliv. (cxlv.) 2 καὶ αἰνέσω τὸ ὄνομά σου. See also 1 Chron. xvi. 35 τοῦ αἰνεῖν τὸ ὄνομα τὸ ἅγιόν σου. On the other hand we find in 2 Chron. vi. 13 αἰνεῖν τῷ κυρίῳ.

ἐν ἀγαλλιάσει, Ps. xli. (xlii.) 5, cf. Ps. xliv. (xlv.) 16, xlvi. (xlvii.) 2.

ἐν μέσῳ ἐπισταμένων τὰ κρίματά σου τὰ δίκαια. The phrase undoubtedly contrasts the Pharisee with the scornful Sadducee and the impatient zealot. The Pharisees alone are ἐπιστάμενοι τὰ κρίματα. Compare ii. 37 εὐλογεῖτε τὸν θεὸν οἱ φοβούμενοι τὸν κύριον ἐν ἐπιστήμῃ.

For τὰ κρίματα τὰ δίκαια cf. ii. 12, viii. 29, ix. 4.

2 χρηστὸς καὶ ἐλεήμων. Cf. x. 8. Ps. lxxxv. (lxxxvi.) 5 ὅτι σὺ κύριε χρηστὸς καὶ ἐπιεικὴς καὶ πολυέλεος πᾶσιν τοῖς ἐπικαλουμένοις σε. cxliv. (cxlv.) 8, 9 οἰκτίρμων καὶ ἐλεήμων ὁ κύριος, μακρόθυμος καὶ πολυέλεος· χρηστὸς κύριος τοῖς ὑπομένουσιν.

καταφυγὴ τοῦ πτωχοῦ. Cf. Ps. ix. 9 καὶ ἐγένετο κύριος καταφυγὴ τῷ πένητι. xiv. 6 βουλὴν πτωχοῦ κατῃσχύνατε ὅτι κύριος ἐλπὶς αὐτοῦ ἐστιν.

πτωχός in the LXX. is the commonest rendering of עָנִי as πένης is of אֶבְיוֹן. Thus we find πτωχὸς used in such passages as Ps. xxxiv. 6 'This poor man cried, and the LORD heard him, and saved him out of all his troubles.' xxxv. 10 'LORD, who is like unto thee, which deliverest the poor from him that is too strong for him?' lxxii. 2 'He shall judge ...thy poor with judgement.' ver. 4 'He shall judge the poor of the people.' cxl. 12 'I know that the LORD will maintain the cause of the afflicted.'

The words καταφυγὴ τοῦ πτωχοῦ are the echo of such passages. But taken in connexion with τὰ κρίματά σου τὰ δίκαια in the previous line and the epithets χρηστὸς καὶ ἐλεήμων, they very probably contain a side-thrust at the mismanagement of justice in the writer's own time and country. The Sadducees were harsh and cruel (iv. 1, 2) and unjust (iv. 28). The LORD, the people's great Judge (iv. 28), judges righteously and is full of mercy. The poor will find redress from him and shall find in him protection from the oppression of the rich.

3 ἐν τῷ κεκραγέναι με πρὸς σέ. Cf. Ps. iv. 4 κύριος εἰσακούσεταί μου ἐν τῷ κεκραγέναι με πρὸς αὐτόν.

μὴ παρασιωπήσῃς ἀπ' ἐμοῦ. This expression is used in the LXX. of 1 Sam. vii. 8 'Cease not to cry unto the LORD our God for us' (μὴ παρασιωπήσῃς ἀφ' ἡμῶν τοῦ μὴ βοᾶν πρὸς κύριον θεόν σου).

The language of the verse is based upon Ps. xxvii. (xxviii.) 1 πρὸς σὲ ἐκέκραξα, ὁ θεός μου, μὴ παρασιωπήσῃς ἐπ' ἐμοί, where ἐπ' ἐμοί is the reading of B (Cod. Vat.), but ἀπ' ἐμοῦ is read by ℵ and A (Codd. Sin. and Alex.) and by R, T and U (Psalt. Veronense, Turicense and Fragm. Londin.).

The present passage renders valuable support to the reading ἀπ' ἐμοῦ. For, although our Psalms were no more free than other writings from the tampering of scribes, the obscurity of the work afforded its text a certain degree of immunity from a fruitful source of error in transcription; and we think there is good reason for assigning the Greek translation to the 1st cent. A.D.

For παρασιωπᾶν cf. also Gen. xxiv. 21, xxxiv. 5; Num. xxx. 5 &c.; 1 Sam. xxiii. 9; Ps. xxxiv. 25, xxxviii. 17, xlix. 3, cviii. 1; Hab. i. 13.

⁴οὐ γὰρ λήψεται cκῦλα ἄνθρωπος παρὰ ἀνδρὸς δυνατοῦ.
⁵καὶ τίς λήψεται ἀπὸ πάντων ὧν ἐποίησας, ἐὰν μὴ σὺ δῷς;
⁶ὅτι ἄνθρωπος καὶ ἡ μερὶς αὐτοῦ παρὰ σοὶ ἐν σταθμῷ,
οὐ προσθήσει τοῦ πλεονάσαι παρὰ τὸ κρίμα σου, ὁ θεός.

⁷Ἐν τῷ θλίβεcθαι ἡμᾶc ἐπικαλεcόμεθά cε εἰς βοήθειαν,
καὶ σὺ οὐκ ἀποστρέψεις τὴν δέησιν ἡμῶν,
ὅτι σὺ εἷς ὁ θεὸς ἡμῶν.

7 εἷς A, V: εἶ K, P, M: εἷς Hilg.

---

4 οὐ γὰρ λήψεται. The sentence is based upon Isai. xlix. 24 'Shall the prey be taken from the mighty?' The LXX. rendering is μὴ λήψεταί τις παρὰ γίγαντος σκῦλα. It is possible that the translator reproduces the substance of the Hebrew without reference to any existing Greek Version. Otherwise he either quotes loosely by memory from the LXX. or combines the LXX. rendering with that of some other well-known version. In favour of the first alternative is the fact that though γίγας is occasionally found (Gen. vi. 4, x. 8, 9; 1 Chr. i. 10; Ps. xviii. 6; Isai. iii. 2, xiii. 3; Ezek. xxxii. 12, 26, xxxix. 18, 20), the regular word in the LXX. to translate גִּבּוֹר is δυνατός. Quoting from memory the translator would naturally use the most familiar word.

On the other hand there might be cited the version of Symmachus which gives: μὴ ληφθήσεται παρὰ δυνατοῦ λῆψις. But the resemblance is limited to the words παρὰ δυνατοῦ, and no conclusion can be drawn from it.

It seems to us most probable that the translator made use of the LXX., but inadvertently substituted δυνατοῦ for γίγαντος.

The passage has a further special interest. The force of the sentence suggests that the words of the prophet had become a proverbial expression. Not more than a century later we find it used and expanded by our Lord in His parable of 'the strong man.' Matt. xii. 29 ἢ πῶς δύναταί τις εἰσελθεῖν εἰς τὴν οἰκίαν τοῦ ἰσχυροῦ καὶ τὰ σκεύη αὐτοῦ ἁρπάσαι, ἐὰν μὴ πρῶτον δήσῃ τὸν ἰσχυρόν; καὶ τότε τὴν οἰκίαν αὐτοῦ διαρπάσει. Mark iii. 27.

The argument of this and the succeeding verse is from the less to the greater. You cannot wrest booty from a warrior by force; neither can you claim it from him as a right: but he will be ready to give of it spontaneously and generously. How much more may you not trust in the goodness and kindness of God? He who has made all and given us all we have, surely will give according to our needs.

5 ἐὰν μὴ σὺ δῷς. Compare for this thought 1 Cor. iv. 7 τί δὲ ἔχεις ὃ οὐκ ἔλαβες;

6 ὅτι ἄνθρωπος. The verse completes and expands the argument. The portion of each man is weighed as it were in the balances before God. None can add to it save by Divine decree.

The literal translation 'Because man and his portion are weighed in the balances before thee, (therefore) he will not add to his abundance contrary to thy judgement,' gives a very tautological process of reasoning. It is also an objection that ἄνθρωπος and ἡ μερὶς αὐτοῦ should thus be treated as separate items placed in the same scale.

According to our translation ὅτι ἄνθρωπος introduces the whole explanatory sentence which concludes with παρὰ τὸ κρίμα σου, ὁ θεός. The words καὶ ἡ μερὶς αὐτοῦ...ἐν σταθμῷ are first introduced to describe the limitation of human powers in their relation to the divine, under a well-known metaphor.

The same thought is repeated in its direct and concrete form by οὐ προσθήσει ...κρίμα σου. The substantive ἄνθρωπος stands at the head of the sentence, which falls into two coordinate clauses.

This construction reproduces the common Hebrew idiom, which for the sake of emphasis places the subject absolutely at the head of a sentence, and repeats it under the form of a pronoun. Cf. Ps. xviii. 31 'As for God, his way is perfect.' civ. 17 'As for the stork, the fir-trees are her nest.'

v. 7]   ΨΑΛΜΟΙ ΣΑΛΟΜΩΝΤΟΣ.   55

4 For no man taketh spoil from a mighty man;
5 And who shall receive aught of all the things that thou hast made, except thou give it?
6 *Verily as for* man—his portion[1] is *laid* in the balance before thee—he addeth not *thereto* nor increaseth[2] contrary to thy judgement, O God.

7 In our distress we will call upon thee for help, and thou wilt not turn away our petition, for thou art our God.

[1] Gr. *a man and his portion are...*
[2] Gr. *to increase*

ἐν σταθμῷ. Not a common word in the LXX. version. Cf. Is. xxviii. 17 ἡ δὲ ἐλεημοσύνη μου εἰς σταθμούς (לְמִשְׁקָלֶת). xl. 12 τίς ἔστησε τὰ ὄρη σταθμῷ καὶ τὰς νάπας ζυγῷ; (בְּפֶלֶס). Ezek. iv. 16 φάγονται ἄρτον ἐν σταθμῷ (בְּמִשְׁקָל). Ecclus. xvi. 25 ἐκφαίνω ἐν σταθμῷ παιδείαν. xxvi. 16 οὐκ ἔστι σταθμὸς πᾶς ἄξιος ἐγκρατοῦς ψυχῆς. Wisd. xi. 21 πάντα μέτρῳ καὶ ἀριθμῷ καὶ σταθμῷ διέταξας. Cf. Aq. Prov. xvi. 11 σταθμὸς καὶ ζύγια δίκαια. The citation from the book of Wisdom it is important to observe is included by Hilgenfeld in the list of passages which he adduces (*Messias Judaeor. Prolegg.* p. xvii.) as evidence that the writer of the Psalms of Solomon was acquainted with the book of Wisdom. Upon the general question the reader is referred to the Introduction. But it seems obvious, (1) that beyond the fact that in both passages σταθμῷ occurs where the Almighty is being addressed, there is no similarity of thought between our context and Wisd. xi. 21; (2) that the word itself is used in different senses in the two passages; in Wisd., as in Ezek., it has the meaning of 'weight' as a method of computation by the side of 'measure,' 'number': in Ps. Sol. it has the meaning of 'the instrument for weighing,' the balance or scale.

The more general term would be ἐν ζυγῷ. Cf. Job xxxi. 6 ἔσταμαι γὰρ ἐν ζυγῷ δικαίῳ. Ps. lxi. (lxii.) 10 ψευδεῖς οἱ υἱοὶ τῶν ἀνθρώπων ἐν ζυγοῖς τοῦ ἀδικῆσαι. Dan. v. 27 (Theodot.) θεκέλ, ἐστάθη ἐν ζυγῷ. The passage in Wisdom is much more like Test. Nephth. 2 πάντα γὰρ ἐν τάξει ἐποίησεν ὁ θεὸς καλά κ.τ.λ.

οὐ προσθήσει τοῦ πλεονάσαι. For this common Hebrew idiom cf. Gen. viii. 12 οὐ προσέθετο τοῦ ἐπιστρέψαι πρὸς αὐτὸν ἔτι. Deut. xxv. 3 ἐὰν δὲ προσθῇς μαστιγῶσαι. Acts xii. 3 προσέθετο συλλαβεῖν.

For παρά in the sense of 'contrary to' cf. παρὰ νόμον Acts xviii. 13. Here, however, the παρά probably represents the Hebrew מִן with the meaning of the comparative. This idiom, which is perhaps more generally found with ὑπέρ (e.g. Eccles. iv. 9 ἀγαθοὶ οἱ δύο ὑπὲρ τὸν ἕνα), is common enough in this dialect. The preposition, denoting excess, is added to the comparative to give 'greater expressiveness.' (Winer, § 35.) Cf. Luke iii. 13 μηδὲν πλέον παρὰ τὸ διατεταγμένον ὑμῖν πράσσετε.

If this explanation is correct, the translation of πλεονάσαι παρὰ τὸ κρίμα σου will be 'to increase *beyond* that which thou ordainest.'

7 ἐν τῷ θλίβεσθαι ἡμᾶς. Cf. i. 1. The reference is probably to the drought (cf. ver. 11) or famine (cf. vv. 10, 12), which is the occasion of the supplicatory Psalm.

εἰς βοήθειαν. Cf. Ps. xxxiv. (xxxv.) 2 ἀνάστηθι εἰς βοήθειάν μου. lxix. (lxx.) 1 ὁ θεὸς εἰς τὴν βοήθειάν μου πρόσχες.

ἀποστρέψεις τὴν δέησιν. This phrase does not occur in the LXX.; but ἀποστρέφειν is very frequent in the sense of 'refusing' or 'rejecting' when coupled with πρόσωπον.

The same thought however is expressed by different verbs in the LXX., e.g. Ps. liv. (lv.) 1 καὶ μὴ ὑπερίδῃς τὴν δέησίν μου. lxv. (lxvi.) 20 εὐλογητὸς ὁ θεὸς ὃς οὐκ ἀπέστησεν τὴν προσευχήν μου. ci. (cii.) 18 καὶ οὐκ ἐξουδένωσεν τὴν δέησιν αὐτῶν.

δέησις is here the most appropriate word for prayer, expressing petition for the relief of material wants.

ὅτι σὺ εἶς ὁ θεὸς ἡμῶν. Cf. ix. 16. For εἶ (not εἷς) we may quote the parallel passages, Ps. cxxxix. (cxl.) 7 εἶπα τῷ κυρίῳ θεός μου εἶ σύ. cxli. (cxlii.) 10 ὅτι θεός μου εἶ σύ.

Hilgenfeld's conjecture εἷς is quite out of keeping with the thought and argument of the Psalm.

⁸ μὴ βαρύνῃς τὴν χεῖρά σου ἐφ' ἡμᾶς,
ἵνα μὴ δι' ἀνάγκην ἁμάρτωμεν.
⁹ καὶ ἐὰν μὴ ἐπιϲτρέψῃϲ ἡμᾶϲ, οὐκ ἀφεξόμεθα,
ἀλλὰ ἐπὶ σὲ ἥξομεν.
¹⁰ ἐὰν γὰρ πεινάσω, πρὸς σὲ κεκράξομαι, ὁ θεός,
καὶ σὺ δώσεις μοι.
¹¹ τὰ πετεινὰ καὶ τοὺϲ ἰχθύαϲ σὺ τρέφεις
ἐν τῷ διδόναι σε ὑετὸν ἐν ἐρήμοις εἰς ἀνατολὴν χλόηϲ,
ἑτοιμάϲαι χορτάϲματα ἐν ἐρήμῳ παντὶ ζῶντι.
¹² καὶ ἐὰν πεινάσωσι, πρὸϲ ϲὲ ἀροῦϲι πρόσωπα αὐτῶν,
¹³ τοὺς Βαϲιλεῖϲ καὶ τοὺς ἄρχονταϲ καὶ λαοὺϲ σὺ τρέφεις, ὁ
θεός,

8 ἁμαρτάνωμεν (? K) Fab.: ἁμάρτωμεν A (Cerda) V, P, M.
9 ἡμᾶς Codd.: πρὸς ἡμᾶς Fritzsch. Pick.
11 χιλόης A (Cerda: εἰς ἀνατολὴν χιλόης=ad orientem pascis).

---

8 μὴ βαρύνῃς τὴν χεῖρά σου ἐφ' ἡμᾶς. See on ii. 24 ἱκάνωσον...τοῦ βαρύνεσθαι χεῖρά σου ἐπὶ Ἱερουσαλήμ. From the passages there referred to, it will be seen that the active voice in this metaphor is not found in the O.T. The Psalmist, who obviously bases his use of the metaphor on such O.T. passages as Job xxxiii. 7; Ps. xxxii. 4, would here reproduce their idiom. We conjecture therefore that the Hebrew ran אַל תִּכְבַּד יָדְךָ μὴ βαρυνθείη (or μὴ βαρυνέσθω) ἡ χείρ σου instead of אַל תַּכְבֵּד יָדְךָ, which represents the reading of the vowels followed by the Greek translator. As the vowels were not written, this was a very likely mistake to occur.

ἵνα μὴ...ἁμάρτωμεν. The aor. has better MS. authority than the present ἁμαρτάνωμεν.

Cf. Ps. cxviii. (cxix.) 11 ἐν τῇ καρδίᾳ μου ἔκρυψα τὰ λόγιά σου ὅπως ἂν μὴ ἁμάρτω σοι.

δι' ἀνάγκην, i.e. on account of the pressure of necessity arising from want of food. The thought seems to be that extreme physical suffering tempts men to lose their faith in God and seek relief in sinful ways. Such was the temptation of Job (Job ii.). The verse will then best be illustrated by Prov. xxx. 8, 9 'Feed me with the food that is needful for me...lest I be poor, and steal, and use profanely the name of my God.' Is. viii. 21 'it shall come to pass that, when they shall be hungry, they shall fret themselves, and curse by their king and their God.'

It seems however to us that this explanation does not exhaust the full meaning of the passage. The Psalmist's prayer for relief from the scourge of famine, lest in this dire extremity he should sin against God, contains a hidden allusion to the laws of cleanliness in matters of food, concerning which the Pharisees were minutely particular. In times of scarcity, the difficulty of keeping to the letter the rules which regulated their food became increasingly formidable; and the liability 'to sin,' i.e. to transgression of the law, was proportionately aggravated.

ἀνάγκην. Cf. Ps. cvi. (cvii.) 6, 13, 19, 28 καὶ ἐκέκραξαν πρὸς κύριον ἐν τῷ θλίβεσθαι αὐτούς, καὶ ἐκ τῶν ἀναγκῶν αὐτῶν ἔσωσαν αὐτούς.

9 καὶ ἐὰν μὴ ἐπιστρέψῃς ἡμᾶς. The phrase is undoubtedly based on the refrain of Ps. lxxix. (lxxx.) 7, 14, 19 'turn us again' (ἐπίστρεψον ἡμᾶς), where it is doubtful whether the meaning 'restore us to prosperity' or 'bring us back from captivity' is most appropriate. In the present passage it can only carry the former meaning. For ἐπιστρέφειν used of Divine *restoration* after discipline, cf. Ecclus. xviii. 12 ἔλεος δὲ

8 Make not thy hand heavy upon us, that we sin not by reason of *our sore* necessity.

9 Even if thou turn us not again, yet will we not cease *from thee*—nay, we will come unto thee.

10 For if I be an hungered, unto thee will I cry, O God, and thou wilt give unto me.

11 The fowls of the air and the fishes dost thou feed, when thou givest showers in the desert places that the green grass may grow up, to prepare food³ in the wilderness for every living thing. ³ Gr. *fodder*

12 And if they be hungry, unto thee will they lift their face.

13 Kings and rulers and nations dost thou feed, O God;

κυρίου ἐπὶ πᾶσαν σάρκα ἐλέγχων καὶ παιδεύων καὶ διδάσκων, καὶ ἐπιστρέφων ὡς ποιμὴν τὸ ποιμνίον.

Fritzsche, by his conjectural reading πρὸς ἡμᾶς, gives a different turn to the clause i.e. 'If you incline not unto us, &c.' and is followed by Pick.

But as the reading gives a good sense and is supported by the analogy of the LXX. version of Ps. lxxix. (lxxx.) and lxxxiv. (lxxxv.) 4, we see no sufficient reason for introducing the preposition.

It is possible that the original Hebrew may have had the sense which Fritzsche proposes, since the LXX. in Ps. cxviii. (cxix.) 79 give ἐπιστρεψάτωσάν με as the rendering of יְשֻׁבוּ-לִי 'convertantur ad me.'

οὐκ ἀφεξόμεθα. Cf. viii. 38 'We will not hold off or abstain from approaching thee in prayer.' For ἀπέχομαι, cf. Job i. 1, 8 ἀπεχόμενος ἀπὸ παντὸς πονηροῦ πράγματος. Isai. liv. 13 ἀπέχου ἀπὸ ἀδίκου.

ἀλλ' ἐπὶ σὲ ἥξομεν. Cf. Ps. lxiv. (lxv.) 3 εἰσάκουσον προσευχῆς μου, πρὸς σε πᾶσα σὰρξ ἥξει.

10 ἐὰν γὰρ πεινάσω. The thought of this verse recalls Ps. cvi. (cvii.) 9 ὅτι ἐχόρτασεν ψυχὴν κενήν, καὶ ψυχὴν πεινῶσαν ἐνέπλησεν ἀγαθῶν.

11 τὰ πετεινά...τρέφεις...ὑετόν...ἀνατολὴν χλόης...ἑτοιμάσαι χορτάσματα. The occurrence of these words illustrates the influence of the LXX. version on the translator, cf. Ps. cxlvi. (cxlvii.) 8, 9 τῷ ἑτοιμάζοντι τῇ γῇ ὑετόν, τῷ ἐξανατέλλοντι ἐν ὄρεσι χόρτον καὶ χλόην τῇ δουλείᾳ τῶν ἀνθρώπων, καὶ διδόντι τοῖς κτήνεσι τροφὴν αὐτῶν καὶ τοῖς νοσσοῖς τῶν κοράκων τοῖς ἐπικαλουμένοις αὐτόν, Job xxxviii. 25—27. Cf. Matt. vi. 26 for the illustrative detail.

τρέφεις. Cf. Ps. cxliv. (cxlv.) 15, 16 καὶ σὺ δίδως τὴν τροφὴν αὐτῶν ἐν εὐκαιρίᾳ. cxlv. (cxlvi.) 7 διδόντα τροφὴν τοῖς πεινῶσιν.

εἰς ἀνατολὴν χλόης. A picture of the rapid growth of vegetation after a fall of rain in Palestine. ἀνατολή is here used as a verb noun, so that these words are equivalent to ἵνα ἀνατέλλῃ χλόη. ἀνατολή in this sense does not occur in the LXX. or in the N. T.

ἑτοιμάσαι. This might be taken as a fresh clause coordinate with ἐν τῷ διδόναι σε ὑετόν. But we prefer to regard it as explanatory and expressing the purpose of ἐν ἐρήμοις εἰς ἀνατολὴν χλόης. Cf. Ps. lxiv. (lxv.) 10 ἡτοίμασας τὴν τροφὴν αὐτῶν.

χορτάσματα is used for 'provender' Gen. xxiv. 25, 32, xlii. 27, xliii. 24; Jud. xix. 19; for 'grass' (=Aq. χλόην) in Deut. xi. 15, in which sense it may occur here, unless it should receive a perhaps general application in the sense of 'food' as in Acts vii. 11 καὶ οὐχ ηὕρισκον χορτάσματα οἱ πατέρες ἡμῶν.

12 πρὸς σὲ ἀροῦσι πρόσωπα αὐτῶν. The verse expresses in reference to all living creatures the same thought as Ps. ciii. (civ.) 21 'The young lions roar after their prey and seek their meat from God.'

For ἀροῦσι πρόσωπα αὐτῶν cf. 2 Sam. ii. 22 πῶς ἀρῶ τὸ πρόσωπόν μου πρὸς Ἰωάβ; where in a very different context the same thought of trust and confidence underlies the metaphor.

13 βασιλεῖς...ἄρχοντας...λαούς. For this collocation compare Ps. cxlviii. 11 βασιλεῖς τῆς γῆς καὶ πάντες λαοί, ἄρχοντες καὶ πάντες κριταὶ γῆς.

58   ΨΑΛΜΟΙ ΣΑΛΟΜΩΝΤΟΣ.   [V. 13

καὶ πτωχοῦ καὶ πένητος ἡ ἐλπὶς τίς ἐστιν, εἰ μὴ σύ, κύριε;
14 καὶ σὺ ἐπακούσῃ, ὅτι τίς χρηστὸς καὶ ἐπιεικής, ἀλλ᾽ ἢ σύ, εὐφρᾶναι ψυχὴν ταπεινοῦ ἐν τῷ ἀνοῖξαι χεῖρά σου ἐν ἐλέῳ;
15 ἡ χρηστότης ἀνθρώπου ἐν φίλῳ [σήμερον] καὶ αὔριον, καὶ ἐὰν καὶ δευτερώσῃ ἄνευ γογγυσμοῦ, καὶ τοῦτο θαυμάσειας·

15 ἐν φίλῳ Codd.: ἐν φηλῷ Hilg. καὶ ἡ αὔριον Codd.: ἐπ᾽ αὔριον Hilg. ἀνὲκ. A (Cerda). ·

καὶ πτωχοῦ καὶ πένητος ἡ ἐλπὶς τίς ἐστιν. Cf. Ps. xxxiv. (xxxv.) 10 ῥυόμενος πτωχὸν ἐκ χειρὸς στερεωτέρων αὐτοῦ, καὶ πτωχὸν καὶ πένητα ἀπὸ τῶν διαρπαζόντων αὐτόν. lxxi. (lxxii.) 12, 13 ὅτι ἐρύσατο πτωχὸν ἐκ χειρὸς δυνάστου καὶ πένητα ᾧ οὐχ ὑπῆρχεν βοηθός· φείσεται πτωχοῦ καὶ πένητος, καὶ ψυχὰς πενήτων σώσει. lxxiii. (lxxiv.) 21 πτωχὸς καὶ πένης αἰνέσουσιν τὸ ὄνομά σου.

14 χρηστὸς καὶ ἐπιεικής. The same words occur together in Ps. lxxxv. (lxxxvi.) 5 ὅτι σύ, κύριε, χρηστὸς καὶ ἐπιεικής: the probability that the translator was influenced by this Psalm is increased on our observing in ver. 1 εἰσάκουσόν μου ὅτι πτωχὸς καὶ πένης εἰμὶ ἐγώ, in ver. 2 τὸν ἐλπίζοντα ἐπί σε, in ver. 4 εὔφρανον τὴν ψυχὴν τοῦ δούλου σου, words which find their echo in our present context.

ἀλλ᾽ ἤ used after a direct or implied negative. Cf. Job vi. 5 μὴ διακενῆς κεκράξεται ὄνος ἄγριος ἀλλ᾽ ἢ τὰ σῖτα ζητῶν; Luke xii. 51 οὐχί, λέγω ὑμῖν, ἀλλ᾽ ἢ διαμερισμόν. 2 Cor. i. 13 οὐ γὰρ ἄλλα γράφομεν ὑμῖν ἀλλ᾽ ἢ ἃ ἀναγινώσκετε. On ἀλλ᾽ ἤ standing for ἄλλο ἤ (not ἀλλὰ ἤ) and its use as a conjunction see Winer's *Gr. of N.T.* (Moulton's 3rd ed. p. 552, n. 4).

εὐφρᾶναι. The infin. corresponds with ἑτοιμάσαι in ver. 11.

Wellhausen translates εὐφρᾶναι and ἀνοῖξαι as if they had both been Imperatives in the original. But this seems to us to introduce unnecessarily a sentence of entreaty, which would interrupt the description of Divine mercy. The thought of the passage seems to follow an orderly arrangement: ver. 14 God hearkens, for he is gracious and maketh glad the heart of the humble by his bounteous mercy: ver. 15 man's mercy and kindness are shortlived: ver. 16 God's gifts are without stint.

Whatever may have been the precise form of the verbs in the original, it is more natural to suppose that they continue the previous clause than that they introduce a new starting-point in the sentence. We are confirmed in this view when we find the phrase ἀνοίγειν χεῖρα coupled with χρηστότης in the same Psalm ciii. (civ.) from which has been borrowed the substance of these verses 11—15.

ταπεινοῦ. Cf. Ps. ci. (cii.) 17 ἐπέβλεψεν ἐπὶ τὴν προσευχὴν τῶν ταπεινῶν.

ἐν τῷ ἀνοῖξαι χεῖρά σου ἐν ἐλέῳ. Compare ciii. (civ.) 28 ἀνοίξαντος δέ σου τὴν χεῖρα τὰ σύμπαντα ἐμπλησθήσεται χρηστότητος. cxliv. (cxlv.) 16 ἀνοίγεις σὺ τὰς χεῖράς σου καὶ ἐμπιμπλᾷς πᾶν ζῷον εὐδοκίας.

15 ἡ χρηστότης ἀνθρώπου. The gnomic character of this and the following verse is quite in the style of Proverbs. When viewed in conjunction with the proverbial saying in ver. 4 and the practical philosophy of vv. 18—20, as well as with the references to the natural world (cf. 1 Kings iv. 32, 33), this feature in our Psalm may well have been understood to confirm the claim of Solomonic authorship.

ἐν φίλῳ κ.τ.λ. The ἐν φίλῳ literally reproduces the Hebrew בְּאֹהֶב. Hilgenfeld's conjecture ἐν φηλῷ = 'deceitfully,' 'with guile,' from the rare adjective φηλός, which does not occur in LXX. or N. T. Greek, only deserves notice as a remarkable instance of critical perversity. The text gives a fair sense, though the construction is harsh; the conjecture is no sort of improvement.

Conjectural emendation of our Psalmist's text has been confirmed by the discovery

v. 15]   ΨΑΛΜΟΙ ΣΑΛΟΜΩΝΤΟΣ.   59

and who is the hope of the needy and the poor beside thee, O Lord?

14. And thou wilt hearken:—for who is gracious and gentle but thou?

Thou makest[4] glad the soul of the humble by opening thine hand in mercy.

15 The kindness of a man is toward *his* friend [to-day] and to-morrow[5], and if he should do it a second time without grudging, even so thou wouldest marvel.

[4] Gr. *to make*, or, *make*

[5] Gr. *and the morrow*

---

of MSS. (e.g. IV. 31), but the introduction of a lexical curiosity like φηλῷ, which is not found once in the LXX. or the N.T., into a passage where φίλῳ gives a reasonable sense, is indefensible. Hilgenfeld's line, ἡ χρηστότης ἀνθρώπου ἐν φηλῷ καὶ ἐπ' αὔριον, is apparently intended to mean 'man's kindness is deceitful and has an eye to the future; if it is repeated, it is a marvellous exception.'

We feel convinced, however, that the second clause of the sentence becomes almost meaningless unless the first clause be much more favourable in tone than Hilgenfeld's emendation makes it. The general meaning we take to be quite satisfactory as supplied by the present text: 'a man's kindness is short-lived; with repetition it becomes grudging; if not, it is a case for wonderment.'

There are two objections to the present text: (1) the abruptness of the first clause ἡ χρηστότης ἀνθρώπου ἐν φίλῳ, (2) the ungrammatical construction of the following words, καὶ ἡ αὔριον καὶ ἐὰν καὶ...καὶ τοῦτο, emphasized by the repetition of καί.

The difficulty we conjecture to be due either to the error of the translator or to the condition of the Hebrew text.

We believe that the best explanation is to be found in the hypothesis that something has fallen out which formed part of the original text.

Our conjecture is that the word 'to-day' was accidentally omitted from the Hebrew text, and that the Greek should have run ἡ χρηστότης ἀνθρώπου ἐν φίλῳ [σήμερον] καὶ αὔριον. The sense which is thus secured is very appropriate: 'a man's kindness toward his friend is for to-day and to-morrow: but if he ungrudgingly repeats it, this is wonderful.' In favour of the conjecture we may bear in mind

(1) that 'to-day and to-morrow' was a proverbial Jewish expression (cf. Luke xiii. 32, 33; Jas. iv. 13) for the present and immediate future;

(2) that καί before ἡ αὔριον stands in need of some explanation when followed by another καί;

(3) that the probability of the Hebrew word for 'to-day' of four letters dropping out is rendered exceedingly probable by the fact of its two last letters being the same as the two first letters of the Hebrew 'and to-morrow.' The sentence might have run טובת האדם באהב היום ומחר, while the liability to the omission might have been further increased if the Hebrew had read 'towards *his* friend,' when the final letters of that substantive would almost have corresponded with the opening letters of 'to-day'; thus,

טובת איש ברעהו היום ומחר.

This appears to us by far the most satisfactory explanation; and the objection based on the literal rendering of δευτερόω disappears when we find that (1) δευτερόω is used not merely of 'doing a second time' (e.g. 1 Kings xviii. 34), but also of 'repeating' generally (e.g. Ecclus. vii. 25 καὶ μὴ δευτερώσῃς λόγον ἐν προσευχῇ σου): (2) the word שָׁנָה, which it translates, is often used of 'indefinite repetition'; e.g. Prov. xvii. 9 'He that harpeth on a matter' (Sym. = ὁ δὲ δευτερῶν λόγον. Th. = καὶ δευτερῶν ἐν λόγῳ): xxvi. 11 'A fool that repeateth his folly' (Sym. Th. ἀνόητος δευτερῶν ἐπὶ ἀφροσύνῃ αὐτοῦ).

In Deut. vii. 7 Aquila's use of δευτερόω is due to a confusion between שָׁנָה and שְׁנֵי.

Another possible rendering of the MS. text is this: A man's kindness is toward his friend, and extends only to the morrow, *or* is deferred to the morrow, whereas God's kindness is toward all. He maketh

¹⁶ τὸ δὲ δόμα σου πολὺ μετὰ χρηστότητος καὶ πλούσιον, καὶ οὗ ἔστιν ἐπὶ σὲ, κύριε, ἡ ἐλπὶς, οὐ φείσεται ἐν δόματι. ¹⁷ ἐπὶ πᾶσαν τὴν γῆν τὸ ἔλεός σου, κύριε, ἐν χρηστότητι.

¹⁸ Μακάριος οὗ μνημονεύει ὁ θεὸς ἐν συμμετρίᾳ αὐταρκεσίας·

16 τὸ δεὶ V. φείσεται V, K, P, M: φύσται A: φυσαεται Cerda, Fabr. φείσει Fritzsch. Pick.
18 αὐταρκεσίας Codd. : αὐταρκείας Hilg.

---

his sun to shine upon the just and the unjust.

ἄνευ γογγυσμοῦ. γογγυσμὸς is not a common word. It renders תלונה in Ex. xvi. 7, 8, 9, 12; Num. xvii. 5, 10, and און in Isai. lviii. 9, and is found in Wisd. i. 10, 11; Ecclus. xlvi. 10. We have ἄνευ γογγυσμοῦ in 1 Pet. iv. 9, χωρὶς γογγυσμῶν Phil. ii. 14; and elsewhere in the N.T. the word occurs only in John vii. 12; Acts vi. 1.

καὶ τοῦτο θαυμάσειας. Cf. Ps. cxvii. (cxviii.) 23 καὶ ἔστιν θαυμαστὴ ἐν ὀφθαλμοῖς ἡμῶν.

For the Aeolic aorist cf. ψηλαφήσειαν Acts xvii. 27.

16 οὐ φείσεται ἐν δόματι. Upon our explanation of these words must turn our explanation of the argument in this and the following verses. There are two main alternatives of explanation:

A. According to the first, the argument is: as contrasted with man's goodness, Divine goodness is rich and bountiful; the gifts of God will always be plentifully showered upon the man whose trust is in Him; yea and more than that, the whole earth partakes of them. This seems to be the view of

(a) Fritzsche, who conjecturing φείσει would apparently prefer the reading 'And towards him, whose trust is in Thee, O LORD, Thou wilt not be sparing in gifts.'

(b) Wellhausen, who, if he reads φείσεται, must regard it as a mistranslation of the original Hebrew, translates as if it should have been rendered οὐχ ὑστερήσει, 'und wessen Hoffnung auf dich steht, Herr, wird keinen Mangel haben an Gute.' This gives a better grammatical sense than Fritzsche's, inasmuch as the antecedent to the relative clause is the subject and not the unexpressed object of the main verb.

B. The alternative explanation of the verse may be expressed as follows: God's gifts and mercy are bountiful; and they who trust in Him have more than enough, for they can give abundantly out of the store which He has granted them. Those who trust in Him imitate His goodness.

οὐ φείσεται is taken in its literal sense, 'And he whose trust is in thee, O LORD, will not be sparing in his gifts.' So Geiger, who however wrongly refers to xi. 2. This rendering of φείδομαι in the sense of 'I am parsimonious' is not common, but might be defended from Jer. xxvii. (l.) 14 μὴ φείσησθε ἐπὶ τοῖς τοξεύμασιν ὑμῶν, and Aq. Sym. Prov. xi. 24 ὁ δὲ φειδόμενος יחשׂך. The thought also might be illustrated from the description of the opposite character in Prov. xxi. 14 δώρων δὲ ὁ φειδόμενος θυμὸν ἐγείρει ἰσχυρόν.

Out of these rival methods of translation we incline to that represented by Wellhausen A (b). The sense which his rendering gives agrees best in our belief with the context. We are not, however, aware how Wellhausen arrives at his translation.

Our own belief is (1) that φείσεται is the right Greek reading, and that the varieties in the text are due to the difficulties in the way of its interpretation: (2) that φείσεται is the translator's rendering of an inaccurate Hebrew text: (3) that whereas φείσεται would be the natural rendering of יחום 'he will spare,' cf. Deut. vii. 16 οὐ φείσεται לא־תחום: Ezek. ix. 10 καὶ οὐ φείσεται (לא־תחום), יחום was presumably in the text before the translator: (4) that יחום was a copyist's blunder for יחסר 'he will want,' the final letters having been transposed, and ו read for ר: (5) that on the supposition of the original text

ΨΑΛΜΟΙ ΣΑΛΟΜΩΝΤΟΣ.

16 But thy gifts, according to thy loving-kindness, are bounteous and rich;
and he whose hope is in thee, O Lord, standeth not in need of gifts[6].

17 Thy mercy, O Lord, is upon all the earth in loving-kindness.

18 Blessed is the man whom God remembereth with a sufficiency convenient *for him;*

[6] Or, as Greek, *will not be sparing in gift*

---

having been יחסר, the Greek rendering should have been ὑστερήσει or ἀπορήσει.
Our explanation of the verse then becomes 'God's gifts are rich and plentiful; the man who trusts in the Lord shall be well provided for, he will need gifts no more: but God restricts not His love; His mercy is toward all the world.'
Pick's translation of this verse is 'But thy gift is large with benevolence, and rich. And whoso putteth his trust, O Lord, in Thee, shall have no need of anything.' φείσει (the reading followed) is here rendered as if there were a word φείδω 'I have need of,' with φείσει 3 sing. fut. 'he shall have need of.'
For δόμα...πλούσιον cf. xviii. 2 ἡ χρηστότης σου μετὰ δόματος πλουσίου ἐπὶ Ἰσραήλ. Prov. xix. 17 κατὰ δὲ τὸ δόμα αὐτοῦ ἀνταποδώσει αὐτῷ. Sym. Prov. xix. 6 καὶ πᾶς φίλος ἀνδρὸς δόματος.

17 ἐπὶ πᾶσαν τὴν γῆν τὸ ἔλεός σου. We more often find the power than the mercy of the Lord described as universal. Compare for this expression Ps. xxxii. (xxxiii.) 5 τοῦ ἐλέους κυρίου πλήρης ἡ γῆ.
For the comparison of Divine and human mercy our Psalmist shows a close agreement with Ecclus. xviii. 12 ἔλεος ἀνθρώπου ἐπὶ τὸν πλησίον αὐτοῦ· ἔλεος δὲ κυρίου ἐπὶ πᾶσαν σάρκα.

18 οὗ μνημονεύει ὁ θεός. The verb for 'to remember' applied to God is generally μιμνήσκω. An exception is Rev. xviii. 5 καὶ ἐμνημόνευσεν ὁ θεὸς τὰ ἀδικήματα αὐτῆς.
The meaning of the clause seems to be 'blessed is the man who is the recipient of Divine favour with a humble but contented lot. On the other hand a man sins who seeks to exceed, apparently by unrighteous means, the limit which God has assigned him' (cf. ver. 6). According to this explanation ἐν συμμετρίᾳ αὐταρκεσίας is opposed to ἐὰν ὑπερπλεονάσῃ, and μακάριος οὗ μνημονεύει ὁ θεός to ἐξαμαρτάνει. The latter contrast is not very evident at first sight. But it is implied that the man whom God remembers is a holy man.

ἐν συμμετρίᾳ αὐταρκεσίας. We cannot be far wrong in supposing that the general sense of these words is 'contentment in circumstances sufficing for daily needs.' But it is not so easy to determine more narrowly their precise significance.
συμμετρία does not occur in the LXX. or in the N.T. σύμμετρος is found in Jer. xxii. 14 ᾠκοδόμησας σεαυτῷ οἶκον σύμμετρον.
αὐταρκεσίας is probably introduced as an additional interpretative rendering to explain συμμετρίᾳ. Cf. iv. 20 ἀτεκνίας, xvi. 1 ὕπνου. αὐταρκεσία appears to be a ἅπαξ λεγόμενον. Hilgenfeld reads αὐταρκείας, and Geiger suggests αὐταρεσκίας.
αὐταρκεσία however seems to stand in the same relation to αὐτάρκεια and αὐταρκεῖν as ἀποικεσία to ἀποικία and ἀποικεῖν, and is certainly not to be rejected from the text as an impossible compound, with the meaning of 'sufficiency.' The word, and indeed the whole phrase, seems to be based on Prov. xxx. 8 'Give me neither poverty nor riches; Feed me with the food that is needful for me.' (πλοῦτον δὲ καὶ πενίαν μή μοι δῷς, σύνταξον δέ μοι τὰ δέοντα καὶ τὰ αὐτάρκη = Aq. ἄρτον ἀκριβασμῶν μου. Sym. δίαιταν ἱκανήν.)
It is interesting to find this proverbial maxim so prominently asserted in this Psalm. The Pharisees, whose Sadducee opponents numbered amongst them the wealthiest of the race, probably dwelt with special satisfaction on the blessings of humble station with contentment. It was, we may believe, a recollection of his early training, which gives to us St Paul's teaching on the subject of 'contentment' in the words of Phil. iv. 11 ἐγὼ γὰρ ἔμαθον ἐν οἷς εἰμὶ αὐτάρκης εἶναι, 1 Tim. vi. 6, 8 ἔστιν δὲ πορισμὸς μέγας ἡ εὐσέβεια

¹⁹ ἐὰν ὑπερπλεονάσῃ ὁ ἄνθρωπος, ἐξαμαρτάνει.
²⁰ ἱκανὸν τὸ μέτριον ἐν δικαιοσύνῃ,
καὶ ἐν τούτῳ ἡ εὐλογία κυρίου εἰς πλησμονὴν ἐν δικαιοσύνῃ.
²¹ εὐφράνθησαν οἱ φοβούμενοι κύριον ἐν ἀγαθοῖς,
καὶ ἡ χρηστότης σου ἐπὶ Ἰσραὴλ ἐν τῇ βασιλείᾳ σου.
²² εὐλογημένη ἡ δόξα κυρίου,
ὅτι αὐτὸς βασιλεύς ἡμῶν.

21 εὐφράνθησαν Codd. : εὐφρανθείησαν Fritzsch. Pick.

μετὰ αὐταρκείας.. ἔχοντες δὲ διατροφὰς καὶ σκεπάσματα τούτοις ἀρκεσθησόμεθα. Very similar is the sentence, perhaps derived from the same source, in the *Pirqe Aboth* IV. 3 'Who is rich? He that is contented with his lot; for it is said, When thou eatest the labour of thy hands, happy art thou, and it shall be well with thee' (Ps. cxxviii. 2). 'Happy art thou' sc. in this world; 'and it shall be well with thee, sc. in the world to come.'

19 ὑπερπλεονάσῃ. With the same meaning probably as ver. 6 πλεονάσαι παρὰ τὸ κρίμα σου, ὁ θεός.

For the use of the word compare 1 Tim. i. 14 ὑπερεπλεόνασεν δὲ ἡ χάρις τοῦ κυρίου ἡμῶν.

ἐξαμαρτάνω is not found in the N.T. In the LXX. it is found intransitively in Neh. ix. 33; Hab. ii. 10; Zeph. i. 18; Song of Three Ch. 5, and often transitively in the sense of 'make to sin,' e.g. 1 Kings xiv. 16.

20 τὸ μέτριον. μέτριος seems only to be found once in the LXX. Ecclus. xxxiv. 20 (=xxxi. 22) ὕπνος ὑγιείας ἐπὶ ἐντέρῳ μετρίῳ. The adverb μετρίως also occurs once, in 2 Macc. xv. 38 εἰ δὲ εὐτελῶς καὶ μετρίως, τοῦτο ἐφικτὸν ἦν μοι. In the N.T. the adverb occurs once, Acts xx. 12 παρεκλήθησαν οὐ μετρίως.

The meaning of τὸ μέτριον can receive no better illustration than Prov. xxx. 8 'Give me neither poverty nor riches.' It represents the position in life freed from the temptations peculiar to extreme poverty and extreme wealth.

τὸ ἱκανόν is the LXX. rendering of די in Lev. xxv. 28.

ἐν δικαιοσύνῃ. Without δικαιοσύνη there is no sufficiency possible; with δικαιοσύνη, 'the golden mean' amply supplies human wants. The purely legal character of the δικαιοσύνη here spoken of is suggested by the other references to 'righteousness' in this book.

The idea of a little with righteousness being better than great wealth and wickedness is frequently mentioned in Hebrew literature. Compare Ps. xxxvii. 16 'Better is a little that the righteous hath than the abundance of many wicked.' It is a common maxim in the Book of Proverbs, e.g. xv. 16 'Better is little with the fear of the LORD, than great treasure and trouble therewith'; xvi. 8 'Better is a little with righteousness than great revenues with injustice.'

ἡ εὐλογία κυρίου. Cf. xvii. 43.

εἰς πλησμονὴν. This phrase is used here in a good sense in connexion with the blessing of the LORD. In the LXX. it occurs frequently, with the sense of 'to the full,' 'unto abundance.' Ex. xvi. 3 ἠσθίομεν ἄρτους εἰς πλησμονήν; ver. 8; Lev. xxv. 19, xxvi. 5.

Thus Ps. lxxviii. 25 'He sent them meat to the full' (ἐπισιτισμὸν ἀπέστειλεν αὐτοῖς εἰς πλησμονήν). Lam. v. 6 'We have given the hand to the Egyptians, and to the Assyrians to be satisfied with bread' (Αἴγυπτος ἔδωκε χεῖρα, Ἀσσοὺρ εἰς πλησμονὴν αὐτῶν).

In the N.T. it is found with a bad sense in the well-known but difficult passage, Col. ii. 23 οὐκ ἐν τιμῇ τινι πρὸς πλησμονὴν τῆς σαρκός. R.V. 'against the indulgence of the flesh.'

The present sentence is not without obscurity. The words ἐν τούτῳ may refer back to τὸ μέτριον or may point forward to εἰς πλησμονὴν ἐν δικαιοσύνῃ. We prefer the latter alternative; the second clause explains and expands the former.

εἰς πλησμονὴν is then equivalent to ἵνα γένηται πλησμονή.

[v. 22] ΨΑΛΜΟΙ ΣΑΛΟΜΩΝΤΟΣ. 63

19 If a man abound beyond measure, he sinneth.
20 Sufficient is a moderate provision with righteousness[7]; and herein is the blessing of the LORD, that *a man* be satisfied in righteousness.
21 They that fear the LORD rejoice in prosperity[8], and thy loving-kindness is upon Israel in thy kingdom.
22 Blessed be the glory of the LORD, for he is our King.

[7] Gr. *unto satisfaction*
[8] Or, *his goodness*

ἐν δικαιοσύνῃ. The 'righteousness' of the true Israelite alone can fill the measure of satisfaction. This 'righteousness' consisted in ἔννομος βίωσις 'living in conformity with the Law.' It was the due performance of duties, cf. Matt. iii. 15 'to fulfil all righteousness' (πληρῶσαι πᾶσαν δικαιοσύνην). Our Lord's ministry was a constant witness against the unspiritual ideal of righteousness set up by the Scribes and Pharisees, e.g. Matt. v. 20 'except your righteousness shall exceed *the righteousness* of the Scribes and Pharisees, ye shall in no wise enter into the kingdom of heaven.' But in the same sermon He recognizes the existence of those whose spiritual yearnings were unsatisfied by the Pharisaic standard of legal performance. 'Blessed are they that hunger and thirst after righteousness (τὴν δικαιοσύνην) for they shall be filled' (Matt. v. 6), where the true satisfaction may be contrasted with the εἰς πλησμονήν of our own verse. Our Lord, like the Pharisee teachers, laid before the people the primary duty of the pursuit of righteousness, 'Seek ye first the kingdom of God and His righteousness.' The difference between His teaching and that of the Pharisees lay in the fundamental conception of 'righteousness,' the Pharisee basing it on obedience to the 'letter,' our Lord on the 'Spirit' of holiness.

The passages in the Gospels where δικαιοσύνη is mentioned are Matt. iii. 15, v. 6, 10, 20, vi. 1(?), 33, xxi. 32; Luke i. 75; John xvi. 8, 10.
It is interesting also to observe how largely St Paul, the Pharisee, deals with the Christian expansion of this Jewish idea of 'righteousness.'

21 εὐφράνθησαν. Fritzsche's emendation εὐφρανθείησαν is very possible; cf. iv. 21 σκορπισθείησαν for σκορπίσθησαν. But the aorist indic. may equally well here state the continuous fact.

οἱ φοβούμενοι κύριον. Cf. ii. 37, iii. 16. The theocratic section of the community. Compare Luke ii. 25 ὁ ἄνθρωπος οὗτος δίκαιος καὶ εὐλαβής.

ἐν ἀγαθοῖς. Considering the context and the subject of the Psalm, we prefer to understand this as an allusion to 'the blessings of prosperity,' as in Ps. cvi. (cvii.) 9 'the hungry soul he filleth with good things,' ψυχὴν πεινῶσαν ἐνέπλησεν ἀγαθῶν (cf. Luke i. 53); Job xxi. 13 συνετέλεσαν δὲ ἐν ἀγαθοῖς τὸν βίον αὐτῶν: so ἀγαθά xvii. 50.
Another possible rendering would be 'in goodness' or 'good deeds,' cf. R.V. in 2 Chron. vi. 41 οἱ υἱοί σου εὐφρανθήτωσαν ἐν ἀγαθοῖς.

ἐπὶ Ἰσραὴλ ἐν τῇ βασιλείᾳ σου. We believe that these two expressions are really intended to be synonymous; for the change of preposition compare xi. 9 ἐπὶ Ἰσραὴλ καὶ ἐν Ἱερουσαλήμ. Israel is thus not a portion of the kingdom, but is the Kingdom of God. The true Israel is coextensive with the Divine Kingdom. 'Thy loving kindness is towards Israel, even Thy Kingdom.' For a description of the Divine Kingdom see Ps. cxlv. 11—13.
It is however quite possible that ἐν τῇ βασιλείᾳ σου may have been used by the translator of our Psalmist, in the sense of ἐν τῷ βασιλεῦσαί σε 'in Thy reign.'

22 εὐλογημένη ἡ δόξα κυρίου. The words are probably taken from Ezek. iii. 12 εὐλογημένη ἡ δόξα κυρίου ἐκ τοῦ τόπου αὐτοῦ.

αὐτὸς βασιλεὺς ἡμῶν. See on xvii. 1, 38, 51.

ϛ΄. ψαλμὸс ἐν ἐλπίδι τῶι caλομών.

VI. Μακάριος ἀνὴρ οὗ ἡ καρδία αὐτοῦ ἑτοίμη ἐπικαλεῖσθαι τὸ ὄνομα κυρίου·
² ἐν τῷ μνημονεύειν αὐτὸν τὸ ὄνομα κυρίου σωθήσεται.
³ αἱ ὁδοὶ αὐτοῦ κατευθύνονται ὑπὸ κυρίου,
καὶ πεφυλαγμένα ἔργα χειρῶν αὐτοῦ ὑπὸ κυρίου θεοῦ αὐτοῦ.
⁴ ἀπὸ ὁράσεων πονηρῶν ἐνυπνίων αὐτοῦ οὐ ταραχθήσεται ἡ ψυχὴ αὐτοῦ,
⁵ ἐν διαβάσει ποταμῶν καὶ σάλων θαλασσῶν οὐ πτοηθήσεται.

Inscript.: ψαλμὸς τῷ Σαλομὼν ἐν ἐλπίδι ϛ΄ A Cerda. Ε΄ ἐν ἐλπίδι τῶι Σαλομὼν (a sinistra parte superscriptum) V, K, P (? om. num.) : deest M.
3 post χειρῶν αὐτοῦ legunt ὑπὸ κυρίου θεοῦ αὐτοῦ K, P, M, om. A, V.
4 ἐνυπνίων A (Cerda). conj. καὶ ἐνυπνίων Hilg. ταραχθήσεται· ἡ ita interpung. Cerd.
5 σαλῶν A: σάλων V, K, P, M, Cerda, Fabr., Geig. σάλῳ conj. Lagarde; ita Hilg. Fritzsch. Pick.

Ps. VI. *Argument*.
A. The Blessing of the Prayerful Man (ver. 1);
In prayer is his salvation; he receives guidance and protection in the affairs of life, he is preserved from mental disquiet, he is upheld in physical peril (2—5).
B. The character of his prayer;
He offers his prayer day by day, in the spirit of constancy and thanksgiving, and omits not intercession for those dependent on him (6, 7).
C. Its answer;
The prayer of the God-fearing man is heard, and so is the request of every soul, whose hope is in the Lord (8).
D. Doxology: the Lord is merciful to those whose love is sincere (9).
There is nothing in the present Psalm, which can be said to reflect in any marked manner the date or position of the writer. It contains no direct allusion to national history, and there are no references to the writer's personal experience.
It is a eulogy on prayer, and, as such, illustrates the importance attached to the performance of personal devotion by the pious Pharisee.
It is interesting to observe how prayer is spoken of as a preservative against superstitious fears (ver. 4).
The prayer of petition is spoken of as certain of receiving its answer; but special prominence is given to its less common aspects, the eucharistic and the intercessory.
The tone of verses 8 and 9 connects it with the religious poetry of the theocratic Jews.
Inscription 'In hope.' This title cannot be said to be very appropriate. It has probably been taken from the words ψυχῆς ἐλπιζούσης in ver. 8.

1 ἑτοίμη. The expression is based upon Ps. lvi. (lvii.) 7 'my heart is fixed' (LXX. ἑτοίμη ἡ καρδία μου) and cxi. (cxii.) 7 'his heart is fixed trusting in the Lord' (ἑτοίμη ἡ καρδία αὐτοῦ ἐλπίζειν ἐπὶ τὸν κύριον).
2 ἐν τῷ μνημονεύειν...τὸ ὄνομα κυρίου. Compare for the sense generally, Ps. xliv. (xlv.) 17 μνησθήσονται (אזכירה) τοῦ ὀνόματός σου: cxviii. (cxix.) 55 ἐμνήσθην (זכרתי)...τὸ ὄνομά σου.
σωθήσεται. The thought is drawn from Joel ii. 32 'And it shall come to pass, that whosoever shall call on the name of the Lord shall be delivered' (LXX. καὶ ἔσται πᾶς ὃς ἂν ἐπικαλέσηται τὸ ὄνομα κυρίου σωθήσεται, quoted by St Peter, Acts ii. 21, and by St Paul, Rom. x. 13).
3 αἱ ὁδοί...κατευθύνονται. Cf. Ps. v. 8 κατεύθυνον ἐνώπιόν σου τὴν ὁδόν μου, xxxvi. (xxxvii.) 23 παρὰ κυρίου τὰ διαβήματα ἀνθρώπου κατευθύνεται, cxviii. (cxix.)

ΨΑΛΜΟΙ ΣΑΛΟΜΩΝΤΟΣ.

PSALM VI.

'In hope.' A Psalm of Solomon.

1 Blessed is the man, whose heart is fixed to call upon the name of the LORD.
2 When he remembereth[1] the name of the LORD, he is[2] saved.
3 His goings are established of the LORD, and the works of his hands are preserved by the LORD his God[3].
4 By the evil visions of his dreams[4] his soul is not disquieted.
5 When he passeth through rivers, yea, through the surge of the seas, he is not affrighted.

[1] Or, *maketh mention of*
[2] Gr. *shall be*
[3] Some MSS. omit
[4] Or, *by evil visions and dreams*

---

5 ὄφελον κατευθυνθείησαν αἱ ὁδοί μου τοῦ φυλάξασθαι τὰ δικαιώματά σου.

πεφυλαγμένα ἔργα χειρῶν. The Psalmist has expanded the thought of Ps. lxxxix. (xc.) 17 καὶ τὰ ἔργα τῶν χειρῶν ἡμῶν κατεύθυνον ἐφ' ἡμᾶς, which contains the phrases of both clauses in this verse.

4 ἀπὸ ὁράσεων πονηρῶν ἐνυπνίων. The expression ὄρασις ἐνυπνίου is familiar from Dan. iv. 6 ἄκουσον τὴν ὅρασιν τοῦ ἐνυπνίου μου, Ecclus. xxxi. (xxxiv.) 3 τοῦτο κατὰ τοῦτο ὅρασις ἐνυπνίων, upon the analogy of which we should here expect ἀπὸ ὁράσεως πονηρῶν ἐνυπνίων.

On the other hand we find in the O.T. the use of 'the vision' side by side with, but distinct from, 'the dream.' Thus Job vii. 14 'Then thou scarest me with dreams, and terrifiest me through visions' (ἐκφοβεῖς με ἐνυπνίοις καὶ ὁράμασί με καταπλήσσεις). xxxiii. 15 'In a dream, in a vision of the night' (ἐνύπνιον ἢ ἐν μελέτῃ νυκτερινῇ). Dan. i. 17 'Daniel had understanding in all visions and dreams' (Δανιὴλ συνῆκεν ἐν πάσῃ ὁράσει καὶ ἐνυπνίοις). On the analogy of these expressions we should expect to find ἀπὸ ὁράσεων πονηρῶν καὶ ἐνυπνίων.

There are therefore three ways of rendering the words:

(a) By the evil visions of his dreams.
(b) By the visions of his evil dreams.
(c) By evil visions (and) by his dreams (subaud. καί).

It is possible that the two words in conjunction may indicate a double rendering of the original or the insertion of an explanatory gloss ἐνυπνίων. For the apparently otiose addition of a qualifying genitive cf. iv. 20 ἀτεκνίας, v. 18 αὐταρκεσίας, xi. 1 σημασίας.

οὐ ταραχθήσεται. Cf. Ps. cxi. (cxii.) 7 ἀπὸ ἀκοῆς πονηρᾶς οὐ φοβηθήσεται: the same passage is quoted in ver. 1.

5 ἐν διαβάσει ποταμῶν καὶ σάλων θαλασσῶν. The reading of the MSS. is probably correct, although the language is certainly unusual. Lagarde's conjecture σάλῳ gives a good sense, and the possibility of an error by the addition of ν to a word standing between ποταμῶν and θαλασσῶν is obvious. But there is no absolute need for alteration; and σάλῳ is not parallel to διαβάσει.

We might conjecture that σάλων represents a wrongly written θαλασσῶν in some early copy, and that the erasure not having been noticed, both words were reproduced in subsequent transcripts. Again, it is not impossible that θαλασσῶν may be a gloss on σάλων, which has found its way into the text. But though σάλων is almost uncommon enough to be glossed, we cannot at present point to any other plain instance of a gloss in our book. Hesychius explains it by ἡ τῆς θαλάσσης κλύδωνος κίνησις. We are inclined, therefore, to give the benefit of the doubt in favour of the MS. text, and so to treat σάλων θαλασσῶν as coordinate with ποταμῶν. The sense then is 'when he crosses rivers and passes through angry seas.'

ἐν διαβάσει ποταμῶν is based upon Isai. xliii. 2 'When thou passest through the waters I will be with thee' (ἐὰν διαβαίνῃς δι' ὕδατος).

For σάλων θαλασσῶν compare Ps. lxxxviii. (lxxxix.) 10 καὶ τὸν σάλον τῶν κυμάτων αὐτῆς (בְּשׂוֹא גַלָּיו) σὺ καταπραΰνεις; Jon. i. 15 καὶ ἔστη ἡ θάλασσα ἐκ τοῦ σάλου αὐτῆς (מִזַּעְפּוֹ). As a translation of סוּד σάλος occurs in Ps. liv. (lv.) 22, lxv. (lxvi.) 9, cxx. (cxxi.) 3; Isai. xxiv. 20.

J. P.

66 ΨΑΛΜΟΙ ΣΑΛΟΜΩΝΤΟΣ. [VI. 6

⁶ ἐξανέστη ἐξ ὕπνου αὐτοῦ,
καὶ εὐλόγησε τὸ ὄνομα κυρίου.
⁷ ἐπ' εὐσταθείᾳ καρδίας αὐτοῦ ἐξύμνησε τὸ ὄνομα τοῦ θεοῦ αὐτοῦ,
καὶ ἐδεήθη τοῦ προσώπου κυρίου περὶ παντὸς τοῦ οἴκου αὐτοῦ·
⁸ καὶ κύριος εἰσήκουσε προσευχὴν παντὸς ἐν φόβῳ θεοῦ,
καὶ πᾶν αἴτημα ψυχῆς ἐλπιζούσης πρὸς αὐτὸν ἐπιτελεῖ κύριος.
⁹ εὐλογητὸς κύριος ὁ ποιῶν ἔλεον τοῖς ἀγαπῶσιν αὐτὸν ἐν ἀληθείᾳ.

Ζ. ψαλμὸς τῶι Σαλομὼν ἐπιστροφῆς.

VII. Μὴ ἀποσκηνώσῃς ἀφ' ἡμῶν, ὁ θεός,
ἵνα μὴ ἐπιθῶνται ἡμῖν οἱ μισήσαντες ἡμᾶς δωρεάν·

7 εὐσταθίᾳ P, M.
9 εὐλογήτω A, Cerda, Fabr. (*benedicatur*, cf. v. 1).
Inscriptio: ψαλμὸς τῷ Σαλομὼν ἐπιστροφῆς ζ' A, Cerda (ϛ' ἐπιστροφῆς Fabr.): τῶι Σαλομὼν ἐπιστροφῆς K, P (K habet ϛ' a sinistra parte scriptum): V, ut Hilg. refert, 'ψαλμός, sed a sinistra parte superscriptum est ϛ' τῶι σαλομὼν ἐπιστροφῆς.'

It is also the rendering of רַעַשׁ in Sym. Job xxxix. 24, in Theodot. Ezek. xii. 18, of רָגְזָה in Sym. Ezek. xii. 18, and of וְיָנַע in Sym. Jer. xv. 4, and perhaps of נָפְלָם in Aq. Jer. xlix. 21 (xxix. 22).

οὐ πτοηθήσεται. Cf. Job xi. 15 οὐ πτοηθήσῃ.
We cannot see much probability in the suggestion that ποταμοί and σάλος θαλασσῶν contain an allusion to 'the flood' of the Roman power passing over Syria. The Psalmist is speaking of the ordinary dangers of travel in the East, and there is no reason to suppose that he is employing metaphor. Geiger understands the passage of floods and rivers as occurring in the righteous man's bad dreams: but this interpretation partakes, to our mind, of the grotesque.

6 ἐξανέστη...εὐλόγησε. The aorist represents the quick succession of acts. Cf. Aq. Sym. Isai. xxix. 8 ἐξυπνίσθη καὶ κενὴ ἡ ψυχὴ αὐτοῦ. Jas. i. 24.

7 ἐπ' εὐσταθείᾳ καρδίας αὐτοῦ. Cf. εὐστάθεια in iv. 11. The idea of the word is 'stability.' It is found in Wisd. iv. 26 βασιλεὺς φρόνιμος εὐστάθεια δήμου. 2 Macc. xiv. 6 οὐκ ἐώντες τὴν βασιλείαν εὐσταθείας τυχεῖν. The verb εὐσταθέω occurs in Jer. xlix. (xxx.) 31 ἀνάβηθι ἐπ' ἔθνος εὐσταθοῦν (v. l. ἡσύχαζον) 'unto a nation that is at ease' (שַׁלְיו). Sym. Jer. xlvii. (xxix.) 27 εὐσταθήσει (וְשַׁאֲנַן); and in 2 Macc. xii. 2 οὐκ εἴων αὐτοὺς εὐσταθεῖν. xiv. 25 ἐγάμησεν, εὐστάθησεν. The adjective εὐσταθής is found in Ecclus. xxvi. 18 καὶ πόδες ὡραῖοι ἐπὶ στέρνοις εὐσταθοῦς, where the text is very doubtful.

This is one of the words occurring also in the Book of Wisdom which Hilgenfeld adduces for his strange argument in behalf of the Greek original for this book. But the fact that εὐστάθεια occurs in Wisdom once, and twice in Ps. S. in a very different context, does not advance his theory. See Introd.

ἐδεήθη τοῦ προσώπου κυρίου. Cf. on ii. 24.

περὶ παντὸς τοῦ οἴκου αὐτοῦ. Compare 'the righteous man' in iv. 8. The present passage representing 'the holy man' offering up intercession for the members of his household is clearly based on Job i. 5.

VII. 1]   ΨΑΛΜΟΙ ΣΑΛΟΜΩΝΤΟΣ.   67

6 He riseth up from his sleep, and blesseth the name of the LORD.
7 In the steadfastness of his heart he singeth praise unto the name of his God, and intreateth the favour of the LORD for all his house.
8 And the LORD hearkeneth unto the prayer of every one that feareth[5] God: and every request of the soul that trusteth in him doth the LORD perform.
9 Blessed is the LORD that showeth mercy unto them that love him in truth.

[5] Or, *that prayeth in the fear of*

PSALM VII.

A Psalm of Solomon. '*Of restoration.*'

1 Remove not thy habitation from us, O God, lest they fall upon us that hate us without a cause:

---

8 παντὸς ἐν φόβῳ θεοῦ. This we take to be equivalent, in the style of our translator, to παντὸς φοβουμένου θεὸν or τοῦ ἐν φόβῳ θεοῦ. For other instances of the substantive with ἐν used as an adjective or participle compare iv. 11 ἀνδρὸς ἐν εὐσταθείᾳ=ἀνδρὸς εὐσταθοῦντος: viii. 20 ἀρνία ἐν ἀκακίᾳ=ἀρνία ἄκακα: ix. 12 ψυχὴν ἐν ἐξομολογήσει=ψυχὴν ἐξομολογουμένην: x. 5 ἡ μαρτυρία ἐν νόμῳ for ἡ μαρτυρία ἡ ἐν νόμῳ: xvi. 3 τῷ ἐλέει αὐτοῦ εἰς τὸν αἰῶνα for τῷ ἐλέει αὐτοῦ τῷ εἰς τὸν αἰῶνα or τῷ αἰωνίῳ.

For ἐν φόβῳ compare Apoc. Bar. xlvi. 'et subjaceatis illis qui in timore sunt sapientes et intelligentes.'

πᾶν αἴτημα. Compare Ps. xix. (xx.) 5 πληρώσαι κύριος πάντα τὰ αἰτήματά σου.

ἐλπιζούσης πρὸς αὐτόν. The title of the Psalm is very probably based upon this mention of 'the hoping' soul. The construction of ἐλπίζειν πρὸς is very unusual. The prepositions ἐν, ἐπί, εἰς are all frequently found with ἐλπίζειν in LXX. and N.T. Greek. But we do not know of an instance where πρὸς is used with this verb. For other grammatical anomalies cf. iv. 25, xvii. 14.

ἐπιτελεῖ. For ἐπιτελεῖν used of Divine completion cf. 1 Sam. iii. 12 ἄρξομαι καὶ ἐπιτελέσω: Phil. i. 6 ὁ ἐναρξάμενος...ἔργον ἀγαθὸν ἐπιτελέσει.

9 εὐλογητός. Cf. ii. 41. The Augsburg MS. apparently had the Imperat. εὐλογήτω [*sic*] for εὐλογείσθω. εὐλογητός used of God in the last verse of the Psalm, corresponds to μακάριος used of man in the first verse.

τοῖς ἀγαπῶσιν...ἐν ἀληθείᾳ. On ἀγαπᾶν cf. iv. 29. ἀγαπᾶν ἐν ἀληθείᾳ cf. 2 John 1 οὓς ἐγὼ ἀγαπῶ ἐν ἀληθείᾳ: 3 John 1 ὃν ἐγὼ ἀγαπῶ ἐν ἀληθείᾳ.

ἐν ἀληθείᾳ. For this phrase defining the character of the love towards God, compare ii. 36 οἱ φοβούμενοι τὸν κύριον ἐν ἐπιστήμῃ: iv. 20 οἱ φοβούμενοι τὸν κύριον ἐν ἀκακίᾳ αὐτῶν.

It occurs again in xiv. 1, and may be illustrated by Tobit xiv. 7 μνημονεύοντες τοῦ θεοῦ ἐν ἀληθείᾳ.

The Psalmist contrasts the sincere love of the pious Jew with the pretence of the worldly Sadducee.

It is interesting to compare with the praise here given to sincere love of God, the passage in the Gospels, where the Scribe, who belonged probably to the Pharisees, asserted that sincere love was more essential than all whole burnt offerings and sacrifices. See Mark xii. 32—34.

The Pharisees, joining with the Herodians, begin their temptation of the LORD by flattering His sincerity. διδάσκαλε οἴδαμεν ὅτι ἀληθὴς εἶ καὶ τὴν ὁδὸν τοῦ θεοῦ ἐν ἀληθείᾳ διδάσκεις (Matt. xxii. 16).

Ps. VII. *Argument.*

The Psalm falls into two marked divisions, Israel's peril and Israel's security.

A. Israel's Peril, 1—4.

(1) A prayer that the Divine presence should not be withdrawn, lest heathen enemies take possession of Zion (1, 2).

(2) Israel will submit to the chastening

5—2

² ὅτι ἀπώσω αὐτούς, ὁ θεός·
μὴ πατησάτω ὁ ποῦς αὐτῶν κληρονομίαν ἁγιάσματός σου.

of the LORD; for He is merciful: but prays not to be given over to the hands of men, who have no mercy and would utterly destroy (3, 4).

B. Israel's Security.

(1) The presence of God is an assurance of mercy, and the hope of defence (5—7).

(2) He will chasten and correct Israel, but not in anger (8).

(3) For when He turns and takes pity upon Israel, He will establish them according to His promise (9).

Owing to the obscurity of the allusions in this Psalm, it is impossible to determine with any certainty the date at which it was composed.

According to Geiger it was written while Pompey was laying siege to the Temple of Jerusalem.

Wellhausen supposes that the events referred to are the attack on Antigonus and the siege of Jerusalem by Sosius and Herod. His opinion is that the theocratic fervour, which this Psalm breathes, is not found in the two Psalms (ii., viii.), which undoubtedly refer to Pompey's capture of Jerusalem and investment of the Temple; and that on the other hand it corresponds to the description of Josephus, *Ant.* XIV. 16. 2 μετὰ πολλῆς δὲ προθυμίας καὶ ἔριδος, ἅτε σύμπαντος ἠθροισμένου τοῦ ἔθνους, οἱ Ἰουδαῖοι τοῖς περὶ τὸν Ἡρώδην ἀντεπολέμουν, καταλειφθέντες ἐντὸς τοῦ τείχους, πολλά τε ἐφήμιζον περὶ τὸ ἱερὸν καὶ πολλὰ ἐπ' εὐφημίᾳ τοῦ δήμου ὡς ῥυσομένου τῶν κινδύνων αὐτοὺς τοῦ θεοῦ.

Wellhausen's reasons are not however in this instance very convincing. It is true that Pompey was received within the walls of Jerusalem with the consent of the citizens (cf. viii. 15—22). But the severity of his measures during and after the siege seem to have filled the writers of both Psalms (ii., viii.) with terror and indignation. The allusion to the honour of the Temple in our Psalm (ver. 2) corresponds to ii. 2, 5, 21; and verses 3, 4 may well refer to the massacre of Jewish citizens described in viii. 23, and implied in ii. 25, 26. The fervour of such passages as ii. 30—35 or viii. 7—14 cannot be said to be less than that which we find here.

It is also an objection to Wellhausen's theory that the writer contemplates the crisis as in the past. Now, if Sosius' attack is intended, he had been already victorious; Herod had been made king; and the last prince of the Asmonean House had been made prisoner and doomed to death. Surely, if the writer had referred to such a period, the fall of the Asmonean dynasty and the rise of the Idumean king would not have been passed over in silence.

What then is the situation described in this Psalm? The 1st pers. plural personal pronoun is found in each verse. The Psalmist speaks in the name of the true sons of Israel, the true house of Jacob (vv. 8, 9). The peril apprehended in the first part of the Psalm (1—4) has passed away, when we come to the second part (5—9). In this concluding portion Israel is still represented as 'under the rod of chastening' (ver. 8); but God's presence is still with Israel, He hears, defends, and will help in His appointed time (ver. 9).

The peril which had menaced Israel had come from those who hated Israel without a cause (ver. 1), from those whom God had cast aside (ver. 2). The writer had feared lest the holy Temple (or city) should utterly fall into their hands (vv. 2—6); and had prayed that God would not deliver the people into the hands of the heathen (ver. 3). Let God, he says, rather scourge us with a pestilence; then shall we fall into the hands of a merciful God, as David of old. Let us not be given over to our enemies, who will utterly consume us. The prayer had been heard, the peril averted, and, though chastened, Israel hoped in her God.

It may be fairly questioned whether those 'who hated Israel without cause, whom God cast off' are to be identified with 'the heathen' of ver. 3. We would hazard the suggestion that ἔθνεσιν in ver. 3 refers to the Romans, and that οἱ μισήσαντες ἡμᾶς δωρεὰν...ἀπώσω αὐτοὺς (vv. 1, 2) describe the High Priest's party, the Sadducees, who hated their countrymen the Pharisees, and were themselves, in the writer's opinion, rejected of God for having usurped the sacred offices.

The recent invasion of Pompey is, we believe, the occasion of the Psalm. The hostility of the Sadducees and the power of the Romans were the immediate cause

2 *Nay,* as for them whom thou hast cast off, O God, let not their foot tread the inheritance of thy sanctuary.

of alarm. But the danger is over. Pompey had not destroyed "their place and nation." The pious Jews may look for the accomplishment of a still greater deliverance, when the necessary chastisement for sin is overpast.

Inscription. Literally 'of turning,' either transitively in the sense of 'restoration' (cf. ἐπιστρέφω in v. 9), or intransitively in the sense of 'conversion' as in xvi. 11 εἰς ἐπιστροφήν (cf. ἐπιστρέφω Luke xxii. 32). In the former alternative it would be an ἐπιστροφὴ θεοῦ, in the latter an ἐπιστροφὴ Ἰσραήλ. See the title τῆς ἐπιστροφῆς Ἀγγαίου καὶ Ζαχαρίου of Ps. cxi. (cxii.). The general sense of the Psalm, and especially the concluding verse, favour the former view, which is supported by the use of ἐπιστρέφω in v. 9.

1 Μὴ ἀποσκηνώσῃς. In the parallelism of the two portions of this Psalm, these words find their counterpart in ver. 5 ἐν τῷ κατασκηνοῦν τὸ ὄνομά σου.

The withdrawal of Divine favour from Israel is expressed under the image of Jehovah's departure from Zion.

Cf. Ps. xxxvii. (xxxviii.) 21 μὴ ἐνκαταλίπῃς με, κύριε· ὁ θεός μου, μὴ ἀποστῇς ἀπ' ἐμοῦ.

ἀφ' ἡμῶν. The pronoun ἡμεῖς occurs *twelve* times in this Psalm, and σύ *thirteen* times.

ἐπιθῶνται ἡμῖν. Cf. i. 1, ix. 16.

οἱ μισήσαντες ἡμᾶς δωρεάν. The phrase μισεῖν δωρεάν is based on Ps. xxxiv. (xxxv.) 19 μὴ ἐπιχαρείησάν μοι οἱ ἐχθραίνοντές μοι ματαίως, οἱ μισοῦντές με δωρεάν (אֹיְבַי שֶׁקֶר) quoted in John xv. 25. A very similar expression occurs in Ps. xxxvii. (xxxviii.) 19 ἐπληθύνθησαν οἱ μισοῦντές με ἀδίκως (שֹׂנְאַי שֶׁקֶר), and as the first clause in our verse recalls Ps. xxxvii. (xxxviii.) 22, it is very possible that our Psalmist here recurs in thought to the same Psalm. If so, the translator has shown his independence of the LXX. version by the use of the word δωρεάν instead of ἀδίκως.

The Hebrew שֶׁקֶר 'wrongfully,' 'falsely,' occurs in both the above passages in the sense of 'without justification,' '*immerito*,' and can thus be represented by δωρεάν 'gratuitously' '*gratis*,' which generally renders חִנָּם e.g. 1 Sam. xix. 5, xxv. 31; 1 Kings ii. 31; Ps. xxxiv. (xxxv.).

7; Aq. Job ii. 3; Aq. Sym. Th. Prov. xxiii. 29, xxvi. 2.

The Psalmist either refers to the Gentiles or, as appears to us more probable, those of his own countrymen, i.e. the Sadducees, who were opposed to the theocratic party.

2 ὅτι ἀπώσω. If the Gentiles generally are intended, the writer speaks of them as 'cast off' or 'rejected by God' in contrast to the Israelites, whom God had chosen to be His own people.

If the Sadducees are intended, the passage implies that the High Priest and his family were virtually rejected by God for having wrongfully usurped possession of the Holy Place. Cf. xvii. 6—8.

The explanation of the words ὅτι ἀπώσω αὐτούς is not quite obvious. We may safely assume that ὅτι translates the Hebrew כִּי. If this conjunction occurs in a causative sense 'seeing that,' 'because' (= ὅτι), μὴ πατησάτω will give the result of the argument, 'therefore let not &c.' But כִּי is also used in an adversative sense equivalent to 'minime vero,' 'nay but,' generally after a negative in the preceding clause.

Both renderings of כִּי are possible in this passage; the translator by his rendering ὅτι selected the one which was more usual and obvious, but far less forcible. The terseness and abruptness of the clauses, given by the adversative rendering of כִּי would have been much more appropriate to words of strong emotion. The sense then of the original was, we believe, 'Nay but thou surely hast rejected them! let not then their foot tread the Holy Ground.'

Instances are frequent in the LXX. where this shade of meaning in the conjunction כִּי has been obscured by the rendering ὅτι, e.g. Job xxxi. 18 'Nay, from my youth he grew up' (ὅτι ἐκ νεότητός μου ἐξέτρεφον); Ps. xliii. (xliv.) 22 'Yea, for thy sake we are killed' (ὅτι ἕνεκα σοῦ θανατούμεθα); cxxix. (cxxx.) 4 'But there is forgiveness with thee' (ὅτι παρὰ σοὶ ὁ ἱλασμός ἐστιν).

For ἀπώσω cf. Ps. xlii. (xliii.) 2 ἵνα τί ἀπώσω με; xliii. (xliv.) 9 νυνὶ δὲ ἀπώσω καὶ κατῄσχυνας ἡμᾶς, lxxiii. (lxxiv.) 1 ἵνα τί ἀπώσω, ὁ θεός, εἰς τέλος;

μὴ πατησάτω ὁ ποῦς αὐτῶν. Cf. viii.

ΨΑΛΜΟΙ ΣΑΛΟΜΩΝΤΟΣ. [VII. 3

³ σὺ ἐν θελήματί σου παίδευσον ἡμᾶς,
καὶ μὴ δῷς ἔθνεσιν.
⁴ ἐὰν γὰρ ἀποστείλῃς θάνατον,
σὺ ἐντελῆι αὐτῷ περὶ ἡμῶν·
ὅτι σὺ ἐλεήμων,
καὶ οὐκ ὀργισθήσῃ τοῦ συντελέσαι ἡμᾶς.
⁵ Ἐν τῷ κατασκηνοῦν τὸ ὄνομά σου ἐν μέσῳ ἡμῶν
ἐλεηθησόμεθα,
⁶ καὶ οὐκ ἰσχύσει πρὸς ἡμᾶς ἔθνος,
ὅτι σὺ ὑπερασπιστὴς ἡμῶν.
⁷ καὶ ἡμεῖς ἐπικαλεσόμεθά σε,
καὶ σὺ ἐπακούσῃ ἡμῶν·
⁸ ὅτι σὺ οἰκτειρήσεις τὸ γένος Ἰσραὴλ εἰς τὸν αἰῶνα,
καὶ οὐκ ἀπώσῃ.
καὶ ἡμεῖς ὑπὸ ζυγόν σου τὸν αἰῶνα,
καὶ [ὑπὸ] μάστιγα παιδείας σου.

4 σὺ ἐντελῆ V, K, -ῇ P, M (ita Hilg. conj., Fritzsch. σὺ ἐντελεῖ) : σὺν ἐντολῇ A, Cerda, Fabr. Geig. (? Wellh.).
8 οἰκτειρήσεις K, P, M, Hilg. Geig. Fritzsch. Pick., οἰκτηρήσεις A, V, Cerda, Fabr.
σου τὸν αἰῶνα (om. εἰς) A, V, K, M, Cerda, Hilg. Geig., σου εἰς τὸν αἰῶνα P, Fabr. Fritzsch. Pick.
καὶ μάστιγα (om. ὑπὸ) Codd. : ὑπὸ μάστιγα conjec. Lagarde, Fritzsch. Pick.

---

13 ἐπάτουν τὸ θυσιαστήριον κυρίου. If the Gentiles are referred to, πατεῖν is used in the sense of καταπατεῖν 'to trample under foot,' as in ii. 2 ἀνέβησαν ἐπὶ τὰ θυσιαστήριόν σου ἔθνη ἀλλότρια, κατεπάτουν.
But supposing, as we prefer to do, that the Sadducees are referred to, then we see the reason of πατεῖν being used rather than καταπατεῖν : it will denote the habitual tread of the Priests in the courts of the Sanctuary, not the downtreading by the heathen. It seems to be used in this way in viii. 13, and may best be illustrated by Isai. i. 12 τίς γὰρ ἐξεζήτησε ταῦτα ἐκ τῶν χειρῶν ὑμῶν; πατεῖν τὴν αὐλήν μου κ.τ.λ., xxvi. 6 καὶ πατήσουσιν αὐτοὺς πόδες πραέων καὶ ταπεινῶν, where πατεῖν renders רמס.
The Psalmist denounces the men, who, having illegally usurped the highest offices, polluted the sacred place by their constant presence.
κληρονομίαν ἁγιάσματός σου. Cf. Ps. lxxviii. (lxxix.) 1 ὁ θεός, ἤλθοσαν ἔθνη εἰς τὴν κληρονομίαν σου, ἐμίαναν τὸν ναὸν τὸν ἅγιόν σου.
The expression κληρονομία ἁγιάσματος does not occur in the LXX., but we may compare τόπος ἁγιάσματος (Ezr. ix. 8; 1 Esd. viii. 80) ; πόλις ἁγιάσματος (Ecclus. xxxvi. 12, xlix. 7); ὄρος ἁγιάσματος Ps. lxxvii. (lxxviii.) 54.
The allusion here is to the Temple.
3 ἐν θελήματί σου παίδευσον ἡμᾶς. For the Divine θέλημα cf. Ps. xxix. (xxx.) 5 ζωὴ ἐν τῷ θελήματι αὐτοῦ, 7 κύριε, ἐν τῷ θελήματί σου παράσχου τῷ κάλλει μου δύναμιν. The best comment on the words is afforded by Jer. x. 24 παίδευσον ἡμᾶς κύριε πλὴν ἐν κρίσει καὶ μὴ ἐν θυμῷ ἵνα μὴ ὀλίγους ἡμᾶς ποιήσῃς.
But the thought both of this and the following verse is drawn from 2 Sam. xxiv. 14. There is the same avowal of sin, and the same readiness to submit to any chastisement inflicted by the Lord rather than to suffer from the cruel vengeance of a human foe. Compare 4 Esdr. v. 30 'Et si odiens odisti populum tuum, tuis manibus debet castigari'; Ecclus. ii.

ΨΑΛΜΟΙ ΣΑΛΟΜΩΝΤΟΣ.

3 Do thou chasten us in thy good pleasure, but give us not over to the Gentiles.
4 For if thou sendest pestilence, thou wilt give charge to it concerning us, for thou art merciful, and wilt not be angry *with us* to consume us altogether.
5 Whilst thy name doth dwell in our midst, we shall find mercy,
6 And no nation shall prevail against us, seeing that thou art our defence.
7 When we call upon thee, thou wilt hearken unto us,
8 For thou wilt have pity for evermore on the house of Israel, and wilt not cast *them* off.
And as for us, we are beneath thy yoke for evermore, and *beneath* the rod of thy chastening.

18 ἐμπεσούμεθα εἰς χεῖρας κυρίου καὶ οὐκ εἰς χεῖρας ἀνθρώπων.
ἔθνεσιν. The Romans are probably referred to.
4 ἐὰν...ἀποστείλῃς θάνατον. θάνατος here represents דֶּבֶר 'pestilence,' as in Lev. xxvi. 25 ἐξαποστελῶ θάνατον. Jer. xxi. 6, Ezek. vi. 12 (θανάτῳ = Aq. Sym. λοιμῷ). xii. 16, xiv. 19. Amos iv. 10. 2 Chr. vii. 13.
σὺ ἐντελῇ. This is probably the right reading; Hilgenfeld's conjecture is confirmed by the Copenhagen and Paris MSS. The cause of the various reading was probably an error in transcription; the medial ε of εντελη having been accidentally changed to ο, συ before εντολη was changed to σὺν. Compare cγεΝΤΕΛΗΙ with cγΝΕΝΤΟΛΗΙ.
For the Greek phrase compare Ps. xc. (xci.) 11 ὅτι τοῖς ἀγγέλοις αὐτοῦ ἐντελεῖται περὶ σοῦ.
οὐκ ὀργισθήσῃ τοῦ συντελέσαι ἡμᾶς. A comparison with ii. 26, καὶ συντελεσθήσονται, ἐὰν μὴ σύ, κύριε, ἐπιτιμήσῃς αὐτοῖς ἐν ὀργῇ σου, gives the contrast between the Divine wrath and the ferocity of human foes.
For the meaning cf. Lev. xxvi. 44 'neither will I abhor them to destroy them utterly.' Baruch iv. 6 ἐπράθητε τοῖς ἔθνεσιν οὐκ εἰς ἀπώλειαν.
For τοῦ συντελέσαι see Ezek. xxii. 31 ἐξέχεα ἐπ' αὐτὴν θυμόν μου ἐν πυρὶ ὀργῆς μου τοῦ συντελέσαι.
5 Ἐν τῷ κατασκηνοῦν τὸ ὄνομά σου. κατασκηνόω is here used intransitively, cf. Ezek. xliii. 7 ἐν οἷς κατασκηνώσῃ τὸ ὄνομά μου ἐν μέσῳ οἴκου Ἰσραὴλ τὸν αἰῶνα, 9 κατασκηνώσω ἐν μέσῳ αὐτῶν τὸν αἰῶνα.

For instances of the transitive use 'cause to dwell,' see Jer. vii. 12; Neh. i. 9.
6 ἰσχύσει πρὸς ἡμᾶς, 'prevail against,' cf. xvii. 44. See Ps. xii. (xiii.) 4 μή ποτε εἴπῃ ὁ ἐχθρός μου Ἴσχυσα πρὸς αὐτόν. Dan. vii. 21 τὸ κέρας ἐκεῖνο ἐποίει πόλεμον μετὰ τῶν ἁγίων καὶ ἴσχυσε πρὸς αὐτούς. 2 Chron. xiv. 11 μὴ κατισχυσάτω πρὸς σὲ ἄνθρωπος.
ὑπερασπιστής, a common word in the LXX., e.g. Ps. xxvii. (xxviii.) 7 κύριος βοηθός μου καὶ ὑπερασπιστής μου (מָגִנִּי). xxx. (xxxi.) 2 γενοῦ μοι εἰς θεὸν ὑπερασπιστήν (לְצוּר מָעוֹז). lxxxiii. (lxxxiv.) 9 ὑπερασπιστὰ ἡμῶν (מָגִנֵּנוּ) ἴδε ὁ θεός.
7 καὶ ἡμεῖς...καὶ σύ. The two co-ordinate clauses beginning with καί probably reproduce the Hebrew idiom of the tenses, = when we...then thou &c., cf. viii. 35.
The thought is based upon Solomon's prayer at the dedication of the Temple, 1 Kings viii. 30 &c.
8 τὸ γένος Ἰσραήλ. Wellhausen's 'des Namens Israel' is presumably a misprint for 'des Samens Israel.'
For τὸ γένος Ἰσρ. = 'the seed of Israel,' instead of τὸ σπέρμα Ἰσρ., see Jer. xxxviii. (xxxi.) 36 καὶ τὸ γένος Ἰσραὴλ (זרע ישראל) παύσεται γενέσθαι.
οὐκ ἀπώσῃ. See on ver. 2.
ὑπὸ ζυγόν σου. Cf. xvii. 32. These words of the Psalmist 'we are beneath thy yoke for evermore' deserve especial attention. The metaphor of the yoke is not found in the O.T. with the possible exception of Lam. iii. 27 'It is good for a man that he bear the yoke in his youth.'

⁹ κατευθυνεῖς ἡμᾶς ἐν καιρῷ ἀντιλήψεώς σου,
τοῦ ἐλεῆσαι τὸν οἶκον Ἰακὼβ εἰς ἡμέραν ἐν ᾗ ἐπηγγείλω
αὐτοῖς.

H. ψαλμὸς τῶι cαλομὼν εἰc νῖκοc.

VIII. Θλῖψιν καὶ φωνὴν πολέμου ἤκουcε τὸ οὖς μου,
φωνὴν cάλπιγγοc ἠχούσης σφαγὴν καὶ ὄλεθρον·

9 κατευθύνεις Codd., Cerda, Fabr. (*diriges*), Geig.: κατευθυνεῖς Lagarde, Hilg. Fritzsch. Pick.
ἐπηγγείλω V, K, P, M: ἐπαγγείλω (? A) Cerda.
Inscriptio: ψαλμὸς τῷ Σαλομών εἰς νίκας η' A, ψ. τ. Σαλ. εἰς νῖκος ζ' V, P, ζ' ψαλμ. τ. Σ. εἰς νῖκος K.

The present passage therefore offers the only certain instance in Jewish literature previous to our Lord's time, in which 'the yoke' is employed as a metaphor for the service of Jehovah.

Our Lord's words 'Take my yoke upon you, and learn of me, &c....For my yoke is easy' (Matt. xi. 29), with which we naturally illustrate our passage, suggest two things, (1) that the metaphor was a proverbial one, (2) that He contrasts His yoke with some other yoke that the Jews were familiar with. For both these observations we find remarkable confirmation. The 'yoke' seems to have been a metaphor especially applied to the service of the Law at least as early as the Christian era. Thus we find in Pirqe Aboth iii. 8 (ed. Taylor) 'R. Nechonyiah ben ha-Qanah said, Whoso receives upon him the yoke of Thorah, they remove from him the yoke of royalty (i.e. burden of taxation) and the yoke of worldly care; and whoso breaks from him the yoke of Thorah, they lay upon him the yoke of royalty and the yoke of worldly care.' The yoke of Thorah clearly here means devoted study of, and attention to, the Mosaic Law.

A similar use of this metaphor for the Jewish law appears in Apoc. Bar. xli. 3 'quia ecce video multos ex populo tuo, qui recesserunt a sponsionibus tuis et projecerunt a se *jugum legis tuae*.' The Apostle St Peter therefore makes use of an almost technical term, when he warns the first Christians not to impose the yoke of the Jewish law upon Gentile converts. Acts xv. 10 'Now therefore why tempt ye God, that ye should put a yoke upon the neck of the disciples, which neither our fathers nor we were able to bear?' St Paul too employs the same metaphor when he reproaches the Galatian Church with their relapse into Judaism, Gal. v. 1 'be not entangled again in a yoke of bondage.'

These passages show that our Lord in Matt. xi. 29, 30 contrasted the service which He offered with the burden of minute legal observance—the yoke, as it was proverbially called—which the Scribes and Pharisees laid upon the people. It is of this yoke that the Pharisee writer of our Psalm is speaking. He claims with pride that the true Israelites are under God's yoke; that yoke is His Law, and under it stands every Jew that fears God.

Schöttgen (*Hor. Hebr.* I. 115—120) quotes other Jewish uses of this metaphor from Rabbinical and Talmudic literature, e.g. 'The yoke of God' Schemoth Rabba 30, fol. 1272. 'Because the ten tribes refused to bear the yoke of God, came Sennacherib on them.' Yalkut Ruben fol. 30, 1. 'The 'Massa' or burden of Agur (Prov. xxx. 1) is so called because he took or bore on himself the yoke of God.' 'The yoke of the kingdom of heaven.' In Berachoth fol. 10. 2 it is said of the man who eats before asking a blessing 'after that he has vaunted himself, he taketh upon him the yoke of the kingdom of heaven.' Cf. 'The yoke of precept,' Berachoth fol. 13. 1. 'Why in the Prayers do the words 'Hear, O Israel,' precede the words 'And it shall be if thou hearkenest, &c.'? Ans. 'Because a man first receives the kingdom of heaven, and afterwards the yoke of the precept.' Targ. in Thren. iii. 17 'It is good for a man that he accustom himself to bear the yoke of precepts in his youth.'

τὸν αἰῶνα for εἰς τὸν αἰῶνα. Cf. Ezek. xliii. 9.

VIII. 1]   ΨΑΛΜΟΙ ΣΑΛΟΜΩΝΤΟΣ.   73

9 Thou wilt establish¹ us in the time appointed, when thou shalt succour us; *and shalt*² have mercy upon the house of Jacob on the day wherein thou didst promise them *help*.

¹ Gr. direct
² Gr. to

PSALM VIII.

A Psalm of Solomon: For the chief Musician.

1 Distress and the sound of war hath my ear heard, the sound of a trumpet proclaiming slaughter and destruction!

καὶ [ὑπὸ] μάστιγα παιδείας σου. If the clause literally reproduces the original, we must clearly supply ὑπὸ before μάστιγα and preserve the parallelism with ὑπὸ ζυγόν σου. Cf. xviii. 8. We suspect that some word had dropped out of the Hebrew text.
Another possible conjecture is to place a full stop after αἰῶνα, and to read καὶ μάστιγι παιδείας σου κατευθυνεῖς ἡμᾶς κ.τ.λ. The syllable παι- immediately following would account for the error of writing; and μάστιγα having once found its way into the text, the words would necessarily be connected with the preceding clause. In favour of this conjecture is the position of τὸν αἰῶνα at the end of the sentence.
μάστιγα παιδείας σου. See xvi. 4. Cf. Prov. xxii. 15 ῥαβδὸς δὲ καὶ παιδεία μακρὰν ἀπ' αὐτοῦ. Ecclus. xxii. 6 μάστιγες δὲ καὶ παιδεία ἐν παντὶ καιρῷ σοφία. The Divine chastisement becomes not only a discipline but a privilege, cf. Tobit xiii. 14 μακάριοι πάντες οἱ ἄνθρωποι οἳ ἐπὶ σοὶ λυπηθήσονται ἐπὶ πάσαις ταῖς μάστιξιν σου.
9 ἐν καιρῷ ἀντιλήψεως σου. For καιρὸς cf. Ps. ci. (cii.) 13 ὅτι καιρὸς τοῦ οἰκτειρῆσαι αὐτήν, ὅτι ἥκει καιρός.
For ἀντίληψις = 'the act of taking another's part,' 'succour,' cf. Ps. xxi. (xxii.) 19 εἰς τὴν ἀντίληψίν μου πρόσχες. lxxxiii. (lxxxiv.) 5. lxxxviii. (lxxxix.) 18. Ecclus. xi. 13 νωθρὸς προσδεόμενος ἀντιλήψεως. 2 Macc. xv. 7 ἀντιλήψεως τεύξασθαι παρὰ τοῦ κυρίου. 1 Cor. xii. 28 ἀντιλήψεις, and the use of the verb ἀντιλαμβάνομαι, e.g. Luke i. 54 ἀντελάβετο Ἰσραὴλ παιδὸς αὐτοῦ (Is. xli. 8, 9). Acts xx. 35. 1 Tim. vi. 2.
τοῦ ἐλεῆσαι τὸν οἶκον, κ.τ.λ. defines ἀντιλήψεώς σου.
Ἰακώβ. Cf. xv. 1 τοῦ θεοῦ Ἰακώβ.

εἰς ἡμέραν. For the preposition cf. xvii. 23 εἰς καιρὸν, xviii. 6 εἰς ἡμέραν ἐλέου...εἰς ἡμέραν ἐκλογῆς.
Ps. VIII. *Argument.*
A. 1—14. The Coming Visitation, and its Cause.
B. 15—26. The Great Delusion, and its Consequence.
C. 27—32. God's Ways justified to the Heathen and to Israel.
D. 33—39. The Prayer of the Saints.
E. 40, 41. Doxology.
There can be little doubt as to the historical events, to which allusion is made in this Psalm. The writer describes the effect produced upon him by the rumour of war, which was sweeping upon Jerusalem from a distance (1—6). The man who is the instrument of the Divine visitation comes 'from the ends of the earth' and his blows are terribly powerful (16). The princes of Judæa receive him with open arms, assist his march into their land, admit him within the walls (18—20). Once established there, he shows his real character by massacring the leading people and carrying off numbers of captives (23, 24).
This description corresponds closely enough with the capture of Jerusalem by Pompey and his conduct after storming the Temple (see on Ps. ii.).
The resemblance of this Psalm to Ps. ii. is very close. Numerous expressions (see espec. 8, 12, 13, 14, 18) are repeated almost verbally from this Psalm by the writer of Ps. ii., which judging from the reference to Pompey's death we assume to be the later composition of the two.
The writer represents the same section of the Jewish community. Speaking of himself in the early portion of the Psalm (1, 3, 4—7), he relapses into the 1st Pers. Plur. in the latter portion (30,

74   ΨΑΛΜΟΙ ΣΑΛΟΜΩΝΤΟΣ.   [VIII. 2

²φωνὴ λαοῦ πολλοῦ ὡς ἀνέμου πολλοῦ σφόδρα,
ὡς καταιγὶς πυρὸς πολλοῦ φερομένου διʼ ἐρήμου.
³καὶ εἶπον [ἐν] τῇ καρδίᾳ μου· ποῦ ἄρα κρινεῖ αὐτὸν ὁ θεός ;
⁴φωνὴν ἤκουσα· ἐν Ἰερουσαλὴμ πόλει ἁγιάσματος.
⁵συνετρίβη ἡ ὀσφύς μου ἀπὸ ἀκοῆς,
παρελύθη γόνατά μου.
⁶ἐφοβήθη ἡ καρδία μου,
ἐταράχθη τὰ ὀστᾶ μου ὡς λίνον.

3 τῇ καρδίᾳ Codd.: ἐν τῇ καρδίᾳ Fritzsch. Pick.
4 πόλιν V, K, P, M, πόλει A.

31—33, 35—39), and practically identifies himself with those whom he calls 'the saints of God' (28).

The mention of the sudden alarm of war, with which the Psalm opens, recalls Ps. i. 1. The writer's denunciation of those, whom he had believed to be righteous (ver. 7) and found to be guilty of secret abominations (9—10) reminds us of Ps. i. 3, 7, and of ii. 13—15. The fact that sinfulness is particularly identified with the profanation of sacred rites and the disregard of sacrificial duties (12, 13, 25, 26), reminds us of such passages as i. 8, ii. 3. At the same time it reveals the priestly function of many of these offending Sadducees, and expresses the horror of the Pharisees at the negligence and impiety of their foes. The reader should notice especially ver. 12, where allusion is made to the illegitimate claim of the Asmonean house to the High Priesthood.

Inscription. **εἰς νῖκος**, a rendering of למנצח, 'To the Chief Musician' which is found in Theodotion's version, Ps. xii. 1, xiii. 1 εἰς τὸ νῖκος, iv. 1, vi. 1.

We conjecture that this title has been borrowed from the Canonical Psalms by copyists.

1 φωνὴν πολέμου. Cf. i. 2.
The passage seems to be based on Jer. iv. 19 οὐ σιωπήσομαι, ὅτι φωνὴν σάλπιγγος ἤκουσεν ἡ ψυχή μου, κραυγὴν πολέμου καὶ ταλαιπωρίας συντριμμὸν ἐπικαλεῖται.

2 ὡς ἀνέμου. Cf. on xvii. 13.
The simile of a storm or whirlwind in the desert is applied to the approach of war by Jer. iv. 12, 13.

For καταιγὶς see Jer. iv. 13 ὡς καταιγὶς τὰ ἅρματα αὐτοῦ, and compare Isai. xxi. 1 ὡς καταιγὶς διʼ ἐρήμου διέλθοι, ἐξ ἐρήμου ἐρχομένη ἐκ γῆς. xxix. 6 ἐπισκοπὴ γὰρ ἔσται μετὰ βροντῆς καὶ σεισμοῦ καὶ φωνῆς μεγάλης καταιγὶς φερομένη καὶ φλὸξ πυρὸς κατεσθίουσα. lxvi. 15 ἰδοὺ γὰρ κύριος ὡς πῦρ ἥξει καὶ ὡς καταιγὶς τὰ ἅρματα αὐτοῦ. Prov. i. 27 ὁμοίως καταιγίδι (כְּסוּפָה).

3 [ἐν] τῇ καρδίᾳ μου. ἐν, which the MSS. omit, has probably dropped out by Homoeoteleuton after εἶπον. ΕΙΠΟΝΕΝΤΗ.

ποῦ ἄρα κρινεῖ αὐτὸν ὁ θεός; (1) A very natural explanation of this and the following verse assumes a dialogue to take place. The Psalmist asks in his heart, where shall be the place of judgement? The reply is given him—by whom, we are not told—that it will be in Jerusalem itself. The φωνὴν of ver. 4 is the voice, which makes answer to his question; the words ἐν Ἰερουσαλὴμ πόλει ἁγιάσματος are the substance of the reply. The ἀκοῆς of ver. 5 refers to the hearing of these words.

(2) A quite different interpretation is suggested by Wellhausen's translation 'gewiss wird uns Gott richten wollen!' 'Einen Laut hörte ich in Jerusalem.' ποῦ ἄρα is then an erroneous rendering of אֻלַי which, instead of asking the question 'where?,' should have been rendered 'surely,' e.g. Gen. xxvii. 33; Jud. ix. 38; Job xix. 23; Is. xix. 2.

On hearing the sounds of the approaching tempest of war, the Psalmist first recognizes what it means; 'Assuredly God sends his judgement upon us.' An alarm within Jerusalem itself reveals to him that the Holy City is to receive the heaven-sent chastisement: he is then overwhelmed with terror.

It is an objection to the interrogative ποῦ ἄρα that the Psalmist should enquire

VIII. 6]   ΨΑΛΜΟΙ ΣΑΛΟΜΩΝΤΟΣ.   75

2 *It is* the sound of a mighty people as of an exceeding mighty wind! *It is* as the tempest of a mighty fire rushing through the wilderness[1].
3 And I said in my heart, Surely[2] God will judge us[3].
4 I heard a sound in Jerusalem, the city of the sanctuary[4].
5 My loins were broken at the hearing *thereof*; my knees were loosed;
6 My heart was afraid; my bones were shaken like flax.

[1] Or, *a dry place*
[2] Gr. *wherewill?*
[3] Gr. *him*, i.e. *the mighty people*
[4] Or, *the Holy City*

---

the *place* of judgement, before he has apparently realised that it is judgement which is being carried out.

On the other hand, the adverb 'assuredly' gives the note of recognition that the storm about to break is judicial. The Hebrew would be the same in each case, אִם־שֹׁפְטֵינוּ; and as the shade of meaning according to this suggestion is preferable, we have no hesitation in supposing that the translator took the wrong alternative by rendering the words interrogatively.

κρινεῖ αὐτόν. We have left to this point the explanation of αὐτόν. Does it refer to λαοῦ πολλοῦ? or to Ἰσραὴλ understood? or to some person undefined? The last alternative we may dismiss at once. The first is obviously not appropriate; it is not the judgement on the Romans or on Pompey, which is contemplated in this Psalm. Can however αὐτὸν refer to Ἰσραήλ, as the dweller in Jerusalem mentioned in the next line? Such an interpretation gives the sense of the passage, but the harshness of the construction constitutes an obvious difficulty.

A probable explanation is afforded by the ambiguity of the Hebrew pronominal suffix, which in the word here used שֹׁפְטֵינוּ would be the same for the 3rd Sing. Masc. as for the 1st Pers. Plur. The Greek translation might be either κρινεῖ αὐτόν or κρινεῖ ἡμᾶς according to the context. If we suppose that the Psalmist meant 'where then shall God judge *us?*' and that the translator mistaking the sense rendered it κρινεῖ αὐτόν, we can see at once how the obscurity has arisen. Now the Psalmist, in prayer and soliloquy at the close of the Psalm, makes frequent use of the 1st Pers. Plur. Pronoun and does not refer to himself individually. Here then, where he records a short soliloquy, he might naturally speak of Israel as 'us,' although in the descriptive narration before and after he speaks of himself in the singular.

πόλει ἁγιάσματος. See on vii. 2. Cf. Ecclus. xlix. 6 ἐνεπύρισαν ἐκλεκτὴν πόλιν ἁγιάσματος.

5 συνετρίβη ἡ ὀσφύς μου. For this and the following clauses cf. Jer. xxiii. 9 συνετρίβη ἡ καρδία μου ἐν ἐμοί, ἐσαλεύθη πάντα τὰ ὀστᾶ μου. Ezek. xxi. 6 καὶ σὺ υἱὲ ἀνθρώπου καταστέναξον ἐν συντριβῇ ὀσφύος σου. Dan. v. 6 καὶ οἱ σύνδεσμοι τῆς ὀσφύος αὐτοῦ διελύοντο καὶ τὰ γόνατα αὐτοῦ συνεκροτοῦντο.

Enoch, ch. lx. 3 'And a great trembling took hold of me, and fear seized me; my loins were bent and were loosened, and my whole being melted together' (trans. Schodde).

The loins were the seat of strength. Cf. Test. XII. Patr. Napht. β′ ἐποίησεν ὁ θεὸς...ὀσφὺν εἰς ἰσχύν.

ἀπὸ ἀκοῆς. Cf. Hab. iii. 1 κύριε εἰσακήκοα τὴν ἀκοήν σου καὶ ἐφοβήθην. For ἀπὸ = 'because of' cf. Isai. vi. 4 ἐπήρθη τὸ ὑπέρθυρον ἀπὸ τῆς φωνῆς (מִקּוֹל).

παρελύθη γόνατά μου. Cf. χεῖρες ἀνειμέναι καὶ γόνατα παραλελυμένα. Isai. xxxv. 3; Ecclus. xxv. 23; Heb. xii. 12.

6 ἐφοβήθη ἡ καρδία μου. Cf. Job xxxvi. 34 (xxxvii. 1) καὶ ἀπὸ ταύτης ἐταράχθη ἡ καρδία μου καὶ ἀπερρύη ἐκ τοῦ τόπου αὐτῆς. Ps. xxvi. (xxvii.) 3 οὐ φοβηθήσεται ἡ καρδία μου.

ἐταράχθη τὰ ὀστᾶ μου. From Ps. vi. 3 ἐταράχθη τὰ ὀστᾶ μοῦ. Cf. Hab. iii. 16 εἰσῆλθε τρόμος εἰς τὰ ὀστᾶ μου καὶ ὑποκάτωθέν μου ἐταράχθη ἡ ἕξις μου.

ὡς λίνον. The Psalmist amplifies the quotation by his own simile. Cf. 1 Kings xiv. 15 κύριος πλήξει τὸν Ἰσραὴλ καθὰ κινεῖται ὁ κάλαμος ἐν τῷ ὕδατι. Matt. xi. 7.

⁷ εἶπον· κατευθυνοῦσιν ὁδοὺς αὐτῶν ἐν δικαιοσύνῃ.
ἀνελογισάμην τὰ κρίματα τοῦ θεοῦ ἀπὸ κτίσεως οὐρανοῦ
  καὶ γῆς,
ἐδικαίωσα τὸν θεὸν ἐν τοῖς κρίμασιν αὐτοῦ τοῖς ἀπ' αἰῶνος.
⁸ ἀνεκάλυψεν ὁ θεὸς τὰς ἁμαρτίας αὐτῶν ἐναντίον τοῦ ἡλίου,
ἔγνω πᾶσα ἡ γῆ τὰ κρίματα τοῦ θεοῦ τὰ δίκαια.
⁹ ἐν καταγαίοις κρυφίοις αἱ παρανομίαι αὐτῶν ἐν παροργισμῷ·
¹⁰ υἱὸς μετὰ μητρός, καὶ πατὴρ μετὰ θυγατρὸς συνεφύροντο·
¹¹ ἐμοιχῶντο ἕκαστος γυναῖκα τοῦ πλησίον αὐτοῦ,
συνέθεντο αὐτοῖς συνθήκας μετὰ ὅρκου περὶ τούτων·

7 κατευθύνουσιν Codd., κατευθυνοῦσιν Fritzsch. Pick., εἶπον κατευθύνουσιν (M), Hilg.
8 τοῦ ἡλίου: om. τοῦ Fabr.
9 ἐν παροργισμῷ jung. cum versu 9, A? V, K, P, Fabr. Geig. Wellh., incip. vers. 10 M et Hilg., ita Fritzsch. Pick. (Cerda et Geig. conj. in notis ἐν παραλογισμῷ ἐν παρορισμῷ Hilg.²
11 πλησίον A (Cerda).
αὐτοῖς Codd.: αὐτοῖς Hilg. Fritzsch. Pick.
μετὰ ὅρκου περὶ τούτων· (V), K, P, M, Hilg. Fritzsch. Wellh. Pick.
μετὰ ὅρκου· περὶ τούτων A (?) Cerda, Fabr. Geig.

---

7 εἶπον· κατευθυνοῦσιν ὁδοὺς αὐτῶν ἐν δικαιοσύνῃ. The Psalmist endeavours to allay his fears by reflecting that the dwellers in Jerusalem 'direct their ways in righteousness,' and that, though they may be tried by temporary discipline, they will be preserved on account of their righteousness and the city saved for the sake of 'the righteous' to be found in it (cf. Gen. xviii.). But the Psalmist is destined to be cruelly undeceived. The people are not 'directing their ways in righteousness': they are given over to secret sin, which had been unknown to him. The position of the writer is therefore the same in this Psalm as that occupied by the writer of the 1st Psalm. In Ps. i. 1, 2 we have the approach of war corresponding to Ps. viii. 1—6; in Ps. i. 3 the writer's security, based on the 'righteousness' of his countrymen, corresponds to the present verse; in Ps. i. 7, 8 the discovery of their secret sins and unsurpassed abominations, which prepares the Psalmist for the inevitable visitation, corresponds to Ps. viii. 9—14.

For κατευθυνοῦσιν see note on vi. 3, and cf. Apoc. Bar. lxxvii. 5 si ergo direxeritis vias vestras, non abibitis etiam vos, sicut abierunt fratres vestri.

The 3rd Pers. Plur. refers to the inhabitants of Jerusalem mentioned in ver. 4.

Wellhausen renders 'Ich sprach: die Frommen—ihre Wege sind Gerechtigkeitswege.' This is plausible, and derives support from αὐτῶν in ver. 8, which seems to presuppose a Plural substantive in a previous clause. The Psalmist then merely consoles himself with the thought that 'the upright' will be preserved on account of 'their righteousness,' for this was the teaching of all the past judgements of God. To obtain this meaning, W. assumes that κατευθυνοῦσιν is a wrong rendering by the translator for the adjective יְשָׁרִים 'the upright.'

The existing rendering however gives a good sense. A comparison with i. 3 ἐλογισάμην ἐν καρδίᾳ μου ὅτι ἐπλήσθην δικαιοσύνης, where Zion is speaking is an exact parallel to the present clause, and renders any change in the reading unnecessary.

The Fut. tense κατευθυνοῦσιν represents the frequentative sense of the Heb. Impf.

For Hilgenfeld's εἶπον κατευθύνουσιν,

VIII. 11] ΨΑΛΜΟΙ ΣΑΛΟΜΩΝΤΟΣ. 77

7 I said, Surely they direct their paths in righteousness⁵.
I considered the judgements of God from the creation of the heaven and the earth; I justified God in his judgements which have been of old.

8 God laid bare their sins in the sight of the sun; all the earth hath learned the righteous judgements of God.

9 In secret places beneath the earth were their iniquities that provoked *him to anger*⁶:

10 The son with the mother, and the father with the daughter wrought confusion:

11 They committed adultery each one with his neighbour's wife; they covenanted thereto with oaths one with another:

⁵ Conj. *The upright, their way is in righteousness*

⁶ Gr. *in provocation*

'I spake to them that directed their ways in righteousness,' we cannot see that anything favourable can be said.

ἀνελογισάμην. ἀναλογίζομαι is not found in the LXX. and occurs once only in the N.T. Heb. xii. 3 ἀναλογίσασθε γὰρ τὸν τοιαύτην ὑπομεμενηκότα...ἀντιλογίαν. Sym. Ps. lxxvi. (lxxvii.) 6 ἀνελογιζόμην (חָשַׁבְתִּי) τὰς ἡμέρας τὰς πρώτας.

ἀπὸ κτίσεως. Cf. Deut. iv. 32; Ezek. xxviii. 15. See xviii. 13, 14.

ἐδικαίωσα τὸν θεόν. Cf. 27, 31, ii. 16, iii. 3.

ἐν τοῖς κρίμασιν αὐτοῦ τοῖς ἀπ' αἰῶνος. Cf. Ps. cxviii. (cxix.) 52 ἐμνήσθην τῶν κριμάτων σου, κύριε, ἀπ' αἰῶνος.

8 ἀνεκάλυψεν ὁ θεὸς τὰς ἁμαρτίας αὐτῶν. See ii. 18 ἀνεκάλυψας τὰς ἁμαρτίας αὐτῶν ἵνα φανῇ τὸ κρῖμά σου.

αὐτῶν. The Pronoun refers to the Jews, of whom the Psalmist spoke in ver. 7, κατευθυνοῦσιν ὁδοὺς αὐτῶν.

ἐναντίον τοῦ ἡλίου. Cf. ii. 13, 14; iv. 21.

ἔγνω, κ.τ.λ. Cf. ii. 12 καὶ γνώσεται ἡ γῆ τὰ κρίματά σου πάντα τὰ δίκαια.

9 ἐν καταγαίοις κρυφίοις. For the sensualities secretly practised by the Jews of Jerusalem, see on i. 7, ii. 13—15.

The word κατάγαια occurs in Gen. vi. 16 κατάγαια διώροφα. For κρυφίοις cf. Wisd. xvii. 3 λανθάνειν γὰρ νομίζοντες ἐπὶ κρυφαίοις ἁμαρτήμασιν.

ἐν παροργισμῷ. We prefer to include these words in the sentence of verse 9, as if they were equivalent to παροργιζόντων. Cf. note on παντὸς ἐν φόβῳ (vi. 7).

(1) The expression is general; secret iniquities provoked the LORD to anger, and, after this preliminary statement, they are described in detail.

(2) A comparison with iv. 1, ἐν παρανομίαις παροργίζων τὸν θεὸν Ἰσραήλ, supports this interpretation. The similarity of the phrase there used and the general correspondence in the wickedness described in Ps. iv. with what is described in these verses shows that the same Sadducee foes are intended.

10 υἱὸς μετὰ μητρὸς...συνεφύροντο. This use of the verb is probably taken by the translator from the LXX. of Hos. iv. 14 αὐτοὶ μετὰ τῶν πορνῶν συνεφύροντο. Cf. Ezek. xxii. 6 ἰδοὺ οἱ ἀφηγούμενοι οἴκου Ἰσραὴλ ἕκαστος πρὸς τοὺς συγγενεῖς αὐτοῦ συνεφύροντο ἐν σοὶ ὅπως ἐκχέωσιν αἷμα.

11 ἐμοιχῶντο. The clause expresses the substance of Jer. v. 8 ἕκαστος ἐπὶ τὴν γυναῖκα τοῦ πλησίον αὐτοῦ ἐχρεμέτιζον. For the change of tense ἐμοιχῶντο...συνέθεντο, cf. ii. 2 ἀνέβησαν...κατεπάτουν.

The verse expresses in more general terms the indictment of iv. 4—6, 11—15.

συνέθεντο αὐτοῖς συνθήκας μετὰ ὅρκου περὶ τούτων. The line repeats the substance of iv. 4 ἡ γλῶσσα αὐτῶν ψευδὴς ἐν συναλλάγματι μεθ' ὅρκου.

The allusion is not quite clear. The meaning may be, as in iv. 4, that they pledged the oaths which belonged to the agreement of lawful marriage.

Or the allusion may be to the test of unfaithfulness described in Num. v., according to which the priest administered 'the water of bitterness' to a woman charged with infidelity. This was accompanied by an oath, ver. 21 'Then the priest shall cause the woman to swear with the oath of cursing, and the priest shall say unto the woman, The LORD make thee a curse and an oath among thy people.'

78   ΨΑΛΜΟΙ ΣΑΛΟΜΩΝΤΟΣ.   [VIII. 12

¹² τὰ ἅγια τοῦ θεοῦ διήρπαζον, οὐκ ὄντος κληρονόμου λυτρουμένου,
¹³ ἐπάτουν τὸ θυσιαστήριον κυρίου ἀπὸ πάσης ἀκαθαρσίας, καὶ ἐν ἀφέδρῳ αἵματος ἐμίαινον τὰς θυσίας ὡς κρέα βέβηλα.
¹⁴ οὐ παρέλιπον ἁμαρτίαν, ἣν οὐκ ἐποίησαν ὑπὲρ τὰ ἔθνη.

13 ἐν ἀφέδρῳ A (Cerda *fluento*), V, K, P. Cerda in scholiis haec habet; 'perperam scriptum a librario ἐν φέδρῳ αἵματος, rescribendum omnino est ἐν ῥεέθρῳ vel ῥείθρῳ αἵματος.' ἐν ἀφαιδρῳ M.

If the priests who administered the curse themselves were the adulterers, the force of this allusion to 'the oath' is greatly intensified, and the fact that priests are clearly alluded to in ver. 12 seems to add probability to this striking explanation.

The meaning of περὶ τούτων remains obscure. Geiger connects περὶ τούτων with the following sentence 'for this cause'; but there is no logical sequence of thought combining sensual vice and sacrilege.

It might be rendered 'for this end' i.e. to compass their evil purpose, εἰς τὸ μοιχᾶσθαι.

On the strength of Ezek. xvi. 59, where ταῦτα is the LXX. rendering for אָלָה, it is tempting to suggest a confusion of

אָלָה = ἀρὰ 'a curse' with אֵלֶּה = ταῦτα

'these things,' especially as in the LXX. of Num. v. 21 the ὅρκος and ἀρά occur together καὶ ὁρκιεῖ ὁ ἱερεὺς τὴν γυναῖκα ἐν τοῖς ὅρκοις τῆς ἀρᾶς ταύτης καὶ ἐρεῖ ὁ ἱερεὺς τῇ γυναικί Δῴη σε κύριος ἐν ἀρᾷ καὶ ἐνόρκιον κ.τ.λ.

Upon this hypothesis either the true rendering would have been μετὰ ὅρκων ἀρᾶς or μετὰ ὅρκου καὶ ἀρᾶς; or, very possibly, περὶ τούτων represents a duplicate rendering of μετὰ ὅρκου.

According to Wellhausen this clause begins a fresh sentence and introduces the subject of the wrongful position of the High-Priestly family. 'Besides this' (zu-dem) they (the Jews) made a covenant, bartering away the Holy things, referring to the agreement between the people and the Asmonean House described in 1 Macc. xiv. 35 καὶ εἶδεν ὁ λαὸς τὴν πίστιν τοῦ Σίμωνος καὶ τὴν δόξαν ἣν ἐβουλεύσατο ποιῆσαι τῷ ἔθνει αὐτοῦ καὶ ἔθεντο αὐτὸν ἡγούμενον αὐτῶν καὶ ἀρχιερέα, διὰ τὸ αὐτὸν

πεποιηκέναι πάντα ταῦτα καὶ τὴν δικαιοσύνην καὶ τὴν πίστιν ἣν συνετήρησε τῷ ἔθνει αὐτοῦ καὶ ἐξεζήτησε παντὶ τρόπῳ ὑψῶσαι τὸν λαὸν αὐτοῦ.

12 τὰ ἅγια τοῦ θεοῦ διήρπαζον. The Psalmist passes away from the charge of sinful sensuality to that of sacrilege.

τὰ ἅγια τοῦ θεοῦ as an object of διαρπάζειν may mean *either* 'the sacred things' in the sense of things dedicated, gifts, sacrifices &c. (cf. τὰ ἡγιασμένα, ver. 26), with which the priests enriched themselves making a spoil of them, or the temple, which the Asmonean Princes had taken violent possession of.

The former interpretation has the support of i. 8 τὰ ἅγια κυρίου, ii. 3 τὰ ἅγια κυρίου...τὰ δῶρα τοῦ θεοῦ, and is favoured by the use of the Imperf. διήρπαζον, denoting continuous practice.

The latter interpretation gives a common meaning of τὰ ἅγια and agrees well with the short following clause, οὐκ ὄντος κληρονόμου λυτρουμένου. It was a principal cause of the hostility of the Pharisees to the Sadducees, that the Asmonean house had set aside the legitimate line of the High Priest and had assumed to themselves the power and dignity, which the office conferred.

οὐκ ὄντος κληρονόμου λυτρουμένου. Geiger surely takes a wrong view of κληρονόμου (which he supposes to translate יוֹרֵשׁ), when he asserts that it can have no meaning here in the sense of 'inheritor'; and supposes the Hebrew word to have been used in the sense of 'disinheritor' or 'expeller.' 'Und keiner war, der vertrieb, der rettete' i.e. there was none to drive out the spoiler, none to save the spoiled.

This rendering loses sight of what seems to us to be the most significant point in the passage.

VIII. 14] ΨΑΛΜΟΙ ΣΑΛΟΜΩΝΤΟΣ. 79

12. The holy things[7] of God they took for spoil; and there was   [7] Or, *the holy place*
no inheritor to deliver *out of their hand*.
13 They went up to[8] the altar of the LORD *when they were*   [8] Gr. *trode*
full of[9] all uncleanness;   [9] Gr. *from*
  yea, even in their separation they polluted the sacrifices, *eating them* like profane meats.
14 They left not a sin undone, wherein they offended not above the heathen.

The κληρονόμος is the true heir; he is the 'go'êl,' the kinsman, who should take upon himself the rights and obligations of the inheritance. The inheritance is represented by τὰ ἅγια τοῦ κυρίου. The true heirs, the rightful lineage of the High Priest, had been ejected. Strangers had entered into violent possession, and there was no 'kinsman,' no 'go'êl' to deliver it out of their hand.

κληρονόμος occurs in the LXX. as a translation of יוֹרֵשׁ in Jud. xviii. 7; 2 Sam. xiv. 7; Jer. viii. 10; Mic. i. 15. The word גֹּאֵל is rendered in Ruth iv. by ἀγχιστεύς, but the verb is reproduced in the LXX. by ῥύομαι (e.g. Is. xlviii. 20; lii. 9 ἀπολυτρόω, and especially λυτροῦμαι e.g. xliii. 1, 14, xliv. 22).

It appears to us very possible that κληρονόμον λυτρουμένου are a duplicate rendering of the same word, κληρονόμον representing the rightful claim of the 'go'êl,' λυτρουμένου his effectual act of deliverance or redemption.

We conclude that the original Hebrew ran either וְאֵין יוֹרֵשׁ גֹּאֵל 'and there was no inheritor redeeming,' or, as seems to us very probable, וְאֵין גֹּאֵל 'and there was no redeemer' or 'go'êl.'

The form of the sentence recalls Ps. vii. 2 μὴ ὄντος λυτρουμένου μηδὲ σώζοντος (פֹּרֵק וְאֵין מַצִּיל). Lam. v. 8 λυτρούμενος οὐκ ἔστιν ἐκ τῆς χειρὸς αὐτῶν (פֹּרֵק אֵין מִיָּדָם).

13 ἐπάτουν. On πατεῖν = 'tread with frequency,' see note on vii. 2. It is evidently here used to denote constant attendance, and has no sense of trampling under foot, such as is found in καταπατεῖν (ii. 2).

ἀπὸ πάσης ἀκαθαρσίας. A harsh construction; the preposition ἀπό seems to suggest the idea of priests *proceeding from* scenes of every possible pollution to their holy avocation. That is, they did their work of sacrifice being full of all uncleanness, coming straight, as it were, *from* that which defiled to the holy altar.

It is possible also to include in this rendering the temporal signification. The work at the altar came immediately after (ἀπό) deeds of uncleanness; there was no intervening period of purification, nay more, even *while* (ἐν) uncleanness was still on them, they partook of consecrated food.

ἐν ἀφέδρῳ αἵματος. The technical expression in the LXX. for the impurity described in Lev. xii. 1—8, xv. 19—33; Ezek. xviii. 6. The ἐν of the actual condition of uncleanness is contrasted with the ἀπό.

ἐμίαινον τὰς θυσίας. The Levitical rule strictly prohibited the attendance of the unclean at the feasts and sacrifices. Cf. Lev. xv. 31 'Thus shall ye separate the children of Israel from their uncleanness; that they die not in their uncleanness, when they defile my tabernacle that is in the midst of them.' The presence of the ceremonially unclean at the feasts and sacrifices was apparently connived at by the Sadducee priests; and such laxity shocked and incensed the strict Pharisees.

κρέα βέβηλα. This phrase occurs once in the LXX., Ezek. iv. 14 οὐδὲ εἰσελήλυθεν εἰς τὸ στόμα μου πᾶν κρέας βέβηλον (v. l. ἕωλον).

14. ὑπὲρ τὰ ἔθνη. Cf. on i. 8 αἱ ἀνομίαι αὐτῶν ὑπὲρ τὰ πρὸ αὐτῶν ἔθνη, ἐβεβήλωσαν τὰ ἅγια κυρίου.

15 ἐκέρασεν αὐτοῖς...πλανήσεως. The words are taken almost literally from the LXX. of Isai. xix. 14 κύριος γὰρ ἐκέρασεν αὐτοῖς πνεῦμα πλανήσεως (רוּחַ עִוְעִים, lit. 'a spirit of perverseness') καὶ ἐπλάνησαν Αἴγυπτον...ὡς πλανᾶται ὁ μεθύων. The folly of the princes of Egypt as depicted by Isaiah is borrowed by our writer as an

80 ΨΑΛΜΟΙ ΣΑΛΟΜΩΝΤΟΣ. [VIII. 15

¹⁵ Διὰ τοῦτο ἐκέρασεν αὐτοῖς ὁ θεὸς πνεῦμα πλανήσεως,
ἐπότισεν αὐτοῖς ποτήριον οἴνου ἀκράτου εἰς μέθην.
¹⁶ ἤγαγε τὸν ἀπ' ἐσχάτου τῆς γῆς, τὸν παίοντα κραταιῶς,
¹⁷ ἔκρινε τὸν πόλεμον ἐπὶ Ἱερουσαλὴμ καὶ τὴν γῆν αὐτῆς.
¹⁸ ἀπήντησαν αὐτῷ οἱ ἄρχοντες τῆς γῆς μετὰ χαρᾶς,
εἶπον αὐτῷ· ἐπευκτὴ ἡ ὁδός σου, δεῦτε, εἰσέλθετε μετ'
εἰρήνης.

15 ἐπότισεν αὐτοῖς A, V, K, M, Fabr.   αὐτοὺς P, Geig. Hilg. Fritzsch. Pick.
16 κρατερῶς A.   κραταιῶς V, K, P, M.
18 ἐπευκτὴ V, K, P, M, conj. Lagarde, ita Hilg. Geig. Fritzsch. Wellh. Pick.
ἐπαυκτή A.

illustration of the perversity of the Jewish nobles in welcoming the representative of Rome.

Test. XII. Patr. Dan 9 τὰ πνεύματα τῆς πλάνης ἀπατᾷ αὐτούς...πᾶν πνεῦμα πλάνης πατηθήσεται.

A strange use of πνεῦμα πλανήσεως occurs in Jer. iv. 11 where it renders רוּחַ צַח 'a hot wind' (Aq. πνεῦμα λαμπηδόνος. Sym. πνεῦμα καύσωνος). Jerome's translation is '*ventus urens* sive *roris*,' where 'roris' is probably a mistake for 'erroris' and is intended to represent the LXX. reading.

ἐπότισεν αὐτοῖς ποτήριον οἴνου ἀκράτου. These words again are based on the LXX. in Ps. lxxiv. (lxxv.) 9 ὅτι ποτήριον ἐν χειρὶ κυρίου οἴνου ἀκράτου πλῆρες κεράσματος, and Jer. xxxii. 1 (=Heb. xxv. 15) λάβε τὸ ποτήριον τοῦ οἴνου τοῦ ἀκράτου τούτου ἐκ χειρός μου, καὶ ποτιεῖς πάντα τὰ ἔθνη. In the first of these passages the R.V. rendering of the Hebrew is 'For in the hand of the LORD there is a cup, and the wine foameth (or, *is red*); it is full of mixture,' where 'the wine foameth' (יַיִן חָמַר) corresponds to οἴνου ἀκράτου. In the passage from Jeremiah the R.V. rendering is, 'Take the cup of the wine of this fury at my hand,' where 'the cup of the wine of this fury' (כּוֹס הַיַּיִן הַחֵמָה הַזֹּאת) suggested the words used by the Psalmist in the present passage.

The translator has given the LXX. rendering of a phrase in familiar use.

εἰς μέθην. This may be rendered either 'with a view to their being drunken' or 'until they are drunken.'

The latter rendering, which is the more probable, may be illustrated by Hag. i. 6 ἐπίετε καὶ οὐκ εἰς μέθην ('ye drink and are not filled with drink').

Ezek. xxxix. 19 καὶ πίεσθε αἷμα εἰς μέθην ('and drink blood until ye be drunken,' R.V.).

16 τὸν ἀπ' ἐσχάτου τῆς γῆς. Pompey the conqueror from Rome is thus referred to. The phrase is used not so much with the purpose of conveying the idea of the remoteness of Italy from Palestine as of reproducing the language of the prophets, in predicting the coming of the Babylonians, e.g. Jer. vi. 23 ἰδοὺ λαὸς ἔρχεται ἀπὸ βορρᾶ καὶ ἔθνη ἐξεγερθήσονται ἀπ' ἐσχάτου τῆς γῆς.

τὸν παίοντα κραταιῶς. We do not find any close parallel in the LXX. to this description of Pompey.

The expression ὁ παίων is used of the king of Assyria, Isai. xiv. 29 'the rod that smote thee is broken'=LXX. συνετρίβη ὁ ζυγὸς τοῦ παίοντος ὑμᾶς.

Ewald, who finds an allusion to Antiochus Epiphanes in this verse, explains ἀπ' ἐσχάτου τῆς γῆς as referring to the departure of Antiochus from Rome to the throne of Syria. If applicable to Antiochus Epiphanes, the description is even more appropriate to Pompey; and the brilliant succession of victories which Pompey won in Asia Minor and Syria deserves the title of ὁ παίων κραταιῶς, a world-conqueror, better than the chequered fortune of Antiochus' campaigns or even the ferocity of his tyranny.

17 ἔκρινε τὸν πόλεμον. In hazarding the translation 'he decreed the war,' we are obliged to confess that we have found no certain authority for it either as a Greek or as a literal rendering of a Hebrew phrase.

ΨΑΛΜΟΙ ΣΑΛΟΜΩΝΤΟΣ.

15 For this cause did God mingle for them a spirit of error, he made them to drink of the cup of unmixed wine until they were drunken.

16 He brought him that is from the utmost part of the earth, whose stroke is mighty[10];

17 He decreed[11] war against Jerusalem and her land.

18 The princes of the land met him with joy; they said unto him, Blessed is thy path! come ye, enter in with peace.

[10] Gr. *that smiteth powerfully*
[11] Conj. *made ready*

κρίνω was commonly used of 'deciding' or 'determining' a contest by arms or litigation. Geiger renders 'beschied den Krieg.' Wellhausen 'beschloss den Krieg.' Pick 'he determined war.'

The unusual phrase may however arise from some early confusion in the reading. In the absence of any confirmation of the usage in our text, we venture to suggest a conjecture which supplies a good explanation of our text.

(*a*) It is evident that ἔκρινε τὸν πόλεμον does not indicate actual hostilities, but the preparation for them. The next verse shows that the conflict was averted by the submission of the ἄρχοντες. The meaning that we should expect would be 'he made ready' or 'declared the war.'

(*b*) ἔκρινε translates יָדִין 'he judgeth or will judge' (e.g. Gen. xlix. 16 and *passim*). But as the word יָכִין 'he maketh ready' is what we should naturally expect in the present passage, we conjecture that יָכִין by an error of a scribe may have been changed to יָדִין; of this very error a probable instance is presented by Ezek. vii. 14 'They have blown the trumpet and made all ready' which is rendered in the LXX. σαλπίσατε ἐν σάλπιγγι καὶ κρίνατε (Sym. Theod. ἑτοιμάσατε; Heb. וְהָכִין).

(*c*) Upon this assumption the right translation of the original Hebrew would have been ἡτοίμαζε τὸν πόλεμον.

18 ἀπήντησαν αὐτῷ οἱ ἄρχοντες τῆς γῆς μετὰ χαρᾶς. These words, according to Ewald, represent the party in Jerusalem who supported the Hellenizing policy of Antiochus Epiphanes and opened to him the gates of Jerusalem, cf. Joseph. *Ant.* XII. v. 3 ἀμαχητὶ λαμβάνει τὴν πόλιν, ἀνοιξάντων αὐτῷ τὰς πύλας, ὅσοι τῆς ἐκείνου προαιρήσεως ἦσαν. Ἐγκρατὴς δὲ οὕτως τῶν Ἱεροσολύμων γενόμενος, πολλοὺς ἀπέκτεινεν τῶν ἐναντία φρονούντων, καὶ χρήματα πολλὰ συλήσας ὑπέστρεψεν εἰς Ἀντιόχειαν.

It cannot be denied that this description by Josephus of Epiphanes' seizure of the city agrees in a remarkable manner with the general impression produced by the main outlines of the present passage 15—24.

But the general description given by the poet applies equally, if not more, closely to the occupation of Jerusalem by Pompey; and various details mentioned by the Psalmist seem to receive their only possible explanation from the supposition of the Pompeian invasion.

In the present verse it should be noted that the meeting of the foreign conqueror and the welcome extended to him by οἱ ἄρχοντες τῆς γῆς are mentioned before the fact of his arrival in Palestine. This small point corresponds with Josephus' description of the action both of the two brothers Hyrcanus and Aristobulus, and of the leading citizens. Each of the rival princes invoked Pompey's aid, while Pompey was still at Damascus; and at the same time a strong deputation arrived from Jerusalem soliciting that Pompey would give the kingdom to neither claimant; for it was contrary to the laws of the people that they should be ruled by a king. These appeals to Pompey will amply explain the term ἀπήντησαν.

See Jos. *Ant.* XIV. iii. 2.

ἐπευκτή. This word occurs in the LXX. Jer. xx. 14 ἡμέρα ἐν ᾗ ἔτεκέ με μὴ ἔστω ἐπευκτή (Aq. Sym. εὐλογημένη= בָּרוּךְ).

It is clearly the preferable reading in this passage. ἐπαυκτή of the Augsburg MS., rendered 'dilatata' (i.e. enlarged) by Cerda and Fabricius, has no other authority and gives a very artificial turn to the words of greeting.

J. P.

82 ΨΑΛΜΟΙ ΣΑΛΟΜΩΝΤΟΣ. [VIII. 19

¹⁹ ὡμάλισαν ὁδοὺς τραχείας ἀπὸ εἰσόδου αὐτῶν,
ἤνοιξαν πύλας ἐπὶ Ἰερουσαλήμ,
ἐστεφάνωσαν τείχη αὐτῆς.
²⁰ εἰσῆλθεν ὡς πατὴρ εἰς οἶκον υἱῶν αὐτοῦ μετ' εἰρήνης,
ἔστησε τοὺς πόδας αὐτοῦ μετὰ ἀσφαλείας πολλῆς,
²¹ κατελάβετο τὰς πυργοβάρεις αὐτῆς καὶ τὸ τεῖχος Ἱερου-
σαλήμ·
²² ὅτι θεὸς ἤγαγεν αὐτὸν μετὰ ἀσφαλείας ἐν τῇ πλανήσει
αὐτῶν.
²³ ἀπώλεσεν ἄρχοντας αὐτῶν καὶ πάντα σοφὸν ἐν βουλῇ,
ἐξέχεε τὸ αἷμα τῶν οἰκούντων Ἰερουσαλὴμ ὡς ὕδωρ ἀκαθαρσίας.

20 μετὰ ἀσφαλείας V, K, P, M, μετ' ἀσφαλείας Α.

---

19 ὡμάλισαν ὁδοὺς τραχείας. Cf. xi. 4. The words of welcome to the foreigner are based on the language of Isaiah xl. 3, 4 ἑτοιμάσατε τὴν ὁδὸν κυρίου... καὶ ἔσται πάντα τὰ σκολιὰ εἰς εὐθεῖαν καὶ ἡ τραχεῖα εἰς πεδία (cf. Luke iii. 5). For ὁμαλίζω cf. Is. xlv. 2 ὄρη ὁμαλιῶ. Sym. Ps. v. 9 ὁμάλισον (הַיָּשָׁר) ἔμπροσθέν μου τὴν ὁδόν σου and ἐν ὁμαλῷ. Sym. Ps. xxv. (xxvi.) 12 for בְּמִישׁוֹר.

ἤνοιξαν πύλας ἐπὶ Ἰερουσαλήμ. The expression πύλας ἐπὶ must be observed. It is not to be regarded as identical with πύλας Ἰερουσαλήμ 'the gates of Jerusalem.' 'The gates to Jerusalem' are the approaches to Jerusalem; the passes and roads, which admitted an army to the capital.

Josephus particularly mentions the surrender of Coreae and Alexandrium by Aristobulus as facilitating the march of Pompey against Jerusalem (*Ant.* XIV. iii. 4 κελεύοντος δὲ Πομπηΐου παραδιδόναι τὰ ἐρύματα καὶ τοῖς φρουράρχοις ἐπιστέλλειν τῇ ἑαυτοῦ χειρί, παραδέχεσθαι δὲ ἄλλως ἀπείρητο, πείθεται μὲν δυσανασχετῶν δὲ ἀνεχώρησεν εἰς Ἱεροσόλυμα).

ἐστεφάνωσαν τείχη αὐτῆς. The festal decoration of the city, as Pompey drew near, is obviously the meaning. The words recall the description of the national celebration at the first feast of Dedication 1 Macc. iv. 57 καὶ κατεκόσμησαν τὸ κατὰ πρόσωπον τοῦ ναοῦ στεφάνοις χρυσοῖς καὶ ἀσπιδίσκοις κ.τ.λ.

Geiger, who admits this more obvious rendering into his translation, expresses his dissatisfaction with it on the ground that the clause presents no adequate parallel to ἤνοιξαν πύλας. He therefore suggests that the Hebrew words should rather have been rendered 'they surrendered the walls or fortresses,' the verb עָטַר 'to crown' having in the Chaldee the sense of 'abstulit.'

20 εἰσῆλθεν ὡς πατήρ. Only at this point do we reach the actual entry of the conqueror within the walls. The writer does not concern himself with the delays caused by the action of Aristobulus and his supporters. Pompey and his army encamped at Jericho. Aristobulus offered to surrender, but had no control over his followers in Jerusalem, who shut the gates against Gabinius, Pompey's lieutenant. Pompey in anger marched upon Jerusalem. Faction within the walls was intensified by fear. The partisans of Aristobulus seized the Temple and its fortifications; the others threw open the gates, and placed in Pompey's hands the possession of their city and the disposal of their crown (οἱ δὲ ἕτεροι δεξάμενοι τὴν στρατιὰν ἐνεχείρισαν Πομπηΐῳ τήν τε πόλιν καὶ τὰ βασίλεια, *Ant.* XIV. iv. 2).

Pompey entered the city as its lord and patron to defend it from those who wished Aristobulus the usurper to be their King and High Priest.

ἔστησε τοὺς πόδας αὐτοῦ. Compare

VIII. 23]   ΨΑΛΜΟΙ ΣΑΛΟΜΩΝΤΟΣ.   83

19 They made the rough paths even before their entering in, they opened the gates that led unto Jerusalem; her walls they crowned *with garlands*.

20 He entered in, as a father *entereth* into his sons' house, in peace.

He established his feet and made them very firm[12].

21 He occupied her strongholds, *yea*, and the wall of Jerusalem.

22 For God led him in safety, because of their blindness.

23 He cut off their princes and every wise councillor; he poured out the blood of the dwellers in Jerusalem like the water of uncleanness,

[12] Lit. *with much safety*

Ps. xxx. (xxxi.) 9 ἔστησας ἐν εὐρυχώρῳ τοὺς πόδας μου. xxxix. (xl.) 3 καὶ ἔστησεν ἐπὶ πέτραν τοὺς πόδας μου.

21 κατελάβετο τὰς πυργοβάρεις αὐτῆς. This brings us to the last stage of Pompey's occupation of Jerusalem. Admitted within the walls, he was compelled to reduce the Temple and the adjacent fortifications by siege (see Ps. ii.). Their capture, it appears to us, is indicated in this line.

κατελάβετο. Cf. Num. xxi. 32; 1 Macc. i. 22; 2 Macc. x. 22.

τὰς πυργοβάρεις αὐτῆς. Cf. Ps. cxxi. (cxxii.) 7 καὶ εὐθηνία ἐν τοῖς πυργοβάρεσίν σου (where πυργόβαρις renders אַרְמוֹן 'palace').

This may possibly refer to the citadel or 'Baris' which lay to the north of the Temple, cf. Neh. ii. 8 στεγάσαι τὰς πύλας τῆς βάρεως.

καὶ τὸ τεῖχος. Cf. ii. 1.

Hilgenfeld quotes Orosius, *Hist.* VI. 6: ipse (Pompeius) continuo subsecutus et a patribus urbe susceptus, sed a plebe muro templi repulsus, oppugnationem ejus intendit.

23 ἀπώλεσεν ἄρχοντας αὐτῶν. After the capture of the Temple Pompey took a bloody revenge upon the leaders of the Aristobulus party. Cf. Jos. *Ant.* XIV. iv. 4 καὶ τοὺς αἰτίους τοῦ πολέμου τῷ πελέκει διεχρήσατο. *Bell. Jud.* I. vii. 6 καὶ τοὺς μὲν αἰτιωτάτους τοῦ πολέμου πελέκει κολάζει.

πάντα σοφὸν ἐν βουλῇ. Leading members of the Sanhedrin are clearly intended. The supporters of Aristobulus must have been largely represented in the National Council. It is impossible otherwise to account for the success and influence of Aristobulus. That they numbered amongst them the most important of the priests, is a natural conclusion to be drawn from the Temple being held by the party, and by the priests having continued their functions throughout the blockade.

ἐξέχεε τὸ αἷμα τῶν οἰκ. Ἱερ. The massacre of the Jews by the Roman soldiers has almost escaped notice in the chronicle of horrors which Jerusalem has experienced. Josephus speaks of 12,000 Jews slaughtered in the siege and capture of the Temple. Jos. *Ant.* XIV. iv. 5 φόνου δὲ ἦν πάντα ἀνάπλεω. καὶ τῶν Ἰουδαίων οἱ μὲν ὑπὸ Ῥωμαίων οἱ δὲ ὑπ' ἀλλήλων ἀνῃροῦντο· εἰσὶ δὲ οἳ καὶ κατὰ κρημνῶν ἑαυτοὺς ἔρριπτον καὶ πῦρ ἀνιέντες εἰς τὰς οἰκίας ἐνεπίμπραντο, τὰ γινόμενα καρτερεῖν οὐχ ὑπομένοντες. ἔπεσον δὲ τῶν μὲν Ἰουδαίων εἰς μυρίους καὶ δισχιλίους Ῥωμαίων δὲ πάνυ ὀλίγοι. Cf. *Bell. Jud.* I. vii. 5.

ἐξέχεε...ὡς ὕδωρ ἀκαθαρσίας. For the metaphor ὡς ὕδωρ, cf. Ps. lxxviii. (lxxix.) 3 ἐξέχεαν τὸ αἷμα αὐτῶν ὡς ὕδωρ κύκλῳ Ἱερουσαλήμ, which passage the Psalmist had probably in his mind.

He has amplified the metaphor from ὡς ὕδωρ to ὡς ὕδωρ ἀκαθαρσίας according to his practice of introducing his own words into the quotations from Scripture, cf. on ὡς λίνον in ver. 5.

For one of the earliest instances of the occurrence of this metaphor, see *Records of the Past*, 2nd Series, vol. I. p. 85 'An Erechite's Lament' line 3, 'Blood is flowing like water in Eulbar, the house of thy oracle.' For ὕδωρ ἀκαθαρσίας = the water used in removing uncleanness, see Num. xix. 9 ὕδωρ ῥαντισμοῦ, xxxi. 23 ὕδωρ ἁγνισμοῦ.

84 ΨΑΛΜΟΙ ΣΑΛΟΜΩΝΤΟΣ. [VIII. 24

²⁴ ἀπήγαγε τοὺς υἱοὺς καὶ τὰς θυγατέρας αὐτῶν, ἃς ἐγέννησαν ἐν βεβηλώσει.
²⁵ ἐποίησαν κατὰ τὰς ἀκαθαρσίας αὐτῶν, καθὼς οἱ πατέρες αὐτῶν,
²⁶ ἐμίαναν Ἱερουσαλὴμ καὶ τὰ ἡγιασμένα τῷ ὀνόματι τοῦ θεοῦ.

²⁷ Ἐδικαιώθη ὁ θεὸς ἐν τοῖς κρίμασιν αὐτοῦ ἐν τοῖς ἔθνεσι τῆς γῆς,
²⁸ καὶ οἱ ὅσιοι τοῦ θεοῦ ὡς ἀρνία ἐν ἀκακίᾳ ἐν μέσῳ αὐτῶν·

24 ἀπήγαγε τοὺς υἱοὺς καὶ τὰς θυγατέρας αὐτῶν. The last detail in the description of the conqueror's dealings is the carrying away into captivity the children of the dwellers in Jerusalem. That Pompey carried away many captives appears from various sources of evidence: e.g. Joseph. *Ant.* XIV. iv. 4 ἐλήφθη δὲ αἰχμάλωτος καὶ Ἀψάλωμος θεῖος ἅμα καὶ πενθερὸς Ἀριστοβούλου. 5 ἐπήγετο δὲ (εἰς Ῥώμην) μετὰ τῆς γενεᾶς καὶ Ἀριστόβουλον δεδεμένον. δύο γὰρ ἦσαν αὐτῷ θυγατέρες καὶ τοιοῦτοι υἱεῖς ὧν εἷς Ἀλέξανδρος μὲν ἀπέδρα, ὁ δὲ νεώτερος Ἀντίγονος συνεκομίζετο εἰς Ῥώμην ἅμα ταῖς ἀδελφαῖς.

The captives from Jerusalem swelled the number who were led in thousands through Rome on the occasion of the celebration of his great triumph (61). Plutarch mentions that 'the captives who walked in the procession (not to mention the chief of the pirates) were the son of Tigranes, king of Armenia, Zosima the wife of Tigranes, Aristobulus the king of Judea, &c. &c.'

We learn also from Philo's *De Legatione ad Caium* how numerous the Jewish captives were in Rome during the reign of Tiberius. And it can hardly be questioned that the great majority of these had been brought to the capital either by Pompey or by his lieutenants. Phil. *Legat. ad Cai.* § 23 πῶς οὖν ἀπεδέχετο τὴν πέραν τοῦ Τιβέρεως ποταμοῦ μεγάλην τῆς Ῥώμης ἀποτομήν, ἣν οὐκ ἠγνόει κατεχομένην καὶ οἰκουμένην πρὸς Ἰουδαίων; Ῥωμαῖοι δὲ ἦσαν οἱ πλείους ἀπελευθερωθέντες· αἰχμάλωτοι γὰρ ἀχθέντες εἰς Ἰταλίαν ὑπὸ τῶν κτησαμένων ἠλευθερώθησαν.

ἐν βεβηλώσει. βεβήλωσις in the LXX. occurs only in Lev. xxi. 4 οὐ μιανθήσεται ἐξάπινα ἐν τῷ λαῷ αὐτοῦ εἰς βεβήλωσιν αὐτοῦ. See i. 8.

ἐν βεβηλώσει seems here to mean 'in the time when they disregarded all laws of ceremonial cleanness.'

Looking back over these nine verses it is worth while noticing how closely we can identify the various details of the description on the assumption that Pompey is the foreign invader.

Thus in ver. 16 we have the far off place of his birth, and his tremendous victories over Tigranes and Mithridates: in ver. 17 he is yet at a distance in Syria when he determines upon a campaign in which Palestine is included; in ver. 18 his attention is attracted to the affairs of Jerusalem by the rival applicants and the representatives of the people, who all load him with gifts and flattery and hail him as their nation's deliverer; in ver. 19 his march into Palestine is conducted without opposition, the fortresses that barred the way are one after another surrendered without a blow, he finally enters Jerusalem amid public acclamation; in ver. 20 he stands among the people as their father to assist them and compose their differences; in ver. 21 he captures by force the Temple and its fortifications; in ver. 22 his success is so complete and the folly of the people so perverse, that it is as if God himself were guiding him on his way; in ver. 23 his relentless character shows itself towards those who tried to thwart him: princes and councillors are put to death, Jerusalem flows with blood; and in ver. 24 the climax is reached in the final scene, where this Deliverer of the people carries off into captivity thousands of their sons and daughters.

25 ἐποίησαν. The connection of

24 He carried away their sons and their daughters whom they had begotten in *their* defilement.

25 They *had done*[13] according to their uncleanness, even as their fathers did,

[13] Gr. *did*

26 They polluted Jerusalem and the things that had been dedicated unto the name of God.

27 God hath been justified in his judgements upon the nations of the earth,

28 And the saints of God are as innocent lambs in their midst.

this and the following verse with the section that has just closed is not obvious. They seem to belong more naturally to the description of Jewish vice in vv. 8—14. The most probable explanation is that the Psalmist here begins a recapitulation of his theme. Verses 25, 26 summarize the provocations of the people, vv. 27—32 testify the equity of Divine visitation. The connecting thought in this verse with the previous sentence is the captivity of 'the sons and daughters' of Jerusalem. Just as 'their fathers' had done wickedly and been carried captive to Babylon, so the Jews of this generation had done according to their uncleanness and had been carried away prisoners to Rome. Wellhausen explains οἱ πατέρες of the preceding generation who had committed the High-Priesthood into the hands of the Asmonean Princes. But so literal an interpretation of οἱ πατέρες αὐτῶν seems to us to be a needless and prosaic limitation of the sense.

26 ἐμίαναν Ἰερουσαλὴμ καὶ τὰ ἡγιασμένα κ.τ.λ. Cf. i. 8 ἐβεβήλωσαν τὰ ἅγια κυρίου. ii. 3 οἱ υἱοὶ Ἱερουσαλὴμ ἐμίαναν τὰ ἅγια κυρίου, ἐβεβήλουν τὰ δῶρα τοῦ θεοῦ. In all these passages a special reference seems to be made to the pollution of the sacrifices and sacred gifts by priests who were neglectful of the Levitical ceremonial. It is therefore interesting to note the similarity of the phraseology of these passages with the LXX. of Levit. xxi. xxii., which deals with the ceremonial purification of the sons of Aaron, e.g. ver. 6 ἅγιοι ἔσονται τῷ θεῷ αὐτῶν καὶ οὐ βεβηλώσουσι τὸ ὄνομα τοῦ θεοῦ αὐτῶν: ver. 12 (ὁ ἱερεὺς ὁ μέγας) οὐ βεβηλώσει τὸ ἡγιασμένον τοῦ θεοῦ αὐτοῦ. xxii. 2 οὐ βεβηλώσουσι τὸ ὄνομα τὸ ἅγιόν μου ὅσα αὐτοὶ ἁγιάζουσί μοι· ἐγὼ κύριος: ver. 3 πᾶς ἄνθρωπος ὃς ἂν προσέλθῃ ἀπὸ παντὸς τοῦ σπέρματος ὑμῶν πρὸς τὰ ἅγια ὅσα ἂν ἁγιάζωσιν οἱ υἱοὶ Ἰσραὴλ τῷ κυρίῳ καὶ ἡ ἀκαθαρσία αὐτοῦ ἐπ' αὐτῷ ᾖ, ἐξολοθρευθήσεται ἡ ψυχὴ ἐκείνη ἀπ' ἐμοῦ.

A good illustration of our passage is afforded by Assumpt. Mos. v. 3, 4 et contaminabunt inquinationibus domum servitutis suae...non enim sequentur veritatem Dei, sed quidam altarium inquinabunt de(decoris) muneribus quae imponent Domino, qui non sunt sacerdotes, sed servi de servis nati. τὰ ἡγιασμένα τῷ ὀνόματι τοῦ θεοῦ are equivalent to τὰ δῶρα τοῦ θεοῦ.

27 ἐδικαιώθη ὁ θεός. Cf. iii. 4, 5; iv. 9.

ἐν τοῖς κρίμασιν αὐτοῦ ἐν τοῖς ἔθνεσι τῆς γῆς, i.e. when He sends His judgements upon the nations of the earth, God's justice is seen and acknowledged, even by His saints who are in the midst of the calamities which He sends. How much more, the Psalmist seems to argue, when He sends His judgements upon His own chosen people, must His saints praise His name and recognize the righteous dealing of His chastisement.

28 οἱ ὅσιοι τοῦ θεοῦ. Cf. on iii. 10, iv. 7. For the expression in the Psalter see xxix. (xxx.) 4, xxx. (xxxi.) 23 &c.

ὡς ἀρνία ἐν ἀκακίᾳ ἐν μέσῳ αὐτῶν. For the translator's use of ἐν ἀκακίᾳ instead of the adjective ἄκακα see note on vi. 8. The words very possibly contain an allusion to Lot (cf. 2 Pet. ii. 7), but the language of the simile is based probably upon Jer. xi. 19 ἐγὼ δὲ ὡς ἀρνίον ἄκακον ἀγόμενον τοῦ θύεσθαι. It was no doubt one in familiar use. Its occurrence here is interesting as affording a nearly contemporary illustration of the figure of speech employed by our LORD when addressing His disciples, Matt. x. 16 ἰδοὺ ἐγὼ ἀποστέλλω ὑμᾶς ὡς πρόβατα ἐν μέσῳ λύκων. Luke x. 3 ὡς ἄρνας ἐν μέσῳ λύκων.

²⁹ αἰνετὸς κύριος ὁ κρίνων πᾶσαν τὴν γῆν ἐν δικαιοσύνῃ αὐτοῦ.
³⁰ ἰδοὺ δὴ, ὁ θεὸς, ἔδειξας ἡμῖν τὸ κρίμα σου ἐν τῇ δικαιοσύνῃ σου.
³¹ εἶδον οἱ ὀφθαλμοὶ αὐτῶν τὰ κρίματά σου, ὁ θεὸς, ἐδικαιώσαμεν τὸ ὄνομά σου τὸ ἔντιμον εἰς αἰῶνας·
³² ὅτι σὺ ὁ θεὸς τῆς δικαιοσύνης, κρίνων τὸν Ἰσραὴλ ἐν παιδείᾳ.

³³ Ἐπίστρεψον, ὁ θεὸς, τὸ ἔλεός σου ἐφ' ἡμᾶς καὶ οἰκτείρησον ἡμᾶς,
³⁴ συνάγαγε τὴν διασπορὰν Ἰσραὴλ μετ' ἐλέου καὶ χρηστότητος·
³⁵ ὅτι ἡ πίστις σου μεθ' ἡμῶν,
καὶ ἡμεῖς ἐσκληρύναμεν τὸν τράχηλον ἡμῶν,
καὶ σὺ παιδευτὴς ἡμῶν εἶ.
³⁶ μὴ ὑπερίδῃς ἡμᾶς, ὁ θεὸς ἡμῶν,
ἵνα μὴ καταπίῃ ἡμᾶς ἔθνη, μὴ ὄντος λυτρουμένου.

31 αὐτῶν Codd. (Wellh. conj. ἡμῶν).
32 σὺ ὁ θεὸς V, K, P, M, om. ὁ A, edd.
33 οἰκτήρησον Fabr. (cf. vii. 8).
34 συνάγαγε V, K, P, M, Fabr. συνήγαγε A? (Cerda). ἐλαίου P.

A similar metaphor is employed by the writer of Enoch, throughout his vision of Israel's history ch. lxxxix. &c.

Schöttgen (*Hor. Heb.* I. 97) cites a Rabbinic saying from Tanch. fol. 10, 2. Hadrian said to Rabbi Jehuda: 'Great is the sheep that stands firm among seventy wolves.' He answered: 'Great is the Shepherd who rescues and protects it, but smiteth the wolves in the presence of the Lord.'

29 αἰνετὸς. Cf. iii. 2 τῷ θεῷ τῷ αἰνετῷ.

ὁ κρίνων πᾶσαν τὴν γῆν. Cf. ii. 36. Possibly a reminiscence of Gen. xviii. 25 ὁ κρίνων πᾶσαν τὴν γῆν, οὐ ποιήσεις κρίσιν. If so, the probability that the example of Lot underlies vv. 27, 28 is greatly increased.

For the contents of the verse cf. Ps. ix. 9 καὶ αὐτὸς κρινεῖ τὴν οἰκουμένην ἐν δικαιοσύνῃ.

30 ἰδοὺ δὴ. Cf. 2 Sam. vii. 2 ἰδοὺ δὴ (רְאֵה נָא) ἐγὼ κατοικῶ ἐν οἴκῳ κεδρίνῳ, the only place in the LXX., according to Tromm, where it occurs. It is not found in the N. T.

Cf. Aq. Job xiii. 15 (הֵן), 18 (הִנֵּה־נָא).

ἡμῖν, emphatic. God who judgeth the whole earth righteously (ver. 29) is righteous when He sendeth judgements upon Israel.

31 οἱ ὀφθαλμοὶ αὐτῶν. All the MSS. read αὐτῶν. At first sight we should have expected ἡμῶν in a sentence occurring between ἔδειξας ἡμῖν and ἐδικαιώσαμεν, and Wellhausen boldly translates 'unsere Augen.' In support of this conjecture may be cited ix. 3, where the MSS. show a confusion between ἡμῶν and αὐτῶν, and the advantage of the reading is obvious, since it maintains the continuity of thought from the preceding verse.

The reading of the MSS. is however capable of a good explanation; 'the eyes of the Gentiles look upon thy judgements, but it is we, the saints of God, who not only beheld but justified his ways.' The αὐτῶν of this verse must then be understood like the αὐτῶν of ver. 28 to refer to the τὰ ἔθνη of ver. 27; or even to the subject of vv. 25, 26, the profane Jews.

29 The LORD is worthy to be praised that judgeth all the earth in his righteousness.

30 Behold now, O God, thou hast shown to us thy judgement in thy righteousness.

31 Our[14] eyes have seen thy judgements, O God; we have justified thy name that is honoured for evermore.

[14] Txt. *their*

32 For thou art the righteous God, that judgeth Israel with chastening.

33 O God, turn thy mercy upon us and have compassion upon us.

34 Gather together the dispersed of Israel with mercy and lovingkindness.

35 For thy faithfulness is with us; and when we stiffen our neck, thou dost chasten us[15].

36 Forsake us not, O our God, lest the heathen should swallow us up, and there be none to deliver:

[15] Gr. *and we have stiffened... and thou art our chastener*

ἐδικαιώσαμεν. See on ver. 27.

τὸ ὄνομα τὸ ἔντιμον. Cf. Dt. xxviii. 58 φοβεῖσθαι τὸ ὄνομα τὸ ἔντιμον. In Ps. lxxi. (lxxii.) 14 καὶ ἔντιμον τὸ ὄνομα αὐτῶν ἐνώπιον αὐτοῦ, either ὄνομα is a corruption of αἷμα or the LXX. and Theodot. read שמם for דמם.

32 ὅτι σύ. This clause may be taken in three different ways; (1) as the summary of the foregoing sentences = 'for thou art the God of righteousness;' (2) as an introduction to ver. 33 = 'Seeing that thou art..., therefore turn;' (3) as epexegetic of ἐδικαιώσαμεν = 'We justified Thy name... that Thou art the God of righteousness.' The last method seems to be most suitable to the context.

ὁ θεὸς τῆς δικαιοσύνης. Cf. Ps. iv. 1 ὁ θεὸς τῆς δικαιοσύνης μου.

ἐν παιδείᾳ. Cf. Ecclus. iv. 17 καὶ βασανίσει (σοφία) αὐτὸν ἐν παιδείᾳ αὐτῆς. See on vii. 3, 4, 8, x. 3.

34 συνάγαγε τὴν διασπορὰν. On the gathering together of 'the dispersed' Israelites see note on xi. 3, 4; and for διασπορά see ix. 2; John vii. 35.

Compare for this passage Is. xlix. 6 τὴν διασπορὰν τοῦ Ἰσραὴλ ἐπιστρέψαι. Ps. cxlvi. 2 τὰς διασπορὰς τοῦ Ἰσραὴλ ἐπισυνάξει.

The general tenour of the passage may be illustrated by Apoc. Bar. lxxxviii. 7 Si enim hæc ita feceritis semper recordabitur vestri is qui omni tempore pollicitus est pro nobis illis qui præstantiores nobis erant, quod non in perpetuum obliviscereretur, aut derelinqueret semen nostrum, sed *misericordia multa colligeret denuo omnes qui dispersi sunt*.

35 ἡ πίστις σου. πίστις is here used in the sense of 'faithfulness,' the quality of one who keeps faith and fulfils a promise: see xiv. 1. In this sense it is not common, but cf. Lam. iii. 23 πολλὴ ἡ πίστις σου, 'great is thy faithfulness.' The Hebrew אמונה is in the Psalter generally rendered ἀλήθεια.

καὶ ἡμεῖς...καὶ σύ. Cf. on vii. 7.

ἐσκληρύναμεν. For the phrase 'to stiffen the neck' הקשה את ערף, cf. 2 Chron. xxx. 8 μὴ σκληρύνητε τὰς καρδίας ὑμῶν (v. 6 τοὺς τραχήλους ὑμῶν, as the Hebr.). Neh. ix. 16 ἐσκλήρυναν τὸν τράχηλον αὐτῶν. Jer. vii. 26, xix. 15. In all these passages the words 'as your fathers' accompany the phrase and point back to its Deuteronomic use, Deut. x. 16 τὸν τράχηλον οὐ σκληρυνεῖτε.

36 μὴ ὑπερίδῃς, lit. 'do not overlook us and neglect us.'

The word ὑπεριδεῖν is found in the LXX. with its natural signification, as in Deut. xxii. 1 μὴ ἰδὼν τὸν μόσχον τοῦ ἀδελφοῦ σου ἢ τὸ πρόβατον αὐτοῦ πλανώμενα ἐν τῇ ὁδῷ ὑπερίδῃς αὐτὰ (וְהִתְעַלַּמְתָּ מֵהֶם). Ps. liv. (lv.) 1 καὶ μὴ ὑπερίδῃς τὴν δέησίν μου (וְאַל־תִּתְעַלַּם מִתְּחִנָּתִי).

It is also used to translate quite a different word, e.g. Deut. iii. 26 'the LORD was wroth with me for your sakes' (καὶ ὑπερεῖδε κύριος = וַיִּתְעַבֵּר יְהֹוָה), where the Greek word is either an intentional modi-

ΨΑΛΜΟΙ ΣΑΛΟΜΩΝΤΟΣ. [VIII. 37

³⁷ καὶ σὺ ὁ θεὸς ἡμῶν ἀπ' ἀρχῆς,
καὶ ἐπὶ σὲ ἠλπίσαμεν, κύριε.
³⁸ καὶ ἡμεῖς οὐκ ἀφεξόμεθά σου,
ὅτι χρηστὰ τὰ κρίματά σου ἐφ' ἡμᾶς.
³⁹ ἡμῖν καὶ τοῖς τέκνοις ἡμῶν ἡ εὐδοκία εἰς τὸν αἰῶνα,
κύριε σωτὴρ ἡμῶν, ογ caλεγθηcομεθα ἔτι τὸν αἰῶνα χρόνον.

⁴⁰ Αἰνετὸς κύριος ἐν τοῖς κρίμασιν αὐτοῦ ἐν στόματι ὁσίων,
⁴¹ καὶ σὺ εὐλογημένος, Ἰσραὴλ, ὑπὸ κυρίου εἰς τὸν αἰῶνα.

θ. ψαλμος τωι cαλομων εις ελεγχον.

IX. Ἐν τῷ ἀπαχθῆναι Ἰσραὴλ ἐν ἀποικεσίᾳ εἰς γῆν ἀλλοτρίαν,
ἐν τῷ ἀποστῆναι αὐτοὺς ἀπὸ κγρίογ τογ λγτρωcαμένογ αὐτοὺς,

37 καὶ A ('pæne deletum' Cerda, qui conj. ἐαὶ vel potius ἐὰ (cf. Job xxv. 6) vel καὶ).
38 οὐκ ἀφεξόμεθα V, K, P, M: om. οὐκ A (Cerda). Fabr. 'forte ἀντεξόμεθα.'
39 σαλευθησόμεθα V, K, P, M, Hilg. Geig. Fritzsch. Pick. σαλευθησώμεθα A, Fabr. Wellh.
40 ἀνετός A, Cerda ('liber,' 'solutus').
1 ἀποικησίᾳ P.

---

fication of the Hebrew or has arisen from a confusion of the root עבר with the preposition ὑπέρ.

ἵνα μὴ καταπίῃ ἡμᾶς ἔθνη. If, as is most probable, the Psalmist alludes to the Romans, we may compare the expression of dread, which the chief priests and the Pharisees uttered at a later period, 'the Romans will come and take away our place and nation' (John xi. 47, 48).

For καταπίῃ, cf. Num. xvi. 34 μήποτε καταπίῃ ἡμᾶς ἡ γῆ. Lam. ii. 16 διήνοιξαν ἐπὶ σὲ στόμα αὐτῶν πάντες οἱ ἐχθροί σου... καὶ εἶπαν κατεπίομεν αὐτήν. Hab. i. 13 ἐν τῷ καταπίνειν ἀσεβῆ τὸν δίκαιον.

μὴ ὄντος λυτρουμένου. See note on ver. 12. Observe μὴ in the hypothetic clause; but in ver. 12 οὐκ ὄντος states the fact.

37 ὁ θεὸς ἡμῶν ἀπ' ἀρχῆς. Possibly a reminiscence of Hab. i. 12 οὐχὶ σὺ ἀπ' ἀρχῆς κύριε ὁ θεὸς ὁ ἅγιός μου.

For ἀπ' ἀρχῆς 'of old' referring to God's earliest dealings with the chosen people, cf. Ps. lxxiii. (lxxiv.) 2 μνήσθητι τῆς συναγωγῆς σου ἧς ἐκτήσω ἀπ' ἀρχῆς.

38 οὐκ ἀφεξόμεθά σου. See on v. 9. The meaning is 'We will not swerve from following thee: we will not cease to call upon thee; for our confidence in Thy righteousness is complete.' Cf. Ps. cxix. 102 'I have not turned aside from thy judgements.'

χρηστά. Cf. Ps. cxviii. (cxix.) 39 τὰ γὰρ κρίματά σου χρηστά.

39 ἡμῖν καὶ τοῖς τέκνοις ἡμῶν ἡ εὐδοκία. The words ἡμῖν καὶ τοῖς τέκνοις ἡμῶν here introduce a blessing. It is striking to compare them with the self-pronounced curse of the people in Matt. xxvii. 25 καὶ ἀποκριθεὶς πᾶς ὁ λαὸς εἶπεν Τὸ αἷμα αὐτοῦ ἐφ' ἡμᾶς καὶ ἐπὶ τὰ τέκνα ἡμῶν. Cf. Acts ii. 39 ὑμῖν γὰρ ἐστιν ἡ ἐπαγγελία καὶ τοῖς τέκνοις ὑμῶν καὶ πᾶσι τοῖς εἰς μακρὰν οὖσι.

ἡ εὐδοκία. εὐδοκία is used here as usual of the Divine favour and good-will. See on iii. 4.

It is not clear whether ἡ εὐδοκία expresses an assertion or a wish, whether we should supply ἔσται (ἐστιν) or εἴη (ἔστω). The point must be determined by the reading to be adopted in the following clause, σαλευθησόμεθα or σαλευθησώμεθα.

κύριε σωτὴρ ἡμῶν. Cf. Isai. xliii. 11 ἐγὼ ὁ θεὸς καὶ οὐκ ἔστι πάρεξ ἐμοῦ σώζων. lx. 16 γνώσῃ ὅτι ἐγὼ κύριος ὁ σώζων σε. Ecclus. li. 1 αἰνέσω σε θεὸν τὸν σωτῆρά

37 And thou art our God from the beginning, and upon thee have we set our hope, O LORD.

38 And we will not depart from thee, for thy judgements are gracious towards us.

39 Upon us and upon our children be thy good pleasure for ever, O LORD our Saviour, that we be not [16] moved again for ever.

[16] Gr. *we shall not be*

40 The LORD is worthy to be praised in the mouth of his saints for the sake of his judgements,

41 And blessed art thou of the LORD, O Israel, for evermore.

PSALM IX.

A Psalm of Solomon: 'For a rebuke.'

1 When Israel was led away captive into a strange land, because[1] they departed from the LORD which redeemed them;

[1] Gr. *when*

μου. Bar. iv. 22 παρὰ τοῦ αἰωνίου σωτῆρος ὑμῶν.

σαλευθησόμεθα. The Ind. is to be expected after οὐ. The form σαλευθησώμεθα is in all probability a mere itacism. For the words cf. Ps. ix. 27 (x. 6) οὐ μὴ σαλευθῶ, xxix. (xxx.) 7. xv. (xvi.) 8 ἵνα μὴ σαλευθῶ εἰς τὸν αἰῶνα. cxi. (cxii.) 6 εἰς τὸν αἰῶνα οὐ σαλευθήσεται.

ἔτι τὸν αἰῶνα χρόνον. Cf. xv. 14 εἰς τὸν αἰῶνα χρόνον. The idiom is found in the LXX. e.g. Ex. xiv. 13; Is. xiii. 20; and is frequent in the other versions, Aq. Symm. Theod.

40 αἰνετὸς κύριος. Cf. ver. 29.

ἐν τοῖς κρίμασιν αὐτοῦ, i.e. on account of the justice of his judgements.

41 καὶ σὺ εὐλογημένος. The usual doxology is expanded by the blessing pronounced on Israel, for which cf. Num. vi. 26, xxiv. 1; Deut. xxvi. 15. So Ps. iii. 9 τοῦ κυρίου ἡ σωτηρία καὶ ἐπὶ τὸν λαόν σου ἡ εὐλογία σου, xxviii. (xxix.) 11.

For εὐλογημένος...ὑπὸ κυρίου cf. Gen. xxiv. 31 εὐλογητὸς κυρίου (v. l. κύριος) where Procop. in *Cat. Niceph.* p. 299 says τὸ Ἑβραϊκὸν ἔχει· ηὐλογημένος ὑπὸ κυρίου (Field's *Hex.* I. 39).

Ps. IX.—*Argument.* The Psalm appears to fall easily into three parts.

I. 1—6.

(*a*) 1, 2. In the first two verses the situation is put before us. Israel is captive, and dispersed.

(*b*) 3—6 give the reason in a rather indirect form.

Israel had sinned, though secretly, and God saw it, as, in fact, He sees all acts, good or bad.

II. 7--15.

(*a*) 7—10. Every man makes his own fate. Righteousness results in life: iniquity in death to the doers.

(β) 11—15. He who has sinned, however,—as Israel has done—may still hope for pardon if he repents.

III. 16—19.

Since, then, God is forgiving will He not have mercy upon Israel, in remembrance of His ancient choice and covenant? God is their hope, may He shew them mercy.

The general character of the Psalm is historical and religious, not political. It deals with very much the same topics, and in much the same strain as the last part (v. 27—41) of Ps. viii.; and it is more retrospective than any of the other Psalms.

1 Whatever the probability that the first Psalm contains a retrospect over a long period of years, there can be no doubt that here the Babylonian captivity is referred to.

ἀπαχθῆναι...ἐν ἀποικεσίᾳ. Cf. 2 Kings xxiv. 15 ἀπήγαγεν εἰς ἀποικεσίαν (הוֹלִיד הִגְלָה). 16 ἤγαγεν αὐτούς...μετοικεσίαν (וַיְבִיאֵם...גּוֹלָה). Cf. 'children of the captivity' υἱοὶ ἀποικεσίας, Ezr. vi. 16.

ἐν τῷ ἀποστ. We have rendered 'because' in preference to 'when' as it seems obvious that the reason for the captivity is being given, not the moment when it took place.

²ἀπερρίφησαν ἀπὸ κληρονομίας ἧς ἔδωκεν αὐτοῖς κύριος
    ἐν παντὶ ἔθνει,
ἐπὶ διασπορᾷ τοῦ Ἰσραὴλ κατὰ τὸ ῥῆμα τοῦ θεοῦ,
³ἵνα δικαιωθῇc, ὁ θεός, ἐν τῇ δικαιοσύνῃ σου ἐν ταῖς
    ἀνομίαις ἡμῶν·
⁴ὅτι σὺ κριτὴς δίκαιος ἐπὶ πάντας τοὺς λαοὺς τῆς γῆς.
⁵οὐ γὰρ κρυβήσεται ἀπὸ τῆς γνώσεώς σου πᾶς ποιῶν κακά,
⁶καὶ αἱ δικαιοσύναι τῶν ὁσίων σου ἐνώπιόν σου, κύριε·
καὶ ποῦ κρυβήσεται ἄνθρωπος ἀπὸ τῆς γνώσεώς σου;

⁷Ὁ θεός, τὰ ἔργα ἡμῶν ἐν ἐκλογῇ καὶ ἐξουσίᾳ τῆς
    ψυχῆς ἡμῶν,
τοῦ ποιῆσαι δικαιοσύνην καὶ ἀδικίαν ἐν ἔργοις χειρῶν
    ἡμῶν·
⁸καὶ ἐν τῇ δικαιοσύνῃ σου ἐπισκέπτῃ γίογc ἀνθρώπων.
⁹ὁ ποιῶν δικαιοσύνην θησαυρίζει ζωὴν ἑαυτῷ παρὰ κυρίῳ,
καὶ ὁ ποιῶν ἄδικα αὐτὸς αἴτιος τῆς ψυχῆς ἐν ἀπωλείᾳ·

2 ἧς ita V, K, P, M, ᾗ A.
3 αὐτῶν edd. Hilg.¹ Fritzsch., corr. Hilg.² ἡμῶν A, V, K, P, M.
6 καὶ ποῦ V, K, P. καὶ οὐ A.
τῆς γνώσεώς σου ὁ θεός V, K.
7 ἐξουσίᾳ V, (?) K, P, M, Hilg. conj., ita Fritzsch. Pick.   ἐξουσία A, Cerda Fabr. Geiger.
ἔργα ἡμῶν ἐν εὐλογῇ A.
8 ἐπισκέπτεις A.
υἱὸς M.

λυτρωσαμένου. Not, as viii. 12 and 36, λυτρωμένου = goël, but as in Deut. xiii. 5 τοῦ λυτρωσαμένου σε ἐκ τῆς δουλείας. The deliverance from Egypt is meant here, as there.

2 ἀπερρίφησαν—ἐν παντὶ ἔθνει. We have taken these words together, in the belief that the passage is a reminiscence of Deut. iv. 27, διασπερεῖ Κύριος ὑμᾶς ἐν παντὶ ἔθνει. This passage is, in fact, the ῥῆμα τοῦ θεοῦ referred to just afterwards, as receiving its fulfilment. The strong word ἀπορρίπτω is probably taken from Jer. xvi. 13 καὶ ἀπορρίψω ὑμᾶς ἀπὸ τῆς γῆς ταύτης. xxii. 26 καὶ ἀπορρίψω σε...εἰς γῆν οὗ οὐκ ἐτέχθης ἐκεῖ.

διασπορά. See on viii. 34.

3 ἵνα δικαιωθῇς, see on ii. 16. The language here closely resembles that of Ps. l. 6 (li. 4), ὅπως ἂν δικαιωθῇς ἐν τοῖς λόγοις σου. Cf. viii. 7.

ἡμῶν. The reading αὐτῶν was a slip of Hilgenfeld's.

4 κριτής, ii. 19, 36, iv. 28.
5 For the omniscience of the Almighty cf. ii. 18, viii. 8, xiv. 5.

The closest parallel is to be found in Job xxxiv. 22 οὐδὲ ἔσται τόπος τοῦ κρυβῆναι τοὺς ποιοῦντας τὰ ἄνομα. The sequence of thought should be noticed.

v. 5, b. God sees sinful actions,
6, a. and righteous ones;
6, b. where then shall a man be hidden from this knowledge?

οὐ...πᾶς. See ii. 11, xiv. 3.

6 Cf. Matt. vi. 1—4 προσέχετε [δὲ] τὴν δικαιοσύνην (v. l. ἐλεημοσύνην) ὑμῶν μὴ ποιεῖν ἔμπροσθεν τῶν ἀνθρώπων....(2) ὅταν οὖν ποιῇς ἐλεημοσύνην κ.τ.λ....(4) καὶ ὁ πατήρ σου ὁ **βλέπων ἐν τῷ κρυπτῷ** ἀποδώσει σοι. This passage finds an interesting illustration in our Psalm, if, as is probable enough, δικαιοσύναι here is used in the special sense of almsgiving. We have preferred to let the more general rendering 'righteous acts' stand in the

2 They were cast away among every nation, from out of the inheritance which the LORD gave them: that Israel might be dispersed according to the word of God;

3 That thou mightest be justified, O God, in thy righteousness by reason of our transgressions.

4 For thou art a just Judge over all the peoples of the earth.

5 For there shall not be hidden from thy knowledge any one that doeth evil,

6 And the righteous acts of thy saints are before thee, O LORD; and where shall a man be hidden from thy knowledge?

7 O God, our works are in our choice, yea, in the power of our own soul: to do either righteousness or iniquity in the works of our hands.

8 And in thy righteousness dost thou visit the sons of men.

9 Whoso doeth righteousness layeth up for himself life at the LORD'S hand: and whoso doeth wickedness is guilty of his own soul to destroy it.

---

text, but as a fact, to the Jewish mind the acts included would be of two kinds principally: (*a*) ceremonial observances, (*b*) works of mercy. When the authors (or author) of 4 Esdras and Apoc. Baruch speak of 'a treasure of works laid up with the most High' (Esdr. vi.ᵃ 50), or 'the treasures wherein is gathered together the *righteousness* (iustitia, doubtless = δικαιοσύνη) of those that have been justified in the world (creatura),' or even when our Lord speaks of 'laying up treasure in heaven,' the works and the treasure would alike mean to their immediate hearers such definite acts of charity as are enumerated in Matt. xxv. 35—46. Similar works are those of which St James speaks (ii. 14 sqq.) as is manifest from the examples he there gives, and the reward which God sends even in this life to the doers of them, forms the main subject of the Book of Tobit. See also v. 9 of this Psalm.

That δικαιοσύνη in Matt. vi. 1 = ἐλεημοσύνη is obvious not only from other considerations, but more particularly from the emphatic οὖν in verse 2, and from the fact that later scribes have conspired to substitute ἐλεημ. for δικ. in verse 1. On the Hebrew equivalents and LXX. renderings see Dr Hatch's statement in *Essays on Biblical Greek*, p. 49 sqq.

δικαιοσύναι in the plural occurs nine times in the LXX. (acc. to Tromm) and once in Ecclus. (xliv. 10). Three of the passages occur in Ezekiel. In seven cases it is the equivalent of צְדָקָה; once (Ez. iii. 20) it stands for צֶדֶק. The passage in Ecclus. is worth quoting. ἀλλ' ἢ οὗτοι ἄνδρες ἐλέους ὧν αἱ δικαιοσύναι οὐκ ἐπελήσθησαν. Here again the idea of ἔλεος occurs in close connection with that of righteousness.

Another document as yet inedited in which the plural occurs with some frequency, is the Greek text of the Testament of Abraham.

The general conclusion of the foregoing is that we seem to be justified in attaching the special meaning of 'works of mercy' to δικαιοσύναι in this passage.

καὶ ποῦ. A reads καὶ οὐ, which is probably a reminiscence of v. 5 οὐ γὰρ κρυβήσεται.

7 See note on p. 95.

8 ἐπισκέπτῃ. The active form read by A never occurs in the LXX. A close parallel to this is Ps. viii. (ix.) 5 τίς ἐστιν ...υἱὸς ἀνθρώπου, ὅτι ἐπισκέπτῃ αὐτόν;

9 The meaning of δικαιοσύνη in this verse seems to differ from that in v. 8. The δικαιοσύνη of God in this latter passage is justice, impartiality. That of the righteous in v. 9 is practically the same as the δικαιοσύναι of v. 6; and the contrast between ὁ ποιοῦν δικαιοσύνην and ὁ ποιῶν ἄδικα will be well illustrated by such chapters as Ezekiel xviii. and xxxiii., where various acts of each kind are specified.

θησαυρίζει ζωήν. See above on v. 6 reff. to Esdras and Baruch. In the O. T.

92   ΨΑΛΜΟΙ ΣΑΛΟΜΩΝΤΟΣ.   [IX. 10

[10] τὰ γὰρ κρίματα κυρίου ἐν δικαιοσύνῃ κατ' ἄνδρα καὶ οἶκον.
[11] τίνι χρηστεύσῃ, ὁ θεός, εἰ μὴ τοῖς ἐπικαλουμένοις τὸν κύριον;
[12] καθαρίσει ἐν ἁμαρτίαις ψυχὴν ἐν ἐξομολογήσει, ἐν ἐξηγορίαις·
[13] ὅτι αἰσχύνη ἡμῖν καὶ τοῖς προσώποις ἡμῶν περὶ ἁπάντων.
[14] καὶ τίνι ἀφήσει ἁμαρτίας, εἰ μὴ τοῖς ἡμαρτηκόσι;
[15] δικαίους εὐλογήσεις καὶ οὐκ εὐθυνεῖς περὶ ὧν ἥμαρτον,
καὶ ἡ χρηστότης σου περὶ ἁμαρτάνοντας ἐν μεταμελείᾳ.

[16] Καὶ νῦν σὺ ὁ θεός, καὶ ἡμεῖς [ὁ] λαὸς ὃν ἠγάπησας,
ἴδε καὶ οἴκτειρον, ὁ θεὸς Ἰσραήλ, ὅτι σοί ἐσμεν,
καὶ μὴ ἀποστήσῃς ἔλεόν σου ἀφ' ἡμῶν,
ἵνα μὴ ἐπιθῶνται ἡμῖν·
[17] ὅτι σὺ ᾑρετίσω τὸ σπέρμα Ἀβραὰμ παρὰ πάντα τὰ ἔθνη,

12 ἐξομολογήσει V, K, P, M.   ὁμολογήσει A.
16 καὶ ἡμεῖς—οἴκτειρον om. A.   Per homœot. ὁ θεός.
σοί V, K, P.   σοῦ A, M (?).
ἀποστήσῃς.   ἀποστήσεις A.
17 ᾑρετίσω V.   Cerda Gr. ἡρέτισε, Lat. elegisti.   Fabr. ἡρέτεσας.
παρὰ om. A, V; supplevit Fabr.

---

we have similar language in Prov. ii. 7 θησαυρίζει τοῖς κατορθοῦσι σωτηρίαν, and similar thought in Tob. iv. 9 (11) à propos of almsgiving, θέμα γὰρ ἀγαθὸν θησαυρίζεις σεαυτῷ εἰς ἡμέραν ἀνάγκης.

παρὰ κυρίῳ is exactly the 'apud altissimum' of Esdras.

αἴτιος τῆς ψυχῆς. The word αἴτιος seems to occur only once in the canonical books, 1 Sam. xxii. 22 ἐγώ εἰμι αἴτιος τῶν ψυχῶν τοῦ οἴκου τοῦ πατρός σου. In Bel and the Dragon, v. 42 we have αἰτίους τῆς ἀπωλείας.

ἐν ἀπωλείᾳ by destroying his soul—because he destroys it.

10 τὰ γὰρ κρίματα. The connection is this: the good man reaps life, the bad man death, *for* God is just and distinguishes between man and man, between house and house. Cf. ii. 38 τοῦ διαστεῖλαι ἀνὰ μέσον δικαίου καὶ ἁμαρτωλοῦ.

κατ' ἄνδρα καὶ οἶκον. See iii. 9, 10, where the ideas are throughout similar to those here and in v. 12. We should get a simpler sequence of thought were we to make v. 12 change places with v. 11, but the MSS. give no support to this.

11 χρηστεύομαι, not found in the LXX., occurs in 1 Cor. xiii. 4 ἡ ἀγάπη ...χρηστεύεται. No earlier authority is quoted for it, so that the occurrence of the word may serve towards determining the date of this Version.

12 καθαρίσει. The subject of the verb is God: this is determined by the closely similar passage iii. 10. Cf. also xviii. 6.

ἐν ἁμαρτίαις, 'in the case of sin.'

ἐν ἐξομολογήσει etc. 'by means of' here practically equivalent to 'on condition of.' The ψυχὴν ἐν ἐξομολογήσει is equivalent to ψυχὴν ἐξομολογουμένην. Cf. ἀνδρὸς ἐν εὐσταθείᾳ iv. 11, παντὸς ἐν φόβῳ vi. 8, ἡ μαρτυρία ἐν νόμῳ x. 5. The reading of A ὁμολογήσει should be noted. This form is not found in the LXX. or N. T. Diod. Sic. (XVII. 68) has it in the sense of 'confession' and it is not unlikely to be correct here, but is unsupported by other MSS. ἐν ἐξηγορίαις is in all probability a duplicate rendering of ἐν ἐξομολογήσει, cf. Job xxii. 22, LXX. ἐξηγορίαν =Symm. ἐξομολόγησιν; xxxiii. 26 LXX. ἐξηγορία=Theodot. μετὰ ἐξομολογήσεως.

ΨΑΛΜΟΙ ΣΑΛΟΜΩΝΤΟΣ.

10 For the judgments of the LORD are in righteousness according to *each* man and his house.

11 With whom wilt thou deal graciously, O God, save with them that call upon the LORD?

12 He will cleanse the soul that hath sinned[2], if it make confession and acknowledgment[2].

[2] Gr. *in sin, in confession, in acknowledgment*

13 For upon us and upon our faces is shame because of all *these* things.

14 And to whom will he forgive sins, save unto them that have committed sin?

15 The righteous thou wilt bless and wilt not correct them for the sins that they have committed: and thy kindness is toward them that sin, *if so be* they repent[3].

[3] Gr. *in repentance*

16 And now thou art *our* God, and we are the people whom thou hast loved: behold and have pity, O God of Israel, for we are thine, and remove not thy mercy from us, that they set not upon us.

17 For thou didst choose the seed of Abraham before all the nations,

---

ἐξηγορία. The word occurs twice in Job (see Index), and the verb ἐξαγορεύω in Ps. xxxi. (xxxii.) 5 ἐξαγορεύσω κατ' ἐμοῦ τὴν ἀνομίαν μου τῷ κυρίῳ. The argument is: God forgives sins. To whom then? Naturally to those who have committed them. There is hope, then, for the sinner.

13 αἰσχύνη. The language seems to be based on Dan. ix. 7 καὶ ἡμῖν ἡ αἰσχύνη τοῦ προσώπου. Another variation is found in Bar. ii. 7 ἡμῖν δὲ καὶ τοῖς πατρίσιν ἡμῶν ἡ αἰσχύνη τῶν προσώπων, where the plural of πρόσωπον occurs as in this passage.

14 ἀφίημι occurs again only in Ps. xvii. There it is found thrice. In v. 29 and 45 it clearly = to allow. In v. 11 two renderings are possible, 'to let go' and 'to forsake.' See further *in loc.* ἀφιέναι ἁμαρτίας occurs with some frequency in the LXX., e.g. Exod. xxxii. 31; Ps. xxv. 19.

15 οὐκ εὐθυνεῖς. The uncompounded verb causes some little difficulty. The meaning required is 'thou wilt not exact the full penalty,' 'wilt correct them with judgment.' In this sense it is also found in 3 Macc. ii. 17 μὴ ἐκδικήσῃς ἡμᾶς ἐν τῇ ἀκαθαρσίᾳ μηδὲ εὐθύνῃς ἡμᾶς ἐν βεβηλώσει (cf. εὐθύνη, 3 Macc. iii. 28 τὴν οὐσίαν τοῦ ἐμπίπτοντος ὑπὸ τὴν εὐθύνην λήψεται).

Elsewhere in the LXX. it is almost synonymous with κατευθύνω, and stands for a process which was eminently desirable, and desired by the just man.

μεταμέλεια. Only in Hos. xi. 9. The ἐν here again expresses the condition under which God's goodness visits the sinner. See note on ver. 12. περὶ ἁμαρτάνοντας ἐν μεταμελείᾳ might have been equally well rendered περὶ ἁμαρτωλοὺς μεταμελομένους.

On the importance of 'repentance' in the doctrinal system of the Rabbins see *Pirqe Aboth* IV. 15, 'R. Li'ezer ben Jacob said...Repentance and good works are as a shield against punishment,' with Taylor's note (*Sayings of the Jewish Fathers*, p. 84). The verse reminds us of the distinction between 'the just' and 'the sinner...that repented' (Luke xv. 7, 10).

16 ἠγάπησας. For the aorist cf. Isai. xliii. 4 ἐγώ σε ἠγάπησα (אֲהַבְתִּיךָ).

ἐπιθῶνται. The subject is not expressed. The 3rd Plur. is here used indefinitely, reproducing the Heb. idiom. Cf. Gen. xxix. 2 ἐπότιζον, 1 Kings i. 2 ζητησάτωσαν.

17 ᾑρετίσω. Only in xvii. 5. The best parallel is in Ez. xx. 5 ἀφ' ἧς ἡμέρας ᾑρέτισα τὸν οἶκον Ἰσραήλ.

ΨΑΛΜΟΙ ΣΑΛΟΜΩΝΤΟΣ.

[18] καὶ ἔθου τὸ ὄνομά σου ἐφ' ἡμᾶς, κύριε,
καὶ οὐ καταπαύσῃ εἰς τὸν αἰῶνα.
[19] ἐν διαθήκῃ διέθου τοῖς πατράσιν ἡμῶν περὶ ἡμῶν,
καὶ ἡμεῖς ἐλπιοῦμεν ἐπὶ σὲ ἐν ἐπιστροφῇ ψυχῆς ἡμῶν.
[20] τοῦ κυρίου ἡ ἐλεημοσύνη ἐπὶ τὸν οἶκον Ἰσραὴλ εἰς τὸν
αἰῶνα καὶ ἔτι.

20 ἡ ἐλεημοσύνη ἡ A, V, Fabr. etc.: delevit Fritzsche. om. ἡ K, P, M : om. τὸν ante οἶκον V, K, P, M.
καὶ ἔτι add. A τέλος.

---

18 καὶ ἔθου τὸ ὄνομά σου ἐφ' ἡμᾶς, κύριε. Cf. Ecclus. xxxiii. 12 (xxxvi. 17) ἐλέησον λαὸν, κύριε, κεκλημένον ἐπ' ὀνόματί σου. Is. xliii. 7, lxiii. 19. Jas. ii. 7. καὶ οὐ καταπαύσῃ εἰς τὸν αἰῶνα. This, the reading of all MSS., can only bear one meaning. Thou wilt not desist for ever—desist, that is, from setting thy name upon us, or from choosing us. Geiger 'und nicht wirst du ablassen ewiglich.' Wellh. 'und wirst nicht ewiglich feiern.' Pick 'wilt not desist for ever.' But it seems exceedingly doubtful if καταπαύομαι will bear this meaning. In the LXX. it is used in several ways, e.g. of God resting from his works (in Gen. i.), of any one leaving off doing a particular thing (but always with a participle, κατέπαυσε λαλῶν etc.), transitively of giving rest from enemies, etc., and of making a thing cease, destroying it. But no close parallel to the sense wanted here is to be found.

There is an obvious correction however which has something ·in its favour. If we read CY for OY, we get the meaning, 'thou wilt abide or rest for ever,' and it is in favour of this, that we find Jerusalem spoken of as the κατάπαυσις of God (Ps. cxxxi. (cxxxii.) 14 αὕτη ἡ κατάπαυσίς μου εἰς αἰῶνα αἰῶνος· ὧδε κατοικήσω, ὅτι ᾑρετισάμην αὐτήν), a passage which is on the whole very like the one before us. Compare also Ecclus. xxxiii. 13, (xxxvi. 18) Οἰκτείρησον πόλιν ἁγιάσματός σου Ἰερουσαλὴμ, πόλιν καταπαύματός σου. In these Psalms again we have a similar expression, vii. 5 ἐν τῷ κατασκηνοῦν τὸ ὄνομα σου ἐν μέσῳ ἡμῶν ἐλεηθησόμεθα. The principal objection to this reading is that we still have to supply something in translation. Nothing is said of the place where God is to dwell. In spite of this we believe that the emendation gives a more intelligible meaning, and with more correct Greek, than the common text.

The reading of the MSS. might be illustrated by Aquila's rendering of Jer. xxxi. (xxxviii.) 36, καίγε τὸ σπέρμα Ἰσραὴλ καταπαύσῃ τοῦ μὴ εἶναι ἔθνος ἐνώπιόν μου. The sense then would be 'and wilt not suffer it (thy name) to cease *from among us* for ever.'

19 ἐν διαθήκῃ διέθου may possibly represent the Hebrew infin. absolute, 'verily Thou didst covenant.'

ἐπιστροφή, again only in xvi. 11. See on v. 19, and the title of vii. Here it has an intransitive sense, = 'the turning again,' not 'the restoration.' The 'covenant' forms, of course, a very common theme with O.T. writers. It occurs most prominently perhaps in Gen. xv. 18 διέθετο κύριος τῷ Ἀβραμ διαθήκην, λέγων, Τῷ σπέρματί σου δώσω τὴν γῆν ταύτην. Cf. also Jer. xxxi. (xxxviii.) 32 οὐ κατὰ τὴν διαθήκην ἣν διεθέμην τοῖς πατράσιν αὐτῶν. xxxiv. (xli.) 13; Neh. ix. 8.

20 The form of this verse gives a possibility of two renderings. It may be either a statement or a wish. But the latter seems most probable. A verse of similar form (xii. 7) is continued by means of optatives.

It is very noticeable that Psalms ix.—xii. each of them contain a verse precisely similar in form. In ix. x. xi. such a verse ends the Psalm. In xii. it is supplemented by a further prayer. In the rest of the collection the endings are dissimilar, only iv. 29 resembles this, and there again it is a wish, not a statement, being introduced with γένοιτο.

τοῦ κυρίου ἡ ἐλεημοσύνη is probably not the same as τοῦ κυρίου τὸ ἔλεος in xi. 9. The ἐλεημοσύνη of the Lord is his *righteousness* displayed in mercy: ἐλεημοσύνη represents צדקה in the original (see note on ver. 6 and the special significance of δικαιοσύνη). Another instance occurs

18 And didst set thy name upon us, O Lord; and thou wilt abide[4] *among us* for ever.

19 *Of a truth* thou didst covenant with our fathers concerning us: and in thee will we trust when our soul is turned unto thee.

20 Let the mercy of the Lord be upon the house of Israel for everlasting and world without end.

[4] Or, *wilt not suffer it to cease*. Gr. *wilt not rest*

---

in this book in xv. 15 where see note. Compare Deut. vi. 25 καὶ ἐλεημοσύνη (וּצְדָקָה) ἔσται ἡμῖν. Ps. xxiii. (xxiv.) 5 οὗτος λήμψεται εὐλογίαν παρὰ κυρίου καὶ ἐλεημοσύνην (וּצְדָקָה) παρὰ θεοῦ σωτῆρος αὐτοῦ. Dan. ix. 16 κύριε, ἐν πάσιν ἐλεημοσύνη σου (בְּכָל־צִדְקֹתֶיךָ). Isai. i. 27, xxviii. 17, lix. 16. So also ἐλεημοσύνη is the rendering of Symmachus in Ps. xxxiv. (xxxv.) 11, and of Aquila in Ex. xv. 13; Apoc. Bar. xliv. 14 'et a misericordia non recesserunt.'

εἰς τὸν αἰῶνα καὶ ἔτι = לְעוֹלָם וָעֶד as in xi. 8, 9. Cf. Ex. xv. 18 ἐπ' αἰῶνα καὶ ἔτι. Dan. xii. 3 εἰς τοὺς αἰῶνας καὶ ἔτι.

Note on v. 7.

7 This is by far the most difficult verse in the Psalm. The text is uncertain, and a doubt attaches to the meaning. Let us first consider the question connected with the text.

First, we find that Cerda's MS. (A) read ἐξουσία, and Hilgenfeld suggested the dative ἐξουσίᾳ which is adopted by Fritzsche. The question is one where we derive little help from MSS. No variants are recorded from Fritzsche's text by any other of our authorities, but the Copenhagen MS. does not insert iotas subscript or adscript: of the Vienna MS. we cannot speak from ocular inspection. The matter must be decided on consideration of intrinsic probability.

What are the two renderings?

α. **τὰ ἔργα ἡμῶν ἐν ἐκλογῇ καὶ ἐξουσίᾳ τῆς ψ. ἡμῶν.** 'Our works are in (depend upon) the choice and are subject to the authority of our soul.'

εἶναι ἐν ἐξουσίᾳ τινὸς would mean, no doubt, 'to be under the control, authority, jurisdiction of some one.' In Acts i. 7 Christ speaks of the times and seasons which the Father hath put ἐν τῇ ἰδίᾳ ἐξουσίᾳ. In Acts v. 4 Peter says to Ananias, of his land, οὐχὶ ἐν τῇ σῇ ἐξουσίᾳ ὑπῆρχε; These instances are, it seems to us, sufficient to show that the dative in this passage will give a sentence which is grammatical and legitimate.

Now turn to the actual reading of the MSS. These give us a different construction.

β. **τὰ ἔργα ἡμῶν ἐν ἐκλογῇ, καὶ ἐξουσία τῆς ψυχῆς ἡμῶν τοῦ ποιῆσαι.** Two renderings are possible. (α) Our deeds are in our own choice, and there is authority (power) belonging to our soul to do good or evil. (β) Our deeds are by the choice (of God) and (at the same time) we have power, etc. The point to be noticed is that (α) gives the same statement in two forms, (β) gives two apparently conflicting statements.

The rendering (α) joins τοῦ ποιῆσαι to ἐξουσία: at least this is the most natural though not the only way of treating the words. This construction is quite possible. We find it e.g. in Luke x. 19 ἐξουσίαν τοῦ πατεῖν ἐπάνω ὄφεων.

Objections which may be brought against the translation are (1) it leaves the words ἐν ἐκλογῇ somewhat obscure, as being without definition or limitation: and (2) it gives *two* coordinate clauses with the auxiliary verb understood in each; which is harsh.

Is the rendering (β) possible? Can the simple words *ἐν ἐκλογῇ* mean 'dependent on God's choice' = predestined? In favour of this translation is the fact that in *Pirqe Aboth* III. 24 (ed. Taylor, p. 73) we have the same paradox very similarly expressed. 'Everything is foreseen; and freewill is given. And the world is judged by grace: and everything is according to work.' It will, we think, also appear that the use of the word ἐκλογή elsewhere in this book, and in N.T., points in the same direction. ἐκλογή is not a LXX. word at all. It occurs in Aquila, Isa. xxii. 7, once in Symm. Isa. xxxvii. 24 and once in Theod., ibid., each time meaning 'the choicest,' but Tromm does not quote it. It occurs

ī. ὕμνος τῶι ϲαλομών.

X. Μακάριος ἀνήρ, οὗ ὁ κύριος ἐμνήσθη ἐν ἐλέγχῳ, καὶ ἐκυκλώθη ἀπὸ ὁδοῦ πονηρᾶς ἐν μάστιγι, καθαρισθῆναι ἀπὸ ἁμαρτίας τοῦ μὴ *πληθυνθῆναι*.

1 ἐλέγχῳ. ἐλεγμῷ K, P, M.
ἐκυκλώθη. ἐκωλύθη venit in mentem Fr.
καὶ καθαρισθῆναι codd. Hilg. Geig. Fr. Pick. τοῦ καθαρισθῆναι conj. Hilg.[2]
πληθῦναι P: πληθύναι V, K, M: πληθῆναι A: πλησθῆναι Hilg. Fr. Pick.

once more in this book, xviii. 6 εἰς ἡμέραν ἐκλογῆς, where the reference can only be to God's choice, whether the words mean 'for the day which God shall choose' or 'for the day when God chooses Israel.' In N.T. it is found seven times, and in each case it is the Divine choice not the human choice that is alluded to. Four of the seven passages are in the Epistle to the Romans, the work of one who had been a Pharisee of the Pharisees and whose evidence is therefore of importance in this connection. Rom. ix. 11 speaks of ἡ κατ' ἐκλογὴν πρόθεσις τοῦ θεοῦ, xi. 5 λίμμα κατ' ἐκλογὴν χάριτος γέγονεν. Similarly in xi. 7 and 28 God's ἐκλογή of Israel is referred to. In 1 Thess. i. 4 εἰδότες...τὴν ἐκλογὴν ὑμῶν, 2 Pet. i. 10 βεβαίαν τὴν κλῆσιν καὶ ἐκλογὴν ὑμῶν ποιεῖσθαι. Lastly, Acts ix. 15 gives the well-known phrase σκεῦος ἐκλογῆς. It is, then, a word applied to God's choosing or predestination, and to that only, in the N.T. On the other side we have the fact that where the verb ἐκλέγομαι is used in the LXX. it applies indifferently to man's choice or God's (e.g. 2 Sam. xxiv. 12 and 1 Chr. xxi. 10, 11, ἐκλέξαι σεαυτῷ). But this does not seem very convincing against the evidence adduced above from N.T. The one objection which, to our mind, really has force lies in the extremely unemphatic, cursory way in which the doctrine would be stated, coupled with the doubt whether the words ἐν ἐκλογῇ *must* not of necessity have been so defined as to prevent the possibility of their being joined to ἐξουσία.

It may be well however to cite some passages from Jewish literature which bear on the question of free will.

Jos. *B. J.* II. viii. 14 says Φαρισαῖοι... εἱμαρμένῃ τε καὶ θεῷ προσάπτουσι πάντα καὶ τὸ μὲν πράττειν τὰ δίκαια, καὶ μὴ, κατὰ τὸ πλεῖστον ἐπὶ τοῖς ἀνθρώποις κεῖσθαι,

βοηθεῖν δὲ εἰς ἕκαστον καὶ τὴν εἱμαρμένην. *Ant.* XIII. v. 9, οἱ μὲν οὖν Φαρισαῖοι τινὰ καὶ οὐ πάντα τῆς εἱμαρμένης εἶναι λέγουσιν ἔργον, τινὰ δ' ἐφ' ἑαυτοῖς ὑπάρχειν, συμβαίνειν τε καὶ οὐ γίνεσθαι. XVIII. i. 3 Πράσσεσθαι δὲ εἱμαρμένῃ τὰ πάντα ἀξιοῦντες (οἱ Φαρισαῖοι) οὐδὲ τοῦ ἀνθρωπείου τὸ βουλόμενον τῆς ἐπ' αὐτοῖς ὁρμῆς ἀφαιροῦνται· δοκῆσαν τῷ θεῷ κρᾶσιν γενέσθαι καὶ τῷ ἐκείνης βουλευτηρίῳ καὶ τῶν ἀνθρώπων τῷ θελήσαντι προσχωρεῖν μετὰ ἀρετῆς ἢ κακίας. Ecclus. xv. 11—20 Μὴ εἴπῃς ὅτι διὰ κύριον ἀπέστην. ἃ γὰρ ἐμίσησεν, οὐ ποιήσεις· Μὴ εἴπῃς, ὅτι αὐτός με ἐπλάνησεν...καὶ ἀφῆκεν αὐτὸν ἐν χειρὶ διαβουλίου αὐτοῦ. xvii. 6 Διαβούλιον καὶ γλῶσσαν καὶ ὀφθαλμοὺς ὦτα καὶ καρδίαν ἔδωκε διανοεῖσθαι αὐτοῖς. xxxvi. 13—15 ὡς πηλὸς κεραμέως ἐν χειρὶ αὐτοῦ, πᾶσαι αἱ ὁδοὶ αὐτοῦ κατὰ τὴν εὐδοκίαν αὐτοῦ· οὕτως ἄνθρωποι ἐν χειρὶ τοῦ ποιήσαντος αὐτούς, ἀποδοῦναι αὐτοῖς κατὰ τὴν κρίσιν αὐτοῦ.

The passages from Josephus express exactly the view of the words quoted from *Pirqe Aboth*, and also that which our rendering of the verse would give. They go therefore to increase the probability that this rendering is the correct one.

Ps. X.—*Argument.*

Here again a threefold division of the Psalm is obvious. The fifth verse stands by itself, but may be taken to lead over from what precedes to what follows.

Verses 1—4. Chastening is a true blessing: and God will not alway be chiding.

5. This is the teaching of the written Law, and this is the meaning of God's care for men.

6—8. At present the chastening is heavy upon Israel, but the day of gladness will come, and all will acknowledge at once the justice and mercy of God.

9. May that day of gladness come to us.

Title. It is probably the hopeful tone

ΨΑΛΜΟΙ ΣΑΛΟΜΩΝΤΟΣ.

PSALM X.

A Hymn of Solomon.

1 Blessed is the man whom the LORD remembereth with reproving: and he is fenced about[1] from the way of evil by affliction, that he may be cleansed from sin, lest he abound therein[2].

[1] Or, *turned aside*

[2] Or, *to the end that it be not multiplied*

---

of the third division of the Psalm that has led the (later) writer of these titles to call it a Hymn.

1 The words closely resemble two passages in O.T., Job v. 17 μακάριος δὲ ἄνθρωπος ὃν ἤλεγξεν ὁ κύριος, and Ps. xciii. (xciv.) 12 μακάριος ὁ ἄνθρωπος ὃν ἂν σὺ παιδεύσῃς, κύριε. Cf. Prov. iii. 11, 12. The blessedness of affliction is the subject of iii. xiii. 6 sqq. and xiv. Is not this a theme singularly suitable to a time when resistance to the Roman power was in constant contemplation? The pious Pharisee recognised it as a higher duty to accept the troubles of his lot as coming by Divine appointment and working together for his good: the Zealot party, though not regarded by him with hatred and abhorrence as were the Sadducees, have yet, to his mind, not chosen this better part. They are not οἱ ὑπομένοντες παιδείαν, but still they are not οἱ ἁμαρτωλοί.

ἔλεγχος only here and in ix. *Tit.* ἐλεγμός, the reading of Par. in this place, is very nearly as common in the LXX. as ἔλεγχος.

ἐκυκλώθη. Fritzsche had thought of substituting ἐκωλύθη, but on second thoughts refrained from correcting what was a translator's error. He does not explain further. Of the renderings given above 'he is turned away from' finds favour with Cerda, who renders 'deviavit.' His note is ingenious: he compares the fashion of turning a person round and round in order to confuse him and make him forget a path. This, he says, was done to a bride in Roman times, when she left her father's house. What must really decide the question, however, is the evidence of the LXX. The word occurs a good many times and is used in several senses. Those which favour Cerda's interpretation are the following: Exod. xiii. 18 'God led the people about,' καὶ ἐκύκλωσεν ὁ Θεὸς τὸν λαόν, Deut. xxxii. 10 ἐκύκλωσεν αὐτόν, καὶ ἐπαίδευσεν αὐτόν—a strong instance, as the idea of chastening is connected with it. There may be possibly one or two others which have escaped us. On the other hand, by far the commonest meanings of the words are

α. to surround, usually in a hostile manner, like besiegers, but sometimes by way of defence, e.g. Ps. xxxi. (xxxii.) 10 τὸν δὲ ἐλπίζοντα ἐπὶ κύριον ἔλεος κυκλώσει, xc. (xci.) 4 ὅπλῳ κυκλώσει σε ἡ ἀλήθεια αὐτοῦ.

β. to go round, as Jos. vi. 7 κυκλῶσαι τὴν πόλιν.

The N.T. uses of the word all come under one of these two heads. As far as numbers go then, the passages in which κυκλόω = to encompass are much the strongest, but the parallel in Deuteronomy is extremely suggestive, and the idea of 'turning aside by means of a scourge' entails no mixture of metaphor. The same cannot be said of 'encompassing or fencing about with a scourge.'

καθαρισθῆναι. The succession of moods gives a hardly tolerable construction, ἐκυκλώθη—καθαρισθῆναι, but Hilgenfeld's substitute ἐκαθαρίσθη entails a rather violent altering of letters. καὶ καθαρισθήσεται would be nearer to the MSS. The omission of καὶ may be defended on the ground of the similarity existing between και and καθ. The epexegetic Inf. is quite in character with the Greek of this book. We prefer either of these to ἐκαθαρίσθη, but are unwilling to introduce any alteration into our text.

πληθῦναι. If this reading be accepted, that of A (πληθῆναι) may be attributed to itacism, and in any case Hilg.'s conjecture is less satisfactory than the text given here. πληθύνω is used intransitively quite often in the LXX., and especially often does the word occur in connection with ἀδικίαι, ἀνομίαι or ἁμαρτίαι: cf. Prayer of Manass. 9 ἐπλήθυναν αἱ ἀνομίαι μου, κύριε.

If the reading πληθῦναι must be changed

² ὁ ἑτοιμάζων νῶτον εἰς μάστιγας καθαρισθήσεται,
χρηστὸς γὰρ ὁ κύριος τοῖς ὑπομένουσι παιδείαν·
³ ὀρθώσει γὰρ ὁδοὺς δικαίων,
καὶ οὐ διαστρέψει ἐν παιδείᾳ.
⁴ καὶ τὸ ἔλεος κυρίου ἐπὶ τοὺς ἀγαπῶντας αὐτὸν ἐν ἀληθείᾳ,
καὶ μνησθήσεται κύριος τῶν δούλων αὐτοῦ ἐν ἐλέει.

⁵ Ἡ μαρτυρία ἐν νόμῳ διαθήκης αἰωνίου,
ἡ μαρτυρία κυρίου ἐπὶ ὁδοὺς ἀνθρώπων ἐν ἐπισκοπῇ.
⁶ δίκαιος καὶ ὅσιος ὁ κύριος ἡμῶν ἐν κρίμασιν αὐτοῦ εἰς τὸν αἰῶνα,
καὶ Ἰσραὴλ αἰνέσει τὸ ὄνομα κυρίου ἐν εὐφροσύνῃ·
⁷ καὶ ὅσιοι ἐξομολογήσονται ἐν ἐκκλησίᾳ λαοῦ,
καὶ πτωχοὺς ἐλεήσει ὁ θεὸς ἐν εὐφροσύνῃ Ἰσραήλ·
⁸ ὅτι χρηστὸς καὶ ἐλεήμων ὁ θεὸς εἰς τὸν αἰῶνα,
καὶ συναγωγαὶ Ἰσραὴλ δοξάσουσι τὸ ὄνομα κυρίου.

4 αὐτόν. Cerda αὐτῶν mendose.
6 ὅσιος ὁ κύριος V, P, M, om. ὁ A, K.
κρίμασιν, ita codd. omisso ἐν, quod ab Hilg. quem sequitur Fr. suppletur.

---

at all, surely it would be better to read πληθυνθῆναι, which unites the characteristics of both πληθῦναι and πληθῆναι, cf. 2 Sam. xiv. 11 πληθυνθῆναι (v. l. πληθῦναι), Ecclus. xvi. 2 πληθύνωσι (v. l. πληθυνθῶσι), xxii. 3. Ps. xxxix. (xl.) 12 ἐπληθύνθησαν (αἱ ἀνομίαι) ὑπὲρ τὰς τρίχας τῆς κεφαλῆς μου.

2 'A voluntary submission to God's chastening is the true way to realising the uses of it.' The language here is modelled on Is. l. 6 τὸν νῶτόν μου ἔδωκα εἰς μάστιγας (cf. Prov. xix. 29), and the Greek recalls the LXX. version of 'I am ready to halt.' Ps. xxxvii. (xxxviii.) 18 ἐγὼ εἰς μάστιγας (לצלע) ἕτοιμος. For the latter clause of the verse compare ii. 40, xiv. 1, xvi. 15.

3 The affliction sent will not be so severe as to force the righteous into sin, cf. v. 8.

ὀρθώσει. Cf. Prov. iii. 6 ἵνα ὀρθοτομῇ τὰς ὁδούς σου, x. 9 διαστρέφων τὰς ὁδοὺς αὐτοῦ. The thought is not unlike that of 1 Cor. x. 13 'God is faithful, who will not suffer you to be tempted above that ye are able.'

4 The qualifying ἐν ἀληθείᾳ is characteristic of these shorter religious psalms, vi. 9, xiv. 1, xv. 3.

τῶν δούλων αὐτοῦ, cf. ii. 41.

5 The inner connection and meaning of this verse are not obvious at first sight. It is especially the second clause which causes difficulty. 'The Lord,' it has just been said, 'will have mercy on His servants.' This is the fact to which the law of the everlasting covenant bears witness. The Lord will yet choose Israel. This is plain enough: with regard to the second half (ἡ μαρτ.—ἐπισκοπῇ) we are at liberty to take it either as a separate statement, or as explanatory of ἡ μαρτ. in the line before. This latter rendering we prefer. The verse may then be paraphrased after this sort, 'The ultimate purpose of God's constant watching over (and visitation of) men is that he may test and have mercy upon His servants, and to this the law of the Eternal Covenant bears witness.'

μαρτυρία. The use of this form as opposed to μαρτύριον may possibly supply something towards determining the

x. 8]	ΨΑΛΜΟΙ ΣΑΛΟΜΩΝΤΟΣ.	99

2 He that prepareth his back for stripes shall be cleansed: for the LORD is gracious unto such as patiently abide chastening.

3 For he will make straight the ways of the righteous: and will not pervert *them* by his chastening.

4 And the mercy of the LORD is upon them that love him in truth: and the LORD will remember his servants in mercy.

5 The testimony is in the law of the everlasting covenant: the testimony of the LORD is over the ways of men, when he visiteth³ *them*.

6 Righteous and holy is our LORD in his judgments for ever: and Israel shall praise the name of the LORD in gladness.

7 The saints also shall give thanks in the assembly of the people: and God will have mercy upon the needy in the *day of gladness of Israel*.

8 For gracious and merciful is God for ever: and the congregations of Israel shall glorify the name of the LORD.

³ Gr. *in visitation*, or *in overseeing*.

---

date of this Version. According to Tromm, it occurs six times in the LXX. (Gen., Ps., Prov., Sirach, and 4 Macc.), whereas μαρτύριον is used well over 100 times.

In the N.T. on the other hand the use of μαρτυρία considerably exceeds that of μαρτύριον. It is an especially Johannine word, occurring 14 times in the Gospel, 7 times in the Epistles and 7 times in the Apocalypse. The only passage in the LXX. resembling this is in Ps. xviii. (xix.) 8 ἡ μαρτυρία κυρίου πιστή.

The later versions often use μαρτυρία where the LXX. has μαρτύριον, e.g. Ps. xcii. (xciii.) 5, LXX. τὰ μαρτύριά σου = Sym. αἱ μαρτυρίαι σου, cxviii. (cxix.) 15, LXX. μαρτυρίων = Aq. Sym. μαρτυριῶν.

διαθήκη αἰώνιος. Ps. cx. (cxi.) 9 ἐνετείλατο εἰς τὸν αἰῶνα τὴν διαθήκην αὐτοῦ. Ecclus. xiv. 17 ἡ γὰρ διαθήκη ἀπ' αἰῶνος, θανάτῳ ἀποθανῇ. Bar. ii. 35 στήσω αὐτοῖς διαθήκην αἰώνιον. 4 Esdr. iii. 15 disposuisti ei testamentum æternum et dixisti ei ut non umquam derelinqueres semen eius.

ἐν ἐπισκοπῇ, 'oversight' or 'visitation' are the two possible renderings here. In both LXX. and N.T. the latter meaning is the commoner. In the first sense it occurs several times in Numbers, e.g. iv. 16 ἡ ἐπισκοπὴ τῆς σκηνῆς. The difference in essential meaning is not very great here. God oversees the ways of men and this implies some kind of 'visitation' according to their works. In xi. 2, 7 the rendering 'visitation' is undoubtedly the correct one.

6 Cf. Ps. cxviii. (cxix.) 142 τὰ μαρτύριά σου δικαιοσύνη εἰς τὸν αἰῶνα.

For δίκαιος καὶ ὅσιος κύριος cf. Ps. cxlv. 17 δίκαιος κύριος ἐν πάσαις ταῖς ὁδοῖς αὐτοῦ καὶ ὅσιος ἐν πᾶσιν τοῖς ἔργοις αὐτοῦ.

7 We take these verses to apply to a somewhat vague and distant future. The εὐφροσύνη Ἰσραήλ is the 'day of gladness' for Israel to which all the later Jews looked forward. See for the expression, Ps. cv. (cvi.) 5 τοῦ εὐφρανθῆναι ἐν τῇ εὐφροσύνῃ τοῦ ἔθνους σου.

ἐν ἐκκλησίᾳ λαοῦ. The clause is very similar to Ps. cvi. (cvii.) 31, 32 ἐξομολογησάσθων τῷ κυρίῳ τὰ ἐλέη αὐτοῦ...ὑψωσάτωσαν αὐτὸν ἐν ἐκκλησίᾳ λαοῦ (בקהל עם), where Cod. ℵ reads ἐκκλησίαις.

ἐκκλησία occurs here only in the Psalms. No technical sense attaches to it, cf. Ps. cxlix. 1 ἡ αἴνεσις αὐτοῦ ἐν ἐκκλησίᾳ ὁσίων.

πτωχοὺς ἐλεεῖν, only of men in the LXX.

For the reference to 'the poor' cf. v. 2, 13; xv. 2; xviii. 3.

8 συναγωγή recurs xvii. 18, 48, 50. In the two former places it simply means 'assemblies,' 'gatherings.' In xvii. 50 it = the gathering together of the tribes out of the dispersion. Here it is purely general.

7—2

100 ΨΑΛΜΟΙ ΣΑΛΟΜΩΝΤΟΣ. [X. 9

⁹τοῦ κυρίου ἡ σωτηρία ἐπ' οἶκον 'Ισραὴλ εἰς εγφροcγΝΗΝ
αἰώΝΙΟΝ.

ιαˉ. τῶι ϲαλομῶν εἰc προcδοκίαν.

XI. Σαλπίϲατε ἐν Σιὼν ἐν cάλπιγγι cημαϲίαϲ ἁγίων,
²κηρύξατε ἐν 'Ιερουσαλὴμ φωνὴν εγαγγελιζομένογ,
ὅτι ἠλέησεν ὁ θεὸς 'Ισραὴλ ἐν τῇ ἐπισκοπῇ αὐτῶν.
³στῆθι, 'Ιερουσαλήμ, ἐφ' ὑψΗλοῦ,
καὶ ἴδε τὰ τέκνα σου ἀπὸ ἀνατολῶν καὶ δγcμῶν ϲγνΗΓμένα
εἰσάπαξ ὑπὸ κυρίου·

9 εὐφροσύνην, ita Cerda et edd.   σωφροσύνην A, V, K, P, M (cωφρ. pro εγφρ.).
2 ἐν Ἰσραήλ codd.: Fab. Geig.   τὸν Ἰσραήλ Hilg. Fr. Pick (Ἰσρήλ!!).
3 εἰς ἅπαξ V, K.

---

9 See on ix. 20. For τοῦ κυρίου ἡ σωτηρία cf. iii. 9.

εὐφροσύνην. Cf. Is. xxxv. 10 εὐφροσύνη αἰώνιος ὑπὲρ κεφαλῆς αὐτῶν, and Baruch iv. 29 ἐπάξει ὑμῖν τὴν αἰώνιον εὐφροσύνην μετὰ τῆς σωτηρίας ὑμῶν.

The reading of the MSS. σωφροσύνην is inadmissible, and must be explained as an 'insigne mendum' (Cerda) in the archetype of our MSS. σωφροσύνη in the LXX. seems only to occur in 2 Macc. iv. 37 and 4 Macc. i. 31 (σωφροσύνη ἐστὶν ἐπικράτεια τῶν ἐπιθυμιῶν): in the N.T. only Acts xxvi. 25 and 1 Tim. ii. 9, 15. We should not expect to find it coupled with αἰώνιος in a doxology.

Ps. XI.—*Argument.*
The Return of the Dispersed ones.
1, 2. The news announced.
3. Call to Jerusalem.
4—7. The return described.
8. Jerusalem bidden to rejoice in God.
9. A prayer for the speedy realisation of these hopes.

For a discussion of the relation of this Psalm to the conclusion of the Book of Baruch, see Introd. p. lxviii.

The subject of the Psalm—the restoration of Israel—is one of great interest, and this particular document occupies a middle position between two forms of treating it. This is not the place for an exhaustive essay upon the development of the idea. We can only point here to several documents which represent different stages of it. Amos (ix.), the two parts of the Book of Isaiah, Zephaniah (iii.), Jeremiah, the Deuteronomist, Ezekiel, Haggai are among those who have spoken most clearly on the subject, and among them all it is, of course, the 'second Isaiah' who stands preeminent.

These seers all of them speak of a dispersion or captivity, either generally or in certain definite regions (as Is. xi.), which is to be gathered again. The captive tribes are not thought of as being collected together in any one place.

A further class of writings still deals in general terms and copies the old models, but adds certain supernatural details. To this belong our Psalm and the 2nd part of Baruch.

Next, we find certain documents which presuppose a popular belief that the ten (or nine and a half) tribes would all return together from some distant land where they lived as a well-defined and independent community. Such are 4 Esdras xiii. 40—50, Apoc. Baruch lxxvii. 19 etc. (for the present situation of the 9½ tribes), Commodianus, *Instruct.* II. i., *Carmen Apologeticum* 934 sqq., Sib. Orac. II. 170, Ethiopic Conflict of St Matthew (Malan, *Conflicts of the Holy Apostles*, p. 45) [A slight error of the translator has long obscured the meaning of this very important passage. Instead of 'nine and a half orders [of angels],' we should read 'nine and a half tribes'], Wright, Cat. MSS. Eth. Brit. Mus. Cod. 390. 3, p. 309, Zotenberg, Catal. MSS. Aeth. Paris Cod. 146, no. 6.

For mediaeval Jewish developments of this last belief, where less emphasis is laid on the restoration than on the glory

XI. 3]   ΨΑΛΜΟΙ ΣΑΛΟΜΩΝΤΟΣ.   101

9 Let the salvation of the LORD be upon the house of Israel unto everlasting joy⁴.

⁴ The MSS. give *prudence*

PSALM XI.

A Psalm of Solomon: 'Unto expectation.'

1 Blow ye the trumpet in Sion, *yea* the holy trumpet of Jubilee.

2 Proclaim ye in Jerusalem with the voice of him that bringeth good tidings, that¹ God hath had mercy upon Israel: he hath visited them.

¹ Or, *for*

3 Stand up on high, O Jerusalem: and behold thy children gathered from the East and the West together by the LORD.

---

and prosperity of the separated tribes, see Eisenmenger, *Entdecktes Judenthum* II. cap. x. The passages there quoted from a certain 'Book of Eldad the Dante' (printed at Venice in 1544 along with a 'Chronicle of Moses') are particularly instructive. The title of this book is suggestive of older relationships.

The lines in Commodian's *Carm. Apol.* afford so close a parallel to the words of our Psalm in some cases that we may as well quote them here in a connected form.

952. Hic erit populus, qui nunc est extra repostus;
Siccato fluvio repetet in terra Judæa:
Cum ipsis et Dominus veniet implere promissa,
Qui per totum iter exsultant Deo præsente.
Omnia virescunt ante illos, omnia gaudent,
Excipere sanctos ipsa creatura lætatur:
Omni loco fontes exsurgunt e se parati,
Qua graditur populus Summi cum errore cælesti.
Umbram illis faciunt nubes, ne vexentur a sole,
Et ne fatigentur, substernunt se montes et ipsi;
Præmittitur enim ante illos angelus Alti,
Qui ducatum eis pacificum præstet mundo.

If Commodian is quoting either of our two documents here it is almost certainly Baruch, and not the Psalm, especially as in l. 367 he quotes Bar. iii. 36, 37. But it is plain from the lines that precede those quoted above, that he had some other Apocryphal source by him as well.

1 σάλπιγγι σημασίας ἁγίων. σημασία is in Lev. xxv. 10 etc. the LXX. rendering of יוֹבֵל. In Num. xxi. 6 we have the phrase αἱ σάλπιγγες τῶν σημασιῶν, cf. 2 Chr. xiii. 12; 1 Macc. vii. 45. In Jos. vi. 7 the same Hebrew word is rendered by ἱεράς,—ἑπτὰ σάλπιγγας ἱεράς. The juxtaposition of these expressions suggests the question whether the two words σημασίας and ἁγίων here may not be both equivalents of one word יוֹבֵל in the Hebrew. See on viii. 12.

In any case the sense is obvious 'the great year of Jubilee for Israel has come.' Joel ii. 1, 'Blow ye the trumpet in Zion and sound an alarm (κηρύξατε) in my holy mountain' is the original of the verse.

2 φωνήν, the accus. after κηρύξατε, is peculiar. It is probably a literal reproduction of the Hebrew phrase הַעֲבִיר קוֹל, cf. Ex. xxxvi. 6, Ezr. i. 1, x. 7.

εὐαγγελιζομένου. So Is. xl. 9 ὁ εὐαγγελιζόμενος Σιών, and Nahum i. 15. Cf. Is. lii. 7 ὡς πόδες εὐαγγελιζομένου ἀκοὴν εἰρήνης, ὡς εὐαγγελιζόμενος ἀγαθά.

ἐπισκοπή, see on x. 5. This ἐπισκοπή is such an one as Zacharias means when in Luc. i. 68 he says 'God hath *visited* and redeemed His people' (also i. 78). Cf. 1 Pet. ii. 12 ἐν ἡμέρᾳ ἐπισκοπῆς, Wisd. iii. 7 ἐν καιρῷ ἐπισκοπῆς. See also iii. 14; xv. 14, and Assumpt. Mos. i. 17 in respectu quo respiciet illos Dominus in consummatione exitus dierum.

ἠλέησεν...Ἰσραήλ. Hilgenfeld corrects ἐν to τὸν quoting Isai. xliv. 23 ὅτι ἠλέησεν ὁ Θεὸς τὸν Ἰσραήλ. As the verb

ΨΑΛΜΟΙ ΣΑΛΟΜΩΝΤΟΣ. [XI. 4

⁴ ἀπὸ βορρᾶ ἔρχονται τῇ εὐφροσύνῃ τοῦ θεοῦ αὐτῶν,
ἐκ νήϲων μακρόθεν συνήγαγεν αὐτοὺς ὁ θεός.
⁵ ὄρη ὑψηλὰ ἐταπείνωϲεν εἰς ὁμαλισμὸν αὐτοῖς,
⁶ οἱ βουνοὶ ἔφυγον ἀπὸ εἰσόδου αὐτῶν,
οἱ δρυμοὶ ἐσκίασαν αὐτοῖς ἐν τῇ παρόδῳ αὐτῶν·
⁷ πᾶν ξύλον εὐωδίας ἀνέτειλεν αὐτοῖς ὁ θεός,
ἵνα παρέλθῃ Ἰσραὴλ ἐν ἐπισκοπῇ δόξης θεοῦ αὐτῶν.
⁸ ἔνδυϲαι, Ἱερουϲαλήμ, τὰ ἱμάτια τῆς δόξης ϲου,
ἑτοίμασον τὴν στολὴν τοῦ ἁγιάσματός σου,
ὅτι ὁ θεὸς ἐλάλησεν ἀγαθὸν Ἰσραὴλ εἰς τὸν αἰῶνα καὶ ἔτι.
⁹ ποιῆσαι κύριος ἃ ἐλάλησεν ἐπὶ Ἰσραὴλ καὶ ἐν Ἱερουσαλήμ,
ἀναστῆσαι κύριος τὸν Ἰσραὴλ ἐν ὀνόματι δόξης αὐτοῦ.
τοῦ κυρίου τὸ ἔλεος ἐπὶ τὸν Ἰσραὴλ εἰς τὸν αἰῶνα καὶ ἔτι.

ιβ. τῶι ϲαλομὼν ἐν γλώϲϲηι παρανόμων.

XII. Κύριε, ῥῦϲαι τὴν ψυχήν μου ἀπὸ ἀνδρὸς παρανόμου
καὶ πονηροῦ,
ἀπὸ γλώϲϲης παρανόμου καὶ ψιθυροῦ,
καὶ λαλούϲης ψευδῆ καὶ δόλια.

6 δρομοί A.   ἐσκίρτησαν P.
8 ἀγαθά P, M.
9 A per homœotel. omittit verba ἐν ὀνόματι δόξ.—ἰσραηλ.

ἐλεῶ is not elsewhere found with the prep. ἐν, we must suppose that ἐν either represents the translator's attempt to render a Hebrew preposition (e.g. אֶל, בְּ), or has carelessly been substituted for τὸν, the eye of the scribe passing on to ἐν τῇ ἐπισκοπῇ, or being confused by the last syllable of ἠλέηϲεν. If ἐν be retained, we must explain the words as = 'had compassion in respect of' or 'among Israel.' Cf. ὁμολογεῖν ἐν, Mt. x. 32 and Winer's note in *Gram. of N.T. Gr.* Pt. iii. sec. xxxii. 3.

3 εἰσάπαξ, cf. ii. 8.

4 ἔρχονται τῇ εὐφροσύνῃ. The use of the dative is very peculiar. We should expect either ἐν εὐφροσύνῃ (cf. x. 7) or μετ' εὐφροσύνης (cf. xiv. 18), as always apparently in the LXX. e.g. 2 Chron. xx. 28 ἐπέστρεψε πᾶς ἀνὴρ Ἰούδα ἐν εὐφροσύνῃ, Isai. xxxv. 10 ἥξουσιν εἰς Σιὼν μετ' εὐφροσύνης. Perhaps our text is defective: the τῇ may be the repetition of the last syllable of ἔρχονται, and ἐν may have fallen out before εὐφρ.

For the sense cf. Isai. lxi. 7 καὶ εὐφροσύνη αἰώνιος ὑπὲρ κεφαλῆς αὐτῶν.

5 εἰς ὁμαλισμὸν, cf. Isai. xlv. 2 ὄρη ὁμαλιῶ (יָשָׁר), Sym. Ps. v. 2 ὁμάλισον (הַיְשֵׁר), Ecclus. xxi. 10 ὁδὸς...ὡμαλισμένη ἐκ λίθων. In Mic. vii. 12 εἰς ὁμαλισμὸν is a mistranslation.

6 ἐσκίασαν, cf. 5 Esdr. i. 20 'propter æstus foliis arborum vos texi.'

For σκιάζω cf. Job xl. 17 σκιάζονται δὲ ἐν αὐτῷ δένδρα μεγάλα σὺν ῥαδάμνοις καὶ κλῶνες ἀγροῦ.

7 ξύλον εὐωδίας. Only here and Baruch. But cf. Enoch, c. 24 'fragrant trees,' a sign of Divine blessing.

8 The disrobing of Jerusalem (ii. 22) has been already casually referred to Baruch (see above) seems to unite these two passages.

στολὴν τοῦ ἁγιάσματος. ἁγιασμ[ὸς] usually in these Psalms means the sanc[tuary]

XII. 1] ΨΑΛΜΟΙ ΣΑΛΟΜΩΝΤΟΣ. 103

4 From the North they come in the gladness of their God: from the islands afar off hath God gathered them.

5 Lofty mountains did he make low: *yea even* unto the plain before them.

6 The hills fled before their entering in, the woods gave them shelter as they passed by.

7 Every tree of sweet savour did God make to spring up before them: that Israel might pass by in *the day when* the glory of their God shall visit them.

8 Put on, O Jerusalem, the garments of thy glory: make ready thine holy apparel, for God hath spoken comfortably unto Israel, world without end.

9 The LORD perform that which he hath spoken concerning Israel and concerning Jerusalem.

The LORD raise up Israel in the name of his glory.

The mercy of the LORD be upon Israel, world without end.

PSALM XII.

Of Solomon: 'Concerning the tongue of the wicked.'

1 O LORD, save my soul from the wicked and evil man: from the tongue that is wicked and lying, and that speaketh false and deceitful words.

tified place vii. 2, viii. 4. ἁγιασμός (xvii. 33) the process of sanctification. Here 'holiness' is probably a just rendering, 'the robe that is a sign of thy holiness.'

ἁγία στολή is the regular expression for the priest's robe in Exodus.

ἐλάλησεν ἀγαθὸν Ἰσραήλ. Generally with a preposition e.g. Num. x. 29 κύριος ἐλάλησε καλὰ περὶ Ἰσραήλ. 1 Sam. xxv. 30 ἐλάλησεν ἀγαθὰ ἐπί σε. Ps. lxxxiv. (lxxxv.) 9. Jer. xxxix. (xxxii.) 42 πάντα τὰ ἀγαθὰ ἃ ἐλάλησα ἐπ' αὐτούς.

9 ἐπί...ἐν. We believe that no distinction of meaning between these prepositions can be maintained here. Cf. v. 21.

ἐν ὀνόματι δόξης, 'by once more making his name to dwell among them' seems to be the meaning of this phrase. Cf. vii. 5.

For ὄνομα δόξης cf. Ps. lxxi. (lxxii.) 19; Is. lxiii. 14; Dan. Add. iii. 29.

Ps. XII.—*Argument.*

1—4ª. A Prayer for protection against the slanderers. Their ways are described.

4ᵇ—8. May they reap that they have deserved, while the peaceable and God-fearing inherit the promises.

The text of this Psalm presents some extremely difficult problems. We have succeeded, we think, in presenting a coherent whole, but we cannot pretend that we are entirely satisfied with our restorations.

The Psalmist, or some friend of his, has evidently suffered at the hands of some accuser, as did the son of Sirach at an earlier time. It is natural enough to suppose that this accuser was a Sadducee, and that he had brought ruin and perhaps death on some prominent Pharisee by laying information against him at the court. Further than this we cannot undertake to go.

1 The thought and form of this verse as well as of v. 2 is taken from Ps. cxix. (cxx.). In v. 2 of that, we have Κύριε, ῥῦσαι τὴν ψυχήν μου ἀπὸ χειλέων ἀδίκων καὶ ἀπὸ γλώσσης δολίας. Further on in v. 4 the 'coals of fire' are connected with the deceitful tongue, and in v. 5 the words οἴμοι ὅτι ἡ παροικία μου ἐμακρύνθη contain two coincidences of vocabulary with our Psalm. The last resemblance we shall cite is that of ἐπολέμουν με δωρεάν (v. 7) with ἐν πολέμῳ v. 4 here.

104   ΨΑΛΜΟΙ ΣΑΛΟΜΩΝΤΟΣ.   [XII. 2

²ἐν ποιήσει διαστροφῆς οἱ λόγοι τῆς γλώσσης ἀνδρὸς
    πονηροῦ·
ὥσπερ ἐν ἅλῳ πῦρ ἀνάπτον καλάμην αὐτοῦ
ἡ παροικία αὐτοῦ, ³*ἐμπρῆσαι* οἴκους ἐν γλώσσῃ ψευδεῖ,
ἐκκόψαι δένδρα εὐφροσύνης, φλογιζούσης [γλώσσης] παρα-
    νόμου,

2 ἄλλῳ P.
3 παροινία conj. Hilg.: ita Wellh.
  ἐμπρῆσαι conj. Hilg.² Wellh. ἐμπλῆσαι A, V, Fab. Geig. Hilg. ἐμπλῆσαι
K, P, M, Fr.
  φλογιζούσης codd.: φλογὶ ζήλους conj. Hilg.² Wellh.(?). φλογιζούσης γλώσσης
nos conj.

ψιθυρός. Ecclus. v. 14 Μὴ κληθῇς ψιθυρός, xxviii. 13 ψιθυρὸν καὶ δίγλωσσον
καταράσθαι, but nowhere else in LXX.
See on v. 3. ὁ ψιθυρίζων occurs in Ecclus.
xxi. 28.
  2 ἐν ποιήσει διαστροφῆς. It is not
impossible, though we have not adopted
the arrangement, that these words ought
to be joined to the preceding verse, 'the
tongue that speaketh deceitfully for the
accomplishment of perversity.' So Wellhausen, 'Zunge die redet...mit ihrer
Verdrehungskunst.' We have in this particular instance retained the punctuation
of earlier editors. For other clauses beginning with ἐν, see iv. 7, vi. 5, viii. 9
etc. and v. 5 of this psalm.
  διαστροφή only occurs (in LXX.) in
Prov. ii. 14 χαίροντες ἐπὶ διαστροφῇ κακῇ,
and nowhere in N.T.
  ὥσπερ πῦρ. The comparison of the
tongue to fire is a commonplace of most
literatures. See the commentators on
James iii. 5 (ἰδοὺ ἡλίκον πῦρ ἡλίκην ὕλην
ἀνάπτει· καὶ ἡ γλῶσσα πῦρ), and particularly a fragment of Euripides (Ino 6, ap.
Stob. Flor. xli. 1).
  Cf. Prov. xvi. 27 ἐπὶ τῶν ἑαυτοῦ χειλέων θησαυρίζει πῦρ.
  καλάμην. For this metaphor cf. Joel
ii. 5 ὡς φωνὴ φλογὸς πυρὸς κατεσθιούσης
καλάμην. Zech. xii. 6 ὡς λαμπάδα πυρὸς
ἐν καλάμῃ. Wisd. iii. 7 ὡς σπινθῆρες ἐν
καλάμῃ.
  2, 3 ἡ παροικία αὐτοῦ. These
words we join on to the preceding verse.
The division adopted by earlier editors
is perfectly justifiable, but we venture to
think that our use of παροικία gives more
point to that word. The vicinity of the
evil man is like that of fire to a threshing-
floor, destructive and dangerous to the
last degree, and the three clauses that
follow expand the statement in different
ways. Each of them is introduced by
what might be either an optative or infinitive, but we venture to think that the
infinitive gives by far the best sense here.
It is to be taken as epexegetical of the
preceding verse.
  A similar doubt as to the mood of various verbs exists in several places in
these Psalms, notably in xvii. 26, 27,
xviii. 5, 9. But in passages such as xv.
7, 14 the infinitive is understood.
  Cf. also ii. 40, iv. 11, v. 11, 14, vii.
34. Imperatives and optatives which
are undoubted occur iv. 25, 26, and in
this Psalm (xii.) 4, 6, xvii. 51, xviii. 6,
but it is noticeable that here the nomina-
tive is carefully supplied.
  Now what sense does the text of earlier editors attribute to v. 3? Cerda renders thus 'Vicinia eius implebit domos
in lingua falsa, ut percutiat arbores
inflammante laetitia transgressoris. 4.
Confunde domos iniquas etc.'
  Fritzsche by his punctuation joins the
sentence συγχέαι—ψιθυροῖς to the infinitives which precede it, and this arrangement we have, with some hesitation,
adopted. Probably his translation would
have been something of this kind. 'Let
his vicinity fill houses with his false
tongue. Let it cut down the trees which
his wicked delight setteth on fire. Let
it confound the houses of transgressors in
strife with slanderous lips.'
  We submit that this is confused and
inadequate, that ἐμπλῆσαι gives no tolerable sense, and that the words εὐφρ.
φλογ. παραν. are also extremely strained:
εὐφροσύνη not occurring elsewhere in
this book save in a good sense. We

2 The words of the tongue of the evil man are for the accomplishment of frowardness: even as fire in a threshing-floor, that burneth up the straw thereof, *so is* his sojourning *among men*:
3 That he may set fire to houses with *his* lying tongue, *and* cut down the trees of gladness with the flame of *his* wicked[1] tongue,

[1] Gr. *of wicked gladness that setteth on fire*

do not doubt that Hilgenfeld's emendation ἐμπρῆσαι is correct. It is simple, for it only alters one letter, substituting one liquid sound for another; and seems obvious, for it carries on the metaphor of the preceding verse, and ranges far better with the following verbs, which are both of a 'hostile' sense.

His other conjecture, however, παροινία for παροικία, which Wellhausen adopts ('seine Lust'),-is no improvement on the present text.

Further, we consider it almost certain that the words δένδρα εὐφροσύνης form one expression and that they signify the same thing as the ξύλα τῆς ζωῆς of xiv. 2, i.e. the saints. The exact expression does not occur in the LXX., but cf. Ez. xxxi. 16, 18 ξύλα ὡραῖα, παράδεισος τῆς τρυφῆς. The proximity of the wicked man tends to cut down and burn up these trees of gladness—the saints of God.

But, if we join the two words δένδρα εὐφρ. closely together, the two that follow—φλογιζούσης παρανόμου—are left without a visible governing noun. It would be possible to translate—and perhaps Fr. means this—'the trees of wicked inflammatory joy,' but this explanation does not commend itself to us. So rendered, the clause would correspond to what follows, but not to what precedes.

An alteration in the text appears to us inevitable, and there are two which are more possible than the rest: (a) we may read παρανόμους (a final ς having dropped out before συγχέαι) and render 'trees of gladness which set on fire the wicked:' (β) we may suppose that the original subject of φλογ. παραν. has accidentally disappeared, and that that subject was γλώσσης. This is, as a matter of fact, what we do adopt: the rendering of (a) is so very like nonsense that we are unwilling to attribute it to the writer; while on the other hand a copyist may easily have been induced, by the occurrence of four genitives in a row, εὐφρ. φλογ. παραν. γλώσσ., and by the frequent recurrence of γλῶσσα in various parts of the Psalm, to suspect that the last word in the line had crept in by mistake, and to cut it out.

Hilgenfeld's conjecture φλογὶ ζήλους is a very ingenious one. It contains almost all the elements of φλογιζούσης, and has only one thing against it—that it imports a new word, though by no means an uncommon one, into the vocabulary of our Psalmist.

We are by no means sure that the clause συγχέαι—ψιθυροῖς forms part of the same sentence with the above. It is a little difficult at first to see why the παράνομος should confound the παρανόμους οἴκους, and accordingly Wellhausen proposes to read παρανόμως ('heimtückisch'): but, if it is to be joined to v. 3, the sense may very well be that the slanderer will not scruple to set those of his own party by the ears (ἐν πολέμῳ), and that there is no real 'honour among thieves.'

παροικία. The word occurs again in these Psalms, xvii. 19, where it seems undoubtedly to bear the meaning of 'a body of sojourners' (see *in loc.*). In the LXX. it is fairly common, and is used in several ways of the *household* of Jacob, of the *dwelling-place* of the wicked, and of a *sojourn* in any spot. In N.T. it twice means sojourn. Any of these senses will suit our passage: that which we have adopted is agreeable to the literal meaning of the word.

Ecclus. xxi. 28 has a very similar thought. Μολύνει τὴν ἑαυτοῦ ψυχὴν ὁ ψιθυρίζων καὶ ἐν παροικήσει μισηθήσεται.

ἐμπρῆσαι οἴκους. That a verb of hostile sense is required here is suggested by such a passage as iv. 23 ἠρήμωσαν οἴκους πολλοὺς ἀνθρώπων, and cf. Ecclus. xxviii. 14 γλῶσσα τρίτη οἰκίας μεγιστάνων κατέστρεψε. Prov. xxix. 8 ἄνδρες ἄνομοι ἐξέκαυσαν πόλιν.

ἐκκόψαι. Cf. Dan. iv. 11 ἐκκόψατε τὸ δένδρον. Jer. vi. 6 ἔκκοψον τὰ ξύλα αὐτῆς. The ideas of cutting down and burning occur together in Matt. iii. 10 δένδρον...

⁴συγχέαι παρανόμους οἴκους ἐν πολέμῳ χείλεσι ψιθυροῖς.

Μακρύναι ὁ θεὸς ἀπὸ ἀκάκων χείλη παρανόμων ἐν ἀπορίᾳ,
καὶ cκορπιcθείη ὀcτᾶ ψιθύρων ἀπὸ φοβουμένων κύριον·
⁵ἐν πυρὶ φλογὸς γλῶσσα ψιθυρὸς ἀπόλοιτο ἀπὸ ὁσίων.
⁶φυλάξαι κύριος ψυχὴν ἡσύχιον μισοῦσαν ἀδίκους,
καὶ κατευθύναι κύριος ἄνδρα ποιοῦντα εἰρήνην ἐν οἴκῳ.
⁷τοῦ κυρίου ἡ σωτηρία ἐπὶ Ἰσραὴλ παῖδα αὐτοῦ εἰς τὸν αἰῶνα,
⁸καὶ ἀπόλοιντο οἱ ἁμαρτωλοὶ ἀπὸ προcώπογ κυρίου ἅπαξ,
καὶ ὅσιοι κυρίου κληρονομήσαιεν ἐπαγγελίας κυρίου.

ιΓ. ψαλμὸc τῶι cαλομών, παράκλΗcιc τῶν Δικαίων.

XIII. Δεξιὰ κγρίογ ἐσκέπασέ με,
δεξιὰ κγρίογ ἐφείσατο ἡμῶν·

4 παρανόμως conj. Wellh.
ἀπὸ κακῶν M.
χείλη παρανόμων—φοβουμένων om. A.
κύριον. πύριον conj. Cerda.
8 ἅπαξ. εἰσάπαξ conj. Hilg.
1 ἐσκέπασε V, K, M, P, Hilg. Fr. ἐσπέσασε A (Cerda 'conciliauit'). ἐπέσπασε conj. Fabr. ἐξέσπασε conj. Geig. ἐπήσπισε conj. Wellh.

ἐκκόπτεται καὶ εἰς πῦρ βάλλεται, and Joh. xv. 6.
4 σκορπισθείη. Cf. iv. 21.
5 πῦρ φλογός. 5 times in LXX. e.g. Is. lxvi. 15, also 2 Thess. i. 8 ἐν πυρὶ φλογὸς διδόντος ἐκδίκησιν.
Ps. xi. (xii). 4. 3 ἐξολοθρεύσαι κύριος πάντα τὰ χείλη τὰ δόλια καὶ γλῶσσαν μεγαλορρήμονα.
Orac. Sib. iii. 760 αὐτὸς καὶ πυρὶ φλέξειεν χαλεπὸν μένος ἀνδρῶν.
ἀπόλοιτο ἀπὸ ὁσίων. ἀπὸ = 'from among,' where ἐξ might have been expected; but the sense of separation is emphasized.
6 φυλάξαι. Cf. Ps. lxxxv. (lxxxvi.) 2 φύλαξον τὴν ψυχήν μου.
ἡσύχιος. Isai. lxvi. 2 ἐπὶ τὸν ταπεινὸν καὶ ἡσύχιον. Compare the contrast of ἥσυχος and γλωσσώδης in Ecclus. xxv. 19 οὕτως γυνὴ γλωσσώδης ἀνδρὶ ἡσύχῳ.
ποιοῦντα εἰρήνην, cf. Jas. iii. 18 ἐν εἰρήνῃ σπείρεται τοῖς ποιοῦσιν εἰρήνην.
7 Wellhausen conjectures that this verse should change places with the following one on the analogy of Psalms ix.—xi.

Ἰσραὴλ παῖδα αὐτοῦ. Cf. Luc. i. 54 ἀντελάβετο Ἰσραὴλ παιδὸς αὐτοῦ. The common expression is Ἰακὼβ παῖς μου. Cf. also Is. xli. 8.
8 ἀπόλοιντο. Apparently here again we have an intimation that the wicked have no part in 'the life' to come. See on iii., xiv. 6. The words of this curse recall Ps. ix. 3 ἀπολοῦνται ἀπὸ προσώπου σου, and Ps. lxvii. (lxviii.) 2 ἀπόλοιντο οἱ ἁμαρτωλοὶ ἀπὸ προσώπου τοῦ θεοῦ.
ἅπαξ. In the sense of ἅμα, cf. εἰσάπαξ ii. 8.
κληρονομήσαιεν ἐπαγγελίας. A phrase savouring more of N.T. phraseology. It does not occur in the LXX., but cf. Heb. vi. 12 τῶν διὰ πίστεως...κληρονομουμένων τὰς ἐπαγγελίας (see Westcott ad loc.). Also xi. 9 (13) and Gal. iii. 29 κατ' ἐπαγγελίαν κληρονόμοι. Clem. 1 Cor. 10 Ἀβραάμ...ὅπως κληρονομήσῃ τὰς ἐπαγγελίας τοῦ θεοῦ.
Have we not here the first instance in extant Jewish literature where the expression 'the promises of the Lord' sums up the assurances of the Messianic Redemption?

4 And put to confusion the houses of the wicked by *kindling* strife with slanderous lips.

Let God remove far from the innocent the lips of the wicked by bringing them to want: and let the bones of slanderers be scattered far from them that fear the LORD.

5 Let the slanderous tongue perish from among the saints in flaming fire.

6 The LORD preserve the quiet soul that hateth the unrighteous: and the LORD direct the man that worketh peace in his house.

7 The salvation of the LORD be upon Israel his servant for ever:

8 And let the sinners be destroyed from before the face of the LORD together: and let the saints of the LORD inherit the promises of the LORD.

PSALM XIII.

A Psalm of Solomon: 'To comfort the righteous.'

1 The right hand of the LORD overshadowed me: the right hand of the LORD spared us.

Ps. XIII.—*Argument*.

1—3. The righteous were preserved when the sinners were slain by a sudden visitation: for this mercy they return thanks.

4—8. The ungodly prince was in fear. For trouble means very different things to the ungodly and to the righteous.

9—11. Their ultimate fates, too, differ widely. Life is in store for one, destruction for the other.

In this Psalm we come back to the now familiar contrast between the δίκαιοι and ἁμαρτωλοί, or, as we prefer to put it, between Pharisee and Sadducee. But here a new feature is introduced. Besides the mention of the sinners in general terms we have one particular representative singled out—ὁ ἀσεβής.

If this reading be the right one—and there seems no sufficient reason to doubt it—it is natural to suppose that some prince or great man among the 'sinners' is meant, in other words some leader of the Sadducean party. Can we fix upon any individual who seems to be pointed at more than another? The Psalm affords us certain data. The sinners have been attacked by some divine visitation, which is described as sword, famine, pestilence and noisome beasts—in the phraseology of Ezekiel. Now these words are susceptible either of a literal interpretation—in which case any closer approximation to dating the document is out of the question—or of a metaphorical one. And if this latter be the case then it is natural to fix, as for example Wellhausen has fixed, upon the Roman invasion as the event here alluded to. If, again, the Romans are intended by the 'noisome beasts' then one of the two Asmonean princes, whose contest brought on their invasion, may well be ὁ ἀσεβής. And of the two Aristobulus, whose supporters shut themselves up in the Temple and for three months defied the armies of Pompey, is more obviously appropriate than his brother and rival, John Hyrcanus. There is little local colour in the Psalm, and its chief object seems to be to point out that, though Pharisee and Sadducee had alike borne the brunt of the visitation in varying degrees, whatever it was, yet, in the case of the Pharisee, all would work together for good, while for the Sadducee the result would be death here and annihilation hereafter.

108   ΨΑΛΜΟΙ ΣΑΛΟΜΩΝΤΟΣ.   [XIII. 2

²ὁ βραχίων κυρίου ἔcωcεν ἡμᾶς ἀπὸ ῥομφαίας διαπορευο-
        μένης,
ἀπὸ λιμοῦ καὶ θανάτου ἁμαρτωλῶν.
³θηρία ἐπέδραμον αὐτοῖς πονηρά,
ἐν τοῖς ὀδοῦσιν αὐτῶν ἔτιλλον σάρκας αὐτῶν,
καὶ ἐν ταῖς μύλαις αὐτῶν ἔθλων ὀστᾶ αὐτῶν·
καὶ ἐκ τούτων ἁπάντων ἐρρύσατο ἡμᾶς κύριος.

⁴Ἐταράχθη ὁ ἀσεβὴς διὰ τὰ παραπτώματα αὐτοῦ,
μήποτε cυμπαραληφθῇ μετὰ τῶν ἁμαρτωλῶν·
⁵ὅτι δεινὴ καταστροφὴ τοῦ ἁμαρτωλοῦ,
καὶ οὐχ ἅψεται δικαίου ἐκ πάντων τούτων οὐδέν·
⁶ὅτι οὐχ ὁμοία ἡ παιδεία τῶν δικαίων ἐν ἀγνοίᾳ,
καὶ ἡ καταστροφὴ τῶν ἁμαρτωλῶν.
⁷ἐν περιστολῇ παιδεύεται δίκαιος,
ἵνα μὴ ἐπιχαρῇ ὁ ἁμαρτωλὸς τῷ δικαίῳ.

3 ὀδοῦσιν. Cerda vertit 'viis.'
4 ἀσεβής, conj. (?) Wellh. εὐσεβής.   5 ἅψεται. ἄψεται V.
6 καταστροφή V, K, P, M. καταρροφή A sed Cerda ubique 'subuersio.'

The opening verses indicate that the 'righteous' had been shielded from the fiercest shock of the visitation, and it may be noted that the priestly order—identical with the Sadducee—had been those who had suffered most in the Pompeian invasion.

1 Hilgenfeld cites in illustration Wisd. v. 17 ὅτι τῇ δεξιᾷ σκεπάσει αὐτοὺς καὶ τῷ βραχίονι ὑπερασπιεῖ αὐτῶν, xix 8 οἱ τῇ σῇ σκεπαζόμενοι χειρί. Sib. Orac. iii, 705 αὐτὸς γὰρ σκεπάσειε μόνος. Add to these Ps. xcvii. (xcviii.) 1 ἔσωσεν αὐτῷ ἡ δεξιὰ αὐτοῦ καὶ ὁ βραχίων ὁ ἅγιος αὐτοῦ. cxvii. (cxviii.) 16 δεξιὰ κυρίου ὕψωσέ με, δεξιὰ κυρίου ἐποίησε δύναμιν.

2 θανάτου ἁμαρτωλῶν. A strange expression, suggesting a translator's error. Does not θανάτου = 'pestilence' (דֶּבֶר)? And should not the word 'sinners' open the next clause? 'As for sinners—evil beasts ran upon them.' This gives point to μετὰ τῶν ἁμαρτωλῶν in ver. 4. In this explanation we find that Wellhausen has anticipated us.

2, 3 The list of plagues here is taken from such passages as Ez. xiv. 17 where the expression ῥομφαία διελθάτω ἐπὶ τῆς γῆς explains the διαπορευομένης. Cf. Lev. xxvi. 5 πόλεμος οὐ διελεύσεται. 22 ἀποστελῶ ἐφ' ὑμᾶς τὰ θηρία τὰ ἄγρια τῆς γῆς. Ez. v. 17 ἐξαποστελῶ ἐπί σε λιμὸν καὶ θηρία πονηρά. Ecclus. xl. 9 θάνατος καὶ αἷμα καὶ ἔρις καὶ ῥομφαία, ἐπαγωγαί, λιμὸς καὶ σύντριμμα καὶ μάστιξ. ἐπὶ τοὺς ἀνόμους ἐκτίσθη ταῦτα πάντα.

θηρία πονηρά is a common expression in the LXX. of Ezekiel. Cf. Lev. xxvi. 6. ὀδόντες—μύλαι. Ps. lviii. 6 τὰς μύλας τῶν λεόντων συνέθλασεν ὁ κύριος. Ps. xxx. 14 μαχαίραις τοὺς ὀδόντας ἔχει καὶ τὰς μύλας τομίδας.

4 ὁ ἀσεβής. There is no variant in the MSS. (though we should remember that in many minuscule hands the initial a- and ευ- are almost indistinguishable), but the word is ἅπαξ λεγόμενον in the book. Partly on this account, perhaps, but mainly, no doubt, owing to the difficulties which the retention of it causes, Wellhausen alters it to εὐσεβής 'the pious man.' There is a certain plausibility in this reading. There is a plain allusion in the wording and matter of this and the next verse to the story of Lot: the words μήποτε συμπαραληφθῇ occur only in Gen. xix. 17 εἰς τὸ ὄρος σώζου μήποτε συμπαραληφθῇς, and the word καταστροφή is used to describe the fate of the cities of the plain. Gen. xix. 29 ἐξαπέστειλε τὸν Λὼτ ἐκ μέσου τῆς καταστροφῆς. Cf. the late reading in 2 Pet. ii. 6 καταστροφῇ

XIII. 7] ΨΑΛΜΟΙ ΣΑΛΟΜΩΝΤΟΣ. 109

2 The arm of the LORD saved us from the sword that passed through: from famine and from the plague of the sinners.

3 Noisome beasts ran upon them: with their teeth they rent the flesh of them, and with their jaws they brake their bones in pieces; and out of all these things did the LORD save us.

4 The ungodly man[1] was troubled because of his transgressions: lest he should be taken along with the sinners.

[1] Conj. *The pious man*

5 For fearful is the overthrow of the sinner: and of all these things nothing shall touch the righteous.

6 For the chastening of the righteous which have sinned ignorantly, and the overthrow of the sinners are not alike.

7 The righteous is chastened secretly[2]; that the sinner may not rejoice over the righteous.

[2] Or, *sparingly*

κατέκρινεν. Now, it may be asked, can we suppose that the writer would compare Lot to an ἀσεβής? Is not εὐσεβής far more appropriate to his position?

It is a strong point too that the word παραπτώματα is only used in this book of the sins of the *righteous*. See iii. 8, xiii. 9, which are the only other places where the word occurs.

On the other hand, compare the following coincidences with the text of Job in this and the following verses, Job xv. 20 πᾶς ὁ βίος ἀσεβοῦς ἐν φροντίδι, xxi. 17 οὐ μὴν δὲ ἀλλὰ καὶ ἀσεβῶν λύχνος σβεσθήσεται ἐπελεύσεται δὲ αὐτοῖς ἡ καταστροφή, xxvii. 7 ὥσπερ ἡ καταστροφὴ τῶν ἁμαρτωλῶν. Id. i. 12 ἀλλ' αὐτοῦ μὴ ἄψῃ sc. τοῦ Ἰώβ.

It is difficult to find a historical place for the εὐσεβής, but in other respects the reading gives a far smoother sense. It would, however, be against our critical principles to alter a word which gives an adequate sense and is supported by all MS. evidence.

A similar list of plagues associated with the ἀσεβεῖς occurs in Ecclus. xxxix. 29, 30 πῦρ καὶ χάλαζα, καὶ λιμὸς καὶ θάνατος, ταῦτα πάντα εἰς ἐκδίκησιν ἔκτισται· θηρίων ὀδόντες καὶ σκορπίοι καὶ ἔχεις, καὶ ῥομφαία ἐκδικοῦσα εἰς ὄλεθρον ἀσεβεῖς.

6 ἐν ἀγνοίᾳ. See for this notes on iii. 9.

7 ἐν περιστολῇ. The word occurs nowhere in the LXX. or N.T. and no other instance of its use in Hellenistic Greek is known to us. In Classical Greek its one meaning seems to be the decking out of a corpse for burial.

We have therefore to deduce a probable meaning of the word from the verb περιστέλλω. This has three leading uses, (i) of decking out a corpse, (ii) of wrapping round and so concealing, (iii) of protecting or defending. Either of the last two yield a possible sense for περιστολή.

Previous editors have usually thought that the sense should be 'in secret': and the only objection to this rendering is the difficulty of attaching a real meaning to the sentiment. In other Psalms, e.g. xvii., the sufferings of the righteous are described and dwelt upon. The fact that righteous men like Job had suffered, and that not secretly, was well known to the writer, so that we feel some hesitation in crediting him with an assertion of the contrary here. Still Psalm xv. may be cited to confirm the interpretation.

The only other passage where this writer uses περιστέλλω (xvi. 10) certainly cannot bear the meaning of '*concealment*.'

The alternative rendering derived from the third sense of περιστέλλω would be 'with regard,' i.e. with the view of correcting the righteous and preventing him from erring so that the enemies of the Lord might blaspheme—which would give a clear and practical sense. A collateral sense, whose correctness seems more doubtful, is 'with reservation,' 'sparingly.' This sense is we think confirmed by vii. 34.

It is tempting to suggest that the translator has here rendered the Hebrew text wrongly, perhaps reading מְעֹטֶה 'a covering' (=καταστολὴν Isai. lxi. 3) instead of מְעַט 'a little.' If this conjecture could

110   ΨΑΛΜΟΙ ΣΑΛΟΜΩΝΤΟΣ.   [XIII. 8

⁸ ὅτι νουθετήσει δίκαιον ὡς υἱὸν ἀγαπήσεως,
καὶ ἡ παιδεία αὐτοῦ ὡς πρωτοτόκου·
⁹ ὅτι φείσεται κύριος τῶν ὁσίων αὐτοῦ,
καὶ τὰ παραπτώματα αὐτῶν ἐξαλείψει ἐν παιδείᾳ·
ἡ γὰρ ζωὴ τῶν δικαίων εἰς τὸν αἰῶνα,
¹⁰ ἁμαρτωλοὶ δὲ ἀρθήσονται εἰς ἀπώλειαν,
καὶ οὐχ εὑρεθήσεται μνημόσυνον αὐτῶν ἔτι·
¹¹ ἐπὶ δὲ τοὺς ὁσίους τὸ ἔλεος κυρίου,
καὶ ἐπὶ τοὺς φοβουμένους αὐτὸν τὸ ἔλεος αὐτοῦ.

ΙΔ. ΫΜΝΟC ΤΩΙ CΑΛΟΜΩΝ.

XIV. Πιστὸς κύριος τοῖς ἀγαπῶσιν αὐτὸν ἐν ἀληθείᾳ,
τοῖς ὙΠΟΜΕΝΟΥCΙ παιδείαν αὐτοῦ,
τοῖς πορευομένοις ἐν δικαιοσύνῃ προσταγμάτων αὐτοῦ,
ἐν νόμῳ ὡς ἐΝΕΤΕΙΛΑΤΟ ἡμῖν εἰς ΖΩΗΝ ἡμῶν,
² ὅσιοι κυρίου ζήσονται ἐν αὐτῷ εἰς τὸν αἰῶνα.
ὁ παράδεισος κυρίου, τὰ ΞΎΛΑ ΤΗC ΖΩΗC ὅσιοι αὐτοῦ·

10 οὐκ codd. et edd.: primus Hilg. scripsit οὐχ: ita Geig. Fr. Pick.
ἔτι. ἐπί A.
1 Tit. om. M.
ἐννόμῳ V, M, ut vidʳ. Ita pridem coni. Hilg.¹: jam corr. Hilg.².
ὡς codd. et edd.: fortasse ᾧ.

---

be maintained, we would compare Luke
xiii. 48 θυρήσεται ὀλίγας as giving the
sense of the original in our passage.
ἐπιχαίρω. Cf. Ps. xxxvii. (xxxviii.)
17 Μήποτε ἐπιχαρῶσί μοι οἱ ἐχθροί μου,
also xli. 12, and Ecclus. xxiii. 3.
8 νουθετήσει. No subject is expressed. The Greek requires us to supply ὁ θεός. The translator probably mistook a Passive for an Active verb, reading
יְיַסֵּר for יִוָּסֵר. The clause should have
run νουθετηθήσεται δίκαιος ὡς υἱὸς ἀγαπήσεως. The idea of the verse is drawn
from Deut. viii. 5.
Cf. Wisd. xi. 10 τούτους μὲν γὰρ ὡς
πατὴρ νουθετῶν ἐδοκίμασας: also xvi. 8 and
Judith viii. 27, cf. Joseph. *Ant.* III. xv. 1
Μωϋσῆς...τὸν θεὸν ἐδήλου...λήψεσθαι τιμωρίαν οὐκ ἀξίαν μὲν τῶν ἐξημαρτημένων
οἵαν δὲ οἱ πατέρες ἐπὶ νουθεσίᾳ τοῖς τέκνοις
ἐπιφέρουσι.
υἱὸν ἀγαπήσεως. Cf. Gen. xxii. 2 λάβε

τὸν υἱόν σου τὸν ἀγαπητὸν ὃν ἠγάπησας.
Zech. xii. 10 κόψονται κοπετόν, ὡς ἐπ'
ἀγαπητῷ, καὶ ὀδυνηθήσονται ὀδύνην, ὡς
ἐπὶ τῷ πρωτοτόκῳ, compare also Ps. S.
xviii. 4.
πρωτοτόκου. Cf. Ex. iv. 22 υἱὸς πρωτότοκός μου Ἰσραήλ.
9 ἐξαλείψει. See on ii. 29. Ps. l.
(li.) 3 ἐξάλειψον τὸ ἀνόμημά μου, and 11,
and Is. xliii. 25.
10 μνημόσυνον. Cf. Job xviii. 17 τὸ
μνημόσυνον αὐτοῦ ἀπόλοιτο ἐκ γῆς, Ps. ix.
7 ἀπώλετο τὸ μνημόσυνον αὐτῶν μετ' ἤχου.
11 Here we find a close resemblance
to the words of the Magnificat, Luc. i. 50
καὶ τὸ ἔλεος αὐτοῦ εἰς γενεὰς καὶ γενεὰς
τοῖς φοβουμένοις αὐτόν.
Ps. XIV.—*Argument.*
1—3. God's unchanging faithfulness
to those who are faithful to Him. Their
consequent security from trouble. The
result of God's ancient promise to Israel.

XIV. 2]   ΨΑΛΜΟΙ ΣΑΛΟΜΩΝΤΟΣ.   111

8 For he will admonish the righteous as a beloved son: and his chastening is as *a man chasteneth his* firstborn.

9 For the LORD will spare his saints, and will blot out their transgressions with his chastening: for the life of the righteous is for ever.

10 But sinners shall be taken away unto destruction: and the memorial of them shall no more be found.

11 But upon the saints is the mercy of the LORD: yea[3] upon them that fear him is his mercy.

[3] Gr. *and*

PSALM XIV.

A Hymn of Solomon.

1 Faithful is the LORD unto them that love him in truth: even unto such as abide his chastening; who walk in the righteousness of his commandments, in the law[1] according as[2] he commanded us for our life.

2 The saints of the LORD shall live therein[3] for ever: the garden of the LORD, even the trees of life, such are his saints.

[1] Or, *even the righteousness of the law*
[2] Or, *which*
[3] Or, *in him*

4—7. The insecurity of the sinner. His secrets are known to God, and his end is destruction. In which he affords a contrast to the righteous.

The Psalm is little more than a paraphrase of the 1st canonical Psalm, with which it should be compared. The comparison of the righteous to a tree occurs in both places, as well as in several other Psalms and in Job.

1 Cf. x. 2, 4. The thought is the same as in Deut. vii. 9 καὶ γνώσῃ ὅτι κύριος ὁ θεός σου οὗτος θεός, θεὸς πιστός, ὁ φυλάσσων διαθήκην καὶ ἔλεος τοῖς ἀγαπῶσιν αὐτὸν καὶ τοῖς φυλάσσουσι τὰς ἐντολὰς αὐτοῦ εἰς χιλίας γενεάς.

δικαιοσύνη προσταγμάτων. The righteousness consisting in the observance of the enactments of the law. Cf. Lev. xxvi. 3 ἐὰν τοῖς προστάγμασιν πορεύησθε καὶ τὰς ἐντολάς μου φυλάσσησθε. 1 Kings viii. 62 ὁσίως πορεύεσθαι ἐν τοῖς προστάγμασιν αὐτοῦ καὶ φυλάσσειν ἐντολὰς αὐτοῦ. Ez. xxxiii. 15 ἐν προστάγματι ζωῆς διαπορεύηται, Luke i. 6.

ἐν νόμῳ. Cf. Bar. iv. 1 αὕτη ἡ βίβλος προσταγμάτων τοῦ θεοῦ καὶ ὁ νόμος ὁ ὑπάρχων εἰς τὸν αἰῶνα· πάντες οἱ κρατοῦντες αὐτὴν εἰς ζωήν. Ecclus. xvii. 11, xlv. 6 νόμον ζωῆς.

See also Deut. xxx. 20, Ps. cxxxiii. 4.

Hilgenfeld's conjecture ἐννόμῳ is supported by the reading of M, and the word is used in the Prologue to Ecclus. and in Acts xix. 30, and 1 Cor. ix. 21 ἔννομος Χριστῷ. If adopted it renders our conjecture ᾧ, on which we lay no stress, unnecessary.

But ἐν νόμῳ is a very natural phrase for our Psalmist to use, as an explanation of ἐν δικ. προσ. It is also implied in ver. 2, ζήσονται ἐν αὐτῷ.

εἰς ζωὴν ἡμῶν = 'That we should live therein,' or 'that He might preserve our life.'

2 ἐν αὐτῷ is either ἐν κυρίῳ or ἐν νόμῳ. If ἐννόμῳ is the right reading, there can be no doubt that ἐν αὐτῷ refers to κύριος. The life of the saints is through the mercy and in the presence of the Lord.

But more probably ζήσονται ἐν αὐτῷ refers back to ἐν νόμῳ...εἰς ζωὴν ἡμῶν.

ξύλα τῆς ζωῆς. A not uncommon metaphor in Proverbs, e.g. iii. 18. Cp. also Is. lxv. 22 κατὰ γὰρ τὰς ἡμέρας τοῦ ξύλου τῆς ζωῆς ἔσονται αἱ ἡμέραι τοῦ λαοῦ μου. 4 Macc. xviii. 16.

The παράδεισος τοῦ θεοῦ occurs in Ez. xxxi. 8, and xxviii. 13, and Rev. ii.

³ἡ φυτεία αὐτῶν ἐρρίζωμένη εἰς τὸν αἰῶνα,
ογκ ἐκτιλήϲονται πάϲαϲ τὰϲ ἡμέραϲ τοŷ ογρανοŷ·
ὅτι ἡ μερὶς καὶ ἡ κληρονομία τοῦ θεοῦ ἐστιν ὁ Ἰσραήλ.

⁴Καὶ οὐχ οὕτως οἱ ἁμαρτωλοὶ καὶ παράνομοι,
οἳ ἠγάπησαν ἡμέραν ἐν μετοχῇ ἁμαρτίας αὐτῶν,
ἐν μικρότητι σαπρίας, ἐν ἐπιθυμίᾳ αὐτῶν,
⁵καὶ οὐκ ἐμνήσθησαν τοῦ θεοῦ·
ὅτι ὁδοὶ ἀνθρώπων γνωϲταὶ ἐνώπιον αὐτοῦ διὰ παντός,
καὶ ταμιεῖα καρδίας ἐπίσταται πρὸ τοῦ γενέσθαι.
⁶διὰ τοῦτο ἡ κληρονομία αὐτῶν ᾅδης καὶ ϲκότοϲ καὶ ἀπώλεια,
καὶ οὐχ εὑρεθήσονται ἐν ἡμέρᾳ ἐλέου δικαίων·
⁷οἱ δὲ ὅσιοι κυρίου κληρονομήσουσι ζωὴν ἐν εὐφροσύνῃ.

ιε. ψαλμὸϲ τῷι ϲαλομὼν μετ' ᾠιδῆϲ.

XV. Ἐν τῷ θλίβεϲθαί με ἐπεκαλεϲάμην τὸ ὄνομα κγρίογ,
εἰς βοήθειαν ἤλπισα τοῦ θεοῦ Ἰακώβ καὶ ἐσώθην,
²ὅτι ἐλπὶς καὶ καταφυγὴ τῶν πτωχῶν σύ, ὁ θεός·

3 τοῦ οὐρανοῦ V, K, P. τοῦ ἀνθρώπου (ανου pro ουνου) M: om. A.
κληρονομία. Cerda vitiose πληρονομία.

4 καί om. Cerda: idem in scholiis notat se vocem praetermisisse partim deletam quam pro voce exclamationis habuerit, ut viii. 37.
μικρότητι codd. (A μικρότητε). πικρότητι conj. Hilg. (Fr. Pick.).

---

3 ἐρριζωμένη. Cf. Prov. xii. 3 αἱ δὲ ῥίζαι τῶν δικαίων οὐκ ἐξαρθήσονται, and 19. Jer. xlii. (xlix.) 10 φυτεύσω ὑμᾶς, καὶ οὐ μὴ ἐκτίλω.

τὰς ἡμέρας τοῦ οὐρανοῦ. The expression occurs in Ps. lxxxviii. (lxxxix.) 30 τὸν θρόνον αὐτοῦ ὡς τὰς ἡμέρας τοῦ οὐρανοῦ, and Bar. i. 11 ἵνα ὦσιν αἱ ἡμέραι αὐτῶν ὡς αἱ ἡμέραι τοῦ οὐρανοῦ.

ἡ μερίς. Cf. Ecclus. xvii. 13 μερὶς κυρίου Ἰσραὴλ ἐστίν, and Deut. xxxii. 9.

4 οὐχ οὕτως (לֹא כֵן), a reminiscence of Ps. i. 4 οὐχ οὕτως οἱ ἀσεβεῖς, οὐχ οὕτως.

ἠγάπησαν. The aor. is the commonest rendering in the LXX. of the Heb. אהב. Cf. ix. 16.

ἀγαπᾶν ἡμέραν seems to mean, content themselves with the day's enjoyment, love this present world. The phrase most like it is that in Ps. xxxiii. (xxxiv.) 13 ἀγαπῶν ἡμέρας ἰδεῖν ἀγαθάς. But in our Psalm the stress is laid on the shortness of the pleasure. The ἡμέρα answers to μικρότης in the next clause.

This is why we have preferred to render ἀγαπᾶν to be content with, instead of 'to love.'

ἐν μετοχῇ ἁμαρτίας αὐτῶν, cf. Assumpt. Mos. v. 1 'in reges participes scelerum.'

μικρότης. This is the reading of all MSS. whereas πικρότης gives a doubtful sense and is nowhere found in the LXX. The LXX. version of Susanna v. 56 affords an excellent illustration of what is meant by μικρότης here. Daniel says to one of the elders, τὸ κάλλος σε ἠπάτησεν, ἡ μικρὰ ἐπιθυμία, the lust whose enjoyment lasts so short a time, and whose being as well as its end is corruption. Evidently we have here again an allusion to those secret sins of which the Psalmist has already spoken (iii., iv., viii.).

5 ὅτι may be either a separate statement explaining why they ought to have

3 The planting of them is rooted for ever: they shall not be plucked out all the days of the heaven: for the portion *of the* LORD and the inheritance of God is Israel.

4 The sinners and transgressors are not like them, which were contented with a day while they were partners together in sin: *yea*, with a short space of corruption in fulfilling their lust.

5 And they remembered not God, that[4] the ways of men are known before him continually: and he knoweth the secret chambers of the heart before they had their being. [4] Or, *for*

6 Therefore is their inheritance hell and darkness and destruction: and they shall not be found in the day of mercy for the righteous.

7 But the saints of the LORD shall inherit life in gladness.

PSALM XV.

A Psalm of Solomon: With a song.

1 When I was in trouble I called upon the name of the LORD: I trusted in the God of Israel for help, and I was preserved.

2 For thou art the hope and refuge of the needy, O God;

---

remembered God, or a pointing out what they ought to have remembered about Him. We do not feel that the one rendering is intrinsically less probable than the other, but certainly in a majority of cases the former is the only admissible sense for ὅτι in these Psalms.

ταμιεῖα καρδίας, cf. Apoc. Bar. xx. 3 'in penetralibus mentis tuæ,' and Prov. xx. 27, 30 ταμεῖα κοιλίας.

πρὸ τοῦ γενέσθαι (Gen. ii. 5 πρὸ τοῦ γενέσθαι ἐπὶ τῆς γῆς) may refer either to the man or to the chambers of his heart. Cf. Enoch, cap. 9. 11, 'Thou knowest everything before it comes to pass' (tr. Schodde).

Cf. generally Jer. i. 5 πρὸ τοῦ με πλάσαι σε ἐν κοιλίᾳ ἐπίσταμαί σε.

6 σκότος. Ps. xxxiv. (xxxv.) 6 γενηθήτω ἡ ὁδὸς αὐτῶν σκότος καὶ ὀλίσθημα, see xv. 11.

οὐχ εὑρεθήσονται. Job xx. 8 ὥσπερ ἐνύπνιον...οὐ μὴ εὑρεθῇ, and Ps. ix. 18, xxxvi. (xxxvii.) 38.

ἐλέου δικαίων, transitive as in ii. 8. 'The day of mercy to the righteous' we understand to be the resurrection in the Messianic consummation. The wicked will not partake in it, but their souls will continue in Sheol, in darkness and doom.

7 κληρονομεῖν ζωήν, we find this expression in the mouth of a true Pharisee, the rich young man, in Mk. x. 17 τί ποιήσω ἵνα ζωὴν αἰώνιον κληρονομήσω; cf. Matt. xix. 29.

Ps. XV.—*Argument.*

1, 2. The call to praise God.

3—8. The reward of praise, viz. safety from the destruction that follows sinners.

9—14. The other side of the picture: misfortune in this life and annihilation after it are the lot of sinners,

15. while the righteous inherit eternal life.

The Psalm treats of the same theme as iii. and xiv.: the contrast between the life and destination of the righteous and of the sinner.

1 Cf. Ps. xvii. (xviii.) 7, cxix. (cxx.) 1, and Ps. S. i. 1.

2 Lit. I trusted for the help of the God of Jacob. The trouble in which the Psalmist found himself is not more particularly specified, but very probably the occasion is the same as that of Ps. xiii. In both we have references to famine, sword and pestilence, and in both the righteous have been preserved, while the sinners have suffered. In this Psalm the writer appears to lay special stress on

J. P. 8

114 ΨΑΛΜΟΙ ΣΑΛΟΜΩΝΤΟΣ. [XV. 3

³τίς γὰρ ἰσχύει, ὁ θεός, εἰ μὴ ἐξομολογήσασθαί σοι ἐν ἀληθείᾳ;
⁴καὶ τί δυνατὸς ἄνθρωπος, εἰ μὴ ἐξομολογήσασθαι τῷ ὀνόματί σου;
⁵ψαλμὸν καὶ αἶνον μετ' ᾠδῆς ἐν εὐφροσύνῃ καρδίας,
καρπὸν χειλέων ἐν ὀργάνῳ ἡρμοσμένῳ γλώσσης,
ἀπαρχὴν χειλέων ἀπὸ καρδίας ὁσίας καὶ δικαίας·
⁶ὁ ποιῶν ταῦτα οὐ σαλευθήσεται εἰς τὸν αἰῶνα ἀπὸ κακοῦ,
φλὸξ πυρὸς καὶ ὀργὴ ἀδίκων οὐχ ἅψεται αὐτοῦ,
⁷ὅταν ἐξέλθῃ ἐπὶ ἁμαρτωλοὺς ἀπὸ προσώπου κυρίου,
ὀλοθρεῦσαι πᾶσαν ὑπόστασιν ἁμαρτωλῶν·
⁸ὅτι τὸ σημεῖον τοῦ θεοῦ ἐπὶ δικαίους εἰς σωτηρίαν,
λιμὸς καὶ ῥομφαία καὶ θάνατος μακρὰν ἀπὸ δικαίων·
⁹φεύξονται γὰρ ὡς διωκομένου *πολεμίου* ἀπὸ ὁσίων,
καταδιώξεται δὲ ἁμαρτωλοὺς καὶ καταλήψεται.
καὶ οὐκ ἐκφεύξονται οἱ ποιοῦντες ἀνομίαν τὸ κρίμα κυρίου,
ὡς ὑπὸ πολεμίων ἐμπείρων καταληφθήσονται,

3 τίς codd. Fr. τί.
9 πολεμίου nos conj., λιμοῦ codd. et edd.

---

praise as a means whereby safety may be secured. 'Praise' in the mouth of a Pharisee may well be taken to mean liturgical praise—attention, in fact, to the religious duties which the sinners had neglected.

ἐλπίς. Cf. v. 2.

3 Fritzsche's correction of τί for τίς is quite uncalled for, and though assimilating the clauses in form does, in fact, destroy their parallelism. There is here, too, a general resemblance to the opening verses of the fifth Psalm (v. 5).

4 τί δυνατός. Bar. iv. 17 ἐγὼ δὲ τί δυνατὴ βοηθῆσαι ὑμῖν;

5 αἶνος only occurs five times in the LXX. (Tromm), viz. in Esdr., Neh., Sap. and Ecclus. Cp. Ps. lxviii. (lxix.) 31 αἰνέσω τὸ ὄνομα τοῦ θεοῦ μου μετ' ᾠδῆς.

A comparison with Ps. S. iii. 1, 2 suggests the conjecture that καὶ αἶνον here should be καινὸν as there: the change is infinitesimal, but, however probable, we do not venture to introduce it into the text.

καρπὸν χειλέων (נִיב שְׂפָתַיִם). Is. lvii. 19 (Theodot.) κτίζων καρπὸν χειλέων. Hos. xiv. 3 ἀνταποδώσομεν καρπὸν χειλέων ἡμῶν.

Cf. Prov. xviii. 20, xxxi. 31. Also Heb. xiii. 15 θυσίαν αἰνέσεως...τουτέστιν καρπὸν χειλέων ὁμολογούντων τῷ ὀνόματι αὐτοῦ.

ὄργανον. 2 Sam. vi. 5 ἐν ὀργάνοις ἡρμοσμένοις ἐν ἰσχύϊ. In Job xxi. 12 Aquila gives ὀργάνου for עוּגָב, where the LXX. has ψαλμοῦ, and Symmachus κιθάρας. In Ps. cxxxvi. (cxxxvii.) 2 τὰ ὄργανα ἡμῶν = בְּנוֹרוֹתֵינוּ 'our harps.'

ἀπαρχὴν χειλέων, not synonymous with καρπὸν χειλέων: it is the *sacrificial offering* of the first-fruits (=תְּרוּמַת שְׂפָתַיִם), to which we have a parallel in Ecclus. xxxii. 8 μὴ σμικρύνῃς ἀπαρχὴν χειρῶν σου.

ἀπὸ καρδίας. In this usage we more generally find ἐκ...καρδίας (cf. Ps. S. iii. 2) or ἐν...καρδίᾳ.

καρδίας ὁσίας. Prov. xxii. 11 κύριος ἀγαπᾷ ὁσίας καρδίας.

6 ταῦτα. Our punctuation here differs from that of Fritzsche. He connects the whole of ver. 5 with ver. 4, at the end of which he places a comma. We make the question end with ver. 4, and the accusatives of ver. 5 will then depend on ποιῶν, being all in apposition to ταῦτα.

οὐ σαλευθήσεται. From Ps. ix. 27 (x. 6) οὐ μὴ σαλευθῶ ἀπὸ γενεᾶς εἰς γενεὰν ἄνευ

ΨΑΛΜΟΙ ΣΑΛΟΜΩΝΤΟΣ.

3 For who, O God, is strong save to praise Thee in truth?
4 And wherein is a man able, save to give thanks unto thy name?
5 A psalm and praise with a song in gladness of heart: the fruit of the lips with the well-tuned instrument of the tongue: the firstfruits of the lips from a holy and righteous heart;
6 He that doeth these things shall not be removed for ever by evil: flaming fire and the wrath against[1] the ungodly shall not touch him,   [1] Or, *of*
7 When it goeth forth against the sinners from before the face of the LORD, to destroy all the substance[2] of the sinners.   [2] Or, *hope*
8 For the mark of the LORD is upon the righteous unto their salvation. Famine and the sword and pestilence shall be far from the righteous.
9 For they shall flee from the saints as an enemy that is pursued: but it shall pursue after the sinners and shall overtake *them:* and they that work wickedness shall not escape the judgment of the LORD; they shall be overtaken as it were by mighty men of war.

κακοῦ. There can be little doubt that ἀπὸ really = ὑπὸ here. Hardly any use of a preposition need surprise us in dealing with a writer of this stamp. Cf. Ps. xiv. (xv.) 5 ὁ ποιῶν ταῦτα οὐ σαλευθήσεται εἰς τὸν αἰῶνα.

φλὸξ πυρός. See xii. 5 for the converse, and cf. Is. xliii. 52 φλὸξ οὐ κατακαύσει σε. An allusion to the Story of the Three Children may underlie this.

ὀργὴ ἀδίκων. Gen. object, exactly parallel to ἔλεος δικαίων xiv. 6. But ἀδίκων may also be understood as a genitive of the subj.; 'the wrath of the ungodly' would then allude to the fury of Nebuchadnezzar (Dan. iii. 19).

οὐχ ἅψεται, xiii. 5.

7 ὑπόστασις. In the LXX. this word occurs some 19 times in very various senses. Twice it means a camp, elsewhere a firm ground or foundation: once ὑπόστασις ζωῆς = means to support life. None of these meanings are admissible here. Two which are given in our text and margin do both appear possible. The first, *substance,* is confirmed by Jer. x. 17 Συνήγαγεν ἔξωθεν τὴν ὑπόστασίν σου, and especially Deut. xi. 6 καὶ πᾶσαν αὐτῶν τὴν ὑπόστασιν (קוּמָם) τὴν μετ' αὐτῶν, of Korah. The second, *confidence* or *expectation,* is the commoner sense in N.T., and is found in LXX. Ps. xxxviii. (xxxix.) 8 καὶ ἡ ὑπόστασίς μου παρὰ σοί ἐστιν. Ruth i.

12 ἔστι μοι ὑπόστασις τοῦ γενηθῆναι με ἀνδρί. See also 2 Cor. ix. 4, xi. 17; Heb. iii. 14. A third, *remnant,* might be suggested. It is important because it occurs in Job (xxii. 20) εἰ μὴ ἠφανίσθη ἡ ὑπόστασις αὐτῶν.

The word occurs again in our Psalms (xvii. 26) in a connection so similar to this passage that the meaning may fairly be taken as identical with this.

8 τὸ σημεῖον, from Ez. ix. 4 δὸς σημεῖον ἐπὶ τὰ μέτωπα τῶν ἀνδρῶν τῶν καταστεναζόντων. This in its turn may be a reminiscence of Ex. xii. 13 ἔσται τὸ αἷμα ὑμῖν ἐν σημείῳ, of the blood on the lintel. Cf. Rev. vii. 3 ἄχρι οὗ σφραγίσωμεν τοὺς δούλους τοῦ θεοῦ ἡμῶν ἐπὶ τῶν μετώπων αὐτῶν, and ix. 4.

λιμὸς, etc. See on xiii. 2. iv. (v.) Esdr. xv. 5 gladium et famem et mortem et interitum.

9 We have to justify the somewhat startling emendation introduced into the text. It will readily, we think, be acknowledged that the text, as it has been hitherto read, is unsatisfactory. It would be very tame to say that a famine and other things would flee from the righteous, as if they (the righteous) were a famine being pursued; so that it seems some change is required. We believe that the key to the requisite alteration is to be looked for in the following verse, which

¹⁰ τὸ γὰρ cHMεῖον τῆς ἀπωλείας ἐπὶ τοῦ μετώπογ αὐτῶν,
¹¹ καὶ ἡ κληρονομία τῶν ἁμαρτωλῶν ἀπώλειά καὶ ϲκότοϲ.
καὶ αἱ ἀνομίαι αὐτῶν διώξονται αὐτοὺς ἕως ᾅδου κάτω,
¹² ἡ κληρονομία αὐτῶν οὐχ εὑρεθήσεται τοῖς τέκνοις αὐτῶν·
¹³ αἱ γὰρ ἀνομίαι ἐξερημώσουσιν οἴκους ἁμαρτωλῶν,
καὶ ἀπολοῦνται οἱ ἁμαρτωλοὶ ἐν Ημέρᾳ κρίϲεωϲ κγρίογ εἰς
    τὸν αἰῶνα,
¹⁴ ὅταν ἐπισκέπτηται ὁ θεὸς τὴν γῆν ἐν κρίματι αὐτοῦ,
ἀποδοῦναι ἁμαρτωλοῖς εἰς τὸν αἰῶνα χρόνον.
¹⁵ οἱ δὲ φοβούμενοι τὸν κύριον ἐλεηθήσονται ἐν αὐτῇ,
καὶ ζήσονται ἐν τῇ ἐλεημοσύνῃ τοῦ θεοῦ αὐτῶν.

ιε̄. ψαλμὸϲ τῶι ϲαλομών εἰϲ ἀντίληψιν.

XVI. Ἐν τῷ νγϲτάζαι ψγχήν μογ ἀπὸ κυρίου,
παρὰ μικρὸν ὠλίσθησα ἐν καταφορᾷ ὕπνου·

10 τῆς ἀπωλείας. A om. τῆς.
11 ἀνομίαι αὐτῶν codd.: A ins. αὐτῶν, non, ut dicit Fr., omittit. Fabr. om.
    Inscriptio deest in M.
1 καταφθορᾷ A, V, K, M, Cerda.
    καταφορᾷ P, Cerda conj. quem seqq. Fabr. Lagarde Hilg. Geig. Fritzsch.
Wellh. Pick.

---

points the contrast between the righteous and the sinner. The case of the latter is the opposite of that of the righteous. The sense clearly is, that while plagues flee from the righteous as if they (the plagues) were being pursued, they will pursue the ungodly as does an enemy in war. We believe then that the point of comparison between the clauses lies in πολεμίων. The plagues which follow the sinners like enemies are themselves chased away from the righteous as if by enemies, and some case of the word πόλεμιος must underlie the λιμοῦ of the present text. Several forms are possible. The simplest mode of expression would be ὡς διωκόμενοι πολέμιοι, the most elaborate (suggested by Mr W. G. Headlam) ὡς διωκόμενοι ὑπὸ πολεμίου. That which we print in the text stands midway between the two. We conjecture the genesis of the present reading to have been something of this kind:
ΔιωκοΜεΝΟΥΠΟΛεΜΙΟΥ
mistaken for
ΔιωκοΜεΝΟΥ ΥΠΟ ΛεΜΙΟΥ,
which being nonsense, ὑπὸ is cut out, and we get
ΔιωκοΜεΝΟΥ Λ(ε)ΙΜΟΥ.
The same, almost, holds good for the reading διωκόμενοι ὑπὸ πολεμίου, which has the further advantage of not suddenly and harshly introducing a genitive absolute.
For the reading of the MSS. cf. Job v. 20 ἐν λιμῷ ῥύσεταί σε ἐκ θανάτου.
καταδιώξεται. Cf. Ps. xvii. (xviii.) 38 καταδιώξω τοὺς ἐχθρούς μου καὶ καταλήψομαι. xxxiv. (xxxv.) ὁ ἄγγελος κυρίου καταδιώκων αὐτούς. lxx. (lxxi.) 11 καταδιώξατε καὶ καταλάβετε αὐτόν. Prov. xiii. 21 ἁμαρτάνοντος καταδιώξεται κακά, τοὺς δὲ δικαίους καταλήψεται ἀγαθά.
ἐμπείρων. For the habit of this writer to change his verbs from plural to singular without changing his subject, compare iv. 7—15.
ἔμπειρος occurs once in Tobit (v. 5). For the meaning of πολεμίων ἐμπείρων cf. δεδιδαγμένοι πόλεμον Cant. iii. 8; 1 Chr. v. 18; διδακτὸς πολέμου 1 Macc. iv. 7.
10 Compare Ez. ix. 4 (cited above) and Gen. iv. 18 ἔθετο κύριος ὁ θεὸς σημεῖον τῷ Καΐν.

10 For the mark of destruction is upon their forehead,
11 And the inheritance of the sinners is destruction and darkness: and their iniquities shall pursue them as far as hell beneath.
12 Their inheritance shall not be found of their children.
13 For their iniquities shall lay waste the houses of sinners: and the sinners shall perish in the day of the LORD's judgment for ever,
14 When God visiteth the earth with his judgment to recompense the sinners unto everlasting.
15 But they that fear the LORD shall find mercy therein: and shall live in the righteousness³ of their God.   ³ Gr. *mercy*

PSALM XVI.

A Psalm of Solomon: 'For help.'

1 When my soul slumbered *and fell away* from the LORD, then had I well nigh slipped in the heaviness of sleep:

---

11 ἕως ᾅδου κάτω. Cf. Ps. lxxxv. (lxxxvi.) 13 ἐξ ᾅδου κατωτάτου מִשְּׁאוֹל תַּחְתִּיָּה. Prov. xv. 24 'from hell beneath' (מִשְּׁאוֹל מָטָּה). Is. xiv. 9 (שְׁאוֹל מִתַּחַת). Ecclus. li. 6 σύνεγγυς ᾅδου κάτω.
Cp. xiv. 6. The future of διώκω is the only one of the middle tenses used in an active sense.
12 οὐχ εὑρεθήσεται with the dat. 'shall not be found of.' Cf. Ex. xxxv. 23 πᾶς ᾧ εὑρέθη βύσσος.
13 οἴκους ἐξερημοῦν. See iv. 23, xii. 4.
ἡμέρα κρίσεως κυρίου. We find ἡμέρα κρίσεως denoting the Final Judgement in Judith xvi. 17 κύριος παντοκράτωρ ἐκδικήσει αὐτοὺς ἐν ἡμέρᾳ κρίσεως, and often in the N.T. (e.g. Matt. x. 15, xi. 22; 2 Pet. iii. 7; 1 John iv. 17). The commoner phrase is ἡμέρα κυρίου, as in Amos v. 18; Joel ii. 11; 1 Cor. v. 5; 2 Pet. iii. 10, 12. Here the two phrases are combined; but it is not improbable that the translator, finding יוֹם יְהוָה, introduced the explanatory κρίσεως.
14 ὅταν ἐπισκέπτηται, iii. 14.
ἀποδοῦναι, ii. 38.
εἰς τὸν αἰῶνα χρόνον. Cf. viii. 39.
15 ἐλεημοσύνη. No doubt a rendering of צְדָקָה. As is well known, the LXX. fluctuate between ἐλεημοσύνη and δικαιοσύνη as equivalents for this word. See for further remarks the note on ix. 6 and Hatch, *Essays in Biblical Greek*, p. 49 sqq. We have here preferred to render the word 'righteousness.'

Ps. XVI.—*Argument*.
1. Thanksgiving for deliverance.
  (a) 1, 2. The Psalmist's peril; the apathy of some deadly sin.
  (b) 3—5. He had perished, if the LORD by timely chastisement had not roused to consciousness, and delivered him.
2. Prayer for continuance in holy living.
  (a) 6—8. That the thought of God may reign in the heart and overcome all fleshly lusts.
  (b) 9. That the Divine rule may order life and practice.
  (c) 10. That truth may ever adorn speech, and anger be put away.
  (d) 11, 12. That under trial there may be no murmuring, but a spirit of patience and brightness.
3. Poverty a Divine chastisement.
  (a) 13, 14. Heavy is the chastisement by poverty which assails a man's bodily comforts.
  (b) 15. The righteous will endure the test and will find mercy.
This Psalm contains no allusion to events of national importance. The use of the 1st Pers. Sing., which is found in each of the first twelve verses, relates to

118　　　　　ΨΑΛΜΟΙ ΣΑΛΟΜΩΝΤΟΣ.　　　　[XVI. 2

²[ἐν] τῷ μακρὰν ἀπὸ θεοῦ,
παρ' ὀλίγον ἐξεχύθη ἡ ψυχή μου εἰc θάνατον·
σύνεγγυc πυλῶν ᾅδου μετὰ ἁμαρτωλοῦ,
³ἐν τῷ διενεχθῆναι ψυχήν μου ἀπὸ κυρίου· θεοῦ Ἰσραὴλ,
εἰ μὴ ὁ κύριοc ἀντελάβετό μου τῷ ἐλέει αὐτοῦ εἰc τὸν αἰῶνα.

2 τῷ μακρὰν ἀπὸ θεοῦ codd. Geig. Hilg. ἐν τῷ μακρῦναί με (vel ἐν τῷ μακράν με εἶναι) conj. Fritzsch., ita Pick. ἐν τῷ ναρκᾶν conj. Schmidt, (Hilg.² Wellh.).
ἐξεχύθη V, K, P, M, Hilg. (conj.), Fritzsch. Pick. ἐξεχώθη A, Fabr.
Post σύνεγγυς Fritzsch. conj. ἦν.
3 μοι (post ἀντελάβετο) M.

the feelings and experience of the writer. It does not impersonate the nation. This is shown not so much by the penitential character of the Psalm as by the description of the temptations to which the writer is exposed in daily life (7—11).

We may gather that the Psalmist, like David of old, had fallen into some deadly sin. He might well have been condemned to perdition along with the sinners (2, 5). His conscience slept (1): his soul had wandered far from God (2, 3). But the LORD had mercy on him: by the sharp spur of trial the LORD restored him to wakefulness and delivered him from utter downfall (3, 5). We may suppose that perhaps the Psalmist's sin, like David's or Solomon's, had been one of sensuality, and accordingly the Prayer which he offers opens with special supplication that he might be saved from such a fall (7, 8).

The trial, which had awakened the Psalmist to a sense of his sin, had been that of sudden poverty (12—15). Like the patriarch Job, his faith was tested by discipline in the flesh and by the removal of bodily comforts. But 'the righteous' is sustained by the thought that trouble is of God to prove his soul and that even in adversity he will find mercy.

It is possible that the poverty and privation to which the Psalmist alludes may have resulted from the capture and occupation of Jerusalem by Pompey, or again they may have been inflicted upon the pious Pharisee by his opponents the Sadducees (cf. iv. 13, 23).

Either explanation would account for its inclusion in our collection.

Professor Stanton, in his *Jewish and Christian Messiah*, points to this Psalm as one which might be fitly put into the mouth of Solomon, and as being the strongest instance of personification in the book. We should, however, bear in mind that the ultimate repentance of Solomon was always a matter of grave dispute among the Jews.

Inscription. The title εἰς ἀντίληψιν has probably been taken from the words ἀντελάβετο, ἀντιλήπτωρ, ἀντελάβου in vv. 3—5.

1 ἐν τῷ νυστάξαι ψυχήν μου. These words are taken from Ps. cxviii. (cxix.) 28 ἐνύσταξεν (דָּלְפָה A.V. and R.V. *melteth.* Heb. *droppeth*) ἡ ψυχή μου ἀπὸ ἀκηδίας. The verb νυστάζειν denotes the torpor of oppressive drowsiness. It is used in Ps. lxxv. (lxxvi.) 7 ἀπὸ ἐπιτιμήσεώς σου, ὁ θεὸς Ἰακώβ, ἐνύσταξαν οἱ ἐπιβεβηκότες τοὺς ἵππους...Prov. xxiv. 33 ὀλίγον νυστάξω (מְעַט שֵׁנוֹת). Jer. xxiii. 20 νυστάξοντας νυσταγμὸν αὐτῶν (a different reading from the Heb.): Prov. vi. 4 μηδὲ ἐπινυστάξῃς. Aq. Sym. Theo. νυσταγμόν (תְּנוּמָה).

The preposition ἀπὸ is used by a 'constructio prægnans.' The clause combines the double thought of the soul's lethargy and its removal from God.

παρὰ μικρὸν ὠλίσθησα. The idea comes from Ps. lxxii. (lxxiii.) 2 ἐμοῦ δὲ παρὰ μικρὸν ἐσαλεύθησαν οἱ πόδες. παρὰ μικρόν, cf. Ezek. xvi. 47.

ἐν καταφορᾷ ὕπνου. καταφορά is Cerda's conjecture for the reading of the text of the MSS. καταφθορᾷ. The latter was a much commoner word, and was very likely to be substituted by accident.

καταφορά is Aquila's translation of תַּרְדֵּמָה 'a deep sleep' in Gen. ii. 21; Prov. xix. 15; Isai. xxix. 10. It reproduces the thought of being 'borne or weighed down' with sleep, a sense in which καταφέρω occurs e.g. in Acts xx. 9 καταφερόμενος ὕπνῳ βαθεῖ.

XVI. 3]   ΨΑΛΜΟΙ ΣΑΛΟΜΩΝΤΟΣ.   119

2 When *I was* far from God, within a little had my soul been poured out unto death, *yea I had been* hard unto the gates of hell in the company of the sinner
3 What time my soul was departed from the LORD the God of Israel,
If the LORD had not helped me through his mercy that abideth for ever.

2 [ἐν] τῷ μακρὰν ἀπὸ θεοῦ. The MSS. agree in the reading τῷ μακρὰν ἀπὸ, which is extremely harsh.
If we may draw any conclusions from the parallelism of vv. 1 and 3, the clause should begin with ἐν τῷ and an Inf. corresponding with ἐν τῷ νυστάξαι and ἐν τῷ διενεχθῆναι. We accept the conjecture that ἐν has fallen out after ὕπνου.
Fritzsche conjectures ἐν τῷ μακρῦναί με ἀπὸ or ἐν τῷ μακρὰν με εἶναι ἀπό. Against μακρῦναι it may be objected that the aor. of μακρύνω is used in this Psalm (ver. 11) with a transitive meaning, and that in the Active this is by far its commonest use in the LXX.
M. Schmidt makes an ingenious conjecture in his suggestion of ἐν τῷ ναρκᾶν. The similarity of the letters is certainly in its favour, and the meaning of the word 'to be numb' corresponds well with ἐν τῷ νυστάξαι. We are not however prepared to adopt it, partly perhaps because it is almost too ingenious, but chiefly because the word in the LXX. is very rare (Gen. xxxii. 25, 32; Job xxxiii. 19 only according to Tromm; also Theodot. in Job xxxiii. 19), and in none of these passages is employed in a metaphorical sense.
If ἐν τῷ μακρὰν ἀπὸ θεοῦ needs conjectural amplification, we would suggest that words have dropped out which included the verb that was qualified by μακράν. The verbs that are commonly associated with μακράν are ἀπέχειν and ἀφιστάναι. An error of sight may have occasioned a scribe to pass from ἀπο- to ἀπὸ in such a clause as ἐν τῷ μακρὰν ἀποστῆναι ἀπὸ τοῦ θεοῦ: and the omission of the verb would have facilitated the dropping of the ἐν after ὕπνου.
παρ' ὀλίγον ἐξεχύθη. The reference is still to Ps. lxxiii. (lxxiv.) 2 παρ' ὀλίγον ἐξεχύθη τὰ διαβήματά μου.
On the expansion of the quotation by the words εἰς θάνατον, see note on our Psalmist's method viii. 6.
For παρ' ὀλίγον (=בִּמְעַט) cf. Prov. v. 14 παρ' ὀλίγον ἐγενόμην.

For ἐξεχύθη ἡ ψυχὴ cf. Lam. ii. 12 ἐν τῷ ἐκχεῖσθαι ψυχὰς αὐτῶν εἰς κόλπον μητέρων αὐτῶν. The passage Isai. liii. 12, 'he poured out his soul unto death,' may have originated the phrase in our verse. But in that case the translator has followed the Hebrew and not the LXX. (παρεδόθη εἰς θάνατον ἡ ψυχὴ αὐτοῦ).
σύνεγγυς. Fritzsche says "post σύνεγγυς fortasse addendum ἦν." The verb must be supplied for purposes of translation.
The thought is taken from Ps. cvi. (cvii.) 18 καὶ ἤγγισαν ἕως τῶν πυλῶν τοῦ θανάτου, and closely resembles Ecclus. li. 6 ἤγγισεν ἕως θανάτου ἡ ψυχή μου, καὶ ἡ ζωή μου ἦν σύνεγγυς ᾅδου κάτω. Cf. Ps. lxxxvii. (lxxxviii.) 4 καὶ ἡ ζωή μου τῷ ᾅδῃ ἤγγισε.
For πύλαι ᾅδου compare Job xxxviii. 17 ἀνοίγονται δέ σοι φόβῳ πύλαι θανάτου πυλωροὶ δὲ ᾅδου ἰδόντες σε ἔπτηξαν. Ps. ix. 14 ὁ ὑψῶν με ἐκ τῶν πυλῶν τοῦ θανάτου. Is. xxxviii. 10 ἐγὼ εἶπα ἐν τῷ ὕψει τῶν ἡμερῶν μου Ἐν πύλαις ᾅδου, καταλείψω τὰ ἔτη τὰ ἐπίλοιπα.
Though Hades is here mentioned as virtually a synonym for death, the addition of the words μετὰ ἁμαρτωλοῦ show that it is not used in its neutral sense of a place of departed spirits, but as a description of the future abode of the wicked. Cf. xiv. 6.

3 ἐν τῷ διενεχθῆναι. A rare use of the word, which may be illustrated by the difficult passage in Wisd. xviii. 2 καὶ τοῦ διενεχθῆναι χάριν ἐδέοντο (A.V. 'and besought them pardon for that they had been enemies,' where some render 'and asked a favour of them that they would withdraw'). The idea is that of 'estrangement from' as the result of 'difference with;' it may be exemplified by 2 Macc. iii. 4 Σίμων δέ τις...διενέχθη τῷ ἀρχιερεῖ περὶ τῆς κατὰ τὴν πόλιν ἀγορανομίας, where 'difference' has developed into 'conflict.' Our version, 'departed,' is to be taken in its older sense, which long survived in the well-known words 'till death us depart.'
ἀντελάβετο. See on ἀντίληψις vii. 9.

120   ΨΑΛΜΟΙ ΣΑΛΟΜΩΝΤΟΣ.   [XVI. 4

⁴ ἔνυξέ με ὡς κέντρον ἵππου ἐπὶ τὴν γρηγόρησιν αὐτοῦ,
ὁ cωτὴρ κὰὶ ἀντιλήπτωρ μογ ἐν παντὶ καιρῷ ἔσωσέ με.
⁵ ἐξομολογήcομαί coι, ὁ θεός, ὅτι ἀντελάβογ μογ ἐὶc cωτηρίαν,
καὶ οὐκ ἐλογίcω με μετὰ τῶν ἁμαρτωλῶν εἰς ἀπώλειαν·
⁶ μὴ ἀποστήσῃς τὸ ἔλεός σου ἀπ᾽ ἐμοῦ, ὁ θεός,
μηδὲ τὴν μνήμην σου ἀπὸ καρδίας μου ἕως θανάτου.
⁷ ἐπικράτησόν μου, ὁ θεός, ἀπὸ ἁμαρτίας πονηρᾶς,
καὶ ἀπὸ πάσης γυναικὸς πονηρᾶς σκανδαλιζούσης ἄφρονα·

5 ἐλογίσω V, K, P, M, Hilg. (conj.), Geig. Fritzsch. Pick. ἐλλογίσω A, Fab.

τῷ ἐλέει αὐτοῦ εἰς τὸν αἰῶνα. There can be very little doubt that εἰς τὸν αἰῶνα should be taken with ἐλέει, and that the reference is to the well-known refrain 'For his mercy endureth for ever,' ὅτι εἰς τὸν αἰῶνα τὸ ἔλεος αὐτοῦ, e.g. Ps. cxxxv. (cxxxvi.).

Strictly therefore the Greek should have run τῷ ἐλέει αὐτοῦ τῷ εἰς τὸν αἰῶνα. On the absence of the article as a characteristic of our translator's style, see note on vi. 8.

4 ἔνυξε. The Psalmist represents his being aroused from torpor by the prick or spur of trial and suffering.

For νύσσω compare Ecclus. xxii. 19 ὁ νύσσων ὀφθαλμὸν κατάξει δάκρυα, καὶ ὁ νύσσων καρδίαν ἐκφαίνει αἴσθησιν.

ὡς κέντρον ἵππου. It seems to us very probable that the word ἵππου has been added by the translator as an explanatory gloss on κέντρον, just as in ver. 1 ὕπνου seems to have been added to explain καταφορά, and in xv. 13 κρίσεως to explain ἡμέρα κυρίου.

We associate the κέντρον or 'goad' with the ox or the ass but not with the horse. Cf. Prov. xxvi. 3 ὥσπερ μάστιξ ἵππῳ καὶ κέντρον ὄνῳ: Ecclus. xxxviii. 25 καυχώμενος ἐν δόρατι κέντρου, βόας ἐλαύνων: Eccles. xii. 11 λόγοι σοφῶν ὡς τὰ βούκεντρα.

We are disposed to think (1) that the Hebrew had the meaning 'He pricked me as *with* a goad;' but that, as is often the case, the preposition of the instrument not being expressed, it was overlooked by the translator: (2) that the translator's addition of the ἵππου changed the image from that of the ox, driven by the goad, to that of the horse, urged by the spur.

But the simile ὡς κέντρον ἵππου 'as a horse's spur' applied to the Almighty is obviously repugnant to the poetical treatment of the subject, even if it could be granted that κέντρον was ever used for a spur.

It is found in Prov. xxvi. 3 as a translation of מֶתֶג 'bridle.'

We believe that the Psalmist's meaning would have been expressed by ἔνυξέ με ὡς ἐν κέντρῳ.

The Psalmist describes himself as the ox at the plough, that needed to be pricked on with the goad.

ἐπὶ τὴν γρηγόρησιν αὐτοῦ. See on iii. 2. The meaning is clear. The goad is applied that the beast of burden may be alert and wakeful to obey the master's will.

On σωτήρ cf. viii. 39.

ἀντιλήπτωρ. Cf. Ps. xvii. (xviii.) 3 κέρας σωτηρίας μου καὶ ἀντιλήμπτωρ μου: liii. (liv.) 6 καὶ ὁ κύριος ἀντιλήμπτωρ τῆς ψυχῆς μου: lxxxviii. (lxxxix.) 27 θεός μου καὶ ἀντιλήμπτωρ τῆς σωτηρίας μου.

5 ἐξομολογήσομαί σοι...ὅτι. Cf. Matt. xi. 25 ἐξομολογοῦμαί σοι πάτερ κύριε τοῦ οὐρανοῦ καὶ τῆς γῆς ὅτι ἔκρυψας κ.τ.λ.

There is a very similar passage to this in Ps. cxvii. (cxviii.) 21 ἐξομολογήσομαί σοι ὅτι ἐπήκουσάς μου καὶ ἐγένου μοι εἰς σωτηρίαν.

εἰς σωτηρίαν corresponding to εἰς ἀπώλειαν in the next clause. For the opposition of the two words see Phil. i. 28 ἥτις ἐστὶν αὐτοῖς ἔνδειξις ἀπωλείας ὑμῶν δὲ σωτηρίας.

οὐκ ἐλογίσω με μετὰ τῶν ἁμαρτωλῶν εἰς ἀπώλειαν. The 'destruction' here spoken of as the portion of the sinners can hardly be distinguished from the violent end, which was regarded as their just retribu-

XVI. 7]   ΨΑΛΜΟΙ ΣΑΛΟΜΩΝΤΟΣ.   121

4 He pricked me as *a man* pricketh his horse, that I might watch unto him.
He that is my saviour and helper at all times preserved me.

5 I will praise thee, O God, because thou didst help me unto salvation, and didst not reckon me with the sinners for destruction.

6 Withdraw not thy mercy from me, O God, and *take* not the remembrance of thee from my heart until I die.

7 Keep me, O God, from abominable sin[1], and from every wicked woman that layeth a snare for the simple;

[1] Conj., *from the strange woman in her wickedness*

tion: see especially xiii. 2 θανάτου ἁμαρτωλῶν: 5, 6 καταστροφὴ τοῦ ἁμαρτωλοῦ: 10 ἁμαρτωλοὶ δὲ ἀρθήσονται εἰς ἀπώλειαν.
This thought appears in the phraseology of St Paul in such passages as Rom. vi. 21 τὸ τέλος ἐκείνων θάνατος. Phil. iii. 19 ὧν τὸ τέλος ἀπώλεια, where the Apostle employs the current terms of Pharisee theology without adding any precise definition of their development in Christian teaching.
The language is based upon Isai. liii. 12 παρεδόθη εἰς θάνατον ἡ ψυχὴ αὐτοῦ καὶ ἐν τοῖς ἀνόμοις ἐλογίσθη. Ps. lxxxvii. (lxxxviii.) 5 προσελογίσθην μετὰ τῶν καταβαινόντων εἰς λάκκον.

6 μὴ ἀποστήσῃς τὸ ἔλεός σου. See ix. 16.

τὴν μνήμην σου, 'the memory and recollection of thy goodness.' The Hebrew זֵכֶר is more often rendered by μνημόσυνον, but the use of μνήμη may be illustrated by Ps. xxix. (xxx.) 5, xcvi. (xcvii.) 12 καὶ ἐξομολογεῖσθε τῇ μνήμῃ τῆς ἁγιωσύνης αὐτοῦ, cxliv. (cxlv.) 7 μνήμην τοῦ πλήθους τῆς χρηστότητός σου ἐξερεύξονται. Aq. Ps. vi. 6 μνήμη σου (LXX. ὁ μνημονεύων σου).

7 ἐπικράτησόν μου. For ἐπικρατεῖν see on xvii. 17. A strange word to occur in the present context. Its use in the LXX. is either intransitive in the sense of prevailing, e.g. of the flood, Gen. vii. 18, 19; Sym. Gen. VII. 20, 24; of famine, Gen. xli. 58, xlvii. 20: or transitive, with a gen. in the sense of ruling over, e.g. Ezr. iv. 20 ἐπικρατοῦντες ὅλης τῆς ἑσπέρας τοῦ ποταμοῦ. 1 Macc. x. 52, xiv. 17 ἐ. τῆς χώρας. Aq. Gen. i. 26 καὶ ἐπικρατείτωσαν (וְיִרְדּוּ) and 28. Ps. cix. (cx.) 2 ἐπικράτει (רְדֵה) ἕνεκα τῶν ἐχθρῶν σου. Hos. xi. 12 (xii. 1) ἐπικρατῶν (רָד).

If the text is correct, the word is used here in the sense of 'hold fast,' 'strengthen,' 'protect,' translating חֲזַק־נָא. It occurs in the versions of Aq., Sym. and Th. in Isai. li. 18 ἐπικρατῶν, translating מַחֲזִיק (LXX. ἀντιλαμβανόμενος). Cf. Aq. Sym. Jer. li. (xxvii.) 12 ἐπικρατήσατε φυλακῆς.

We should rather have expected a word like ἐγκράτησον (cf. Ex. ix. 2 ἀλλὰ ἔτι ἐγκρατεῖς αὐτοῦ) with the appropriate meaning 'withhold,' 'keep back,' or συγκράτησον. Cf. Sym. Ps. xvi. 5.

ἀπὸ ἁμαρτίας πονηρᾶς, καὶ ἀπὸ πάσης γυναικὸς κ.τ.λ. A little awkwardness arises from the words καὶ ἀπὸ πάσης γυναικὸς πονηρᾶς following after ἀπὸ ἁμαρτίας πονηρᾶς. The expression 'and from every wicked woman' seems to presuppose some reference to a specific class just mentioned.

The passage reminds us of Proverbs vii. 5 ἵνα σε τηρήσῃ ἀπὸ γυναικὸς ἀλλοτρίας καὶ πονηρᾶς: and it is a suggestion, which seems to us very plausible, that instead of ΑΜΑΡΤΙΑϹ we should read ΑΛΛΟΤΡΙΑϹ, the error arising from the confusion between Μ and ΛΛ and from the transposition of ΡΤ for ΤΡ.

If this reading were accepted, the Psalmist would first have singled out 'the wicked strange woman,' before he passed on to speak of 'every wicked woman that layeth snares for the simple.'

In favour of this suggestion it will be remembered that the term 'strange wives' is especially used with reference to Solomon, 1 Kings xi. 1 καὶ ἔλαβε γυναῖκας ἀλλοτρίας, and ver. 8. See Ezr. x. 2, 10, &c.; Neh. xiii. 26, 27. Again ἀλλοτρία is used absolutely as an equivalent of πόρνη in Prov. v. 20 μὴ πολὺς ἴσθι πρὸς ἀλλοτρίαν: vi. 24 ἀπὸ διαβολῆς γλώσσης ἀλλοτρίας (R.V. 'from the flattery of the stranger's tongue'). Cf. Prov. v. 3 γυναικὸς πόρνης (זָרָה), where Aq., Sym. and Theodot.

122   ΨΑΛΜΟΙ ΣΑΛΟΜΩΝΤΟΣ.   [XVI. 8

⁸ καὶ μὴ ἀπατησάτω με κάλλος γυναικὸς παρανομούσης,
καὶ *πᾶν τὸ συγκείμενον* ἀπὸ ἁμαρτίας ἀνωφελοῦς.
⁹ τὰ ἔργα τῶν χειρῶν μου κατεγθγνον ἐν *λόγῳ* σου,
καὶ τὰ Διαβήματά μου ἐν τῇ μνήμῃ σου Διαφγλαξον·

   8 παντὸς ὑποκειμένου codd. et edd.: ὑποκαιομένου conj. Hilg.²: πᾶν τὸ συγκείμενον nos conj.
   9 τόπῳ A, V, K, P, Fab. Geig. φόβῳ M, Hilg. (conj.), Fritzsch. Pick.
τύπῳ conj. Hilg. (Wellh.). λόγῳ nos conj.

---

have ἀλλοτρίας : xxii. 14 στόμα παρανόμου (זָרוֹת׳פִּ) Aq. Th. ἀλλοτρίας.

σκανδαλιζούσης. The verb σκανδαλί-ζειν in the LXX., according to Tromm, is found only in Ecclus. ix. 7, xxiii. 7, xxxii. 16. But see Dan. xi. 41 καὶ πολλαὶ σκανδαλισθήσονται (יִכָּשְׁלוּ). Aq. Prov. iv. 12. Is. xl. 30, lxiii. 13. Cf. Ps. cxl. (cxli.) 9 ἀπὸ σκανδάλων τῶν ἐργαζομένων τὴν ἀνομίαν. Sym. Ps. lxiii. (lxiv.) 9 καὶ ἐσκανδάλισαν αὐτὴν (וַיַּכְשִׁילֻהוּ) ἐπ᾿ αὐτοὺς αἱ γλῶσσαι αὐτῶν. Is. viii. 21.

ἄφρονα, 'the simpleton.' See Prov. vii. 7 ὃν ἂν ἴδῃ τῶν ἀφρόνων τέκνων νεανίαν ἐνδεῆ φρενῶν: ix. 16 ὅς ἐστιν ὑμῶν ἀφρονέστατος ἐκκλινάτω πρὸς μέ.

8 μὴ ἀπατησάτω με κάλλος γυναικός. Numerous illustrations of this sentiment might be taken from gnomic writings, e.g. Prov. vi. 25 μή σε νικήσῃ κάλλους ἐπιθυμία, Ecclus. ix. 8 ἀπόστρεψον ὀφθαλμὸν ἀπὸ γυναικὸς εὐμόρφου, καὶ μὴ καταμάνθανε κάλλος ἀλλότριον· ἐν κάλλει γυναικὸς πολλοὶ ἐπλανήθησαν, xxv. 21 μὴ προυπέσῃς ἐπὶ κάλλος γυναικός, Susan. 56 τὸ κάλλος ἐξηπάτησέ με.

πᾶν τὸ συγκείμενον ἀπὸ ἁμαρτίας ἀνωφελοῦς. The reading of the MSS. παντὸς ὑποκειμένου cannot in our opinion be retained. Geiger renders 'Noch Jemands, der sich von heilloser Sünde beherrschen lässt,' and is followed by Pick 'Nor of any, who is controlled by unprofitable sin.' But it is clear that the words παντὸς ὑποκειμένου ἀπὸ ἁμαρτίας ἀνωφελοῦς are extremely periphrastic if dependent upon κάλλος, and introduced as a parallel to γυναικὸς παρανομούσης.

Wellhausen renders freely 'und keine Eingebung nichtsnütziger Sünde,' as if he would read πᾶν τὸ ὑποκείμενον in the sense of 'every submission or surrender to,' literally, 'and everything subdued by.'

It does not appear to us that 'that which is subject to or subdued by vanity' constitutes a natural parallel to κάλλος γυναικός, and a further minor objection arises from the use of ἀπό.

In conjecturing πᾶν τὸ συγκείμενον we introduce a very slight change into the text, i.e. παντοσυγκ for παντοσυποκ. The reading we adopt gives a wide and appropriate meaning to the clause. The sentence then runs: 'Let not the beauty of woman deceive me, nay, let not anything deceive me that is composed (that consists) of empty vanity.' As in the preceding verse, the specific source of danger is mentioned before the general class to which it belongs; while the preposition ἀπὸ reproduces the Hebrew מִן in its partitive sense.

It may be objected that σύγκειμαι does not occur in this sense in either the LXX. or the N.T. But its use in this sense is so general in Greek writers that we cannot admit the force of an objection, which in the case of an unusual word would be decisive against its introduction as a conjectural reading.

ἀπὸ ἁμαρτίας ἀνωφελοῦς. The preposition ἀπὸ, which here represents מִן, here takes the place of ἐκ (ἐξ), which is the ordinary construction after σύγκειμαι.

ἀνωφελὴς in the sense of 'unprofitable' occurs in the LXX. only in Prov. xxviii. 3 ὥσπερ ὑετὸς λάβρος καὶ ἀνωφελής, Jer. ii. 8 καὶ ὀπίσω ἀνωφελοῦς ἐπορεύθησαν, Isai. xliv. 10 καὶ γλυπτὸν χωνεύσει εἰς ἀνωφελῆ, Wisd. i. 11 φυλάξασθε τοίνυν γογγυσμὸν ἀνωφελῆ.

The expression 'unprofitable sin' calls for some remark.

It is noticeable that אָוֶן is rendered by Aquila in Ps. v. 6 ἀνωφέλειαν (LXX. ἀνομίαν), vi. 9 ἀνωφελὲς (LXX. ἀνομίαν), xiv. 4, xxxvi. 13, lv. 4, lvi. 8, Job iv. 8. (LXX. τὰ ἄτοπα), Prov. xxii. 8 (LXX. κακά), xxviii. 3 ἀνωφελὲς (LXX. ἀδικίαν), lxvi. 18.

XVI. 9]   ΨΑΛΜΟΙ ΣΑΛΟΜΩΝΤΟΣ.   123

8 And let not the beauty of an ungodly woman beguile me, nor aught that consisteth in sinful vanity[2].

9 Establish thou the works of my hands in thy word[3], and preserve my goings in the remembrance of thee.

[2] Lit. *unprofitable sin*
[3] Gr. *in thy place;* others, *in thy fear*

Aq. Is. lviii. 9 λαλοῦντα ἀνωφελές, Hos. xii. 8 (9) ἀνωφελὲς αὐτῷ, reading אָוֶן for אִין, Am. i. 5 ἀνωφελοῦς (LXX. ὤν), Jer. iv. 14 ἀνωφελείας σου (אוֹנֵךְ).

On the strength of this evidence it seems to us probable that either ἁμαρτίας ἀνωφελοῦς is a double rendering of אָוֶן, or the translator has added the adjective ἀνωφελοῦς in order to define ἁμαρτίας more closely in accordance with the shade of meaning attaching to אָוֶן.

9 τὰ ἔργα τῶν χειρῶν μου. Cf. Sym. Ps. xviii. 2.

ἐν λόγῳ σου. The reading in this passage is very uncertain. (1) The Augsburg, Vienna, Copenhagen and Paris MSS. agree in reading ἐν τόπῳ σου. It may be questioned whether any satisfactory sense can be obtained from this reading. Geiger adopts it and translates 'in deiner Gegenwart,' on the assumption that τόπος is here employed to translate מָקוֹם 'space' or 'place' in its Rabbinical application to the Deity. Dr Taylor in his note on 'maqom' (*Sayings of the Jewish Fathers*, p. 53) quotes from *Jalqut* 117 where it is said that God is called 'Place,' because He is the 'PLACE of the world and not the world His place.' He also mentions the fact that the Rabbins laid stress on the numerical values of the letters of the Tetragrammaton, and of the word 'maqom' being identical, i.e. 186.

The passage from Philo *De Somn.* Lib. I. (vol. I. p. 630, ed. Mangey), which he quotes, indicates that τόπος was interpreted by Jewish teachers in this mystical sense at a time very little later than the date of the composition of our Psalms. The passage deserves close attention : τριχῶς δὲ ἐπινοεῖται τόπος· ἅπαξ μὲν χώρα ὑπὸ σώματος ἐκπεπληρωμένη· κατὰ δεύτερον δὲ τρόπον ὁ θεῖος λόγος, ὃν ἐκπεπλήρωκεν ὅλον δι' ὅλων ἀσωμάτοις δυνάμεσιν αὐτὸς ὁ θεός. 'εἶδον' γάρ, φησί, 'τὸν τόπον, οὗ εἱστήκει ὁ θεὸς τοῦ Ἰσραήλ.' ...κατὰ δὲ τρίτον σημαινόμενον αὐτὸς ὁ θεὸς καλεῖται τόπος, τῷ περιέχειν μὲν τὰ ὅλα περιέχεσθαι δὲ πρὸς μηδενὸς ἁπλῶς, καὶ τῷ καταφυγὴν τῶν συμπάντων αὐτῶν εἶναι, καὶ ἐπειδήπερ αὐτός ἐστι χώρα ἑαυτοῦ κεχωρηκὼς ἑαυτὸν καὶ ἐμφερόμενος μόνῳ ἑαυτῷ....ὁ ἀσκητής, οὐχ ὑπαντᾷ τόπῳ, οὔτε τῷ ἐκπεπληρωμένῳ ὑπὸ σώματος θνητοῦ...οὔτε τῷ τρίτῳ καὶ ἀρίστῳ...ἀλλὰ τῷ μέσῳ λόγῳ θείῳ τὰ ἄριστα ὑφηγουμένῳ καὶ ὅσα πρόσφορα τοῖς καιροῖς ἀναδιδάσκοντι.

If τόπῳ is to be retained as a translation of the Rabbinical 'maqom,' we should prefer to explain it not (as Geiger) as denoting 'the Almighty' (ὁ θεός), but, in accordance with this passage of Philo, as a term for the Divine Logos (ὁ θεῖος λόγος). The sense then would be, 'Establish the works of my hands by Thy Divine Logos.'

To this rendering there are obviously two strong objections: (a) it is not to be expected that the technical terms of Philo's teaching would be introduced in our Psalm, whose religious tone is of a simple and practical character; (b) a Rabbinic explanation of 'maqom' fails to make κατεύθυνον ἐν τόπῳ σου a suitable parallel to ἐν τῇ μνήμῃ σου διαφύλαξον.

(2) Hilgenfeld's conjecture, ἐν φόβῳ σου, adopted by Fritzsche and Pick, has the support of the Moscow MS. Here, however, as elsewhere, the Moscow MS. seems to have adopted an emendational reading.

φόβῳ gives an excellent meaning, and corresponds quite suitably to μνήμῃ. But it appears to us that the weight of transcriptional probability tells against φόβῳ being the right reading. A parallel might be cited from iv. Esdr. xvi. 71, where the MSS. read 'eritque locis locus.' Here an original φόβος for τόπος is probable.

(3) Hilgenfeld's conjecture, ἐν τύπῳ σου 'nach deiner Regel' is ingenious. In the LXX. τύπος occurs in Ex. xxv. 40; Am. v. 26, and frequently in the New Test.; but such an expression as ἐν τύπῳ σου addressed by a Jew to God, in the sense of κατὰ τὴν εἰκόνα σου, or κατὰ τὴν ὁμοίωσιν σου will require more authority than we have been able to find before its admission into the text could be justified.

¹⁰ τὴν γλῶσσάν μου καὶ τὰ χείλη μου ἐν λόγοις ἀληθείας
περίστειλον,
ὀργὴν καὶ θυμὸν ἄλογον μακρὰν ποίησον ἀπ' ἐμοῦ,
¹¹ γογγυσμὸν καὶ ὀλιγοψυχίαν ἐν θλίψει μάκρυνον ἀπ' ἐμοῦ,
ἐὰν ἁμαρτήσω ἐν τῷ σε παιδεύειν εἰς ἐπιστροφήν.
¹² εὐδοκίᾳ δὲ μετὰ ἱλαρότητος στήριξον τὴν ψυχήν μου,
ἐν τῷ ἐνισχῦσαί σε τὴν ψυχήν μου ἀρκέσει μοι τὸ δοθέν·
¹³ ὅτι ἐὰν μὴ σὺ ἐνισχύσῃς, τίς ὑφέξεται ἐν πενίᾳ παιδείαν,
¹⁴ ἐν τῷ ἐλέγχεσθαι ψυχὴν ἐν χειρὶ σαπρίας αὐτῆς;
ἡ δοκιμασία σου ἐν σαρκὶ αὐτοῦ καὶ ἐν θλίψει πενίας·

11 καιδεύειν A (Cerda).
12 εὐδοκίᾳ (om. ἐν) codd. Fab. Geig.
ins. ἐν Fritzsch. Pick. (sine notâ).
ἰσχύσαι P.
ἀρκέσαι Fabr.

13 ἐν πενίᾳ παιδείαν K, P, M.   ᴮ ᴬ
παιδείαν ἐν πενίᾳ A, edd.   ἐν πενίᾳ παιδείαν V.
om. ἐν πενίᾳ Wellh. conj.

But see Orig. Hex. (ed. Field) Gen. xlvii. 26 חֹק Statutum. O'· εἰς πρόσταγμα. Ἄλλος· εἰς τύπον. Ex. xii. 43 חֻקַּת. O'· ὁ νόμος. Ἄλλος· ὁ τύπος.

(4) We venture to conjecture ἐν λόγῳ (or λογίῳ) σου. In favour of this reading we may fairly claim transcriptional probability. There is a well-established instance in 2 Kings xx. 13 οὐκ ἦν τόπος (Heb. דָּבָר) ὃν οὐκ ἔδειξεν αὐτοῖς Ἐζεκίας, where the various reading λόγος is surely the original rendering: τόπος might indeed be there regarded as an interpretative rendering, but it is more natural to assume that it is a transcriber's error for λόγος (λογος . τοποc). If λογω or λογιω were accidentally changed to λοπω, the alteration to τοπω would follow naturally. Another possible suggestion is ΝΟΜω, a word often interchanged in the MSS. with λογω.

διαβήματα. Cf. Ps. cxviii. (cxix.) 133 τὰ διαβήματά μου κατεύθυνον κατὰ τὸ λόγιόν σου.

10 περίστειλον. See note on περιστολή xiii. 7.

ἄλογον, in the sense of unreasoning, is found in the LXX. only in Wisd. xi. 17 ἄλογα ἑρπετά...ἀλόγων ζῴων, and in the N.T. in 2 Pet. ii. 12; Jude 10. Cf. Acts xxv. 27.

But ὀργὴν ἄλογον probably represents the same Hebrew words as ὀργὴ ἄφρονος in Prov. xxvii. 3.

11 γογγυσμός. Cf. Joh. vii. 12; Acts vi. 1; Phil. ii. 14; 1 Pet. iv. 9.

ὀλιγοψυχία. This word renders the Hebrew expression 'shortness of spirit,' i.e. impatience. Ex. vi. 9 οὐκ εἰσήκουσαν Μωϋσῆ ἀπὸ τῆς ὀλιγοψυχίας. Num. xxi. 4 καὶ ὠλιγοψύχησεν ὁ λαὸς ἐπὶ τῇ ὁδῷ.

The ὀλιγόψυχος is the קְצַר רוּחַ 'brevis spiritu,' i.e. 'hasty of spirit' in Prov. xiv. 29. Cf. 1 Thess. v. 14. ὀλιγόψυχος meaning 'fainthearted' renders רוּחַ נְכֵאָה in Prov. xviii. 14, and ὀλιγοψυχεῖν 'to faint' occurs in Jonah iv. 8 (וַיִּתְעַלָּף). Cf. Isai. liv. 6.

The Psalmist prays that a complaining spirit may be taken from him, that he may not offend by murmuring, and impatience at the discipline and chastisement which is sent him on account of his sin in order to reclaim him. This is clearly the meaning of the passage; and it can hardly be doubted that the translator has tended to confuse the sense by placing ἐὰν ἁμαρτήσω before ἐν τῷ σε παιδεύειν.

For the thought generally, cf. Ecclus. x. 28 (Lat.) vir prudens et disciplinatus non murmurabit correptus.

ἐπιστροφή. See ix. 19.

12 εὐδοκίᾳ μετὰ ἱλαρότητος. The union of willingness and cheerfulness

XVI. 14] ΨΑΛΜΟΙ ΣΑΛΟΜΩΝΤΟΣ. 125

10 My tongue and my lips do thou guard about with the words of truth; anger and senseless wrath put thou far from me.

11 Murmuring and faintheartedness in the time of affliction remove thou far from me, when for my sin[4] thou dost chasten me to the end I may be restored.

[4] Or, *if I sin when*

12 But with goodwill and cheerfulness uphold thou my soul; when thou strengthenest my soul, I shall be satisfied with that thou givest me.

13 For if thou strengthenest not, who can abide chastisement in poverty?

14 Seeing that a soul is rebuked by the corruption thereof; thou dost prove a man in his flesh and in the affliction of poverty:

---

forms the counterpart to the murmuring and faintheartedness mentioned in the previous verse.

εὐδοκίᾳ = בְּרָצוֹן. Cf. e.g. Prov. xxxi. 13. Aq. Th. ἐν βουλῇ. Sym. ἐν θελήματι.

ἱλαρότης. Cf. Prov. xviii. 22 ἔλαβε δὲ παρὰ θεοῦ ἱλαρότητα (רָצוֹן), where Aq. Sym. Th. render εὐδοκίαν (xix. 12 τὸ ἱλαρὸν αὐτοῦ = Aq. Sym. Th. εὐδοκία).

στήριξον. Luke xxii. 32 ἐπιστρέψας στήρισον τοὺς ἀδελφούς σου.

ἀρκέσει μοι. Cf. Num. xi. 22 μὴ πρόβατα καὶ βόες σφαγήσονται αὐτοῖς καὶ ἀρκέσει αὐτοῖς; ἢ πᾶν τὸ ὄψος τῆς θαλάσσης συναχθήσεται αὐτοῖς καὶ ἀρκέσει αὐτοῖς;

13 τίς ὑφέξεται ἐν πενίᾳ παιδείαν. The Psalmist here specifies the chastisement which God had sent upon him, the sudden loss of riches. The MSS. differ as to the position of the words ἐν πενίᾳ, whether they should follow or precede παιδείαν.

(*a*) According to the reading of the Copenhagen, Paris and Moscow MSS., ἐν πενίᾳ follows ὑφέξεται: the sense then is 'Who, being already in poverty, will be able to abide chastisement?'

(*b*) According to the reading of the Augsburg and Vienna MSS., ἐν πενίᾳ follows παιδείαν: the sense then is, 'Who will be able to abide the chastisement which comes through poverty?'

We prefer the former rendering: ἐν πενίᾳ = πενὴς ὤν. It suits better the preceding verse. That verse ended with the thought, 'if Thou givest strength, I shall be satisfied with the lot, however poor it be, which Thou ordainest.' The present verse replies: 'but if Thou dost not give strength, where is the hope of the poor man, when correction cometh upon him, yea when his soul is rebuked by the recollection of his frail mortal nature?'

There is no reason to follow Wellhausen, who would omit ἐν πενίᾳ altogether.

14 ἐλέγχεσθαι. Compare for the whole passage Heb. xii. 4—13.

ἐν χειρὶ σαπρίας αὐτῆς. Cf. Job viii. 4 ἀπέστειλεν ἐν χειρὶ ἀνομίας αὐτῶν. For σαπρία see xiv. 4.

δοκιμασία. This word is found in the LXX. in Ecclus. vi. 21 ὡς λίθος δοκιμασίας ἰσχυρὸς ἔσται ἐπ' αὐτῷ, and in the N.T., Heb. iii. 9 οὗ ἐπείρασαν οἱ πατέρες ὑμῶν ἐν δοκιμασίᾳ (= in Ps. xciv. (xcv.) 9 ἐδοκίμασαν), Sym. Ezek. xxi. 13 (18) καὶ τί ἡ δοκιμασία;

ἐν σαρκὶ αὐτοῦ. The pronoun αὐτοῦ following after ψυχή may be illustrated, as Geiger suggests, by Lev. ii. 1 ἐὰν δὲ ψυχὴ προσφέρῃ δῶρον..., σεμίδαλις ἔσται τὸ δῶρον αὐτοῦ, v. 1 ἐὰν δὲ ψυχὴ ἁμάρτῃ ...καὶ οὗτος μάρτυς, Num. xv. 28. The masc. in these passages literally reproduces the Hebrew.

It is possible that αὐτοῦ implies in the present passage the use of נֶפֶשׁ as a masc. substantive (cf. Gen. ii. 19, xlvi. 25, Num. xxxi. 28). But it seems to us more probable that it is an instance of a 'constructio κατὰ σύνεσιν.' The word ψυχή is used for an individual; and in close connexion with σάρξ the translator naturally passes to the use of the personal pronoun.

ἐν θλίψει πενίας. The example of the

¹⁵ ἐν τῷ ὑπομεῖναι δίκαιον ἐν τούτοις ἐλεηθήσεται ὑπὸ κυρίου.

ιζ. ψαλμὸς τῶι Cαλομὼν μετ' ᾠδῆς τῷ Βαςιλεῖ.

XVII. Κύριε, σὺ αὐτὸς Βαςιλεὺς ἡμῶν εἰς τὸν αἰῶνα καὶ ἔτι,
ὅτι ἐν σοὶ, ὁ θεός, καυχήσεται ἡ ψυχὴ ἡμῶν.

Inscriptio deest in M.

---

patriarch Job is clearly the point of the allusion.

It may be objected that ἐν θλίψει πενίας does not balance ἐν σαρκὶ αὐτοῦ, and that we should have expected some such expression as ἐν τοῖς ἀγαθοῖς αὐτοῦ.

But the preposition ἐν does not refer to the sphere of trial so much as to its appointed instrument. A man is tried by his own frail nature and by the sufferings of want.

15 ἐν τῷ ὑπομεῖναι δίκαιον. For the reward of mercy vouchsafed to the righteous that patiently endure, cf. Is. lxiv. 4 ἀπὸ τοῦ αἰῶνος οὐκ ἠκούσαμεν οὐδὲ οἱ ὀφθαλμοὶ ἡμῶν εἶδον θεὸν πλὴν σοῦ καὶ τὰ ἔργα σου ἃ ποιήσεις τοῖς ὑπομένουσιν ἔλεον, Dan. xii. 12 μακάριος ὁ ὑπομένων, Lam. iii. 25 ἀγαθὸς κύριος τοῖς ὑπομένουσιν αὐτόν. The opposite of this spirit of patient endurance is expressed by Ps. cv. (cvi.) 13 ἐτάχυναν, ἐπελάθοντο τῶν ἔργων αὐτοῦ, οὐχ ὑπέμειναν τὴν βουλὴν αὐτοῦ.

For the attitude of the δίκαιος under chastisement cf. iii. 3—6. If the writer has the instance of Job before his mind as the typical righteous man who patiently endured suffering, we should compare Jas. v. 11 τὴν ὑπομονὴν Ἰὼβ ἠκούσατε καὶ τὸ τέλος κυρίου εἴδετε, ὅτι πολύσπλαγχνός ἐστιν ὁ κύριος καὶ οἰκτίρμων.

ἐν τούτοις, not with ὑπομεῖναι, but with ἐλεηθήσεται. Even in the midst of these troubles, the 'righteous' man, like Job of old, shall find that the Lord is merciful.

Ps. XVII.—*Argument.* 1—4. *Introduction.* The Lord is King. The hopes of men generally resemble their own life, short and fleeting: the hopes of the true Israel are in their God and Saviour, whose kingdom is everlasting.

5—22. *The overthrow of David's dynasty.*

(*a*) 5—12. The Lord made choice of David and his seed to reign over Israel. Sinners made the Divine decree of none effect. They have desolated David's throne. God will recompense them and will not utterly forsake His elect.

(*b*) 13—22. The instrument of Divine visitation is the 'ungodly' man; he will massacre and banish foes. As a stranger, he will practise idolatries in Jerusalem, and Jews shall surpass the heathen in abominations. The saints flee for their lives and are despoiled: the heavens and the earth stand aghast at the wickedness from which none either high or low are exempt.

23—49. *The Kingdom of the Messiah.*

(*a*) 23—31. Prayer for the reign of David's Son, to destroy the heathen from out of the land and gather together again the true Israelites.

(*b*) 32—46. The description of His reign and rule.

Its holiness will be the wonder and glory of the world.

Its strength will not be in material force but in the trust in God.

Wise, strong and sinless, the King shall prevail, and in His righteousness will suffer none of His subjects to be oppressed.

(*c*) 47—49. *Résumé.* Such is the Majesty of Israel's King; His words will be pure and just.

50 and 51. *Epilogue.* Such are the days of the Messiah: the Lord hasten His coming. The Lord is King.

This long Psalm is the most important in the whole collection. The special interest attaching to it turns upon the historical allusions in the earlier portion (5—22) and the description of the Messianic King and Kingdom, which occupies the whole of the latter portion of the Psalm (23—51).

The historical allusions are as follows: sinful men have usurped the throne of David (6, 7); for this God sends punishment upon them by the hand of a stranger, who will render to them according to their deeds (8—10). But God's

XVII. I] ΨΑΛΜΟΙ ΣΑΛΟΜΩΝΤΟΣ. 127

15 The righteous man, if he continue steadfast, shall therein find mercy of the LORD.

PSALM XVII.

A Psalm of Solomon: with a Song unto the King.

1 O LORD, thou art our King henceforth and even for evermore, for in thee, O God, our soul exulteth.

---

mercy is still shown, they are not utterly forsaken (11). This man of lawlessness devastates Israel, slaying some, exiling others to 'the far west' (13, 14); because he is a stranger, he is guilty of presumption and idolatry; the Jews themselves emulate and surpass the heathen in wickedness (15—17). The pious are scattered far and wide (18, 19); famine and drought add to the horrors of the time (20, 21). All are sinful; common people, judges, and the king himself.

These references are best understood, when they are explained as follows: the usurpers are the house of the Asmoneans, who took to themselves the throne of David as well as the High Priesthood of Aaron, Aristobulus I. (105—104) being the first who assumed the royal title. The 'stranger' who carried out the Divine wrath is Pompey; he spared Hyrcanus II. (ver. 11), the capture of the Temple led to a terrible slaughter (ver. 13), Aristobulus and his family were led prisoners to Rome, where they adorned Pompey's triumph (14). Pompey violated the Temple, but his presumption was due to the ignorance of a foreigner (16, 17). The mention of drought and famine about this time agrees with the statements in Pss. S. ii. 10, v. 11, 12 &c. The title of 'king' in ver. 22 refers to Hyrcanus II.

No other identifications can be reconciled with the various statements contained in this passage. The 'lawless' man has been said to be Antiochus, Herod or Titus. The allusion to a Jewish king makes a reference to Antiochus Epiphanes and Titus impossible: the mention of banishment to 'the far west' does not agree with the action of Antiochus or Herod: the estrangement from the Jewish religion (15) is not applicable to Herod; the mention of mercy (ver. 11), and the implied survival both of city and people (25 &c.), conflicts with the view that Titus is referred to.

We conclude then that this Psalm, like others in this collection, was composed not long after the capture of Jerusalem by Pompey.

The allusions to the Messianic King give a vivid description of the hopes of the Pharisees half a century before the coming of Christ. The details will come under observation in the commentary. The reader however should carefully observe (1) the two external characteristics of the Messianic reign, the overthrow and exclusion of the heathen (25, 27, 31 &c.) and the restoration and reunion of the tribe (28, 30, 48), (2) the weapons of the Messiah's power, holiness, faith, wisdom and justice (25, 27, 33, 39, 42 &c.).

The writer identifies himself with the true Israel (cf. the 1st Pers. Pron. 1—4, 6, 9, 13, 15, 51). He implies the existence of corruption and wickedness in his own people; the oppression by the Gentiles; the persecution of the pious; and the general oppression.

The prayer for the days of the Messiah contains no insinuation of a resort to physical force or insurrection. The faith of the pious Pharisee has not degenerated to the fanaticism of the zealot.

How it shall come to pass is not a matter for consideration. But the kingdom of Israel shall be established through holiness over the whole world. The throne of David shall be set up, and 'the Son of David,' the Anointed of the Lord, shall administer justice, a holy prince of a holy people, ruling as it were on behalf of God the King of kings.

The picture is ideal, and is based on the thought, which is the refrain of the whole Psalm (1, 4, 38, 51), that the LORD himself is Israel's King, that He is faithful, His kingdom is for everlasting, and in the appointed day He will restore the throne to Israel.

Inscription. For μετ' ᾠδῆς see note on xv. (Inscript.).

² καὶ τίς ὁ χρόνος ζωῆς ἀνθρώπου ἐπὶ τῆς γῆς;
κατὰ τὸν χρόνον αὐτοῦ καὶ ἡ ἐλπὶς αὐτοῦ ἐπ' αὐτόν.
³ ἡμεῖς δὲ ἐλπιοῦμεν ἐπὶ θεὸν τὸν σωτῆρα ἡμῶν,
ὅτι τὸ κράτος τοῦ θεοῦ ἡμῶν εἰς τὸν αἰῶνα μετ' ἐλέου,
⁴ καὶ ἡ βασιλεία τοῦ θεοῦ ἡμῶν εἰς τὸν αἰῶνα ἐπὶ τὰ
    ἔθνη ἐν κρίσει.

⁵ Σύ, κύριε, ᾑρετίσω τὸν Δαυὶδ βασιλέα ἐπὶ Ἰσραήλ,
καὶ σὺ ὤμοσας αὐτῷ περὶ τοῦ σπέρματος αὐτοῦ εἰς τὸν
    αἰῶνα,
τοῦ μὴ ἐκλείπειν ἀπέναντί σου βασιλείαν αὐτοῦ.
⁶ καὶ ἐν ταῖς ἁμαρτίαις ἡμῶν ἐπανέστησαν ἡμῖν ἁμαρτωλοί,
ἐπέθεντο ἡμῖν καὶ ἔξωσαν ἡμᾶς·
οἷς οὐκ ἐπηγγείλω, μετὰ βίας ἀφείλοντο,

3, 4 ὅτι τὸ κράτος τοῦ θεοῦ ἡμῶν ἐς τὸν αἰῶνα ἐπὶ τὰ ἔθνη ἐν κρίσει. M (omissis per homœotel. verbis μετ' ἐλέου—αἰῶνα).
5 βασιλείαν A, P, Cerd. Fab. Fritzsch. Pick.
βασίλειον V, K, M, Hilg. Geig.
6 ἐπαγγείλω A (Cerd.).

τῷ βασιλεῖ might be taken in apposition to τῷ Σαλομών, but it is better to regard it as a reference to the chief feature of the Psalm, the Messianic King (ver. 23).

1 σὺ αὐτὸς βασιλεὺς ἡμῶν. The αὐτὸς reproduces the Hebrew idiom. Cf. Ps. xliii. (xliv.) 4 σὺ εἶ αὐτὸς ὁ βασιλεύς μου (אתה־הוא מלכי). 1 Chron. xvii. 26 κύριε σὺ εἶ αὐτὸς θεὸς (אתה־הוא יהוה האלהים).

The thought of the Kingship of Jehovah over Israel is found in numerous places in the O.T.: Ex. xv. 18; Ps. xliv. 4, lxxiv. 12, xciii. 1, xcvii. 1, xcix. 1; Is. xliii. 22.

In the present Psalm cf. vers. 4, 38, 51.

ὅτι ἐν σοί. The ὅτι in this clause is not wanted. It is perhaps a transcriber's accidental repetition of the preceding ἔτι. But the loose insertion of ὅτι is common in the LXX.

καυχήσεται. The fut. probably reproduces the Hebr. Imperf. The rendering by the Fut. makes good sense, as it would denote the future exultation of the faithful. But in a clause parallel to σὺ αὐτὸς βασιλεὺς ἡμῶν, the tense employed will naturally indicate a corresponding continuity.

For καυχᾶσθαι ἐν 'to glory in,' see especially St Paul's usage, e.g. Rom. ii. 17, 23, v. 3, 11; 1 Cor. i. 31, iii. 21;

2 Cor. v. 12, x. 17, xi. 12, xii. 9; Gal. vi. 13; Phil. iii. 3; 2 Thess. i. 4. In two of these passages, 1 Cor. i. 31; 2 Cor. x. 17, he refers to the passage in the LXX. version, where καυχᾶσθαι renders ב התהלל. Jer. ix. 23, 24 τάδε λέγει κύριος Μὴ καυχάσθω ὁ σοφὸς ἐν τῇ σοφίᾳ αὐτοῦ, καὶ μὴ καυχάσθω ὁ ἰσχυρὸς ἐν τῇ ἰσχύι αὐτοῦ, καὶ μὴ καυχάσθω ὁ πλούσιος ἐν τῷ πλούτῳ αὐτοῦ, ἀλλ' ἢ ἐν τούτῳ καυχάσθω ὁ καυχώμενος συνιεῖν καὶ γινώσκειν ὅτι ἐγώ εἰμι κύριος κ.τ.λ.

In the Psalms it is found but seldom in the LXX. version. It occurs with the simple meaning of exultation as a translation of עלץ in Ps. v. 12 καὶ καυχήσονται ἐν σοὶ οἱ ἀγαπῶντες τὸ ὄνομά σου, and of עלז in cxlix. 5 καυχήσονται ὅσιοι ἐν δόξῃ καὶ ἀγαλλιάσονται (cf. xciii. (xciv.) 3).

2 ὁ χρόνος...τὸν χρόνον. χρόνος in the LXX. is very generally used for ימים 'days,' e.g. Isai. xxxviii. 5 'behold, I will add unto thy days fifteen years' = ἰδοὺ προστίθημι πρὸς τὸν χρόνον σου δεκαπέντε ἔτη: lxv. 20 'nor an old man that hath not filled his days' = καὶ πρεσβύτης ὃς οὐκ ἐμπλήσει τὸν χρόνον αὐτοῦ.

καὶ ἡ ἐλπὶς...ἐπ' αὐτόν. The meaning of this line is obscure.

XVII. 6] ΨΑΛΜΟΙ ΣΑΛΟΜΩΝΤΟΣ. 129

2 And what is the time of man's life upon the earth? Even according to the measure of his time, so is his hope in him[1]. ¹ Text corrupt, perh. *thereon*
3 But as for us, we will hope in God, our saviour, for the might of our God endureth unto everlasting with mercy.
4 And the kingdom of our God is unto everlasting over the heathen in judgement.
5 Thou, O LORD, didst choose David to be king over Israel, and didst swear unto him touching his seed for ever, that his kingdom should not fail before thee.
6 But when we sinned, sinners rose up against us; they fell upon us and thrust us out: even they, to whom thou madest no promise, took away *our place* with violence[2].

² Or, *that which thou didst not promise to them, they took with violence*

(1) Geiger, who carries on the question καὶ τίς to the end of the verse, and puts a comma after χρόνον αὐτοῦ, renders 'Und was ist des Menschen Lebenszeit auf Erden im Vergleich zu seiner Zeit, dass er seine Hoffnung auf sie setzt?' ἐπ' αὐτὸν then refers to ὁ χρόνος ζωῆς ἀνθ. But this distinction between ὁ χρόνος ζωῆς 'the mortal life,' and τὸν χρόνον αὐτοῦ 'his time' (=his eternal life), is quite arbitrary, and has no support from other writings.

(2) Wellhausen gives 'Was ist die Dauer von eines Menschen Leben auf Erden! Ebenso kurz ist auch die Hoffnung auf ihn!' In proportion as man's life on earth is short, so limited is the hope or trust which can be placed in a man. ἐπ' αὐτὸν is then equivalent to ἐπ' ἄνθρωπον, just as ἐλπὶς αὐτοῦ is for ἐλπὶς ἀνθρώπου. In other words, 'men generally put their hope in man; but the hope is transitory, for every man's life is short.' This seems better than to refer αὐτὸν to χρόνος, since ἐπ' ἄνθρωπον supplies the natural antithesis to ἐπὶ θεὸν (ver. 3). The text however is probably corrupt; or the translator was in difficulties.

3 ἡμεῖς δὲ. The true Israel is distinguished from mankind (ἄνθρωπος) generally by the fact of resting their hope upon God.

θεὸν τὸν σωτῆρα ἡμῶν. Cf. iii. 7, viii. 39. The title of 'Saviour' is here used in the sense of 'National Deliverer,' as is evident by the reference to τὰ ἔθνη ἐν κρίσει in the next verse.

4 ἡ βασιλεία τοῦ θεοῦ ἡμῶν εἰς τὸν αἰῶνα. These words reproduce such passages as Ps. cxliv. (cxlv.) 13 ἡ βασιλεία σου βασιλεία πάντων τῶν αἰώνων. Dan. vii. 27 καὶ ἡ βασιλεία αὐτοῦ βασιλεία αἰώνιος. If we may assume that these words are a quotation, the strange position of ἐπὶ τὰ ἔθνη ἐν κρίσει after εἰς τὸν αἰῶνα becomes intelligible. They represent our Psalmist's addition to his citation. Cf. viii. 6.

The conception of the universal and eternal Kingdom has been illustrated from the Sibylline Oracles: *Sib. Orac.* III. 47 βασιλεία μεγίστη Ἀθανάτου βασιλῆος ἐπ' ἀνθρώποισι φανεῖται: 766 καὶ τότε δ' ἐξεγερεῖ βασιλήϊον εἰς αἰῶνας Πάντας ἐπ' ἀνθρώπους.

5 ἡρετίσω. Cf. ix. 17.

τὸν Δαυὶδ βασιλέα. The promise of an Eternal throne to David, ratified by an oath, is referred to in numerous passages. See especially 2 Sam. vii.; Ps. lxxxviii. (lxxxix.) 4, 5 ὤμοσα Δαυεὶδ τῷ δούλῳ μου ἕως τοῦ αἰῶνος ἑτοιμάσω τὸ σπέρμα σου καὶ οἰκοδομήσω εἰς γενεὰν καὶ γενεὰν τὸν θρόνον σου: cxxxi. (cxxxii.) 11, 12 ὤμοσεν κύριος τῷ Δαυεὶδ ἀλήθειαν, καὶ οὐ μὴ ἀθετήσει αὐτήν Ἐκ καρποῦ τῆς κοιλίας σου θήσομαι ἐπὶ τὸν θρόνον σου...καὶ οἱ υἱοὶ αὐτῶν ἕως αἰῶνος καθιοῦνται ἐπὶ τὸν θρόνον σου. 1 Macc. ii. 57 Δαυὶδ ἐν τῷ ἐλέῳ αὐτοῦ ἐκληρονόμησε θρόνον βασιλείας εἰς αἰῶνα αἰῶνος. Ecclus. xlv. 25.

For the house of David cf. *Orac. Sibyll.* III. 288 Ἔστι δέ τις φυλὴ βασιλήϊος, ἧς γένος ἔσται Ἄπταιστον.

περὶ τοῦ σπέρματος κ.τ.λ. Cf. *Assumptio Mosis* III. et jusjurandum quod jurasti eis per te, ne unquam deficiat semen eorum a terra quam dedisti illis.

6 ἁμαρτωλοί. It is important for the understanding of the whole passage to determine the application of this word. See note on i. 1.

It is not used of Antiochus Epiphanes and his army, nor of Pompey and the Romans, nor of Herod and his followers;

J. P.

130 ΨΑΛΜΟΙ ΣΑΛΟΜΩΝΤΟΣ. [XVII. 7

⁷καὶ οὐκ ἐδόξασαν τὸ ὄνομά coy τὸ ἔντιμον ἐν δόξῃ,
ἔθεντο βασίλειον ἀντὶ ὕψους αὐτῶν,
⁸ἠρήμωσαν τὸν θρόνον Δαυὶδ ἐν ὑπερηφανίᾳ ἀλαλάγματος.
καὶ σύ, ὁ θεὸς, καταβαλεῖς αὐτοὺς,
καὶ ἀρεῖς τὸ σπέρμα αὐτῶν ἀπὸ τῆς γῆς,
⁹ἐν τῷ ἐπαναστῆναι αὐτοῖς ἄνθρωπον ἀλλότριον γένους ἡμῶν.
¹⁰κατὰ τὰ ἁμαρτήματα αὐτῶν ἀποδώσεις αὐτοῖς, ὁ θεός·
εὑρεθείη αὐτοῖς κατὰ τὰ ἔργα αὐτῶν.

7 τὸ ἔντιμον ἐν δόξῃ· ἔθεντο A, V, K, M, Cerd..Fab. Hilg. Geig.
τὸ ἔντιμον· ἐν δόξῃ ἔθεντο. P, Fritzsch. Pick.
9 γένους A, (Cerd.), V, P, M, Hilg. Fritzsch. Geig. Pick. : γένος K, (?) Fab.
ἡμῶν V, K, P, M, Hilg. Geig. Fritzsch. Pick. : ἡριτῶν A, (Cerd.), Fab. Cerd. conj. θηριτῶν.

for the 'sinners' are carefully distinguished in ver. 9 from the foreigners.

It is clearly used of native Jews, who (1) usurped power which did not belong to them (ver. 6), (2) did not give the due honour to the nation's God, which was to have been expected from them (ver. 7), (3) grasped at monarchical authority (ver. 8). This description exactly tallies with the Asmonean house, who, having usurped the High Priesthood, made it subserve their political purposes, and in the reign of Aristobulus assumed the title of King, to the great offence of the Theocratic party.

In what way however are we to understand the Psalmist's statement that the 'sinners' rose up against 'us,' attacked 'us,' &c.? We believe that he represents not only the Pharisees, but the priests, who had been alienated by the setting aside of the legitimate line of the High Priesthood. It is noteworthy that the fourfold repetition of the 1st Pers. Pron. is followed by the mention of this spoliation οἷς...ἀφείλοντο.

For the possibility of the writer belonging to a priestly house see note on iii. 7, viii. 12, 13.

οἷς οὐκ ἐπηγγείλω...ἀφείλοντο. We make no doubt that by this clause is intended the assumption of the High Priest's office and of the royal title by the Asmonean Princes.

The literal translation of the clause is 'they to whom thou madest no promise, with violence took away from us our honour' (subaud. ἡμᾶς τὴν τιμὴν ἡμῶν). The sense is obvious; those who were not of the house of Aaron took by force the position and privileges of the sacred family. The Greek however is not without difficulty in consequence of the absence of (a) the antecedent to the relative clause, (b) the object of the verb ἀφείλοντο.

The awkwardness of the construction affords good ground for the conjecture that οἷς is the rendering of אֲשֶׁר לְהֶם..., which in this case should have been translated by ὅ or ἅ...αὐτοῖς, 'that which thou didst not promise unto them, they took by force.' This explanation accounts for the dative οἷς, gives a suitable object to ἀφείλοντο, and preserves the general sense of the passage.

7 ἐδόξασαν...ἐν δόξῃ. Fritzsche, followed by Pick, connects δόξῃ with ἔθεντο in the following clause.

For ἐδόξασαν...ἐν δόξῃ compare i. 8 ἐβεβήλωσαν...ἐν βεβηλώσει: ix. 19 ἐν διαθήκῃ διέθου.

τὸ ὄνομά σου τὸ ἔντιμον. Cf. Dt. xxviii. 58 φοβεῖσθαι τὸ ὄνομα τὸ ἔντιμον τὸ θαυμαστὸν τοῦτο.

In Ps. lxxi. (lxxii.) 14 καὶ ἔντιμον τὸ ὄνομα αὐτῶν ἐνώπιον αὐτοῦ, ὄνομα seems to be an error for αἷμα.

ἔθεντο βασίλειον ἀντὶ ὕψους αὐτῶν. We understand these words to mean, that the Sadducee party preferred a worldly monarchy to the Kingdom of Jehovah. The Theocratic party considered that Jehovah was the King of Israel, and that no mere man should receive the title.

βασίλειον is here used for the office and power of the King. Cf. 2 Macc. ii. 17 τὸ βασίλειον καὶ τὸ ἱεράτευμα. Wisd. i. 14 οὔτε ᾅδου βασίλειον ἐπὶ γῆς. It is some-

XVII. 10]   ΨΑΛΜΟΙ ΣΑΛΟΜΩΝΤΟΣ.   131

7 And they esteemed not thy glorious name in any honour; they preferred a kingdom to that which was their excellency.
8 They laid waste the throne of David with a tumultuous shout of triumph.
But thou, O God, didst³ cast them down, and remove their seed from off the earth,
9 When there arose⁴ against them a man that was a stranger to our race.
10 According to their sins didst³ thou recompense them, O God! *yea*, it befell⁵ them according to their works.

³ Gr. *wilt*
⁴ Conj. *When thou didst raise up*
⁵ Gr. *may it befall*

---

times used for the emblems of the regal power, the crown or the throne. Cf. 2 Sam. i. 10; 1 Kings xiv. 8 (A); 2 Chron. xxiii. 11; Wisd. v. 17.

ἀντὶ ὕψους αὐτῶν. Literally, 'in the place of that which was their exaltation.' Cf. 1 Macc. ii. 40 καὶ τὸ ὕψος αὐτῆς ἐστράφη εἰς πένθος. ὕψος would then be used almost in the sense of ὁ ὕψιστος.

Our rendering gives its full meaning to ἀντί, which other translators have taken to mean 'because of' or 'in,' as if = בְּ. Thus Geiger, 'setzten sich die Krone auf in ihrem Uebermuthe.' Wellhausen, '...in ihrem Stolz.' Pick, 'because of their pride.' Geiger quotes Gen. xlvii. 29. But the author of the Greek version of these Psalms, who shows such a predilection for the preposition ἐν, is not likely to have rendered בְּ by ἀντί. His use of ἀντί in other passages, ii. 3, 13, 15, 21, is rare, but always with the full sense of 'instead of,' or 'in the place of' (= תַּחַת).

8 ἠρήμωσαν. This may possibly refer to the conflict between Hyrcanus II. and Aristobulus, which preceded the advance of Pompey into Palestine. But it is better to explain it more generally as an allusion to the vain and ambitious policy of the Asmonean princes, impoverishing the country and weakening their own resources.

For ἐρημόω cf. Ps. lxxviii. (lxxix.) 7 κατέφαγον τὸν Ἰακώβ, καὶ τὸν τόπον αὐτοῦ ἠρήμωσαν.

ὑπερηφανίᾳ ἀλαλάγματος. A difficult phrase to reproduce in English. The two words combine the ideas of insolent pride and the clamour of victory. While they shouted for triumph, the princes were desolating the city of David. ἀλάλαγμα does not seem to occur in the LXX., except, acc. to Tromm, 1 Sam. iv. 6 (v. l.). We have ἀλαλαγμός = תְּרוּעָה Ps. lxxxviii. (lxxxix.) 16 μακάριος ὁ λαὸς ὁ γι-

νώσκων ἀλαλαγμόν. Cf. Ps. xxvi. 11, xxxii. 3, xlvi. 5, cl. 5.

καταβαλεῖς...ἀρεῖς. These future tenses are almost certainly examples of the translator's inability to render the Hebrew Impf. accurately. For (1) they stand between the ἠρήμωσαν of ver. 8 and the ἐξηρεύνησε...οὐκ ἀφῆκεν of ver. 11, (2) they refer to the time mentioned in ver. 9, ἐν τῷ ἐπαναστῆναι αὐτοῖς κ.τ.λ.

καταβαλεῖς. The Asmonean monarchy practically ceased after the capture of Jerusalem by Pompey.

9 ἐπαναστῆναι. The previous clause would have led us to expect the transitive ἐπαναστῆσαι, explanatory of καταβαλεῖς and ἀρεῖς.

ἄνθρωπον ἀλλότριον γένους ἡμῶν. Not unnaturally these words have been taken to allude to Herod or his father Antipater, who were Idumeans. But the description lower down (15, 16) makes this identification out of the question, if, as we think, the same person is indicated there as here.

Pompey is clearly referred to.

For ἄνθρωπον ἀλλότριον cf. Dt. xvii. 15 οὐ δυνήσῃ καταστῆσαι ἐπὶ σεαυτὸν ἄνθρωπον ἀλλότριον.

The γένους ἡμῶν is not wanted after ἀλλότριον and follows awkwardly after αὐτοῖς. It has all the appearance of a translator's addition.

10 ἀποδώσεις. For the tense note on ver. 8. For the thought of retribution see ii. 7, 17.

εὑρεθείη αὐτοῖς. The optative is in all probability to be regarded as an erroneous rendering of the Heb. Impf., cf. i. 4, iv. 9. The two verbs are coordinate.

In the LXX. the Pass. of εὑρίσκω followed by the dat. often renders the Hebrew idiom 'to be found of' = 'to be present to.' Cf. 1 Chron. xxviii. 9 ἐὰν ζητήσῃς αὐτόν, εὑρεθήσεταί σοι, Is. lxv. 1 εὑρέθην τοῖς ἐμὲ μὴ ζητοῦσιν, Jer. xxix.

ΨΑΛΜΟΙ ΣΑΛΟΜΩΝΤΟΣ. [XVII. 11

¹¹ κατὰ τὰ ἔργα αὐτῶν ἐλεήσει αὐτοὺς ὁ θεός,
ἐξηρεύνησε τὸ σπέρμα αὐτῶν καὶ οὐκ ἀφῆκεν αὐτούς.
¹² πιστὸς ὁ κύριος ἐν πᾶσι τοῖς κρίμασιν αὐτοῦ οἷς ποιεῖ
ἐπὶ τὴν γῆν.

¹³ Ἠρήμωσεν ὁ ἄνεμος τὴν γῆν ἡμῶν ἀπὸ ἐνοικούντων
αὐτήν,
ἠφάνισαν νέον καὶ πρεσβύτην καὶ τέκνα αὐτῶν ἅμα·
¹⁴ ἐν ὀργῇ κάλλους αὐτοῦ ἐξαπέστειλεν αὐτὰ ἕως ἐπὶ δυσμῶν,
καὶ τοὺς ἄρχοντας τῆς γῆς εἰς ἐμπαιγμὸν, καὶ οὐκ ἐφείσατο.

12 οἷς V, K, P, M, Hilg. Geig. Fritzsch. Pick.   τὰ A, (Cerd.), Fab.
13 ἄνεμος codd. Fab. Geig.   ἄνομος conj. Ewald, quem seq. Hilg. Fritzsch. Pick.
   ἠφάνισαν A, V, K, Fab. Geig.   ἠφάνισεν P, M, Hilg. Fritzsch. Pick.
14 ἐν ὀργῇ ζήλους conj. Hilg.² (Pick.).

14. But this usage seems to occur especially in a good sense.

Here εὑρεθείη αὐτοῖς seems to be equivalent to εὑρεθήσεται αὐτοῖς or εὑρήσουσιν, cf. Deut. xxi. 17 ἀπὸ πάντων ὧν ἂν εὑρεθῇ αὐτῷ.

11 ἐλεήσει...ἐξηρεύνησε. The uncertainty of the tenses is here well exemplified.

There are two ways of interpreting this verse, according as ἐλεήσει is understood ironically or literally. (1) *Ironically.* His mercy towards them is according to their works; their works are evil; therefore he punishes them. He searches out all their race; none can escape; he letteth none of them go (οὐκ ἀφῆκεν αὐτούς). Thus the Lord is just in all his judgements.

(2) *Literally.* But where their works are not evil, he sheweth mercy; he trieth and searcheth out the whole race. If there is any good in them, he spareth them, and doth not forsake them utterly (οὐκ ἀφῆκεν αὐτούς). Thus the Lord's justice is shown in all his judgements.

In favour of (1), it should be observed that the tone of denunciation in vv. 8—10 is maintained; ἐξερευνάω is commonly used in a hostile sense; e.g. 1 Macc. iii. 5 καὶ ἐδίωξεν ἀνόμους ἐξερευνῶν, ix. 26 καὶ ἐξεζήτουν καὶ ἐξηρεύνων τοὺς φίλους Ἰούδα.

For οὐκ ἀφῆκεν αὐτοὺς cf. Ps. civ. 19 καὶ ἔλυσεν αὐτὸν ἄρχων λαοῦ καὶ ἀφῆκεν αὐτὸν, 1 Macc. xiii. 19 καὶ οὐκ ἀφῆκεν τὸν Ἰωνάθαν. (In the sense of 'to forgive' ἀφίημι is only found with the dative of the person forgiven.)

We prefer (2) however, on the ground that the tone of irony does not appear to correspond with the general style of our Psalmist, and that the transition from denunciation to the declaration of mercy is explained by Pompey's treatment of Hyrcanus II, who was left in occupation of the High Priesthood.

ἐξερευνάω is used of careful inquisitive search Ps. lxiii. (lxiv.) 7 ἐξηρεύνησαν ἀνομίαν, ἐξέλιπον ἐξερευνῶντες ἐξερευνήσει, not always in a hostile sense, Prov. ii. 4 καὶ ὡς θησαυροὺς ἐξερευνήσῃς αὐτήν, Lam. iii. 39 ἐξερευνήθη ἡ ὁδὸς ἡμῶν, 1 Pet. i. 10. For ἀφίημι in the sense of 'desert,' 'abandon' cf. Jer. xii. 7 ἀφῆκα τὴν κληρονομίαν μου, Eccl̇us. vi 26 καὶ ἐγκρατὴς γενόμενος μὴ ἀφῆς αὐτήν.

If it were not for ἐλεήσει we should prefer the sense given by (1), which derives support from the use of ἐξερευνᾶν and ἀφιέναι.

The difficulty is not lessened by the transition from the 2nd Pers. Sing. to the 3rd Pers. Sing. ἐλεήσει.

13 ὁ ἄνεμος. All the MSS. read ὁ ἄνεμος. Ewald's conjecture ὁ ἄνομος has commended itself generally to the Editors. The change from ε to ο is very slight, and the application of the title ὁ ἄνομος to Pompey as the representative of the heathen adversaries of Jerusalem would be quite appropriate. Cf. 2 Thess. ii. 8 τότε ἀποκαλυφθήσεται ὁ ἄνομος.

For ἄνομος used technically of the Gentiles, i.e. those without law, cf. Acts ii. 23 διὰ χειρῶν ἀνόμων: 1 Cor. ix. 21: Is. i. 7 ἠρήμωται κατεστραμμένη ὑπὸ λαῶν ἀλλοτρίων.

In our opinion the reading of the MSS.

XVII. 14] ΨΑΛΜΟΙ ΣΑΛΟΜΩΝΤΟΣ. 133

11 According to their works God had[3] compassion upon them; he sought out their seed diligently and forsook them not.

12 Faithful is the LORD in all his judgements, which he doeth upon the earth.

13 The tempest[6] hath laid waste our land that none should inhabit it; they destroyed both young and old and their little ones together.

14 In the fury of his wrath[7] he sent them away even unto the west.

And the princes of the land he *turned* into derision, and spared them not.

[6] Conj. *lawless one*

[7] Gr. *beauty*

ὁ ἄνεμος should be adhered to. The Psalmist refers to the Roman attack under the similitude of a devastating tempest. Cf. ἀνέμου πολλοῦ, viii. 2. In Is. xxviii. 18, 19, the same metaphor is used of an invader; and in the great wind which in the Conflict of Adam, Bk iii. x. 25, sweeps over the earth to destroy idols, we have a somewhat similar thought.

Compare also the mention in Jos. *Ant.* XIV. ii. 2 of a great tempest of wind which devastated the land shortly before the date of this book.

ἀπὸ ἐνοικούντων αὐτήν. Cf. Jer. li. (xliv.) 2 καὶ ἰδοὺ εἰσὶν ἔρημοι ἀπὸ ἐνοίκων, which expresses generally the sense of 'And, behold, this day they are a desolation, and no man dwelleth therein.'

The use of ἐρημόω with ἀπὸ is not common; it occurs with the sense of 'to deprive' in Bar. iv. 16 καὶ ἀπὸ τῶν θυγατέρων τὴν μόνην ἠρήμωσαν, on the analogy of which passage we might render the present clause 'they robbed our land of her inhabitants.'

But τὴν γῆν ἡμῶν seems to demand the primary meaning of ἠρήμωσεν, 'laid waste.' The ἀπὸ ἐνοικούντων αὐτήν is probably a Hebraism = מֵאֵין יוֹשֵׁב 'without inhabitant,' as in Isai. vi. 11 ἕως ἂν ἐρημωθῶσι πόλεις παρὰ τὸ μὴ κατοικεῖσθαι (מֵאֵין יוֹשֵׁב) καὶ οἶκοι παρὰ τὸ μὴ εἶναι ἀνθρώπους (מֵאֵין אָדָם).

ἠφάνισαν. We prefer this reading to ἠφάνισεν, which has all the appearance of being a mere correction of a harsh construction. The devastating wind is the metaphor for Roman armies, and the Plural is very naturally employed κατὰ σύνεσιν. The transition from ἠρήμωσεν to ἠφάνισαν may be paralleled by other instances of change from Singular to Plural, e.g. iv. 7, 9, 10.

νέον καὶ κ.τ.λ. See ii. 8, where with the exception of εἰσάπαξ for ἅμα the same words occur.

14 ἐν ὀργῇ κάλλους. The combination of κάλλος with ἐν ὀργῇ is very strange. Obviously it is used in quite a different sense from that in which it occurs in ii. 4, 5, 20.

Geiger considers it to be a rendering of תִּפְאֶרֶת used in the sense of זָדוֹן = 'insolence,' quoting Isai. x. 12; cf. Zech. xii. 7. Wellhausen probably explains the word in the same way, 'Im Zorn und Uebermuth.' Pick renders 'in his jealous fury,' without however suggesting the reading ἐν ὀργῇ ζήλους αὐτοῦ which his translation might be taken to indicate. The gen. κάλλους qualifying ὀργῇ may be illustrated by Wisd. v. 16 τὸ διάδημα τοῦ κάλλους = τὸ καλὸν διάδημα.

We suggest another explanation of κάλλους αὐτοῦ. (1) These words literally retranslated give us יָפְיוֹ. (2) After ἐν ὀργῇ we should expect θυμοῦ αὐτοῦ = 'in the fury of his wrath,' cf. Lam. ii. 3 συνέκλασεν ἐν ὀργῇ θυμοῦ αὐτοῦ πᾶν κέρας Ἰσραήλ. (3) It appears to us that אפו 'his wrath' was by an easy error in one letter written יפו 'his beauty.' (4) The translator rightly rendered יפו by κάλλους αὐτοῦ; but if he had the true reading before him, he would have rendered it by θυμοῦ αὐτοῦ. Our translation 'in the fury of his wrath' conjecturally restores the original meaning. Most probably we should supply ὁ θεὸς before ἐξαπέστειλεν.

αὐτὰ ἕως ἐπὶ δυσμῶν. Pompey sent off Aristobulus and his family to adorn the triumph at Rome. See Introd.

Fritzsche says 'scribendum ἕως ἐπὶ

ΨΑΛΜΟΙ ΣΑΛΟΜΩΝΤΟΣ. [XVII. 15

¹⁵ ἐν ἀλλοτριότητι ὁ ἐχθρὸς ἐποίησεν ὑπερηφανίαν,
καὶ ἡ καρδία αὐτοῦ ἀλλοτρία ἀπὸ τοῦ θεοῦ ἡμῶν.
¹⁶ καὶ πάντα ὅσα ἐποίησεν ἐν Ἱερουσαλήμ,
καθὼς καὶ τὰ ἔθνη ἐν ταῖς πόλεσι τοῖς θεοῖς αὐτῶν.
¹⁷ καὶ ἐπεκράτουν αὐτῶν οἱ υἱοὶ τῆς διαθήκης ἐν μέσῳ
  ἐθνῶν συμμίκτων,
οὐκ ἦν ὁ ποιῶν ἐν αὐτοῖς ἐν μέσῳ Ἱερουσαλὴμ ἔλεος καὶ
  ἀλήθειαν.
¹⁸ ἔφυγον ἀπ' αὐτῶν οἱ ἀγαπῶντες συναγωγὰς ὁσίων,
ὡς στρουθία ἐξεπετάσθησαν ἀπὸ κοίτης αὐτῶν·
¹⁹ ἐπλανῶντο ἐν ἐρήμοις, σωθῆναι ψυχὰς αὐτῶν ἀπὸ κακοῦ,
καὶ τίμιον ἐν ὀφθαλμοῖς παροικίας ψυχὴ σεσωσμένη ἐξ
  αὐτῶν·

16 ἐποίησαν conj. Hilg.²

δυσμάς, cf. 1 Macc. v. 28, nisi interpres solœcismum admisit.' But we need not hesitate to retain the reading of the MSS.

καὶ τοὺς ἄρχοντας. Strictly speaking the accusative is by *zeugma* after ἀπέστειλεν. But in all probability this accusative case is due to an error of the translator, who did not perceive that there was a fresh clause, being misled by the absence of a verb.

εἰς ἐμπαιγμόν then does not express that the rulers were sent *to* mockery, but that the rulers *became* a laughing-stock. The εἰς gives a common use of ל, as in εἰς ὀνειδισμόν, εἰς γέλωτα, etc.; cf. ii. 13.

It is possible that ἐμπαιγμόν may refer to the degradation of being led in the conqueror's triumph.

15 ἐν ἀλλοτριότητι. The Psalmist deals leniently with 'the adversary.' His 'insolence' (ὑπερηφανία) is explained to be due to his foreign origin, and to the fact of 'his heart' being strange from, i.e. ignorant of, the Jewish God.

The Psalmist, we make no doubt, is alluding to the presumption of Pompey in entering the Holy of Holies.

But Pompey's freedom from avarice and consideration for the religion and worship of the Jews had commanded the respect of the people. He is therefore not vindictively assailed: his profanity is ascribed to his ignorance.

ἀλλοτρία ἀπὸ τοῦ θεοῦ ἡμῶν. The adj. ἀλλότριος is found with a gen. of the object, and not elsewhere with ἀπό, though the verb ἀλλοτριόω has this construction, e.g. Gen. xlii. 7; 1 Macc. vi. 24. Here the ἀπὸ reproduces the Hebrew מִן.

16 πάντα ὅσα ἐποίησεν. The ὅσα does not seem to be wanted in the clause; for it requires us to supply ἐποίησεν a second time.

Is ὅσα a corruption in the text for ὅσια? And is it intended that Pompey offered sacrifices to the God of Israel in Jerusalem, following the ordinary ritual of the heathen in their own cities?

καθὼς καὶ τὰ ἔθνη. Neither Antipater nor Herod would have acted thus in Jerusalem.

17 ἐπεκράτουν. For ἐπικρατεῖν see note on xvi. 7. Here the sense is that the Jews *outdid* and *surpassed* the heathen in the outrageous excesses of idolatry (perhaps=חֲזַק בְּ).

Another explanation of the word is to regard it as a rendering of "בְּ הֶחֱזִיק with the sense of 'join oneself to.' So Geiger, who quotes 1 Kings ix. 9 'laid hold on other gods;' Prov. iii. 18 'she is a tree of life to them that lay hold upon her;' iv. 13. He however explains the line to mean that the Jews laid hold of (i.e. banded themselves with) the *heathen* against their own countrymen, referring αὐτῶν to ἔθνη. A more natural interpretation would refer αὐτῶν to the heathen gods and practices, which the Jews 'laid hold of.'

οἱ υἱοὶ τῆς διαθήκης. Not a common phrase. Cf. Ezek. xxx. 5 καὶ πάντες οἱ

XVII. 19] ΨΑΛΜΟΙ ΣΑΛΟΜΩΝΤΟΣ. 135

15 In that he was an alien, the adversary wrought insolence, and his heart was alien from our God.

16 And all things whatsoever he did[8] in Jerusalem, *he did* even as do the Gentiles in their cities unto their gods.

17 And the children of the covenant *that dwelt* in the midst of the mingled people surpassed them[9], there was none among them in the midst of Jerusalem that did mercy and truth.

18 They that loved the assemblies of the saints fled from them: they were scattered as sparrows from their nest.

19 They were wandering in desert places, that their lives might be preserved from harm; and precious in the sight of them that were sojourners was *one* life saved from among them.

[8] Conj. *And all the sacred rites performed he*
[9] Or, *clave unto them*, or, *got the mastery over them*

ἐπίμικτοι καὶ τῶν υἱῶν τῆς διαθήκης μου. Acts iii. 25 ὑμεῖς ἐστε υἱοὶ τῶν προφητῶν καὶ τῆς διαθήκης ἧς διέθετο ὁ θεὸς κ.τ.λ.

ἐθνῶν συμμίκτων. Clearly a rendering of עֶרֶב. Cf. Jer. xxxii. (Heb. xxv.) 25 καὶ πάντας τοὺς συμμίκτους, xxvii. (Heb. ii.) 27 καὶ τὸν σύμμικτον τὸν ἐν μέσῳ αὐτῆς. We find for the same word ἐπίμικτος used as a subst. in Ex. xii. 28 καὶ ἐπίμικτος πολὺς συνανέβη αὐτοῖς. Cf. Ezek. xxx. 5 quoted above.

Here it is very possible that ἐθνῶν is either an alternative rendering or introduced explanatorily, cf. xvi. 1 καταφορᾷ ὕπνου, κέντρον ἵππου.

ἔλεος καὶ ἀλήθειαν. Cf. Jos. ii. 14 'deal kindly and truly' (LXX. ποιήσετε... ἔλεος καὶ ἀλήθειαν); Ps. lxxxiii. (lxxxiv.) 12 ὅτι ἔλεον καὶ ἀλήθειαν ἀγαπᾷ κύριος.

18 συναγωγὰς ὁσίων, 'the assemblies of the saints' or 'the gatherings together of the saints.' Cf. Ps. cxlix. 1 ἡ αἴνεσις αὐτοῦ ἐν ἐκκλησίᾳ ὁσίων. συναγωγὰς may refer either generally to collected multitudes, cf. Ecclus. xxiv. 22 συναγωγαὶ Ἰακώβ, or to more formal gatherings, Ecclus. xlv. 18 ἡ συναγωγὴ Κορέ, 1 Macc. xiv. 28.

For the opposite to συναγωγὴ ὁσίων cf. Ecclus. xxi. 9 στυππεῖον συνηγμένον συναγωγὴ ἀνόμων, Apoc. ii. 9, iii. 9 συναγωγὴ τοῦ Σατανᾶ.

ὡς στρουθία. The metaphor is perhaps borrowed from Ps. x. (xi.) 1 μεταναστεύου ἐπὶ τὰ ὄρη ὡς στρουθίον.

ἐξεπετάσθησαν. We should have expected ἐξέπτησαν. Cf. Ecclus. xliii. 14 ἐξέπτησαν νεφέλαι ὡς πετεινά.

ἀπὸ κοίτης. κοίτη here seems to be used for a nest (νοσσιά).

In Jer. x. 22 κοίτην στρουθῶν occurs for 'the dwelling-place of jackals.' It is very probable that our translator confusing στρουθοί and στρουθία has adopted κοίτην from this passage!

19 ἐπλανῶντο. Cf. Heb. xi. 38 ἐν ἐρημίαις πλανώμενοι.

σωθῆναι. The infin. is epexegetic of, but stands in no strict grammatical connexion with, ἐπλανῶντο.

τίμιον ἐν ὀφθαλμοῖς. Cf. Ps. cxv. (cxvi.) 15 τίμιος ἐναντίον κυρίου ὁ θάνατος τῶν ὁσίων αὐτῶν. For τίμιος = 'rare' cf. 1 Sam. iii. 1 ῥῆμα κυρίου ἦν τίμιον ἐν ταῖς ἡμέραις ἐκείναις.

παροικίας for τῶν παροίκων, the abstract for the concrete. The sense is that the community of the Jews dispersed in other countries regarded as a rare and precious thing any one life saved from the perils which Jerusalem offered both from the Romans and from fellow-countrymen.

We have here perhaps the earliest instance of παροικία applied to a *community* temporarily sojourning in a strange land. As a title for the Jewish sojourners in foreign lands, it represents a different shade of thought from διασπορά. As ἡ διασπορά they are described in their relation to their fatherland; as ἡ παροικία they are described in their relation to the countries in which they sojourned for a time until the day of Israel's restoration. Cf. Ecclus. Prol. οἱ ἐν τῇ παροικίᾳ. 1 Pet. i. 1 παρεπιδήμοις διασπορᾶς. Its occurrence in the present passage is of especial interest, since it shows that the use of παροικία for 'a body of sojourners' was an accepted Jewish one before it became generally adopted in the language of the Church. See Bp Lightfoot's note on Clem. *Ep. ad Cor.* i., where however the present passage is not mentioned, and where the earliest instances quoted

²⁰ εἰς πᾶσαν τὴν γῆν ἐγενήθη ὁ σκορπισμὸς αὐτῶν ὑπὸ
ἀνόμων,
ὅτι ἀνέσχεν ὁ οὐρανὸς τοῦ στάξαι ὑετὸν ἐπὶ τὴν γῆν,
²¹ πηγαὶ συνεσχέθησαν αἰώνιοι ἐξ ἀβύσσων ἀπὸ ὀρέων ὑψηλῶν·
ὅτι οὐκ ἦν ἐν αὐτοῖς ποιῶν δικαιοσύνην καὶ κρίμα,
ἀπὸ ἄρχοντος αὐτῶν καὶ [ἕως] λαοῦ ἐλαχίστου ἐν πάσῃ
ἁμαρτίᾳ·
²² ὁ βασιλεὺς ἐν παρανομίᾳ, καὶ ὁ κριτὴς ἐν ἀπειθείᾳ,
καὶ ὁ λαὸς ἐν ἁμαρτίᾳ.

²³ Ἴδε, κύριε, καὶ ἀνάστησον αὐτοῖς τὸν βασιλέα αὐτῶν,
υἱὸν Δαυίδ, εἰς τὸν καιρὸν ὃν οἶδας σύ, ὁ θεός,
τοῦ βασιλεῦσαι ἐπὶ Ἰσραὴλ παῖδά σου,
²⁴ καὶ ὑπόζωσον αὐτὸν ἰσχὺν τοῦ θραῖσαι ἄρχοντας ἀδίκους· Sh

20 ὁ οὐρανὸς P, M; om. ὁ A, V, K.
ἐπὶ τὴν γῆν V, K, P, M. τῆς γῆς A.
21 ἕως nos conj.
22 ἐν ἀπειθείᾳ V, K, P, M: ἐν ἀληθείᾳ A: Hilg. conj. οὐκ ἐν ἀληθείᾳ; ita
Fritzsch. Pick. Conj. ἐν ἀσεβείᾳ Geig.
23 οἶδες V, K. εἶδες A. οἶδας P, M, (Hilg. conj.).
24 ἰσχύν codd. (A ἰχύν, sic), Fabr. ἰσχυῖ.

---

are from Christian sources, *Mart. Polyc.* inscr., Dionys. Corinth. (?) in Eus. *H. E.* IV. 23.

Wahl's *Clavis Apocr.* quotes as examples of παροικία=οἱ πάροικοι, 3 Macc. vi, 36 καὶ κοινὸν ὁμοιώμενοι περὶ τούτων θεσμὸν ἐπὶ πᾶσαν τὴν παροικίαν αὐτῶν εἰς γενεάς, vii. 19 ἐπὶ τὸν τῆς παροικίας αὐτῶν χρόνον εὐφροσύνους; but mistakenly, as in both cases παροικία refers to the period and condition of τὸ παροικεῖν, as in Acts xiii. 17.

In another passage Ecclus. xvi. 8, οὐκ ἐφείσατο περὶ τῆς παροικίας Λώτ, οὓς ἐβδελύξατο, if παροικία=οἱ πάροικοι, it is in the sense of 'neighbours' not of 'temporary sojourners.'

Geiger's conjecture that ἐν ὀφθαλμοῖς παροικίας is a mistranslation of בְּעֵינֵי מְגוּרִים 'im Angesichte der Schrecknisse' does not seem to be either forcible or poetical enough to justify acceptance.

20 σκορπισμός. The substantive does not seem to occur in the LXX. For σκορπίζω, cf. Ecclus. xlviii. 16 ἐσκορπίσθησαν ἐν πάσῃ τῇ γῇ, 1 Macc. vii. 6 καὶ ἡμᾶς ἐσκόρπισαν ἀπὸ τῆς γῆς ἡμῶν.

ἀνέσχεν ὁ οὐρανός. For this drought and consequent famine, see Joseph. *Ant.* XIV. 3.

The same famine here spoken of has been mentioned in ii. 10.

For ἀνέσχεν, cf. Hagg. i. 10 διὰ τοῦτο ἀνέξει ὁ οὐρανὸς ἀπὸ δρόσου, Ecclus. xlviii. 3 ἐν λόγῳ κυρίου ἀνέσχεν οὐρανόν.

21 πηγαί...ἐξ ἀβύσσων. This phrase is a variation of πηγαὶ τῆς ἀβύσσου in Gen. vii. 11, viii. 2 and πηγαὶ τῶν ἀβύσσων Dt. viii. 7, xxx. 13.

The adj. αἰώνιοι probably represents the idea of 'living water' (מַיִם חַיִּים), the 'perennial (אֵיתָנִים) springs,' cf. Ps. lxxiii. (lxxiv.) 15 ἐξήρανας ποταμοὺς Ἠθάμ (נַהֲרוֹת אֵיתָן). Amos v. 24 (מִשְׁפָּט וּצְדָקָה).... (כְּנַחַל אֵיתָן).— The line probably denotes the two sources of water; (1) the springs, which were unfailing in summer and winter alike, (2) the water-courses from the mountains, dry during the hot season.

Cf. Assumpt. Mosis x. 8 Et fontes

20 Over all the earth were they scattered *and driven* by lawless men.

For the heaven ceased to drop rain upon the earth,

21 The fountains were stayed, the everlasting *fountains that spring* out of the great depths *and* from the high mountains: because there was none among them that did righteousness and judgement.

From their ruler to[10] the vilest of the people, they were altogether sinful.   [10] Gr. *and*

22 The king was a transgressor, and the judge was disobedient, and the people sinful.

23 Behold, O LORD, and raise up unto them their king, the son of David, in the time which thou, O God, knowest, that he may reign over Israel thy servant;

24 And gird him with strength that he may break in pieces them that rule unjustly.

---

aquarum deficient, et flumina exarescent. 4 Esdr. vi. 24 Et venæ fontium stabunt. Test. Levi. 4 ὑδάτων ξηραινομένων.

ποιῶν δικαιοσύνην καὶ κρίμα. Cf. Ezek. xviii. 5 ὁ δὲ ἄνθρωπος ὃς ἔσται δίκαιος, ὁ ποιῶν κρίμα καὶ δικαιοσύνην, Ps. cxviii. (cxix.) 121 ἐποίησα κρίμα καὶ δικαιοσύνην.

ἀπὸ ἄρχοντος ... λαοῦ ἐλαχίστου. A very probable instance of a Hebrew idiom imperfectly understood; 'from their prince to the very least of the people,' i.e. both their prince and the dregs of the mob. Cf. Jonah iii. 5 ἀπὸ μεγάλου αὐτῶν ἕως μικροῦ αὐτῶν. Very possibly ἕως should be supplied here; in xviii. 13 it was omitted by A and by older editors. The idiom in the LXX. is generally given by ἀπὸ...καὶ ἕως (cf. Ex. ix. 25, Jos. vi. 21, 1 Sam. xv. 3). Geiger, who also explains the difficulty of the passage as due to a misapprehension of the Heb. prep. מִן, connects ἀπὸ ἄρχοντος αὐτῶν with the previous clause, 'Keiner...übte mehr als ihr Fürst.'

22 ὁ βασιλεὺς. The Asmonean Prince, referring to Hyrcanus II. or Aristobulus II.

ἐν ἀπειθείᾳ. Four of the MSS. give this reading in place of ἐν ἀληθείᾳ, which was so unintelligible that Hilgenfeld's conjectural insertion of οὐκ was accepted by Fritzsche (?), Wellhausen 'in Bestechlichkeit,' and Pick, while Geiger suggested ἐν ἀσεβείᾳ.

ἀπείθεια is not found in the LXX., but ἀπειθεῖν is not uncommon, e.g. Isai. i. 23 οἱ ἄρχοντές σου ἀπειθοῦσι (Symm. ἀπειθής), iii. 8.

23 The Psalmist has described, in the most moving terms he can employ, the state of decay into which the Jewish polity had fallen. To his mind there is only one possible remedy for it: the King promised long before, of the true ancient kingly line.

For the wording of the appeal many parallels can be cited. The promise originally made to David is in 2 Sam. vii. 12. In Jer. xxx. 9 we have τὸν Δ. βασιλέα αὐτῶν ἀναστήσω αὐτοῖς. Cf. Ezek. xxxiv. 23, xxxvii. 25; and, as perhaps the earliest in date, Amos ix. 11 ἀναστήσω τὴν σκηνὴν τοῦ Δ. τὴν πεπτωκυῖαν.

καιρὸν ὃν οἶδας. Cf. Zech. xiv. 7 ἡ ἡμέρα ἐκείνη γνωστὴ τῷ Κυρίῳ. A reference to the old promise is indicated.

24 ὑπόζωσον occurs once in 2 Macc. and in Acts xxvii. 17. The usual LXX. expression is περιζωννύναι δύναμιν, Ps. xviii. 38, 43. In Is. xi. the Messiah is girded with righteousness and faithfulness.

θραῦσαι. Cf. Num. xxiv. 17 θραύσει τοὺς ἀρχηγοὺς Μωάβ. The corrupt Sadducean princes are to be cast down.

138   ΨΑΛΜΟΙ ΣΑΛΟΜΩΝΤΟΣ.   [XVII. 25

²⁵ καθάρισον Ἱερουσαλὴμ ἀπὸ ἐθνῶν καταπατούντων ἐν
    ἀπωλείᾳ,
ἐν σοφίᾳ, ἐν δικαιοσύνῃ·
²⁶ ἐξῶσαι ἁμαρτωλοὺς ἀπὸ κληρονομίας,
ἐκτρίψαι ὑπερηφανίαν ἁμαρτωλῶν,
ὡς cκεύη κεραμέωc ἐν ῥάβδῳ cιδηρᾷ cυντρίψαι πᾶσαν ὑπό-
    στασιν αὐτῶν·
²⁷ ὀλοθρεύσαι ἔθνη παράνομα ἐν λόγῳ cτόματοc αὐτοῦ,
ἐν ἀπειλῇ αὐτοῦ φυγεῖν ἔθνη ἀπὸ προσώπου αὐτοῦ,
καὶ ἐλέγξαι ἁμαρτωλοὺς ἐν λόγῳ καρδίας αὐτῶν.
²⁸ καὶ συνάξει λαὸν ἅγιον, οὗ ἀφηγήσεται ἐν δικαιοσύνῃ,
καὶ κρινεῖ φυλὰς λαοῦ ἡγιασμένου ὑπὸ κυρίου θεοῦ αὐτοῦ.
²⁹ καὶ οὐκ ἀφήσει ἀδικίαν ἐν μέσῳ αὐτῶν αὐλισθῆναι,
καὶ οὐ κατοικήσει πᾶς ἄνθρωπος μετ' αὐτῶν εἰδὼς κακίαν·
³⁰ γνώσεται γὰρ αὐτοὺς ὅτι πάντες υἱοὶ θεοῦ αὐτῶν εἰσι,
καὶ καταμερίσει αὐτοὺς ἐν ταῖς φυλαῖς αὐτῶν ἐπὶ τῆς γῆς.
³¹ καὶ πάροικος καὶ ἀλλογενὴς οὐ παροικήσει αὐτοῖς ἔτι·
κρινεῖ λαοὺς καὶ ἔθνη ἐν σοφίᾳ δικαιοσύνης αὐτοῦ. Διά-
    ψαλμα.

25 Geig. conj. καθαρίσαι.
26 ἐξῶσαι Μ.
    ἁμαρτωλῶν Α, Μ. ἁμαρτωλοὺς V, Κ, Ρ. (Ρ, ὑπερηφανίαν, ἁμαρτωλ. ὡς σκεύη.)
27 ὀλοθρεῦσαι V, P, M.
    ἀπειλῇ V, K, (Hilg. conj.). ἀπέλλῃ Α. (Cerda 'concione.')
    P et M omittunt ἐν ἀπειλῇ......προσώπου αὐτοῦ.
30 καταμερίσει V, P, M, Hilg. Geig. Fritzsch. Pick.
    καταμετρίσει Α, Κ, Fabr.
31 ἔθνη καὶ λαοὺς Α.
    om. διάψαλμα Μ.

25 The Romans are to disappear from the Holy City. Cf. ii. 2.

A noteworthy point in this verse is the apparent coordination of the three words ἀπώλεια, σοφία, δικαιοσύνη. The first does not, and we think was never intended to, range with the other two. It is a striking instance of the translator's fondness for ἐν: here he is led into an extreme awkwardness of expression thereby. The asyndeton adds to the obscurity. Cf. generally, v. 33.

26 ἐξῶσαι. We are again confronted here by the question, Are these verbs to be taken as Optatives or Infinitives? The MSS. usually declare (as here) for the latter. We believe that the former is correct in this place, and that the Optative has really the force of the Future. The Infinitive would be entirely unobjectionable, were it not for the intervening clause v. 27, ἐν ἀπειλῇ...φυγεῖν ἔθνη..., which introduces a new subject. Two MSS. (M, P) have felt the difficulty and met it by omitting the clause. That was not really necessary. We can still retain the words, and construe the verbs as Infinitives: only the resultant text is very clumsy; whereas the Optative gives an easy construction in v. 27, and an easy transition to the Futures of v. 28 sqq.

ἐκτρίψαι. Ecclus. xxxiii. 8, and often elsewhere in this connection.

The punctuation and text of P deserve a passing notice.

ὡς σκεύη κεραμέως, from Ps. ii. 9 ποι-

XVII. 31]   ΨΑΛΜΟΙ ΣΑΛΟΜΩΝΤΟΣ.   139

25 Purge Jerusalem from the heathen that trample her down to destroy her, with wisdom *and* with righteousness.

26 He shall[11] thrust out the sinners from the inheritance, utterly destroy the proud spirit of the sinners, *and* as potter's vessels with a rod of iron shall he break in pieces all their substance[12].

27 He shall destroy the ungodly nations with the word of his mouth, *so that* at his rebuke the nations may flee before him, and he shall convict the sinners in the thoughts of their hearts.

28 And he shall gather together a holy people, whom he shall lead in righteousness; and shall judge the tribes of the people that hath been sanctified by the LORD his God.

29 And he shall not suffer iniquity to lodge in their midst; and none that knoweth wickedness shall dwell with them.

30 For he shall take knowledge of them, that they be all the sons of their God, and shall divide them upon the earth according to their tribes.

31 And the sojourner and the stranger shall dwell with them no more.

He shall judge the nations and the peoples with the wisdom of his righteousness.   Selah.

[11] Gr. *May he*; with other accents, *To*
[12] Or, *confidence*

μανεῖς αὐτοὺς ἐν ῥάβδῳ σιδηρᾷ, ὡς σκεύη κεραμέως συντρίψεις αὐτούς. The translator here, as elsewhere, shows, as we should expect, close familiarity with the LXX.

ὑπόστασις. Cf. on xv. 7.

The clause is from Is. xi. 4. This passage is still more closely copied in v. 39, which see.

27 ἐν ἀπειλῇ. A reason has already been assigned for the omission of this clause by M, P; on the relation between these two MSS. see Introd. Cf. Hab. iii. 11 ἐν ἀπειλῇ ὀλιγώσεις γῆν, and Is. liv. 9.

The 3rd clause is remarkable. Sinners are to be convicted by the 'word of their heart,' i.e. the testimony of their conscience, cf. Luke i. 51 διεσκόρπισεν ὑπερηφάνους διανοίᾳ καρδίας αὐτῶν. The expression, though not the idea, belongs more to the N.T. sphere of thought: cf. the received text of John viii. 9 ὑπὸ τῆς συνειδήσεως ἐλεγχόμενοι. The story of David's conviction, 2 Sam. xii., and the passage Is. xxxiii. 11 are two only of several O.T. illustrations of the thought here.

28 When all the destructive work of the Messiah is over, his constructive functions begin. First his subjects are to be gathered, and then their freedom from alien pollution secured. Is. xi. 12 συνάξει τοὺς ἀπολομένους Ἰσραήλ etc.

ἀφηγήσεται. In Ex. xi. 8 of Moses, πᾶς ὁ λαός σου οὗ σὺ ἀφηγῇ. In Ezekiel ἀφηγούμενος is the regular word for 'prince.'

κρινεῖ φυλάς. Cf. Luke xxii. 30.

29 Cf. Ps. c. (ci.) 7 οὐ κατῴκει ἐν μέσῳ τῆς οἰκίας μου ποιῶν ὑπερηφανίαν, and Job xi. 14.

30 πάντες υἱοὶ θεοῦ. Is. liv. 13 καὶ πάντας τοὺς υἱούς σου διδακτοὺς θεοῦ. Hos. i. 10 καὶ αὐτοῦ υἱοὶ θεοῦ ζῶντος. Also Deut. xiv. 1 Υἱοί ἐστε Κυρίου τοῦ θεοῦ ὑμῶν. We might compare the words of our Lord in John x. 14 ('I know my sheep, and am known of mine'), which are particularly appropriate here, for in v. 45 the metaphor of the good shepherd is employed by this writer.

καταμεριεῖ. Deut. xix. 3 (γῆν) ἣν καταμεριεῖ σοι Κύριος ὁ θεός σου. Also Num. xxxii. 18; Ezek. xlv. 8; Ecclus. xxxvi. 12; Ps. lxvii. 15 (Sym.).

The reading (?) of A καταμετρίσει would be an error by itacism for καταμετρήσει. Cf. Amos vii. 17 ἡ γῆ σου ἐν σχοινίῳ καταμετρηθήσεται.

31 The idea of the 'stranger in the gates' has become intolerable to the Jew

³² Καὶ ἕξει λαοὺς ἐθνῶν δουλεύειν αὐτῷ ὑπὸ ζυγὸν αὐτοῦ,
καὶ τὸν κύριον δοξάσει ἐν ἐπισήμῳ πάσης τῆς γῆς·
³³ καὶ καθαρίσει Ἱερουσαλὴμ ἐν ἁγιασμῷ, ὡς καὶ τὸ ἀπ
ἀρχῆς,
³⁴ ἔρχεσθαι ἔθνη ἀπ' ἄκρου τῆς γῆς ἰδεῖν τὴν δόξαν αὐτοῦ,
φέροντες δῶρα τοὺς ἐξησθενηκότας υἱοὺς αὐτῆς,
³⁵ καὶ ἰδεῖν τὴν δόξαν κυρίου, ἣν ἐδόξασεν αὐτὴν ὁ θεός·
καὶ αὐτὸς βασιλεὺς δίκαιος καὶ διδακτὸς ὑπὸ θεοῦ ἐπ'
αὐτούς.
³⁶ καὶ οὐκ ἔστιν ἀδικία ἐν ταῖς ἡμέραις αὐτοῦ ἐν μέσῳ αὐτῶν,
ὅτι πάντες ἅγιοι, καὶ βασιλεὺς αὐτῶν χριστὸς κύριος·

32 τὸν κύριον δοξάσει V, K, P, M: om. τὸν κύριον A.
34 φέροντες A, V, K, P, Fabr.
φέροντας M (? corr.), conj. Hilg. (Fritzsch. Pick).
Geig. conj. φέροντα.
35 δίκαιος καὶ διδακτός P: rel. om. καί.

---

of this period. He desires nothing more than to see the land reserved for the chosen race alone. That this exclusiveness made a deeply unfavourable impression on the stranger who came in contact with him, is too familiar a topic to bear enlarging upon. For O.T. foreshadowings of this, see Joel iii. 17 (of Jerusalem) ἀλλογενεῖς οὐ διελεύσονται δι' αὐτῆς οὐκέτι.

ἀλλογενής is a very common word in Leviticus, e.g. xxii. 10 where πάροικος also occurs,—another of many cases where our writer seems to show a familiarity with the LXX. version of that book.

We see from the second clause of the verse that the nation are not to be destroyed; though excluded from residing in the land. They will look to Judaea as their centre and to Messiah as their sovereign.

ἐν σοφίᾳ δικαιοσύνης. This is merely another way of writing ἐν σοφίᾳ ἐν δικαιοσύνῃ, v. 28. In these verses the Messiah appears as a second Joshua. In the next division he is a second Solomon, v. supra.

διάψαλμα, omitted by the Moscow MS. Very likely it is not genuine, any more than the other one in Ps. S. xviii. 10, where we believe that a longer pause ought to be expressed. It may have been put in in both places by the man who wrote the titles of our Psalms, in order to assimilate them more closely in outward form to the Davidic collection. Against this is the fact that only two are to be found in the whole book.

If genuine, they point to a liturgical use of these Psalms, of which we have no other trace.

32 This Messianic dominion over the Gentiles is dwelt upon in Ps. lxxii. 11 etc. (πάντα τὰ ἔθνη δουλεύσουσιν αὐτῷ), Is. lxvi.; Zech. xiv.; Dan. vii. (14). Compare for the language, Zeph. iii. 19 τοῦ δουλεύειν αὐτῷ ὑπὸ ζυγὸν ἕνα, and on ζυγόν see notes on Ps. vii. 8.

In the later literature (4 Esdr. xiii.; Apoc. Bar. lxxii.) the fate predicted for the Gentiles is far less mild. Most of them are to perish, and all who are left are to be enslaved. This, too, is the idea of such a writer as Commodian (who draws from Jewish sources), *Instr.* II. 2, *Carm. Apol.* 1012.

ἐν ἐπισήμῳ. Geiger translates 'durch Unterwerfung der ganzen Erde,' and regards ἐπισήμῳ as parallel to ζυγόν just as in Ps. ii. 6 it corresponds to σφραγίς. We cannot agree with him. It seems to us far simpler to assign its usual sense to ἐπισήμῳ of 'conspicuous,' and to regard the clause as an allusion to Is. ii. 2 (Micah iv. 1), 'The mountain of the Lord's house shall be established in the top of the mountains, and shall be exalted above the hills.'

It has been suggested to us that ἐν ἐπισήμῳ both here and in ii. 6 has the

XVII. 36]   ΨΑΛΜΟΙ ΣΑΛΟΜΩΝΤΟΣ.   141

32 And he shall possess the nations of the heathen to serve him beneath his yoke; and he shall glorify the LORD in a place to be seen of the whole earth;

33 And he shall purge Jerusalem and make it holy, even as it was in the days of old.

34 So that the nations may come from the ends of the earth to see his glory, bringing as gifts her sons that had fainted,

35 And may see the glory of the LORD, wherewith God hath glorified her.

And a righteous king and taught of God *is* he *that reigneth* over them;

36 And there shall be[13] no iniquity in his days in their midst, for all *shall be* holy and their king is the Lord Messiah[14].

[13] Gr. *is*
[14] Probably in the original *the Lord's Anointed*

same meaning, that of 'publicity.' We prefer however to think that, while that idea explains the present passage, the word in ii. 6 has a more concrete meaning and is a substantive (=στίγμα).

33 ἁγιασμός means here according to Geiger 'the state, as well as the process, of sanctification.' The cleansing here spoken of refers mainly to the sanctuary. The Messiah, like Judas Maccabaeus, will reestablish the splendour of the old Solomonic worship. Cf. 1 Macc. iv. 36—41.

ὡς καὶ τὸ ἀπ' ἀρχῆς. Cf. Is. i. 26 'I will restore thy judges as at the first and thy counsellors as at the beginning.' ii. 6 (LXX.) ὡς τὸ ἀπ' ἀρχῆς, xliii. 13, lxiii. 19, Hab. i. 12, Zech. xii. 7.

34 This verse is a condensation of several passages in Isaiah, notably lxvi. 18—20 (τὰ ἔθνη...ἥξουσι καὶ ὄψονται τὴν δόξαν μου...καὶ ἄξουσι τοὺς ἀδελφοὺς ὑμῶν ἐκ πάντων τῶν ἐθνῶν δῶρον κυρίῳ). See also ch. lx. and Ezek. xxxvii. 28, 4 Esdr. xiii. aliqui adducentes ex eis qui offerebantur.

ἐξασθενεῖν occurs only (?) in Ps. lxiii. (lxiv.) 9 as a various reading.

The change of the text from φέροντες to φέροντας (Hilgenfeld, Fritzsche) is a needless alteration.

35 διδακτὸς ὑπὸ θεοῦ. See Is. liv. 13 (quoted above on v. 30). The word is not very common. It occurs in 1 Macc. iv. 7 διδακτοὶ πολέμου etc. The merely human nature of the Messiah is here not obscurely indicated. There is, we think, a considerable pause in the sense between the first and second clauses of this verse. The αὐτοί are not the Gentiles; they could not be called πάντες ἅγιοι.

36 The first part of this verse calls for no particular comment. It resembles such prophecies as Jer. xxiii. 6. The ἀδικία may have special reference to the unorthodox practices, or the oppression, of the then reigning dynasty.

But in the expression χριστὸς κύριος, we have perhaps the 'crux' of the whole book. We will attempt to state at once the various views which have been or may be held concerning it.

α. It may be a correct rendering of the original Hebrew.

β. It may be a mistranslation of the Hebrew.

γ. It may be a Christian perversion of the text.

(a) We hold that either this view, or that mentioned next in order, is perfectly tenable. The main difficulty lies in the procuring evidence to show that the word κύριος, which so uniformly represents the name of God, could be applied to one who, as appears from the context here, is merely man. The following passages seem to point to the possibility of this.

(1) Lam. iv. 20 'The breath of our nostrils, the Anointed of the Lord (LXX. χριστὸς κύριος) is taken in their pits.' The LXX. are here guilty of a mistranslation, but their mistake points to the currency of the expression.

(2) Ps. cix. (cx.) 1 εἶπεν κύριος τῷ κυρίῳ μου.

(3) Ecclus. li. 10 ἐπεκαλεσάμην κύριον πατέρα τοῦ κυρίου μου. Here a Christian corruption has been suspected, but perhaps unnecessarily.

(4) Luke ii. 11 (the Angel to the

ΨΑΛΜΟΙ ΣΑΛΟΜΩΝΤΟΣ. [XVII. 37

^{37} οὐ γὰρ ἐλπιεῖ ἐπὶ ἵππον καὶ ἀναβάτην καὶ τόξον,
οὐδὲ πληθυνεῖ αὑτῷ χρυσίον καὶ ἀργύριον εἰς πόλεμον,
καὶ *πλοίοις* οὐ συνάξει ἐλπίδας εἰς ἡμέραν πολέμου.

37 πολλοῖς codd.: ὅπλοις conj. Hilg. (Fritzsch.), idem ἄλλοις, παλτοῖς. πλοίοις nos conj.
ἐλπίδας codd. Hilg.² conj. ἀσπίδας.

Shepherds) σωτήρ, ὅς ἐστιν χριστὸς κύριος. It should be noticed that this part of St Luke's Gospel has a specially hebraistic colouring, and that we are here dealing with an announcement made to men who were expecting a Messiah. It may be argued that the Angel would speak of him in terms corresponding to the expectation of him, and under a name by which he was known.

(5) By way of illustration we may add Is. xlv. 1 οὕτω λέγει κύριος ὁ θεὸς τῷ χριστῷ μου Κύρῳ. For in the Epistle of Barnabas, xii. 11 we find that passage quoted in this form καὶ πάλιν λέγει οὕτως Ἡσαΐας· 'εἶπεν κύριος τῷ χριστῷ μου κυρίῳ.' A corresponding perversion is found in some Latin authorities. Gebhardt and Harnack *in loc.* refer to Tert. *adv. Judaeos* c. 7, *adv. Praxeam* II. 28, Cypr. *Testim.* I. 21. This corruption lends a certain colour to the idea that a Christian scribe has altered a word in our Psalm. It is not absolutely impossible that the change of Κύρῳ to Κυρίῳ may have been made by a Jew, on the authority of Ps. cx.

To summarise our evidence. We find that the expression χριστὸς κύριος is once applied to a king (by mistake), and once to the expected Messiah (in St Luke), that κύριος is possibly twice applied to the Messiah, and, lastly, that χριστὸς κύριος is by no means a distinctively Christian expression, occurring, as it does, only once in N.T.

It may very well be the case, we think, that the phrase is here a correct rendering of the Hebrew, and that the word κύριος represents not, of course, Jehovah, but אדון, a word which might very properly be applied to a supreme conqueror of earthly origin.

(β) The second theory mentioned above has however met with more support than this. It is that the disputed expression is a reminiscence of the LXX. rendering of Lam. iv. 20 (*v. supra*), and that here, as there, the Hebrew original was מְשִׁיחַ יְהוָה, and, consequently, the Greek ought to be χριστὸς κυρίου. The supporters of this theory would for the most part maintain that the *text* should not be altered, but that it is to be regarded as a mistranslation. Those who do not believe in a Hebrew original of the book, see in this mistake a confirmation of their view, holding that the writer is directly quoting the LXX. of Lam. iv. 20. So Hilg., who calls the hypothesis of a mistranslation 'mera hariolatio.'

There is a good deal to be said in favour of this theory. *First*, there is the undoubted rarity of the expression χριστὸς κύριος. *Secondly*, there is the analogy of this same book, Ps. xviii. 6 ἐν ἀνάξει χριστοῦ αὐτοῦ (sc. θεοῦ) and 8. *Thirdly*, the comparative frequency of the phrase χριστὸς κυρίου whether, as in earlier literature, applied to the king (e.g. 2 Sam. i. 14), or, as it was later on, to the Messiah (Luke ii. 26) ἕως ἂν ἴδῃ τὸν Χριστὸν Κυρίου (of Simeon).

This view has the support of Ewald, Hilgenfeld, Geiger, Carrière, Vernes, Wellhausen, Prof. Robertson Smith, and other critics.

(γ) A third hypothesis has to be mentioned. It is that which sees in χριστὸς κύριος either a Christian corruption of χ. κυρίου, or a Christian alteration perhaps of the plain χριστός. This view derives, as we said, a certain support from the quotation found in Barnabas (*v. supra*). But we believe we have shown sufficient reason for thinking that χριστὸς κύριος is by no means an emphatically Christian phrase. It should be borne in mind, moreover, that this is the one and only phrase in the book to which any suspicion of the kind has attached, although few books of the time and class to which this belongs have escaped the charge of Christian interpolation; so that a very strong case would have to be made out before we could admit the validity of the charge here. It would be necessary to show, *inter alia*, why the interpolator did not insert any other single Christian touch into the Psalmist's description: it

XVII. 37]   ΨΑΛΜΟΙ ΣΑΛΟΜΩΝΤΟΣ.   143

37 For he shall not put his trust in horse and rider and bow, nor shall he multiply unto himself gold and silver for war, nor by ships shall he gather confidence for the day of battle.

---

would have been no harder, surely, to insinuate some allusion here to the birth and life of our Lord or to his death, than it was to insert the celebrated words ἀπὸ ξύλου in Ps. xcv. (xcvi.) 10.

It is a little difficult to separate this theory from the last. Several critics (e.g. Geiger) merely believe the translator to have been a Christian; while another (Graetz, *Gesch. d. Juden.* iii. (ed. 2) p. 439 not quoted by Hilg.) used to assign Pss. xvii., xviii. to a Christian author entirely on the strength of this phrase. Obviously the most tenable form is that held by Geiger, although, as we have already said, we do not think that the hypothesis of Christian interference with the text is really needed.

The names Anointed, Christ, Messiah occur with some frequency in the Apocalypses. Enoch 48. 10, 52. 4 (both times in the Parables), 4 Esdr. vii. 28, 9, xii. 32, Apoc. Bar. 29, 3 and often.

37 This verse points to the contrast between the old Solomon and his future antitype, and shows how the latter would obey the letter of the Mosaic Law, and so realise the Pharisaic idea of the good king.

The chief passage in the Law which bears upon this point is Deut. xvii. 16, 17 Διότι οὐ πληθυνεῖ ἑαυτῷ ἵππον...καὶ οὐ πληθυνεῖ ἑαυτῷ γυναῖκας...καὶ ἀργύριον καὶ χρυσίον οὐ πληθυνεῖ ἑαυτῷ σφόδρα.

See also Is. xxxvi. 9 οἱ πεποιθότες ἐπ' Αἰγυπτίοις εἰς ἵππον καὶ ἀναβάτην, and Ps. xliii. (xliv.) 7 οὐ γὰρ ἐπὶ τῷ τόξῳ μου ἐλπιῶ, and, generally, the accounts of Solomon's wealth and splendour in 1 Kings x. Here, as in Deut. xx. 1 and Ezek. xxxix. 20 ἵππον καὶ ἀναβάτην, ἀναβάτην is the rendering of רָכָב 'chariot.'

The last line is the only one which presents any particular difficulty. It will be seen that the MSS. all read πολλοῖς. To this we find ourselves unable to attach a satisfactory sense; it is a very strained phrase if intended to stand for 'multitudes.' Various improvements have been attempted. Geiger's is perhaps as good as any. He thinks the word is a mistranslation of לְרַבִּים = archers, and refers to a similar mistake in Jer. xxvii. (l. Heb.) 29 παραγγείλατε ἐπὶ Βαβυλῶνα πολλοῖς, רַבִּים. We see an objection to this in the fact that it would be a misplaced recurrence to a matter already touched upon (cp. τόξῳ above). Hilgenfeld offers three conjectures, ἄλλοις, παλτοῖς, ὅπλοις, of which the last is adopted by Fritzsche. It may be supported by a reference to 2 Chr. xxxii. 5, where it is said of Hezekiah κατεσκεύασεν ὅπλα πολλά, and to 1 Kings x. where Solomon's ὅπλα χρυσᾶ are described.

We have ventured to suggest πλοίοις as an emendation which comes closest to the 'ductus literarum,' and yields a good sense. The Messiah will not gather 'hopes' (i.e. mercenary troops or supplies) for the day of war in ships.

But we further conjecture that the peculiar expression συνάξει ἐλπίδας is a duplicate rendering, an attempt on the part of the translator to combine the two well known meanings which are found with קוה and its derivatives. Thus συνάξει corresponds to the Niphal usage 'to be gathered together,' ἐλπίδας to the Piel 'to trust.' The substantive מִקְוֶה occurs with the sense of 'hope' in 1 Chron. xxix. 15, Ezr. x. 2, Jer. xiv. 8, xvii. 13, l. 7, and of 'a gathering together' in Gen. i. 10, Ex. vii. 19, Lev. xi. 36, 'a troop' in 1 Kings x. 28. In Jer. l. (xxvii.) 7 מִקְוֵה אֲבוֹתֵיהֶם 'the hope of their fathers,' the LXX. version gives τῷ συναγαγόντι τοὺς πατέρας αὐτῶν, apparently reading מְקַוֶּה. Similarly the present passage preserves the translator's uncertainty between the vocalization of מִקְוֶה (=συνάξει) and מִקְוָה (ἐλπίδας). Compare Zech. ix. 12 אֲסִירֵי הַתִּקְוָה = LXX. δέσμιοι τῆς συναγωγῆς.

Foreign *commerce* had been a foremost source of strength and also of weakness to Solomon, and naval *warfare* had become prominent since his time; to either of these one might expect an allusion here. The various 'sinews of war' would then be all represented in the verse. Recent events would have impressed upon the Jews the importance of naval strength. Pompey's victories in the East had been

⁸⁸κύριος αὐτὸς βασιλεὺς αὐτοῦ, ἐλπὶς τοῦ δυνατοῦ ἐλπίδι θεοῦ,

καὶ ἐλεήσει πάντα τὰ ἔθνη ἐνώπιον αὐτοῦ ἐν φόβῳ·
³⁹πατάξει γὰρ γῆν τῷ λόγῳ τοῦ ϲτόματοϲ αὐτοῦ εἰς αἰῶνα,
⁴⁰εὐλογήσει λαὸν κυρίου ἐν σοφίᾳ μετ' εὐφροσύνης.
⁴¹καὶ αὐτὸς καθαρὸς ἀπὸ ἁμαρτίας τοῦ ἄρχειν λαοῦ μεγάλου, ἐλέγξαι ἄρχοντας καὶ ἐξᾶραι ἁμαρτωλοὺς ἐν ἰσχύϊ λόγου.
⁴²καὶ οὐκ ἀσθενήσει ἐν ταῖς ἡμέραις αὐτοῦ ἐπὶ θεῷ αὐτοῦ, ὅτι ὁ θεὸς κατειργάσατο αὐτὸν δυνατὸν ἐν πνεύματι ἁγίῳ, καὶ ϲοφὸν ἐν βουλῇ ϲυνέϲεωϲ μετ' ἰϲχύοϲ καὶ Δικαιοϲύνηϲ.
⁴³καὶ εὐλογία κυρίου μετ' αὐτοῦ ἐν ἰσχύϊ, καὶ οὐκ ἀσθενήσει ἡ ἐλπὶς αὐτοῦ ἐπὶ κύριον,
⁴⁴καὶ τίς δύναται πρὸς αὐτόν;
ἰσχυρὸς ἐν ἔργοις αὐτοῦ καὶ κραταιὸς ἐν φόβῳ θεοῦ,
⁴⁵ποιμαίνων τὸ ποιμνίον κυρίου ἐν πίστει καὶ δικαιοσύνῃ, καὶ οὐκ ἀφήσει ἀσθενῆσαι ἐν αὐτοῖς ἐν τῇ νομῇ αὐτῶν.

38 ἐλεήσει codd.; στήσει Hilg. conj., ita Fritzsch. Pick. ἐλέγξει Schmidt ap. Hilg.²
41 ἐξάραι codd. ἐξᾶραι, Hilg.
43 οὐκ ἀσθενήσει. ἡ ἐλπὶς (M ita interpung.).
44 δυνατεῖ conj. Hilg.

---

preceded by the success of his armada over the pirates that had been the terror of shipping in the Eastern Mediterranean.

Thus Hyrcanus before Pompey complains that his brother Aristobulus had stirred up 'piratical expeditions by sea' (τὰ πειρατήρια τὰ ἐν θαλάττῃ τοῦτον εἶναι τὸν συστήσαντα, Jos. *Ant.* XIV. iii. 2).

Hilg. refers to 4 Esr. xiii. 9 'non levavit manum suam neque frameam tenebat neque aliquod vas bellicosum.'

A further suggestion (due to Hilgenfeld), that for ἐλπίδας we should read ἀσπίδας, need not be considered more particularly.

38 κύριος αὐτὸς κ.τ.λ., see on v. 1.
ἐλπὶς κ.τ.λ. Here again we have a difficult expression, which, if the Greek may be taken as a fair equivalent of the original Hebrew, can be explained on the analogy of ἀνδρὸς ἐν εὐσταθείᾳ (iv. 11) etc., the words δυνατοῦ ἐλπίδι θεοῦ being taken as one expression, equivalent to δυνατοῦ διὰ τῆς ἐπὶ τὸν θεὸν ἐλπίδος. This may seem a strained construction. Geiger restores the original Hebrew, and renders it 'Gott lässt den Starken ungefährdet weilen.' Wellhausen assumes a different grouping of the words in the original, and renders 'Der Herr ist König, das ist sein Vertrauen, er ist stark in der Hoffnung auf Gott, der wird Gnade geben. Alle Völker werden vor ihm in Furcht sein.'

ἐλεήσει. This, the reading of the MSS., yields, we think, a preferable sense to the less decided στήσει of Hilgenfeld (Fritzsche etc.). The author does not here or elsewhere mean to devote the Gentiles to entire reprobation. This again is a note of early date.

ἐλέγξει, the conjecture of Schmidt, is ingenious; but we find ἐλέγξαι in vv. 27 and 41 used of ἁμαρτωλοί and ἄρχοντες, not of ἔθνη. If any change in the text were needed to give the idea of ver. 27 ὀλοθρεῦσαι ἔθνη παράνομα, we might sug-

38 The LORD himself is his King, and the hope of him that is strong in the hope of God.

And he shall have mercy upon all the nations *that come* before him in fear.

39 For he shall smite the earth with the word of his mouth even for evermore.

40 He shall bless the people of the LORD with wisdom and gladness.

41 He himself also is pure from sin, so that he may rule a mighty people, and rebuke princes and overthrow sinners by the might of his word.

42 And he shall not faint all his days, *because he leaneth* upon his God; for God shall cause[15] him to be mighty through the spirit of holiness, and wise through the counsel of understanding, with might and righteousness.

[15] Gr. *caused*

43 And the blessing of the LORD is with him in might, and his hope in the LORD shall not faint.

44 And who can stand up against him? *he is* mighty in his works and strong in the fear of God,

45 Tending the flock of the LORD with faith and righteousness; and he shall suffer none among them to faint in their pasture.

---

gest ἀλοήσει = triturabit. But the ἔθνη here are not παράνομα, and mercy to the Gentile is an independent and original thought.

39 Verbally taken from Is. xi. 4. For the literal interpretation see 4 Esdr. xiii. and later Apocalypses. The words εἰς αἰῶνα are added after the fashion of our Psalmist, in order slightly to vary the borrowed words.

41 καθαρός. Geiger cites Prov. xx. 9 (τίς παρρησιάσεται καθαρὸς εἶναι ἀπὸ ἁμαρτιῶν;) and Job xiv. 4. Another point of contrast to the old heroes of the Jewish monarchy, David and Solomon. 'He that ruleth over men must be just, ruling in the fear of God.'

ἐλέγξαι. So above, v. 24, and Is. xi. 3, 4.

42 ἐν πνεύματι ἁγίῳ. This expression conveys, as Geiger says, no idea of a personal being; it is explained further on in the same verse by βουλὴ συνέσεως, and most fully by a reference to Is. xi. 2 πνεῦμα τοῦ θεοῦ πνεῦμα σοφίας καὶ συνέσεως, πνεῦμα βουλῆς καὶ ἰσχύος, πνεῦμα γνώσεως καὶ εὐσεβείας. The expression occurs in the LXX. several times, Is. lxiii. 10, 11; Dan. iv. 5, vi. 15; Susanna 44.

The rest of the verse is a paraphrase of Is. xi. 2.

44 τίς δύναται πρός. Cf. xv. 2, 3. κραταιὸς ἐν φ'βῳ κυρίου. Ps. xxv. (xxiv.) 14 κραταίωμα κύριος τῶν φοβουμένων αὐτόν.

45 ποιμαίνων. The King as shepherd of his people. This idea appears not unfrequently in the Old Testament, e.g. in Micaiah's vision, 1 Kings xxii., Zech. xi. Jehovah or the Messiah is more often thought of under this image. Cf. Ps. xxiii., Is. xl. 11 ὡς ποιμὴν ποιμανεῖ τὸ ποίμνιον αὐτοῦ, and Ez. xxxiv. passim. Micah v. 4 καὶ ποιμανεῖ τὸ ποίμνιον αὐτοῦ ἐν ἰσχύϊ κύριος.

It is interesting too to make the obvious comparison between this and our Lord's description of Himself as the shepherd.

In Enoch's vision (c. 90) the Messiah is himself one of the herd, its protector and leader.

ἀσθενῆσαι. Cf. Ps. cv. (civ.) 37 οὐκ ἦν ἐν ταῖς φυλαῖς αὐτῶν ἀσθενῶν.

⁴⁶ ἐν ὁσιότητι πάντας αὐτοὺς ἄξει,
καὶ οὐκ ἔσται ἐν αὐτοῖς ὑπερηφανία τοῦ καταδυναστευθῆναι
  ἐν αὐτοῖς.

⁴⁷ Αὕτη ἡ εὐπρέπεια τοῦ βασιλέως Ἰσραήλ, ἣν ἔγνω ὁ θεός,
ἀναστῆσαι αὐτὸν ἐπ' Ἰσραήλ, παιδεῦσαι αὐτόν.
⁴⁸ τὰ ῥήματα αὐτοῦ πεπυρωμένα ὑπὲρ χρυcίον τίμιον τὸ
   πρῶτον,
ἐν συναγωγαῖς διακρινεῖ λαοὺς, φυλὰς ἡγιασμένων·
⁴⁹ οἱ λόγοι αὐτοῦ ὡς λόγοι ἁγίων ἐν μέσῳ λαῶν ἡγιασμένων.
⁵⁰ μακάριοι οἱ γινόμενοι ἐν ταῖς ἡμέραις ἐκείναις,
ἰδεῖν τὰ ἀγαθὰ Ἰσραὴλ ἐν συναγωγῇ φυλῶν, ἃ ποιήσει ὁ
   θεός.
⁵¹ ταχύναι ὁ θεὸς ἐπὶ Ἰσραὴλ τὸ ἔλεος αὐτοῦ,
ῥύσεται ἡμᾶς ἀπὸ ἀκαθαρσίας ἐχθρῶν βεβήλων.
κγριοc αὐτὸς Βαcιλεγc ἡμῶν εἰc τὸν αἰῶνα καὶ ἔτι.

46 ἄξει A, V, K, M. αὔξει P.
47 ἀναστῆσαι codd. ἀναστῆναι Fabr. ἀναστήσαι Hilg. etc.
51 ῥύσεται codd. Fabr. conj. ῥύσαι. Fritzsch. conj. ῥύσαιτο.

---

46 There will be no further oppression from the wicked Sadducaean 'shepherds.' Cf. Ez. xlv. 8 καὶ οὐ καταδυναστεύσουσιν οὐκέτι οἱ ἀφηγούμενοι τοῦ Ἰσραὴλ τὸν λαόν μου.

πάντας αὐτούς. A literal rendering of כֻּלָּם cf. xviii. 9.

The reading of P, αὔξει for ἄξει, introduces a fresh and a less appropriate metaphor. Num. xxxiv. 7 καὶ αὐξηθήσεται βασιλεία αὐτοῦ.

47 Αὕτη ἡ εὐπρέπεια. Perhaps there is a conscious reference to Samuel's words (1 Sam. viii. 11), 'This will be the manner of the king that shall reign over you.' The word εὐπρέπεια is probably a reminiscence of Ps. xcii. (xciii. 1) ὁ κύριος ἐβασίλευσεν, εὐπρέπειαν ἐνεδύσατο; see Ps. S. ii. 21.

παιδεῦσαι αὐτόν, sc. τὸν οἶκον Ἰσραήλ.

48, 49 are an amplification of the word παιδεῦσαι. The people will be chastened and kept pure by the divine purity of their ruler.

πεπυρωμένα. Cf. 2 Sam. xxii. 31 (Ps. xviii. 31) τὸ ῥῆμα κυρίου κραταιὸν πεπυρωμένον, Prov. xxx. 5. Ps. xviii. (xix.) 11 ἐπιθυμητὰ ὑπὲρ χρυσίον καὶ λίθον τίμιον πολύν. Comp. also Ps. xi. (xii.) 7, cxviii. (cxix.) 139; Prov. viii. 10 ὑπὲρ χρυσίον δεδοκιμασμένον, 19 ὑπὲρ χρυσίον καὶ λίθον τίμιον.

For τὸ πρῶτον, probably a duplicate rendering of τίμιον, cf. Sym. Ps. cxviii. (cxix.) 128 χρυσίον πρωτεῖον (מִזָּהָב וּמִפָּז).

ἐν συναγωγαῖς. 'Assemblies' for the purpose of judgment, instruction, and the like, not technically used. Deut. xxxiii. 5 κληρονομίαν συναγωγαῖς Ἰακώβ. Geiger well compares Ps. lxxxi. (lxxxii.) 1.

διακρινεῖ, as Ps. xlix. (l.) 4. See also Joel iii. 12; Gen. xlix. 16; Ez. xlvii. 22.

φυλάς. Cf. our Lord's promise to the Twelve, Luke xxii. 30.

It may be questioned whether ἐν συναγωγαῖς is not a wrong translation, the translator reading בְּעֵדֹת which, if read בְּעֵדוּת, would give the sense of 'by means of the testimony,' i.e. the Law. This would assert the Law to be the Messianic rule of judgment.

49 λόγοι ἁγίων. No doubt, as former critics have said, ἅγιοι here are the angels. Ps. lxxxviii. (lxxxix.) 6 ἐν ἐκκλησίᾳ ἁγίων, 8 ἐν βουλῇ ἁγίων. Dan. iv. 10, 14 εἱρ καὶ ἅγιος, ῥῆμα ἁγίων. Job v. 1 ἀγγέλων ἁγίων (קְדֹשִׁים), xv. 15 κατὰ

ΨΑΛΜΟΙ ΣΑΛΟΜΩΝΤΟΣ.

46 In holiness shall he lead them all, and there shall no pride be among them that any should be oppressed.

47 This is the majesty of the king of Israel, which[16] God hath appointed[17] to raise him up over *the house of* Israel, to instruct him.

[16] Perh. *whom*
[17] Gr. *knew*

48 His words shall be purified above fine gold, *yea, above* the choicest *gold*.
In the congregations will he judge among the peoples, the tribes of them that have been sanctified.

49 His words shall be as the words of the holy ones in the midst of the peoples that have been sanctified.

50 Blessed are they that shall be born in those days, to behold the blessing of Israel which God shall bring to pass in the gathering together of the tribes.

51 May God hasten his mercy toward Israel! may he[18] deliver us from the abomination of unhallowed adversaries!

[18] Gr. *he will*

The LORD, he is our king from henceforth and even for evermore.

ἁγίων. Deut. xxxiii. 2 'ten thousands of holy ones.' Cf. Enoch i. 9.

50 In this verse Hilg. sees an indication that our author knew the third (oldest) book of the Sibylline oracles, and consequently wrote in Greek. Sib. or. iii. 371 ὦ μακάριστος, ἐκεῖνον ὃς ἐς χρόνον ἔσσεται ἀνήρ. But surely the sentiment is a very common one. It recurs in xviii. 7. Cp. Ps. cxxvii. (cxxviii.) 5 ἴδοις τὰ ἀγαθὰ Ἰερουσαλήμ etc. Dan. xii. 12 μακάριος ὁ ὑπομένων καὶ φθάσας. Eccls. xlviii. 11.

51 There seems no occasion for Fritzsche's correction of ῥύσεται to ῥύσαιτο. Geiger calls the Heb. original a precatory Imperf. יַצֵּל, cf. Ps. xvii. (xviii.) 18—20. Notice the prominence given to the 'uncleanness of the oppressors.'

The Psalm ends with the same thought that began it. The Lord is the true King of Israel, whoever may be its temporary rulers.

Ps. XVIII. *Argument.*
1—5. God is loving to Israel. It is as their Father that He punishes them for their good.
6—10. May this correction avail to cleanse them in the day of visitation, when the Anointed shall rule over them in the fear of God.
(11—14) xix. 1—3. The praise of God, whose might is seen in the order of creation. The stars in their courses obey Him......

This psalm—especially vv. 6—10 of it—is closely connected with the last. The same expressions recur, χριστὸς κυρίου (-ος) xvii. 36. σοφία, δικαιοσύνη, ἰσχὺς xvii. 25, 31, 42. ῥάβδος xvii. 26. καθαρίσαι etc. xvii. 25, 33. μακάριοι etc. xvii. 50. φόβῳ θεοῦ xvii. 44, and compare xviii. 9 with xvii. 38.

The first section of the Psalm (vv. 1—5) reminds us of Ps. v. more particularly. Comp. v. 13, 16, 17 with xviii. 1—3.

In verse 4 we have an expression reminding us of xiii. 8.

The first two sections of the Psalm are logically enough connected. After ver. 10 however there is a complete change of subject. And the new subject is never brought into any semblance of connection with what has preceded, but is left hanging in the air. No one will, we think, be able to resist the impression that the Psalm as it stands is a fragment. The further question has occurred to us: is it one fragment or two? It will be seen that we think this latter alternative highly probable, and have suggested as

ιη. ψαλμὸς τῷι σαλομὼν ἐπὶ τοῦ χριστοῦ κυρίου.

XVIII. Κύριε, τὸ ἔλεός σου ἐπὶ τὰ ἔργα τῶν χειρῶν
σου εἰς τὸν αἰῶνα,
² ἡ χρηστότης σου μετὰ δόματος πλουσίου ἐπὶ Ἰσραήλ·
οἱ ὀφθαλμοί σου ἐπιβλέποντες ἐπ' αὐτά, καὶ οὐχ ὑστερήσει
ἐξ αὐτῶν,
³ τὰ ὦτά σου ἐπακούσει εἰς δέησιν πτωχοῦ ἐν ἐλπίδι·
τὰ κρίματά σου ἐπὶ πᾶσαν τὴν γῆν μετ' ἐλέου,
⁴ καὶ ἡ ἀγάπη σου ἐπὶ σπέρμα Ἀβραάμ, υἱοὺς Ἰσραήλ·
ἡ παιδεία σου ἐφ' ἡμᾶς ὡς υἱὸν πρωτότοκον μονογενῆ,
⁵ ἀποστρέψαι ψυχὴν ὑπήκοον ἀπὸ ἀμαθίας ἐν ἀγνοίᾳ.

⁶ Καθαρίσαι ὁ θεὸς Ἰσραὴλ εἰς ἡμέραν ἐλέου ἐν εὐλογίᾳ,
εἰς ἡμέραν ἐκλογῆς ἐν ἀνάξει χριστοῦ αὐτοῦ.

Inscriptio deest in M.
2 ἐξ αὐτῶν ἕν vel τι ἐξ αὐτῶν conj. Hilg.²
4 codd. υἱοῦ. Fabr. υἱούς, ita edd.
5 ἀμαθίας V, K, P, M, Hilg. ἁμαρτίας A (Cerda 'ab imperitia'). ἁμαρτίας Fabr. (notat "Gr. *a peccato*") Fritzsch.
ἀγνοίᾳ. ἀνοίᾳ M.

much in the text. Against this idea it may be urged that a διάψαλμα is inserted by all MSS. save *one* (M), and that that one's evidence is invalidated by the fact that it omits all titles and subscriptions. We at once admit the practical absence of external support, for we lay little stress on the evidence of M. It seems to treat the verses in question exactly as it does the 2nd half (23—51) of Ps. xvii. But we find it difficult to conceive how the subject of the last verses is to be brought round to that of the first: we cannot help seeing that vv. 1—10 form a complete whole 'teres atque rotundus,' and we find no such complete change of subject introduced in any other of these Psalms as is entailed here. We think it highly probable that at least a leaf had disappeared at the end of the archetype of our present copies, and very likely much more than a leaf. Such an archetype would of course represent an earlier stage of the text than did the Codex Alexandrinus. The one fact we know about that copy is that it contained eighteen Psalms and no more.

We are not however inclined to insist that the 'xix[th]' Psalm must necessarily be divorced from the xviii[th]: we lay far more stress on the assertion that that Psalm as we have it is incomplete.

1 The first five verses are composed chiefly of what may be called the commonplaces of these Psalms. Most of the phrases can be paralleled from the Old Testament, and most of the parallels have already been cited more than once. Thus for ver. 1 we have Ps. cxliv. (cxlv.) 9 οἱ οἰκτιρμοὶ αὐτοῦ ἐπὶ πάντα τὰ ἔργα αὐτοῦ.

2 For verse 2 see Ps. S. v. 16. Ps. xi. 5 οἱ ὀφθαλμοὶ αὐτοῦ εἰς τὸν πένητα ἀποβλέπουσιν. Zech. iv. 10.

The words καὶ οὐχ ὑστερήσει ἐξ αὐτῶν are capable of bearing two meanings, 'there shall none of them come to want,' or 'be lacking.' The latter is perhaps commoner in the LXX. and the former more probable here, cf. Ps. xxii. (xxiii.) 1 οὐδέν με ὑστερήσει, lxxxiii. (lxxxiv.) 11 οὐχ ὑστερήσει τὰ ἀγαθὰ τοῖς πορευομένοις ἐν ἀκακίᾳ, as against Ps. xxxiii. (xxxiv.) 10 οὐκ ἔστιν ὑστέρημα τοῖς φοβουμένοις αὐτόν, which represents what we take to be the sense of the verse before us.

3 Cf. Ps. xxxiii. (xxxiv.) 16 τὰ ὦτα αὐτοῦ εἰς δέησιν αὐτοῦ, 2 Chron. vi. 40 τὰ

PSALM XVIII.

A Psalm of Solomon touching the Lord Messiah.

1 O LORD, thy mercy is upon the works of thine hands for ever.

2 Thy goodness is upon Israel with a bounteous gift: yea thine eyes look upon thy works¹ and none of them shall come to want. [1 Gr. *them* (n. pl.)]

3 Thine ears will hearken unto the prayer of the needy that hopeth *in thee;* thy judgments are upon all the earth with mercy.

4 And thy love is toward² the seed of Abraham, even the sons of Israel: thy chastening is upon us as upon a firstborn son only-begotten, [2 Gr. *upon*]

5 To convert the soul that is obedient from simpleness and from sins of ignorance³.

6 The LORD cleanse Israel for the day when he shall have mercy upon them and shall bless them⁴: even for the day of his appointing when he shall bring back⁵ his anointed.

[3 Gr. *from simplicity (or sin) in ignorance*]
[4 Gr. *day of mercy in blessing.*]
[5 Gr. *day of choosing in bringing back*]

ὦτά σου ἐπήκοα εἰς τὴν δέησιν τοῦ τόπου τούτου.

ἐπακούσει. Strictly we should have expected ἐπακούσεται, but it is probable that the text here is correct. It is known that the active form ἀκούσω is a feature of Alexandrine Greek. It is found—though not universally—in the LXX. (Is. vi. 9 ἀκοῇ ἀκούσετε etc.), and sometimes in N.T. We cannot cite examples of ἐπακούσω, but there is no reason why the form used for the simple verb should not have been extended to its compounds. See Winer, Gr. of N.T. Gk. p. 99.

Hilg. in loc. cites Ex. iv. 22 υἱὸς πρωτότοκός μου Ἰσραήλ, and 4 Esdr. vi. 58 nos autem populus tuus quem vocasti primogenitum, unigenitum, aemulatorem carissimum. This last passage is particularly noteworthy.

πτωχοῦ ἐν ἐλπίδι, probably another parallel to ἀνδρὸς ἐν εὐσταθείᾳ iv. 11, meaning 'the needy that hopeth in thee.'

4 Cf. xiii. 8 and the passages (already cited) in Ps. lxxxviii. (lxxxix.) 27 κἀγὼ πρωτότοκον θήσομαι αὐτόν, xxi. (xxii.) 21 ἐκ χειρὸς κυνὸς τὸν μονογενῆ μου, Ecclus. xxxvi. 12 Ἰσραὴλ ὃν πρωτογόνῳ ὡμοίωσας.

5 ὑπήκοος, used, it seems, only in Proverbs by the LXX. Another instance of parallelism of language between these books.

ἀποστρέψαι, cf. Ez. xxxiii. 14 ἀποστρέψει ἀπὸ τῆς ἁμαρτίας αὐτοῦ.

ἀμαθίας. This is practically the reading of all MSS. If A is correctly represented by Cerda, which may be considered doubtful, still its reading ἁμαρθίας retains the characteristic of ἀμαθίας; and Cerda's rendering 'imperitia' seems to show that he understood this latter word to be intended. Most likely ἁμαρτίας is a misprint. The meaning of ἀπὸ ἀμαθίας ἐν ἀγνοίᾳ seems to be that the unlearnedness of the soul is exemplified by the sins of ignorance which it commits. Here compare xiii. 6.

For ἀμαθία see Sym. Prov. xiv. 24 אִוֶּלֶת, Eccles. ii. 13 סִכְלוּת. Cf. ἀμαθὴς Sym. Ps. xlviii. 11 בַּעַר.

6 The ἡμέρα ἐλέου and ἡμέρα ἐκλογῆς refer to the same thing considered in two different aspects. The first is the ἡμέρα ἐλέου δικαίων of xiv. 6, the day when God will visit and have mercy on the righteous: it is therefore seen here from the point of view of those visited. The other expression refers to the same day looked upon from God's point of view. ἡμέρα ἐκλογῆς = καιρὸς ὃν οἶδας σύ, ὁ θεός (xvii. 23).

ἐν ἀνάξει χριστοῦ αὐτοῦ. The verse just cited (xvii. 23) contains in its earlier clause what is probably the best

⁷ μακάριοι οἱ γινόμενοι ἐν ταῖς ἡμέραις ἐκείναις
Ἰδεῖν τὰ ἀγαθὰ κυρίου, ἃ ποιήσει γενεᾷ τῇ ἐρχομένῃ,
⁸ ὑπὸ ῥάβδον παιδείας χριϲτοῦ κυρίου ἐν φόβῳ θεοῦ αὐτοῦ,
ἐν ϲοφίᾳ πνεύματοϲ καὶ δικαιοϲύνηϲ καὶ ἰϲχύοϲ,
⁹ κατευθῦναι ἄνδρα ἐν ἔργοις δικαιοσύνης φόβῳ θεοῦ,
καταστῆσαι πάντας αὐτοὺς ἐν φόβῳ κυρίου.
¹⁰ γενεὰ ἀγαθὴ ἐν φόβῳ θεοῦ ἐν ἡμέραις ἐλέου. Διάψαλμα.

[**XIX.**] ¹⁽¹¹⁾ Μέγας ὁ θεὸς ἡμῶν καὶ ἔνδοξος ἐν ὑψίστοις κατοικῶν,

9 καταστῆσαι ita A, V, K, P (sed Cerda in Gr. καταστῆπαι). Fabr. καταστῆναι. καταστήσαι M. ita Hilg. Fr. (Pick.).
κυρίου. M κυρίῳ.
10 M om. διάψαλμα sed ita interpungit quasi Psalmus his verbis finiretur, et sequentem versum litera majuscula inchoat.

---

commentary on this interesting phrase. Ἀνάστησον αὐτοῖς τὸν βασιλέα αὐτῶν, υἱὸν Δαυίδ etc. But ἄναξις, the word used here, is a more definite one than the ἀνάστησον of that passage. We are at liberty to assign to it a somewhat more precise meaning, that namely of 'bringing again' or 'bringing up,' which our text and margin suggest. The first of these renderings would indicate a belief on the part of the writer in a doctrine which we know to have been anterior to his time—the pre-existence of the Messiah. Such a belief is first hinted at in Dan. vii. 13, and is plainly stated in the 2nd Parable of Enoch (xlviii. 3), whatever may be the date of that document. 4 Esdr. vii. 28, xii. 32, xiii. 26 etc. intimate a similar belief, without dwelling on it, and later instances might be multiplied. Those given cover our period. The present passage is at most only a hint of the writer's belief.

The Messianic ideas of the xviith Psalm, however, show no trace of any mystical doctrine of the kind, if we except the difficult phrase χριστὸς κύριος. They resemble closely those of Enoch (the First Book, c. xc. 37, 38), among later writers, and of the first part of Isaiah, among earlier ones. The Messiah is, as we have seen, the conquering hero and restorer of the nation, sprung of David's line. He is taught of God, anointed of God, full of the spirit of God, it is true; but of any closer relationship, of any superhuman origin, there is not a word. Yet in the xviith Psalm the Messiah and his times are so fully treated that, if the writer entertained a belief that the deliverer was more than man, he certainly ought to have said so. In the face of such an omission we find it difficult to believe that the single word ἄναξις here contains all that the writer had to say on so important a subject. We are compelled to believe that ἄναξις is simply a rather more detailed equivalent of ἀνάστησον, and that any such thought as that of 'bringing the first-begotten again into the world' is inadmissible here.

χριστοῦ αὐτοῦ. On the relation of this phrase to χριστὸς κύριος see on xvii. 36.

7 Cf. xvii. 50 and reff. there.
γενεᾷ τῇ ἐρχομένῃ. Cf. Ps. xxi. (xxii.) 31, 32 ἀναγγελήσεται τῷ κυρίῳ ἡ γενεὰ ἐρχομένη (לדור: יבוא), lxx. (lxxi.) 18 ἕως ἂν ἀπαγγείλω...τῇ γενεᾷ τῇ ἐρχομένῃ (לדור לכל יבוא), (4) 5 Esdr. i. 35 testor populi venientis gratiam, and 37. The analogy of these expressions and of the technical Hebrew phrase הָעוֹלָם הַבָּא = 'aevum veniens' forbids us to join the three last words of ver. 7 with ver. 8 and construe ἐρχομένῃ ὑπὸ ῥάβδον, as Fritzsche's punctuation would lead us to do.

8 ὑπὸ ῥάβδον. Our objection to Wellhausen's ingenious rendering "An Stelle der Zuchtruthe tritt der Gesalbte des Herrn" (which assumes that ὑπὸ

ΨΑΛΜΟΙ ΣΑΛΟΜΩΝΤΟΣ.

7 Blessed are they that shall be in those days: for they shall see the goodness of the LORD which he shall bring to pass for the generation that cometh,

8 Under the rod of the chastening of the LORD'S anointed[6] in the fear of his God: in the spirit of wisdom and of righteousness and of might,

[6] Or, *Lord Messiah*

9 To direct *every* man in the works of righteousness with the fear of God; to stablish them all in the fear of the LORD,

10 Yea *to make them* a good generation in the fear of God in the days of his mercy. Selah.

[XIX.]

1 (11) Great is our God and glorious, dwelling in the highest,

---

= נחה should have been translated ἀντί) lies in the erroneous conception of the Messiah that results from it. It will be remembered that in Ps. S. xvii. 26, 47 the Messiah is to wield the rod of chastening against Jew and Gentile alike. In our view the verse simply extends the description of "the coming generation" which will be subject to "the rod of chastening," as indeed the subsequent verses clearly indicate. We believe that this clause is connected with the preceding rather κατὰ σύνεσιν than in any more formal way. The best parallel expression is to be found in vii. 8 καὶ ἡμεῖς ὑπὸ ζυγόν σου [εἰς] τὸν αἰῶνα, etc. The auxiliary verb ἔσονται has to be supplied here, and no verb of motion (such as ἐρχομένῃ) is needed.

The grammatical construction is of the loosest kind, and must be explained upon the principle of coordination not of subordination of sentences.

χριστοῦ κυρίου. See on xvii. 36.

ἐν σοφίᾳ πνεύματος. The rendering of these words in their present order is out of the question. Whatever meaning they do yield is practically identical with that in our text. We hardly think that an original reading ἐν πνεύματι σοφίας ever existed, but obviously that is what is required in translating.

9 κατευθῦναι... καταστῆσαι. Hilg. and Fritzsche take these verbs as Optatives. We believe them to be Infinitives, on the ground that, when a wish is expressed, this writer most frequently inserts the subject.

The actions of individuals are to be directed by the coming Deliverer, and thus the whole community is to be brought into the condition of fearing the Lord. The second clause is consequent upon the first.

πάντας αὐτούς. Cf. xvii. 46. A brief indication of the general result.

10 γενεὰ ἀγαθή perhaps in loose apposition to πάντας αὐτούς.

[Ps. XIX.]

1 (11) The theme of the order and regularity of Creation, especially as seen in the movements of the heavenly bodies, is a favourite one with Jewish writers. The conception of any physical law restraining or ordering their movements is not natural to the mind of man in a primitive state. Doubtless the stars were looked upon in the first instance as divinities possessing volition and personality. They went in their particular course because they liked it: and there was no reason why they should not deviate from it or move in another direction. They influenced the minds and destinies of men, and were themselves subject to interruptions in their courses, whether from the attacks of the Great Dragon (Job iii. 8) or from other causes.

But soon it was realised that the movements of the stars could not possibly be regarded as arbitrary, and that some superior intelligence was directing their movements: and the next stage of belief concerning them, which does not materially differ from our own, is probably represented by the familiar name of Jehovah Sabaoth, the Lord of hosts. The hosts are in all probability the sentient armies of heaven marshalled and directed by the constant care of Jehovah. But

² ⁽¹²⁾ ὁ διατάξας ἐν πορείᾳ φωστῆρας εἰς καιροὺς ὡρῶν ἀφ'
    ἡμερῶν εἰς ἡμέρας,
καὶ οὐ παρέβησαν ἀπὸ ὁδοῦ ἣν ἐνετείλω αὐτοῖς.
³ ⁽¹³⁾ ἐν φόβῳ θεοῦ ἡ ὁδὸς αὐτῶν καθ' ἑκάστην ἡμέραν,
ἀφ' ἧς ἡμέρας ἔκτισεν αὐτοὺς ὁ θεὸς καὶ ἕως αἰῶνος,
⁴ ⁽¹⁴⁾ καὶ οὐκ ἐπλανήθησαν ἀφ' ἧς ἡμέρας ἔκτισεν αὐτούς·
ἀπὸ γενεῶν ἀρχαίων οὐκ ἀπέστησαν ἀπὸ ὁδοῦ αὐτῶν,
εἰ μὴ ὁ θεὸς ἐνετείλατο αὐτοῖς ἐν ἐπιταγῇ δούλων αὐτοῦ.

ψαλμοὶ σολομῶντος
ιη· ἔχουσιν ἔπη α.

2 (12) πορείᾳ. κυρείᾳ A.
ἥν. ἧς K, M.
3 (13) καὶ ἕως αἰῶνος V, K, P, M. om. ἕως A, et edd.
4 (14) ἐπιταγῇ. Cerda ἐπεταγῇ.

Subscriptio.

A, V, K, Ψαλμοὶ Σαλομῶντος (Σολ. K), ιη'. ἔχουσιν ἔπη ͺα. τέλος σὺν θεῷ (om. K, V). om. subscriptionem M.

P Ψαλμοὶ σολομῶντος δεκαοκτω ἔχουσιν ἔπη τριάκοντα. (scilicet Λ pro A legit).

---

still they are thought of as possessing life and will of their own, and as being capable of disobedience to their Ruler. Comp. Ps. cxlvii. 4 He telleth the number of the stars: he calleth them all by their names; Is. xl. 26 He calleth them all by name...not one faileth; also Baruch iii. 33—4; Ecclus. xliii. 5—7, 10. For the disobedient stars, the ἀστέρες πλανῆται of Jude 13 see Enoch xviii. 12—16 (15) 'The stars that roll over the fire are they that have transgressed the command of God before their rising, because they did not come forth in their time.' Cf. also xxi. 3—6.

The next stage of the conception is that which regards the stars as in the charge of angels, but as being themselves inanimate bodies. This is the view we find in the second great section of the Book of Enoch, that of the Parables (xliii. 2, 'these come according to the number of angels'). The first writer of Enoch does indeed partly lean towards this theory in so far that he assigns a particular leader, Uriel, to all the heavenly bodies.

It seems at first sight that the view which identified stars with angels must be a reversion to the earliest conception, but we believe that in reality it is a late view and grew out of the belief mentioned just above which assigned particular stars to particular angels. We are not certain how far it is to be pressed as affecting the interpretation of Rev. i. 20 "The seven stars are the angels of the seven churches." But we think that at any rate the view set forth in the Enochian Parables must have some bearing on that verse.

But the main point which deserves notice in connection with this passage of the Psalm is the similarity of the language here with that of the Parables of Enoch, especially c. xli. 5 'I saw...the

XIX. 4]   ΨΑΛΜΟΙ ΣΑΛΟΜΩΝΤΟΣ.   153

2 (12) Even he that hath appointed the lights of heaven in their course unto times of seasons from everlasting unto everlasting[1]: and they have not transgressed from the path which thou didst command them.

[1] Gr. *from day to day*

3 (13) In the fear of God is their course every day, since the day when God created them even unto everlasting,

4 (14) And they have not erred since the day when he created them: from the generations of old they have not departed from their path, except God commanded them at the precept of his servants.

---

sun and moon...and their fixed course, and how they do not leave their course, and how they add nothing to their course, and take nothing from it, and preserve their fidelity one with the other, remaining steadfast in their oaths.' It seems most likely that both writers drew a distinction between the two great luminaries and the body of the stars, regarding the former as personalities, the latter as inanimate. In any case, we feel that the author of the Parables and the author of our Psalm are moving in much the same circle of ideas.

φωστῆρας. This is the word used of the sun and moon in Gen. i. 14, as distinct from the stars. It occurs again (of the moon) in Ecclus. xliii. 7. In Wisd. xiii. 2 we find φωστῆρας οὐρανοῦ distinguished from κύκλον ἄστρων. In Phil. ii. 15 (ὡς φωστῆρες ἐν κόσμῳ), and Rev. xxi. 11 (ὁ φωστὴρ αὐτῆς), the application is less distinct. But in Test. xii. Patr., Levi 14, we have a good instance of the specific use, ὑμεῖς οἱ φωστῆρες τοῦ οὐρανοῦ, ὡς ὁ ἥλιος καὶ ἡ σελήνη. Cp. Judah 25. Aquila uses the word, and had we the Greek of Enoch it would doubtless be common in that book. The passages quoted point to the fact that here our author is referring specially to the sun and moon.

πορεία, used of the sun in Ecclus. xliii. 5. Cf. Hab. iii. 6 πορείας αἰωνίας αὐτοῦ. For the whole verse cf. Apoc. Bar. xlviii. 9, 10 et sapientes facis orbes caelestes ut ministrent in ordinibus suis. Exercitus innumerabiles astant coram te et ministrant in ordinibus suis quiete ad nutum tuum.

3 (13) There can be no doubt that the reading καὶ ἕως αἰῶνος is far superior to the ordinary one, which yields no particular sense. For the construction cf. xvii. 21.

4 (14) Here, as Cerda remarks, is an obvious allusion to the 'factum Josuae,' and also, as Hilg. adds, to the miracle wrought for Hezekiah. Allusions to definite incidents in the O. T. history are sufficiently uncommon in our book to merit notice when they so occur. It is almost inconceivable that the whole book should have ended with this unexplained reference. Not one of the other Psalms is destitute of some sort of doxology or rounding off, save the first, and in that case there is the possibility already alluded to that it ought to be more closely connected with Psalm ii. than it is.

In the case before us, we prefer the suggestion that the last leaf of the archetype had disappeared at a very early date. The Subscription merits a word: it will be noticed that A V K P have a stichometric note; A K and V attributing 1000 ἔπη to the book, P 30. It is obvious, we think, that P or its predecessor was copied from an uncial or semi-uncial archetype; that the scribe mistook Α for Λ and incautiously expanded the numerical sign into τριάκοντα.

APPENDIX.

The Odes of the Pistis Sophia.

THE accompanying five Odes of Solomon have been already referred to in the Introduction. For the sake of completeness, rather than in the hope that we have succeeded in throwing much light upon their meaning, we have included them in this volume, in a new form. It seems appropriate to include them thus in an appendix, inasmuch as we have seen that the evidence points to their having, in company with other compositions of the same sort, originally occupied that position (Introd. p. xx).

They have been already published several times; first by Woide in his (posthumous) *Appendix ad Codicem Alexandrinum*, p. 148 (Thebaic and Latin); next by Fred. Münter, Bishop of Seeland, in 1812, *Odae gnosticae Salomoni tributae*; by Ideler, *Psalterium Coptice* 1837, p. 243; by Max Uhlemann, *Grammaticae Copticae Rudimenta* (Nos. iii. and v.); in Migne's *Dict. des Apocryphes*, i. s.v. *Salomon*, in French only; and in Schwartze and Petermann's edition of the Pistis Sophia (Berlin, 1851) in Thebaic and Latin: probably also by others. In the *Comptes Rendus de l'Académie des Inscriptions*, 1872, p. 347, M. Révillout quotes two of them.

We have attempted to render them into Greek, and have subjoined by way of *apparatus criticus* a statement of the more important differences between the renderings of Schwartze (S.) and Woide (W.). We especially crave the indulgence of our readers for this part of our work: and we should particularly value any suggestions as to the improvement of our renderings.

It is necessary to state, for the benefit of those to whom the Pistis Sophia is unfamiliar, the manner in which these Odes are introduced into the text of that book. They occur at intervals in a long series of hymns (called μετάνοιαι) which are recited by the Pistis Sophia at various stages of her progress upward, through and out of the chaos. Our Lord is represented as detailing the adventures of the Pistis Sophia, and as quoting the hymns of thanksgiving or supplication which she utters. At the end of each, He pauses, and asks for an explanation of the hymn. Hereupon, one of the Apostles, or of the holy women who form His audience, steps forward and says, "Thy power of Light formerly prophesied by means of David (or Solomon) in his (e.g. 55th) Psalm, saying..." Then follows the text of one of the Canonical Psalms or one of these Odes: after which our Lord expresses His approval, expounds the application of the Psalm to the situation, and proceeds with His narrative. It is to be noticed that these five Odes of Solomon are quoted in precisely the same form as the Psalms of David; in the case of these latter the text and number of the Psalm are always correctly given: and no author save these two is referred to. Hence, the impression left with the reader is that a real collection of Solomon's Odes is being used, and that the Odes were not simply written for the occasion. On the question of the possible origin and extent of this collection something has been already said (Introd. l. c.). The idea that the Odes may have been simply written to fill a place in the text of the Pistis Sophia derives slight support from the existence of one or two such Odes in other Coptic Apocrypha, e.g. one sung by David in Hades on the occasion of the Virgin's birth, which will be found in Révillout's *Apocryphes Coptes du Nouveau Testament*, p. 5. Against it is the evidence drawn from Lactantius and the Stichometries (Introd. p. xix), and the lack of any special appropriateness in the Odes themselves.

The spaced words in the Greek are those which are found in Greek in the original text of the Pistis Sophia.

(114). i. Recited by Salome and prefaced with these words: "tua vis ἐπροφήτευσεν olim per Solomonem dicens."

1. ἐξομολογήσομαί σοι, κύριε, ὅτι σὺ εἶ ὁ θεός μου· μή με ἐγκαταλίπῃς, κύριε, ὅτι σὺ εἶ ἡ ἐλπίς μου.

2. ἔδωκάς μοι τὸ κρίμα σου[1] δωρεὰν, καὶ διεφυλάχθην ὑπὸ σοῦ.

3. πέσοιεν οἱ καταδιώκοντές με καὶ μὴ ἴδοιέν με.

4. νεφέλη σκότους καὶ ὁμίχλη ἀέρος ἐπικαλύψαι τοὺς ὀφθαλμοὺς αὐτῶν.

---

[1] or νεφέλη σκότους ἐπικ. τ. ὀφθ. αὐτ. κ. ὀμ. ἀέρ. ἐπισκιάσαι αὐτούς.

THE ODES OF THE PISTIS SOPHIA.

5. σκοτισθείησαν² καὶ μὴ ἴδοιεν τὸ φῶς, μήποτε καταλάβων- ²Ps. lxviii.
ταί με. (lxix.) 24
-ήτωσαν
6. γενηθήτω τὸ διαβούλιον αὐτῶν εἰς ἀσθένειαν· καὶ ἃ τοῦ μὴ
βλέπειν
ἐβούλευσαν ἐπιστρεψάτω ἐπὶ κεφαλὴν αὐτῶν· βουλὴν³ ἐβούλευ- ³ἐν βουλῇ
σαν καὶ μὴ γένοιτο αὐτοῖς.
7. ἐνίκησαν αὐτοὺς δυνατοί, καὶ ἃ παρεσκεύασαν κακῶς συνέπεσαν ἐπ᾽ αὐτούς.
8. ἡ δὲ ἐλπίς μου ἐπὶ κύριον, καὶ οὐ φοβηθήσομαι, διότι σὺ εἶ ὁ θεός μου, καὶ ὁ σωτήρ μου.

ii. Recited by the Virgin: "tua vis luminis ἐπροφήτευσεν p. 75 (116). de his verbis olim per Solomonem in eius decima nona ode et dixit."

1. ὁ κύριος ἐπὶ κεφαλῆς μου ὥσπερ στέφανος καὶ οὐ μὴ χωρισθῶ ἀπ᾽ αὐτοῦ· ἐπλέχθη¹ μοι στέφανος ἀληθείας. ¹ἔπλεξαν
2. οἱ κλάδοι σου ἐφυτεύθησαν ἐν ἐμοί, διότι οὐκ ἐποίησαν στέφανον ξηρὸν καὶ μὴ βλαστάνοντα.
3. ἀλλὰ ζῇς ἐπὶ τῆς κεφαλῆς μου, καὶ αὐξάνῃ ἐπ᾽ ἐμοῦ.
4. οἱ καρποί σου πλήρεις καὶ τέλειοι· ἐπληρώθησαν τῆς σωτηρίας σου.

---

1 or οὐκ ἀποβαλῶ αὐτόν.
2 ἐποίησαν βλαστάνειν τοὺς κλ. κ.τ.λ. S.

---

iii. Recited by Peter: "tua vis luminis ἐπροφήτευσεν olim p. 84 (131). per Solomonem in eius ᾠδαῖς."

1. ἐξῆλθεν ἡ ἀπόρροια καὶ ἐγένετο εἰς ποταμὸν μέγαν καὶ εὐρύν.
2. καὶ ἐπεσπάσατο πάντας αὐτοὺς καὶ ὑπέστρεψεν ἐπὶ τὸν ναόν.
3. καὶ οὐκ ἴσχυσαν τοῦ συγκλεῖσαι αὐτὴν εἰς λάκκους οὐδὲ εἰς τόπους λελατομημένους, οὐδὲ ἠδύναντο συλλαβεῖν αὐτὴν αἱ τέχναι τῶν συλλαμβανόντων τὰ ὕδατα.

---

2 αὐτοὺς sc. fluvios vel aquas W.

4. κατήχθη ἐφ' ὅλην τὴν γῆν, καὶ αὐτὴ ἐπελάβετο πάντων τῶν ὑδάτων.

5. ἔπιον οἱ ἀναστρεφόμενοι ἐν γῇ ἀνύδρῳ. ἐσβέσθη καὶ διελύθη τὸ δίψος αὐτῶν, δοθέντος αὐτοῖς ποτοῦ ἀφ' ὑψηλοῦ.

6. μακάριοι οἱ διάκονοι ἐκείνου τοῦ ποτοῦ, οἷς ἐπιστεύθη τὸ ὕδωρ τοῦ κυρίου.

7. ἐπεστράφησαν τὰ χείλη τὰ ξηρά, ἐνισχύθησαν οἱ ἐκλελυμένοι·
ἐστερεώθησαν αἱ ψυχαὶ τῶν ἀποδιδόντων τὸ πνεῦμα, τοῦ μὴ ἀποθανεῖν.

8. κατεστάθησαν τὰ μέλη τὰ παραλελυμένα· ἐδόθη ἰσχὺς τῇ παρρησίᾳ αὐτῶν, καὶ φῶς τοῖς ὀφθαλμοῖς αὐτῶν.

9. ὅτι πάντες αὐτοὶ ἔπιον τὸ σωτήριον τοῦ κυρίου, καὶ ἐσώθησαν ἐν ὕδατι ζωῆς εἰς τὸν αἰῶνα.

---

4 πάντων τῶν ὑδάτων. eos omnes S. omnes aquas W.
5 οἱ ἀναστρ. biberunt versantes super-arenam aridam S. qui habitabant in W.
7 ψυχὰς. ψυχὰς eiicientes halitum S. animae proiectae a vento W.
9 quod isti omnes cognovere se in Domino S. quia illi biberunt salutem Domini W.

149). iv. Recited by Thomas: "tua vis luminis ἐπροφήτευσεν olim per Solomonem filium Davidis in eius ᾠδαῖς."

1. ἐρρύσθην ἐκ τῶν δεσμῶν μου· ἐπί σε, κύριε, κατέφυγον, ὅτι σὺ ἦς ἐκ δεξιῶν μου, σώζων με· καὶ ἔσωσάς με καὶ ἀντελάβου μου.

2. ἐκώλυσας τοὺς μαχομένους κατ' ἐμοῦ, καὶ οὐχ εὑρέθησαν·

3. διότι τὸ πρόσωπόν σου ἦν μετ' ἐμοῦ καὶ ἐρρύσατό με ἐν τῇ χάριτί σου.

4. κατῃσχύνθην ἐνώπιον τοῦ πλήθους καὶ ἐξεβλήθην·

5. ἐγενόμην ὅμοιος μολύβδῳ ἐνώπιον αὐτῶν.

6. ἐπεγένετό μοι δύναμις παρά σου καὶ ἀντελάβετό μου.

7. ὅτι ἔθηκας λύχνους ἐκ δεξιῶν μου καὶ ἐξ ἀριστερῶν, τοῦ μηδὲν εἶναι σκοτεινὸν κύκλῳ μου.

---

1 ἐκ δεξιῶν=W. dextra S.
7 τοῦ μηδέν. So S. nam nemo mecum est: eram orbatus lumine. W. =διότι οὐκ ἦν μετ' ἐμοῦ οὐδείς, καὶ ἤμην ἄνευ φωτός. This rendering follows the punctuation of the MS.

THE ODES OF THE PISTIS SOPHIA.

8. ἐσκέπασάς με τῇ σκιᾷ τοῦ ἐλέους σου, καὶ ἐπενεδύθην στολὴν τιμίαν.
9. ἡ δεξιά σου ἀνύψωσέ με, καὶ ἀφεῖλεν ἀπ' ἐμοῦ πᾶσαν ἀσθένειαν.
10. ἐνισχύθην ἐν τῇ ἀληθείᾳ σου, καὶ ἐκαθαρίσθην τῇ δικαιοσύνῃ σου. ἐμακρύνθησαν ἀπ' ἐμοῦ οἱ ἐχθροί μου, καὶ ἐδικαιώθην τῇ χρηστότητί σου, ὅτι ἡ ἀνάπαυσίς σου εἰς τὸν αἰῶνα τοῦ αἰῶνος.

---

8 et fui super vestes pelliceas S. et fui coelestis, *indutus* vestimentis honorificis W.
10 ἐκαθαρίσθην. purgatus S. humiliatus W.

---

v. Recited by Matthew: "tua vis luminis ἐπροφήτευσεν p. 99 (155). olim in ᾠδῇ Solomonis."

1. ὁ καταγαγών με ἐκ τῶν ἄνω τόπων τῶν ἐπουρανίων, αὐτός με κατήγαγεν εἰς τοὺς ἐν τῷ κάτω στερεώματι[1]. [1] θεμελίῳ S. φάραγγι W.
2. ὁ τὰ ἐν μέσῳ ἀποστήσας καὶ διδάξας με περὶ αὐτῶν.
3. ὁ διασκορπίσας τοὺς ἐχθρούς μου καὶ τοὺς ἀντιδίκους.
4. ὁ δούς μοι ἐξουσίαν ἐπὶ τὰ δεσμὰ τοῦ λῦσαι αὐτά, ὁ πατάξας ἐν τῇ χειρί μου τὸν δράκοντα τὸν ἑπτακέφαλον.
5. ὁ καταστήσας με ἐπάνω τῆς ῥίζης αὐτοῦ τοῦ ἐκτρίψαι τὸ σπέρμα αὐτοῦ.
6. καὶ [γὰρ] σὺ ἦς μετ' ἐμοῦ τοῦ βοηθεῖν μοι ἐν παντὶ καιρῷ.
7. περιεποιήσατό με τὸ ὄνομά σου.
8. ἡ δεξιά σου ἀπώλεσε τὸ φάρμακον τοῦ βλασφήμου.
9. ἡ χείρ σου ὡμάλισεν ὁδὸν τοῖς πιστοῖς σου.
10. ἐλυτρώσω αὐτοὺς ἐκ τῶν τάφων καὶ ἐξήγαγες αὐτοὺς ἐκ μέσου τῶν πτωμάτων.

---

1 qui deduxit me S. Duxit me W. qui duxit...ille duxit Champollion.
super caelum S. coelestibus W.
et duxit me sursum in locis quae in fundamento inferiori S. et duxit me in loca quae in valle deorsum W.
2 qui abstulit ibi S. Sumpsit huc (προσήγαγεν) W.
erudivit ea W. docuit me ea S.
5 evellerem S. deleam W.
6, 7 in omni loco circumdedit S. W. We join it on to the preceding verse.
9 stravit S. direxit W. = κατεύθυνεν.
10 πτωμάτων. cadaveribus S. sepulchrorum W. μνημείων.

11. ἐπελάβου τῶν ὀστῶν τῶν νεκρῶν. ἐνέδυσας αὐτὰ σώματα, καὶ τοῖς μὴ κινουμένοις ἔδωκας ἐνέργειαν ζωῆς.

12. ἐγένετο ἐν ἀφθαρσίᾳ ἡ ὁδός σου, καὶ ἐν τῷ προσώπῳ σου διέλυσας τὸν αἰῶνά σου·

13. ἵνα διαλυθῶσιν οἱ πάντες καὶ ἀνακαινισθῶσιν καὶ τὸ φῶς σου διπλασιασθῇ ἐπὶ πάντας αὐτούς.

14. κατέστησας ἐν αὐτοῖς τὸ πλοῦτός σου, καὶ ἐγένοντο εἰς κατοίκησιν ἁγίαν.

---

11 qui haud movent se dedisti iis S. ne commoveantur, dedisti iis W.
12 perniciei expers S. incorruptibilitas W.
duxisti tuum αἰῶνα in perniciem S. super pern. W.
14 construxisti tuam opulentiam per eos S. convertisti divitias tuas super eos W. = ἐπέστρεψας ἐπ᾽ αὐτούς.

NOTES.

Ode i. is a colourless composition, containing nothing essentially Gnostic, and resembling to a certain extent the Psalms of Solomon in being almost a cento from the Canonical Psalms. There are, however, few actual coincidences of language. Ver. 3 is taken from Ps. lxviii. (lxix.) 24. The Ode as a whole resembles Ps. xxvi. (xxvii.). It may be originally Jewish.

Ode ii. should be another fragment of that quoted by Lactantius—the 'xixth Ode.'—Here alone is a number given.

The Virgin, be it noted, is the reciter here, and the Virgin is the subject of Lactantius's quotation. Very possibly the present fragment may refer to her, and to the overshadowing of her by the Holy Spirit. The 'fruits of righteousness' might in that case be taken to signify our Lord, the Word full of grace and truth. In any case, this is probably a Christian composition.

Ode iii. is also Christian, and the employment of the term ἀπόρροια seems to stamp it as Gnostic. But we cannot see that there is anything unmistakably Gnostic in the doctrine. The imagery employed is that of Ezek. xlvii., and of our Lord's words concerning the living water: and the thing described seems to be the preaching of the Gospel, which no human effort can avail to hinder, and which brings life and health to the inhabitants of a thirsty heathen world. If our theory of these Odes is correct, we have here a hymn of the second century at latest, and one filled with Johannine phraseology and ideas.

Ode iv. may possibly be Jewish, though the last verse rather militates against such a view.

The original of the curious expression in ver. 8 is ϣⲧⲏⲛ ϣⲁⲁⲣ (shten shaar) meaning literally 'garments of leather': but in a document in Zoega (*Cat. Codd. Copt.* p. 574) it is used of the garments of the wealthy. Hence our freer rendering. As a description of deliverance the Ode may be compared to Ps. S. xiii.

Ode v. The expressions 'heavenly places,' 'the things that were in the midst,' etc. remind us of the phraseology of Colossians and Ephesians. This Ode more than any of its companions has the air of being written to occupy its present place in the text of the Pistis Sophia.

v. 4. Cf. John xx. 23.

ibid. 'The seven-headed dragon.' This verse would be appropriate in the mouth of the 'woman clothed with the sun,' Rev. xii. It carries us into the region of apocalyptic imagery.

v. 10, 11. The original of these verses is to be sought in Ezekiel's vision of the dry bones.

12. Cf. Ps. ciii. (civ.) 30 'when thou lettest thy breath go forth they shall be made, and thou shalt renew the face of the earth.'

We should like to take this opportunity of calling the attention of our readers to two other fragments of the Psalmic literature, which have hitherto received but slight attention. They are to be found among certain apocryphal Syriac Psalms published by the late Professor Wm Wright in the *Proceedings of the Society of Biblical Archaeology* (1887, ix. pp. 257—266). These Psalms are five in number, and are found in two MSS. of the 17th and 18th centuries respectively; the first in the University Library at Cambridge, the second at the Vatican (Cod. Syr. 183). In both they are attached to a work by Elias (Bp of Pērōz-Shabhōr or al-Anbār, cir. 920 A.D.) called the 'Book of Discipline.'

The first of the five is the well-known 'Psalm cli' in a text slightly differing from the ordinary Greek form.

No. 2 is 'the Prayer of Hezekiah when enemies surrounded him.'

No. 3 'when the People obtained permission of Cyrus to return home.'

No. 4 'spoken by David when he was contending with the lion and the wolf which took a sheep from his flock.'

No. 5 'spoken by David when returning thanks to God, who had delivered him from the lion and the wolf, and he had slain both of them.'

Of these Psalms, the two last seem to be modelled on the first. They are quite short, and apply exclusively to the situations indicated in their titles. The 'wolf,' which appears in all three, is a mistake, as the editor points out, for the more familiar bear.

With the second and third of the Psalms, however, the case is different. They are longer compositions, which seem to possess some antiquity and to be originally Jewish in character, and have no particular application to the circumstances which their titles prescribe. They resemble rather markedly the general tone of the Psalms of Solomon.

We had prepared a Greek rendering of them, but have decided not to include it in the present volume.

J. P.

INDEX I.

INDEX VERBORUM IN PSALMIS SALOMONIS.

※ For prepositions see Index II.

Ἀβραάμ ix. 17, xviii. 4
ἄβυσσος xvii. 21
ἀγαθός i. 6, iii. 2, v. 21, xi. 8, xvii. 50, xviii. 7, 10
ἀγαλλίασις v. 1
ἀγαπάω iv. 29, vi. 9, ix. 16, x. 4, xiv. 1, 4, xvii. 18
ἀγάπη xviii. 4
ἀγάπησις xiii. 8
ἁγιάζω viii. 26, xvii. 28, 48, 49
ἁγίασμα vii. 2, viii. 4, xi. 8
ἁγιασμός xvii. 33
ἅγιος i. 8, ii. 3, viii. 12, xi. 1, xvii. 28, 36, 42, 49, xviii. 4
ἄγνοια iii. 9, xiii. 6, xviii. 5
ἄγω viii. 16, 22, xvii. 46
ᾅδης xiv. 6, xv. 11, xvi. 2
ἀδικία ii. 14, iii. 8, iv. 28, ix. 7, xvii. 29, 36
ἄδικος iv. 12, ix. 9, xii. 6, xv. 6, xvii. 24
Αἴγυπτος ii. 30
αἷμα viii. 13, 23
αἰνετός iii. 1, viii. 29, 40
αἰνέω v. 1, x. 6
αἶνος xv. 5
αἱρετίζω ix. 17, xvii. 5
αἴρω v. 12, xiii. 10, xvii. 8
αἰσχύνη ix. 13
αἴτημα vi. 8
αἴτιος iv. 3, ix. 9
αἰχμαλωσία ii. 6
αἰών ii. 38, 41, iii. 13, 15, vii. 8, viii. 7, 31, 39, 41, ix. 18, 20, x. 6, 8, xi. 8, 9, xii. 7, xiii. 9, xiv. 2, 3, xv. 6, 13, 14, xvi. 3, xvii. 1, 3, 4, 5, 39, 51, xviii. 1, 13

αἰώνιος ii. 35, iii. 16, x. 5, 9, xvii. 21
ἀκαθαρσία viii. 13, 23, 25, xvii. 51
ἀκακία iv. 26, viii. 28
ἄκακος iv. 6, 25, xii. 4
ἀκοή viii. 5
ἀκούω i. 2, ii. 9, viii. 1, 4
ἀκρασία iv. 3
ἄκρατος viii. 15
ἄκρος xvii. 34
ἀλδαγμα xvii. 8
ἀλήθεια iii. 7, vi. 9, x. 4, xiv. 1, xv. 3, xvi. 10, xvii. 17
ἀλλά ii. 27, v. 14
ἀλλήλων iv. 11 (?)
ἀλλογενής xvii. 31
ἀλλότριος ii. 2, ix. 1, xvi. 7, xvii. 9, 15
ἀλλοτριότης xvii. 15
ἄλογος xvi. 10
ἅλως xii. 2
ἅμα xvii. 13
ἀμαθία xviii. 5
ἁμαρτάνω iv. 5, v. 8, ix. 14, 15, xvi. 11
ἁμάρτημα xvii. 10
ἁμαρτία i. 7, ii. 7, 17, 18, iii. 7, 12, iv. 3, viii. 8, 14, ix. 12, x. 1, xiv. 4, 8, xvii. 6, 21, 22, 41
ἁμαρτωλός i. 1, ii. 1, 17, 38, 39, iii. 11, 13, iv. 2, 9, 27, xii. 8, xiii. 2, 4, 5, 6, 7, 10, xiv. 4, xv. 7, 9, 10, 13, 14, xvi. 2, 5, xvii. 6, 26, 27, 41
ἀναβαίνω ii. 2
ἀναβάτης xvii. 37
ἀνάγκη v. 8
ἀνακαλύπτω ii. 18, iv. 8, viii. 8
ἀνάληψις iv. 20
ἀναλογίζομαι viii. 7

INDEX I.

ἀναμέσον ii. 38
ἀνάμιξις ii. 15
ἄναξις xviii. 6
ἀναπτέρωσις iv. 15
ἀνάπτω xii. 2
ἀνατέλλω xi. 7
ἀνατολή v. 11, xi. 3
ἄνεμος viii. 2, xvii. 13
ἄνευ iv. 4, v. 15
ἀνέχω xvii. 20
ἀνήρ iii. 10, iv. 11, v. 4, vi. 1, ix. 10,
 x. 1, xii. 1, 2, 6, xviii. 9
ἀνθρωπάρεσκος iv. Tit., 8, 10, 21
ἄνθρωπος ii. 11, 32, iv. 8, 22, 23, 27, v.
 4, 6, 15, 19, ix. 6, 8, x. 5, xiv. 5,
 xv. 4, xvii. 2, 9, 29
ἀνίστημι ii. 35, iii. 13, 16, xi. 9, xvii. 23, 47
ἀνοίγω v. 14, viii. 19
ἀνομία i. 7, ii. 3, 13, ix. 3, xv. 9, 11, 13
ἄνομος xvii. 20
ἀντιλαμβάνομαι xvi. 3, 5
ἀντιλήπτωρ xvi. 4
ἀντίληψις vii. 9, xvi. Tit.
ἀνωφελής xvi. 8
ἀπάγω viii. 24, ix. 1
ἀπαντάω viii. 18
ἅπαξ xii. 8
ἀπαρχή xv. 5
ἅπας ix. 13, xiii. 3
ἀπατάω xvi. 1
ἀπείθεια xvii. 22
ἀπειλή xvii. 27
ἀπέναντι ii. 14, xvii. 5
ἀπέχω v. 9, viii. 38
ἀποβλέπω iii. 5
ἀποδίδωμι ii. 17, 28, 39, xv. 14, xvii. 10
ἀποικεσία ix. 1
ἀπόκρυφος i. 7, iv. 5
ἀπόλλυμι viii. 23, xii. 5, 8, xv. 13
ἀποπίπτω iv. 18
ἀπορία iv. 17, xii. 4
ἀπορρίπτω ii. 4, 23, ix. 2
ἀποσκηνόω vii. 1
ἀποσκοπεύω iii. 6
ἀποστέλλω vii. 4
ἀποστρέφω ii. 8, v. 7, xviii. 5
ἅπτομαι xiii. 5, xv. 6
ἀπωθέω vii. 2, 8

ἀπώλεια ii. 35, iii. 13, ix. 9, xiii. 10, xiv.
 6, xv. 10, 11, xvi. 5, xvii. 25
ἀρά iv. 16
ἄρα viii. 3
ἀργύριον xvii. 37
ἀρκέω xvi. 12
ἁρμόζω xv. 5
ἀρνίον viii. 28
ἅρπαγμα ii. 28
ἀρχαῖος xviii. 14
ἀρχή ii. 34, viii. 37, xvii. 33
ἄρχω xvii. 41
ἄρχων v. 13, viii. 18, 23, xvii. 14, 21, 24, 41
ἀσεβής xiii. 4
ἀσθενέω xvii. 42, 43, 45
ἄστρον i. 5
ἀσφάλεια viii. 20, 22
ἀτεκνία iv. 20
ἀτιμία ii. 23, 29, 32, 35, iv. 16, 21, 23
ἀτιμόω ii. 5
αὐλίζω iii. 7, xvii. 29
αὔριον v. 15
αὐταρκεσία v. 18
ἀφαιρέω iv. 18, xvii. 6
ἀφανίζω xvii. 13
ἄφεδρος viii. 13
ἀφηγοῦμαι xvii. 28
ἀφίημι ix. 14, xvii. 11, 29, 45
ἀφίστημι iv. 1, 13, ix. 1, 16, xvi. 6, xviii. 14
ἄφρων xvi. 7

βαρυθυμέω ii. 10
βαρύνω ii. 24, v. 8
βασίλεια v. 21, xvii. 3, 5
βασίλειον xvii. 7
βασιλεύς ii. 34, 36, v. 13, 22, xvii. 1, 5,
 22, 23, 35, 36, 38, 47, 51, xvii. Tit.
βασιλεύω xvii. 23
βδελύσσω ii. 10
βέβηλος ii. 14, iv. 1, viii. 13, xvii. 51
βεβηλόω i. 8
βεβήλωσις i. 8, ii. 3, viii. 24
βία xvii. 6
βοάω i. 1
βοηθεία xv. 1
βορρᾶ xi. 4
βουλή viii. 23, xvii. 42
βουνός xi. 6

INDEX I.

βραχίων xiii. 2

γενεά xviii. 7, 10, 14
γένεσις iii. 11
γεννάω viii. 24
γένος vii. 8, xvii. 9
γῆ i. 4, ii. 10, 12, 23, 30, 33, 36, iv. 25,
   v. 17, viii. 7, 8, 16, 17, 18, 27, 29,
   ix. 14, xiv. 14, xvii. 2, 8, 12, 13, 14,
   20, 30, 32, 34, 39, xviii. 3
γῆρας iv. 20
γίγνομαι i. 3, iv. 16, 29, xiv. 5, xvii. 20,
   50, xviii. 7
γιγνώσκω ii. 12, 35, viii. 8, xvii. 30, 47
γλῶσσα iv. 4, xii. Tit., 1, 2, 3, 5, xiv. 5,
   xvi. 10
γνῶσις ix. 5, 6
γνωστός xiv. 5
γογγυσμός v. 15, xvi. 11
γόνυ viii. 5
γρηγορέω iii. 2
γρηγόρησις iii. 2, xvi. 4
γυνή iv. 4, viii. 11, xvi. 7, 8

Δαυίδ xvii. 5, 8, 23
δέησις v. 7, xviii. 3
δείκνυμι ii. 30, viii. 30
δεινός xiii. 5
δένδρον xii. 3
δεξιά xiii. 1
δέομαι ii. 24, vi. 7
δεῦρο viii. 18
δευτερόω v. 15
διάβασις vi. 5
διαβῆμα xvi. 9
διαθήκη ix. 19, x. 5, xvii. 17
διακρίνω xvii. 48
διαλύω iv. 11
διαπαντός ii. 40, iii. 8
διαπορεύομαι xiii. 2
διαρπάζω viii. 12
διασπορά viii. 34, ix. 2
διαστέλλω ii. 38
διαστολή iv. 4
διαστρέφω x. 3
διαστροφή xii. 2
διατάσσω xviii. 12
διατίθημι ix. 19

διαφέρω xvi. 3
διαφθείρω ii. 31
διαφυλάττω xvi. 9
διάψαλμα xvii. 31, xviii. 10
διδακτός xvii. 35
δίδωμι v. 5, 10, 11, vii. 3, xvi. 12
διέρχομαι i. 4
δίκαιος ii. 12, 36, 38, iii. Tit., 3, 4, 5, 7,
   8, 14, iv. 9, v. 1, viii. 8, ix. 4, 5, x. 3,
   6, xiii. Tit., 5, 6, 7, 8, xiv. 6, xv. 5, 8,
   xvi. 15, xvii. 35
δικαιοσύνη i. 2, 3, 4, ii. 16, v. 22, viii.
   7, 29, 30, 32, ix. 3, 6, 7, 8, 9, 10, xiv. 1,
   xvii. 21, 25, 28, 31, 42, 45, xviii. 8, 9
δικαιόω ii. 16, iii. 3, 5, iv. 9, viii. 7, 27, 31,
   ix. 3
διώκω xv. 9, 11
δοκιμασία xvi. 14
δόλιος iv. 27, xii. 1
δόλος iv. 10
δόμα v. 16, xviii. 2
δόξα i. 4, ii. 5, 20, 22, 35, v. 22, xi. 7,
   8, 9, xvii. 7, 34, 35
δοξάζω x. 8, xvii. 7, 32, 35
δουλεύω xvii. 32
δοῦλος ii. 41, x. 4, xviii. 14
δράκων ii. 29
δρυμός xi. 6
δύναμαι xvii. 44
δυνατός xv. 4, xvii. 38, 42
δυσμός xi. 3, xvii. 14
δωρεάν vii. 1
δῶρον ii. 3, xvii. 34

ἐάν e.g. ii. 26
ἐγκαταλείπω ii. 7
ἔθνος i. 8, ii. 2, 24, vii. 3, 6, viii. 14, 27,
   36, ix. 2, 17, xvii. 4, 16, 17, 25, 27,
   31, 32, 34, 38
εἰ xviii. 14
εἶπον i. 5, ii. 29, viii. 3, 7, 18
εἰρήνη viii. 18, 20, xii. 6
εἰσακούω vi. 8
εἰσάπαξ ii. 8, 9, xi. 3
εἰσέρχομαι iv. 19, viii. 18, 20
εἴσοδος iv. 6, 16, viii. 19, xi. 6
εἰσπορεύομαι ii. 13
ἕκαστος viii. 11, xviii. 13

ἐκεῖνος xvii. 50, xviii. 7
ἐκκεντέω ii. 30
ἐκκλησία x. 7
ἐκκόπτω iv. 22, xii. 3
ἐκλείπω iii. 16, xvii. 5
ἐκλογή ix. 7, xviii. 6
ἐκπέταμαι xvii. 18
ἐκτίλλω xiv. 3
ἐκτρίβω xvii. 26
ἐκφεύγω xv. 9
ἐκχέω ii. 28, viii. 23, xvi. 2
ἐλάχιστος ii. 30, xvii. 21
ἐλεγμός, x. 1 (?)
ἔλεγχος ix. Tit., x. 1
ἐλέγχω xvi. 14, xvii. 27
ἐλεέω ii. 39, vii. 5, 9, x. 7, xi. 2, xv. 15, xvi. 15, xvii. 11
ἐλεημοσύνη ix. 20, xv. 15
ἐλεήμων v. 2, vii. 4, x. 8
ἔλεος ii. 8, 37, 40, iv. 29, v. 14, 17, vi. 9, viii. 33, 34, ix. 16, xi. 9, xii. 11, xiv. 6, xvi. 3, 6, xvii. 3, 17, 51, xviii. 1, 3, 6, 10
ἐλλιπής iv. 19
ἐλπίζω vi. 8, viii. 37, ix. 19, xv. 1, xvii. 3, 37
ἐλπίς v. 13, 16, vi. Tit., xv. 2, xvii. 2, 37, 38, 43, xviii. 3
ἐμπαιγμός ii. 13, xvii. 14
ἐμπαίζω ii. 13, 25
ἔμπειρος xv. 9
ἐμπίμπλημι iv. 15, 19
ἐμπίμπρημι xii. 3
ἐνάντιον iii. 4, viii. 8
ἔνδοξος xviii. 11
ἔνδυμα ii. 21
ἐνδύομαι xi. 8
ἕνεκεν ii. 4, iv. 13
ἐνισχύω xvi. 12, 13
ἐνοικέω xvii. 13
ἔνοχος iv. 3
ἐνταῦθα iv. 15
ἐντέλλομαι vii. 4, xiv. 1, xviii. 12, 14
ἔντιμος viii. 31, xvii. 7
ἐνύπνιον vi. 4
ἐνώπιον i. 2, ii. 5, 40, 41, iv. 16, ix. 6, xiv. 5, xvii. 38
ἐξαίρω iii. 8, iv. 7, 9, 25, 28, xvii. 41
ἐξαλείφω ii. 19, xiii. 9

ἐξαμαρτάνω v. 19
ἐξανίστημι vi. 6
ἐξάπινα i. 2
ἐξαποστέλλω xvii. 14
ἐξασθενέω xvii. 34
ἐξέγερσις iv. 17
ἐξερευνάω xvii. 11
ἐξερημόω xv. 13
ἐξέρχομαι xv. 7
ἐξηγορία ix. 12
ἐξιλάσκω iii. 9
ἔξοδος iv. 16
ἐξομολογέομαι x. 7, xv. 3, 4, xvi. 5
ἐξομολόγησις iii. 3, ix. 12
ἐξουδενόω ii. 30, 32
ἐξουθενέω ii. 5
ἐξουσία ix. 7
ἐξυβρίζω i. 6
ἐξυμνέω vi. 7
ἐξωθέω xvii. 6, 26
ἐπαγγελία xii. 8
ἐπαγγέλλομαι vii. 9, xvii. 6
ἐπαγωγή ii. 24
ἐπακούω i. 2, v. 14, vii. 7, xviii. 3
ἐπανίσταμαι xvii. 6, 9
ἐπευκτός viii. 18
ἐπιβλέπω xviii. 2
ἐπιγινώσκω ii. 33
ἐπιεικής v. 14
ἐπιθυμία ii. 27, iv. 12, 13, 23, xiv. 4
ἐπικαλέομαι ii. 40, v. 7, vi. 1, vii. 7, ix. 11, xv. 1
ἐπικρατέω xvi. 7, xvii. 17
ἐπίσημος ii. 6, xvii. 32
ἐπισκέπτομαι iii. 8, 14, ix. 8, xv. 14
ἐπισκοπή x. 5, xi. 2, 7
ἐπίσταμαι v. 1, xiv. 5
ἐπιστήμη ii. 37
ἐπιστρέφω v. 9, viii. 33
ἐπιστροφή vii. Tit., ix. 19, xvi. 11
ἐπιταγή xviii. 14
ἐπιτελέω vi. 8
ἐπιτίθημι i. 1, vii. 1, ix. 16, xvii. 6
ἐπιτιμάω ii. 26
ἐπιτρέχω xiii. 3
ἐπιχαίρω xiii. 6
ἔργον ii. 17, 38, iv. 8, vi. 3, ix. 7, xvi. 9, xvii. 10, 11, 44, xviii. 19

INDEX I.

ἔρημος v. 11, viii. 2, xvii. 19
ἐρημόω iv. 13, 23, xvii. 8, 13
ἔρχομαι xi. 4, xvii. 34, xviii. 7
ἔσχατος i. 4, viii. 16
ἕτερος iv. 15
ἔτι iii. 16, ix. 20, xi. 8, 9, xiii. 10, xvii. 1, 51
ἑτοιμάζω v. 11, x. 2, xi. 8
ἕτοιμος vi. 1
εὐαγγελίζομαι xi. 2
εὐδοκία iii. 4, viii. 39, xvi. 12
εὐθηνέω i. 3
εὐθύνω ix. 15
εὐθύτης ii. 16
εὐλογέω ii. 37, iii. 1, v. 22, vi. 6, viii. 41, ix. 15, xvii. 40
εὐλογητός ii. 41, vi. 9
εὐλογία v. 20, xvii. 43, xviii. 6
εὐοδόω ii. 4
εὐπρέπεια ii. 21, xvii. 47
εὑρίσκω xiii. 10, xiv. 6, xv. 12
εὐστάθεια iv. 11, vi. 7
εὐφραίνω v. 14, 21
εὐφροσύνη x. 6, 7, 9, xi. 4, xii. 3, xiv. 7, xv. 5, xvii. 40
εὐωδία xi. 7
ἐχθρός xvii. 15, 51
ἔχω xvii. 32
ἕως i. 4, 5, iv. 13, xvi. 6, xvii. 14

ζάω iv. 7, v. 11, xiv. 2, xv. 15
ζῆλος ii. 27, iv. 3, 7, 17
ζυγόν vii. 8, xvii. 32
ζωή iii. 11, 12, 16, iv. 7, 17, ix. 9, xiii. 9, xiv. 1, 2, 7, xvii. 2

ἥκω iii. 6, v. 9
ἥλιος ii. 13, 14, iv. 21, viii. 8
ἡμέρα iii. 11, vii. 9, xiv. 2, 4, 5, xv. 13, xvii. 36, 37, 42, 50, xviii. 6, 7, 10, 12, 13, 14
ἡσύχιος xii. 6
ἠχέω viii. 1

θάλασσα ii. 30, 33, vi. 5
θάνατος vii. 4, xiii. 2, xv. 8, xvi. 2, 6
θάπτω ii. 31

θαυμάζω ii. 19, v. 15
θέλημα vii. 3
θεός i. 1, ii. 3, 13, 16, 19, 22, 28, 30, 33, 37, iii. 2, 5, 7, iv. 1, 7, 8, 9, 24, 25, 28, v. 1, 6, 7, 10, 13, 18, vi. 7, 8, vii. 1, 2, viii. 3, 7, 8, 12, 15, 22, 26, 27, 28, 30, 31, 32, 33, 36, 37, ix. 2, 3, 7, 11, 16, x. 7, 8, xi. 2, 4, 7, 8, xii. 4, xiv. 3, 5, xv. 1, 2, 3, 8, 14, 15, xvi. 2, 3, 5, 6, 7, xvii. 1, 3, 4, 8, 10, 11, 15, 16 (θεοί), 23, 28, 30, 35, 38, 42, 44, 47, 50, 51, xviii. 6, 8, 9, 10, 11, 13, 14
θηρίον iv. 22, xiii. 3
θησαυρίζω ix. 9
θλάω xiii. 3
θλίβω i. 1, v. 7, xv. 1
θλῖψις viii. 1, xvi. 11, 14
θραύω xvii. 34
θρόνος ii. 20, xvii. 8
θυγάτηρ ii. 6, 14, viii. 10, 24
θυμός ii. 25, xvi. 10
θυσία viii. 13
θυσιαστήριον ii. 2, viii. 13

Ἰακώβ xv. 1
ἰδεῖν ii. 24, 36, viii. 30, ix. 16, xi. 3, xvii. 23, 34, 35, 50, xviii. 7
Ἱερουσαλήμ ii. Tit., 3, 14, 15, viii. 4, 17, 19, 21, 23, 26, xi. 2, 3, 8, 9, xvii. 16, 17, 25, 33
ἱκανός v. 20
ἱκανόω ii. 24
ἱλαρότης iv. 6, xvi. 12
ἱμάτιον xi. 8
ἵνα ii. 18, v. 8, vii. 1, viii. 36, ix. 3, 16, xi. 7, xiii. 7
ἱνατί iii. 1, iv. 1
ἵππος xvi. 4, xvii. 37
Ἰσραήλ iv. 1, v. 21, vii. 8, viii. 34, 41, ix. 12, 16, 20, x. 6, 7, 8, 9, xi. 2, 7, 9, xii. 7, xiv. 3, xvi. 3, xvii. 5, 23, 47, 50, 51, xviii. 3, 4, 6
ἵστημι ii. 13, viii. 20, xi. 3, xvii. 38
ἰσχυρός xvii. 44
ἰσχύς ii. 33, 40, xvii. 24, 41, 42, 43, xviii. 8
ἰσχύω xv. 3

ἰχθύς v. 11

καθά ii. 14
καθαρίζω iii. 10, ix. 12, x. 1, 2, xvii. 25, 33, xviii. 6
καθαρός xvii. 41
κάθημαι iv. 1
καθίστημι xviii. 9
καθώς viii. 25, xvii. 16
καινός iii. 2
καιρός vii. 9, xvi. 4, xvii. 23, xviii. 12
κακία iv. 6, xvii. 29
κακός ix. 5, xv. 6, xvii. 19
καλάμη xii. 2
κάλλος ii. 5, 20, 22, xvi. 8, xvii. 14
καρδία i. 3, iii. 2, iv. 1, vi. 1, 7, viii. 3, 6, xiv. 5, xv. 5, xvi. 6, xvii. 15, 27
καρπός xv. 5
καταβάλλω ii. 1, xvii. 8
κατάγαιος viii. 9
καταγέλως iv. 8
καταδιώκω xv. 9
καταδυναστεύω xvii. 46
καταιγίς viii. 2
κατακρίνω iv. 2
καταλαμβάνω viii. 21, xv. 9
καταμερίζω xvii. 30
καταπατέω ii. 2, xvii. 25
καταπάτησις ii. 20
καταπαύω ix. 18
καταπίνω viii. 36
καταράομαι iii. 11
κατασκηνόω vii. 5
κατασπάω ii. 20
καταστροφή xiii. 5, 6
καταφορά xvi. 1
καταφυγή v. 2, xv. 1, xvi. 1
κατέναντι ii. 13, iv. 21
κατεργάζω xvii. 42
κατευθύνω vi. 3, vii. 9, viii. 7, xii. 6, xvi. 9, xviii. 9
κατισχύω ii. 7
κατοικέω xvii. 29, xviii. 11
κάτω xv. 11
καυχάω xvii. 1
κενός iv. 19
κέντρον xvi. 4
κεραμεύς xvii. 26

κεράννυμι viii. 15
κεφαλή ii. 21, 28
κηρύσσω xi. 1
κληρονομέω xii. 8, xiv. 7
κληρονομία vii. 2, ix. 2, xiv. 3, 6, xv. 11, 12, xvii. 26
κληρονόμος viii. 12
κοιλία ii. 15
κοιμίζω ii. 35
κοίτη xvii. 18
κόραξ iv. 22
κράζω v. 3, 10
κραταιός ii. 33, iv. 28, xvii. 44
κραταιῶς viii. 16
κράτος xvii. 3
κραυγή 1, 2
κρέας viii. 13
κρίμα ii. 12, 14, 16, 18, 36, 37, iii. 3, iv. 9, v. 1, 6, viii. 7, 8, 27, 30, 31, 38, 40, ix. 10, x. 6, xv. 9, 14, xvii. 12, 21, xviii. 3
κρίνω ii. 34, 36, iv. 14, viii. 3, 17, 29, 32, xvii. 28, 31
κριός ii. 1
κρίσις iv. 2, xv. 13, xvii. 4
κριτής ii. 19, iv. 28, ix. 4, xvii. 22
κρόταφος iv. 18
κρύπτω ix. 5, 6
κρύφιος viii. 9
κτίζω xviii. 13, 14
κτίσις viii. 7
κυκλόω x. 2
κῦμα ii. 21
κύριος i. 1, ii. 3, 24, 26, 33, 36, 37, 40, 41, iii. 1, 3, 4, 5, 10, 16, iv. 1, 16, 17, 26, 27, 29, v. 1, 13, 16, 17, 21, 22, vi. 1, 2, 3, 6, 7, 8, 9, viii. 13, 29, 37, 39, 40, 41, ix. 1, 2, 6, 9, 10, 11, 18, 20, x. 1, 2, 4, 5, 6, 8, 9, xi. 3, 9, xii. 1, 4, 6, 7, 8, xiii. 1, 2, 3, 9, 11, xiv. 1, 2, 7, xv. 1, 7, 9, 13, 15, xvi. 1, 3, 15, xvii. 1, 5, 12, 23, 28, 32, 35, 36, 38, 43, 45, 51, xviii. 1, 7, 8, 9, Tit. (ii. 33 of a man).
κωλύω ii. 1

λαλέω iv. 5, 10, 11, xi. 8, 9, xii. 1
λαμβάνω v. 4, 5

INDEX I.

λαός v. 13, viii. 2, ix. 4, 16, x. 7, xvii.
21, 22, 27, 28, 31, 32, 40, 41, 48, 49
λιμός xiii. 2, xv. 8
λίνον viii. 6
λογίζομαι i. 3, ii. 32, xvi. 5
λόγος iv. 2, 11, 12, 14, 15, xii. 2, xvi.
9, 10, xvii. 27, 39, 41, 49
λυτρόω viii. 12, 36, ix. 1

μακάριος iv. 26, v. 18, vi. 1, x. 1, xvii.
50, xviii. 7
μακράν ii. 4, iv. 1, xv. 8, xvi. 10
μακρόθεν xi. 4
μακρύνω xii. 4, xvi. 2, 11
μαρτυρία x. 5
μάστιξ vii. 8, x. 1, 2
μέγας ii. 33, iv. 28, xvii. 41, xviii. 11
μεγιστάν ii. 36
μέθη viii. 15
μερίς iii. 15, iv. 6, v. 6, xiv. 3
μεσός ii. 38, vii. 5, viii. 28, xvii. 17, 29,
36, 49
μεταμέλεια ix. 15
μετοχή xiv. 4
μέτριος v. 20
μέτωπον xv. 10
μηδέ xvi. 6
μήνισις ii. 25
μήποτε xiii. 4
μητήρ viii. 10
μιαίνω ii. 3, 15, viii. 13, 26
μικρός xvi. 1
μικρότης xiv. 4
μιμνήσκω iii. 14, iv. 24, x. 1, 4, xiv. 5
μισέω vii. 1, xii. 6
μίτρα ii. 22
μνήμη xvi. 6, 9
μνημονεύω iii. 3, v. 18, vi. 2
μνημόσυνον ii. 19, xiii. 10
μοιχάω viii 11
μονογενής xviii. 4
μόνωσις iv. 20
μυκτηρισμός iv. 8
μύλη xiii. 3

νέος ii. 8, xvii. 13
νῆσος xi. 4
νηστεία iii. 9

νικάω iv. 13
νῖκος viii. Tit.
νομή xvii. 45
νόμος iv. 10, x. 5, xiv. 1
νουθετέω xiii. 8
νῦν ii. 36, ix. 16
νύξ iv. 5, 18
νύσσω xvi. 4
νυστάζω xvi. 1
νῶτον x. 2

ξύλον xi. 7, xiv. 2

ὁδός vi. 3, viii. 7, 18, 19, x. 1, 3, 5, xiv. 5,
xviii. 12, 13
ὀδούς xiii. 3
ὀδύνη iv. 17
ὅθεν iii. 6
οἶδα i. 7, xviii. 23, 29
οἰκέω viii. 23
οἰκία iv. 6
οἶκος iii. 7, 8, 10, iv. 15, 19, 23, vi. 7,
vii. 9, viii. 20, ix. 10, 20, x. 9, xii. 3,
4, 6, xv. 13, xvii. 47
οἰκτείρω vii. 8, viii. 33, ix. 16
οἶνος viii. 15
ὄλεθρος viii. 1
ὀλίγος xvi. 2
ὀλιγοψυχία xvi. 11
ὀλιγωρέω iii. 4
ὀλισθαίνω xvi. 1
ὀλοθρεύω iv. 15, xv. 7, xvii. 27
ὅλος iii. 2
ὁμαλίζω viii. 19
ὁμαλισμός xi. 5
ὄμνυμι xvii. 5
ὅμοιος xiii. 6
ὀνειδίζω ii. 20
ὄνομα v. 1, vi. 2, 6, 7, vii. 5, viii. 26, 31,
ix. 18, x. 6, 8, xi. 9, xv. 1, 4, xvii. 7
ὅρασις vi. 4
ὁράω iv. 5, 14, viii. 30, 31
ὄργανον xv. 5
ὀργή ii. 25, 26, 28, xv. 6, xvi. 10, xvii. 14
ὀρθόω x. 3
ὅρκος iv. 4, viii. 11
ὅρος ii. 30, xi. 5, xvii. 21
ὀρφανία iv. 13

ὅσιος iii. 10, iv. 7, 9, viii. 28, 40, ix. 6, x. 6, 7, xii. 5, 8, xiii. 9, 10, xiv. 2, 7, xv. 5, 9, xvii. 18
ὁσιότης xvii. 46
ὅσος ii. 11, xvii. 16
ὀστέον iv. 21, viii. 6, xii. 4, xiii. 3
ὀσφύς viii. 5
ὅταν iii. 14, xv. 7, 14
οὐρανός ii. 10, 34, 36, viii. 7, xvii. 20
οὖς viii. 1, xviii. 3
οὕτως xiv. 4
ὀφθαλμός iv. 4, 5, 11, 15, 22, viii. 7, xvii. 19, xviii. 2
ὄφις iv. 11
ὀχυρός ii. 1

παιδεία vii. 8, viii. 32, x. 2, 3, xiii. 6, 8, 9, xiv. 1, xvi. 13, xviii. 4, 8
παιδευτής viii. 35
παιδεύω iii. 4, vii. 3, xiii. 6, xvi. 11, xvii. 47
παῖς xii. 7, xvii. 23
παίω viii. 16
παραβαίνω xviii. 12
παραδειγματίζω ii. 14
παράδεισος xiv. 2
παράκλησις xiii. Tit.
παραλείπω viii. 14
παραλογίζομαι iv. 14
παραλογισμός iv. 12, 25
παραλύω viii. 5
παρανομέω xvi. 8
παρανομία iv. 1, 15, viii. 9, xvii. 32
παράνομος iv. 11, 13, 21, 27, xii. Tit., 1, 3, 4, xiv. 4, xvii. 27
παραπορεύομαι ii. 13
παράπτωμα iii. 8, xiii. 4, 9
παρασιωπάω v. 3
παρέρχομαι xi. 7
παρίστημι ii. 40
πάροδος xi. 6
παροικέω xvii. 31
παροικία xii. 3, xvii. 19
πάροικος xvii. 31
παροξύνω iv. 25
παροργίζω iv. 1, 25
παροργισμός viii. 10
πᾶς i. 4, ii. 40, iii. 4, viii. 8, 13, 23, 29, ix. 2, 4, 5, 17, xi. 7, xiii. 5, xiv. 3, 5,
xv. 7, xvi. 4, 7, 8, xvii. 16, 20, 21, 26, 29, 30, 32, 36, 46, xviii. 3, 9
πατάσσω xvii. 39
πατέω vii. 2, viii. 13
πατήρ viii. 10, 20, 25, ix. 19
πεινάω v. 10, 12
πένης v. 13
πενία iv. 7, 17, xvi. 13, 14
περιαιρέω ii. 22
περιζώννυμι ii. 21
περισσός iv. 2
περιστέλλω xvi. 10
περιστολή xiii. 6
περιτίθημι ii. 22
πετεινός v. 11
πήγη xvii. 21
πίμπλημι i. 2, 3, iv. 25
πίπτω i. 5, iii. 5, 13
πίστις viii. 35, xvii. 45
πιστός xiv. 1, xvii. 12
πλανάω xvii. 19, xviii. 14
πλάνησις, viii. 15, 22
πλεονάζω v. 6
πληθύνω x. 1, xvii. 37
πλησίον viii. 11
πλησμονή v. 20
πλοῖον xvii. 37
πλούσιος v. 16, xviii. 2
πλοῦτος i. 4
πνεῦμα viii. 15, xvii. 42, xviii. 8
πνέω ii. 7, iii. 5, iv. 28, viii. 14, 25, ix. 5, 7, 9, xi. 9, xii. 6, xv. 6, 9, xvi. 10, xvii. 12, 15, 16, 17, 21, 50, xviii. 7
ποίησις xii. 2
ποικιλία iv. 4
ποιμαίνω xvii. 45
ποιμνίον xvii. 45
πολέμιος xv. 9
πόλεμος i. 2, viii. i. 17, xii. 4
πόλις viii. 4, xvii. 16
πολύς i. 4, ii. 31, viii. 2, 20
πονέω ii. 15
πονηρός ii. 6, 9, iii. 13, vi. 4, x. 1, xii. 1, 2, xiii. 3, xvi. 7
πορεία, xviii. 12
πορεύομαι xiv. 1
πόρνη ii. 13
ποταμός vi. 5

INDEX I.

ποτήριον viii. 15
ποτίζω viii. 15
ποῦ viii. 2, ix. 6
ποῦς vii. 2, viii. 20
πρᾶξις iv. 12
πρεσβύτης ii. 8, xvii. 13
προσδοκία xi. Tit.
προσευχή vi. 5
προσκόπτω iii. 5, 11
πρόσταγμα xiv. 1
προστίθημι iii. 12, v. 6
πρόσωπον ii. 8, 19, 24, iv. 9, v. 12, vi. 7, ix. 13, xii. 8, xv. 7, xvii. 27
πρῶτος iv. 3, xvii. 48
πρωτότοκος xiii. 8, xviii. 4
πτοέω vi. 8
πτῶμα iii. 13
πτωχός v. 2, 13, x. 7, xv. 2, xviii. 3
πύλη viii. 19, xvi. 2
πῦρ viii. 2, xii. 2, 5, xv. 6
πυργόβαρις viii. 21
πυρόω xvii. 48

ῥαβδός xvii. 26, xviii. 8
ῥῆμα ix. 2, xvii. 48
ῥιζόω xiv. 3
ῥομφαία xiii. 2, xv. 8
ῥύω iv. 27, xii. 1, xiii. 3, xvii. 51

σάκκος ii. 21
σαλεύω viii. 39, xv. 6
σάλον vi. 5
σάλπιγξ viii. 1, xi. 1
σαλπίζω xi. 1
σαπρία xiv. 4, xvi. 14
σάρξ iv. 7, 21, xiii. 3, xvi. 14
σημασία xi. 1
σημεῖον xv. 8, 10
σημείωσις iv. 2
σιδήρεος xvii. 20
Ϲιών xi. 1
σκανδαλίζω xvi. 7
σκάνδαλον iv. 27
σκεπάζω xiii. 1
σκεῦος xvii. 26
σκιάζω xi. 6
σκληρός iv. 2
σκληρύνω viii. 35

σκορπίζω iv. 13, 21, xii. 4
σκορπισμός xvii. 20
σκότος xiv. 6, xv. 11
σκῦλον v. 4
σοφία iv. 11, xvii. 25, 31, 40, xviii. 8
σοφός viii. 23, xvii. 42
σπέρμα ix. 17, xvii. 5, 8, 11, xviii. 4
σπλάγχνα ii. 15
σταθμός v. 6
στάζω xvii. 20
στεναγμός iv. 16
στέφανος ii. 21
στεφανόω viii. 19
στηρίζω xvi. 12
στολή xi. 8
στόμα viii. 40
στρουθίον xvii. 18
συγκεῖμαι xvi. 8
συγχέω xii. 4
συμμετρία v. 18
σύμμικτος xvii. 17
συμπαραλαμβάνω xiii. 4
συμφύρω viii. 10
συνάγω viii. 34, xi. 3, 4, xvii. 28, 37
συναγωγή x. 8, xvii. 18, 48, 50
συνάλλαγμα iv. 4
σύνεγγυς xvi. 1
συνέδριον iv. 1
σύνεσις xvii. 42
συνέχω xvii. 21
συνθήκη viii. 11
συνταγή iv. 6
συντελέω ii. 26, vii. 4
συντίθημι viii. 11
συντρίβω viii. 5, xvii. 21
σφαγή viii. 1
σφόδρα ii. 17, viii. 2
σφραγίς ii. 6
σχοινίον ii. 21
σώζω vi. 2, xiii. 2, xv. 1, xvi. 4, xvii. 19
σῶμα ii. 31
σωτήρ iii. 7, viii. 39, xvi. 4, xvii. 3
σωτηρία iii. 6, x. 9, xii. 7, xv. 8, xvi. 5

ταμιεῖον xiv. 5
ταπεινός v. 14
ταπεινόω iii. 9, xi. 5
ταπείνωσις ii. 39

ταράσσω vi. 4, viii. 6, xiii. 4
ταχύνω xvii. 51
ταχύς iv. 6
τεῖχος ii. 1, viii. 19, 21
τέκνον i. 3, ii. 8, viii. 39, xi. 3, xv. 12, xvii. 13
τέλος i. 1, ii. 5
τίθημι ix. 18, xvii. 7
τίλλω xiii. 3
τίμιος xvii. 19, 48
τίς iii. 5, ix. 11, 14, xv. 3, 4, xvii. 1, 44
τόξον xvii. 37
τράχηλος ii. 6, viii. 25
τραχύς viii. 19
τρέφω v. 11, 13

ὕβρις ii. 30, 31
ὕδωρ viii. 23
ὑετός v. 11, xvii. 20
υἱός ii. 3, 6, 13, viii. 10, 20, 24, ix. 8, xiii. 8, xvii. 17, 23, 30, 34, xviii. 4
ὕμνος iii. 2, x. Tit., xiv. Tit.
ὑπερασπιστης vii. 6
ὑπερηφανεύομαι ii. 1
ὑπερηφανία ii. 2, 29, xvii. 8, 15, 26, 46
ὑπερήφανος ii. 35, iv. 28
ὑπεροράω viii. 36
ὑπερπλεονάζω v. 19
ὑπέχω xvi. 13
ὑπήκοος xviii. 5
ὕπνος iv. 17, 18, vi. 6, xvi. 1
ὑπνόω iii. 1
ὑπόδημα ii. 2
ὑποζώννυμι xvii. 24
ὑποκρίνομαι iv. 22, 25
ὑπόκρισις iv. 7
ὑπομένω x. 2, xiv. 1, xvi. 15
ὑπομονή ii. 40
ὑπόστασις xv. 7, xvii. 26
ὑστερέω xviii. 2
ὕστερον ii. 32
ὑψηλός xi. 3, 5, xvii. 21
ὕψιστος xviii. 11
ὕψος xvii. 7
ὑψόω i. 5

φαίνω ii. 18
φείδομαι ii. 25, v. 16, xiii. 1, 9, xvii. 14

φέρω i. 6, viii. 2, xvii. 34
φεύγω xi. 6, xv. 9, xvii. 18, 27
φθορά iv. 7
φίλος v. 15
φλογίζω xii. 3
φλόξ xii. 5, xv. 6
φόβος vi. 8, xvii. 34, 38, xviii. 8, 9, 10, 13
φοβοῦμαι ii. 37, iii. 16, iv. 24, 26, v. 21, viii. 6, xii. 4, xiii. 11, xv. 15
φυλάσσω vi. 3, xii. 6
φυλή xvii. 28, 30, 50
φυρμός ii. 15
φυτεία xiv. 3
φωνή viii. 1, 2, 4, xi. 1
φῶς iii. 16
φωστήρ xviii. 12

χαρά viii. 18
χεῖλος xii. 4, xv. 5, xvi. 10
χείρ ii. 7, 24, iv. 3, 18, 19, v. 8, 14, vi. 3, ix. 7, xvi. 9, 14, xviii. 1
χλόη v. 11
χόρτασμα v. 11
χρηστεύω ix. 11
χρηστός ii. 40, v. 2, 14, viii. 38, x. 2, 8
χρηστότης v. 15, 16, 17, viii. 34, ix. 15, xviii. 2
χριστός xvii. 36, xviii. Tit., 6, 8, *always with* κύριος -ου
χρονίζω ii. 28, 30
χρόνος viii. 39, xv. 14, xvii. 2
χρυσίον xvii. 37, 48

ψάλλω iii. 2
ψαλμός iii. 2, xv. 5, Tit. i. ii. iii. iv. v. vi. vii. viii. ix. xiii. xv. xvi. xvii. xviii.
ψευδής iv. 4, xii. 1, 3
ψιθυρός xii. 1, 4, 5
ψυχή ii. 27, iii. 1, 9, iv. 15, 25, v. 14, vi. 4, 8, ix. 7, 9, 12, 19, xii. 1, 6, xvi. 1, 2, 3, 12, 14, xvii. 1, 19, xviii. 5

ᾠδή xv. Tit., 5, xvii. Tit.
ὠδίν iii. 11
ὥρα xviii. 12
ὡς iv. 3, 5, 11, 13, viii. 2, 6, 13, 23, 28, xiv. 1, xv. 9, xvii. 26, 33, xviii. 4
ὥσπερ xii. 2

INDEX II.

PREPOSITIONS.

ἀνά. ἀνὰ μέσον ii. 38
ἀντί ii. 13, 21, xvii. 7; ἀνθ' ὧν ii. 3, 15, 39
ἀπό ii. 4, 8, 19, 20, 39, iv. 1, 9, 18, 19, 25, 27, v. 3, 5, vi. 4, vii. 1, viii. 5, 7, 13, 16, 19, 37, ix. 1, 2, 5, 6, 16, x. 1, xi. 3, 4, 6, xii. 1, 4, 5, 8, xiii. 2, xv. 5, 6, 7, 8, 9, xvi. 1, 2, 3, 6, 7, 8, 10, 11, xvii. 8, 13, 15, 18, 19, 21, 25, 26, 27, 33, 34, 41, 51, xviii. 5, 12, 13, 14
διά. διὰ παντός ii. 40, iii. 3, 4, 8, xiv. 5
Acc. v. 8, viii. 15, xiii. 4, xiv. 6
Gen. viii. 2
εἰς i. 1, 4, ii. 4, 7, 12, 27, 35, 38, 41, iii. 13, 15, 16, iv. 6, 12, 19, 20, v. 7, 11, 20, vii. 8, 9, viii. 15, 20, 31, 39, 41, ix. 1, 18, 20, x. 2, 6, 8, 9, xi. 5, 8, 9, xii. 7, xiii. 9, 10, xiv. 1, 2, 3, xv. 1, 6, 8, 13, 14, xvi. 2, 3, 5, 11, xvii. 1, 3, 5, 14, 20, 23, 37, 39, 51, xviii. 1, 3, 6, 12
ἐκ, ἐξ iii. 2, vi. 6, xi. 4, xiii. 3, 5, xvii. 19, 21, xviii. 2
ἐν i. 1, 3, 6, 7, 8, ii. 1, 2, 3, 4, 6, 12, 15, 16, 20, 23, 24, 25, 26, 27, 28, 29, 31, 32, 33, 35, 37, 40, iii. 3, 7, 8, 9, iv. 1, 2, 3, 4, 5, 6, 7, 8, 9, 11, 13, 14, 15, 16, 17, 18, 20, 21, 23, 24, 26, 28, 29, v. 1, 3, 6, 7, 11, 14, 15, 16, 17, 18, 20, 21, vi. 2, 5, 8, 9, vii. 3, 5, 9, viii. 7, 9, 13, 22, 23, 24, 27, 28, 29, 30, 32, 40, ix. 1, 2, 3, 7, 8, 9, 10, 12, 15, 19, x. 1, 3, 4, 5, 6, 7, xi. 1, 2, 4, 6, 7, 9, xii. 2, 3, 4, 5, 6, xiii. 3, 6, 7, 9, xiv. 1, 2, 4, 6, 7, xv. 1, 3, 5, 13, 14, 15, xvi. 1, 3, 4, 9, 10, 11, 12, 13, 14, 15, xvii. 1, 4, 6, 7, 8, 9, 12, 14, 15, 16, 17, 19, 21, 22, 25, 26, 27, 28, 29, 30, 31, 32, 33, 36, 38, 40, 41, 42, 43, 44, 45, 46, 48, 49, 50, xviii. 3, 5, 6, 7, 8, 9, 10, 11, 12, 13, 14
ἐπί Acc. ii. 2, 23, 24, 37, iii. 2, 7, 12, iv. 3, 4, 15, 29, v. 8, 9, 15 (?), 16, 17, 21, viii. 17, 19, 33, 37, 38, ix. 4, 18, 19, 20, x. 4, 5, 9, xi. 9, xii. 7, xiii. 11, xv. 7, 8, xvi. 4, xvii. 2, 3, 4, 5, 12, 23, 35, 37, 44, 47, 51, xviii. 1, 2, 3, 4
Gen. ii. 11, 30, 31, 34, xi. 3, xv. 10, xvii. 2, 14, 20, 30
Dat. ii. 15, vi. 7, ix. 2, xvii. 42
ἕως Gen. i. 4, 5, xv. 11, xvi. 6
κατά Acc. ii. 7, 14, 17, 38, 40, viii. 25, ix. 2, 10, xvii. 2, 10, 11, xviii. 13
μετά Gen. ii. 25, 37, 40, iv. 4, 7, 10, v. 16, viii. 10, 11, 18, 20, 22, 34, 35, xiii. 4, xv. 5, xvi. 2, 5, 12, xvii. 6, 29, 40, 42, 43, xviii. 2, 3
παρά Acc. v. 6, ix. 17, xvi. 2
Gen. iii. 7, v. 4
Dat. v. 6, ix. 17
περί Acc. ii. 21, ix. 15
Gen. iii. 9, vi. 7, vii. 4, viii. 12, ix. 13, 15, 19, xvii. 5
πρό xiv. 5
πρός Acc. i. 1, v. 3, 10, 12, vi. 8, vii. 6, xvii. 44
ὑπέρ Acc. i. 8, iv. 2, viii. 14, xvii. 48, xviii. 8
ὑπό Acc. ii. 36, vii. 8, xvii. 32
Gen. ii. 30, iii. 4, iv. 21, vi. 3, viii. 41, xi. 3, xv. 9, xvi. 15, xvii. 20, 28, 35

INDEX III.

PASSAGES IN THE LXX. VERSION REFERRED TO IN THE PSALMS OF SOLOMON.

Genesis	i. 14	xviii. 12	2 Sam.	vii. 12	xvii. 23
	viii. 2	xvii. 21		xii. 11, 12	ii. 13, 14
	ix. 26	ii. 41		xxii. 7	i. 1
	xix. 17	xiii. 4		,, 31	xvii. 48
Exodus	ix. 34	xvii. 20	1 Chron.	xxviii. 10	,, 5
	xi. 8	,, 29			
	xv. 16	xi. 7	2 Chron.	vi. 16	,, 5
	xvii. 14	ii. 19		,, 40	xviii. 3
	xxxii. 8	xviii. 13		,, 41	v. 21
Levit.	v. 18	iii. 9	Job	vi. 11	xvii. 2
	xxi. 6	i. 8, ii. 3, viii. 26		xi. 14	,, 29
	xxii. 10	xvii. 31		xxvii. 7	xiii. 5
	xxvi. 5, 6, 22	xiii. 2, 3, xv. 8		xxxiii. 30	iii. 16
Numb.	xxi. 6	xi. 1	Psalms	i. 4, 6	xiv. 4, 5
	xxiv. 17	xvii. 24		ii. 9	xvii. 26
	xxv. 4	ii. 14		iii. 5	xvi. 3
				iv. 4	v. 3
Deut.	vi. 5	iii. 2		v. 9	vi. 3
	vii. 9	xiv. 1		vi. 3	viii. 5
	ix. 29	ll. 33		vii. 3	,, 12
	x. 8	,, 40		,, 12	ii. 19
	,, 17	,, 19		ix. 2	iii. 2
	xiii. 9	iv. 3		,, 23	ii. 1
	xvii. 7	,, 3		,, 27	xv. 6
	,, 15	xvii. 9		,, 32	ii. 8
	,, 16, 17	,, 37		xi. 7	xvii. 48
	xviii. 5, 8	,, 7		xiii. 1	,, 1
	xxxii. 9	xiv. 3		xiv. 5	xv. 6
	xxxiii. 13	xvii. 21		xvii. 3	xvi. 4
				,, 7	i. 1, v. 7, xv. 1
1 Sam.	ii. 8	ii. 35		,, 31	xvii. 48
	vii. 8	v. 3		,, 38	xv. 9
	xii. 12	v. 22, xvii. 1, 51		xxiii. 5	iii. 7
				xxviii. 10	xvii. 1
2 Sam.	ii. 22	v. 12		xxx. 11	iv. 17
	vi. 5	xv. 5		xxxiii. 16	xviii. 3

INDEX III.

Psalms	xxxiv. 6	xiv. 6, xv. 11	Psalms	cxviii. 28	xvi. 1
	,, 19	vii. 1		,, 52	viii. 7
	xxxv. 13	iii. 9		,, 121	xvii. 21
	xxxvi. 23	vi. 3		,, 133	xvi. 9
	xxxvii. 17	xiii. 7		,, 140	xvii. 48
	,, 18	x. 2		cxix. 1	i. 1, v. 7, xv. 1
	xliii. 5	xvii. 1		,, 2	iv. 27
	,, 7	,, 37		,, 2, 4, 5	xii. 1, 3
	,, 24	iii. 1		cxx. 1	iii. 6
	xlvi. 7	xvii. 4		cxxvii. 5	xvii. 50, xviii. 7
	l. 3	xiii. 9		cxxxii. 3	xiv. 1
	lii. 6	iv. 21, xii. 4		cxxxv. 1, etc.	xvi. 3
	liii. 5	xvii. 9		cxxxix. 2	i. 3
	lvi. 8	vi. 1		cxliv. 9	ii. 40, xviii. 1
	lxi. 3, 7	xvi. 4		,, 13	xvii. 1
	lxiv. 10	v. 11		,, 16	v. 14
	lxvii. 3	xii. 8		,, 17	x. 6
	lxviii. 25	ii. 28		,, 18	ii. 40
	,, 31	xv. 5		cxlvi. 8, 9	v. 11
	lxxii. 2	xvi. 2		cxlviii. 11	,, 13
	lxxiii. 13	xvii. 1			
	,, 14	ii. 29	Proverbs	iii. 11	iii. 4
	lxxiv. 9	viii. 15		iv. 16	iv. 18
	lxxviii. 1	ii. 2, 3		viii. 10, 19	xvii. 48
	,, 3	,, 31		xiii. 18	xvi. 13
	lxxix. 8, 19, 20	v. 9		,, 21	xv. 9
	lxxxiii. 12	xviii. 2		xx. 27	xiv. 5
	lxxxv. 5	v. 14		xxii. 11	xv. 5
	lxxxviii. 3, 4, 35, 36	xvii. 5		xxiv. 52	iv. 22
	,, 27	xvi. 4	Isaiah	i. 4	iv. 1
	,, 28	xviii. 4		ii. 6	xvii. 33
	,, 30	xiv. 3		iii. 24	ii. 21
	,, 40	i. 8		xi. 2, 3	xvii. 42, xviii. 8
	lxxxix. 17	vi. 3, xvi. 9		,, 4	,, 27, 38
	xc. 11	vii. 4		xiv. 19	ii. 30
	xcvii. 1	xiii. 2		xix. 14	viii. 14
	c. 7	xvii. 29		xxi. 1	,, 2
	cii. 10	ii. 7, 17, xvii. 10		xxix. 6	,, 2
	ciii. 28	v. 14		,, 13	iv. 1
	cv. 27	xvii. 8		xxx. 1	iii. 7, 12
	cvi. 3	xi. 3		xxxv. 10	x. 9
	,, 31, 32	x. 7		xxxvi. 9	xvii. 37
	cx. 9	,, 5		xl. 4, 11	xi. 5
	cxi. 7	vi. 7		,, 9	,, 2, 3
	cxvii. 16	xiii. 1		,, 11	xvii. 45
	,, 21	xvi. 5		xlii. 10	iii. 2
	cxviii. 5	vi. 3		xliii. 5, 6	xi. 3

Isaiah	xlix. 24	v. 4	Ezekiel	xviii. 6	viii. 13
	l. 6	x. 2		xxi. 6	,, 5
	lii. 1	xi. 8		xxii. 26	ii. 38
	liii. 12	xvi. 2, 5		xxiii. 38	,, 3
	liv. 13	xvii. 35		xxix. 3	,, 29
	lv. 12	xi. 6, 7		xxxiii. 14	xviii. 5
	lvii. 15	xviii. 11		xlv. 8	xvii. 46
	,, 19	xv. 5			
	lx. 19, 20	iii. 16	Daniel	xii. 2	iii. 16
	lxi. 10	ii. 22		,, 12	xviii. 7
	lxv. 22	xiv. 2			
	lxvi. 18—20	xvii. 34, 35	Hosea	i. 10	xvii. 30
				xiv. 3	xv. 5
Jerem.	iv. 13	viii. 2			
	,, 19	i. 2, ii. 15, viii. 1	Joel	ii. 1	xi. 1
	v. 8	viii. 11		,, 5	xii. 2
	xiii. 20	xi. 3		,, 11	xv. 13
	xxiii. 9	viii. 5		,, 32	vi. 2
	xxviii. 9	i. 5			
	xxxii. 1	viii. 15	Amos	v. 18	xv. 13
	xxxiv. 5	ii. 33		ix. 11	xvii. 23
	xxxvii. 9	xvii. 23			
	xxxviii. 8, 10	xi. 3, 4	Micah	v. 4	,, 45
	xlix. 10	xiv. 3			
	li. 2	xvii. 10	Nahum	i. 7	ii. 40
				,, 15	xi. 2
Lament.	i. 10	ii. 2, 3			
	iii. 25	xiv. 1	Habak.	iii. 12	xvii. 27
	v. 8	viii. 12			
			Haggai	i. 10	,, 20
Ezekiel	iii. 12	v. 22			
	v. 11	ii. 3	Zechar.	iv. 10	xviii. 2
	,, 17	xiii. 2, 3, xv. 8		xii. 6	xii. 2
	ix. 4	xv. 8, 10			
	xiv. 17	xiii. 2, 3	Malachi	ii. 11	i. 8
	xviii. 5	xvii. 21			

www.ingramcontent.com/pod-product-compliance
Lightning Source LLC
Chambersburg PA
CBHW062005220426
43662CB00010B/1238